WITNESS TO
WAR

Images from the Persian Gulf War
from the staff of the Los Angeles Times

Los Angeles Times
A Times Mirror Company

PROJECT DIRECTOR	**Angela Rinaldi** Los Angeles Times Syndicate
GRAPHICS/PHOTO EDITOR	**Terry Schwadron** Assistant Managing Editor for Graphics
TEXT EDITOR	**Simon Li** Deputy Foreign Editor
DESIGN/PRODUCTION/ **PRINTING**	**I.P.A. Graphics Management, Inc.** **Patricia McCormick Moritz** Book Design **Bill Dorich** Production Supervision **Posanke & Associates** Color Separations **Color Litho** Cover Printing **Humboldt** Text Printing
COMPUTER GRAPHICS/ **PRODUCTION**	**Mike Chaplin** Los Angeles Times Graphics Editor **Bill Dunn** Associate Graphics Editor **Helene Webb, Susan Mondt** Staff Artists
GRAPHIC RESEARCH	**Sara Lessley** Metro Graphics Editor **Victoria McCargar** Graphics News Editor **Michael Meyers, Nina Green** Staff Researchers, Los Angeles Times Library **Cary Schneider, Supervisor** Reference and Research, Los Angeles Times Library **Tom Lutgen** Information Specialist
PHOTO EDITORS	**Larry Armstrong** Picture Editor **Jerome McClendon** Picture Editor
PHOTO CAPTIONS	**Jane Engle** Assistant Foreign News Editor

ISBN # 0-9619095-6-0
Copyright ©1991, Los Angeles Times
Published in May, l991 by Los Angeles Times,
Times Mirror Square, Los Angeles, California 90053

A Times Mirror Company

Cover Photo
The cover photo which depicts Kuwaiti oil fires flaring beyond
the combat zone was taken by Patrick Downs/Los Angeles Times

Map reproduced from Hammond World Atlas
Printed in the USA

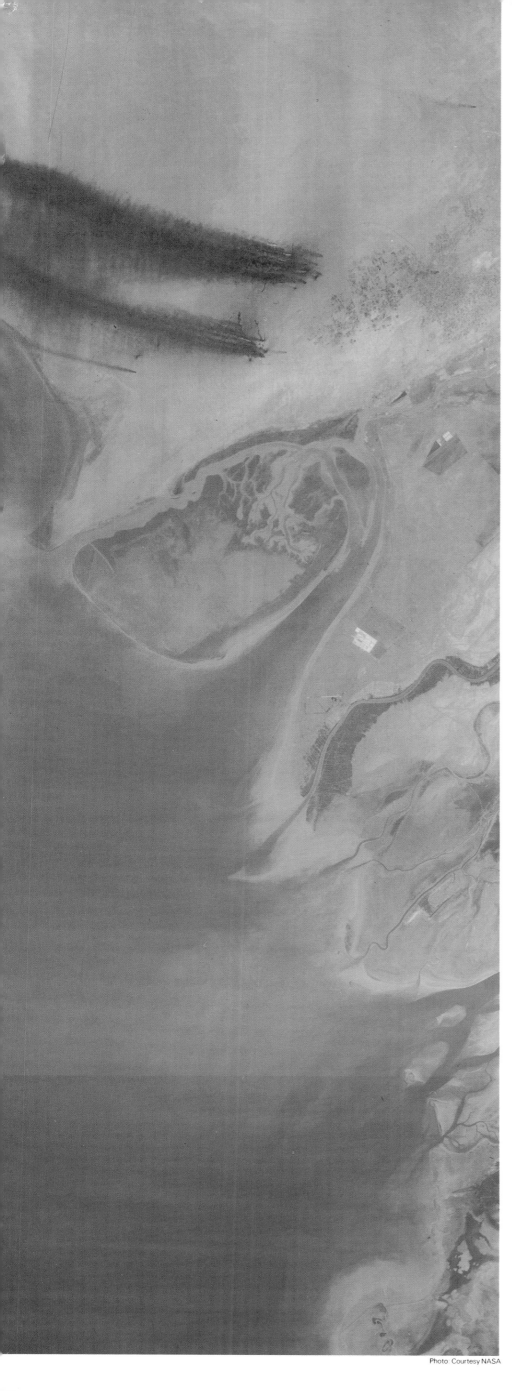

CONTENTS

Smoke from burning oil wells, the aftermath of Iraqi occupation.

On these pages you will find a detailed account of the Persian Gulf War as seen in the pages of the Los Angeles Times, the nation's largest metropolitan daily newspaper.

The Times documented the story from the beginning of the crisis when Iraqi troops under Saddam Hussein invaded neighboring Kuwait, to the dramatic allied military triumph seven months later. This book records the coverage of the war, provides a day-to-day history of the conflict and chronicles the dedication and courage of more than 500,000 American servicemen and women, many from the Southern California area.

The Gulf War coverage was one of the Los Angeles Times' most important journalistic achievements. Time magazine said: "The Los Angeles Times has been offering the most extensive and informative coverage of the war."

Our coverage reflected the extraordinary resources of the Los Angeles Times. With 33 reporters in 27 international bureaus in 25 countries and 44 in Washington, The Times could quickly field a worldwide team to report on unfolding events. We positioned more than a dozen reporters and photographers in the Middle East, moving them from New Delhi, Bangkok, Cairo, London, Rome, Washington, Seattle, Houston and Los Angeles to cover the war from Jordan, Saudi Arabia, Israel, Bahrain, Cyprus and Turkey.

Each day The Times front pages and open pages told the story of the war in words, photos and graphics. This then is an historic record of those unfolding events from the pages of the Los Angeles Times.

David Laventhol, Publisher
Shelby Coffey III, Editor

5

Carey Goldberg drove. Ninety miles an hour, Larry Davis noticed. But Davis had a bigger worry. "Should I be wearing my gas mask?" he wondered. He put it on. The goggles fogged up. He took it off. Goldberg put hers on. She took it off.

Goldberg, a correspondent for the Los Angeles Times, and Davis, a Times photographer, had been dispatched from Jerusalem to Tel Aviv by Foreign Editor Alvin Shuster to cover the first Scud missile attack against Israel in the Persian Gulf War.

"Then," Shuster recalls, "we find out the Scuds may be gas. So we're back on the phone as quickly as possible to Jerusalem, saying: 'Stop Carey!'"

But that was like trying to catch the wind.

Shuster, Shelby Coffey III, editor of

war and issues surrounding it—at home and abroad. It was a commitment that shaped the paper from the first day of the bombing of Baghdad until the United States and its allies drove Iraqi forces out of Kuwait.

The commitment began with Coffey and David Laventhol, The Times' publisher, who decided to send reporters into the Persian Gulf early.

Correspondents flew into the war zone from the United States, Britain, the Soviet Union, Thailand, the Philippines, India, Italy and El Salvador. To cover the home front, reporters, photographers and researchers were enlisted from cities such as Washington, Seattle, Miami, San Francisco, Chicago, Los Angeles, Denver, Houston and Atlanta.

When they got to the war zone, the

On Jan. 16, a day after the deadline set by the United Nations for Iraq to get out of Kuwait, Williams headed for Israel to relieve William Tuohy. That allowed Tuohy to return to London so he could cover Britain, a key ally in the coalition. Williams' wife, Lucia Annunziata, a reporter for La Repubblica, went to Jordan, where she, like Times correspondents Mark Fineman and Nick B. Williams Jr., covered Baghdad from Amman.

Within six days, the Iraqis themselves had ordered reporters for all foreign media but the Cable News Network to leave.

The commitment to full coverage made The Times grow in size. Laventhol approved additional pages—an average of six each day—without advertising.

The Times, and Simon Li, deputy foreign editor in charge of war coverage, sat and suffered the fears of the helpless. Li, for his part, thought about four brass memorials on a wall in the newspaper's lobby, one for each Times reporter killed over the years in the line of duty. "There was great concern," he says, "that there be no cause to add a fifth or sixth."

There was no poison gas, of course; it was never used during the war. Goldberg and Davis telephoned with a story and pictures. They told for the first time of the terror that came to be the special quality of every Iraqi missile attack against Israel and Saudi Arabia until the war was over. But the possibility that they could have been killed gave their editors in Los Angeles some of their worst moments of the war.

To Goldberg and Davis, it was all part of the job. Their work and the work of dozens of other reporters, editors, writers, photographers, artists and researchers was at the heart of a commitment by The Times to provide full coverage of the

correspondents positioned themselves in Saudi Arabia, Jordan, Israel, Bahrain, Cyprus, Egypt, Turkey . . .

What about Iraq?

Daniel Williams, The Times' bureau chief in Jerusalem, was in Baghdad. If war came, Li and Shuster thought, the city was likely to be hit by heavy allied bombardment. And if the danger was not from the bombs, perhaps then angry Iraqis.

"Shelby and I talked about whether to let Dan stay," Shuster says. "We came to the conclusion that the chances were it wouldn't be safe. Virtually all the other American print journalists already had flown out.

"But Dan was still there with his wife—a journalist for an Italian paper. They wanted to stay.

"On that end of the phone, Dan was saying, 'I want to see what happens.' On this end of the phone, we were afraid of what would happen. We leaned on him quite heavily to get out. He finally agreed."

Shuster and Managing Editor George Cotliar had selected Li to run things. In a rush of telephones and computer terminals, he set up what came to be known as the War Desk.

Li consulted with Shuster, National Editor Norman C. (Mike) Miller, Metropolitan Editor Craig Turner and editors in the Washington bureau, led by Jack Nelson. From their staffs and other departments throughout the paper, Li recruited editors to help him. He scheduled them around the clock. He orchestrated arrangements both large and small and directed coverage as U.S. troops began arriving in Saudi Arabia in ever growing numbers.

The war started with a rumor.

Photographer Bernie Boston in the Washington bureau heard it first: Congressional leaders had been called to the White House.

A White House press aide said it wasn't true.

"But I decided to head over anyway," says White House correspondent David

Lauter. "The aide's denial, it turned out, was correct by a preposition. The leaders had been called *by* the White House, not *to* it."

Lauter and other reporters heard the first bombs fall on Baghdad over CNN. Finally, Marlin Fitzwater, the President's spokesman, announced the obvious: The fighting had begun.

Afterward, Lauter says, "We clustered outside Fitzwater's office. At about 8:30 p.m., he opened the door, and we all poured in, crowding around his desk and standing on top of chairs, on his couch and on his coffee table as he gave us a lengthy rundown about how the President had decided to go to war."

With the additional pages came a commitment by The Times to illustrate the war with large graphic displays every

against the Iraqis at home and in occupied Kuwait, the United States and its allies said they would mount a ground assault to drive them out—down to the last soldier. It would be one of the largest ground assaults since World War II.

Pentagon correspondents John M. Broder and Melissa Healy learned that allied ground commanders would open the assault once the air bombardment had destroyed 50% of Iraq's armored units. The question was: When would that be?

Broder and Healy turned to their best sources.

One was an Air Force general. He had rich, sky-blue carpeting, befitting a commander with four stars. On tripods in front of his desk were two graphic displays, each of them four feet square. One

Some of the files stood alone, as individual stories. Others were combined: Editors and writers inserted analysis from Washington into reports from Moscow, for instance; they added reaction from Jerusalem to events in Amman; they topped background from Riyadh with action on the Saudi border.

On the 21st day after The Times published a forecast of about 20 days to the ground war, White House correspondent James Gerstenzang noticed that his sources, usually quick to return his calls, were nowhere to be found.

Just as suddenly, the White House announced that President Bush would return early from a weekend at his Camp David retreat. His helicopter would land behind the White House at 9:30 p.m.

Gerstenzang dashed out of the Washington bureau. He saw a cab. "It's crazy," he thought, "to take a taxi just four blocks"—but he grabbed it. He handed the driver $5 and didn't wait for change.

Washington seemed empty. "There are guys going across the line into the ground war right now," Gerstenzang thought to himself, "and look around: The capital. All is quiet, and there's no sign of anything out of the ordinary."

Across Pennsylvania Avenue from the White House, an anti-war demonstrator was beating a drum. Otherwise the street was as still as the winter night. The drum was muffled. Its sound tumbled over the sidewalk and drifted across the President's lawn.

Bush's helicopter touched down at 9:34 p.m., and Gerstenzang was there. Along with other reporters, he stood in the dark along a driveway behind the Rose Garden. Also on hand were Fitzwater, Vice President Dan Quayle and Brent Scowcroft, the President's national security adviser.

At 10 p.m., Bush announced that America and its allies had, indeed, begun the final phase of the liberation of Kuwait.

Because it featured head-to-head combat against some of the most feared of Iraqi forces, this was likely to be the most intense phase of the war. In pitched competition for places in news pools, The Times got a double hit: two reporters.

The pools were groups of correspondents permitted to accompany ground troops into battle. Even in pools, however, reporters were severely restricted in their access to the fighting. In addition, all pool reports were censored.

Despite these restrictions, Douglas Jehl and John Balzar provided eyewitness coverage of the ground war. Jehl had spent virtually every day since the beginning of the war waiting with American troops for the ground action to start.

And now the troops began to move.

Balzar was with the 18th Airborne Corps, riding in a CH-47 Chinook helicopter. The helicopter was carrying 2,500 gallons of fuel in a rubber bladder. One well-placed missile—and the helicopter would explode.

"Over that rise is Iraq," intoned the chopper captain. "Gunners, get ready." But there were only isolated strands of resistance. The Iraqis were quick to surrender.

Jehl, for his part, found much the same.

He rode with the 1st Armored Division, in the aft hatch of a Bradley Fighting Vehicle. The division rumbled north, then wheeled east.

Three brigades fighting abreast, the 1st Armored became a nightmare of

flash and fire. In the distance, tiny specks that were the enemy erupted in flame. Within hours, the Iraqis were in full retreat.

As U.S. tanks moved in for the kill, the allied coalition called an end to hostilities. The allies owned the skies. They had freed Kuwait. And they had taken a piece of Iraq that was even bigger. The ground assault had lasted only 100 hours.

"In the end," thought Balzar, who had been a Marine in the Vietnam War, "it came down to that same old low-tech ingredient, the one that gave the Viet Cong and North Vietnamese their grinding victory a generation ago—and the one that dealt the Iraqis their smashing defeat this time. It was the spirit of the troops in battle."

Iraqis, Balzar figured, didn't have the heart to fight.

Kuwait had been liberated, and reporters rushed into Kuwait city.

Kim Murphy was part of a six-person news pool escorted by the military. But now the pool had grown to a convoy of 54 assorted vehicles—and guards had halted it at the border between Saudi Arabia and Kuwait. Murphy bolted. She and a jeep full of reporters hit the gas, broke out of the convoy and roared through the border station.

Full throttle and a few minutes later, and she and her colleagues were in Kuwait. Murphy, who had been covering the Arab world from Cairo long before the war started, was joined by Bob Drogin, who had managed to make it into Kuwait as well.

Firsthand, they documented the scars of Iraqi occupation.

As they returned home, reporters and photographers recounted some memorable experiences.

Balzar told of eating in a Saudi restaurant one evening when another reporter at his table dived out of a chair and sent dishes flying. Balzar looked up. The reporter had tackled a small Saudi girl at a nearby table. She had been playing with a machine gun slung over her father's shoulder. The muzzle was pointed toward Balzar's table—and the child had her finger inside the trigger guard.

Correspondent J. Michael Kennedy told of getting so accustomed to air raid sirens in Saudi Arabia that he took to rolling over in bed and putting a pillow over his head. It was not until 28 American soldiers were killed when a Scud struck their barracks that he realized how foolish he'd been.

Thomas B. Rosenstiel, who wrote about media coverage of the war, told of being at CNN in Atlanta when it insured the life of its people in Baghdad with Lloyd's of London. The fee: more than $30,000 per policy per week.

One day, Simon Li was asked about model tanks, aircraft and warships that littered the art department. "They're useful aids to drawing weapons," he replied, "not evidence of arrested development."

Mike Miller will never forget a holiday message he received from correspondent David Lamb in Saudi Arabia, where alcohol is banned.

"Forget cookies," Lamb said. "Send whiskey. Merry Christmas."

From the Staff of the Los Angeles Times

day. As American and allied bombs fell on the Iraqis day after day, these graphics pictured weapon technology, diagrammed Iraqi bunkers under the desert, showed how allied commanders planned strategy.

Besides filling the pages with war stories and graphics, the editors topped them with boxes containing pertinent facts and interesting information:

A statistical description of Chinook helicopters . . . Persian Gulf weather reports . . . a short history of tank warfare . . . an anecdote about bicycling in Baghdad—there was no more gasoline . . . a vignette about a mouse that took up residence in the cockpit of a Harrier jet and flew along on several missions against the Iraqis . . .

The boxes included the origin of one of Iraqi President Saddam Hussein's favorite phrases: "the mother of battles." It came from the Arabic phrase"um al-ma'arik,"where *um* means *mother* and connotes *source* or *origin*.

After weeks of nonstop air attacks

was a map of Iraq, peppered with dots of different colors. The other was a photo of metropolitan Baghdad taken by a spy satellite and enlarged to make every detail plain. It, too, was covered with dots. Each dot represented a target for allied bombing.

The bombing, the general pronounced, was proceeding on schedule.

So when would the ground war start?

The general refused to say.

But he agreed to play a guessing game. His responses left a clear impression: Ground combat was about 20 days away.

By now the interdepartmental team handling war stories was at peak performance.

Reporters from the foreign, national and metro staffs were covering the war. The home front was being covered by the national and metro staffs, the feature sections and the suburban daily and zone editions. All were filing comprehensive reports to a War Desk that was staffed by a wide array of foreign, national, metro and feature editors.

Los Angeles Times
SPECIAL REPORT

The Line in the Sand

The Fate of Kuwait and Beyond

You could see it in George Bush's eyes, one of those closest to him said. "Those eyes are scary. Very calm. Very cool. You look at his eyes—there is an angry man there, and every week I think he gets more angry."

He was angry enough to draw a line in the sand—verbally, at first, in the days following the Iraqi invasion of Kuwait. Now he reaffirmed it physically by spending Thanksgiving Day with American troops at the front, in the Saudi desert.

The U.S. military commitment was already enormous and still growing. And already it was painfully clear that America's capability to quickly project its force across thousands of miles of ocean was deficient.

America had allies, but comparatively speaking, their military contribution was small and their stomach for a fight often uncertain. At home, Vietnam veterans and others protested against the U.S. military presence in the Gulf.

Still, there was a growing sense among Americans that maybe this latest Middle East crisis would not just blow over, after all. Bush seems so determined!

Oh, the critics may have shouted that this was really only about oil. But not for the President. To him, the invasion was more even than a question of power. It was a moral outrage. And this was the first test of the "new world order" he saw emerging after the end of the Cold War.

The crisis was Bush's crucible. Always, he had seemed such an odd mix of pedigree and ambition, a nondescript figure even after 30 years of public life. He appeared to blend with everything, like a primary color.

Yet now he had found a great cause that steeled him. It was George versus Saddam, each waiting for the other to flinch, the old-line, in-the-chips Ivy Leaguer and the peasant-born, gun-toting Butcher of Baghdad. At their command were ordinary soldiers, men—their moms would call them boys—such as Marc Langlois...

Associated Press

How the Crisis in the Persian Gulf Developed

July 18
Iraqi Foreign Minister Tarik Aziz accuses Kuwait of stealing Iraqi oil.

July 24
Iraq deploys thousands of troops on the Kuwaiti border. U.S. warships in the area are put on alert.

Aug. 1
Iraq walks out of negotiations with Kuwait over Iraqi grievances.

Aug. 2
Iraq's powerful army overruns Kuwait in a blitzkrieg invasion before dawn, seizing

Iraqi Foreign Minister Aziz

the emir's palace and other government buildings. The emir flees to safety in Saudi Arabia, but his brother dies defending the royal palace. U.S., Britain and France freeze Iraqi and Kuwaiti assets and President Bush says the United States will place an economic embargo against Iraq. U.N. Security Council issues a resolution condemning the invasion and demands the immediate and unconditional withdrawal of Baghdad's forces.

Aug. 3
Gunfire echoes through Kuwait city as Kuwaiti

George Bush

forces mount a last-ditch resistance.

An estimated 100,000 Iraqi troops and 300 tanks gather along Kuwait's southern border with Saudi Arabia. Bush warns that "the integrity of Saudi Arabia" is a vital U.S. concern.

U.S. and Soviet officials in Moscow issue a joint statement condemning the invasion and calling for an immediate Iraqi withdrawal from Kuwait.

State Department says 14 Americans working in Kuwaiti oil fields are missing and presumed captured by invading Iraqi troops.
Arab League members meeting late into the night in Cairo agree to condemn the invasion,

Iraqi tanks invade Kuwait city

Jordan's King Hussein and President Bush

but five nations vote against condemnation or abstain.

Japan, West Germany, Italy, Belgium and Luxembourg also freeze Kuwaiti assets.

Aug. 4
Iraq announces new military government for Iraqi-occupied Kuwait.

Bush, at Camp David, Md., meets with advisers and then calls Saudi Arabia's King Fahd to offer American military aid.

Aug. 5
Defense Secretary Dick Cheney leaves for Saudi Arabia to discuss deploying American troops there.

Aug. 6
U.N. Security Council votes overwhelmingly to impose a worldwide embargo on trade with Iraq.

Cheney shows Saudi leaders picture of Iraqi troop concentrations on the Saudi border and King Fahd agrees to permit the deployment of American troops on Saudi soil to deter an attack.

Iraqi soldiers round up more than 200 foreigners — including 28 Americans — from two hotels in Kuwait and begin transporting them to Iraq.

Aug. 7
Bush orders an initial contingent of U.S. combat troops and warplanes to Saudi Arabia,

Refugees from Saudi Arabia and Kuwait are stranded in Jordan

'Believe me, no Arab will side with the Americans against the Iraqis. The majority of Arabs support Saddam. No other Arab leader has challenged the outside powers. If I had the ability, yes, I would fight for him.'

RIAD AASSI

American M-60 tanks fire live rounds from 105-millimeter guns in exercises in Saudi desert

Saddam Hussein talks peace with Tehran

cans and other Westerners from two hotels in Kuwait.

King Hussein of Jordan secretly meets with Saddam Hussein in Baghdad.

Aug. 14
King Hussein flies to Washington to meet with Bush.

Aug. 15
In an effort to secure Iraq's eastern border with Iran, Hussein capitulates to all of Tehran's peace demands — including withdrawing from Iranian territories and releasing prisoners of war — bringing the eight-year-long Iran-Iraq war to a formal close.

Aug. 17
Bush decides to call up military reserves to ease shortages of doctors, cargo handlers and other specialists. He commandeers 38 commercial jets to ferry them to the Middle East.

Aug. 18
The first shots of the crisis are fired in warning across the bows of two Iraqi oil tankers in the Gulf of Oman and the Persian Gulf. The tankers do not appear to alter course.

Aug. 20
Bush abandons diplomatic euphemism and declares that the 3,000 Americans remaining in Iraq and Kuwait "are, in fact, hostages."

Iraq orders all embassies in Kuwait to close by the end of the week.

Iraq announces it has carried out a plan to move Western hostages to vital military installations to use as "human shields" to deter any U.S. attack.

Aug. 22
Bush signs an order placing 40,000 American reservists on active duty by Sept. 1.

The U.S. announces that along with other countries, it will defy Iraqi orders to close its embassy in Kuwait.

Jordan, overwhelmed by refugees, announces that it is closing its borders and asks the United Nations for relief.

Aug. 24
Iraq warns that Kuwaitis who harbor foreigners face the death penalty.

Iraqi troops surround the embassies of several Western countries and cut off electricity and water to those inside.

beginning Operation Desert Shield.

State Department says 3,500 Americans are trapped in Iraq and Kuwait because all the airports and border crossings are closed, but avoids using the word "hostage" because "we don't want to use red-flag words."

Aug. 8
Other oil-producing nations indicate they will step up production to make up for embargoed Iraqi and Kuwaiti oil.

Aug. 9
U.N. Security Council unanimously declares Iraqi annexation of Kuwait "null and void."

Aug. 10
Arab leaders meet in Cairo, where 12 of 20 Arab League members vote to send all-Arab

Austria's Kurt Waldheim meets with Hussein in Baghdad

military force to join Americans in defense of Saudi Arabia.

Hussein makes an emotional television appeal to Arab masses to "revolt against oppression"

in a holy war against foreigners who desecrate Islam's holy shrines.

Bush leaves for Kennebunkport, Me., to begin a scheduled three-week vacation.

Aug. 11
Thousands of Arabs in Yemen and Jordan demonstrate against the United States.

Aug. 12
The United States says it will use force if necessary to interdict all trade with Iraq.

Aug. 13
Iraqi troops in Kuwait round up more Ameri-

Burning buildings in Kuwait city

Reuters

'I believe that President Bush is a man of his word. We trust the United States....God willing, we will be victorious.'
KING FAHD

Hussein stages television appearance with a group of hostages. The image of Iraqi strongman with his arm around a 7-year-old British boy enrages Western world, particularly the British public. Prime Minister Margaret Thatcher calls the staged display "sickening."

British Prime Minister Margaret Thatcher

Aug. 25
By a vote of 13 to 0, with Cuba and Yemen abstaining, the U.N. Security Council grants the U.S. and other nations the right to enforce the embargo by military means.

Aug. 28
Hussein announces that he will permit all

foreign women and children to leave Iraq.

U.S. expels 36 Iraqi Embassy personnel and places tight travel restrictions on remaining Iraqi officials.

Bush returns from Kennebunkport to Washington to brief 170 members of Congress, who indicate their overwhelming support for his conduct of the crisis.

Aug. 29
U.S. intelligence reports say Iraqi troops in Kuwait now number 265,000.

Aug. 30
Bush says he will request cash from other nations — including Saudi Arabia, Germany and Japan — to help cover the enormous costs of economic sanctions and military operations in the gulf.

Sept. 6
Iraq imposes a new law mandating life imprisonment for those caught fleeing Kuwait.

Sept. 7
First U.S. evacuation flight carries 167 American hostages home from Kuwait.

Sept. 9
Bush and Soviet President Mikhail S. Gorbachev hold a quickly called summit meeting in Helsinki, Finland, where they declare unconditional support for international sanctions against Iraq. They warn that if current steps fail they are "prepared to take additional ones."

Camels contrast with armored personnel carrier in Saudi desert

Sept. 11
Bush, addressing a joint session of Congress, warns that the siege of Iraq may be long but vows that American resolve will not falter.

Sept. 13
U.N. Security Council decides to permit humanitarian food shipments to Iraq provided that they are distributed by third parties such as the Red Cross.

Sept. 14
Iraqi troops storm the French ambassador's residence in Kuwait and capture four French citizens.

Sept. 15
Flight carrying 285 American and Canadian citizens arrives in the United States.

Sept. 16
A videotaped message from President Bush to the Iraqi people is broadcast over Iraqi television.

Sept. 17
Cheney fires Air Force Chief of Staff Michael J. Dugan for disclosing "top secret" information about the Pentagon's Persian Gulf military strategy.

Iraqi women demonstrate
in the streets of Baghdad

Sept. 18
Pentagon reports that the number of Iraqi troops in Kuwait has grown to 360,000.

Sept. 21
Iraq expels three U.S. diplomats and the military attaches of 11 European embassies in Baghdad. The United States in turn expels three Iraqi diplomats from Washington. Bush warns that international sanctions "are going to take some time to work," and Administration officials tell members of Congress to prepare for a long standoff.

U.S. Ambassador W.
Nathaniel Howell III,
who stayed in
Kuwait

Sept. 22
A U.S.-chartered flight of American citizens leaves Baghdad for London, bringing to 2,000 the number of Americans evacuated from Iraq and Kuwait.

Sept. 25
U.N. Security Council imposes an air embargo against Iraq and Kuwait.

Sept. 28
Bush holds the first meeting in Washington with the Kuwaiti emir, who tells him that Iraq is pillaging his country and repopulating it with outsiders. The next day U.S. officials say the timetable for possible military action against Iraq is shortening.

Gen. Michael J.
Dugan

Oct. 3
The Senate overwhelmingly approves a resolution supporting Bush's Persian Gulf policy.

Oct. 4
Hussein reportedly pays a visit to Kuwait for the first time since Aug. 2.

Oct.12
A planeload of 250 Americans and their dependents arrives in Raleigh, N.C., from Kuwait.

Oct. 13
Kuwait's exiled rulers, meeting in Saudi Arabia, promise to institute democratic reforms when they liberate their country from Iraqi occupation.

Oct. 14
Pentagon announces that the United States

Members of the 1st Cavalry Division move out through the dust of the Saudi Arabian desert.

Nov. 1
Bush, escalating his verbal offensive against Iraq, says Hussein is more brutal than Adolf Hitler.

Iraq announces that family members of Western hostages will be permitted to visit during the Christmas holidays.

Nov. 2
Bush announces that he will visit American troops in Saudi Arabia on Thanksgiving Day.

Jordanian children shout anti-U.S. slogans
during a demonstration held in front of the
U.S. Embassy

Nov. 5
Secretary of State James A. Baker III and King Fahd reach a new military command and control agreement. It guarantees that American troops will be under the command of American officers if they launch an offensive operation against Iraq.

Nov. 6
Pentagon releases figures showing U.S. troop deployment for Operation Desert Shield has reached 230,000.

Cars line up at Baghdad gas station after Iraqi
government announced gasoline would be
rationed

now has more than 200,000 troops in the gulf region, along with 1,000 tanks, nearly 500 combat aircraft and 59 Navy warships.

Oct. 16
On a campaign trip to Iowa, Bush says Hussein will be held accountable for "unprecedented acts of brutality in Kuwait." Bush's speech is interrupted by three hecklers protesting U.S. policy in the gulf.

Oct. 19
Iraq orders foreigners in Kuwait to register with authorities by Nov.5.
Baghdad government announces that it will begin rationing gasoline.

Oct. 20
Canada abandons its embassy in Kuwait, leaving only the United States. Britain and France with diplomatic missions.

Oct. 21
On a private mission to Baghdad, former British Prime Minister Edward Heath wins the release of 70 sick and older Britons.

Hussein shakes hands with an Iraqi soldier during inspection visit in occupied Kuwait

In Paris, Defense Secretary Cheney says the United States believes it has all the authority it needs from the United Nations to justify an attack on Iraqi forces in Kuwait.

Oct. 24
14 American hostages newly released from Iraq say their captors starved them and refused them medical attention.

Oct. 30
Ten U.S. sailors are killed when a steam line explodes on the assault ship Iwo Jima in waters off Bahrain. The incident raises the U.S. military death toll in Operation Desert Shield to 42.

The aircraft carrier Eisenhower goes through the Suez Canal

Associated Press

" . . . And Lord, one other thing. Please watch over our beloved Marc, who is somewhere in the desert today. Please keep him safe from harm. Please don't let him be killed in the war. Amen."

As the oldest of four children, Marine Lance Cpl. Marc Langlois of Coral Springs, Fla. would normally have been carving the family turkey this Thanksgiving. But like 250,000 others, he was poised for battle halfway around the planet as those who loved him most said grace and tried to cope with the empty place at the table.

"I go for hours feeling nothing but pride, then I get a fear that runs up and down what I call my motherhood bone," said Marc's mom, Donna Langlois, her thin voice choking to a trickle. "Like at that very instant he's dead. Or hurt. Or made not whole."

Donna wanted to think America was right to send troops to the Persian Gulf. But who knew? What do Americans really know of these places anyway? Donna's idea of the Middle East came from "Lawrence of Arabia." Recently she found out that Kuwait was not even a democracy. Donna figured if she didn't tell George Bush what she thought, she'd never have a right to criticize.

"The Vietnam conflict took from my generation untold numbers of Einsteins, Picassos,Kennedys, and, yes, even George Bushes . . . " she wrote the President. "[My son] values beyond reason the uniform he wears. He will without hesitation . . . march into glory at your direction. For he is a Marine!!

"It is I who sees the ultimate waste in a future without his contributions as a husband, a father, a brother and a son."

Of course, in their hearts mothers know they can't protect their offspring forever. "Roots and wings, that's all you can give your children. Teach them where they came from—teach them what they'll need to know to be on their own. From the very beginning, you're teaching them how to leave you."

That was what Donna had tried to do, although she was not sure she had taught her Marc quite enough. The line in the sand was like a crack across her heart.

Nov. 8
Bush announces plans to double U.S. forces in the gulf. The move significantly raises the stakes in the standoff.

Nov. 16
Bush leaves Washington on trip to Europe and the Middle East. Baker, in Brussels, rejects a Soviet suggestion that the solution to crisis be linked to the problems of Israel's occupation of land claimed by Palestinians.

Nov. 18
Hussein offers to begin releasing all Western hostages on Christmas Day. U.S. officials quickly rejected the overture.

Nov. 19
Iraq announces it will pour 250,000 more troops into Kuwait.

U.S. Secretary of State James A. Baker III gives troops of the 1st Cavalry Division the thumbs up shortly after he addressed them in the Saudi desert

Gorbachev declines to back a new U.N. resolution authorizing an attack to drive Iraq from Kuwait.

Rough seas force U.S. to cancel Marine landing exercise using Hovercraft on beach in eastern Saudi Arabia.

About 75 Americans who had been held hostage arrive on flight to Washington.

Nov. 20
Hussein orders all German hostages freed.

Nov. 22
Bush visits American soldiers in Saudi Arabia on Thanksgiving Day.

Syrian troops unload from cargo ship at Saudi port

DAY 1

JANUARY 17, 1991

Right from the beginning, it seemed to me odds-on that the Iraqi invasion of Kuwait was going to end in war. I was in Abu Dhabi, in the lower Persian Gulf, when the first Kuwaiti refugees came out in early August. I had coffee with one of them, an oil technician. He was no sheik dripping with money but an ordinary middle-class man who had gotten out by the skin of his teeth.

"I'm going back as soon as I get my wife and kids set up," he said—a cold, flat statement you almost had to believe. He said his brother was in the resistance, already active in the first weeks of the crisis. "My brother and I will have our revenge," he said.

—Nick B. Williams Jr., in Abu Dhabi, United Arab Emirates

GULF: U.S. Warplanes Attack Iraq
PEACE NOW

The Images of War

Los Angeles Times

CIRCULATION: 1,225,189 DAILY / 1,514,096 SUNDAY

THURSDAY, JANUARY 17, 1991

COPYRIGHT 1991 / THE TIMES MIRROR COMPANY / CC† / 166 PAGES

DAILY 25¢ DESIGNATED AREAS HIGHER

U.S. Bombs Baghdad

Allied Jets Raid Targets Across Iraq

■ **Gulf war:** Explosions and fires are reported in the capital. 'The liberation of Kuwait has begun,' Bush says. Hussein declares that 'Iraq will never surrender.'

By JACK NELSON, TIMES WASHINGTON BUREAU CHIEF

WASHINGTON—War with Iraq began today as hundreds of American, British, Kuwaiti and Saudi Arabian warplanes bombed strategic targets in Iraq and occupied Kuwait.

Led by U.S. F-15 fighter-bombers based in Saudi Arabia, the massive air offensive was launched about 1:50 p.m. PST Wednesday—early today, Persian Gulf time—and within three hours explosions and fires were reported in Baghdad, the Iraqi capital.

"The liberation of Kuwait has begun," President Bush announced from the White House shortly afterward in a statement read by his spokesman.

Iraqi President Saddam Hussein, in an address on Baghdad Radio, declared that "the big confrontation has begun in the mother of all battles between the right and the wrong." Calling on his people to resist the onslaught, he declared, "Iraq will never surrender."

Early reports indicated that the carefully orchestrated air raids, beginning only a day after a United Nations deadline for an Iraqi withdrawal from Kuwait had expired, succeeded in hitting at least some Iraqi radar and communications facilities in Baghdad. The Pentagon said the attacks struck at Iraqi air bases and aircraft, chemical and nuclear plants and missile sites.

There were reports that the raids inflicted massive damage, but there was no official confirmation of the extent of it. The Pentagon also declined to comment on casualties.

The attacks began in darkness after 2:30 a.m. today, Baghdad time, and the Saudi military described the raids as "mammoth."

Hundreds of American warplanes and at least 150 Saudi aircraft roared into the night sky as wave after wave of bombers carried out the attacks.

Bush, in a televised address to the nation at 6 p.m. PST, declared "we will not fail" to free Kuwait. He also said the assault is "determined to knock out Iraq's vast military arsenal."

The neutralization of Hussein's war machine has been a major objective of the United States, its Persian Gulf allies and Israel since Iraqi forces invaded Kuwait Aug. 2 and seized control of the oil-rich sheikdom.

Bush said, "Saddam Hussein's forces will leave Kuwait and the legitimate government of Kuwait will be restored." Although Hussein had threatened that if attacked he would retaliate quickly against Israel, no such assault was reported hours afterward, and the Saudi oil fields—considered another prime target—were also reported safe.

■ **RELATED STORIES,** A5-A25, D1, F1

As the bombers swarmed over Baghdad, Iraqi antiaircraft batteries opened fire with booming volleys that could be heard on live news broadcasts from Baghdad. Bursts of light from explosions and tracers lit up the night sky.

Defense Secretary Dick Cheney, appearing at a late briefing at the Pentagon, said preliminary reports indicated that the operation had gone "very well" in its first stages, encountering only limited Iraqi resistance. He declined to comment on casualties or whether there

Please see GULF, A6

COLUMN ONE

U.S. Stakes Hopes on Quick End

■ If Hussein can hold out for even a few days, analysts say, he could establish himself as a leader of the Arab world even if the price is a fearful mauling for his country.

By NORMAN KEMPSTER and ROBIN WRIGHT, TIMES STAFF WRITERS

WASHINGTON—Beyond the immediate military goals of the punishing pre-dawn air attack on Baghdad and the wave after wave of raids to follow, President Bush hopes to sting President Saddam Hussein into reconsidering his adamant refusal to relinquish Kuwait.

And, senior U.S. officials made clear, their war plan was also designed to assure that—if Hussein should capitulate soon—his nuclear and chemical weapons facilities and other offensive capabilities would already have been crippled or destroyed.

For the U.S. strategy of battering Hussein into submission to succeed, however, many analysts believe it must succeed very quickly.

If Hussein can hold out against the massive firepower arrayed against him for even a few days, in this view, he could establish himself as a leader of the Arab world even if the price is a fearful mauling for his people and his country.

And a Saddam Hussein transformed into popular hero among the Arab masses could become a long-term nightmare for Washington and its Arab allies even if they ultimately prevail on the battlefield. Indeed, some Administration officials believe something close to that is Hussein's current strategy: to ride out the initial attack, proving his courage and showing the Arab world and others that he cannot be intimidated. Afterward, he could offer to negotiate peace terms.

The longer Hussein can hold out, the more effective his strategy would become.

"If it's a quick war, if we are able to strengthen Saudi Arabia and Egypt, and if we get rid of Saddam, and if we come with some imaginative diplomacy on the Palestinian issue, then we could come out ahead in the region and the world," said Geoffrey Kemp, a National

Please see STRATEGY, A18

United Press International

President Bush, flanked by White House press secretary Marlin Fitzwater, left, and Secretary of State James A. Baker III, walks toward the Oval Office prior to the launching of Operation Desert Storm.

Had 'No Choice' Other Than War, Bush Says

■ **Military:** Raids were to knock out Iraq's nuclear arms potential and chemical arsenal, the President declares.

By JAMES GERSTENZANG, TIMES STAFF WRITER

WASHINGTON—President Bush, asserting that the United States and its allies had "no choice" other than war, said Wednesday night the massive bombing raids on Iraq were intended to knock out Saddam Hussein's nuclear weapons potential and to destroy his chemical weapons arsenal.

As wave after wave of bombers and fighters began a massive 28-nation military operation to free Kuwait from more than five months of Iraqi occupation, Bush declared: "Saddam Hussein's forces will leave Kuwait. The legitimate government of Kuwait will be restored to its rightful place and Kuwait will once again be free."

"We will not fail," he said.

Bush emphasized that the aerial assault was designed to reduce U.S. and allied casualties to the lowest possible levels and to achieve military success in the shortest possible time.

"Our operations are designed to best protect the lives of all the coalition forces by targeting Saddam's vast military arsenal," the President said, adding that initial reports from Gen. H. Norman Schwarzkopf, the senior U.S. military commander in Saudi Arabia, indicated that "our operations are proceeding according to plan."

Showing little emotion and none of the fidgeting he has displayed in recent public appearances as the Persian Gulf crisis grew ever tenser, Bush told the nation in a broadcast speech from the Oval Office:

"Five months ago, Saddam Hussein started this cruel war against Kuwait. Tonight, the battle has been joined."

"As I report to you, air attacks are under way against military targets in Iraq," he declared, barely two hours after the air raids began.

He said that ground forces had not been engaged. Under military plans, they are unlikely to be sent into battle against the 540,000 Iraqi

Please see BUSH, A24

World Hears War Begin Live From Baghdad

By ERIC MALNIC and THOMAS B. ROSENSTIEL, TIMES STAFF WRITERS

It began almost abstractly, with the muffled crunch of bombs.

But as the sound rose to an earth-shuddering roar and streams of antiaircraft tracers arced upward through the night sky toward unseen airplanes, the war in Baghdad became a reality.

For Iraqis being hammered by waves of U.S. warplanes, it was a time of terror. The world heard the Persian Gulf war begin live over telephones from the Rashid Hotel, and the terror was palpable.

"The sky is lighting up to the south with antiaircraft fire and red and flashes of yellow light," CNN correspondent Peter Arnett reported from his sixth-story room. "There's another attack coming in. . . . It looks like the Fourth of July."

"It's like the center of hell," his associate, John Holliman, said qui-

Please see BAGHDAD, A23

Bombardment Will Go On for Weeks, Pentagon Says

By MELISSA HEALY and JOHN M. BRODER, TIMES STAFF WRITERS

WASHINGTON—Pentagon officials said Wednesday that the massive aerial bombardment of Iraq "will continue around the clock for perhaps weeks" following the initial wave of attacks on chemical and nuclear facilities, air fields, military communications sites and mobile missile launchers.

Defense Secretary Dick Cheney said Iraq had barely responded to the surprise U.S. air assault and suggested that losses of U.S. aircraft and crews had been minimal.

But military officials told lawmakers that the air campaign that began with a swarm of U.S., British, Saudi and Kuwaiti warplanes would likely halt briefly during daylight hours in the Middle East today while intelligence analysts assess the extent of damage to targets.

"The air part will continue until it is finished," said Gen. Colin L. Powell, chairman of the Joint Chiefs of Staff. Officials indicated that hundreds of key military targets would be destroyed before the air campaign would turn to an attack on Iraqi ground troops, tanks and artillery massed in Kuwait and southern Iraq.

No U.S. ground troops have been committed to the initial assault, Cheney said. Officials said that ground attacks on fortified Iraqi

Please see BOMBARD, A6

Southern California Tunes In, Absorbs News of War

■ **Reaction:** Schools, businesses, government agencies and families are all a bit stunned by developments.

By TRACY WILKINSON, TIMES STAFF WRITER

It promises to become one of those moments frozen in time—Jan. 16, 1991, 3:35 p.m., PST. It was at that moment a war was announced.

At the Los Feliz Elementary School, teachers converged around a radio and television set in the office of Principal Betty Castaneda.

"Everyone is on the edge of their chair," she said. "We don't understand it yet. It hasn't hit."

Downtown, in Los Angeles Superior Court, Judge Harvey Schneider interrupted a civil case. "Well, . . . I can tell you we have started bombing Baghdad."

A gasp was heard in the courtroom, and Schneider urged lawyers to wrap up their arguments for the day.

"I think we all want to get home," the judge said, "and see what is happening to our world."

Minutes later, the courthouse emptied.

A few floors down, 10 couples waiting in line to be married before a justice of peace changed their plans on the spot. It was not a good day to celebrate.

"Everybody just cleared out. . . . They just walked away," said Sally Chavez, deputy commissioner of marriages.

War had begun, and all over Los Angeles and throughout its neigh-

Please see REACT, A16

DELIVERING A BLOW

U.S.-led air strike targets nearly all chemical and nuclear sites in Iraq, with the goal of decimating its air force. Ground-to-ground Scud missiles, capable of striking Saudi or Israeli cities, were hit early. There was no official confirmation of the extent of damage.

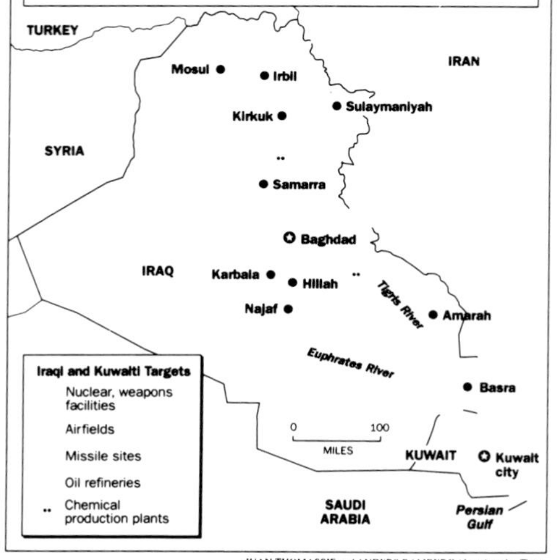

TURKEY
IRAN
SYRIA
IRAQ
Mosul
Irbil
Kirkuk
Sulaymaniyah
Samarra
Baghdad
Karbala
Hillah
Najaf
Tigris River
Amarah
Euphrates River
Basra
0 100
MILES
KUWAIT
Kuwait city
SAUDI ARABIA
Persian Gulf
Iraqi and Kuwaiti Targets
Nuclear, weapons facilities
Airfields
Missile sites
Oil refineries
•• Chemical production plants

JUAN THOMASSIE and ANDERS RAMBERG / Los Angeles Times

MORE WAR COVERAGE

THE POLITICAL MOTIVE
Political considerations may have been foremost on President Bush's mind when he ordered the swift attack, U.S. officials and experts said. **A8**

MILITARY STRATEGY
A military specialist says it appears Iraqi leader Saddam Hussein has already made a fatal error: He underestimated his enemy. **A10**

PROTESTERS REACT
Anti-war activists in Los Angeles reacted instantly to news that war in the gulf had begun, blocking traffic and staging rallies at federal buildings. **A11**

WEATHER: Mostly sunny and windy today and Friday. Fair skies tonight. Civic Center low/high today: 55/75. Details: B5.

■ TOP OF THE NEWS ON A2

ISRAEL ON ALERT
Israel declared a formal state of national emergency shortly after U.S. warplanes hit Iraq. But by dawn the Jewish state had not been attacked by Iraq. **A14**

BUSH TAKES GAMBLE
In ordering U.S. troops into war against Iraq, President Bush has taken one of the biggest gambles any American chief of state has ever taken. **A24**

ARAB WORLD SURPRISED
The opening of the war caught much of the Arab world by surprise, with many officials in the region saying they had no advance notice. **A26**

OIL PRICES GYRATE
Oil prices zoomed up to $6 a barrel on news of the Mideast war but fell back rapidly—in some instances to below pre-attack levels. **D1**

U.S. MILITARY MUSCLE

Air and Naval Forces in the Persian Gulf

The enormous concentration of U.S. weapons in the gulf features some of the world's most advanced airplanes and helicopters. Deployed from land bases and U.S. aircraft carriers in the Persian Gulf region, these aircraft offer allied forces decisive first-strike capabilities.

NAVY

F-14 Tomcat
Launched from aircraft carriers, the F-14 is designed as a fleet defense fighter. Its superior avionics permit the F-14 to track 24 targets and selectively engage six targets simultaneously. In the Persian Gulf, it can defend the U.S. and allied naval forces and engage Iraqi fighters in air-to-air combat.

Armament
- Sparrow, Sidewinder or Phoenix air-to-air missiles

F/A-18 Hornet
Defensively, the carrier-based Hornet can protect naval ships from enemy fighters and missiles. Offensively, the F/A-18 can function as a fighter escort and also deliver 17,000 pounds of gravity and laser-guided bombs with high accuracy.

Armament
- Sparrow and Sidewinder air-to-air missiles
- HARM anti-radar missiles
- Harpoon radar-guided anti-ship missiles
- SLAM stand-off land-attack missiles
- 500-pound gravity bombs
- GBU-10 and -12 laser-guided bombs

A-6 Intruder
The A-6 is designed as an all-weather long-range attack plane able to deliver up to 18,000 pounds of bombs with pinpoint accuracy. Launched from carriers, the A-6 has a maximum speed of 610 m.p.h. and an operational radius of 316 nautical miles.

Armament
- Harpoon missiles
- HARM missiles
- Gravity bombs

EA-6B Prowler
The Prowler is basically an extended A-6 loaded with all-weather electronic warfare equipment. It is designed to accompany fighters/bombers and use its electronic broad-band jammers to locate and confuse enemy radar.

Armament
- HARM missiles

MARINES

AV-8B Harrier
Capable of vertical takeoffs and landings, the fixed-wing fighter can get aloft from a short airfield, deliver thousands of pounds of ordnance, and then land vertically on an unimproved forward site.

Armament
- 25mm gun
- Sidewinder air-to-air missiles
- Maverick air-to-ground missiles
- Laser-guided and gravity bombs
- Rocket launchers

AIR FORCE

E-3 AWACS
The Airborne Warning and Control System (AWACS) is a modified Boeing 707 designed to track and identify up to 600 aircraft simultaneously. It is identified by the 30-foot-by-6-foot rotordome above the fuselage. The rotordome rotates every 10 seconds and projects a radar beam that picks up every moving target from ground to sky.

JSTARS
The new, high-tech JSTARS radar plane—short for Joint Surveillance and Targeting Acquisition Radar System—was designed to monitor troops and tanks in Europe as they moved to engage NATO forces. Two of the modified Boeing 707s—bristling with electronic surveillance equipment that can scan up to 130 miles and spot vehicles moving on the ground—are in Saudi Arabia. The planes may play a critical role in helping detect and target about 70 Iraqi mobile missile launchers.

AIR FORCE

F-117A Stealth
Designed to be virtually undetectable to enemy radar, the F-117A is a first-strike fighter that can attack Iraqi runways, ammunition depots and command centers in the initial stages of a military confrontation.

Armament
- Unspecified missiles
- Guided and gravity bombs

A-10 Thunderbolt
Military sources consider the A-10 to be the primary tank fighter of the Air Force. A-10's operate at low altitude to counter defensive systems, and can fly and fight effectively under low clouds and in poor visibility.

Armament
- 30mm high-speed cannon
- Maverick missiles
- Guided and gravity bombs

F-4G Wild Weasel
Loaded with electronic radar-jamming equipment, the F-4G is designed to detect and destroy enemy radar and ground-to-air missile sites.

Armament
- Shrike anti-radar missile
- HARM anti-radar missile

F-15E Eagle
An all-weather strike fighter, the Eagle has long-range (670 miles) strike capability. It can operate from short stretches of damaged runways in combat situations.

Armament
- Sparrow, Sidewinder or AMRAAM air-to-air missiles
- Maverick TV-guided missiles
- GBU-12/-24 laser-guided bombs
- GBU-15 TV-guided bombs
- Gravity bombs

F-16 Fighting Falcon
One of the smaller, lighter and less expensive fighters, the Falcon is able to carry heavy ordnance loads on long-range missions. It is superior in close-combat "dogfight" situations.

Armament
- Sparrow, Sidewinder or AMRAAM air-to-air missiles
- Maverick TV-guided missiles
- GBU-12/-14 laser-guided bombs
- GBU-15 TV-guided bombs
- Gravity bombs

F-111A Aardvark
Recognized for its pivoting swing-wings, the F-111 is a long-range tactical fighter capable of delivering up to 25,000 pounds of bombs.

Armament
- SRAM missiles
- Nuclear bombs
- Sparrow, Sidewinder or AMRAAM air-to-air missiles
- Maverick TV-guided missiles
- GBU-12/-24 laser-guided bombs
- GBU-15 TV-guided bombs
- Gravity bombs

B-52 Stratofortress
The long-range B-52 bomber is capable of delivering a devastating 50,000 pounds of bombs. In recent years it has been equipped with cruise missiles and sophisticated software giving the capability of delivering both nuclear and conventional bombs.

Armament
- SRAM nuclear attack missiles
- AGM-86 nuclear cruise missiles
- Nuclear gravity bombs, 500-pound and 2,000-pound conventional bombs

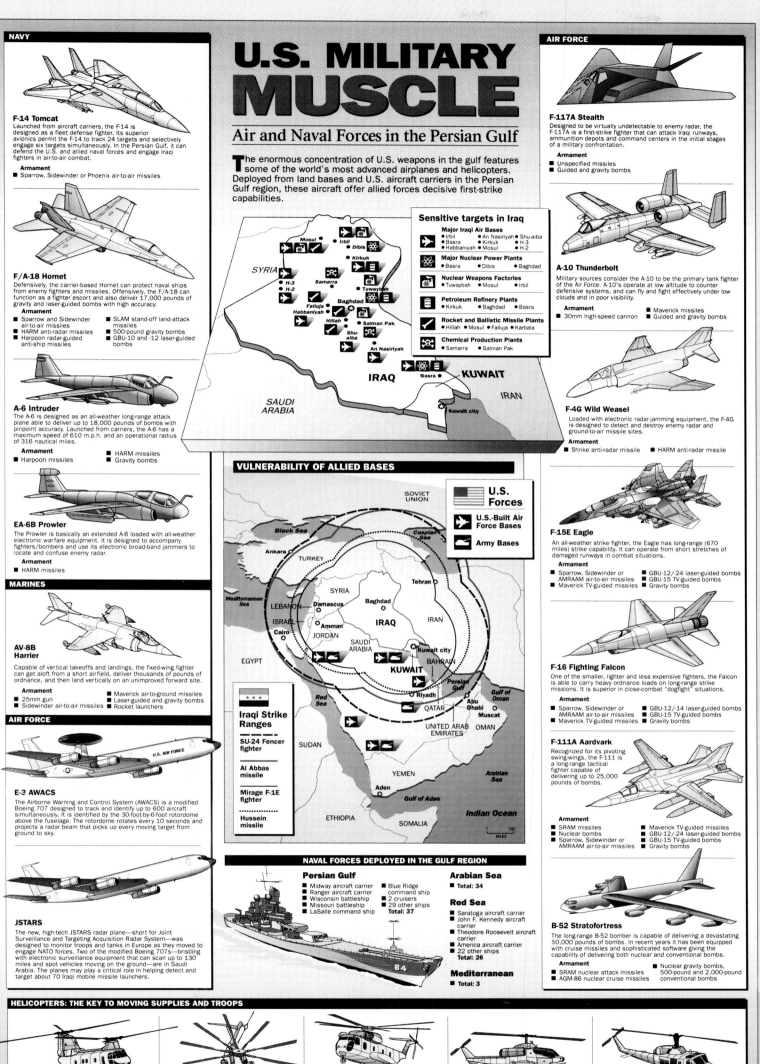

Sensitive targets in Iraq

Major Iraqi Air Bases
- Irbil
- Basra
- Habbaniyah
- An Nasiriyah
- Kirkuk
- Mosul
- Shu-aiba
- H-3
- H-2

Major Nuclear Power Plants
- Basra
- Dibis
- Baghdad

Nuclear Weapons Factories
- Tuwaybah
- Mosul
- Irbil

Petroleum Refinery Plants
- Kirkuk
- Baghdad
- Basra

Rocket and Ballistic Missile Plants
- Hillah
- Mosul
- Falluja
- Karbala

Chemical Production Plants
- Samarra
- Salman Pak

VULNERABILITY OF ALLIED BASES

U.S. Forces
- U.S.-Built Air Force Bases
- Army Bases

Iraqi Strike Ranges
- SU-24 Fencer fighter
- Al Abbas missile
- Mirage F-1E fighter
- Hussein missile

NAVAL FORCES DEPLOYED IN THE GULF REGION

Persian Gulf
- Midway aircraft carrier
- Ranger aircraft carrier
- Wisconsin battleship
- Missouri battleship
- LaSalle command ship
- Blue Ridge command ship
- 2 cruisers
- 29 other ships
- **Total: 37**

Arabian Sea
- **Total: 34**

Red Sea
- Saratoga aircraft carrier
- John F. Kennedy aircraft carrier
- Theodore Roosevelt aircraft carrier
- America aircraft carrier
- 22 other ships
- **Total: 26**

Mediterranean
- **Total: 3**

HELICOPTERS: THE KEY TO MOVING SUPPLIES AND TROOPS

CH-46 Sea Knight
Often referred to as the workhorse of the Marine Corps, the double-rotor Sea Knight carries Marines during both land and sea assaults. It can also be used to move equipment, weapons and supplies and engage in search and rescue.

CH-53E Super Stallion
The heavy-lift Marine helicopter—it is the largest built outside of the Soviet Union—is used to carry trucks, 155-millimeter howitzers and light armored vehicles and to ferry them from position to position. It is one of the few helicopters capable of lifting its own weight—16 tons.

CH-53D Sea Stallion
Smaller than the Super Stallion, the Sea Stallion carries troops, equipment and ammunition and can be launched from amphibious assault ships. Used extensively during the Vietnam War, it can carry 37 combat-equipped troops or 24 injured soldiers and four attendants.

AH-1T Sea Cobra
Just 58 feet long, the Cobra provides close air support for amphibious invasions and ground maneuvers. The helicopter's pilot and gunner control a 20-millimeter gun and a variety of small rockets, including the laser-guided, tank-killing Hellfire missile.

UH-1N Huey
One of the most durable and versatile utility helicopters ever built—the distinctive "whop" of its rotor blades is often associated with Vietnam—the Huey is used for moving troops, light equipment and for battlefield medical evacuations. It can carry eight to 10 combat-equipped Marines or six wounded soldiers with one attendant.

Source: Times Wire Services; Los Angeles Times

Airplanes not to scale

ANDERS RAMBERG, SANDY KAY, DAVID PUCKETT, JUAN THOMASSIE, PAUL GONZALES, JIM OWENS and MATT MOODY / Los Angeles Times

Military: War against Iraq begins at 2:30 a.m. Baghdad time as hundreds of American, British and Saudi warplanes bomb strategic targets in Iraq and occupied Kuwait. Early reports indicate that the air raids inflict enormous damage.
- Defense Secretary Dick Cheney says Iraq barely responds to the surprise assault. American pilots meet "no air resistance."
- Another wave of warplanes launches fresh attacks after the initial assault. Pentagon officials say Operation Desert Storm's massive aerial bombardment "will continue around the clock for perhaps weeks."

White House: President Bush says in a televised address: "Saddam Hussein's forces will leave Kuwait, and the legitimate government of Kuwait will be restored." The United States and its allies had "no choice other than war. . . . We will not fail."

Iraq: President Saddam Hussein, in an address on Baghdad Radio, declares, "The big confrontation has begun in the mother of all battles between the right and the wrong." He tells his people: "Iraq will never surrender."

Diplomacy: Thomas R. Pickering, U.S. ambassador to the United Nations, promises that Iraq can avoid further punishment by unconditionally withdrawing from Kuwait.

Baghdad: Western journalists report damage to Arab Baath Socialist Party headquarters, the Defense Ministry and a large oil refinery along the Tigris River. CNN correspondent Peter Arnett says by satellite telephone from the Rashid Hotel: "It looks like the Fourth of July."

Energy: The White House announces it will open the U.S. Strategic Petroleum Reserve. Oil prices gain up to $6 a barrel but fall back rapidly.

Home front: Anti-war activists launch a wave of protests nationwide, blocking traffic and staging rallies at federal buildings.

Los Angeles Times

CIRCULATION:
1,225,189 DAILY / 1,514,096 SUNDAY

FRIDAY, JANUARY 18, 1991
COPYRIGHT 1991 THE TIMES MIRROR COMPANY CC† 146 PAGES

DAILY 25¢
DESIGNATED AREAS HIGHER

Iraqi Missiles Strike Israel
Massive Air Attacks by Allies Continuing

Israelis were jolted from their beds by the wail of air-raid sirens. Iraqi Scud missiles had hit Tel Aviv, Haifa and other sites. Saddam Hussein had kept his promise to bring the Gulf War to the Jewish state.

The highway between Jerusalem and Tel Aviv is usually the busiest in Israel, often looking like the San Diego Freeway at rush hour. But in the early morning darkness, it was deserted. Fear and uncertainty kept everyone in the sealed rooms that their government had warned them to prepare against chemical weapons. Had Iraq used such weapons?

As [Times reporter] Carey Goldberg and I left Jerusalem and sped towards Tel Aviv, the only other car on the road was a government Volvo with four men in chemical-protection suits and gas masks—going the other way. If not for the radio, it would have seemed that we were the only living people around.

—Larry Davis, in Israel

COLUMN ONE
High-Tech Warfare— A New Era

■ The success of the once-controversial Tomahawk cruise missile is emblematic, experts say, of improvements in electronic weaponry. But many remain skeptical.

By SARA FRITZ and RALPH VARTABEDIAN
TIMES STAFF WRITERS

WASHINGTON—When the first Tomahawk cruise missile hit Baghdad at 3:01 a.m. Thursday, it ushered in a new era of warfare in which U.S. forces take advantage of sophisticated electronic weaponry developed since the Vietnam War to strike their targets with unprecedented precision.

In its wartime debut, the Tomahawk appears to have proved every bit as accurate as its proponents have long insisted it would be. According to Navy officials, more than 90 of the 100 missiles fired from U.S. warships in the Persian Gulf hit their targets in Iraq.

The success of the Tomahawk was emblematic, to many military experts, of the vast improvements made in electronic weaponry over the past two decades. If the early reports of such successes are borne out, that could mitigate the costly failures of high-technology weapons programs that have become so controversial in recent months.

Many weapons experts and even defense executives were cautious Thursday in trumpeting the weapons' success, because preliminary reports often do not stand up under close scrutiny—and because the fighting has just begun. The missile attack launched against Israel early this morning made it clear that Iraq has not been crushed just yet.

The battle against Iraq is hardly the ultimate test of American equipment that was designed to fight the technically advanced forces of the Soviet Union. Nonetheless, the completion of 1,000 bombing sorties by U.S. and allied fighters in the first day of fighting in the Persian Gulf War with just one American loss is considered a tremendous success by itself.

"If we can come back with minimum losses, that shows that technology pays," said Ben Rich, who retired two weeks ago as the head of Lockheed Corp.'s "Skunk Works," its famed secret aircraft unit in Burbank. Although Rich remains cautious about jumping to quick conclusions, it appears that
Please see CRUISE, A9

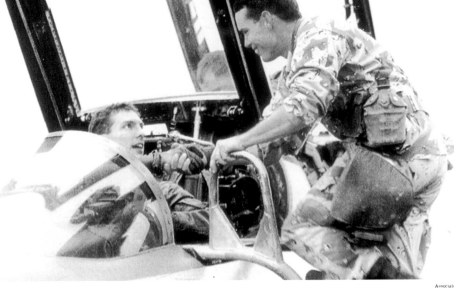

The pilot of an F-4 Phantom fighter-bomber is welcomed back with a handshake from a ground crew member after returning from a raid on Iraq.
Associated Press

Pilots Relive 1st Combat: 'Most Scary Thing…'

By KIM MURPHY
TIMES STAFF WRITER

DHAHRAN, Saudi Arabia— They lifted off on a moonless night on runways etched in the Arabian desert from the Persian Gulf to the Red Sea, bound for a rendezvous in Iraq that would mark the beginning of war.

The aerial armada that sped toward Baghdad just after midnight Wednesday played out a deadly ballet choreographed to tip the combat balance in favor of allied forces in the gulf even before the rolling of the first tank—and marked a new chapter in the most timeless saga of warfare: a man, a machine and a faceless enemy.

The stories of the pilots who flew more than 1,000 sorties that night and the next day, showering Iraqi military targets in a deadly firestorm, provide the only first-hand accounts so far of the showdown between Iraqi troops in Kuwait and a 28-nation international alliance that overnight became the Persian Gulf War.

"It's an exciting one to have under my belt," said U.S. Air Force Capt. Genter Drummond of the
Please see PILOTS, A18

Allied Raids Achieve 2 Goals but Miss Scuds

■ **Military:** Air dominance is established over Iraq, and many vital sites are hit. But some missiles evade attack.

By JOHN M. BRODER
TIMES STAFF WRITER

WASHINGTON—The opening day of the air war against Iraq apparently succeeded in two of its key objectives—the establishment of air dominance over Iraq and Kuwait and the destruction of many critical military and industrial facilities, military officials said Thursday.

But a critical Iraqi capability—its medium-range Scud missiles that were used to attack Israel early today—evaded the U.S. aerial onslaught.

Allied warplanes responded immediately to Iraq's launching of Scud missiles against Israel, taking retaliatory raids against the surface-to-surface missile launchers that are among the most difficult military targets in Iraq.

"This particular effort, to go after those missiles involved in the attack on Israel, is a new mission," Pentagon spokesman Pete Williams said.

Although the Iraqi missile attacks failed to draw Israel into the war, they succeeded in puncturing a mood of near-invincibility among U.S. war strategists after the first night, during which allied warplanes met little resistance when they went after 159 targets in Iraq and Kuwait.

Among those targets were President Saddam Hussein's bunker and residence in Baghdad, said Rep. Bill Dickinson (R-Ala.) after a briefing from Gen. Colin L. Powell, chairman of the Joint Chiefs of Staff. Powell told lawmakers that the two sites were on the list because of command-and-control facilities at each place, but there was no reason to believe that Hussein was present at the time of the attacks.

Dickinson quoted Powell as saying: "We're not chasing the guy. We're going after military targets."

Before the Iraqi missile assault on Israel, U.S. officials said that fixed missile launch sites known as H-2 and H-3 in western Iraq, bases for the Scud missiles targeted on Israel, had been destroyed. But
Please see MILITARY, A22

Israelis Awaken to Harsh Impact of Iraqi Missiles

By CAREY GOLDBERG
TIMES STAFF WRITER

TEL AVIV—There had been a false sense of security throughout much of Israel on Thursday, prompted by initial reports that U.S. warplanes had knocked out the Iraqi missile launchers that threatened Israel.

And then, early this morning, Saddam Hussein's missiles came.

Residents of this city's impoverished Ezra neighborhood awoke to the brutal impact of an Iraqi Scud missile within yards of their homes. It was but one of several to strike their country.

Those who ventured outside found an immense pit—60 feet across and 20 feet deep—surrounded by about 100 yards of rubble.

Houses nearby were stripped to their frames, littered with the debris of mangled furnishings. Cars were crushed. Shards of glass and splintered shutters littered the streets.

Some of the residents were injured; all of them were stunned. But amazingly, despite the force of the explosion, none of them died.
Please see SCENE, A9

■ **Gulf war:** Although Jerusalem says it retains the right to retaliate, there is no immediate counterattack.

By WILLIAM TUOHY and JACK NELSON
TIMES STAFF WRITERS

JERUSALEM—Iraq fired missiles into the civilian populations of Tel Aviv and Haifa early today in a thunderous retaliation as the United States and its allies bombed Iraq and occupied Kuwait for a second day with relentless fury.

The Iraqi missiles injured six or seven Israelis, none seriously, officials said. Although Israel reserved the right to respond, it mounted no immediate counterattack. President Bush, "outraged" by the Iraqi attack, reportedly counseled vengeance. The White House said a fresh wave of bombers was dispatched against the Iraqis.

Eight explosions rocked Israel, said a spokesman at the Israeli Embassy in Washington. Two shattered buildings in Tel Aviv. At least one of those buildings was a dwelling. At least two other explosions rattled the port city of Haifa. Three more were reported in a rural area. And still another, officials said, exploded at an undisclosed location.

Damage was extensive. According to Israeli radio, one death was caused indirectly by the Iraqi missile fire when an Israeli died of a heart attack.

The Israeli government urged citizens to put on gas masks and protect themselves against the possibility that some of the missiles carried chemical warheads. But officials said later that all carried conventional explosives.

At least one additional Iraqi Scud missile was fired at the Saudi Arabian city of Dhahran. In Washington, the Pentagon said a U.S. Patriot surface-to-air missile shot down the Scud before it hit its target. This marked the first firing of a Patriot missile in combat. A French television reporter said a second Scud hit the Dhahran airport, but that report could not be immediately confirmed.

By striking at Israel in his first major counterattack of the Persian Gulf war, Iraqi President Saddam Hussein clearly intended to provoke an Israeli response, American officials and military experts said. By their reckoning, he hoped that such a retaliation by the Jewish state would shatter the Western-Arab alliance.

Whether Hussein succeeds, they said, now depends on what Israel does—and on Arab reaction.

The Iraqi missiles, apparently all of them Scuds, began falling in Tel Aviv at about 2 a.m. today (4 p.m. PST Thursday). Sirens sounded moments before the attack, and Israelis fled to rooms they had sealed against the possibility of gas warfare. They donned gas masks and heard early reports on TV that the missiles carried chemical
Please see WAR, A6

Dow Up 114, Oil Falls 33% on Early Signs of Short War

■ **Markets:** But Iraqi attack on Israel sobers investors worldwide. Japanese stocks falter, then close higher.

By JONATHAN PETERSON
TIMES STAFF WRITER

The Dow Jones industrial average leaped 114.60 points Thursday and the price of oil tumbled by more than $10 a barrel in New York—its biggest one-day drop ever—as financial markets throughout the world responded with glee and, later, fear to news from the Middle East.

For most of the day, investors in the skittish financial markets were electrified by reports of successful allied bombing raids on Iraq. They bid up prices of stocks and bonds, apparently assuming that Saudi oil facilities would not suffer major damage and that stability would soon return to the Persian Gulf.

Crude oil prices fell by an extraordinary one-third in value on the New York Mercantile Exchange, closing at $21.44 a barrel. In Europe and the United States, gold and the U.S. dollar—which usually rise in times of crisis—plunged, as speculators concluded that a U.S. victory was close at hand. Gold dropped more than $30 an ounce to $397 in New York trading.

"The statement by investors is pretty much the same across the globe—and it is one of euphoria," said Gavin R. Dobson, president of Murray Johnstone International, an investment firm in Chicago. But he added prophetically: "My gut feeling is that it's not going to last."
Please see MARKETS, A29

MORE WAR COVERAGE

CHALLENGE IN THE SKIES
The U.S. and allied air attack on Iraq choreographed 24 kinds of aircraft and relied on a complex system of air traffic control and combat management. **A7**

TURKEY OPENS FRONT
Officials in Turkey authorized U.S. warplanes to take off from the country's Incirlik air base if needed to open a second air front against Iraq. **A11**

BUSH STANDS FIRM
President Bush said "we are not going to stop" attacks until Saddam Hussein pulls his troops out of Kuwait. He avoided calling for the Iraqi's surrender. **A11**

WEATHER: Sunny and warm today and Saturday with clear skies tonight. Civic Center low/high today: 50/78. Details: B5

■ **TOP OF THE NEWS ON A2**

OUTLOOK IN 'THE NEW ORDER'
The assault on Iraq suggests military conflict will be as much a part of what President Bush calls the "new world order" as it was in the past, experts say. **A11**

ALLIANCES ENDORSE ACTION
The U.S. military operation received strong backing from key economic and defense alliances. Meanwhile, war protests took place in some countries. **A12**

AIRPORT SECURITY TIGHT
Federal officials tightened security at U.S. airports. New rules suspended curbside baggage check-in and ordered unattended bags impounded. **A16**

PROTESTS AT UCLA, USC
The second day of the gulf war ignited student protests at UCLA, USC and campuses nationwide. Street protests widened across the country. **A17**

Hussein Now Seen as Near Messianic, More Menacing

■ **Politics:** His speech, attack on Israel underscore anti-Western attitude like Khomeini's, experts say.

By KAREN TUMULTY and MARK FINEMAN
TIMES STAFF WRITERS

WASHINGTON—If there was any thought that Saddam Hussein could be vanquished by the first waves of allied bombardment, it was shattered early today as the first Iraqi missile hurtled into Israel.

In Hussein's actions and in his rhetoric since the war began, many analysts have seen a fundamental change that makes him potentially more menacing.

As recently as a few days ago, the Iraqi leader was almost universally viewed as a secular pragma-
Please see SADDAM, A14

Saddam Hussein in prayer.
Iraqi TV via CNN

Radar Choreographed the Allies' Aerial Ballet

WAR: Iraq's Scud Missiles Hit Israeli Casualties Light

With Rumors of War Comes Anxiety, Pride and Chemical Jitters

SCENE: Israelis Awaken to Chaos Missile Crater

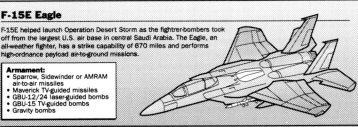

Missiles: Iraqi Scud missiles explode in Tel Aviv, Haifa and unpopulated areas of Israel during the early morning. Radio stations order residents to put on gas masks and go into rooms sealed against gas attack. Early reports on TV that the missiles carried chemicals prove false.
■ Israeli authorities say 12 people suffered minor injuries; three elderly women and a 3-year-old Arab girl apparently suffocated in their gas masks.
■ Iraq fires a single Scud missile toward allied forces in Saudi Arabia, but it is intercepted and destroyed by a Patriot missile.
■ Prime Minister Yitzhak Shamir summons his Cabinet to decide whether Israel will retaliate.

White House: President Bush says he is "outraged" by the missile attack but declares the air offensive against Iraq is "going well."

Military: Air strikes by the United States and allies establish air dominance over Iraq and Kuwait and destroy critical military and industrial facilities.
■ Two Marines and one Navy corpsman are slightly injured after Iraqi artillery shells hit their bunkers near the Saudi border with Kuwait. Iraqi artillery shells hit a Saudi Arabian oil facility.
■ One U.S. plane, an F-18 fighter, is officially confirmed as a loss. Two British, one Kuwaiti and an Italian plane are also reported downed.
■ Defense Secretary Dick Cheney says, "So far, so good." He says 1,000 U.S. and allied air strikes and more than 100 ship-launched cruise missiles caused heavy damage. But he adds that the war could last for a "significant period."

Baghdad: Iraq claims it shot down 44 allied jet fighters, while 23 Iraqis were killed in U.S.-led air strikes. President Saddam Hussein declares that "success is assured."

Markets: The Dow Jones industrial average leaps 114.60 points, its second-biggest gain in history, and the price of oil tumbles by more than $10 a barrel, its biggest one-day drop.

Diplomacy: The Soviet ambassador to Iraq delivers a message from the Kremlin for Saddam Hussein. President Mikhail S. Gorbachev appeals to Hussein to announce immediately that he will pull his forces out of Kuwait.

Terrorism: The FBI warns that known terrorists have entered the United States.

Lucky break: Scud hit this Israeli bunker, but it was vacant.

LARRY DAVIS / Los Angeles Times

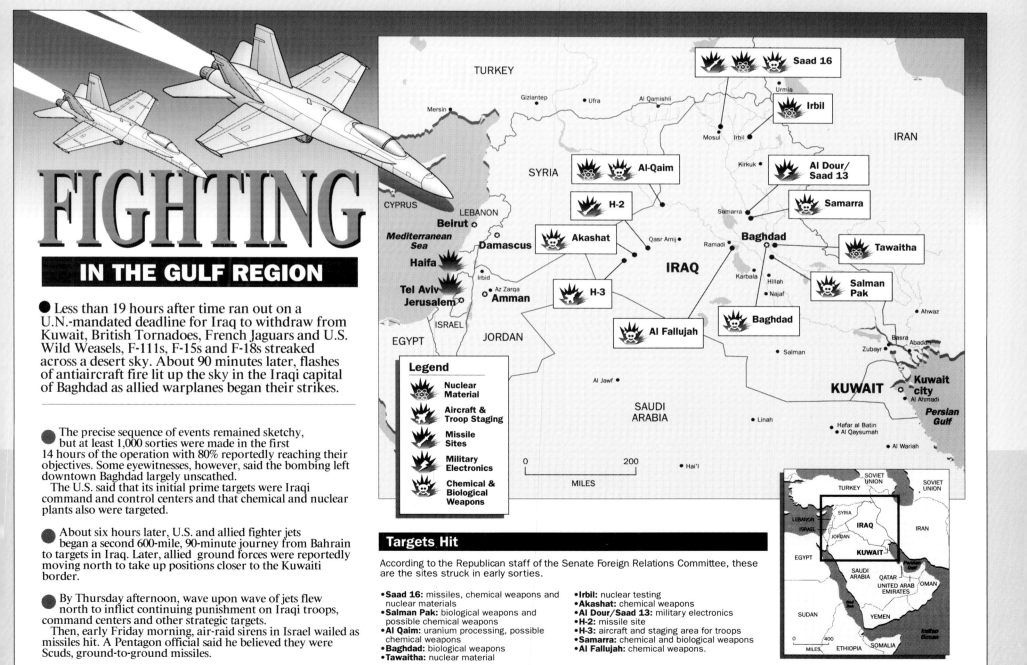

FIGHTING
IN THE GULF REGION

● Less than 19 hours after time ran out on a U.N.-mandated deadline for Iraq to withdraw from Kuwait, British Tornadoes, French Jaguars and U.S. Wild Weasels, F-111s, F-15s and F-18s streaked across a desert sky. About 90 minutes later, flashes of antiaircraft fire lit up the sky in the Iraqi capital of Baghdad as allied warplanes began their strikes.

● The precise sequence of events remained sketchy, but at least 1,000 sorties were made in the first 14 hours of the operation with 80% reportedly reaching their objectives. Some eyewitnesses, however, said the bombing left downtown Baghdad largely unscathed.
The U.S. said that its initial prime targets were Iraqi command and control centers and that chemical and nuclear plants also were targeted.

● About six hours later, U.S. and allied fighter jets began a second 600-mile, 90-minute journey from Bahrain to targets in Iraq. Later, allied ground forces were reportedly moving north to take up positions closer to the Kuwaiti border.

● By Thursday afternoon, wave upon wave of jets flew north to inflict continuing punishment on Iraqi troops, command centers and other strategic targets.
Then, early Friday morning, air-raid sirens in Israel wailed as missiles hit. A Pentagon official said he believed they were Scuds, ground-to-ground missiles.

Source: Associated Press, Senate Foreign Relations Committee

Legend

☢ Nuclear Material
✈ Aircraft & Troop Staging
➤ Missile Sites
⚡ Military Electronics
☣ Chemical & Biological Weapons

TURKEY
Gizianteap • Ufra • Al Qamishli
Mersin •
Mosul • Irbil
SYRIA
CYPRUS
LEBANON
Beirut ○
Mediterranean Sea
Damascus ○
Halfa
Tel Aviv ●
Jerusalem ●
Irbid •
ISRAEL
EGYPT
Az Zarqa •
Amman ○
JORDAN

Saad 16
Irbil
Urmia
IRAN
Al-Qaim
Al Dour/ Saad 13
Kirkuk •
H-2
Samarra
Akashat
Qasr Amij •
Ramadi •
Baghdad
Samarra •
Tawaitha
IRAQ
Karbala •
Hillah •
H-3
Najaf •
Salman Pak
Baghdad
Al Fallujah
Ahwaz •
Al Jawf •
Salman •
Basra •
Abadan
Zubayr •
KUWAIT
Kuwait City
Al Ahmadi •
Persian Gulf
SAUDI ARABIA
Linah •
Hafar al Batin •
Al Qaysumah •
Al Wariah •
0   200
MILES
Hai'l •

Targets Hit

According to the Republican staff of the Senate Foreign Relations Committee, these are the sites struck in early sorties.

•**Saad 16:** missiles, chemical weapons and nuclear materials
•**Salman Pak:** biological weapons and possible chemical weapons
•**Al Qaim:** uranium processing, possible chemical weapons
•**Baghdad:** biological weapons
•**Tawaitha:** nuclear material

•**Irbil:** nuclear testing
•**Akashat:** chemical weapons
•**Al Dour/Saad 13:** military electronics
•**H-2:** missile site
•**H-3:** aircraft and staging area for troops
•**Samarra:** chemical and biological weapons
•**Al Fallujah:** chemical weapons

SOVIET UNION
TURKEY
SYRIA
LEBANON
ISRAEL
JORDAN
IRAQ
KUWAIT
IRAN
EGYPT
SAUDI ARABIA
QATAR
UNITED ARAB EMIRATES
OMAN
SUDAN
YEMEN
ETHIOPIA
SOMALIA
0   400
MILES

DAY 3

JANUARY 19, 1991

The Pentagon summoned us to Andrews Air Force Base, Md., at 4 a.m. for the flight to Saudi Arabia. At the loading area, there was an amazing array of outfits worn by the more than 120 media people, from jeans and jackets to khaki uniforms that would have done any soldier proud. I admit to having made a trip to Banana Republic myself, where the saleswoman told me that the looming war had been a huge boost to business.

Then, Sam Donaldson, the ABC correspondent, made his appearance—in a white stretch limo. An underling dutifully held a flashlight so that Donaldson could read the Washington Post while standing in line to check in.

—J. Michael Kennedy, in Maryland

Los Angeles Times

CIRCULATION: 1,225,189 DAILY / 1,514,096 SUNDAY | SATURDAY, JANUARY 19, 1991 | COPYRIGHT 1991 THE TIMES MIRROR COMPANY CC†† / 112 PAGES | DAILY 25¢ DESIGNATED AREAS HIGHER

More Iraqi Missiles Hit Israel

Allied Jets Pound Targets at Sortie-a-Minute Pace

■ **Gulf war:** President Bush vows to find and destroy mobile Scud launchers terrorizing the Jewish state from desert hiding places.

By CAREY GOLDBERG and KIM MURPHY
TIMES STAFF WRITERS

TEL AVIV—Iraq shot a new round of conventional missiles into Israel early today—the second salvo in as many days—while American and allied warplanes pounded the Iraqis with bombs at the rate of more than a sortie a minute.

The new missile attack rocked Tel Aviv on the Jewish Sabbath with at least two explosions. It put intense pressure on the Israeli government to retaliate against Iraqi President Saddam Hussein and came shortly after President Bush vowed to find and destroy mobile Scud missiles terrorizing Israel from hiding places in the Iraqi desert.

The new missiles fell shortly after 7:20 a.m., moments after air raid sirens sounded a warning. After an all-clear at 8:05 a.m., a temporary Army Information Office in Tel Aviv said there were no immediate reports of serious casualties. Because of the Sabbath, Tel Aviv buildings were virtually empty.

There were no reports of chemical gas. But a plume of smoke could be seen over part of the city. Mayor Shlomo Lahat said two missiles landed in Tel Aviv. He said that there were no deaths but that three persons had been slightly wounded. Asked about structural damage, Lahat replied that it was "not serious."

The new attack, which followed a missile barrage on Friday that hurt a dozen Israelis and caused heavy damage, came as U.S. ground forces in Saudi Arabia moved into potential striking positions against Iraqi troops. The deployment put them in place for an assault as soon as allied commanders decide that Iraqi resistance has been softened sufficiently by air strikes. But it appeared this would take a while.

Such a delay might be necessary because Pentagon officials in Washington said Iraqi air power had not, in fact, been totally crippled by the first two days of allied bombing. These officials said they could confirm that only about 10 Iraqi fighters have been destroyed or damaged—although other aircraft in the 700-plane Iraqi air force may have been hit in their hardened concrete bunkers.

Moreover, about 30 mobile Scud missile launchers survived the initial air attacks. It was those launchers, secreted in the desert, that Iraq used early Friday to strike Tel Aviv, Haifa and other parts of Israel—and may have been used to fire their new attack.

Israel, for its part, did not mount any immediate retaliation—but kept the option open. The United States fears that Israeli involvement in the war could prompt defection by Arab members of the

Please see ISRAEL, A6

COLUMN ONE

Tensions High for U.S. Jews

■ The community has anguished over this war. After the attacks on Israel and with American soldiers at risk, many worry about how others will view their role.

By ALAN C. MILLER
TIMES STAFF WRITER

WASHINGTON—For the past quarter-century, America's Jewish community has been decidedly dovish. By and large, American Jews opposed U.S. military involvement in Southeast Asia and, subsequently, in Central America.

But the Persian Gulf conflict—which has pitted America and its allies against a well-armed expansionist who has been compared to Adolf Hitler and who threatens Israel's survival—has created extraordinary tensions for many American Jews.

Ever since Iraq invaded Kuwait on Aug. 2, the American Jewish community has felt deep anguish. It felt caught in the middle when some critics suggested war could be averted and lives of American soldiers spared if Israel showed more flexibility on Palestinian issues.

And now, in the wake of Iraqi missile attacks on Israel, it feels caught in the middle over another question: Whether Israel should sit still to protect an allied coalition that includes some of its worst enemies, particularly Syria, or retaliate, possibly set off a far wider war and then be viewed as a spoiler of America's carefully crafted strategy against Iraq.

"The Jewish community's being whipsawed just like everybody else," says Joel H. Meyers, executive director of The Rabbinical Assembly, the international association of Conservative rabbis. "Everybody at this moment feels the anxiety of the war."

To be sure, major Jewish organi-

Please see JEWISH, A28

Associated Press

A Tomahawk missile is launched in a burst of light from the battleship Wisconsin in the Persian Gulf early Friday as attack on Iraq continued.

THE TIMES POLL

Americans Back Bush Decision Overwhelmingly

By RONALD BROWNSTEIN
TIMES POLITICAL WRITER

Americans overwhelmingly support President Bush's decision to attack Iraq, a new Los Angeles Times Poll found.

But after the first searing flash of combat, Americans hold high expectations that may create political complications for the President if the war drags on or fails to depose Iraqi leader Saddam Hussein, the poll found. And nearly half of those surveyed are worried that Israel will be drawn into the war and fracture the delicate coalition assembled to confront Hussein.

The poll revealed that Americans hold equivocal views on how Israel should respond to missile attacks from Iraq. Over three-fourths of those surveyed agreed that Israel would be "justified in retaliating" against Iraq; but by more than 2 to 1 they believed Israel should let the United States respond rather than attacking Iraq itself.

Please see POLL, A16

Eastern Airlines Calls It Quits

Eastern Airlines halted operations at 9 p.m. Friday after 62 years in the air. Although it has been in Chapter 11 bankruptcy proceedings, the Miami-based carrier had operated 800 flights daily.

Details in Business

Bush Praises Israelis for Restraint Over Attack

■ **Reaction:** Pentagon officials fear that second Iraqi onslaught may provoke a military response.

By JAMES GERSTENZANG and NORMAN KEMPSTER
TIMES STAFF WRITERS

WASHINGTON—After an intense round of diplomacy to keep Israel out of the Persian Gulf War, President Bush praised Israeli restraint Friday in response to the first Iraqi missile attack and pledged an exhaustive effort to hunt down and destroy Saddam Hussein's missile launchers.

In his first news conference since the war began early Thursday morning, Bush also warned, as he has in other settings, that "there will be losses" in the gulf conflict. "There will be obstacles along the way. War is never cheap or easy," he said.

The Administration appeared to go to great lengths to head off an Israeli military response after Iraq fired eight Scud missiles at Israel with five of them hitting populated areas in the cities of Tel Aviv and Haifa on Friday morning.

The attack "was purely an act of terror—it had absolutely no military significance," Bush said.

"Our defense people are in touch with our commanders to be sure that we are doing the utmost we can to suppress any of these missile sites that might wreak havoc not just on Israel but on other countries that are not involved in this fighting.

"We are going to be redoubling our efforts in the darnedest search-and-destroy effort that's ever been undertaken out in that area," Bush said. "And I hope that that is very reassuring to the citizens of Israel."

The President's remarks reflected the Administration's concern that Israel not take matters into its own hands by retaliating, a step that could prompt some Arab nations to abandon the anti-Iraq coalition rather than fight a war on the same side as Israel.

Pentagon officials have expressed concern that a second round of Iraqi attacks on Israel—which did occur this morning Tel Aviv time—would be certain to invite an Israeli military response.

Bush went to the Pentagon for a military briefing before flying to

Please see AFTERMATH, A26

Hunt for Mobile Launchers Seen as Most Difficult

By DAVID LAUTER and KAREN TUMULTY
TIMES STAFF WRITERS

WASHINGTON—In the skies over Iraq, a deadly chase is being played out, a race pitting America's highest technology—from spy satellites to laser-guided bombs—against Iraqi missile crews desperate to stay alive and protect Saddam Hussein's most fearsome weapon.

At stake are the lives of American troops, the safety of thousands of Israeli civilians and the survival of the fragile but persistent Western-Arab coalition that upholds the current war effort.

The hunt for Iraq's mobile Scud missile launchers—what President Bush on Friday called "the darnedest search-and-destroy effort that's ever been undertaken"—is "as difficult as any military mission there is," said David Ochmanek, a leading U.S. military analyst.

"Suppose you were told to find three dozen trucks somewhere in the state of Wyoming, and the owner of those trucks was determined to hide them. I think that

Please see SCUD, A25

Flying Was Not Just 'Job' to America's First MIA

■ **Military:** Model Navy pilot disappeared in gulf sortie. He grew up in sight of an air base, always hoping to soar.

By PATT MORRISON
TIMES STAFF WRITER

JACKSONVILLE, Fla.—If he stands back a ways from the high fence and looks up through the legs of the longleaf pines, a boy can watch as the narrow, keening jets pull themselves off the Earth and out into the glaze-white sky above the sea.

Scott Speicher was one of the boys who stood and watched and hoped. And Scott Speicher learned the art himself, and in time, pulled his own jet off the wide, hot path to the sky.

This week, on another path into a different sky, Navy Lt. Cmdr. Michael Scott Speicher and his jet vanished in a bright burst. He is believed to be the first American casualty in the war against Iraq.

If someone had to be first, this man, from this place, fits as neatly as the flawless dress uniforms on the Navy people who came Thursday afternoon to Joanne Speicher's front door, where the Christmas poinsettias still blazed in a tub.

In this neighborhood—a raucous ground zero below the flight paths of two air stations—yellow ribbons and tricolor bunting have fluttered and faded from carriage-lamp posts for five months. Here, everyone knows what those dark dress uniforms mean.

Linda Hucks, the nurse coming home from work, saw them and

Please see MIA, A11

MORE WAR COVERAGE

Baghdad's a Ghost Town, Fleeing Journalists Report

■ **Iraq:** In the bomb shelters, the mood among residents changes literally overnight. Some feel betrayed.

By MARK FINEMAN
TIMES STAFF WRITER

AMMAN, Jordan—After nearly 48 relentless hours of surgical cruise missile strikes and bombing runs, Baghdad resembles a ghost town, its inhabitants having fled or in hiding, its sprawling residential districts largely intact but empty.

According to more than a dozen journalists who fled the embattled Iraqi capital and arrived in Jordan by land Friday, the regime of President Saddam Hussein still appears very much in control, despite more than a dozen direct hits on key government installations throughout the city.

The president's main palace was destroyed in a cruise missile attack that Hussein survived, several of the journalists said. The Soviet ambassador to Iraq, Viktor V. Posuvalyuk, said he met with the Iraqi leader in his command bunker Friday.

The journalists, virtually all of them television journalists and the only Western eyewitnesses to leave Baghdad since the war began, confirmed that Hussein's Defense Ministry has been demolished and that the satellite dishes on his main communications tower have been disabled. At least two military airfields in the city were also taken out of operation.

The eyewitness accounts, more than likely the last independent and uncensored descriptions of the

Please see BAGHDAD, A14

MAZ-543 Scud-B Transport

The Soviet-built, 8-wheel transports launched Iraqi Scud-B missiles against Israel and Saudi Arabia. The MAZ-543, is powered by a 525-horsepower engine mounted between twin, two-man cabs. It combines the function of transporter and erector, usually travels with a command-control vehicle and a tanker-pumper unit. It can fuel a Scud with liquid propellent and launch in about an hour.

- Top speed: 45 m.p.h.
- Range: 300 miles
- Max Load: 33,374 pounds
- Length 38 ft.
- Width 10 ft.

Patriot missile, slicing through night, became a familiar Tel Aviv sight.

LARRY DAVIS / Los Angeles Times

Missiles: Three missiles launched from western Iraq hit Tel Aviv in an early morning barrage, injuring as many as 16. Baghdad Radio says Iraq launched 11 missiles "at the enemy."
■ The attack puts intense pressure on the Israeli government to retaliate.
■ President Bush praises Israeli restraint and pledges an exhaustive effort to wipe out Iraq's missile launchers.

Military: Pentagon officials say 10 of an estimated 700 Iraqi warplanes have been destroyed. The rest of Iraq's air force has dispersed to the north or is protected in concrete bunkers.
■ Allied air attacks begin targeting troop formations and equipment in the field.
■ A Pentagon briefer says 2,107 combat missions have been flown and 196 Tomahawk cruise missiles have been fired in 48 hours of war.
■ U.S. losses grow to four warplanes and seven crew members.
■ Heavy cloud cover disrupts daytime bombing of Iraqi targets.
■ U.S. aircraft fly night missions from southern Turkey to bomb targets in northern Iraq. Turkish opposition parties voice fear that raids could bring Turkey into war with Iraq.

Terrorism: Iraq broadcasts a call for terrorism, telling Muslims to attack "interests, facilities, symbols and figures" of the United States, Britain, France, the Netherlands, Saudi Arabia, followers of the emir of Kuwait and their allies.
■ The State Department warns travelers of a " terrorist threat in Thailand.

International: Students hurl rocks through windows at a U.S. Embassy annex in Berlin. Protests draw more than 200,000 Germans into the streets around the country.

Home front: A Los Angeles Times poll shows Americans overwhelmingly support President Bush's decision to attack Iraq.

THE WAR OF
MISSILES

More than 50 types of tactical missiles and precision-guided munitions have been deployed on aircraft, ships and ground units in the Persian Gulf War, providing troops with the mainstay of their firepower so far.

The missiles can cost up to $1.25 million each, but their high cost accompanies the capability to deliver warheads with pinpoint accuracy from long distances.

Although fighter aircraft get greater publicity, it is the missiles that provide their fighting capability. The kinds include:

■ Air to-air missiles: used to shoot down enemy aircraft
■ Ground-to-air: used to shoot down enemy aircraft or enemy missiles
■ Air-to-ground: used to attack tanks, runways or buildings.

The missiles depend on mechanical and electronic guidance systems including: radar, infrared sensors, inertial measuring units, television cameras, terrain following devices.

■ **The Sparrow missile,** a radar guided air-to-air missile, is credited with shooting down an Iraqi aircraft Thursday.
■ **The Tomahawk cruise missile,** a ship-launched missile guided with a combination of inertial and terrain following systems, provided surgical strikes against Iraqi ground targets.
■ **And the Patriot missile,** a ground-launched missile, successfully shot down an incoming ballistic missile Thursday. It was the first time the missile had been fired in combat.

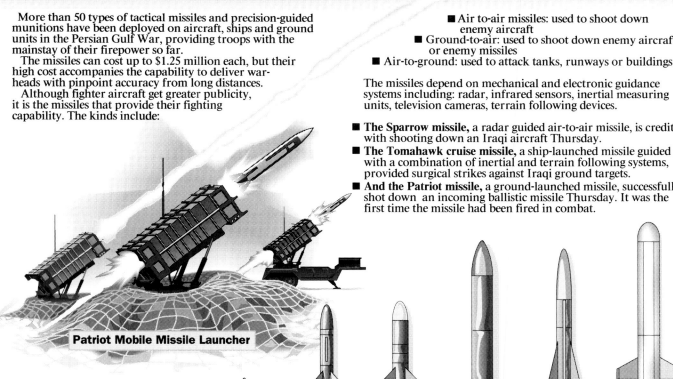

Patriot Mobile Missile Launcher

Six foot tall man to scale

■ HELLFIRE	■ TOW	■ SEAWOLF	■ SEA SPARROW	■ HARPOON	■ PATRIOT	■ I/HAWK	■ TOMAHAWK
Anti-tank	Anti-tank	Shipborne surface-to-air	Shipborne surface-to-air	Air-to-surface	Landmobile surface-to-air	Land mobile surface-to-air	Shipborn Surface-to-surface

Source: U.S. Defense Dept.; Jane's Weapons Systems, Jane's Soviet Intelligence Review.

Iraqi Long-Range Missiles

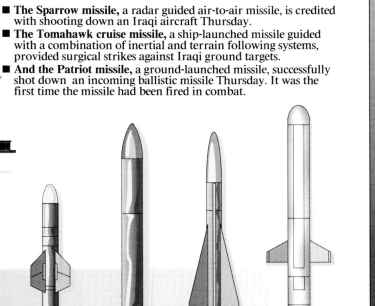

■ SCUD B
Length: 37 feet
Diameter 3 feet
Launch weight: 7 tons
Payload: One 2,172-lb. warhead, conventional or chemical.
Propulsion: Liquid propellant
Accuracy: Within 1,476 feet

■ AL HUSSEIN
Length: 40 feet
Diameter: 3 feet
Launch weight: 7.7 tons
Payload: One 1,102-lb. warhead, conventional or chemical.
Propulsion: Liquid propellant
Accuracy: Within 3,281 feet

ANDERS RAMBERG AND MICHAEL HALL / Los Angeles Times

DAY 4

JANUARY 20, 1991

The huge explosion seemed to detonate right above the car. The sky lit up and the windows rattled. Newsweek photographer Bill Gentile had been here before. He knew what it was immediately. "An Iraqi Scud!" he shouted. "Get to the hotel fast!"

This was my welcome to Dhahran. We had driven 200 miles across the desert from Riyadh and were about three miles from the Dhahran International Hotel when the first Scud exploded. Before we made the hotel parking lot, two more giant explosions had illuminated the night sky.

Driving the rented Toyota up over the curb, I yanked the gas mask from my luggage. Gentile and I joined a crowd of Saudis and journalists streaming into the hotel, down the stairs to the basement. Only an hour later, after huddling in gas masks in this makeshift air raid shelter, did we learn that all three Scuds had been intercepted and destroyed by U.S. Army Patriot missiles.

—Douglas Frantz, in Dhahran, Saudi Arabia

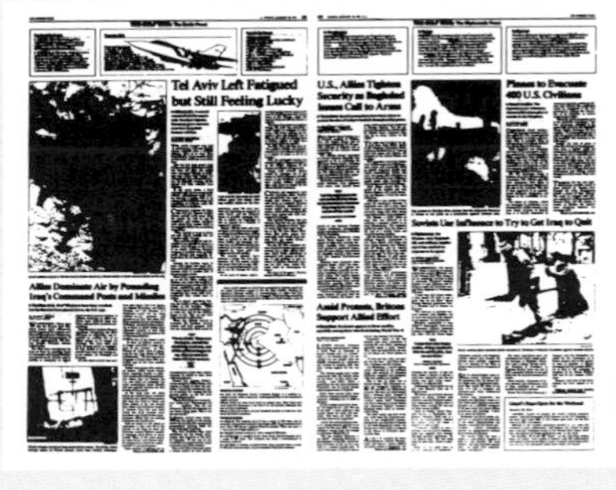

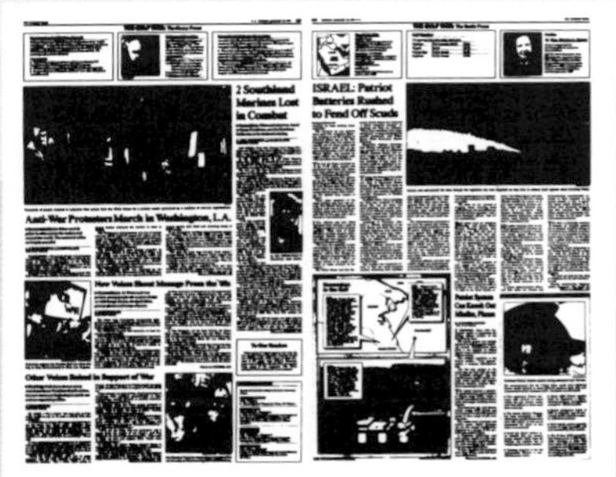

Los Angeles Times

Sunday Final

CIRCULATION: 1,225,189 DAILY / 1,514,096 SUNDAY

SUNDAY, JANUARY 20, 1991

COPYRIGHT 1991 THE TIMES MIRROR COMPANY

CC†/492 PAGES

SUNDAY $1.25 DESIGNATED AREAS HIGHER

U.S. Rushes Defenses to Israel

American Troops to Operate Two Patriot Batteries

■ **Gulf war:** The move may forestall an immediate retaliatory strike by the Jewish state after two attacks on Tel Aviv. Allied warplanes step up the search for Scud mobile launchers.

By MELISSA HEALY and J. MICHAEL KENNEDY
TIMES STAFF WRITERS

WASHINGTON—In an urgent effort to keep Israel from plunging into the Persian Gulf War, the United States on Saturday dispatched American soldiers and two Patriot missile batteries to Israel to stand guard against any new Iraqi missile attacks.

Israeli leaders, reversing their longstanding public insistence on military self-reliance, requested the U.S. assistance after Iraq fired 10 Scud missiles toward Israel in two separate attacks, causing a number of injuries and extensive property damage but no fatalities.

The Bush Administration's decision to provide the advanced surface-to-air missiles and the personnel to operate them appeared to forestall an immediate Israeli retaliatory attack, a development that could splinter the Arab-Western coalition opposing Iraq. It also marked the first time that U.S. combat troops have been assigned to duty in Israel.

The effort to bolster Israel's anti-missile defenses came as U.S. and allied warplanes continued to scour Iraq and Kuwait for elusive Scud mobile missile launchers and escalated their bombardment campaign against Iraqi ground troops and their logistic support sites.

Iraq's elite Republican Guard, considered the most capable of President Saddam Hussein's troops, came under heavy fire in their positions in southern Iraq and northern Kuwait, while U.S. B-52 bombers began attacking Iraqi defenses farther south. Pentagon officials said American and allied pilots had flown 4,700 sorties during the first three days of the conflict. A total of 216 Tomahawk cruise missiles had been fired from U.S. warships at targets in Iraq and Kuwait.

Meanwhile, the first Iraqi prisoners of war were taken by the allied coalition. In a joint operation off the coast of Kuwait, American and Kuwaiti forces captured 12 Iraqi soldiers who had been using oil platforms to fire antiaircraft guns at allied aircraft.

The U.S. frigate Nicholas, in conjunction with a Kuwaiti patrol boat, captured the 12 Iraqis on nine platforms, U.S. officials said. Saudi Arabia, as the host country for the allied forces, is expected to care for all prisoners of war taken in the conflict.

U.S. Marines also engaged in minor skirmishes with Iraqi troops on the Kuwaiti border, prompting air strikes against positions north of the border that reportedly killed at least 40 Iraqis.

Two Marines were also wounded

Please see ISRAEL, A4

First Iraqi Prisoners of War

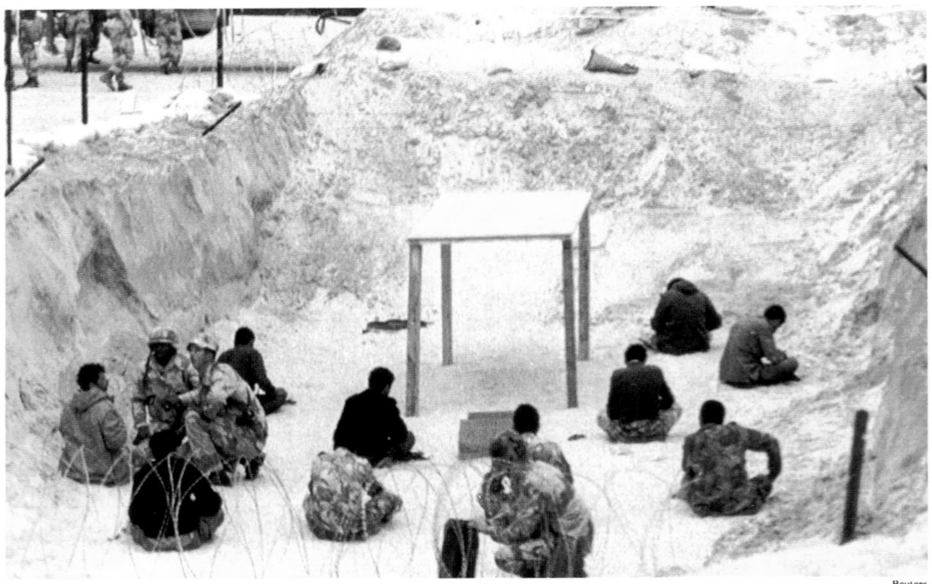

Reuters

Iraqi soldiers seized in attack on oil platforms off Kuwait are inspected by Marines, in helmets and hats, at holding area in Saudi Arabia.

COLUMN ONE

War Affects Ecology—But How?

■ Scenarios range from oil field fires threatening the atmosphere to damage to agriculture and fisheries. Environmentalists are split over whether to oppose the conflict.

By MAURA DOLAN
TIMES ENVIRONMENTAL WRITER

A growing and unprecedented effort is under way to measure the environmental consequences of the Persian Gulf War, spawned in part by the devastation of Vietnam and increased understanding of the global ramifications of pollution.

The scenarios being painted by scientists, oil analysts and environmentalists vary in their extremes. They range from predictions of destructive climate anomalies around much of the world because of smoke pollution to massive oil spills in the gulf's waters.

At the very least, many scientists and environmentalists warn, the conflict threatens the region's fisheries, water supplies and agriculture. Some of the consequences could be felt for years.

"War in the Middle East could result not only in the loss of many thousands of human lives but extend to a scorching of the Earth," Michael S. Clark, president of Friends of the Earth, warned in a letter last month to Secretary of State James A. Baker III.

Some oil industry experts have downplayed the threats, arguing that they are based on worst-case scenarios. Environmental groups have been divided over whether to speak out against the war.

The more dire forecasts stem from fears that the region's oil wells could burn for months at a time if they are ignited. Military experts believe that the Iraqis have wired Kuwait's hundreds of oil wells with explosives. Some oil industry experts concede that

Please see EFFECTS, A7

Experience Varies in 1st District Race

The four major candidates for the 1st District Los Angeles County Board of Supervisors seat bring varied backgrounds in their quest to become the first Latino elected to the powerful body this century.

Details in Metro

Don't Mistreat Prisoners, U.S. Warns Baghdad

By DOYLE McMANUS
TIMES STAFF WRITER

WASHINGTON—The Bush Administration, acting on increasing fears that Iraq may have captured downed U.S. airmen, warned the Baghdad government Saturday that it will be held responsible for treating any prisoners of war humanely.

The United States does not know whether Iraq has captured any of the 16 allied airmen, including nine Americans, listed as missing in action, a senior Administration official said. But he added, "We clearly have that possibility in mind."

Iraq has said that its forces have captured several airmen, but it has provided no clear evidence to support the claim. Two Jordanians who traveled from Iraq to neighboring Jordan on Saturday told the Baltimore Sun that they saw two men identified as American prisoners displayed on Iraqi television Friday evening. However, their report could not be immediately confirmed.

Please see POW, A14

U.S. Jets Now Aiming at Dug-In Iraq Soldiers

■ **Strategy:** After battering the command network, air attacks are to focus on troop concentrations.

By RUDY ABRAMSON and MELISSA HEALY
TIMES STAFF WRITERS

WASHINGTON—It has already become a routine.

Early every morning, the office of Lt. Gen. Charles A. Horner, the U.S. Air Force commander in Saudi Arabia, issues a computerized document half the size of the Orange County phone book. It is by all odds the most compelling reading in the kingdom.

With unerring government instinct for the prosaic, it is entitled the daily ATO, the Air Tasking Order. It's really a hit list, a catalogue, a shoppers guide to Iraqi assets marked for destruction in the following 24 hours.

On the fourth day of the air campaign against Saddam Hussein, Horner's select readers could discern a shift in the ATO plot. More targets now belong to planes such as the A-10 Warthog, a low-flying tank killer with an armored cockpit to protect its pilot from ground fire.

After an opening assault bestowing credibility on the long-maligned term "surgical strike," air raids are about to be turned more heavily on Iraqi troop concentrations, according to military sources. With Saddam Hussein's command and control network evidently in shambles, the killing is about to begin.

The unexpected is to be expected in war, and it can force changes in the best of plans. Thus far, however, in spite of the Scud missile attacks on Israel, the elusiveness of their mobile launchers and the hiding of the Iraqi air force, the war in the desert has been strikingly methodical.

And it has been shaped by one central principle: keeping American casualties to an absolute minimum. The goal of limiting casualties, not a timetable, will now determine how the coming weeks will unfold, sources said Saturday.

"Their air defense system is no longer effective," Lt. Gen. Thomas W. Kelly, director of operations for the Joint Chiefs of Staff Organiza-

Please see STRATEGY, A17

Ground Combat Flares Between U.S. and Iraq

By KIM MURPHY
TIMES STAFF WRITER

DHAHRAN, Saudi Arabia—U.S. forces have engaged in minor skirmishes with Iraqi troops on the Kuwaiti border, prompting air strikes against positions north of the border that reportedly killed at least 40 Iraqis.

Reports from U.S. Marine units deployed near the Saudi-Kuwaiti border city of Khafji indicate Iraq's most sustained counterattack so far. And they indicate movement by the U.S. forces to engage the enemy along the border in possible preparation for a ground assault into Kuwait.

■ **CALIF. MARINES MISSING**
Two from Camp Pendleton are listed as lost in combat. A3

Though apparently very minor, the skirmishes represent the first known ground combat between Iraqi troops and the large coalition of allied forces poised to move into Kuwait.

Commanders in the field said the

Please see COMBAT, A16

Americans Feel the Touch of War Half a World Away

■ **Home front:** Weddings are moved up, there's a run on maps, flags and food, callers clog phone lines.

By LIANNE HART and JUDY PASTERNAK
TIMES STAFF WRITERS

War has lobbed itself into American lives from half a globe away, bollixing up plans and separating lovers and generally keeping everyone on edge. It has turned a quick buck for some and picked the pockets of others.

Suzanne Mackay got married Friday, a long way on the calendar from the fairy-tale wedding she had planned for August. But her fiance was being called up for active duty. "If Brad goes to war, we may never see each other again," she reasoned. And so the wedding was hurriedly moved up.

There was barely time to get a license, reserve a church and invite 40 of their closest relatives and friends. Mackay, a 21-year-old student at the University of Houston, managed the best she could.

On Wednesday, she hastily selected a white, off-the-shoulder wedding dress, hired a photographer, ordered a two-tiered wedding cake and a bouquet of pink and white carnations. By Friday, all the rushing had upset her stomach.

"I am stressing," she said, sitting nervously in a hairdresser's chair, an elaborate Victorian bouffant being shaped out of her long, blonde curls. It was four hours before she exchanged vows. "This has been a pretty rough week," she

Please see TOUCH, A26

MORE WAR COVERAGE

■ **WAR STORIES, PHOTOS: A3-33; B1; D1-6; M1-8**

■ **MORE PROTESTS IN U.S.**
War protesters marched in several anti-war rallies around the nation. In Los Angeles, a crowd estimated between 3,000 and 10,000 rallied in Westwood. **A3**

■ **SUPPORTERS SPEAK OUT**
Some backers of the U.S. military action in the Persian Gulf are growing more vocal in their support, and sales at flag stores have increased. **A3**

■ **ISRAEL'S LUCK HOLDING**
With only 16 light injuries reported after at least three Scud missiles hit Tel Aviv on the Sabbath morning, Israel's good fortune is continuing. **A5**

WEATHER: Patchy morning low clouds near the coast. Civic Center low/high today: 50/67. Details: B2

■ TOP OF THE NEWS ON A2

■ **SOVIETS APPEAL TO IRAQ**
The Soviet Union, in an unusual behind-the-scenes diplomatic role, is trying to persuade Iraqi President Saddam Hussein to end the fighting. **A6**

■ **BRACING FOR TERRORISM**
From the Sphinx in Egypt to a football stadium in Buffalo, N.Y., the United States and its allies prepared for the possible outbreak of terrorist acts. **A6**

■ **ARAB DEMONSTRATIONS**
The split in the Muslim world over the war deepened as tens of thousands of demonstrators took to the streets of their capitals. **A7**

■ **KING HUSSEIN'S CONCERNS**
Jordan's King Hussein called the world's attention to the devastation in Iraq, but said he could not condone or condemn the attacks on Israel. **A13**

Patriot Move Not Likely to Split Fragile Coalition

■ **Missiles:** The Arab world reacts with public alarm, private relief to historic U.S.-Israeli decision.

By ROBIN WRIGHT
TIMES STAFF WRITER

NEWS ANALYSIS

WASHINGTON—The decision to send U.S. crews to Israel with sophisticated Patriot anti-missile batteries, a historic first in the long and deep alliance between the two nations, has elicited public alarm and private relief in the Arab world.

As a result, the deployment—aimed at countering Iraqi missile attacks on Israeli cities—is unlikely to split the fragile 28-nation coalition arrayed against Saddam Hussein in the Persian Gulf.

And that could spell failure for the Iraqi leader's last desperate bid to draw Israel into the gulf crisis and thereby shift its focus from Iraq's seizure of Kuwait to the broader Arab-Israeli conflict—in effect, to achieve with his Scud missiles what he failed to achieve in more than five months of diplomacy.

"Hussein is still fighting to win," said Edward Peck, former U.S. chief of mission in Baghdad. "But the only way he has left to win is to get Israel involved. Otherwise, he's as good as finished."

Arab envoys and U.S. analysts expect Hussein to continue trying to split his foes by using whatever resources he has left to provoke Israeli retaliation. That, as much as

Please see ASSESS, A22

Tornado GR1

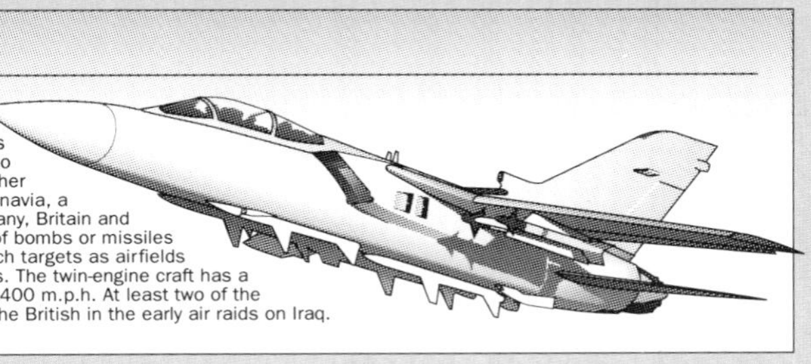

Flown by British forces in the gulf, the Tornado is a two-seat, all-weather interceptor built by Panavia, a joint venture by Germany, Britain and Italy. It carries a mix of bombs or missiles suitable for hitting such targets as airfields and command centers. The twin-engine craft has a maximum speed of 1,400 m.p.h. At least two of the fighters were lost by the British in the early air raids on Iraq.

Patriot crews were first U.S. troops ever deployed in Israel.

Encounters in the Gulf

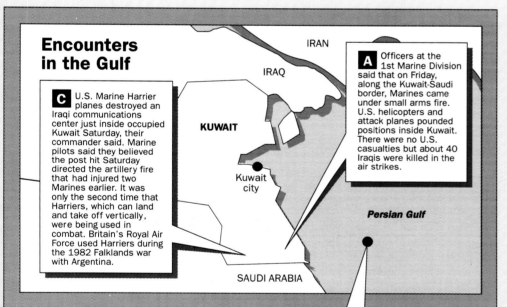

A Officers at the 1st Marine Division said that on Friday, along the Kuwait-Saudi border, Marines came under small arms fire. U.S. helicopters and attack planes pounded positions inside Kuwait. There were no U.S. casualties but about 40 Iraqis were killed in the air strikes.

C U.S. Marine Harrier planes destroyed an Iraqi communications center just inside occupied Kuwait Saturday, their commander said. Marine pilots said they believed the post hit Saturday directed the artillery fire that had injured two Marines earlier. It was only the second time that Harriers, which can land and take off vertically, were being used in combat. Britain's Royal Air Force used Harriers during the 1982 Falklands war with Argentina.

IRAN

IRAQ

KUWAIT

Kuwait city

Persian Gulf

SAUDI ARABIA

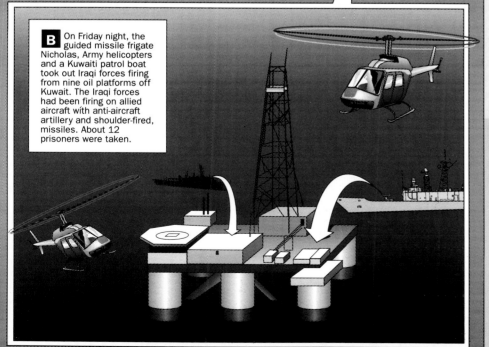

B On Friday night, the guided missile frigate Nicholas, Army helicopters and a Kuwaiti patrol boat took out Iraqi forces firing from nine oil platforms off Kuwait. The Iraqi forces had been firing on allied aircraft with anti-aircraft artillery and shoulder-fired missiles. About 12 prisoners were taken.

Source: International Petroleum Encyclopedia

PATRICIA MITCHELL / Los Angeles Times

DAY IN THE GULF

Missiles: The U.S. government dispatches American soldiers and two Patriot missile batteries to Israel to shoot down Iraqi Scud missiles.

■ The Patriot deployment is greeted by public alarm and private relief in the Arab world; the 28-nation coalition against Iraq is considered unlikely to split apart.

■ Air raid sirens sound again in Jerusalem and Tel Aviv, but they are false alarms.

Military: Pentagon officials say American and allied pilots flew 4,700 sorties during the first three days of conflict. U.S. warships have fired more than 216 Tomahawk cruise missiles.

■ American and Kuwaiti forces take their first Iraqi prisoners in an operation against Iraqi antiaircraft positions on Kuwaiti oil platforms in the Persian Gulf.

■ U.S. forces engage in minor skirmishes with Iraqi troops along the Kuwaiti border.

White House: The Administration warns the Baghdad government that the United States expects "humane treatment" of any prisoners of war.

■ President Bush authorizes the military to call up 170,000 more reservists and National Guard members to serve for one year.

Arab reaction: King Hussein calls the world's attention to the devastation in Iraq and urges a temporary cease-fire.

■ Thousands of demonstrators take to the streets in Arab capitals; Algeria's ruling party calls for an uprising against the United States.

Home front: Anti-war protesters march from the White House through the streets of Washington; estimates of numbers of participants range from 25,000 to 100,000.

■ Small gatherings of war supporters appear spontaneously in some communities as more people begin to speak out against Iraq.

Terrorism: A bomb explodes near a U.S. government library in Manila, injuring two people who may have been carrying it. An Iraqi passport is recovered at the scene.

■ The United States and its allies brace worldwide for possible outbreaks of terrorist attacks.

■ Abul Abbas, leader of the Palestine Liberation Front, calls on his followers over Baghdad Radio to "take up arms" against the United States and its allies.

DAY 5

JANUARY 21, 1991

Just a few days before the war began, I noticed Saddam Hussein's portrait go up in the window of Uncle Sam's Bar and Restaurant. The menu and location seemed to explain the name. The fare: burgers, pizza, hot dogs and the rest. The location: Just 20 yards from the U.S. Embassy in Amman. But why the poster?

"The name? Oh no, that's me. My name's Sam—Samir, actually," said the 80-year-old owner, sitting Sphinx-like, sipping coffee. "The poster? Well, I'm from Palestine, a village near Haifa. I had to leave in '48, like all the others. . . . Never even been to America. Won't go there. Never."

After the bombs and missiles had started raining on Baghdad, Sam was still in his window-front booth. But the name on the marquee was simply, "Bar and Restaurant."

—Mark Fineman,
in Amman, Jordan

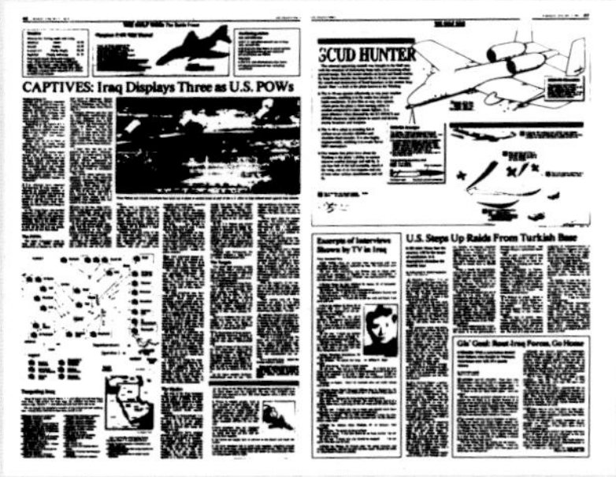

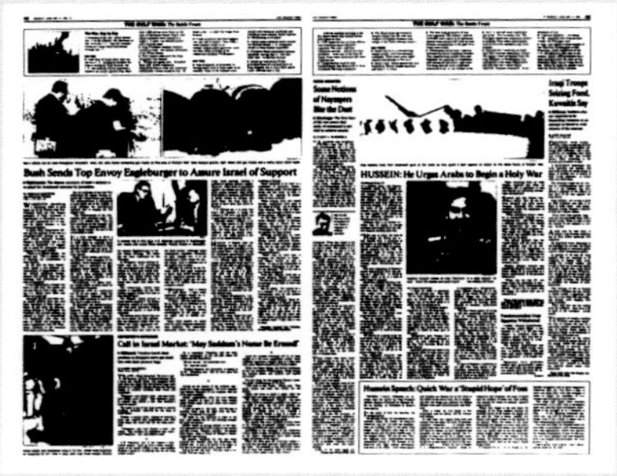

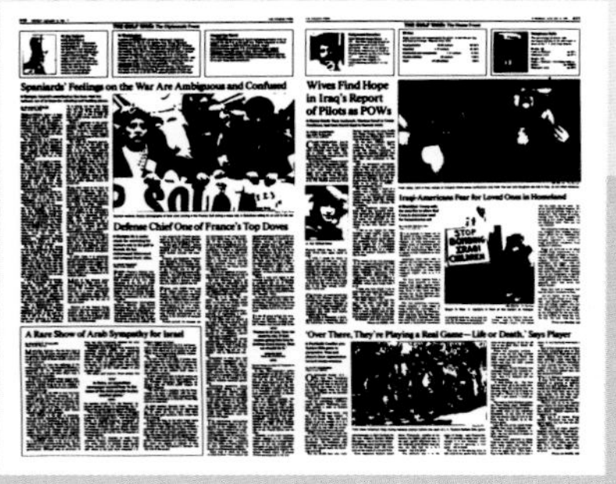

Los Angeles Times

CIRCULATION: 1,225,189 DAILY 1,514,096 SUNDAY | MONDAY, JANUARY 21, 1991 | DAILY 50¢

COPYRIGHT 1991 THE TIMES MIRROR COMPANY CC 102 PAGES
DESIGNATED AREAS HIGHER

Iraq Displays American POWs

9 Scud Missiles Aimed at Saudi Arabia Shot Down

COLUMN ONE

Held in the Grip of the Enemy

■ There are strong suspicions that POWs in Iraq have been abused. Mental health experts also worry about how prisoners may be treated after they come home.

By EDWIN CHEN
and ROBERT W. STEWART
TIMES STAFF WRITERS

WASHINGTON—They spoke haltingly into the Iraqi microphones, obviously under duress. One by one, the seven allied pilots—three of them Americans—uttered the words softly, giving their names and ranks and quietly asserting that the allies had been mistaken in attacking Iraq.

To many, the staged event brought back wrenching memories of the barbaric treatment that other American POWs had received during the Korean and Vietnam wars—paraded blindfolded in public and then beaten into "confessing" their "crimes."

Since the brainwashing fears that surfaced in the Korean War, U.S. service personnel have begun receiving strict do's and don'ts about how to behave as prisoners of war—as well as rigorous training exercises that have sought to simulate captivity under harsh circumstances.

"The training that the military, especially aviation personnel, go through will stand them in good stead," Larry Spencer, a Navy airman held captive for seven years in Vietnam, asserts.

Yet, despite the 1949 Geneva Convention requiring the humane treatment of POWs, experience has shown that POWs—especially in the hands of ruthless dictators—are often subject to enormous and sometimes inhumane pressures, and even torture.

Please see POW, A26

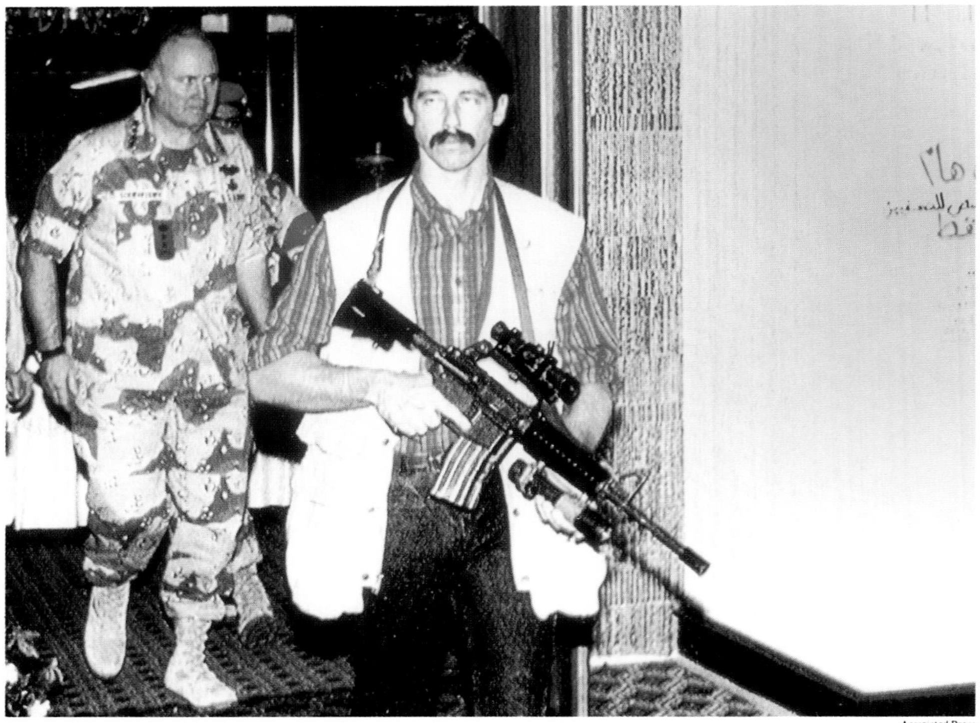

Associated Press

Gen. H. Norman Schwarzkopf, commander of U.S. forces, is escorted as he leaves a hotel in Riyadh, Saudi Arabia, after television interview.

■ **Gulf War:** Three from U.S. are among seven allied fliers shown in Baghdad. Gen. Schwarzkopf says forces may have knocked out Iraqi nuclear capability.

By J. MICHAEL KENNEDY
and DAVID LAUTER
TIMES STAFF WRITERS

RIYADH, Saudi Arabia—Iraqi television, offering the first official reports of American prisoners of war, displayed seven uniformed men Sunday—among them three Americans—whom it identified as captured allied fliers.

Speaking in halting and exhausted tones, the captured men sent messages of reassurance to their families. Several captives also made brief anti-war statements in stilted language that implied that they may have been coerced into reading scripts.

Meanwhile, U.S. Patriot missiles downed nine more Iraqi Scud missiles, including five fired toward the American base at Dhahran, Saudi Arabia, and four aimed at Riyadh, the Saudi capital, the Pentagon announced.

And as the massive allied bombardment of Iraq and occupied Kuwait continued, Gen. H. Norman Schwarzkopf, the commander of U.S. forces, who appeared Sunday in television interviews on each of the major networks, declared that the allied forces may have achieved one prime objective—destroying Iraq's nuclear and chemical warfare programs.

In other developments as the Gulf War moved into its fifth day:

• U.S military officials said that as of Sunday evening, one American flier had been killed and 12 others were considered missing in action in the air war over Iraq and Kuwait.

• Deputy Secretary of State Lawrence S. Eagleburger arrived in Israel for meetings with Israeli officials aimed at reassuring the Israeli government that it can count on continued U.S. support and to plead for continued Israeli restraint in the Gulf conflict.

• Finance ministers and central bankers from the United States and six other leading industrial nations—Britain, Canada, France, Germany, Italy and Japan—met to discuss a U.S. request that the allies contribute more in financial aid for the war effort.

• The Army announced it is calling up about 20,000 members of the Individual Ready Reserve—mostly medical personnel, truck drivers, mechanics, supply specialists and artillery presonnel—to join forces in the gulf. They must report by Jan. 31 for up to one year.

• The Navy made preparations to send a seventh aircraft carrier to the region. The Forrestal, now in Mayport, Fla., will soon be moved to the central Mediterranean. Officials said the ship, with its 80 warplanes, would not initially be involved in attacks against Iraq but

Please see CAPTIVES, A6

Raiders, 49ers Lose Title Games

The Raiders threw six interceptions, five by Jay Schroeder, and lost to the Buffalo Bills, 51-3, in the AFC championship game. The Bills will play the New York Giants, 15-13 winners over the San Francisco 49ers, in Super Bowl XXV in Tampa, Fla., next Sunday.

Details in Sports

Hussein on Air, Whereabouts Aren't Known

By RUDY ABRAMSON
TIMES STAFF WRITER

WASHINGTON—The voice of Saddam Hussein was heard on Iraqi Radio on Sunday for the first time since the deluge of missiles and bombs descended upon his military machine. His whereabouts remain unknown, but U.S. officials suggested that he has taken refuge within the civilian populace.

He called upon Iraqis and their Arab brethren to mount a jihad, or holy war, and promised he will use massive forces that he has held in reserve.

"When the deaths and dead mount on them, the infidels will leave, and the flag of *Allahu akbar* [God is great] will fly over the mother of all battles," Hussein said in the seven-minute message. There was no way to tell whether it was live or recorded earlier.

The rhetoric was more like that of Iran's late Ayatollah Ruhollah Khomeini than the secular leader of a modern army, and Hussein-

Please see HUSSEIN, A9

Scud Attack on Saudis Is Thwarted, U.S. Says

■ **Missiles:** At least 10 are launched at two cities. Reporters spot some damage in Riyadh.

By MELISSA HEALY
and DOUGLAS FRANTZ
TIMES STAFF WRITERS

DHAHRAN, Saudi Arabia—Iraq stepped up its missile attacks Sunday and early today by firing at least 10 Scuds at two Saudi Arabian cities, including the capital of Riyadh. American Patriot air-defense batteries "engaged and destroyed" all missiles threatening the cities, according to a military spokesman.

But reporters challenged the account, obviously surprising the military spokesman by saying they had surveyed damage apparently caused by a missile. Several said they saw the aftermath of an explosion that blew out the backside of a building and created a 10-foot-deep crater in the southeast section of Riyadh.

One thing was clear, however: The hunt for Scud mobile missile launchers was far from over, even though the mission had top priority. The missiles that had terrorized Israel for two nights were now forcing Saudis into shelters and gas masks.

U.S. surveillance satellites and aircraft first detected a launch of three Iraqi Scud missiles from Kuwait about 9:50 p.m. Saudi time, Pentagon officials said.

Patriot air defense radars hunkered into positions near the port city of Dhahran swiveled to pick up the red-hot plumes of the incoming Scuds. Five specially designed Patriot missiles were sent streaking into the night sky to intercept them.

With a series of three bright flashes, a shower of sparks and volley of concussions just seconds later, the engagement was over.

The meeting of high-tech Patriots and low-tech Scuds was another dramatic reminder that even as the Iraqi military is being pum-

Please see SCUD, A16

Baghdad Grits Its Teeth and Runs for Cover

By MARK FINEMAN
TIMES STAFF WRITER

AMMAN, Jordan—When the air raid sirens wail every few hours each day, the shell-shocked residents of Iraq's embattled capital panic and dive into bomb shelters.

"The only real casualties among the civilians so far appear to be their nerves," said one eyewitness who arrived in Jordan from Baghdad on Sunday.

And every night, as allied bombers approach and American cruise missile begin streaking above Baghdad's city streets, surgically searching out their strategic targets, the electricity is cut throughout the city, adding to the isolation of a people living without running water, flushing toilets, telephones or other utilities for the past four days.

"When the raid comes, the Iraqis just turn off the lights and begin blasting away with antiaircraft guns at planes they never see,

Please see BAGHDAD, A12

Soviet Commandos Seize Latvian Interior Ministry

■ **Baltics:** Four die in Riga fighting. Anti-independence 'black beret' troops later leave bullet-scarred building.

By MICHAEL PARKS
TIMES STAFF WRITER

MOSCOW—Soviet commandos shot their way into the headquarters of the Latvian Interior Ministry on Sunday night, seizing the building in a gun battle that raged in central Riga, the Latvian capital, for 90 minutes. Four people were killed and at least nine wounded, according to initial reports.

The 30 "black berets" from the Soviet Interior Ministry's elite special forces apparently met unexpected resistance from the armed headquarters guards and other officers on duty and used stun grenades and then machine-gun fire to capture the five-story building, which they held for five hours.

Red and green tracers shot across the night sky, the explosion of grenades echoed through the capital and several cars, perhaps set on fire as a diversion, burned brightly and filled the air with smoke. Much of the battle was broadcast by Latvian television later in the evening.

The fighting, which began slightly after 9 p.m. local time, spread for a time to the square in front of the Parliament building as other commandos in armored vehicles reportedly opened fire to prevent Latvians from rushing to the Interior Ministry to assist guards.

Latvian authorities said two local policemen and two civilians, one reported to be a local television

Please see LATVIA, A29

MORE WAR COVERAGE

■ **WAR STORIES, PHOTOS: A1-27; B1; D1-3, D5**

■ **HOLY WAR REJECTED**
Saddam Hussein's call for a holy war against the United States and its Arab allies in the Persian Gulf was rejected by powerful Muslim religious leaders. **A5**

■ **MESSAGE FOR ISRAEL**
President Bush has sent Deputy Secretary of State Lawrence S. Eagleburger to Jerusalem to provide new assurances of U.S. support for Israel. **A8**

■ **ARAB MOOD SHIFTS**
For the first time in more than 40 years, the people of Israel are getting a sympathetic hearing in the Arab world in the wake of Iraq's missile attacks. **A10**

WEATHER: Partly cloudy with a chance of showers. Civic Center low/high: 50/63. Details: B2

■ TOP OF THE NEWS ON A2

■ **APPEAL FROM IRAQIS**
A diverse Southland coalition of Iraqi-Americans appealed for a one-day cease-fire to allow the International Red Cross to assess Iraqi civilian casualties. **A11**

■ **THE FOOTBALL FRONT**
To the thousands of fans at the NFL playoffs in Buffalo and San Francisco, the football games took on the mood of a second war front. **A11**

■ **WEEKEND PRAYERS**
The war hovered over services at U.S. churches, synagogues and mosques as congregants sought spiritual help and tried to cope with emotions. **A19**

■ **HIGH-TECH BOOST**
The success of high-tech weapons is likely to prompt Congress to revamp the military budget to put more money toward such weaponry, Democrats said. **A20**

Pool Reporting: There's Good News and Bad News

■ **Media:** A look at the process reveals the difficulty of evaluating dispatches from the battlefield.

By JOHN BALZAR
TIMES STAFF WRITER

DHAHRAN, Saudi Arabia—They number 99, the combat pool reporters who bring to the world the action stories and pictures of American and coalition forces on the battle lines in the Persian Gulf.

About 700 war correspondents and photographers from around the globe have been given credentials by the military's Joint Information Bureau. Most made their way to key Saudi cities before commercial air flights were suspended in the zone of conflict. Another planeload of American correspondents arrived here Friday aboard a Military Airlift Command C-141.

Of those with credentials, only a limited number—99 by one count on Saturday—are actually deployed with coalition combat soldiers, Marines, sailors and fliers. In itself, the number of journalists covering such a big event is small, roughly a third the size of the press contingent at a typical political convention or Summer Olympics.

In the language of news reporters, now becoming familiar to everyday Americans, these men and women serve as "pool" correspondents for all the news agencies covering the war. In this case, it refers to pooled effort and pooled results.

This is the most elaborate and sustained pool effort in modern

Please see PRESS, A23

Phantom F-4G Wild Weasel

A U.S. Air Force version of the oft-modified, Phantom attack plane that has been in use by the Navy and numerous nations around the world for over 20 years. Built by McDonnell Douglas Corp., the Weasel was designed to dart across a front line and knock out defenses. Weasels often hunt in pairs and are equipped with radar-seeking missiles to detect and destroy enemy radar and ground-to-air missile sites.

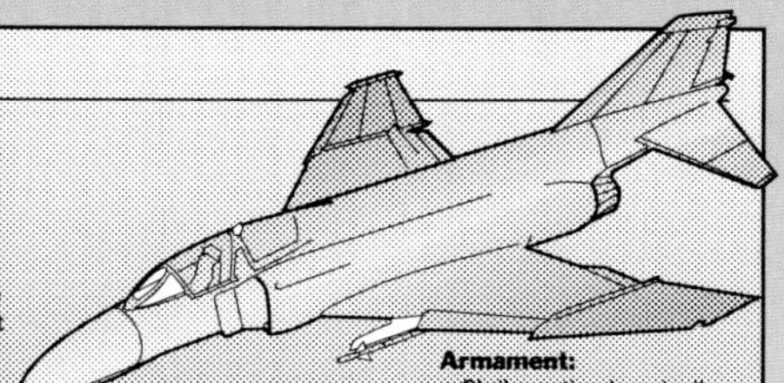

Armament:
• Shrike anti-radar missile
• HARM anti-radar missile

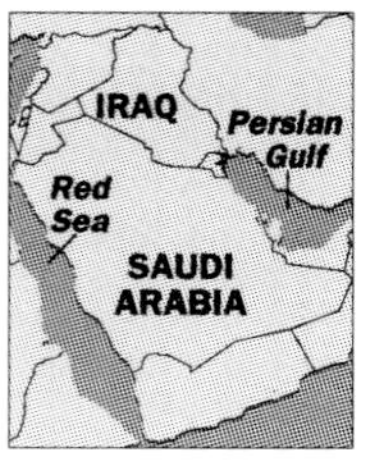

Saudi Arabia

Capital: Riyadh
Area: One-third the size of the U.S.
Topography: The 9,000 foot-tall highlands on the west slope as an arid, barren desert to the gulf.
Population: 16,758,000
Ethnic groups: Arab tribes, emigrants from other Arab and Muslim countries.
Language: Arabic
Religion: 99% Muslim.
Industry: Oil.
Head of State: King Fahd, came to power in June 1982.

Israel's anti-aircraft missiles were ready but never needed.

LARRY DAVIS / Los Angeles Times

DAY IN THE GULF

Prisoners of war: Iraqi television displays seven uniformed men, including three Americans, identified as captured allied fliers. They speak in halting and exhausted tones and use language that suggests they have been coerced.

Missiles: Iraq launches 10 Scuds at Saudi Arabia. Patriot missiles destroy nine, and Pentagon officials say the 10th fell into the Persian Gulf, but journalists report seeing damage in Riyadh.

■ American military crews staff Patriot missile batteries in Israel.

■ Deputy Secretary of State Lawrence S. Eagleburger arrives in Israel to provide assurances of U.S. support for Israeli security.

Military: Gen. H. Norman Schwarzkopf, U.S. commander of allied forces in the Gulf, declares the allied forces may have destroyed Iraq's nuclear and chemical warfare programs.

■ The Pentagon says allied aircraft have flown more than 7,000 combat missions.

■ The allied forces report the loss of 16 planes, including eight American planes shot down and one lost because of mechanical failure; U.S. combat casualties, most of them listed as missing in action, stand at 14.

■ The Army begins activating about 20,000 more reservists.

■ A U.S. Navy submarine fires the first sub-launched cruise missile.

Iraq: The voice of Saddam Hussein is heard on Baghdad Radio urging Arabs to mount a jihad, or holy war. He promises he will use massive forces that he has held in reserve.

■ The call for a holy war is rejected by powerful Muslim religious leaders.

■ Iraqi troops in Kuwait reportedly grow demoralized and experience food shortages.

■ Iraq says it shot down 12 more allied warplanes, raising its claimed toll to 154 planes.

A-10A THUNDERBOLT II

SCUD HUNTER

This unusual appearing aircraft was brought to the Gulf area with the intention of destroying Iraqi tanks and assisting allied ground troops. But the recent attacks on Israel and Saudi Arabia by Iraqi Scud missiles has forced the A-10 into a new mission — the search and destruction of Scud launchers in the remote Iraqi desert. Here's a look at the plane known as the Warthog.

■ The A-10 can operate effectively in very poor weather conditions, enabling it to fly under low clouds in battle conditions. It also flies at very slow speeds, which gives the plane a short turning radius in combat compared to other attack fighters. It is most effective when directed by the E3-AWACS and JSTAR electronic radar planes to search and destroy enemy locations and weapons.

■ The A-10 is adept at avoiding SA-8 surface-to-air missiles (SAMs) and shoulder-fired missiles. It is also highly maneuverable, enabling it to evade Soviet MIG interceptors.

■ One feature that pilots love about the Warthog is the plane's ability to sustain massive combat damage and still fly. It can lose half of the tail assembly, much of the wing, one of its two engines and one of four other surface attachments and still fly.

Wingspan: 57 ft. 6 in.
Length: 53 ft. 4 in.
Max speed: 423 mph

AGM-65 Maverick

This precision air-to-surface guided missile has a range of 25 miles, giving the pilot much greater standoff distances. It can be fitted with a camera, laser or infrared guidance system.

GAU-8A Avenger

This 30-mm, 7-barrel revolving cannon is so accurate that even when fired from 4,000 ft., over 80% of the rounds fired will hit within 20 feet.

■ Its armor-piercing shells are made of depleted uranium, which is extremely hard and slices through even the heaviest tank armor. Upon impact, the force of each shell has the energy to lift a 30-ton tank one foot in the air.

■ The depleted uranium ignites, sending a jet of flame into the tank.

Armor-piercing incendiary shell
Length: 11.4 inches
Weight: 2.05 pounds

Steel windscreen

Aluminum case   Depleted uranium penetrator

HOW THE SYSTEM WORKS

1 A Boeing 707 outfitted with JSTART radar detects motion or radar emissions from Scud missiles as they prepare for launch and radios location to the A-10.

3 Pilot ascends and fires a Maverick missile or a burst from the 30-mm cannon at the Scud missile.

5 The A-10 returns and fires at a second target and flies away.

2 The A-10 flies low toward targets — below 100 ft. — to avoid radar detection.

4 Makes a 2,700-foot-radius turn — tighter than a pursuing aircraft could make — flying close to the ground towards its next target.

JUAN THOMASSIE, SANDY KAY AND ANDERS RAMBERG / Los Angeles Times

DAY 6

JANUARY 22, 1991

Mary Hunter opened her front door at 3:45 p.m. and found three somber-faced Marine officers standing there. Her husband, Chief Warrant Officer Guy L. Hunter, was missing in action, they told her.

I spoke with Mary Hunter while her grief was still raw. She sobbed and sobbed.

"I don't want to think about him being tortured; I don't want him to die a slow death. I just want to wake up and it would be a bad dream," she said through her tears. "Tell me he's OK. Just tell me he's all right."

And I couldn't.

—Nora Zamichow,
in San Diego County

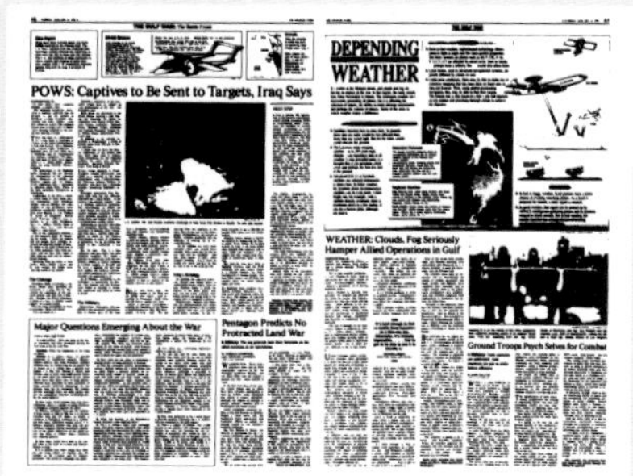

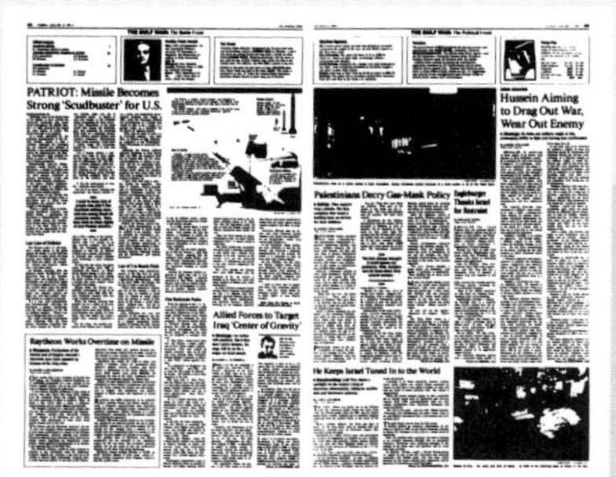

Los Angeles Times

CIRCULATION: 1,225,189 DAILY 1,514,096 SUNDAY | TUESDAY, JANUARY 22, 1991 | DAILY 25¢ DESIGNATED AREAS HIGHER

COPYRIGHT 1991 THE TIMES MIRROR COMPANY CC 110 PAGES

POWs to Be Shields, Iraq Says

Placing Them at Targets Is War Crime, U.S. Charges

COLUMN ONE

High-Tech Missile Hits Bull's-Eye

■ After 25 years and $5 billion, the Patriot, first designed to destroy aircraft, is an overnight success as the 'Scudbuster' of the Persian Gulf War.

By MELISSA HEALY
TIMES STAFF WRITER

WASHINGTON—For five months, the 360 men and women of Lt. Col. Lee Neel's Patriot air defense battalion swaddled their electronic equipment in damp face-cloths to keep it cool, cleaned sand and dust from its air filters with cotton swabs and stared into the cathode rays of its radar screens for signs of an Iraqi air attack that seemed as if it would never come.

But just before 3 a.m. last Friday, a single winking "track" on the Patriot's radar display announced that months of tedium—and two years of training—had come to an end. As an Iraqi Scud missile sped toward the Saudi Arabian port city of Dhahran, Neel's Patriot operators, overcoming an agonizing moment of terror, executed a well-rehearsed, split-second response, and the Patriot—a system that cost almost $5 billion and took 25 years to develop—did the rest.

Seconds later, a 17-foot Patriot missile sped 17,000 feet into the sky, caught the Scud as it arced its way earthward and, in a shower of sparks, detonated on impact.

The age of "Star Wars" had arrived.

The Patriot missile, which started life in the dowdy world of air-defense artillery—weapons that shoot down aircraft—has suddenly turned into the Pentagon's hottest commodity and promises to become one of America's premier exports after the war in the gulf has spent its fury. It is the U.S. arsenal's silver bullet against what so far has been Iraq's most feared weapon—the inaccurate and unpredictable Scud missile, 22 of which have so far been hurled toward Saudi Arabia and Israel.

Please see PATRIOT, A8

Yeltsin Says He'll Side With Baltics

Russian President Boris N. Yeltsin, siding with the rebellious Baltic republics, pledged that he would use the power and resources of the Soviet Union's largest republic to prevent the country from returning to its totalitarian system. A4

Grim Display in Baghdad

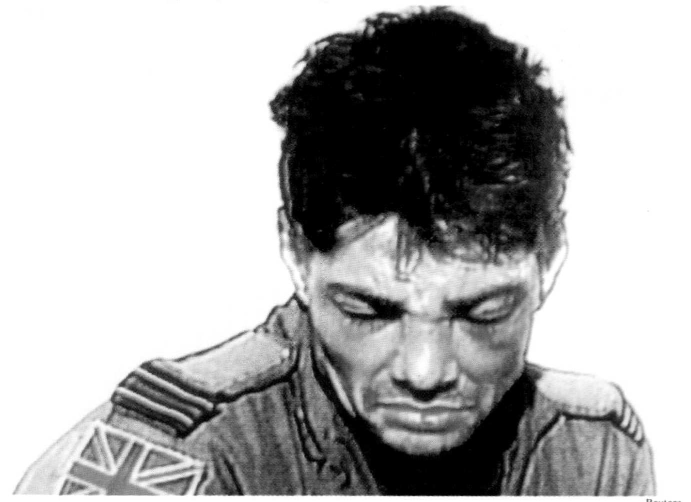

Reuters

Flight Lt. John Peters: British pilot flew a Tornado GR1 jet. Navigator Adrian Nichol is also held.

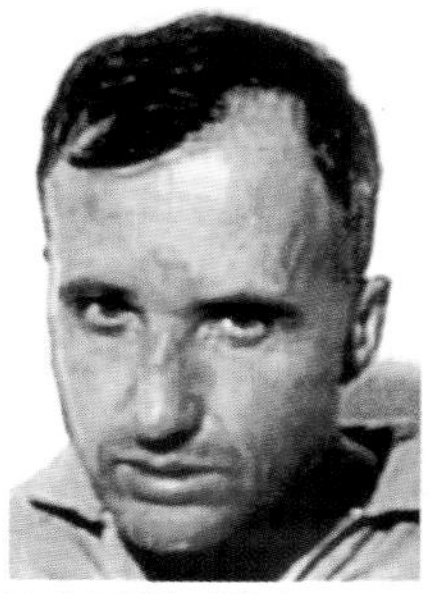

Lt. Col. Clifford M. Acree: Marine flew reconnaissance.

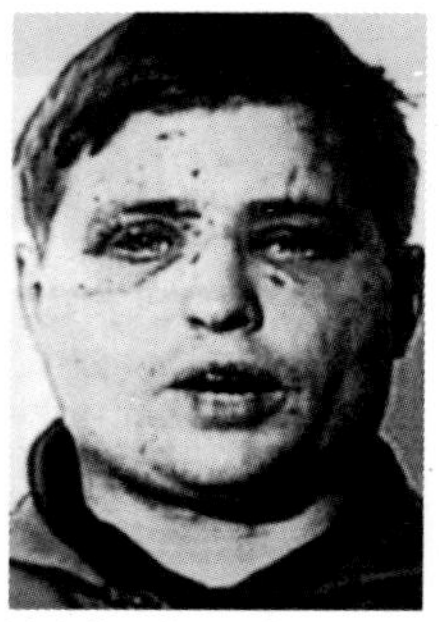

Lt. Jeffrey Norton Zaun: Navy pilot flew A-6E Intruder.

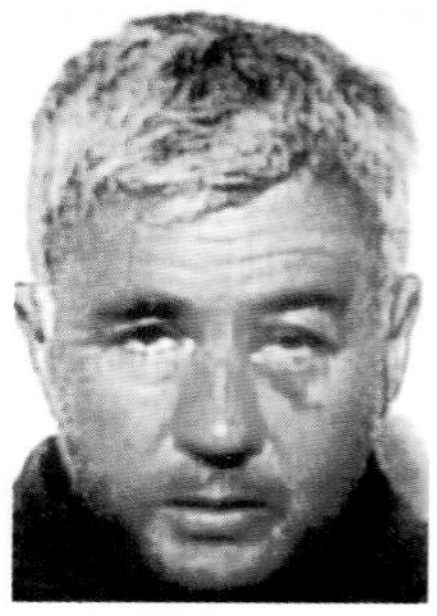

Warrant Officer Guy Hunter: Marine flew Bronco spotter.

■ **Gulf conflict:** Bush says America is angry and that he will press the offensive. Weather hampers air raids. The Pentagon says a 'protracted ground war' is unlikely.

By MARK FINEMAN and JAMES GERSTENZANG, TIMES STAFF WRITERS

AMMAN, Jordan—Iraq announced Monday that it will use its captured American and allied airmen as human shields against the relentless air attack on Iraqi targets, prompting U.S. officials to accuse Saddam Hussein of committing war crimes.

"America is angry about this," said President Bush, who vowed that the threat will not prompt him to relax the U.S. offensive.

The world got its first glimpses Monday of Iraqi Television videotapes showing cut, bruised and dazed allied pilots condemning the allied assault on Iraq and Kuwait.

Meanwhile, one downed Navy pilot stranded in the desert, apparently since Friday, was saved in a daring rescue Monday. An Air Force search-and-rescue team made a dash over the Iraqi border to pick up the A-6 Intruder pilot.

As the Persian Gulf war entered its sixth day, there were these other developments:

- The Pentagon said that a "protracted ground war" lasting months or years "can be avoided." But Defense Secretary Dick Cheney said the conflict could last for "months."
- Iraq said allied aircraft raided Baghdad three times and bombarded other cities, including Tikrit, President Hussein's hometown.
- Iraq launched two Scud missiles toward Saudi Arabia in the last 24 hours—a significant reduction from the barrage of the previous day. The Pentagon said one missile fell harmlessly into the Persian Gulf north of Dhahran. A second attack was reported early this morning but was apparently intercepted by a Patriot anti-missile missile as it neared the capital city of Riyadh.
- The Pentagon said the number of sorties flown over Iraq and Kuwait by allied forces had climbed to 8,100.
- Allied commanders said that the Iraqis had been setting up cardboard and plywood decoys of mobile Scud missile launchers, complicating the task of eliminating the Scud threat. "They do use decoys and they use them well," said Lt. Gen. Thomas W. Kelly, director of operations for the Joint Chiefs of Staff.

The Baghdad announcement that captives would be moved to strategic sites as protection against allied bombing made it clear that Iraq was resurrecting its nightmarish human shield policy from the early period of the Persian Gulf crisis. There was an immediate storm of international protest.

The Outrage

President Bush, returning to the White House after spending the weekend at Camp David, Md., said that Saddam Hussein's treatment of the prisoners would have no impact on "the prosecution of the war."

"If he thought this brutal treatment of pilots is a way to muster world support, he is dead wrong," the President said.

Will Hussein be held accountable?

Please see POWS, A6

Daring Raid Rescues U.S. Pilot in Iraq

By KIM MURPHY
TIMES STAFF WRITER

DHAHRAN, Saudi Arabia—Two U.S. Air Force pilots Monday launched a daring, eight-hour mission into Iraq, locating a downed Navy pilot in the desert and directing his successful rescue, military authorities said.

The operation, conducted as the drawn, frightened images of captured U.S. pilots in Iraq flickered on television sets all over the world, began about 8 a.m. and concluded when the pilot was found at midafternoon in a featureless stretch of the Iraqi desert.

A helicopter swept down to pick up the pilot, who

Please see RAID, A14

Clouds and Fog Curtail Allied Air Operations

By DAVID LAMB
and ALAN C. MILLER
TIMES STAFF WRITERS

EASTERN SAUDI ARABIA—An Air Force squadron sent to attack Iraq's Republican Guard over the weekend returned to its base with a full payload of bombs because heavy clouds had rendered its target invisible.

Intelligence officers say the intensive hunt for Iraqi President Saddam Hussein's mobile Scud launchers has been hampered by fog, which makes it harder for American pilots to spot the truck-mounted launchers as they scuttle away after firing.

And, said Maj. Tim Rush, an F-16A pilot from Columbia, S.C., "We haven't taken out [Iraq's air defense systems] yet due to the weather. I think personally it will take days to weeks."

Weather—chiefly in the form of clouds and fog—has suddenly become a significant nemesis in the 5-day-old U.S. and allied war against Iraq. Clouds and fog over Iraq, not unusual during the desert winter, are hampering efforts to

Please see WEATHER, A7

Israel Lacked U.S. Codes to Protect Its Jets

By RONALD J. OSTROW
and ROBIN WRIGHT
TIMES STAFF WRITERS

WASHINGTON—When Iraq fired its first Scud missiles into Tel Aviv, Israel faced a major obstacle to mounting a retaliatory strike because the United States did not provide electronic identification codes that would have prevented accidental attacks on its jets by U.S. and allied planes, government sources said Monday.

As a precaution before war began, Israel had put pilots in the cockpits of warplanes around the clock so that protection or retaliation missions could be launched instantaneously if the nation were attacked.

However, when the attack came Thursday, the lack of the appropriate "IFF" (Identification Friend or Foe) codes meant that Israeli aircraft could have been mistaken for enemy fighters had they entered Iraqi airspace.

The withholding of the codes indicates that the Bush Administration may have used more than pleas and promises of additional defense equipment to persuade the Israelis not to strike back and risk damaging the gulf coalition.

The United States is continuing to withhold the codes, but it did agree to clear an air corridor for a possible raid if future missile attacks were to cause serious casualties or deaths. It is not clear what the threshold is, or who would determine it.

The arrangement for allowing a possible Israeli aerial mission into Iraq was made only Friday after a longtime Israeli supporter in the United States complained to Sen. Arlen Specter (R-Pa.). Specter in turn contacted the White House, according to sources familiar with the "understanding."

Israel has been praised for its restraint in past days. It is unclear how many factors besides the lack of IFF codes may have influenced its government's decision not to retaliate immediately.

White House Press Secretary

Please see CODES, A15

Skills of Coalition Fliers Give Air Campaign a Lift

■ **Military:** Americans get most of the publicity, but other pilots are busy proving their mettle.

By KIM MURPHY
TIMES STAFF WRITER

DHAHRAN, Saudi Arabia—As the sun climbed over Kuwait in the early hours of last Thursday, Cmdr. Youssef could see a dull glint to the northeast, near the horizon. It was Kuwait city, catching the morning light. For the first time in more than five months, he was seeing home.

For the Kuwaiti pilots who flew their A-4 Skyhawks toward Kuwait city that morning, the dawning of war has brought both the joy of once again flying over Kuwait and a new kind of pain: part of their mission would be to destroy their own airfields.

"There is a lot of emotion going on, especially that first day," said Youssef, who, like most Kuwaiti military officers, asked that his last name be withheld. "When we have to drop bombs on our own fields, we feel frustrated. But we have to take the dirt out of it, anyway. It's a cancer. We need to take it out."

Kuwait's tiny air force, equipped with the 20 A-4s that pilots managed to rush out of the country in the face of the Iraqi invasion, has flown an average of 24 combat sorties a day. It is part of a coalition of forces from Britain, France, Canada, Italy and Saudi Arabia whose exploits have not been widely documented on international television but who nonetheless make up a significant part of the

Please see ALLIES, A13

MORE WAR COVERAGE

■ **WAR STORIES: A5-27; B3; C2, C4; D1, D4-6; E1; F1-2, F-10; H1-5, H-8**

■ **PENTAGON OUTLOOK**
The Pentagon predicted that there will be no protracted ground war in the gulf. The Iraqi army seems immobilized, U.S. military briefers said. **A6**

■ **PALESTINIAN STAND**
Palestinians in Israeli-occupied territories support Iraq's missile attacks on Israel but complain that gas-mask distribution is slow and excludes children. **A9**

■ **TERRORISM WATCH**
Governments worldwide expelled Iraqi diplomats and others suspected of terrorism. In California, two men were arrested in bomb threats. **A10**

WEATHER: Partly cloudy with a chance of showers. Civic Center low/high today: 54/68. Details: C7

■ **'SANCTUARY' REACTS**
A City Council vote making Arcata a sanctuary for deserters and others against the war set off a social convulsion in the northern California city. **A11**

■ **LONG WAR PREDICTED**
Despite the success of the high-tech air war, a long and bloody ground war appears inevitable, leading analysts in this country agree. **A20**

■ **TOLL ON BUSINESS**
The Gulf War has hurt some airlines, darkened auto makers' short-term prospects and added uncertainty to business and consumer spending plans. **D1**

■ **CAN COALITION HOLD?**
If history's lessons hold true, Gulf War alliances could fall apart once the shooting stops and the postwar diplomacy begins, World Report finds. **H1**

U.S. May Add Removal of Hussein to Its War Goals

■ **Policy:** Until now, this has not been a primary aim. But anger over treatment of POWs could change that.

By DOYLE McMANUS
TIMES STAFF WRITER

WASHINGTON—Saddam Hussein's decision to use prisoners of war as human shields, coming on the heels of other actions that U.S. officials see as the equivalent of Nuremberg war crimes, has intensified discussion within the Bush Administration over whether U.S. war aims should expand to include removing the Iraqi leader from power, officials said Monday.

Officially, the Administration says it will still deal with Hussein as a chief of state if he complies with United Nations resolutions and withdraws his army from Kuwait. But President Bush has already gone beyond that original, narrow goal by ordering U.S. warplanes to attack Iraq's nuclear and chemical weapons facilities.

Now, after terror attacks by Iraqi Scud missiles and Baghdad's announcement that allied prisoners of war are being held at military targets inside Iraq as human shields, the grim logic of events is pushing the Administration toward toughening its terms still further.

"America is angry, and I think the rest of the world [is also]," Bush said. Asked whether he would hold Hussein personally accountable for the fate of American prisoners, Bush replied: "You can count on it."

Defense Secretary Dick Cheney added that Iraq's actions constitute

Please see POLICY, A18

OV-10 Bronco

Used primarily as a armed reconnaissance plane for for pinpointing targets for long-range artillery and naval guns. The Bronco can also be employed for low-level photography or as an escort for helicopters over enemy territory. There are about eight in the Gulf with half from Camp Pendleton. Two Bronco crew members are among the American POWs being held in Iraq. They are Marine Chief Warrant Officer Guy L. Hunter, 46 and Lt. Col. Clifford M. Acree, 39.

- **Crew:** Two
- **Power plant:** Two 715 hp turboprops.
- **Performance:** Max. speed 280 mph at sea level, operational ceiling 26,000 ft., flight time 3.85 hrs.
- **Load:** Four .303 inch machine guns, plus up to 3,200 lb. of ordnance/fuel and/or sensors.

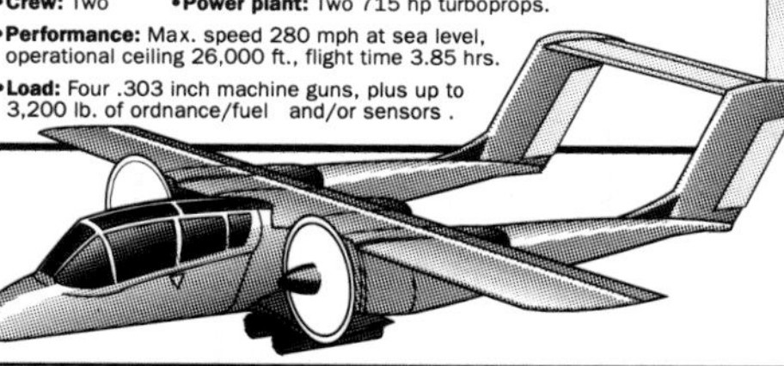

Los Angeles Times

PATRIOT: KEY SCUD DEFENSE

The Patriot, a mobile missile system, was designed to defend U.S. ground forces from air attacks. The Patriots have successfully downed at least nine Iraqi Scud missiles fired at Saudi Arabia.

The Patriot missile, first used in combat in the current crisis, is one of the world's only workable defenses against surface-to-surface guided weapons.

Patriot missile
Missile length: 18 feet
Missile diameter: 16 inches
Range: About 50 miles
Speed: 2,900 m.p.h.
Payload: High-explosive fragmentation warhead

MAN TO SCALE
PATRIOT
SCUD

Ground Radar

How it works:

Typically, a single missile battery has between 4 and 8 launchers and a command station. The command station also monitors the radar, which tracks missiles and planes in the area and calculates missile trajectories. The Patriot uses radar signals transmitted from the ground unit to seek out and destroy missiles and aircraft.

Launchers carry four guided missiles that intercept their targets at high and low altitudes. Missiles are powered by a single-stage solid propellant rocket engine and carry conventional warheads.

Command station:
A truck in a remote area contains display screens and controls. Missiles can be fired by an operator or by computer.

Mobile Patriot Launcher

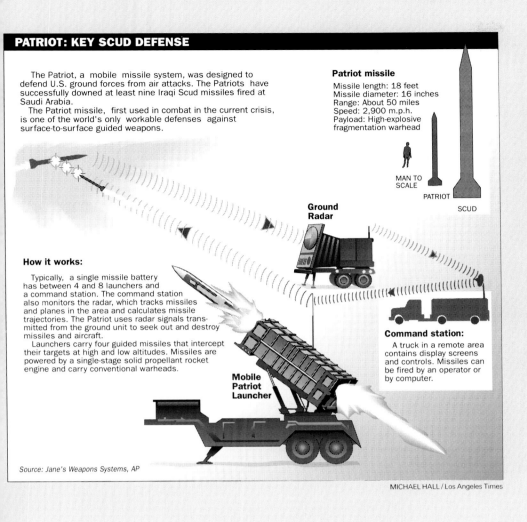

Source: Jane's Weapons Systems, AP

MICHAEL HALL / Los Angeles Times

Prisoners of war: Iraq announces it will use more than 20 allied POWs as human shields at "civilian, economic, education and other targets."
■ Iraqi television shows videotape of cut, bruised and dazed allied pilots condemning the allied air bombardment.
■ President Bush says Saddam Hussein is "dead wrong" if he thinks brutal treatment of pilots will muster world support.
■ World leaders condemn Hussein's use of the captured pilots as human shields and propaganda tools; Britain demands that Baghdad observe the Geneva Convention regarding treatment of prisoners.

Missiles: Iraq launches at least two Scud missiles toward Riyadh. One is downed by a Patriot missile and falls into a street; one or two others fall in the desert.
■ Government sources say Israel has been unable to retaliate against Scud attacks because the United States would not provide electronic identification codes that would have prevented accidental attacks by U.S. and allied planes.
■ Allied warplanes are "nowhere near" eliminating all Iraqi missile launchers, a military official says.

Military: The Pentagon says bad weather and wooden decoy missile launchers hamper its air war over Iraq, leaving U.S. military commanders in doubt about how the bombing campaign is faring.
■ Iraq says allied aircraft raided Baghdad three times in 24 hours and bombarded other cities, including Tikrit, President Hussein's hometown.
■ About 8,100 sorties have been flow, briefers say.
■ The Pentagon predicts the allied effort will not require a ground war that "takes weeks or months."

Terrorism: Governments around the world begin expelling Iraqi diplomats and other foreign nationals suspected of terrorism.

DEPENDING ON THE WEATHER

It's winter in the Mideast desert, and clouds and fog are having an impact on the war. In this region, the rainy season lasts from November to March. The inclement weather isn't necessarily grounding all planes, but it is affecting the selection of targets, the ability to make damage assessments and perhaps the volume of attacks. Some of the areas in which weather makes a difference:

SATELLITES AND RADAR

■ Satellites function best in clear skies. In general, those that use radar would be less affected than those that use visual light. But for the latter, clouds could obscure the ground.

■ The Lacrosse radar-imaging satellite—at its 495-mile-high altitude—can reproduce data in all weather. Using powerful radar, it is thought that it can penetrate cloud cover and perhaps the first few feet of the ground.

■ Advanced KH-11 or Keyhole satellites use infrared instruments to detect heat. In better weather, the Keyhole photo reconnaissance satellites can do even more. Under bright sun, for example, with a satellite directly overhead, there is resolution down to a few inches. It can see a license plate, although not read it.

PLANES

■ Even in bad weather, sophisticated technology allows pilots to fight at night and fire laser-guided projectiles. But those systems on planes such as the F-15E, F-16, F-111, F-117 are affected by cloud cover. Soot or smoke — perhaps from a refinery fire — would also affect them.

■ Laser beams, used in advanced navigational systems, are greatly diffused by clouds or soot.

■ Under poor conditions, fliers may be able to make use of extensive mapping that has been done on fixed sites in Iraq and Kuwait. Then, using global-positioning navigation, they may be able to find their targets. The bottom line is that much of a flier's job still depends on eye contact and punching through clouds to achieve the objective.

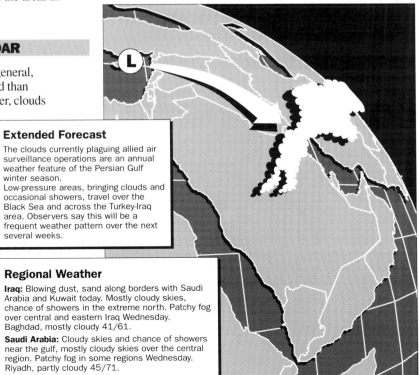

Extended Forecast
The clouds currently plaguing allied air surveillance operations are an annual weather feature of the Persian Gulf winter season.
Low-pressure areas, bringing clouds and occasional showers, travel over the Black Sea and across the Turkey-Iraq area. Observers say this will be a frequent weather pattern over the next several weeks.

Regional Weather
Iraq: Blowing dust, sand along borders with Saudi Arabia and Kuwait today. Mostly cloudy skies, chance of showers in the extreme north. Patchy fog over central and eastern Iraq Wednesday. Baghdad, mostly cloudy 41/61.
Saudi Arabia: Cloudy skies and chance of showers near the gulf, mostly cloudy skies over the central region. Patchy fog in some regions Wednesday. Riyadh, partly cloudy 45/71.

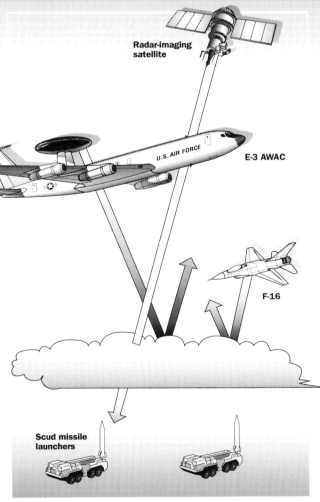

Radar-imaging satellite

U.S. AIR FORCE   E-3 AWAC

F-16

Scud missile launchers

MISSILES

■ In bad or foggy weather, Scud gunners have a better chance of evading searching planes. As a Scud is prepared for launch, a radar signal is emitted.

■ In good weather, that signal can be picked up by AWACS intelligence-gathering planes and its location relayed to attack aircraft. But in bad weather, the missile launcher has a better chance of evading attackers by moving after firing.

JUAN THOMASSIE AND ANDERS RAMBERG / Los Angeles Times

DAY 7

JANUARY 23, 1991

Despite all the criticism of Cable News Network's Peter Arnett for staying in Baghdad and acquiescing to Iraqi censorship, a senior Pentagon official later told me that the Pentagon found his broadcasts an invaluable source of information about the war.

"We loved that stuff. He told us things we could get no other way," the official said.

But the Bush Administration encouraged in the media the idea that it was angry about Arnett carrying Saddam Hussein's messages to the United States precisely so that Baghdad would continue allowing Arnett to broadcast.

—Thomas Rosenstiel, in Washington

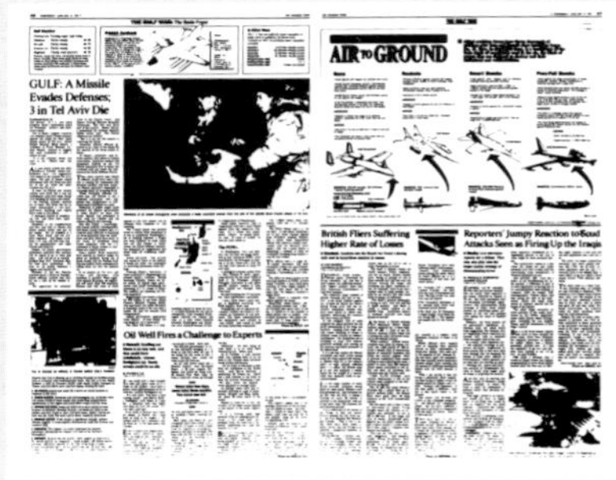

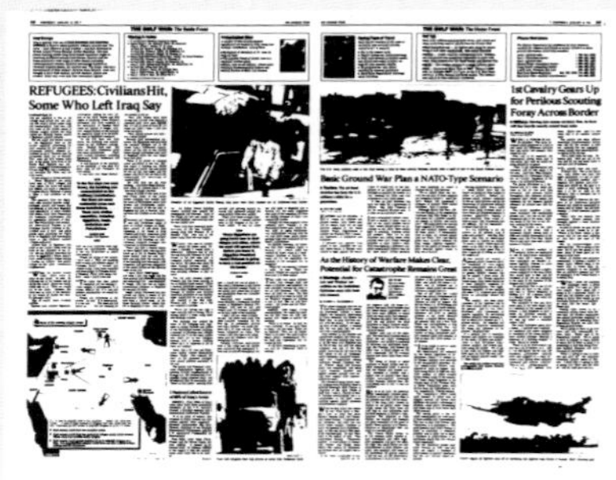

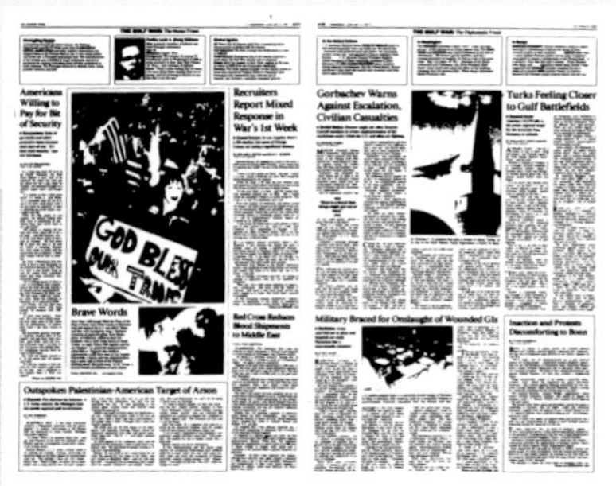

Los Angeles Times

CIRCULATION: 1,225,189 DAILY / 1,514,096 SUNDAY | WEDNESDAY, JANUARY 23, 1991 | COPYRIGHT 1991 THE TIMES MIRROR COMPANY CC† 86 PAGES | DAILY 25¢ DESIGNATED AREAS HIGHER

Missile Strikes Tel Aviv; 3 Die

96 Hurt as Scud Devastates Apartment House Area

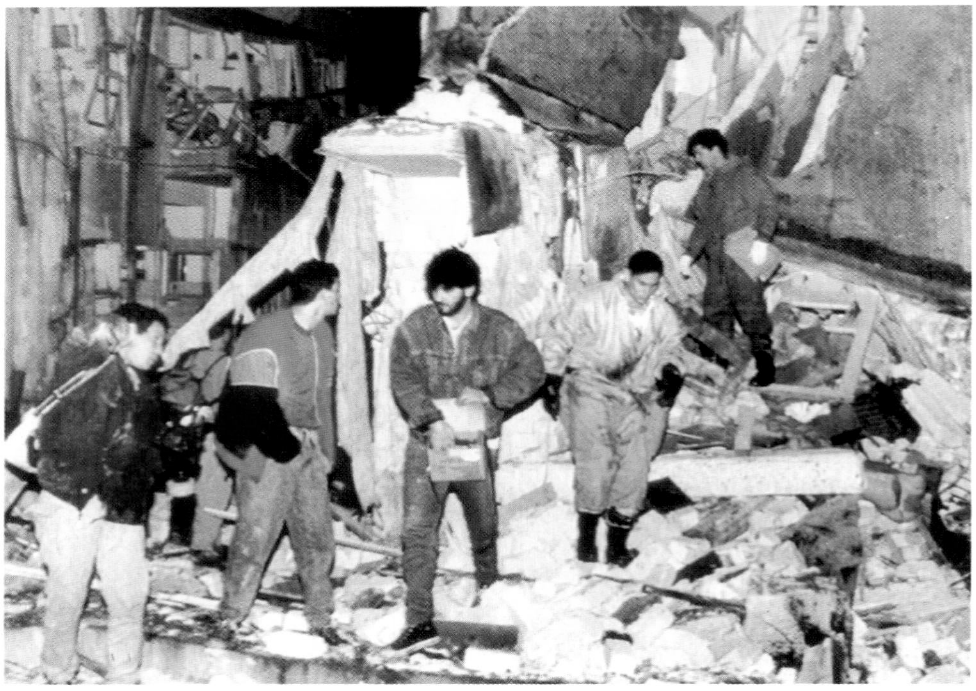

Reuters

Israeli emergency workers and neighbors search through the ruins of a Tel Aviv residence demolished during an Iraqi Scud missile attack.

■ **Gulf War:** Sorties by allied warplanes pass the 10,000 mark. Iraqis torch oil facilities in Kuwait and thick smoke hampers aircraft.

By DANIEL WILLIAMS and CAREY GOLDBERG
TIMES STAFF WRITERS

TEL AVIV—A deadly Iraqi Scud missile slipped past U.S.-manned Patriot interceptor batteries Tuesday and thundered into a densely populated neighborhood of Tel Aviv, bringing death to three people and injury to 96 others.

It was the third and gravest attack on Israel since the Persian Gulf War began six days ago. The high number of casualties raised anew the question of whether the Jewish state would retaliate—and risk splintering the U.S.-Arab coalition against Iraq.

The Scud missile crashed into an area of apartment buildings. The three dead were elderly residents who apparently suffered heart attacks. Three of the wounded, including a baby girl, were critically injured while the rest received light to moderate wounds. The warhead carried a conventional explosive, and government spokesmen said there was no trace of poison gas.

A short time earlier, Iraqi forces had fired four Scud missiles into eastern Saudi Arabia. They were aimed at Dhahran, site of a major allied air base. But all were destroyed by Patriot missiles before they reached their targets.

There were these other developments:

- The missile attacks came as allied warplanes streaked over mist and drizzle along the northern Saudi front lines and passed a new mark in air power—10,000 sorties in six days since the war began, surpassing what is often cited as history's greatest concentration of air power: the 6,151 sorties flown against Germany during six days of 1944.
- In the Persian Gulf itself, U.S. Navy planes sank an Iraqi minelayer and another ship and chased away two other boats.
- The Iraqis displayed two more men on television whom they identified as American prisoners of war. They were identified by the Iraqis as U.S. Air Force Maj. Jeffrey Scott Tice and Capt. Harry Michael Roberts. The allies expressed concern that they would be sent to join other POWs as human shields at strategic Iraqi facilities.
- The Iraqis torched oil facilities in occupied Kuwait, sending thick, black smoke over the desert and hampering allied aircraft. In all, three facilities were burned, military and oil company executives said. Although there was no immediate drop in oil supplies, world oil prices jumped $2.88 a barrel.
- President Bush's spokesman said the commander in chief would like to receive better damage assessments from his commanders. A Pentagon spokesman conceded that "we don't have a fully accu-

Please see GULF, A6

COLUMN ONE

CNN: The Channel to the World

■ The Gulf War certifies it's the first true international news network. Critics worry about its instant reporting, but global leaders have made it a new diplomatic conduit.

By THOMAS B. ROSENSTIEL
TIMES STAFF WRITER

ATLANTA—A few days after the United States made its only offer for direct talks with Iraq last November, the Emir of Bahrain met President Bush in a private Oval Office session and offered at least a partial explanation for why the offer was stalemated: Cable News Network.

"CNN is operating against us," the emir said of the Atlanta-based news organization, one senior Administration official present recalls.

Saddam Hussein watches the debate over gulf policy in America on CNN, the emir said, but he doesn't understand it—he thinks the United States will not do anything and that the President is paralyzed.

While the emir's concern did not fully convince the Administration, it did highlight what the parade of live Saudi Arabian air raid alerts, Patriot missile intercepts and Iraqi communiques has made dizzyingly plain: The Persian Gulf War has certified CNN's unique role as the first true international news network, with all the advantages and drawbacks that implies.

It has become a new channel for world diplomacy, often supplanting the diplomatic cable and the ambassadorial meeting. It has unique influence on international stories, despite the limitation of being aired live in the United States only on cable systems. As the only Western TV network seen in Baghdad, for instance, CNN correspondent Peter Arnett was invited to remain in Iraq, while other news organizations were thrown out.

Please see CNN, A12

Gorbachev Firm on Reform Policy

Soviet President Gorbachev disclaimed responsibility for the deaths of nationalists in the Baltics and promised an investigation. He said reform policies would continue. A19

Molina, Torres Head for Runoff in 1st District

By RICHARD SIMON and JILL STEWART
TIMES STAFF WRITERS

City Councilwoman Gloria Molina and state Sen. Art Torres were headed for a runoff after a historic election Tuesday that will give Los Angeles County its first Latino supervisor this century and end a decade of conservative control of the board.

With all precincts reporting in the 1st District, Molina collected 34.8% of the vote but fell short of the majority required to avoid a Feb. 19 runoff against Torres, a fellow liberal Democrat who finished second with 25.7%.

Sarah Flores, the lone Republican among the leading candidates, polled 20.5%, followed by state Sen. Charles Calderon with 15.9%. The remaining vote was split among five other candidates.

Election officials reported that 21.3% of the new district's 371,611 voters cast ballots in the special election that followed a short, hard-fought campaign overshad-

Please see ELECTION, A20

Refugees Carry Tales of Terror From Baghdad

■ **Escape:** As they reach Jordan, some curse America and tell of bombs hitting homes in poorer suburbs.

By MARK FINEMAN
TIMES STAFF WRITER

TRANSIT CAMP T1-28, Jordan—The human face of war rolled into Jordan's no-man's-land Tuesday in battered buses and broken taxis, with eyes drawn from horror and wet with fury. And with it came the first credible accounts of widespread civilian damage and casualties from allied bombing raids on military targets in Baghdad.

Most of the refugees were Egyptians who had lived in Baghdad, where, before the war, they were among the harshest and most vocal critics of Iraqi President Saddam Hussein and his ruthless regime. But then, as they tell it, the allied bombs began to fall around their homes a week ago, occasionally crushing children, maiming adults and paralyzing all of them with fear.

And now, angry young men like Majid Mohammed, a car mechanic whose government in Cairo is a key Arab member of the anti-Iraq alliance, curses the Americans even more than he does Hussein.

"This is not a war. This is an annihilation of a people," he shouted at two American journalists as he tugged angrily at his red-checkered kaffiyeh, or head scarf, in a crowd of nodding heads at the Red Cross transit camp for war refugees here. "Yes, I am Egyptian, but, please, take your hands off of Iraq. This is an Arab problem now.

"You are taking revenge on Iraq, on its children. . . . The revenge should not be taken on us, not on the Arabs. It should be taken on Saddam. What is the sin of all these people?"

Majid Mohammed was among more than 1,500 Egyptians to arrive Monday and Tuesday in the 43-mile-wide strip of desert between Iraq and Jordan known as the No-Man's-Land, and his was clearly the opinion of the others.

They are among the first of the tens of thousands of war refugees

Please see REFUGEES, A8

Images of Chaos, Pain, Surprise Amid the Debris

By CAREY GOLDBERG and DANIEL WILLIAMS
TIMES STAFF WRITERS

TEL AVIV—Once again, a Tel Aviv street was the scene of images of surprise, chaos and pain that are becoming familiar here: An injured woman, her arm covered with blood, being carried out on a stretcher; another stretcher patient, a man clutching his dog and rubbing a head wound; a young woman dazed and lightly bleeding from the head.

It was the third Iraqi missile attack on Israel and the most serious yet, leaving three dead and 70 injured, demolishing an apartment building and damaging dozens of neighboring houses.

Windows and shutters were blown out blocks away. Balconies along main and side streets were mangled, and broken pipes gushed water onto the street. Scores of ambulances, their red and blue lights spinning, and hundreds of police rushed to the site, which under Israeli censorship rules cannot be specifically located in print.

Please see SCENE, A14

Bush, Gorbachev Dealings Reach Impasse Over Baltics

■ **Diplomacy:** U.S. plans to file charges of rights abuse in Lithuania, one of many issues bedeviling relationship.

By DOYLE McMANUS
TIMES STAFF WRITER

WASHINGTON—The telephone call between the Oval Office and the Kremlin last week lasted 45 long minutes, not counting the 25-minute delay when the secure line went down. First, President Bush and Soviet President Mikhail S. Gorbachev talked about the war in the Persian Gulf and the conversation went well, according to an official who was present.

Then Bush changed the subject, warning Gorbachev, politely but frankly, that the Soviet army's crackdown in Lithuania is unacceptable to the United States. It would freeze the progress in U.S.-Soviet relations that both presidents had worked so hard to build, Bush said.

From the other end of the telephone line came a silence—and then, in Russian, a perfunctory acknowledgement that Bush's views had been heard.

The exchange—or, rather, the absence of one—was symptomatic of an impasse that has brought Bush to an unhappy watershed in his dealings with Gorbachev. After two years of optimism about an expanding "partnership" with Moscow—a link that Bush described as an important part of his vision of a new world order—the U.S.-Soviet honeymoon has abruptly ended, crushed under the

Please see DIPLOMACY, A18

MORE WAR COVERAGE

Iraq Could Be Saving Its Air Force for a Surprise

■ **Strategy:** But with airfields cratered and radar in ruins, an effective attack is viewed as improbable.

By DAVID LAUTER
TIMES STAFF WRITER

WASHINGTON—With its airfields pockmarked by bomb craters and its control radar reduced to rubble, the Iraqi air force seems to have been eliminated as a military force.

Or has it?

U.S. military officials have made confident statements about the destruction they have wreaked on Iraq's air power. At the same time, however, they concede that Saddam Hussein may well have more than 600 planes hidden in hardened shelters.

While many airfields have been devastated, others are still operable, and military officials say Iraqi forces are working overtime to repair the damage where they can. Allied forces have shot down only 18 Iraqi planes, military briefers say. And of those in shelters, as

NEWS ANALYSIS

few as a dozen may have been destroyed, British military officials have said.

At least some analysts suggest that Hussein may yet try to use his remaining planes to alter the course of battle—or at least give his foes a nasty jolt.

The scenarios vary: an attack on Israel, an attack on U.S. ground forces, strikes against ships in the Persian Gulf. But all assume that

Please see PLANES, A15

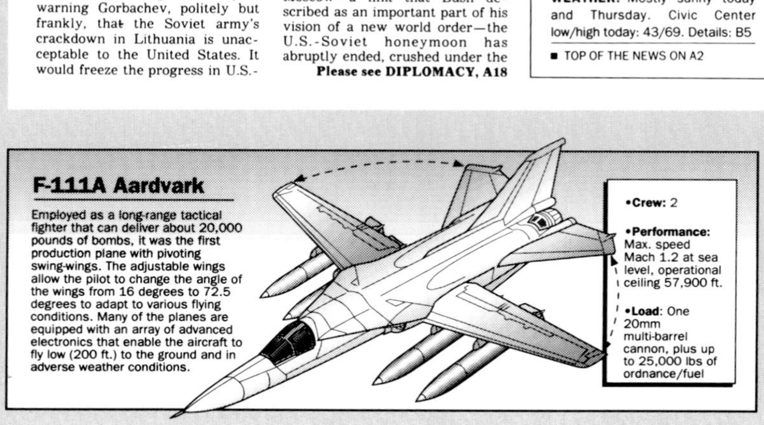

Missiles: An Iraqi Scud missile slips past U.S.-staffed Patriot interceptor batteries and lands outside Tel Aviv; three people die of heart attacks and nearly 100 others are injured.
■ Iraq also fires four Scud missiles into eastern Saudi Arabia in an attempt to hit Dhahran; all are destroyed by Patriot missiles.

Military: More than 10,000 sorties have been flown. Losses include 18 allied planes, 15 in combat — nine American, four British, one Kuwaiti and one Italian.
■ Relatively high British losses are attributed to the pilots' daring flying style and their hazardous mission of destroying runways in Iraq and Kuwait.
■ The allied command says 18 Iraqi planes have been destroyed in dogfights but more than 600 planes may be hidden in hardened shelters.
■ Twenty-four service members are reported missing in action, including 13 Americans, eight Britons, two Italians and one Kuwaiti.
■ Low cloud cover limits visibility for pilots for third straight day.
■ Navy planes sink an Iraqi minelayer in the Persian Gulf.

Environment: Kuwaiti oil facilities are set on fire, apparently by Iraqi forces, sending thick black smoke over the desert.
■ Oil fire experts say the region's wells could burn for months.

International: Soviet President Mikhail S. Gorbachev distances himself from Washington, warning against taking the conflict deep into Iraq and causing extensive civilian casualties.
■ A chorus of voices across the political spectrum in Germany warns against a growing anti-Americanism that has accompanied protests in the country against the Gulf War.

Prisoners of war: Two more men identified as POWs are displayed on Iraqi television.

Scud missiles claimed at least two Israelis and wounded scores.

LARRY DAVIS / Los Angeles Times

FIGHTING
AIR TO GROUND

■ Allied coalition forces have flown thousands of missions over Iraq and Kuwait since hostilities began Jan. 17. Here, in simplified form, is a breakdown of the basic kinds of armaments used in the air, the kinds of targets they are designed to destroy and their limitations and vulnerabilities.

Guns

• Used against soft targets such as vehicles and trucks.

• AH-64 Apache helicopter carries a 30-millimeter rapid-fire chain gun, primarily effective against vehicles and armored personnel carriers that do not have thick armor.

• AV-8B Marine Harrier carries 25-millimeter cannon for use against soft targets.

• A-10 Thunderbolt, a dedicated tank-killer, fires 30-millimeter cannon in its nose. Its extremely powerful shells are about the size of milk bottles.

LIMITATIONS

• Attacker is drawn into range of air defense systems, especially the A-10, which flies low and slowly.

ALTITUDE

• Has to fly in as low as 500 feet in order to see and hit target.

• The helicopter can come in even lower and can use ground terrain to conceal itself.

A-10 Thunderbolt

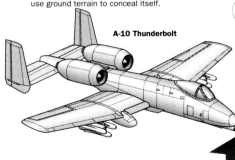

EXAMPLE: GAU-8A Avenger 30-millimeter, 7-barrel revolving cannon.

Armor-piercing incendiary shell
Length: 11.4 inches
Weight: 2.05 pounds

Steel windscreen

Aluminum case   Depleted uranium penetrator

Rockets

• Primarily effective against massed soft targets: vehicles, troops, cluster of frame buildings, radar installations.

• Most commonly used are high explosive 70-millimeter rocket, fired in salvos of 20-30.

• Carried by Cobra AH-1 aircraft or Apache AH-64 helicopters.

LIMITATIONS:

• Subject to enemy ground fire and not effective on hard targets, such as tanks and bunkers.

ALTITUDE:

• Can come in as low as 2,000 feet; helicopter would come in even lower.

AH-64A Apache

EXAMPLE: 2.75 inch (70mm) FFAR rocket (folding fin aerial rocket)

Rocket can carry different warheads

Fins fold out when rocket leaves launch tube

Smart Weapons

• Used against "point" targets, such as individual buildings requiring precision bombing.

• Warheads most commonly used are range in weight from 145 pounds to 2,000 pounds and are television, infra-red or laser-guided to the target.

• Aircraft are medium-range fighter-bombers: the F-16 Fighting Falcon, F-15E Eagle, A-6 Intruder, and F-111A Aardvark.

LIMITATIONS

• Subject to enemy ground fire, antiaircraft missile or cannon.

ALTITUDE

• Depending on target and cloud cover, they can range from 2,000-5,000 feet.

F-15E Eagle

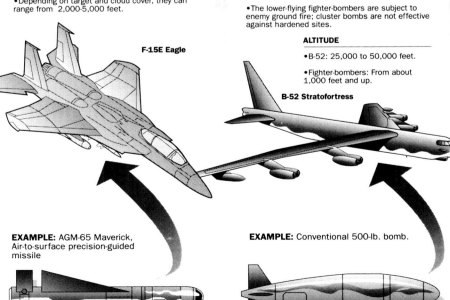

EXAMPLE: AGM-65 Maverick, Air-to-surface precision-guided missile

Free-Fall Bombs

• Used against any large concentration of troops, equipment, vehicles, airfield installations to maximize damage over a large area.

• B-52 Stratofortress can deliver 50,000 pounds of bombs to maximize destruction. This strategy is called "carpet bombing."

• Medium-range fighter-bombers such as the A-6, A-10, A-18 and F-16 can drop "cluster bombs" — clusters of little bomblets that are packed into a larger bomb, similar to shotgun pellets.

LIMITATIONS

• The B-52 is a strategic asset that requires protective escort and high enough altitude to avoid hostile ground fire to assure it is not lost.

• The lower-flying fighter-bombers are subject to enemy ground fire; cluster bombs are not effective against hardened sites.

ALTITUDE

• B-52: 25,000 to 50,000 feet.

• Fighter-bombers: From about 1,000 feet and up.

B-52 Stratofortress

EXAMPLE: Conventional 500-lb. bomb.

Not to scale

Source: Jane's All the Worlds Aircraft, Jane's Weapon Systems, military analyst Gregory Grant.

ANDERS RAMBERG, JUAN THOMASSIE, SANDY KAY AND MATT MOODY / Los Angeles Times

DAY 8

JANUARY 24, 1991

An Iraqi missile landing in the Tel Aviv suburb of Ramat Gan killed one man, injured scores of people and left hundreds homeless, including many traumatized children. One of these, a dark-haired, shiny-eyed girl of 8, described for Israeli Television the terrified confusion that she and her little brother experienced when the blast blew out the windows of their home and cut the power.

What would she say to Saddam Hussein if she could? the interviewer asked.

"That we are all human beings," she replied, and that he should not fire missiles at defenseless people.

I was impressed. No talk of revenge? No warnings of retaliation? Could this girl's generation be the one to break the long cycle of hatred in the Middle East?

Then the interviewer asked the girl what she would do if she met Hussein.

Well, she said, probably take a gun and kill him.

—Carey Goldberg, in Tel Aviv

Los Angeles Times

CIRCULATION: 1,225,189 DAILY 1,514,096 SUNDAY

THURSDAY, JANUARY 24, 1991

COPYRIGHT 1991 THE TIMES MIRROR COMPANY CC† 160 PAGES
DAILY 25¢ DESIGNATED AREAS HIGHER

Iraq Defeat Certain, U.S. Says

Hussein's Army to Be Cut Off, Killed, Powell Asserts

■ **Gulf War:** General and Cheney assess the conflict and cite foe's resilience. Bush says the attacks have put Baghdad out of the 'nuclear bomb-building business.

By MELISSA HEALY, TIMES STAFF WRITER

WASHINGTON—Iraqi President Saddam Hussein and his military forces are "hunkering down" in an effort to ride out the massive allied air assault, but sooner or later they will be crushed by Operation Desert Storm, U.S. officials declared Wednesday.

"There can be no doubt: Operation Desert Storm is working," President Bush said in his first speech since the earliest days of the allied offensive. "There can be no pause now that Saddam has forced the world into war. We will stay the course—and we will succeed."

Defense Secretary Dick Cheney and Joint Chiefs of Staff Colin L. Powell, assessing the first week of the Persian Gulf War, acknowledged that Iraq's Scud missiles have been more elusive than expected and the elite Republican Guard has remained a credible fighting force.

But the two officials warned bluntly that despite its resilience under fire, Hussein's military machine faces certain defeat at the hands of the more than 700,000 American and allied troops deployed in Saudi Arabia and elsewhere in the region.

"He is a man who will use any means at his disposal to break up the coalition and avoid defeat," Cheney said. But, he added, Hussein "cannot change the basic course of the conflict. He will be defeated."

The Iraqi army is "waiting to be attacked, and attacked it will be," said Gen. Powell. "Our strategy for dealing with this army is very simple: First we're going to cut it off, then we're going to kill it."

The President, speaking to a group of retired military officers, said the intensive allied bombardment of military and industrial targets in Iraq and Kuwait is "right on schedule" and praised its success in meeting key strategic objectives.

"We have dealt a severe setback to Saddam's nuclear ambitions," said Bush. "Our pinpoint attacks have put Saddam out of the nuclear bomb-building business for a long time to come. Allied aircraft enjoy air superiority, and we are using that superiority to systematically deprive Saddam of his ability to wage war effectively."

Despite the setbacks caused by heavy cloud cover over Iraq and Kuwait and the necessity of diverting aircraft to search for Scud missiles and launchers, Cheney and Powell insisted that allied forces have the upper hand and ultimately will prevail over Hussein's army.

"Time is clearly on our side," Cheney insisted. "Each day, each week that goes by, he gets weaker and we get stronger."

"There's no question that [Hussein's] force will become progressively weaker," Powell added. "It's absolutely mathematical."

Cheney and Powell said allied military officials are fully prepared to expand the allied campaign to the ground to drive Hussein's forces from occupied Kuwait. Even so,

Please see GULF, A6

Reuters

Gen. Colin L. Powell, during briefing on allied strategy, indicates area in Iraq where aircraft have been lost.

COLUMN ONE

Muslims a Growing U.S. Force

■ But despite the rise in numbers, they feel their beliefs are misconstrued as hostile to the West. Now they fear they will be held responsible for a war most say they didn't want.

By TERRY PRISTIN and JOHN DART
TIMES STAFF WRITERS

Draped in a floor-length black garment, her head covered in a white scarf, and with only her hands and face exposed, Majida Salem cuts an exotic figure even in ethnically diverse Los Angeles. When she emigrated from Jordan seven years ago, she was prepared to encounter stares from puzzled Americans.

Now, however, curiosity has evolved into hostility and "the looks are different," Salem said a few days before war erupted in the Persian Gulf. "At first they questioned my appearance," she explained in near-fluent English, "but they didn't have those hateful looks."

These are wrenching times for Salem and millions of other Muslims living in the United States. Through immigration, a high birth rate and conversion, especially among American blacks, Islam is one of the fastest-growing faiths in America. Yet Muslims say their beliefs are widely misconstrued as

ISLAM IN AMERICA
Time of Opportunity and Trial
One in a series

war-prone and hostile to Western ideals. Isolated in a culture that makes little effort to understand them, they fear their neighbors will hold them responsible for a war most say they did not want.

"When the bodies of American youth come back, [people] are going to blame the Muslims," predicted Zaheer Uddin, editor of a Muslim magazine in Jamaica, N.Y. "It will give a very negative picture [of us]."

War has come just as many Muslims have begun building bridges to mainstream America by, for example, participating in interfaith services and entering political life for the first time. Now some worry these fledgling efforts will be undermined.

Please see MUSLIMS, A24

Analyst Calls Wilson Budget Too Optimistic

By DOUGLAS P. SHUIT
TIMES STAFF WRITER

SACRAMENTO—In a report sure to increase pressure for higher taxes, the Legislature's nonpartisan analyst said Wednesday that the gap between state revenues and expenditures has widened to nearly $10 billion and that Gov. Pete Wilson's budget estimates "significantly underestimate" the magnitude of the problem.

Wilson and analysts in the Department of Finance had built the $55.7-billion budget on the assumption of a $7-billion shortfall for the remainder of this fiscal year and for the 1991-92 fiscal year, which begins July 1.

Legislative Analyst Elizabeth G. Hill disputed Wilson's contention that the economy will come out of the recession later this year, produce a strong recovery in 1992 and lead to increased tax revenue. Rather, she said, economic recovery will take longer and revenues will rise more slowly. The analyst also suggested that the governor underestimated the cost of welfare and other programs by about $300 million.

Please see TAXES, A22

Signs of Iraqi-Trained Terror Network Found

■ **Security:** Manila case prompts a global alert amid evidence that Baghdad's embassies abroad handle arms.

By BOB DROGIN and RONALD J. OSTROW
TIMES STAFF WRITERS

MANILA—Using diaries, a photo album and passports from two would-be bombers directed by the Iraqi Embassy here, Western intelligence agencies say they have found key leads to what they believe is a network of terrorists trained in Baghdad and sent to countries around the world.

The clues here led to the arrests Wednesday of two Iraqis and two Jordanians in Bangkok, Thailand, as well as an international police and immigration alert for Iraqis or other potential Arab terrorists using passports and travel patterns similar to those detected here.

Evidence also is growing that Iraqi embassies have used diplomatic pouches to import arms and explosives. Hundreds of armed Thai troops were deployed to embassies, airline offices and other potential terrorist sites in Bangkok last weekend after authorities received credible reports that the Iraqi Embassy had smuggled in and distributed weapons, C-4 military explosives and sophisticated timers to terrorist teams.

"The volume is quite large," said one official here. "They're talking about crates of weapons."

The authorities especially fear the Iraqis may have smuggled in Soviet SA-16 shoulder-fired missiles, similar to American-made Stinger missiles, which can be used to shoot down an airliner.

The official said Bangkok appears to be a "logistics center" for Iraqi terrorist attacks in Asia. "They're bringing people in," he said. "They're bringing supplies in. And they're expert at making fake passports."

Anomalies in passports used by two Iraqis involved in a bungled bombing Saturday near a U.S. library here provided what another official called a "major break" in the search for Iraqi terrorists. "Now we have something to go on, to look for in other countries," he said.

He said the search will be "most intensive" in countries with known concentrations of Iraqis, Lebanese and Palestinians, "places where

Please see TERROR, A18

Foe Skilled at Trickery, Decoys Show

By PAUL RICHTER
TIMES STAFF WRITER

WASHINGTON—Decoy missile launchers. Phony weapons factories. "Cratered" runways that are really intact.

Iraq may not have impressed the world with its war machine so far, but its military technicians are showing consummate skill at fraud and trickery, according to U.S. military officials.

The tactics are all part of the science of deception—*maskorovka*—that the Iraqis learned from their longtime Soviet advisers and honed during eight years of bloody war with Iran.

"They're quite good at

Please see DECOYS, A18

Scud Downing Fails to Blunt Israelis' Anger

By DANIEL WILLIAMS
TIMES STAFF WRITER

JERUSALEM—A day after a stinging failure, Patriot anti-missile rockets shot down a Scud in flight Wednesday night as it bore down on Israel's north coast, but the successful interception did little to ease official talk that Israel must at some point strike back at Iraq.

While expressing satisfaction with the Patriot's performance, which was signaled by a flash and boom in the misty skies near Haifa, Israeli officials insisted that Israel will not sit back and passively accept being a target for Iraqi missiles.

"We will have to do something eventually," said government spokesman Yossi Olmert. "This doesn't change anything. The attacks persist."

"Every person in the state of Israel would say to you that we must hit them back so hard that their screams of pain will be heard

Please see ISRAEL, A19

Gorbachev Money Decree Stirs Panic Among Savers

■ **Soviet Union:** Large-denomination ruble bills are declared worthless. Besieged banks refuse to open.

By MICHAEL PARKS
TIMES STAFF WRITER

MOSCOW—Angry crowds, afraid that most of their savings would be lost under a government monetary reform, besieged banks across the Soviet Union on Wednesday in a new panic threatening the country's fragile economy.

With wads of bank notes clutched in their hands, they pounded on the doors and windows of neighborhood savings banks, demanding that the money, large-denomination bills declared worthless the night before, be replaced with smaller bills.

But the banks, caught unawares by President Mikhail S. Gorbachev's decree, refused to open although customers had begun lining up before dawn. Most banks had no instructions on how to carry out the exchange—the decree said only limited amounts of large bills could be exchanged without question—and no cash to do so.

Gorbachev's decree had been intended to strengthen the ruble, the Soviet currency, to dampen inflation and, above all, to drain all available cash from the black market, but in its first day the measure appeared to have accelerated the disintegration of the country's economy.

"The utter immorality of this decree is bound to cost the central

Please see SOVIETS, A21

MORE WAR COVERAGE

■ **WAR STORIES, PHOTOS: A5-19; D1, D4-5; F1-2, F7**

■ **BUSH'S STYLE IN CRISIS**
In managing the war crisis, the President is steering a middle course between Reagan-style detachment and Lyndon Johnson's immersion in detail. **A5**

■ **JAPAN BOOSTS AID**
Japan announced plans to add $9 billion to its support of the allied forces in the Middle East and to supply military cargo aircraft to transport refugees. **A6**

■ **GIs HURT IN SKIRMISH**
Two American soldiers were slightly wounded and six Iraqi soldiers were taken prisoner in one of the first small-arms skirmishes of the week-old war. **A7**

WEATHER: Mostly sunny today, Friday. Civic Center low/high today: 44/69. Details: B5

■ TOP OF THE NEWS ON A2

■ **CAIRO EXPERTS WARY**
Egyptian military planners believe that Iraq is waiting for an allied ground offensive before it commits its air force and chemical weapons to the conflict. **A7**

■ **ANXIETY IN CONGRESS**
The prospect of a prolonged war has shifted the mood in Congress from an initial giddy euphoria to anxiety, frustration and even depression. **A10**

■ **FRIENDLY SKIES**
Travelers seem to be more comforted than put out by the new federal precautions against terrorism imposed at 435 airports across the country. **A11**

■ **HOME FRONT MORALE**
In separate public appearances, President Bush and Vice President Dan Quayle opened a coordinated campaign to bolster home-front morale. **A11**

FBI Quest Leaves Many Arab-Americans Fearful

■ **Investigation:** Officials say interviews are designed to protect as well as gather information.

By LAURIE BECKLUND and DAVID FREED
TIMES STAFF WRITERS

Paul Bohn had a full load of dirt in the dump truck he drives for the city of Grapevine, Tex., when his dispatcher called earlier this week with orders to report to the police station.

There, an FBI agent flashed a badge, took out a tape recorder, and asked Bohn if he had any Arab-American friends. The truck driver mentioned Victor Nasser, the manager of a San Diego law firm and an active Republican whom Bohn hadn't seen in four years. The agent produced a file on Nasser and started questioning Bohn about his views on Israel, and those of his friend.

"What's this all about?" Bohn said he demanded after 30 minutes. "Victor's no terrorist. You act like he's going to start throwing hand grenades."

Agents in the past three weeks have conducted dozens of such interviews with Arab-Americans and their friends, part of what the FBI calls a nationwide investigation to "interdict terrorists." The conversations have taken place over pancakes at Denny's in Dallas, in doctors' offices in Orange County, between sips of Arabian coffee served in living rooms in Los Angeles—polite, though often unsettling exchanges, that have pro-

Please see FBI, A11

Gas Masks

Television viewers around the world have been treated to the startling sight of correspondents in the Middle East conducting live broadcasts from behind their gas masks. While the image may be bizarre, it points up the very real possibility that citizens and correspondents alike could be exposed to chemical or biological weapons at any time. The mounting threat of Iraqi-led terrorism in the United States has sent gas mask sales soaring at $20 a copy and up; some consumers are spending hundreds of dollars to outfit themselves with chemical suits and bullet-proof vests as well.

How It Works

Inhaled air passes through valves into replaceable filters over the cheeks. The filters remove chemical or biological agents from the air being inhaled. The filtered air then passes across the inner surface of the lenses to keep them free of condensation. Air then passes through to the nose, and the exhaled air is discharged through outlet valves.

Artilleryman sported graffiti-covered helmet and shells.

PATRICK DOWNS / Los Angeles Times

ASSESSING THE AIR WAR

Under criticism, the Pentagon offered the first detailed, official assessment Wednesday on targets hit in the week-long air war against Iraq. Gen. Colin Powell, chaiman of the Joint Chiefs of Staff, said the allied forces have seized air superiority, but that the Iraqis are proving a resourceful enemy. Among the highlights:

IRAQI AIRCRAFT: More than 12,000 allied sorties have destroyed 41 Iraqi aircraft, either in air-to-air combat or on the ground. Iraq has an estimated 700 planes. Powell said the United States has lost at most one plane in air-to-air combat. Total U.S. aircraft losses are 10.

AIRFIELDS: Iraq is using only five of 66 airfields struck by bombing raids in the last day, Powell said. He acknowledged that Iraqis have been repairing damaged airfields.

NUCLEAR/CHEMICAL: Air raids have destroyed two operating nuclear reactors, caused "considerable damage" to chemical weapons facilities and to several biological warfare plants, Powell said.

PRISONERS: U.S. forces report holding 29 Iraqis prisoner, including six captured in the first skirmish in Saudi Arabia. Egypt is said to have accepted an unspecified number of Iraqi defectors.

CLEARING THE WAY: The air power now is intended to focus on bombing runs against Iraqi ground forces around Kuwait.

THE MILK PLANT: U.S. officials denied that allied planed had bombed a baby formula manufacturing plant, as charged by Iraq, saying that the plant was linked to production of biological weapons.

IRAQI AIRFIELDS HIT BY ALLIES

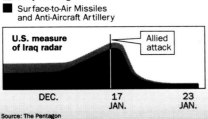

TURKEY

SYRIA

IRAN

Baghdad

0   100

IRAQ

KUWAIT

SAUDI ARABIA

🔥 Main operating bases

🔥 Crude, secondary airfields

🔥 Bases where activity has been detected in the last 24 hours

▨ Scud launch areas

ASSESSING IRAQI RESPONSE

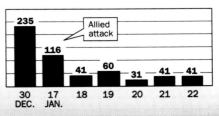

RADAR ACTIVITY

■ Early Warning

■ Surface-to-Air Missiles and Anti-Aircraft Artillery

U.S. measure of Iraq radar

Allied attack

DEC.   17 JAN.   23 JAN.

FLIGHT ACTIVITY

U.S. count of Iraqi sorties.

| 235 | 116 | 41 | 60 | 31 | 41 | 41 |

Allied attack

30 DEC.   17 JAN.   18   19   20   21   22

Source: The Pentagon

COLIN POWELL:

"We're dealing with an enemy that is resourceful, and enemy that knows how to work around problems, an enemy that is ingenious. We are not getting complacent."

"The Iraqi Army in the field is, for the most part, sitting there waiting to be attacked. And attacked it will be. First, we're going to cut it off. Then kill it."

Associated Press

Gen. Colin Powell

THE NUMBERS

Refugees: 12,000 in Jordan
Allied sorties: 12,000
Allied losses:
    20 planes
    10 American
    4 British
    1 Kuwait
    1 Italian
Iraqi losses: 41 planes
Missing in action: 24
    13 Americans
    8 Britons
    2 Italians
    1 Kuwait
Iraqi POWs: 29
Iraqi claims:
    178 allied aircraft downed
    20 prisoners of war held
    40 civilians killed
    31 soldiers killed

ALLIED AIRCRAFT LOST

U.S. Navy F-18C, one killed
Each aircraft: $30.8 million
2 U.S. Navy A-6 Intruders, 3 airmen missing, one rescued
Each aircraft: $22 million
U.S. Air Force F-15E Strike Eagle, crew of two missing
Each aircraft: $50.4 million
U.S. Air Force F-4G Wild Weasel, (mechanical problems, not a combat loss), crew of two rescued
Each aircraft: $15.7 million
U.S. Marine Corps OV-10A Bronco, crew of two captured
Unit: out of production
2 U.S. Air Force F-16s, each with one-man crew
Each aircraft: $18.4 million
U.S. Air Force F-15E Strike Eagle, crew of two missing
Each aircraft: $50.4 million
UH-60 Blackhawk helicopter crash within Saudi Arabia, non-combat incident
Each aircraft: $6.5 million
Saudi Arabia Tornado with two crewmen missing
1 U.S. Navy F-14
Each aircraft: $71.9 million
1 U.S. AH-64 helicopter, non-combat
Each aircraft: $11.7 million

31

JUAN THOMASSIE AND VICTOR KOTOWITZ / Los Angeles Times

DAY 9

JANUARY 25, 1991

Researching a column shortly after war began, I phoned James Akins, former U.S. ambassador to Iraq and Saudi Arabia and now a consultant in Washington, and was taken aback when he came on like the proverbial voice of doom.

"We are destroying 1,000 years of civilization in Iraq. Ruin shall follow," said Akins. "The Arabs are comparing Bush to Hulagu, the Mongol who sacked Baghdad in 1258. If Iraq is destroyed, the whole world will be engulfed in war."

He continued in that vein, worrying about the breakup of Iraq, which he said would preclude a real peace.

Akins has a history of taking the Arab side, so I discounted his worries. But then I called Josh Epstein of the Brookings Institution and found his chief worry also to be the breakup of postwar Iraq, along with the trouble in the power vacuum that would follow.

Well, the fighting's over now, and we seem to be getting the breakup, and I'm staying tuned.

—James Flanigan, in Los Angeles

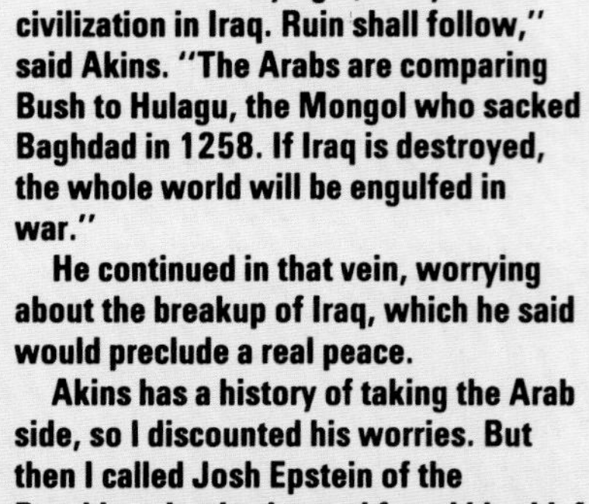

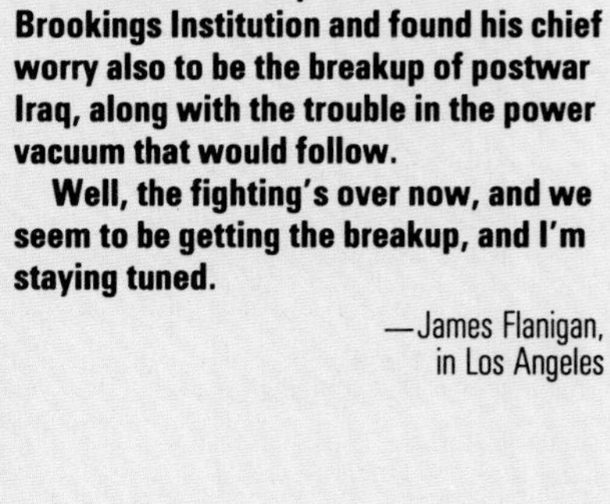

Los Angeles Times

CIRCULATION: 1,225,189 DAILY / 1,514,096 SUNDAY | FRIDAY, JANUARY 25, 1991 | DAILY 25¢ DESIGNATED AREAS HIGHER

COPYRIGHT 1991 / THE TIMES MIRROR COMPANY / CC† / 136 PAGES

COLUMN ONE

War Mood Shapes Pop Culture

■ Songs and slogans have always helped mold America's attitude toward a conflict. But this time, media tastemakers can respond instantly to shifts in the public psyche.

By STEPHEN BRAUN
TIMES STAFF WRITER

Long after the war machines are stilled and killing grounds revert to tourist haunts, some of the most enduring images and sounds of the Persian Gulf conflict may well linger in the debris of popular culture.

By the start of the aerial assault on Iraq last week, many of America's organs of pop culture already were geared for war. For six months, Saddam Hussein has been vilified by novelty songs on the radio and effigies burned at shopping centers and crushed at sports truck rallies. Disc jockeys have led blood bank drives and yellow ribbon campaigns. Before the first 2,000-pound bomb was even dropped on Baghdad, a Hollywood studio finished filming its own version of Operation Desert Shield.

Vivid fragments of war songs, movie battle scenes and home-front humor and slogans have shaped American attitudes toward war from the Revolution forward.

—The First World War's legacy included "Over There," the first modern propaganda campaign and the brief renaming of the German-sounding "hamburger" as "Salisbury steak."

—The Second World War honed popular culture into a propaganda weapon, injected phrases like "victory gardens" and "blackouts" into the dictionary and spawned an entire genre of war films.

—The Vietnam War, the first rock 'n' roll conflict, is still fought 25 years later in stage-prop rice paddies on film and television, its Big Chill-era songs pricking at baby boom memories.

The imprint that the Persian Gulf War leaves on contemporary culture will likely depend, as it has in wars past, on the conflict's duration and the depth of its popular support. What promises to be different this time, social critics say, is the ability of tastemakers to respond almost instantly to subtle changes in the public psyche.

"The impact of technology is the new card that hasn't been played yet," said culture critic Christopher Lasch. "It will heighten the air of unreality and keep pace with every shift in our mood."

In the first week of fighting, radio and television moved quickly to tailor the tone and content of programming to fit America's dawning awareness of the gravity of war. Radio personalities who had ridiculed Iraqis in rock parodies like "Who'll Stop Hussein" suddenly muted their broadcasts. A planned installment of ABC's new "Under Cover" spy drama, which had featured a Persian Gulf storyline the week before, was scuttled.

At the same time, the war spilled into the most obscure crevices of pop culture. Pro wrestling villain

Please see CULTURE, A28

Syria Stalls Iraqi Bid to Widen War

By NICK B. WILLIAMS Jr.
TIMES STAFF WRITER

DAMASCUS, Syria—Every Iraqi Scud missile that crashes into Tel Aviv echoes politically here in Damascus, testing Syria's determination to stand with the allied forces in the Persian Gulf War.

But President Hafez Assad's regime calculates that it has nothing to gain—and plenty to lose—by getting dragged into an Arab-Israeli conflict engineered by Saddam Hussein. It's furious at Hussein's attempts to light the fuse and scramble to stamp it out.

So far, while anticipating Israeli reprisal attacks against Baghdad, Assad has shown no sign of

Please see SYRIA, A9

Ground Assault Could Clog U.S. Supply Lines

By ROBERT W. STEWART and EDWIN CHEN
TIMES STAFF WRITERS

WASHINGTON—The massive, 9,000-mile-long supply line now providing war materiel to the Persian Gulf has been functioning—under strain—without major hitches, but experts fear it could begin to suffer breakdowns, particularly if U.S. forces become involved in a protracted land war.

So far, the effort has gone smoothly. With hundreds of aircraft and ships ferrying massive amounts of supplies, the Pentagon is managing to restock the vast arsenal of munitions and equipment that American forces are expending in the Persian Gulf.

"The effort has been going extremely well, and continues to go extremely well," says Vice Adm. Francis R. Donovan, commander of the U.S. Military Sealift Command. "It's been a staggering effort, and I think it's realistically beyond what we could have expected."

But some military and transportation experts fear that the well-oiled machine could break down if the gulf conflict turns into a lengthy ground war in which the military is forced to rely less on high-tech weaponry and more on massive, old-fashioned cannon fire.

"If you're going to fight for a long time, it's going to be tight," says R. B. Costello, who served as undersecretary of defense for acquisitions from 1986 to 1989. "The logistics are going to be a tough row to hoe."

Lawrence J. Korb, a former assistant secretary of defense for logistics, says one reason the venture has gone so smoothly is that U.S. logistics planners have amassed huge amounts of spare parts in Saudi Arabia, enabling the military to stay well ahead of resupply efforts.

But Korb cautions that even with supply lines continually pouring materiel into the area, the surplus is bound to be eroded if

Please see LOGISTICS, A22

French in 1st Iraq Air Strike; Allied Planes Step Up Attack

Associated Press

Reporters surround Saudi pilot after his return from mission in which he shot down two Iraqi jet fighters.

■ **Gulf War:** Mitterrand responds to criticism of half-hearted effort. U.S. troops free first chunk of Kuwait—a tiny 'bird sanctuary' island—but it gives emirate's citizens a psychological boost.

By J. MICHAEL KENNEDY and KIM MURPHY
TIMES STAFF WRITERS

RIYADH, Saudi Arabia—French warplanes screamed into Iraq for the first time Thursday in a stepped-up air assault on the elite Republican Guard, and allied troops liberated the first chunk of Kuwait—a tiny island in the Persian Gulf.

The decision to attack Iraq, made personally by French President Francois Mitterrand in reply to criticism that France was waging a half-hearted war, loosed Jaguar fighter-bombers against mechanized units of the Republican Guard. The guard took some of their heaviest pounding so far at allied hands.

"We are hitting them with all our assets," said Army Lt. Col. Greg Pepin, the spokesman for American forces. U.S. pilots and military commanders said bombs and missiles inflicted heavy damage on the Republican Guard, the backbone of Iraqi military strength, but they could not provide casualty figures.

While the liberation of the island of Qaruh, 22 miles off the shore of Kuwait, had only limited military value, it was of great psychological significance to Kuwaitis. The island is so small that it has no permanent residents and is often under water. A Kuwaiti spokesman, Hasan Abdul-Aziz, called it "a bird sanctuary."

But he added, "It is the first piece of land liberated from the Iraqis."

Qaruh fell during a U.S. Navy assault that killed three Iraqis, sank an Iraqi minesweeper and took 51 Iraqis prisoner, military officials reported. They said another minesweeper tried to flee—and exploded and sank when it apparently hit a mine.

In the eighth day of the Persian Gulf War, there were these additional developments:

- A U.S. Marine battery, heavily outnumbered and under nagging fire along the Kuwaiti border, struck back with a daring hit-and-run artillery raid—the latest in a series of conflicts sputtering along the Saudi border as the air war raged overhead.
- A Saudi pilot shot down two Iraqi jet fighters, reportedly loaded with bombs and Exocet missiles and headed for the gulf, where American ships are stationed. It was the first report of an Iraqi attempt to enter Saudi airspace—and the first dogfight of the war to end in a double kill.
- Marine Corps Maj. Gen. Martin L. Brandtner told reporters at the Pentagon that the United States does not plan "at this time" to use chemical weapons to retaliate against any Iraqi chemical attack

Please see WAR, A6

Saudi Pilot Downs 2 Iraqi Jets Over the Gulf

■ **Aerial combat:** Incident marks the first such enemy incursion. Planes were carrying Exocet anti-ship missiles.

By KIM MURPHY
TIMES STAFF WRITER

DHAHRAN, Saudi Arabia—A Saudi pilot shot down two Iraqi F-1 Mirage jets over the Persian Gulf just south of the Kuwait border, Saudi officials said Thursday.

The incident marked the first time Iraqi planes have crossed into Saudi territory since the beginning of the war in the gulf and apparently signaled Iraq's intention to attack targets in the gulf or along the coast of Saudi Arabia, the officials said.

The two Iraqi jets, loaded with French-made Exocet anti-ship missiles and possibly bombs as well, were flying south along the Saudi coastline about 200 feet above the water when a Saudi F-15C swung in behind them and fired two AIM-9 Sidewinder missiles, downing both of them.

There were unconfirmed reports that a third Iraqi jet in the area turned back, possibly after firing or dumping an Exocet missile.

"I cannot tell you exactly which part of the gulf [they were headed for], but I am sure they were going to attack us, because their route was heading toward us," said the 30-year-old pilot who shot down the two aircraft, identified only as Capt. Ayedh. "You know, the whole coast is filled with oil fields, refineries, even the [air] base is located on the coast. But they were in my territory; that's what I care about."

An official from the Saudi F-15 squadron investigating the incident said it appeared that allied ships in the gulf were within range of the Iraqi jets' Exocets, the powerful, sea-skimming, anti-ship missiles that have a range of more than 40 miles.

But U.S. military officials in Riyadh said they could not confirm how close the Iraqi planes came to U.S. or other allied ships, and British officers who were tracking the jets on radar said no warships came within range of the missiles.

"He can be pretty far away and still be within range," said a U.S.

Please see PILOT, A20

Arabs Growing Concerned for Iraq's Survival

By ROBIN WRIGHT
TIMES STAFF WRITER

WASHINGTON—After a week of heavy bombing by U.S. and coalition warplanes, the survival of Iraq has begun to replace the liberation of Kuwait as the focus of Arab reaction—and growing anger.

While word of 15,000 allied sorties plays well in U.S. and European nations, the specter of a relentless blitzkrieg on Iraqi cities is galvanizing increasing anti-Americanism and threatening to undermine governments, including some members of the 31-nation coalition.

"The fate of Iraq is becoming an increasingly emotional issue, even among people who don't support [Iraqi President] Saddam [Hussein]," a U.S. official conceded.

"The nature of the attack is now making Iraq more visible than Saddam as the issue in these countries. People are becoming as concerned about saving Iraq as liberating Kuwait," said Clovis Maksoud, former Arab League

Please see ARABS, A29

Latinos Lagging on Every School Level, Study Finds

■ **Education:** From preschool to college, they are under-represented and losing ground nationally.

By JEAN MERL
TIMES EDUCATION WRITER

From enrollment in preschool to attainment of graduate degrees, the nation's Latinos are "grossly under-represented at every rung of the educational ladder" and, by many measures of academic achievement, are losing ground, according to a study by the American Council on Education.

The study, released in Washington this week, showed that the proportion of Latino students completing high school slid from 60.1% in 1984 to 55.9% in 1989. By contrast, the completion rate for blacks rose slightly during the same period—from 74.7% to 76.1%. While the rate for Anglos dipped somewhat, down to 82.1% in 1989, it remained dramatically higher than those of the two minority groups. Based on census data, the report did not provide separate completion rates for Asians and American Indians.

Educators and some political leaders have long been concerned about Latinos' acute lack of success in the schools system, and President Bush recently launched a special effort to improve the educational lot of this group.

But the ACE study, its Ninth Annual Status Report on Minorities in Higher Education, paints the most detailed—and perhaps the darkest—picture to date.

"It's not just that there is no

Please see LATINOS, A30

MORE WAR COVERAGE

■ **WAR STORIES:** A5-23; B3; D1, D4, D15; E1; F2, F15, F23

■ **DOUBTS ABOUT SCUDS**

Military analysts doubt that Iraq has the technology necessary to carry out effective attacks with Scud missiles armed with chemical warheads. **A6**

■ **ISRAELI RESTRAINT**

The Israeli government is weighing the wisdom of a retaliatory attack on Iraq. For now, analysts say, Israel sees more political benefits in restraint. **A7**

■ **IRAQ ASSAILS JAPAN**

Iraq declared Japan a hostile nation in response to Tokyo's decision to supply military cargo planes and an additional $9 billion to the allied coalition. **A8**

■ **EUROPEAN SECURITY**

Europe is taking seriously Iraqi President Saddam Hussein's threat of terrorism. But despite extraordinary measures, there have already been lapses. **A8**

■ **CBS CREW MISSING**

CBS confirmed that four of its newsmen in the gulf, including veteran combat correspondent Bob Simon, have been missing for more than three days. **A9**

■ **TERROR ASSESSMENT**

The risk of domestic terrorism is relatively low, the director of the FBI said, but his agency continues to monitor individuals aligned with terror groups. **A10**

■ **POLITICAL UPROAR**

A top Republican has created an uproar by declaring that Democrats who voted against authorizing war should be held accountable at the polls. **A10**

WEATHER: Cloudy this morning. Civic Center low/high today: 49/64. Details: B5

■ TOP OF THE NEWS ON A2

New Breed of Warriors—Women—Closer to Front

■ **Military:** They still aren't allowed in combat, but gulf marks a turning point in sexual integration of services.

By DAVID LAMB
TIMES STAFF WRITER

EASTERN SAUDI ARABIA—They are America's new breed of warriors, preparing jet fighters for bombing runs on Iraq, hauling ammunition to the front, guarding gates to military installations. They carry themselves with pride and their weapons with authority.

Never before in a major U.S. war have women been so close to the front lines or played such a varied role in warfare. Although prohibited from serving on attack planes, warships and in ground combat units, women are performing most of the same tasks as their male counterparts. And by all accounts they are performing them well, having experienced only minor problems as the military services integrated sexually.

Tescha Shipp, 21, of Dallas, Ga., and her brother Jason joined the Marine Corps about a year ago and went through boot camp at Parris Island, S.C., together. Today, she is one of 130 women Marines at a logistics outpost within artillery range of the Kuwaiti border, working as a "wire dog," climbing telephone poles in a communications outfit.

"I'm here in the desert with a rifle on my shoulder and Jason is at Camp Pendleton in California playing with a computer," she said with a laugh. "Jason wishes it was him over here instead of me, but I'm

Please see WOMEN, A12

Howitzer M198/155mm

Marine Corps 155 mm howitzers, which carry projectiles that weigh about 19 pounds and can penetrate 3 inches of armor, saw their first action of the Persian Gulf War on Monday.

The six-minute salvo of 71 shells was unleashed at an Iraqi artillery unit inside Kuwait that had been shelling the Marines. Field weapons such as the 155mm Howitzer M198 support advancing tanks and ground troops.

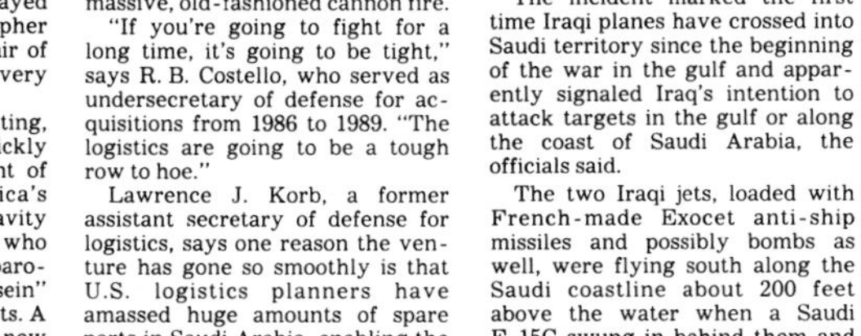

GUN STATISTICS
Caliber: 155 millimeter
Barrel length: 20 feet
Rate of fire: 4 rounds a minute
Maximum range: 20 miles
Crew: 11
Towed by 5-ton truck

Israeli draftees got a chilling lesson in countering chemical warfare.

LARRY DAVIS / Los Angeles Times

SHIFTING FOCUS TO

ISRAEL

Saddam Hussein knows that if he can draw Israel into the war, he will automatically win the sympathy, if not the military support, of many Arabs. The rulers of such U.S. allies as Egypt and Syria may well stick with the coalition despite an Israeli entry, knowing that it resulted from a calculated provocation by the Iraqi leader. But the populations of those countries, as well as most others in the Arab world, undoubtedly support any Arab leader ready to take on the Jewish state.

HISTORY: Technically, most of the Arab world—including Iraq—has been at war with Israel since 1948, when an Arab coalition attacked the newly formed Jewish state in support of the Palestinians. Anti-Israeli sentiment is particularly high in those Arab countries that have significant Palestinian populations—Jordan, Lebanon, Syria.

INTIFADA: Since December, 1987, an overwhelming majority of the 1.7 million Palestinians living on the occupied West Bank of the Jordan River and in the Gaza Strip have supported the so-called *intifada*, or uprising, against Israeli occupation, which has resulted in the deaths of more than 1,000 Palestinians and about 60 Israelis and Jewish tourists.

IMMIGRATION: With Soviet Jews now pouring into Israel at the rate of about 200,000 or more per year, there is Arab concern that the Jewish population of the occupied territories will increase sharply from the current 70,000, putting even more pressure on the Palestinians still there.

HEROES: The issues have changed little during much of the last century in a land that two peoples see as their historic right. And Saddam Hussein understands better than most that the leaders his people recognize as heroes—from the 12th Century sultan Saladin to Egypt's Gamal Abdel Nasser—enjoy their stature because they stood up to outside influence.

PALESTINIANS AROUND THE WORLD

Country/Region	Estimated Population	Country/Region	Estimated Population
Israel and the Occupied Territories	2,300,000	Saudi Arabia	171,145
Jordan	1,297,550	United States	114,402
Lebanon	492,240	Egypt	37,668
Syria	245,288	Iraq	22,712
Kuwait	336,530	Other areas:	297,237

Source: Palestine Yearbook

ISRAEL TODAY

LEBANON
Mediterranean Sea
GOLAN HEIGHTS
Haifa
Tiberias
Nazareth
Nablus
Tel Aviv
WEST BANK
Jerusalem
Hebron
Gaza
GAZA STRIP
Dead Sea
Beersheba
ISRAEL
NEGEV

0 ——— 30
MILES

PRE 1967

LEBANON
Jerusalem International Administration
SINAI

	1947 Mandate
	New territory 1948-49

1967

LEB.
Mediterranean Sea
ISRAEL
EGYPT
SINAI
JORDAN
SAUDI ARABIA

Pre 1967 area and boundaries
1967 cease-fire lines and area
Israeli forces in response to attack

1973

Mediterranean Sea
SYRIA
ISRAEL
JORDAN
SINAI
EGYPT
SAUDI ARABIA

Pre 1973 boundaries
Occupied areas
Israeli forces in response to attack

LEBANON
SYRIA
Mediterranean Sea
ISRAEL
IRAQ
SINAI
EGYPT
JORDAN
SAUDI ARABIA

Israeli - Palestinian Peace Proposals

Here are some of the peace proposals that have been offered in recent years to resolve the Israeli-Palestinian conflict.

■ **NOV. 29, 1947: U.N. VOTES FOR PARTITION OF PALESTINE**
After World War II, the British, frustrated by their attempts to reach a compromise in the region, turned the issue over to the United Nations. Despite strong Arab opposition, the U.N. voted in favor of partition.

Result: The British remained in Palestine until May 14, 1948, the day the mandate expired. The same day, the Jewish National Council proclaimed the state of Israel. The next day, Egypt and Jordan invaded the new state.

■ **NOVEMBER, 1967: U.N. SECURITY COUNCIL RESOLUTION 242**
After Israel's victory in the 1967 Six-Day War, the United Nations Security Council adopted the resolution which has formed the basis of virtually every Mideast peace proposal ever since. It called for withdrawal of Israeli forces from territories occupied in the war and respect for the right of all states in the region to live in peace within secure and recognized boundaries.

■ **SEPTEMBER, 1978: CAMP DAVID ACCORDS**
Egyptian President Anwar Sadat and Israeli Prime Minister Menachem Begin signed an agreement providing for a five-year transition during which inhabitants of the Israeli-occupied West Bank and Gaza Strip would obtain full autonomy and self-government.

Result: Negotiations fell apart because of conflicting definitions of what Palestinian autonomy should be, with Israel opting for an administrative self-governing plan of limited autonomy, while Egypt and the Palestinians called for an independent Palestinian state.

■ **APRIL, 1989: ISRAELI PROPOSALS**
Prime Minister Yitzhak Shamir proposed free elections in the West Bank and Gaza to elect delegates who could then be empowered to negotiate the terms of self-rule under Israeli authority—all contingent on an end to ongoing violence in the occupied territories.

Result: The proposal was rejected by many Palestinian activists because it excluded the Palestine Liberation Organization. However, some observers thought that there was hope that meaningful negotiations could come out of it. These hopes were soon dampened, when in July, Shamir added conditions that ruled out the possibility of a Palestinian state on the West Bank and contained provisions for a continuation of Jewish settlement in the occupied territories.

—Compiled by MICHAEL MEYERS

33

DON CLEMENT / Los Angeles Times

DAY 10

JANUARY 26, 1991

Bahrain quickly became blase about Iraq's Scud missiles. They had been fired at Israel and Saudi Arabia but not at us. Then one night, at about 3 a.m., Patriot anti-Scud missiles started exploding. In a hotel disco, now a makeshift air-raid shelter, half-dressed journalists, Marines in T-shirts and rich Kuwaitis in designer workout clothes squatted on the dance floor as the terrifying detonations boomed overhead. A radio repeatedly blared a warning in Arabic: "Danger! Danger! Danger! An air raid is in progress."

Just then, the door of the disco opened and a Pakistani bellboy with a little chalkboard and a bicycle bell marched in, paging a Mr. Summers. He pushed through the crowd politely, went back up the stairs and closed the door of the shelter behind him, oblivious to the danger.

—Charles P. Wallace, in Bahrain

Los Angeles Times

CIRCULATION: 1,225,189 DAILY / 1,514,096 SUNDAY | SATURDAY, JANUARY 26, 1991 | COPYRIGHT 1991 THE TIMES MIRROR COMPANY CC† 112 PAGES | DAILY 25¢ DESIGNATED AREAS HIGHER

Iraq Unleashing Oil Into Gulf

11 Missiles Fired at Tel Aviv, Saudi Arabia; 2 Killed

Associated Press

The wing of a building in Riyadh, Saudi Arabia, lies in ruins Friday after an Iraqi missile attack that killed one person and wounded 30 others.

Gulf War

■ **Gulf War:** U.S. decries 'environmental terrorism,' says spill off Kuwait is 12 times bigger than the Exxon Valdez disaster. Water supplies threatened; military impact unclear.

By JOHN M. BRODER and MAURA DOLAN
TIMES STAFF WRITERS

WASHINGTON—A defiant Iraq has loosed millions of barrels of crude oil into Persian Gulf waters off Kuwait over a period of several days in what the Bush Administration on Friday branded "environmental terrorism" of an "immense and shocking magnitude."

U.S. officials said that Iraqi forces have opened the valves on an oil-loading pipeline at the Sea Island terminal of the Al Ahmadi refinery. The terminal is about 10 miles off the Kuwaiti coast, pouring an estimated 100,000 barrels of slippery brown crude into the strategic waterway each day.

The Iraqis have also emptied the crude from five large tankers that have been moored off Kuwait city since last October, U.S. government spokesmen said. Each tanker held several hundred thousand barrels of oil.

The resulting spill has created "an enormous mess in the Persian Gulf of rather frightening consequences," said Pentagon spokesman Pete Williams. Military officials insisted, however, that the oil spill would have no impact on the progress of Operation Desert Storm.

Iraqi President Saddam Hussein has long threatened to set the sea afire to thwart an allied amphibious assault. But U.S. military planners appear to have been taken by surprise by the spill and were scrambling to assess the size and danger of the spreading oil plume and to find ways to combat it.

Government officials estimated that, as of Friday, the spill involved a dozen times more crude than the Exxon Valdez disaster, the largest oil spill in U.S. history. The Valdez drenched the shores of Alaska's Prince William Sound with 258,000 barrels of crude oil in March, 1989.

"Saddam Hussein continues to amaze the world," President Bush said at a White House news conference.

"There's no rationality to it," he said. "It looks desperate; it looks last gasp. . . . It's kind of sick."

Bush echoed military officials in insisting that Hussein would gain "no military advantage" from the oil spill.

"It's not going to help him at all," the President said.

Asked whether the oil would interfere with possible Marine amphibious landings, Bush said, "No, it doesn't interfere with anything."

Although the President and Pentagon officials discounted the impact on military operations, the spill clearly has the potential to force allied warships to alter their sailing patterns, impede amphibious landings and foul the Saudi desalination plants that provide

Please see SPILL, A6

COLUMN ONE

Decade of Digging Aids Iraq

■ Hussein imported state-of-the-art bunker-building techniques. Now much of his military punch—and the leader himself—may be protected.

By LEE DYE and MARK FINEMAN
TIMES STAFF WRITERS

A small French fishing net company was thrilled a decade ago to sell millions of dollars worth of its material to Iraq for use as military camouflage.

There was nothing wrong with the decision, company officials would lament later, because Iraq was then at war with the Western World's personification of evil, Iran's Ayatollah Ruhollah Khomeini.

The same reasoning made it easy for a Belgian construction company, along with a government-controlled Yugoslav firm, to build hundreds of underground bunkers across Iraq.

And a British nonprofit company that had been established to teach people how to construct bomb shelters provided Iraq with detailed plans for large bunkers that today can house combat troops by the hundreds.

And thus did Saddam Hussein acquire the technical expertise, the plans and even some of the materials to build a network of bomb shelters and reinforced jet fighter hangers that apparently has protected his troops and air force, and even himself, from one of the most intense aerial assaults in history. U.S. officials concede that the concrete cocoons have allowed Hussein, at a critical time, to maintain control and command of his forces.

In interviews this week, engineers, contractors and material

Please see BUNKERS, A5

USAir Trims Flights in State

USAir, reeling from huge losses brought on by high fuel costs and a West Coast fare war, announced plans to eliminate most of its flights within California.

The airline's dramatic retrenchment comes two weeks after American Airlines all but pulled out of California's north-south corridor. D1

Combat Troops to Patrol Streets in Soviet Cities

By MICHAEL PARKS
TIMES STAFF WRITER

MOSCOW—Armed troops will join police in patrolling the streets of the Soviet Union's major cities next week to combat rising street crime, the Kremlin announced Friday.

In a joint order by the Soviet ministers of defense and of internal affairs, the government said that law and order are deteriorating even more rapidly than before, that criminals are now well armed and that "grave crimes of a vicious and cynical nature" are increasing.

The new directive from Defense Minister Dmitri T. Yazov and Interior Minister Boris K. Pugo said that the measure is a "concrete answer to demands of Soviet people for strengthening legality and order in the country, faithfully ensuring the safety of every citizen."

But the deployment of armed combat troops, who will be supported by armored cars and other military units, is certain to heighten the fear of further clashes between the army and civilians, particularly in the country's troubled areas such as the Baltic re-

Please see SOVIET, A25

Patriots Shoot Down 6 of 7 Scuds Over Israel

■ **Iraqi attacks:** Israel holds off on any retaliation. Saudis suffer their first fatality from missiles.

By DANIEL WILLIAMS and J. MICHAEL KENNEDY
TIMES STAFF WRITERS

TEL AVIV—Iraq fired a rain of seven Scud missiles into Israel on Friday, and one crashed into a house in Tel Aviv, killing a neighbor next door. But Israel refrained from retaliating, despite complaints that allied Scud-killing in Iraq has been too slow.

A barrage of Patriot interceptors blew apart the other six Iraqi Scuds in the air, scattering debris over greater Tel Aviv and near Haifa. Shutters shattered, windows broke and shingles fell on city streets. None of the Scuds carried poison gas. But 66 Israelis were injured, authorities said—most of them slightly.

At about the same time, Iraq fired another four Scuds into Saudi Arabia. One destroyed a wing of a building near downtown Riyadh. Witnesses said the missile hit with a bright orange flash. One person was killed and another 30 were injured, Interior Ministry officials said. The death was Saudi Arabia's first Scud fatality.

Two of the other three missiles fired into Saudi Arabia were destroyed by Patriots. One exploded in the air over Riyadh. The other was intercepted over the Dammam-Dhahran area on the Persian Gulf coast. The fourth missile also was aimed at the Dammam-Dhahran area, but witnesses said it apparently went astray.

As the missiles flew, round-the-clock assaults by allied warplanes "hit heavily" at Iraq's defensive line in Kuwait, allied military officials said. Maj. Gen. Robert B. Johnston, chief of staff of the U.S. Central Command, cited evidence that the bombing is affecting Iraqi supply lines.

He said allied forces had taken prisoners and encountered defectors who were eating one meal a day and were covered with lice.

There were these additional developments:

- Defense Secretary Dick Cheney said in Washington that he would not be surprised to learn that President Saddam Hussein's troops had suffered as many as 10,000 casualties, "given the effort we have mounted against his [Republican] Guard."
- Hussein had his top air force and air-defense commanders shot

Please see MISSILES, A4

Key U.S. Goal: Rout of Elite Iraqi Troops

By MELISSA HEALY and JOHN M. BRODER
TIMES STAFF WRITERS

WASHINGTON—Bush Administration officials have concluded that the outcome of the Persian Gulf War—and the long-term stability of the Middle East—hinges on the destruction of the elite Republican Guard units, which remain under round-the-clock bombardment from allied warplanes.

Administration strategists believe that crushing the 150,000-man Republican Guard will drive a stake through the heart of Iraqi President Saddam Hussein's regime and lead to the collapse of the rest of Iraq's million-man army.

Lt. Gen. Thomas W. Kelly, director of operations for the Joint Chiefs of Staff in Washington, said Friday that initial assessments indicate that the aerial assault on guard units is beginning to produce results.

"We believe we are having a significant impact on them, but we can't prove that from the type of information that we have in front of us right now," he said.

The guard, which is entrenched and dispersed throughout northern

Please see GUARD, A10

Largest Cities Reflect Shift to West, 1990 Census Finds

■ **Population:** Los Angeles beats out Chicago as No. 2 in U.S. California lists 18 of 29 places reaching 100,000.

By KEVIN RODERICK and ANNE C. ROARK
TIMES STAFF WRITERS

Six of the nation's 10 largest cities are now west of the Mississippi River, and most of the 29 cities to reach a population of 100,000 in the last decade are California suburbs, according to final 1990 census data released Friday.

With the news that the country's westward shift has enlarged the suburbs and shuffled the roster of major cities, the Census Bureau also confirmed for the first time that Los Angeles—up half a million people since 1980, to nearly 3.5 million—is the nation's second-largest city.

Chicago, which had been No. 2, was among several cities in the East and Midwest to slip in population. Chicago dropped below 3 million people for the first time since the 1930 census, and in the past 40 years it has lost 837,000 people—23% of its populace.

New York, meanwhile, remained No. 1 and grew by a quarter-million people to 7.3 million, reversing a decline that began in the 1970s.

The trend toward population loss plagued many older cities in the East and Midwest in the 1980s, but not in California and the rest of the Sun Belt West.

Houston edged past Philadelphia to become the fourth-largest city.

Please see CENSUS, A32

INSIDE TODAY'S TIMES

Conflict of Patriotism, Dissent Grips Congress

■ **Politics:** Debate has been less partisan than many expected, but it is already shaping 1992 elections.

By CATHLEEN DECKER
TIMES POLITICAL WRITER

No one questioned Douglas Peterson's patriotism a war ago, when he resided in the successive squalor of two North Vietnamese prisoner-of-war camps. But the Democratic congressman's anguished decision earlier this month to oppose the use of American military force against Iraq undammed a flood of telephone calls from his anxious Florida constituents.

And some of them pointedly rebuked Peterson for what they defined as a lack of patriotic will.

"There is a mind-set that if you're not for war . . . then you're not a patriot," said Peterson, a former Air Force pilot. "If I haven't proven my patriotism by now, I'm not going to try."

Colliding again, as they did during the long and wrenching political debate over the Vietnam War, are the rush to patriotism and the right to dissent. At the vortex are politicians who chose up sides this month in one of the most heart-rending debates in recent history, men and women whose electoral futures may ride on the conduct of the Gulf War.

With the war riding a wave of popularity, the politicians who opposed initial military involvement are taking pains to define their dissent as patriotic. In private talks with constituents and lengthy ad-

Please see CONGRESS, A14

AH-64A Apache Helicopter

The AH-64 Apache helicopter, an attack copter, carries laser-guided anti-tank missiles and night vision sights.It is designed to lurk behind trees and ridges, to pick off tanks three miles away. But the flat and arid waste of the desert doesn't offer many hiding places. Some specialists are concerned about the level of maintenance required by the craft.

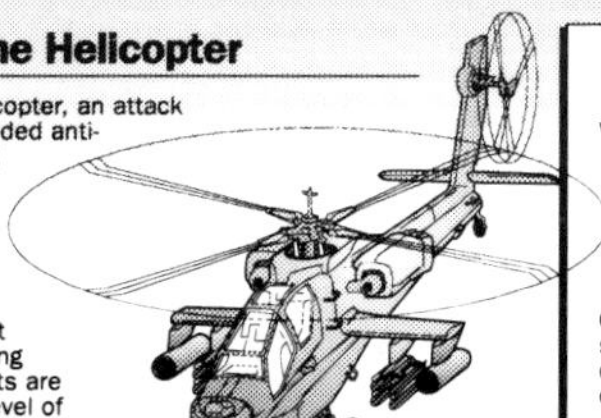

- **Crew:** Pilot and co-pilot/weapons operator
- **Maximum range:** 300 miles; 1,175 miles with external fuel tanks.
- **Maximum cruising speed:** 184 m.p.h.
- **Armaments:** 30-mm gun: fires 625 rounds per minute, carries up to 1,200 rounds; 8 laser-guided Hellfire missiles; 36 aerial rockets, 18 per launcher.
- **Tracking and night vision systems:** Camera target detection and tracking system, laser range finder and target designator. Information is displayed inside of pilots' and co-pilots' helmets.

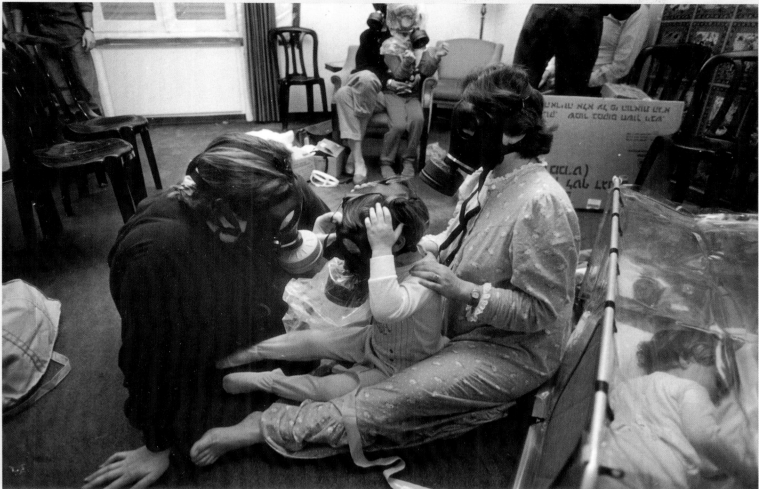

Legacy of the Scuds: Many Israeli children were traumatized.

LARRY DAVIS / Los Angeles Times

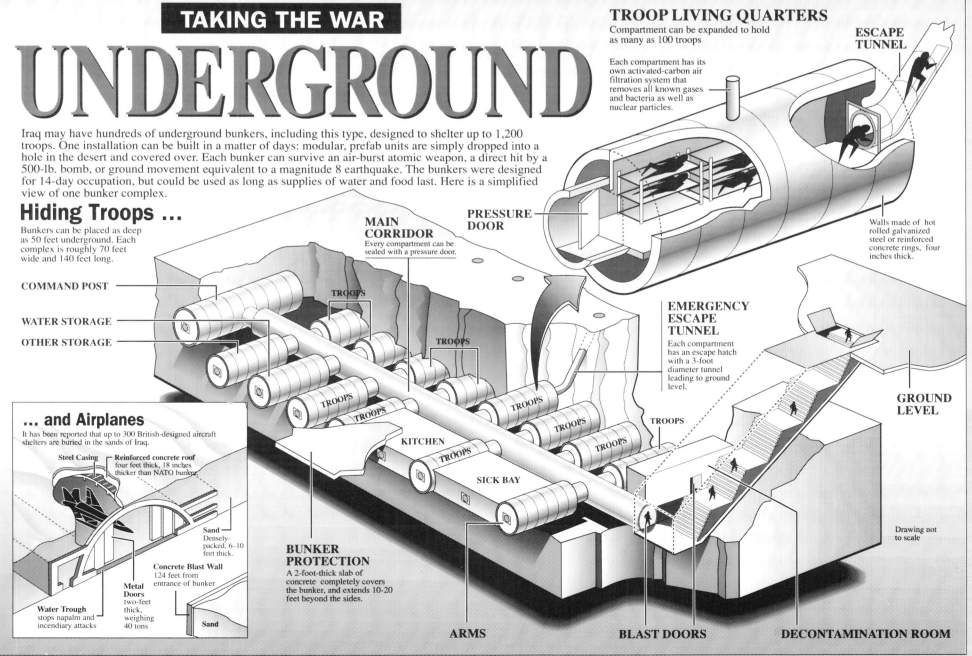

TAKING THE WAR
UNDERGROUND

Iraq may have hundreds of underground bunkers, including this type, designed to shelter up to 1,200 troops. One installation can be built in a matter of days: modular, prefab units are simply dropped into a hole in the desert and covered over. Each bunker can survive an air-burst atomic weapon, a direct hit by a 500-lb. bomb, or ground movement equivalent to a magnitude 8 earthquake. The bunkers were designed for 14-day occupation, but could be used as long as supplies of water and food last. Here is a simplified view of one bunker complex.

Hiding Troops ...

Bunkers can be placed as deep as 50 feet underground. Each complex is roughly 70 feet wide and 140 feet long.

COMMAND POST
WATER STORAGE
OTHER STORAGE
TROOPS

TROOP LIVING QUARTERS
Compartment can be expanded to hold as many as 100 troops.

Each compartment has its own activated-carbon air filtration system that removes all known gases and bacteria as well as nuclear particles.

ESCAPE TUNNEL

MAIN CORRIDOR
Every compartment can be sealed with a pressure door.

PRESSURE DOOR

Walls made of hot rolled galvanized steel or reinforced concrete rings, four inches thick.

EMERGENCY ESCAPE TUNNEL
Each compartment has an escape hatch with a 3-foot diameter tunnel leading to ground level.

GROUND LEVEL

Drawing not to scale

... and Airplanes
It has been reported that up to 300 British-designed aircraft shelters are buried in the sands of Iraq.

Steel Casing — Reinforced concrete roof four feet thick, 18 inches thicker than NATO bunker.

Sand Densely-packed, 6–10 feet thick.

Concrete Blast Wall 124 feet from entrance of bunker.

Metal Doors two-feet thick, weighing 40 tons

Water Trough stops napalm and incendiary attacks

Sand

BUNKER PROTECTION
A 2-foot-thick slab of concrete completely covers the bunker, and extends 10-20 feet beyond the sides.

KITCHEN
TROOPS
SICK BAY
TROOPS

ARMS

BLAST DOORS

DECONTAMINATION ROOM

Source: Federation of Nuclear Shelter Consultants & Contractors, Associated Press

DAVID PUCKETT / Los Angeles Times

DAY 11

JANUARY 27, 1991

This war, with the possible exception of its last few days, was a stage manager's delight, a war of talking heads. It was as if some great black shroud had been placed over the battlefield. Death, the ultimate result of war, was never shown save through the cameras in Baghdad.

There we sat, our televisions tuned to Cable News Network, our radios to the Armed Forces Network, our computers able to pick up the wire services from half a world away. Yet, we really didn't know much more than what the people in the uniforms wanted us to know. And they wanted to portray this as a quick, clean war, which war never is.

—J. Michael Kennedy, in Riyadh, Saudi Arabia

Los Angeles Times

Sunday Final

CIRCULATION: 1,225,189 DAILY / 1,514,096 SUNDAY

SUNDAY, JANUARY 27, 1991

COPYRIGHT 1991 THE TIMES MIRROR COMPANY CC† 474 PAGES

SUNDAY $1.25 DESIGNATED AREAS HIGHER

Nations Rally to Curb Oil Spill

Iraqi Warplanes Land in Iran; 5 Scuds Intercepted

COLUMN ONE

Obeying the Rules of Warfare

■ The U.S. wants to avoid being accused of waging a barbaric campaign against Iraq. Meanwhile, it is amassing evidence that Hussein has violated international standards of wartime behavior.

By PHILIP HAGER
TIMES LEGAL AFFAIRS WRITER

As allied air forces fly thousands of bombing missions and ground troops stand ready for combat, scores of U.S. military lawyers are on hand to make sure the rules of war are observed in the Persian Gulf.

Meanwhile, in Washington, officials are compiling data that, should the opportunity arise, could be used as evidence of war crimes against Iraqi President Saddam Hussein and his lieutenants.

Although inevitably overshadowed by the fury of battle, the laws of warfare are playing both a symbolic and practical role in the Gulf War.

Lawyers from all branches of the service are on the scene rendering advice on how to tailor battle plans to minimize civilian casualties, how to properly treat enemy prisoners of war, how to conform to the law of the sea and how to prepare and negotiate international agreements. A Pentagon legal specialist noted last week that the lawyers confer almost daily with officials in the United States about bombing-target lists.

This detailed attention to the laws of war arises in the aftermath of the Vietnam War and the My Lai massacre, in which scores of Vietnamese civilians were killed by U.S. Army troops. Now, every member of the military receives some training in the legal aspects of war that relate to their duties. Combat troops carry cards reminding them how to treat prisoners.

"Marines do not harm enemies who surrender. They must disarm them and turn them over to their superiors. Marines do not kill or torture prisoners. Marines collect and care for the wounded, whether friend or foe," one such card reads.

"The military was accused of acting barbarously in Vietnam and is determined not to be accused again," said Tom Farer, professor of international law and international relations at American University. "And this is a case where being right and being prudent coincide. If we were seen as being the butchers of Iraqi citizens, the coalition [opposing Iraq] would crumble. The war is unpopular

Please see RULES, A30

A Tel Aviv resident sits in his ruined apartment the morning after Iraq's Friday night Scud missile attack. Iraq fired more missiles Saturday.

■ **Gulf War:** Bush orders U.S. experts to the region to help the Saudis protect vital facilities. The incident could produce history's worst oil disaster.

By KIM MURPHY
and CHARLES P. WALLACE
TIMES STAFF WRITERS

DHAHRAN, Saudi Arabia—An international containment effort was under way Saturday to hold back a massive surge of crude oil unleashed from Kuwaiti oil facilities into the Persian Gulf in what officials say may be the worst oil disaster in history.

The 30-mile-long, eight-mile-wide oil slick, already more than 20 times larger than the Exxon Valdez oil spill in Alaska and spreading at an alarming rate, potentially threatens petrochemical and water desalination plants throughout the region and could upset the ecological balance of the entire Persian Gulf, authorities said.

Saudi officials said they are racing to protect key facilities with booms. In Washington, President Bush ordered a team of oil pollution

■ **STEMMING THE OIL TIDE**
Cleaning up the gulf is a near-impossible job, experts say. A6

and environmental experts, led by the U.S. Coast Guard, to fly to Saudi Arabia immediately "to assist the Saudis in their efforts to contain the oil slick," said Sean Walsh, an assistant White House press secretary.

Allied officials are also studying the possibility of igniting the slick, or portions of it, to minimize its impact.

By Saturday evening, as much as 6 million barrels of crude oil had been pumped into the gulf. U.S. officials said they believe Iraq deliberately unleashed the oil from five huge oil tankers moored off the Kuwaiti coast, loaded with an estimated 3 million barrels of crude, and opened the taps on a major pipeline connecting Kuwait's Sea Island loading terminal 10 miles offshore with the Al Ahmadi loading facility.

Please see SPILL, A26

Associated Press

Oil coats a cormorant in surf at Khafji in northern Saudi Arabia.

Iran's Nuclear Plans Worry U.S. Officials

By JIM MANN
TIMES STAFF WRITER

WASHINGTON—If U.S. military officials are correct, Iraq's nuclear facilities now lie in ruins, hopelessly damaged by a relentless barrage of American bombs and missiles. But that doesn't eliminate the danger that a nuclear-armed nation may come to dominate the Persian Gulf.

Over the last few weeks, some Bush Administration officials and independent nuclear specialists here have grown increasingly worried about new signs that Iran may be starting down the same path as Iraq, its Persian Gulf rival, with secret efforts to buy nuclear technology and build nuclear weapons.

"It looks like there's a really active program in Iran," said Leonard S. Spector, a nuclear specialist at the Carnegie Endowment for International Peace. "It picked up over the past eight or 10 months, after they saw and read about what was going on in Iraq."

Now, the Bush Administration and its allies are quietly launching a new international effort aimed at

Please see NUCLEAR, A28

U.S. Says Tehran Will Hold the Iraqi Aircraft

■ **Air action:** American officials are mystified at pilots' intentions in flying to Iran. Patriots down more Scuds.

By NICK B. WILLIAMS Jr.
and JOHN M. BRODER
TIMES STAFF WRITERS

AMMAN, Jordan—Iraqi aircraft slipped past allied radar, crossed the border and landed in neighboring Iran on Saturday, and the United States said Tehran promised to keep them—at least until the Gulf War ends.

The fugitive planes were combat aircraft, Tehran Radio reported, and the Iranians counted seven of them. But at the Pentagon, U.S. officers said the seven had joined at least 17 additional Iraqi aircraft—both civilian and military—already in Iran. These other planes, an American officer said, had left Iraq during the past several days.

Senior American intelligence officials professed to be mystified about why the Iraqis had gone to Iran.

"It's unclear whether they are husbanding their resources" by flying to a haven in an officially neutral country—or defecting, said Rear Adm. John (Mike) McConnell, director of intelligence for the Joint Chiefs of Staff. He said American estimates of the number of Iraqi aircraft flown to Iran are expected to climb.

In the 10th day of the Persian Gulf War, there were these other developments:

●Iraq fired four Scud missiles at Israel and one at Saudi Arabia. All were intercepted by Patriot missiles. None carried poison gas. There were no immediate reports of any injuries or serious damage from falling debris. The missiles were aimed at Tel Aviv and Haifa in Israel and Riyadh in Saudi Arabia.

●In what pilots call a "fur ball"—a hectic tangle of aerial dogfights—U.S. Air Force F-15s shot down three Iraqi MIG-23s. No allied planes were lost. Pilots returning from furious bombardment of Iraqi positions in Kuwait said the landscape below was ablaze with countless fires.

●On the ground, elements of the 1st Marine Division staged the largest artillery attack of the war. They hit Iraqi targets 27 miles southwest of Kuwait city. But it appeared that a full-scale ground war was not yet imminent because U.S. forces at the Saudi border

Please see PLANES, A8

Soviets Trying New Steps to End Conflict

By MICHAEL PARKS
TIMES STAFF WRITER

MOSCOW—The Soviet Union, afraid that the war in the Persian Gulf could spread through the Middle East and become protracted with mounting casualties, is stepping up its diplomatic efforts to secure a political resolution, probably based on a cease-fire and Iraq's withdrawal from Kuwait, a senior member of the Soviet leadership said Saturday.

Alexander S. Dzasokhov, a member of the Communist Party's Politburo, said that Moscow is trying in new contacts with the United States, the European Community and Arab states to shape an initiative that would attempt to end the war quickly through negotiations at the United Nations and to promote an overall settlement of the Middle East conflict on this basis.

"We need to complement our efforts, both in substance and in intensity, with something extra, something new," Dzasokhov told The Times in an interview.

"I can't say that we have a new formula for such a Soviet initiative,

Please see SOVIETS, A20

Psychological Impact of War Affects Home Front

■ **Emotions:** Steady flow of news intensifies feelings. Fallout ranges from anxiety and guilt to depression.

By TRACY WILKINSON
TIMES STAFF WRITER

While the war's psychological impact on relatives of Americans sent to the battlefront is obvious and well-documented—a time of apprehension and dread—it also has worked in numerous, more subtle ways on the minds of Americans whose connection to the conflict is less direct.

Never before has the American public been so steadily bombarded with immediate news of a war. The constant images of people clumsily donning gas masks or running for cover from bombs serves as unflinching reminder of potential death and destruction. Consequently, the psychological repercussions of this war, even in its early days, threaten to extend deeper and wider than ever before.

"In Vietnam, you saw it on the nightly news. But this is every day, every [hour]," said sociologist John Sibley Butler of the University of Texas at Austin. "It's put constantly on your mind. . . . That's got to have an impact."

With war comes uncertainty. Some people experience feelings of impotence and helplessness, their ability to have complete control over their destiny challenged. With uncertainty come rumors and fears: A college-age San Francisco man prepares his passport for a draft-evading trip to Canada; a Los Angeles construction contractor

Please see IMPACT, A16

INSIDE TODAY'S TIMES

Agence France-Presse

Wang Dan in 1989 speech.

■ **DISSIDENT SENTENCED**
Wang Dan, the top student leader of China's 1989 pro-democracy Tian An Men Square demonstrations, was sentenced to four years in prison. **A5**

■ **WAR STORIES, PHOTOS: A1-31; B1; D1-3, D8-9; M1-8**

■ **JAPAN AID QUESTIONED**
The additional $9 billion pledged by Japan to support the multinational forces in the gulf may be restricted by political opposition to noncombat purposes. **A7**

■ **FRUSTRATION IN ISRAEL**
Two Iraqi missile attacks on Israel caused little damage and no injuries, but they fueled frustration and talk of retaliation in the Jewish state. **A10**

■ **DEAR MOM & DAD**
Army Pfc. Alexander N. Porter of Camarillo wrote to his parents before leaving for the gulf. The letter has touched the hearts of many people. **M1**

WEATHER: High clouds today after morning cloudiness. Civic Center low/high today: 47/68. Details: B2

■ TOP OF THE NEWS ON A2

For Hussein, Stalemate in War Could Be a Victory

■ **Strategy:** He apparently hopes to inflict heavy casualties on the allies and emerge a political winner.

By DOYLE McMANUS
TIMES STAFF WRITER

WASHINGTON—To understand Saddam Hussein's position today, American and British experts say, go back to his meeting last summer with U.S. Ambassador April Glaspie. The Iraqi dictator abruptly declared: "Yours is a society which cannot accept 10,000 dead in one battle."

Today, Saddam Hussein, his back against the wall, is defiantly preparing for a bloody test of that theory.

Scholars who have studied the man for more than a decade warn that from the Iraqi leader's viewpoint, the war has only just begun. Hussein can still "win," in terms of increasing his long-term power and prestige in the Arab world, if circumstances break his way. And if things go wrong for Iraq—as the Pentagon promises—Hussein has few good options beyond ordering his army to fight to the last Iraqi.

"Saddam was convinced—and he is still convinced—that we can't take casualties," says David G. Newton, who served as U.S. ambassador to Iraq from 1984 until 1988. "He appears to believe his forces can take a pounding, inflict casualties on us in a ground war and then force us to draw back."

"Saddam has very few options left," agrees Christine Helms, a scholar who has served as a government consultant. "He knows

Please see HUSSEIN, A18

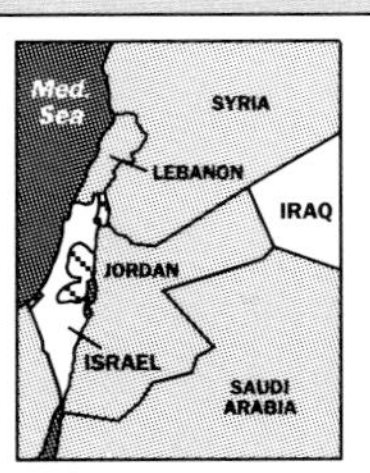

Profile: Israel

Although not part of the allied coalition, Israel has come under eight Iraqi missile attacks:

Capital: Jerusalem; but most countries recognize Tel Aviv.
Area: 7,847 square miles
Population: 5,224,000
Languages: Hebrew, Arabic and English
Ethnic groups: Jewish 83%, Arab 16%
Head of state: Chaim Herzog, president, 1983

Kuwait's oil well fires may take three years to put out.

PATRICK DOWNS / Los Angeles Times

DAY IN THE GULF

Environment: A 30-mile-long oil slick, part of it ablaze and being fed by more crude, threatens the Gulf's petrochemical and desalination plants and its ecological resources.

■ President Bush orders an interagency team of oil pollution and environmental experts to Saudi Arabia to deal with the spill.

■ Experts and military officials say the dangers of war severely limit cleanup options.

Iran: Tehran Radio says seven Iraqi warplanes crossed the border and landed in Iran. U.S. officials say Tehran promised to keep them, at least until the war ends.

■ U.S. briefers say the seven combat aircraft joined 17 Iraqi aircraft—both military and civilian—already in Iran.

Missiles: Iraq fires four Scud missiles at Israel and one at Saudi Arabia. All are intercepted.

■ Continued attacks on Israel fuel frustration and talk of retaliation.

Military: Marines unload their heaviest artillery barrage yet on forward Iraqi positions. Iraqis fire off short-range missiles that fall harmlessly in the desert.

■ Allies report more than 18,500 missions flown since the start of the war. The tally includes 23 allied planes lost, 17 in combat; 45 Iraqi planes destroyed; 27 allied personnel missing in action; 110 Iraqis taken prisoner.

■ Clear skies enable bombers to hit military support targets in southern Iraq and Kuwait, as well as the dug-in positions of the Republican Guard.

Terrorism: The Australian government orders the expulsion of Iraq's charge d'affaires for "security reasons."

■ The Philippines expels two Iraqi nationals linked to an attempted bombing of a U.S. library.

■ A bomb explodes outside the headquarters of the liberal French newspaper Liberation, causing considerable damage to the building's entrance but no injuries.

■ U.S. government agents interview thousands of Arab-Americans.

■ Pan American World Airways turns away Iraqi passengers.

Home front: Anti-war demonstrators return to Washington for the second consecutive weekend. Their ranks swell to at least 150,000.

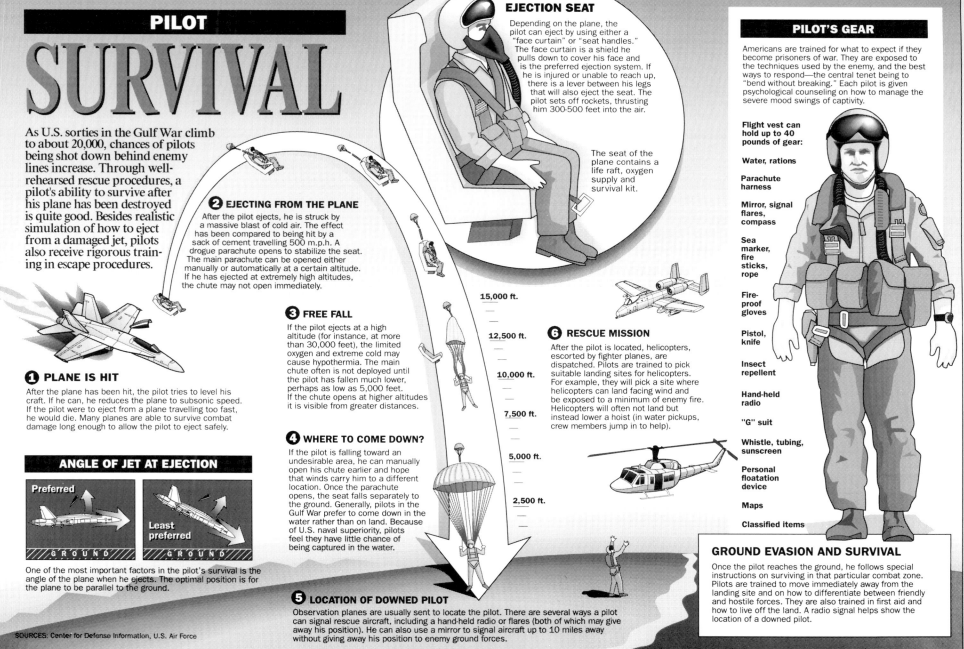

PILOT

SURVIVAL

As U.S. sorties in the Gulf War climb to about 20,000, chances of pilots being shot down behind enemy lines increase. Through well-rehearsed rescue procedures, a pilot's ability to survive after his plane has been destroyed is quite good. Besides realistic simulation of how to eject from a damaged jet, pilots also receive rigorous training in escape procedures.

❶ PLANE IS HIT

After the plane has been hit, the pilot tries to level his craft. If he can, he reduces the plane to subsonic speed. If the pilot were to eject from a plane travelling too fast, he would die. Many planes are able to survive combat damage long enough to allow the pilot to eject safely.

ANGLE OF JET AT EJECTION

Preferred

Least preferred

GROUND   GROUND

One of the most important factors in the pilot's survival is the angle of the plane when he ejects. The optimal position is for the plane to be parallel to the ground.

SOURCES: Center for Defense Information, U.S. Air Force

❷ EJECTING FROM THE PLANE

After the pilot ejects, he is struck by a massive blast of cold air. The effect has been compared to being hit by a sack of cement travelling 500 m.p.h. A drogue parachute opens to stabilize the seat. The main parachute can be opened either manually or automatically at a certain altitude. If he has ejected at extremely high altitudes, the chute may not open immediately.

❸ FREE FALL

If the pilot ejects at a high altitude (for instance, at more than 30,000 feet), the limited oxygen and extreme cold may cause hypothermia. The main chute often is not deployed until the pilot has fallen much lower, perhaps as low as 5,000 feet. If the chute opens at higher altitudes it is visible from greater distances.

❹ WHERE TO COME DOWN?

If the pilot is falling toward an undesirable area, he can manually open his chute earlier and hope that winds carry him to a different location. Once the parachute opens, the seat falls separately to the ground. Generally, pilots in the Gulf War prefer to come down in the water rather than on land. Because of U.S. naval superiority, pilots feel they have little chance of being captured in the water.

❺ LOCATION OF DOWNED PILOT

Observation planes are usually sent to locate the pilot. There are several ways a pilot can signal rescue aircraft, including a hand-held radio or flares (both of which may give away his position). He can also use a mirror to signal aircraft up to 10 miles away without giving away his position to enemy ground forces.

EJECTION SEAT

Depending on the plane, the pilot can eject by using either a "face curtain" or "seat handles." The face curtain is a shield he pulls down to cover his face and is the preferred ejection system. If he is injured or unable to reach up, there is a lever between his legs that will also eject the seat. The pilot sets off rockets, thrusting him 300-500 feet into the air.

The seat of the plane contains a life raft, oxygen supply and survival kit.

15,000 ft.

12,500 ft.

10,000 ft.

7,500 ft.

5,000 ft.

2,500 ft.

❻ RESCUE MISSION

After the pilot is located, helicopters, escorted by fighter planes, are dispatched. Pilots are trained to pick suitable landing sites for helicopters. For example, they will pick a site where helicopters can land facing wind and be exposed to a minimum of enemy fire. Helicopters will often not land but instead lower a hoist (in water pickups, crew members jump in to help).

PILOT'S GEAR

Americans are trained for what to expect if they become prisoners of war. They are exposed to the techniques used by the enemy, and the best ways to respond—the central tenet being to "bend without breaking." Each pilot is given psychological counseling on how to manage the severe mood swings of captivity.

Flight vest can hold up to 40 pounds of gear:

Water, rations

Parachute harness

Mirror, signal flares, compass

Sea marker, fire sticks, rope

Fire-proof gloves

Pistol, knife

Insect repellent

Hand-held radio

"G" suit

Whistle, tubing, sunscreen

Personal floatation device

Maps

Classified items

GROUND EVASION AND SURVIVAL

Once the pilot reaches the ground, he follows special instructions on surviving in that particular combat zone. Pilots are trained to move immediately away from the landing site and on how to differentiate between friendly and hostile forces. They are also trained in first aid and how to live off the land. A radio signal helps show the location of a downed pilot.

Written by SCOTT BROWN / Los Angeles Times

DENNIS LOWE / Los Angeles Times

37

DAY 12

JANUARY 28, 1991

On a brilliant winter's day, Al Turner of Laurens, S.C., came to the Vietnam Memorial to look for a friend's name—and for a little peace in time of war, another war.

"I'm a sad dude, buddy," said Turner. "I just came down here looking to regroup."

A former Army private in the Vietnam War who recently lost his wife in an accident, Turner said he loved America. But his manner bespoke one of this country's lost souls: His eyes were hidden by dark glasses, his voice was gravelly and his words were rambling.

Turner found the name he was looking for, schoolmate James Clifford McKittrick, an All-American farm boy lost in Vietnam on June 18, 1967. But the name had a cross beside it: McKittrick was still listed as missing in action more than 23 years later.

"This war," Turner said of the Gulf conflict, "I think they're going to do this one a little different. They're going to win this one. In Vietnam, we would have hauled some ass if they'd let us. But here I am, 20 years later, an old dude crying about my buddies."

—Alan C. Miller,
in Washington

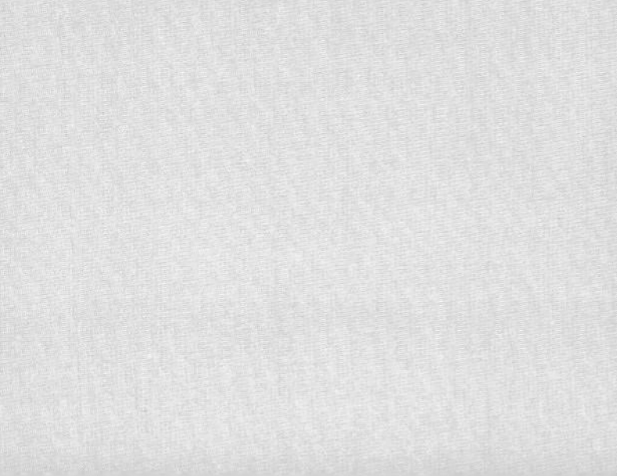

Los Angeles Times

CIRCULATION: 1,225,189 DAILY 1,514,096 SUNDAY | MONDAY, JANUARY 28, 1991 | COPYRIGHT 1991 THE TIMES MIRROR COMPANY CC† 104 PAGES | DAILY 25¢ DESIGNATED AREAS HIGHER

Pipelines Bombed to Halt Spill

No Need to Rush Into Ground Conflict, Cheney Says

■ **Gulf War:** U.S. jets target oil-flow regulators in Kuwait. 'I think that we've been successful, but only time will tell,' Schwarzkopf says. The slick spreads into Saudi waters.

By KIM MURPHY
TIMES STAFF WRITER

DHAHRAN, Saudi Arabia—In a dramatic bid to check a gush of oil into Persian Gulf waters, U.S. warplanes swept into Kuwait and dropped precision glider bombs on two inland pipeline devices that direct crude toward the offshore Sea Island loading station, U.S. military officials said Sunday.

They said it would take a full day to determine whether the nighttime raid by F-111 fighter-bombers on key parts of Kuwait's premier oil facility was successful.

"I think that we've been successful, but only time will tell," Gen. H. Norman Schwarzkopf, commander of allied forces in the Persian Gulf, told reporters in Riyadh.

U.S. officials have accused Iraq of releasing millions of barrels of Kuwaiti crude into the gulf, draining moored oil tankers and opening an offshore pipeline. Baghdad claims the oil spill is the result of U.S.-led bombing raids on Kuwait.

Oil was said to be surging into the gulf at a rate of more than 1.2 million barrels a day—more than four times the amount discharged during the entire Exxon Valdez oil disaster.

By Sunday, the slow-moving slick had widened to at least 350 square miles and crept into Saudi Arabian waters off Ras al Mishab, about 30 miles south of the Kuwaiti border. Winds kept most of it two to three miles offshore, and a decidedly uphill effort was under way to lessen the impact on the gulf's already fragile marine life.

"It is apparent that Saddam Hussein has chosen not only to threaten and destroy the resources of this generation, but also the resources of the future generation," said Abdulbar Gain, president of Saudi Arabia's Meteorology and Environmental Protection Agency. "An oil spill of this magnitude is completely unimaginable. It is catastrophic in terms of the possible damage it might cause."

Schwarzkopf said U.S. intelligence detected the spill last Thursday, observing first that five tankers moored at the Kuwaiti oil complex of Al Ahmadi were conspicuously lighter in the water, and then that a black patch was moving from an offshore buoy at the Sea Island supertanker loading terminal, located about eight miles offshore.

Hasty briefings with military and oil experts followed, and U.S. officials were counseled to attack the spill in two ways: Set fire to the source, the Sea Island terminal, to burn off any crude moving through its tanks and pipes, and launch an air strike designed to halt the flow of new oil toward the gulf facility.

Please see SPILL, A8

Military photo via Associated Press

Kuwait's Sea Island oil terminal, set ablaze by naval action Friday, was still burning after Saturday's U.S. raid on pipeline feeding oil to terminal.

COLUMN ONE

This War Stirs Pains of the Last

■ News from the gulf brings back agonizing memories to many Vietnam veterans. Some are heartened by the level of public support.

By ALAN C. MILLER and MILES CORWIN
TIMES STAFF WRITERS

WASHINGTON—Under a wintry blue sky, former artilleryman Carlis Ragland stands before the black granite Vietnam Memorial and solemnly stares up at the name of his partner, etched in small white letters.

An Army gunner in Vietnam, Ragland has come—along with other patients in a New Jersey post-traumatic-stress disorder program—to help himself deal with the reality of the Persian Gulf conflict. In the five months Ragland's son has been serving in Saudi Arabia with the Air Force, the Vietnam veteran's own nightmares and flashbacks—from the earlier war—have become more frequent.

"Every time I have to look at the 6 o'clock news and they're talking about the war, automatically I'm back in Vietnam," said Ragland, silhouetted against the wall in the midday sun. "You see the babies, the kids dying, the dead bodies. . . ." His voice trails off.

For America's three million Vietnam veterans, the Persian Gulf War has produced myriad emotional conflicts.

Some are actively protesting U.S. involvement in the Gulf War. Others salute the American military response, saying the rationale for *this* war is very different from that of Vietnam. Many, confronted with a flood of news reports from the Middle East, simply are trying to cope with having to think about war again. As the bombs fell on Baghdad last week, veterans' counseling and rehabilitation centers across America were inundated with calls and visits from Vietnam veterans seeking solace.

"Guys fall on all sides of the fence on this issue," Louis Valente, supervisor of a Washington, D.C., veterans center, said. "There's a lot of searching of souls right now as to where they stand."

What makes the Gulf War even more difficult for some Vietnam veterans is that it has come just as America seemed to be healing the wounds of Vietnam. However belatedly, Vietnam veterans *have* been recognized, and many of them felt they had finally begun to put

Please see VETERANS, A22

N.Y. Wins 20-19; Security Tight at Super Bowl

By MIKE KUPPER
TIMES ASSISTANT SPORTS EDITOR

Scott Norwood missed a 47-yard field goal attempt with four seconds remaining Sunday at Tampa, Fla., and the New York Giants won the closest game in Super Bowl history, 20-19.

In the 25th Super Bowl, a game the National Football League had considered postponing because of

MORE STORIES, PICTURES: A11, C1, C11-C21.

the Persian Gulf War, Norwood's pressure kick for the Buffalo Bills sailed about three feet wide to the right.

The game was played under tight security, with such trademarks as the ubiquitous blimp missing, and meticulous checks of bags and packages at gates.

Fans had to pass through X-ray machines and metal detectors to get into Tampa Stadium, which was surrounded by a six-foot fence and concrete barriers. About 20 security guards in yellow windbreakers were stationed about 10 feet from each gate, checking each spectator who passed through gaps in yellow restraining ropes.

Please see SUPER, A25

Defense Chief Dampens Speculation on Assault

■ **Military:** More Iraqi planes fly into Iran. Whether it's a Hussein scheme or a series of defections is unknown.

By DAVID LAUTER and J. MICHAEL KENNEDY
TIMES STAFF WRITERS

WASHINGTON—The United States and its allies will not launch a ground attack against Iraqi positions in Kuwait until "absolutely certain that we have gained everything we can from the air campaign," Defense Secretary Dick Cheney said Sunday.

Although roughly half a million U.S. troops will be "combat ready" before the end of February, "there is no reason for us to rush into a ground conflict that would mean unnecessary American and allied casualties," Cheney said.

The Pentagon chief's remarks, made in a television interview, seemed to be aimed at dampening speculation by some U.S. government figures and Saudi Arabian officials that a potentially bloody ground assault is imminent.

Meanwhile, more Iraqi planes have flown into Iran, bringing the total to more than 40, U.S. officials said, adding that they still do not know whether the flights are the result of defections or a deliberate plan by Iraqi President Saddam Hussein.

Cheney, Gen. H. Norman Schwarzkopf, the U.S. commander in the gulf, and other U.S. officials, however, insisted that they have no reason to doubt Iranian assurances that the planes will be kept on the ground until the war is over.

In other developments:

• Bush Administration budget chief Richard G. Darman said the war is now costing roughly $500 million a day. But officials insist that pledges from other countries—$45 billion so far—will make the overall cost "manageable" and a war tax unnecessary. So far, Saudi Arabia and Kuwait each have pledged $13.5 billion and Japan has pledged $9 billion toward the war effort. U.S. allies pledged between $8 billion and $9 billion toward the cost of Operation Desert Shield before war began.

• Two U.S. fighter jets shot down four Iraqi MIG-23s near Baghdad, bringing to 26 the number of Iraqi planes claimed to have been shot down in air-to-air battles. No allied planes have been lost in the last 48 hours, Schwarzkopf said.

• Iraq vowed to deliver a crushing blow against allied forces, saying once again that its full strength

Please see WAR, A6

Schwarzkopf Says Political Reins Add Risks

By MELISSA HEALY
TIMES STAFF WRITER

WASHINGTON—Orders from the White House to minimize civilian casualties in Iraq require U.S. commanders to use tactics that increase the risk of American casualties and place some military targets off-limits to allied bombers, a senior U.S. military official said Sunday for the first time.

The official, Gen. H. Norman Schwarzkopf, the senior allied commander in the Persian Gulf, did not challenge the White House dictum. His comments were intended to defuse Iraqi claims that the allies were targeting civilians, and he praised the "young men who are out there and doing that in order to minimize damage" to civilians and to cultural sites.

But Schwarzkopf's admission is the first indication to date that the U.S. military is facing political constraints on its operations in the Persian Gulf.

The acknowledgment that political considerations are sometimes overriding military priorities raises questions about President Bush's ability to keep his pledge that the Gulf War "will not be another Vietnam." Repeatedly in the days

Please see RESTRAINTS, A18

What's Next on Hussein's War Agenda? Just Listen

■ **Strategy:** Analysts say he has telegraphed all his moves—and that surrender is the last thing on his mind.

By MARK FINEMAN
TIMES STAFF WRITER

AMMAN, Jordan—Iraqi President Saddam Hussein already has distributed chemical weapons to his front-line troops in Kuwait and plans to bombard allied troops with artillery firing poison-gas projectiles soon after the ground war begins.

Iraq will also unleash a squadron of kamikaze pilots known as the Ali Brigade. Armed with incendiary bombs, some will attempt to strike the largest Saudi Arabian oil fields, while others will make suicide runs against Israel-in long-range SU-24 bombers equipped with chemical-bomb tanks.

Meantime, Hussein's huge military force, most of which remains intact, will hunker down and wait for the real war to begin—the ground war the Iraqi leader has dubbed "the mother of all battles."

The source for all of the above: President Hussein himself.

Eleven days into the Persian Gulf War, Middle East analysts, diplomats and statesmen who know Hussein best say the Iraqi leader has emerged as the most accurate source for predicting his own future battle plan.

Since the war began, said Jordan's Crown Prince Hassan, an acquaintance and sympathetic neighbor, Hussein has done precisely "what he said he would do—attack Israel, blow up the oil

Please see HUSSEIN, A20

MORE WAR COVERAGE

■ **WAR STORIES, PHOTOS: A3, A5-23; B1; C18; D1; E1; F1**

■ **DEFENSE BUDGET BATTLE**
U.S. officials have reached a variety of conclusions as they ponder a revamped defense budget shaped by the successes of high-tech weaponry. **A5**

■ **MORALE LIFT FOR GIs**
Allied troops in the war zone are in a brighter mood as they hear news of defections and reports that the enemy may be more miserable than they are. **A7**

■ **DEATH IN BASRA**
Lying on a strategic Iraqi waterway, the city of Basra is again a killing ground, this time the result of constant air strikes by allied forces. **A7**

WEATHER: Patchy morning and late night low clouds. Civic Center low/high today: 46/65. Details: B2

■ TOP OF THE NEWS ON A2

■ **CAUTION FROM EGYPT**
Cairo's concerns about the war's aims may reflect a divergence of views between the United States and Arab members of the allied coalition. **A9**

■ **ANXIOUS SPOUSES**
Throughout western Germany, spouses of soldiers deployed in the Gulf War describe a feeling of anxious dislocation and intense isolation. **A10**

■ **U.N. CHIEF ASSAILED**
Iraq blamed U.N. Secretary General Javier Perez de Cuellar for sponsoring what it called an "indiscriminate" war to "destroy Iraq." **A10**

■ **WEAPONS TRIGGER DEBATE**
The war's high-tech weapons have raised questions about whether the U.S. can afford to depend on foreign suppliers for key technologies. **D1**

Environmentalists' Worst Predictions Coming True

■ **Ecology:** The massive oil spill, well fires and other signs point to a bleak scenario.

By MAURA DOLAN and JOHN BALZAR
TIMES STAFF WRITERS

An oil slick spreading across the Persian Gulf endangers wildlife populations already teetering from the effects of previous spills. Onshore, columns of smoke rise from Kuwait's oil wells, and Iranian radio reports a fallout of black rain and soot from the faraway fires.

At once, environmental terror that had seemed a relatively distant and extreme war scenario is unfolding with alarming rapidity throughout the gulf.

With a major oil spill, numerous well fires and U.S. bombing runs on Iraqi nuclear reactors and chemical plants, the gulf conflict—only in its second week—already has fulfilled some of environmentalists' darkest prewar predictions. Looking ahead, they can only surmise that, from their perspective, things will get worse.

"This is no longer a military war between nations," said Sue Merrow, president of the Sierra Club. "This has turned into a war on the environment."

At present, most attention is placed on the oil slick in the gulf. To a lesser degree, there is concern that oil-well fires could produce temporary, but potentially significant, changes in the region's climate.

The oil spill already appears likely to become the world's worst.

Please see ECOLOGY, A8

Battleship Wisconsin

The Wisconsin, one of the largest warships in the gulf, has been central to the allied naval contingent. It has fired a steady flow of Tomahawk missiles at targets inside Iraq and Kuwait since the war began. Launched in 1943, the Wisconsin saw action in the South Pacific during World War II and again in the Korean War. Mothballed in 1958, it was recommissioned in 1983. The 57,000-ton vessel has up to 19 inches of forged steel in some places, designed to withstand a hit from an anti-ship missile.

- **Crew:** More than 1,500
- **Missiles:** 32 Tomahawk cruise missiles
- **Guns:** Three 16-inch gun turrets with 66-foot long barrels
- **Shells:** A one-ton weight; range of more than 20 miles.

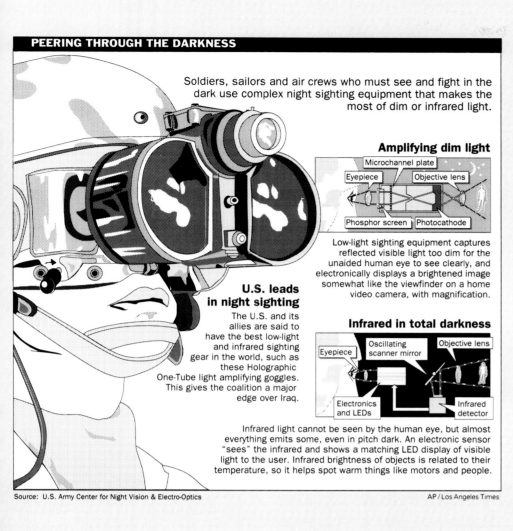

Soldiers, sailors and air crews who must see and fight in the dark use complex night sighting equipment that makes the most of dim or infrared light.

Amplifying dim light

Microchannel plate
Eyepiece — Objective lens
Phosphor screen — Photocathode

Low-light sighting equipment captures reflected visible light too dim for the unaided human eye to see clearly, and electronically displays a brightened image somewhat like the viewfinder on a home video camera, with magnification.

U.S. leads in night sighting

The U.S. and its allies are said to have the best low-light and infrared sighting gear in the world, such as these Holographic One-Tube light amplifying goggles. This gives the coalition a major edge over Iraq.

Infrared in total darkness

Eyepiece — Oscillating scanner mirror — Objective lens
Electronics and LEDs — Infrared detector

Infrared light cannot be seen by the human eye, but almost everything emits some, even in pitch dark. An electronic sensor "sees" the infrared and shows a matching LED display of visible light to the user. Infrared brightness of objects is related to their temperature, so it helps spot warm things like motors and people.

Source: U.S. Army Center for Night Vision & Electro-Optics

AP / Los Angeles Times

Environment: The flow of oil into the Persian Gulf reportedly slows after a nighttime U.S. bomb strike in Kuwait hits two inland pipelines that feed oil to an offshore oil station.
■ The slick widens to at least 350 square miles, U.S. officials say.
■ Saudi Arabia's state oil company charters a Norwegian-owned anti-pollution ship to help mop up the oil slick.

Military: Defense Secretary Dick Cheney says a ground attack will not be launched until allies are "absolutely certain that we have gained everything we can from the air campaign."
■ Allied planes have flown more than 22,000 sorties, chalking up 26 air-to-air kills, Gen. H. Norman Schwarzkopf says. Eighteen Iraqi vessels have been sunk or badly damaged, he adds.
■ U.S. forces continue to enter Saudi Arabia; Cheney says the total will peak at about 500,000.
■ A Marine commander says at least half a million mines have been strung along the Kuwaiti-Saudi border.
■ Two U.S. F-15s down four Iraqi MIG-23s near Baghdad.

Iraq: Baghdad says it holds U.N. Secretary General Javier Perez de Cuellar personally responsible for allied raids and deaths of civilians in Iraq. A scathing letter by Iraqi Foreign Minister Tarik Aziz refers to "ugly crimes" designed solely to "destroy Iraq."
■ More than 5,000 refugees from Iraq remain trapped at the Jordanian border, enduring bitter cold on the open desert. The stranded include Vietnam's ambassador to Iraq, 116 Indian nurses, three Jordanian journalists, and scores of Egyptians, Pakistanis, Vietnamese, Jordanians, Sudanese and other non-Iraqi nationals.

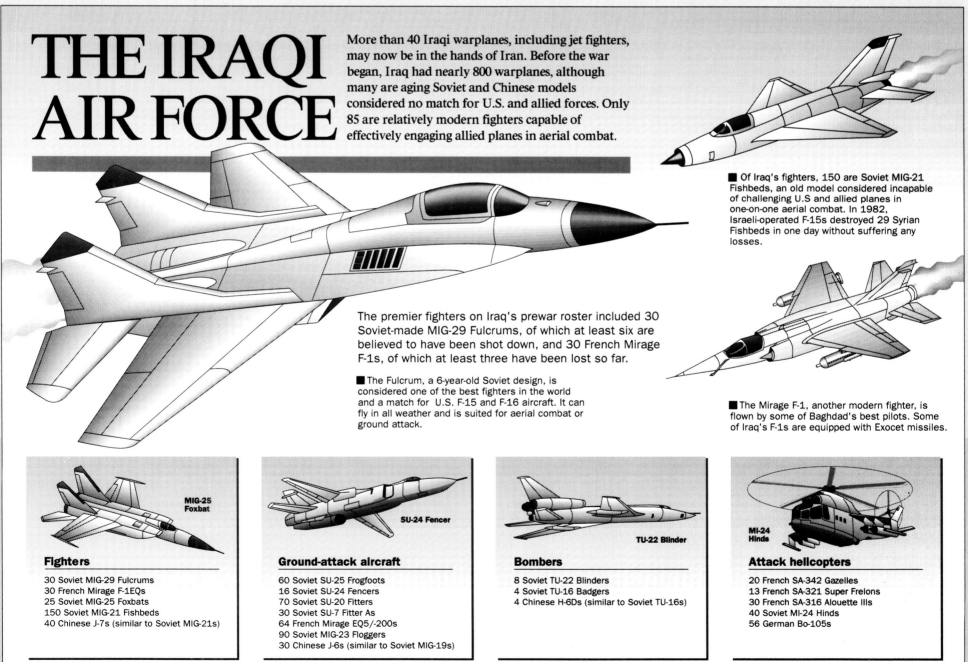

THE IRAQI AIR FORCE

More than 40 Iraqi warplanes, including jet fighters, may now be in the hands of Iran. Before the war began, Iraq had nearly 800 warplanes, although many are aging Soviet and Chinese models considered no match for U.S. and allied forces. Only 85 are relatively modern fighters capable of effectively engaging allied planes in aerial combat.

■ Of Iraq's fighters, 150 are Soviet MIG-21 Fishbeds, an old model considered incapable of challenging U.S and allied planes in one-on-one aerial combat. In 1982, Israeli-operated F-15s destroyed 29 Syrian Fishbeds in one day without suffering any losses.

The premier fighters on Iraq's prewar roster included 30 Soviet-made MIG-29 Fulcrums, of which at least six are believed to have been shot down, and 30 French Mirage F-1s, of which at least three have been lost so far.

■ The Fulcrum, a 6-year-old Soviet design, is considered one of the best fighters in the world and a match for U.S. F-15 and F-16 aircraft. It can fly in all weather and is suited for aerial combat or ground attack.

■ The Mirage F-1, another modern fighter, is flown by some of Baghdad's best pilots. Some of Iraq's F-1s are equipped with Exocet missiles.

MIG-25 Foxbat

SU-24 Fencer

TU-22 Blinder

MI-24 Hinds

Fighters

30 Soviet MIG-29 Fulcrums
30 French Mirage F-1EQs
25 Soviet MIG-25 Foxbats
150 Soviet MIG-21 Fishbeds
40 Chinese J-7s (similar to Soviet MIG-21s)

Ground-attack aircraft

60 Soviet SU-25 Frogfoots
16 Soviet SU-24 Fencers
70 Soviet SU-20 Fitters
30 Soviet SU-7 Fitter As
64 French Mirage EQ5/-200s
90 Soviet MIG-23 Floggers
30 Chinese J-6s (similar to Soviet MIG-19s)

Bombers

8 Soviet TU-22 Blinders
4 Soviet TU-16 Badgers
4 Chinese H-6Ds (similar to Soviet TU-16s)

Attack helicopters

20 French SA-342 Gazelles
13 French SA-321 Super Frelons
30 French SA-316 Alouette IIIs
40 Soviet MI-24 Hinds
56 German Bo-105s

Source: International Institute for Strategic Studies

PAUL GONZALES / Los Angeles Times

DAY 13

JANUARY 29, 1991

For days, the allied bombardment had been carving up the Iraqi capital. For days, there had been no witnesses to tear aside the heavy veil of Baghdad's secrecy, the sterile blanket of American "surgical-strike" videos. Now, on a frigid morning, across a black-rock desert, they came by the thousands, refugees pouring across a border open for the first time since Jan. 17.

The human face of war was Egyptian Ahmad Said, near tears as he cradled his 13-year-old son, Hamad:

"The bombing is so bad, we leave our houses. Maybe it is safer on the street, we think. But the bombs are louder there, and there is no light. Everything is blackness. So we run for the shelter. But there is no room in the shelter. So we squat near the door, trying to lean close to it. We feel safer there. Every night, this is what the war is like in Baghdad."

—Mark Fineman, in Ruweished, Jordan

Los Angeles Times

CIRCULATION: 1,225,189 DAILY / 1,514,096 SUNDAY

TUESDAY, JANUARY 29, 1991

COPYRIGHT 1991 / THE TIMES MIRROR COMPANY / CC† / 104 PAGES

DAILY 25¢ DESIGNATED AREAS HIGHER

Count Tops 80 as More Iraqi Planes Fly to Shelter in Iran

■ **Gulf War:** Some captured allied pilots have been injured by strikes on civilian targets, Iraq says. Bombing has stemmed the oil spill, U.S. reports.

By J. MICHAEL KENNEDY and DAVID LAUTER
TIMES STAFF WRITERS

RIYADH, Saudi Arabia—The unexplained exodus of Iraqi planes to shelter in Iran topped 80 Monday as U.S. officials said they are considering flying fighter patrols over northern Iraq to detect, and perhaps intercept, the jets.

Army Lt. Gen. Thomas W. Kelly, director of operations for the Joint Chiefs of Staff, said in Washington that the more than 60 fighter-bombers and more than 20 transport planes that have flown to Iran are "top-of-the-line aircraft."

The planes have eluded sporadic allied sorties in Iran-Iraq border areas, and the Iranians "appear to be letting them in, letting them land," Kelly said.

"They say they are going to impound them," he said. "But if they don't . . . [and the planes return to the war] . . . we will deal with them."

In Riyadh, British Group Capt. Naill Irving said that with scores of Iraqi planes on the ground in Iran and hundreds more apparently hidden, out of action, in underground hangars in Iraq, "the extent to which the Iraqi air force can operate is hardly worth talking about."

But "we are not forgetting they are there," the U.S. Army's Brig. Gen. Pat Stevens IV added.

In other developments on the 12th day of the war:

- Iraq claimed in a radio broadcast Monday that some captured allied pilots have been wounded in Desert Storm air strikes on "populated and civilian targets in Iraq." The broadcast, monitored in Nicosia, Cyprus, gave no further details, saying only that "the responsible military headquarters did not indicate whether any of the injured pilots have died." Iraq, which claims that it has captured 20 downed fliers, has said it would place some of them as human shields at potential air strike targets.
- Iraq launched two more Scud missiles, one toward Tel Aviv, the other toward Riyadh, bringing the total number of Scuds fired at Israel and Saudi Arabia to at least 53. Officials said a Patriot interceptor missile destroyed the Scud aimed at Riyadh. In Israel, no Patriots were launched, but the Scud appeared to have broken up short of its target, with debris raining down on Palestinian villages in the occupied West Bank. There were no reports of injuries in either of Monday's attacks.
- The torrent of oil pouring into Persian Gulf waters was "down to a trickle, if at all," after U.S. bombs destroyed the valves and pumps that control the flow, American officials said. This main spill now covers about 350 square miles of the gulf but has not yet touched shore, said Capt. David Herrington,

Please see WAR, A6

Associated Press

A crew of the 2nd Marine Division, stationed a few miles from Kuwait, fires an eight-inch howitzer at Iraqi positions. U.S. officials described the attack as the largest ground shelling yet by allied forces.

COLUMN ONE

Dhahran Adapts to Wartime

■ The hub of the Eastern Province owes its existence to oil. Now comes conflict to reshape its peaceful character.

By DAVID LAMB and JOHN BALZAR
TIMES STAFF WRITERS

DHAHRAN, Saudi Arabia—Along the corniche, when the sky is blue and the Persian Gulf is as smooth as glass, it is as though nothing has changed. Life is as it always has been, abundant and peaceful and full of uncomplicated pleasures.

The beachside carnival at the foot of 28th Street is ablaze with lights, its miniature Ferris wheel turning lazily in the evening dusk. The call to prayer echoes from the minarets that rise like spikes out of the squat city skyline.

Across town, a Saudi enters a jewelry shop, briefly examines a diamond ring and says, "Yes, I'll take it." He counts out $50,000 in cash.

But, like so much of what one sees in the Arab world, these scenes of normalcy in Dhahran are an illusion. Life is normal in Saudi Arabia's Eastern Province only in the sense that the government says everything is fine. Beneath the facade, the character of this one-time oil boom town is being shaped by a war that no one thought would happen. Nothing again will ever be as it was.

Though the carnival rides spin gaily, the amusement park is empty, save for a solitary custodian. The wide, spotless beach that seems to stretch all the way to Kuwait is virtually empty, as it usually is even in peacetime, and the sole figure who walks it appears as a white-robed apparition, off in the distance near the Gulf Meridien Hotel.

In the lobby of the hotel, an American boy wears a T-shirt that says on the front, "Scud Bait" and on the back, "This isn't hell but you can see it from here."

Dhahran and the surrounding area, including the port city of Dammam and the shopping district of Al Khubar, have a population exceeding 300,000, making it the kingdom's sixth-most-populated region, after Riyadh, Jidda, Mecca, Medina and Taif.

Like most of Saudi Arabia's other population centers, Dhahran and its sister cities sprang out of nothing in the span of two generations, the product of boundless oil wealth and the kingdom's desire to dash pell-mell into the 21st Century.

Al Khubar was a sleepy fishing village in 1931 when the U.S. extended diplomatic recognition to Saudi Arabia, five years after the Soviet Union and Britain had granted it. Dhahran didn't even exist. Then in 1938, Saudi Arabia made its first oil strike here and, by the 1950s, the region was booming. American oilmen poured in by the thousands, followed by a legion of Asian laborers.

Life, though, remained primitive, and for years the only decent restaurant in Al Khubar was on an old barge pulled in from Bahrain.

Please see DHAHRAN, A10

U.S., Soviets Agree to Put Off Summit

By ROBERT C. TOTH
TIMES STAFF WRITER

WASHINGTON—President Bush and Soviet President Mikhail S. Gorbachev on Monday postponed "by mutual agreement" their scheduled Moscow summit meeting—the most tangible sign so far of the cooling relations between Moscow and Washington.

The meeting, slated to begin Feb. 11, instead will take place at "a later date in the first half of this year," according to a joint U.S.-Soviet statement. Not since the 1960 downing of an American U-2 spy plane over the Soviet Union has a scheduled U.S.-Soviet meeting at the highest lev-

Please see SUMMIT, A22

State's AAA Credit Status in Jeopardy

By DOUGLAS P. SHUIT
TIMES STAFF WRITER

SACRAMENTO—California officials were warned by the Standard & Poor's credit-rating agency Monday that they must come up with a better plan to deal with the "rapidly developing [budget] deficit" or face a downgrading of the state's highly valued AAA bond rating.

State officials cautioned that the agency's announcement—officially placing California on its "credit watch"—does not carry an immediate cost to state taxpayers. But they conceded that if the AAA rating is lowered, the state's cost to borrow money could increase by millions.

The development came in the wake of assessments by various state officials that California faces a budgetary shortfall of $7 billion to $10 billion over the next 18 months.

Standard & Poor's was particularly concerned about a $1.8-billion shortfall it projects for the remainder of this fiscal year, which ends June 30.

California's credit rating dropped twice in the last decade, once in 1980 after passage of the property tax limitation measure Proposition 13 in 1978 and voter approval a year later of strict spending limits. In 1983, two credit-rating agencies, including Standard & Poor's, further lowered California's rating. The rating climbed back from AA to AAA about three years later, a move that lowered interest rates the state paid to borrow money.

About 30 other states are said to be in a financial bind similar to California's. States facing the most severe problems are in the Northeast. New York, Connecticut, and Massachusetts have all had their credit ratings lowered in recent months.

The threat to California is not immediate. Standard & Poor's said it would give state officials several months to come up with a budget plan before taking action to down-

Please see CREDIT, A27

Experts 'Dumbstruck' by Iraqi Planes in Iran

■ **Air war:** Theories run from mass defection to murky deal that would allow Hussein to use them in later strike.

By JOHN M. BRODER and ROBIN WRIGHT
TIMES STAFF WRITERS

WASHINGTON—Iraq and Iran have added a new twist to the labyrinthine politics of the Middle East with the flight of scores of top-line Iraqi aircraft to officially neutral Iran.

What are these two bitter enemies up to?

U.S. analysts say they are "dumbstruck" by this latest surprise, and a frantic effort is under way in official circles to unravel the mystery.

Has a desperate or cagey Saddam Hussein sent his best fighters to an Iranian haven intending to use them against U.S.-led forces in

NEWS ANALYSIS

a later battle? Has a significant faction of the Iraqi air force abandoned the regime, choosing safety over loyalty? Or has Iran struck a deal with its erstwhile foe, agreeing to shelter the aircraft for the duration of the war in exchange for later political concessions, arms, cash or other considerations?

A high-level Iraqi delegation was in Tehran just before the Gulf War began, and U.S. officials have not yet deciphered what was discussed or agreed to. The delegation included Baghdad's minister of transportation and the second-ranking official on the ruling Revolutionary Command Council.

But the escape of Iraqi civilian airliners to two commercial airports in Iran began two days *before* the war broke out, U.S. officials said.

The flights halted briefly, then

Please see MYSTERY, A14

U.S. Bombing Appears to Halt Gulf Oil Spill

By KIM MURPHY
TIMES STAFF WRITER

DHAHRAN, Saudi Arabia—A gush of crude oil feeding a major slick in the Persian Gulf apparently was halted by a U.S. bombing raid on oil pumping facilities in Kuwait, but not before it dumped a record 11 million barrels of oil into the fragile waterway, military and government officials said Monday.

As experts from the United States and Britain arrived in Saudi Arabia to combat the spill, a U.S. military spokesman said the Saturday night attack on inland pipeline complexes that direct crude toward the giant Sea Island loading termi-

Please see SPILL, A7

Hussein Issues Boasts, Threats in TV Interview

By MARK FINEMAN
TIMES STAFF WRITER

AMMAN, Jordan—A boastful and confident President Saddam Hussein indicated Monday that he will use chemical weapons only as a last resort, and he asserted that he and his military have maintained "our balance" by employing only conventional weapons thus far in the Persian Gulf War.

But, he added menacingly, the type of missiles that his forces have already fired at Israel and Saudi Arabia can be fitted with nuclear, chemical and biological warheads.

"We pray that not a lot of blood will be shed from any nation," the Iraqi strongman said in his first public comments since the first week of the war. But, in a seeming inconsistency, he commented later that in the fighting to come, "Lots of blood will be shed . . . the Americans, the French, Saudi blood and Iraqi."

Hussein's remarks came during a 90-minute interview with Cable News Network correspondent Peter Arnett, the only Western journalist the Iraqis have permitted to remain in Baghdad while the U.S.-led allies wage their war on Iraq.

Asked how long the war will last, Hussein said, "Only God knows," Arnett related. Arnett quoted him as adding that there is "not even one in a million" chance that Iraq will lose the war.

Please see HUSSEIN, A16

Proposal by Ethics Panel to Punish Cranston Seen

■ **Congress:** Sources expect him to face serious penalty, but not expulsion from Senate, for links to Keating S&L.

By SARA FRITZ
TIMES STAFF WRITER

WASHINGTON—The Senate Ethics Committee is likely to recommend that Sen. Alan Cranston (D-Calif.) be disciplined by the full Senate for his actions on behalf of former Lincoln Savings & Loan owner Charles H. Keating Jr., knowledgeable sources said Monday.

The sources indicated that they expect Cranston to face something short of expulsion but more serious than a letter of reprimand—probably censure, denouncement or some step that would condemn his actions without forcing him from office.

The six-member committee, which completed 26 days of public hearings earlier this month, is scheduled to begin its final closed deliberations in the so-called "Keating Five" case later this week. A decision by the committee is expected in March.

Five senators are accused of improperly trying to influence federal regulators on behalf of Lincoln in exchange for contributions from Keating to their campaigns and their favorite political causes.

William W. Taylor III, Cranston's attorney, said that he cannot predict how the committee will vote on the case against his client. "I don't have any information that the committee has decided any-

Please see CRANSTON, A24

INSIDE TODAY'S TIMES

■ **WAR STORIES, PHOTOS: A5-21; D1, D3, D6; E1; F1-2, F9**

■ **ISRAEL SEEKS GO-AHEAD**
The Israeli government is pressing hard to get Washington's approval for retaliation against Iraq. **A8**

■ **REGULATORY JUNGLE**
Defense experts are worried that federal contract regulations could bottle up production for the Gulf War or leave contractors in the lurch. **D1**

■ **WAGING A LAND WAR**
The possibility that a ground war will settle the Persian Gulf conflict begs the questions: How and when will it be waged and at what cost? **In World Report**

WEATHER: Sunny today with gusty canyon winds. Civic Center low/high today: 50/75. Details: B5

■ TOP OF THE NEWS ON A2

Associated Press

Red Grange in 1920s.

■ **RED GRANGE DIES**
Red Grange, perhaps the most gifted and certainly the most publicized football player of all time, died after a lengthy hospital stay in Florida at 87. **C1**

Anguished Refugees From Iraq Pouring Into Jordan

■ **Frontier:** A crossing is reopened by Baghdad. Victims tell of war terror and suffering at border.

By MARK FINEMAN
TIMES STAFF WRITER

RUWEISHED, Jordan—Shell-shocked and half-frozen, hundreds of war-weary refugees began pouring across the Iraqi border here Monday, after remaining nearly a week with little food and no shelter at a desert frontier crossing that Iraqi authorities had closed without explanation six days ago.

Many of them, like Jordanian high school teacher Abdulaziz Fares, who had lived 26 years in Kuwait, brought with them credible eyewitness accounts of life inside occupied Kuwait city—human sagas that begin with the tragedy of invasion six months ago, continue with the terror of a week inside bomb shelters under continuing allied assault on Kuwait and culminate in the horror of children freezing to death at the closed Iraqi border outpost.

Others, like Indian refugee A. K. Nayak, who worked as a contract laborer on the construction of a new palace for President Saddam Hussein in the southern Iraqi city of Basra, told of nighttime allied bombing runs pounding that city and also the main highway from Baghdad to Jordan. That artery is now all but severed by bomb craters and burning trucks and buses, refugees said.

Still others, like Kheirieh Salman, expressed sheer joy at having

Please see BORDER, A9

M-3 Bradley Infantry Fighting Vehicle

The Bradley, an armored personnel carrier with a crew of three, will play a key role in any action against Iraqi ground forces. It also carries seven fully equipped infantrymen. The Bradley is armed with cannons and TOW missiles—which can damage enemy armor at a distance of 3,000 yards and is fully amphibious. Maximum speed is about 42 m.p.h. on land and 5.6 m.p.h. in water. An estimated 600 Bradley vehicles are in the Middle East.

Armament:
One 25mm cannon
One 7.62mm machine gun
One dual-tube TOW missile launcher

Saddam Hussein—for all you do, this one's for you.

PATRICK DOWNS / Los Angeles Times

DAY IN THE GULF

Iran: At least 80 Iraqi planes have flown to Iran for shelter, U.S. officials say, including more than 60 fighter-bombers and 20 transport planes.

■ A British military official says that with that number of planes in Iran and scores more apparently out of action in underground hangars "the extent to which the Iraqi air force can operate is hardly worth talking about."

Missiles: Iraq launches two more Scud missiles, one toward Tel Aviv and one toward Riyadh. The Israel-bound missile breaks up short of its target, showering debris on Palestinian villages. The missile aimed at Saudi Arabia is intercepted.

■ The Israeli government presses hard to get Washington to approve retaliation against Iraq because of the increased threat of chemical attack.

■ At least 53 Scuds have been fired at Israel and Saudi Arabia.

Iraq: Baghdad Radio launches a bitter attack against Egyptian President Hosni Mubarak, accusing the pro-American Arab leader of selling out for dollars and predicting he will be assassinated.

■ Iraq's boastful and confident President Saddam Hussein indicates in a CNN interview that he will use chemical weapons only as a last resort.

■ An Iraqi radio broadcast claims that some captured allied pilots have been wounded in allied strikes on "populated and civilian targets in Iraq."

■ Iraq tells the United Nations that 345 people have been killed and 450 wounded in the first days of the war.

■ Hundreds of refugees pour into Jordan after Iraq drops exit visa requirements.

Military: A U.S. warplane is shot down in combat, the first allied loss in more than three days. The Marine Corps AV-8 Harrier jet is the 11th American aircraft lost. Its pilot is listed as missing.

Home front: The American Civil Liberties Union challenges FBI assertions that Arab-Americans will suffer no consequences if they refuse to be interviewed about possible terrorism.

CONTROLLING THE

OIL SPILL

U.S. military officials said Monday that the bombing of the Iraqi oil storage facilities in Kuwait seems to have lessened the flow of opened oil pipes into the Persian Gulf. Still, those involved in the clean-up effort said there are lots of problems ahead. Among the developments:

■ **Saudi Oil Minister** Hisham Nazir reported the Iraqis have pumped about 460 million gallons of oil, or more than 11 million barrels of oil, into the gulf, easily making it the world's worst oil slick. The previous record oil spill sent about 175 million gallons into the Gulf of Mexico in 1979.

■ **Help was en route** from Danish and Norwegian experts, the British and American environmentalists. Hundreds have volunteered to help with the oil mop-up, but it has been deemed too dangerous for them to be in the war zone.

■ **The U.N. Environmental Program** appealed Monday both to Iraq and the coalition forces to to provide information on damage being caused by the massive oil spill and to allow U.N. environmental experts into the area.

■ **Iraq renewed charges** Monday that the oil spill was caused by allied bombing of oil facilities in Kuwait.

■ **The official word** from Army Brig. Gen. Pat Stevens IV in Saudi Arabia: ``The extent of that slick remains a little bit unclear. I assure you it is being monitored. It appears that we have stopped the flow of oil, but we continue to seek positive confirmation of that fact."

■ **Mines floating** in the region may make it next to impossible for a cleanup operation at sea.

Saudi Arabia desalination plant threatened by the oil slick.   Associated Press

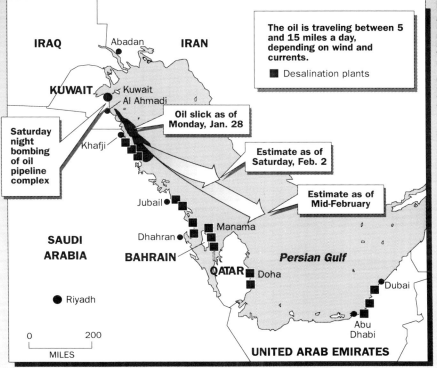

IRAQ Abadan **IRAN**

The oil is traveling between 5 and 15 miles a day, depending on wind and currents.

■ Desalination plants

KUWAIT Kuwait Al Ahmadi

Saturday night bombing of oil pipeline complex

Oil slick as of Monday, Jan. 28

Khafji

Estimate as of Saturday, Feb. 2

Estimate as of Mid-February

Jubail

Manama

Dhahran

SAUDI ARABIA

BAHRAIN

Persian Gulf

QATAR Doha

● Riyadh

Dubai

0   200

MILES

Abu Dhabi

UNITED ARAB EMIRATES

How to Fight the Spill

According to some estimates, it will take more than six months to clean up the spill, and at best less than 20% of the oil will be removed. Here are the techniques:

Contain the spill. Floating partitions, already on site in the gulf, are deployed around the spill to keep it from reaching the coast.

Skim the oil. The Al Wassid, a Norwegian-Danish skimmer, can skim oil from the surface and store 350,000 gallons a day. From there it is pumped into an oil tanker.

Vacuum the oil. A special chemical powder is sifted over the surface oil, which thickens it and enables a vacuum to suck it into a storage tank.

Use chemical dispersants. These behave like household detergents and suspend the oil in droplets, which are less harmful to wildlife.

Encourage oil-eating bacteria. Employed in the later stages of cleanup, specialized bacteria that occur naturally in oceans eat a remarkable volume of spilled oil. The existing populations are enhanced with fertilizers and nutrients.

Booms and Skimmers

The tried-and-true method of cleanup is corralling the oil with booms and then skimming the contained oil. The system works as long as the oil has not dispersed too far, but high seas, wind and time act to thin the oil, making it harder to pick up.

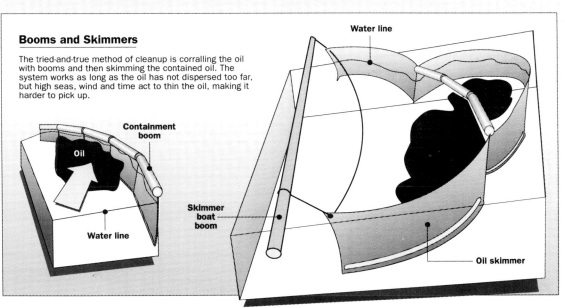

Water line

Containment boom

Oil

Water line

Skimmer boat boom

Oil skimmer

PATRICIA MITCHELL / Los Angeles Times

DAY 14

JANUARY 30, 1991

A high-school geography class in Baghdad was reciting the truth according to Iraqi President Saddam Hussein for a visiting reporter: The Kuwaitis are cheats, the British are colonialists, the Americans are Zionist tools, etc.

I decided to see what else was being stuffed into the students' heads. Picking up a pointer, I asked a young girl to identify a few places on the wall map. She got them all, better than an American kid her age—or older—could do. There is more to Iraq than Saddam Hussein.

—Nick B. Williams Jr.
in prewar Baghdad

Los Angeles Times

CIRCULATION: 1,225,189 DAILY 1,514,096 SUNDAY

WEDNESDAY, JANUARY 30, 1991

COPYRIGHT 1991 THE TIMES MIRROR COMPANY CC† 86 PAGES

DAILY 25¢ DESIGNATED AREAS HIGHER

'We Will Succeed,' Bush Says

U.S. Softens Terms for an Iraqi Pullout to Stop War

'Unequivocal' Pledge by Hussein Is Needed

■ **Diplomacy:** A U.S.-Soviet statement also promises 'to promote Arab-Israeli peace.' Moscow gives assurances of a partial Baltic troop pullout.

By DAVID LAUTER and DOYLE McMANUS
TIMES STAFF WRITERS

WASHINGTON—The allied assault on Iraq could end now if Iraqi President Saddam Hussein makes an "unequivocal commitment" to withdraw from Kuwait, the United States and Soviet Union declared Tuesday, softening the previous U.S. insistence that only an actual withdrawal would stop the war.

The statement also pledged joint U.S.-Soviet efforts "to promote Arab-Israeli peace" once the war is over, the closest the Bush Administration has come to linking the war with the Palestinian issue and an unusual bow to Moscow's desire to take a more central role in Middle East diplomacy.

At the same time, the White House announced that Moscow has promised Bush that at least some Soviet troops would be withdrawn from the restive Baltic republics of Lithuania, Latvia and Estonia. The statement appeared to be the first concrete pledge by the Soviet Union to remove troops from the Baltics, although Administration officials indicated that neither the number of troops nor the timing of the withdrawal was specified.

The announcements came at the close of a four-day visit to Washington by Alexander A. Bessmertnykh, the new Soviet foreign minister, aimed at ending a sudden chill in U.S.-Soviet relations caused by Moscow's moves against the independence-seeking governments in the Baltic states and signs of Soviet backtracking on several arms control agreements.

President Bush, in his State of the Union address Tuesday evening, assessed the superpower relationship in more guarded, cautious terms than he might have used last year, when the idea of a U.S.-Soviet "partnership" was in full flower.

"Our relationship with the Soviet Union is important, not only to us but to the world," Bush said. "But like many other nations, we have been deeply concerned by the violence in the Baltics, and we have communicated that concern to the Soviet leadership. . . . If it is possible, I want to continue to build a lasting basis for U.S.-Soviet cooperation, for a more peaceful future for all mankind."

During his meetings with Bush and Secretary of State James A. Baker III, Bessmertnykh delivered a letter from Soviet President Mikhail S. Gorbachev outlining in detail a new set of Soviet peace proposals for the gulf, a government spokesman announced in Moscow.

According to the spokesman, Gorbachev press secretary Vitaly N. Ignatenko, the Soviets are seeking comments from other countries before formally presenting their

Please see POLICY, A17

Marines Pound Iraqi Bunkers, Lookout Posts

By J. MICHAEL KENNEDY and ROBIN WRIGHT
TIMES STAFF WRITERS

RIYADH, Saudi Arabia—Ground action in the war intensified Tuesday as elements of the 1st Marine Division pounded Iraqi targets in Kuwait with artillery, mortars, anti-tank missiles and automatic cannon fire.

Firing from as close as 1,100 yards from the border, a task force of Marine light armored vehicles, artillery and other equipment hit Iraqi bunkers and observation posts with a 300-round barrage, according to military sources here.

Officers said at least one complex of Iraqi bunkers and outposts was destroyed during the 15-minute bombardment. Iraqi units did not return the fire, and there were no reports of Marine casualties. Despite the action, there was no indication that a full-scale ground offensive was under way.

In the air war, U.S. forces hammered targets in round-the-clock bombing they said is gradually destroying President Saddam Hussein's elite Republican Guard.

Allied planes flew more than 2,600 combat sorties against Iraqi targets Tuesday. The American command said attacks on roads, fuel depots, command posts and a wide range of other targets close to the Iraqi-Kuwaiti border are making it increasingly difficult for Iraq to supply its army in occupied Kuwait.

In other developments:

- Iraq said that a downed allied pilot being used as a human shield was killed during a bomb attack on the Ministry of Industry building in Baghdad.
- Allied warplanes caught an Iraqi military convoy moving across the open desert and, in the largest "confirmed" destruction of enemy armored vehicles, knocked out 24 tanks, armored personnel carriers and supply vehicles. "They were sloppy and they were

Please see WAR, A6

United Press International

Vice President Dan Quayle and House Speaker Thomas S. Foley lead applause for President Bush before his State of the Union address.

Smuggling Into Iraq Continues Despite War

■ **Embargo:** Officials cite 700 cases worldwide of attempts to sell goods to Baghdad. There are 20 in U.S.

By KAREN TUMULTY and RONALD J. OSTROW
TIMES STAFF WRITERS

WASHINGTON—Law enforcement and intelligence agencies have detected more than 700 cases in which firms and individuals worldwide have attempted to sell munitions and other goods to Iraq, including at least 20 cases since August in the United States, government sources have told The Times.

The efforts to circumvent the 5-month-old international embargo are believed to be continuing even in the midst of war—hostilities that pose greater dangers to smugglers, but also potentially higher profits.

The current estimates represent a marked increase from only a few weeks ago, when the sources said they had evidence of about 500 violations.

"There are sleazeballs out there who are out to make a buck," said U.S. Customs Service spokesman Dennis Shimkoski. "It's even more than [breaking the overall] embargo. We've got people trying to profit by sending munitions."

Officials say that the cases they have detected may represent only a fraction of the violations.

It is unclear how many of the cases being investigated in the United States involve American businesses attempting to profit by trade with Iraq. Officials say they believe that foreign firms—particularly in Western Europe—are responsible for the vast majority of embargo violations.

"We have a long way to go to make these economic sanctions effective," said Rep. Doug Bereuter (R-Neb.), a member of the House Intelligence Committee. "It is clear to me, on the basis of information that I have seen, that companies have violated the embargo in important ways."

Nonetheless, officials insist, the embargo is proving tighter than any similar international effort in recent history, cutting off 90% of Iraq's imports and 97% of its

Please see EMBARGO, A16

■ **State of the Union:** The nation is 'at a defining hour,' the President says of the gulf conflict. He declares that 'Iraq's capacity to sustain war is being destroyed.'

By JAMES GERSTENZANG, TIMES STAFF WRITER

WASHINGTON—President Bush, delivering his State of the Union address to a nation in the midst of war, called on Americans on Tuesday night to "accept our responsibility to lead the world away from the dark chaos of dictators."

In the Persian Gulf War, he said, the United States stands "at a defining hour."

"We will succeed," he declared of the allied commitment to expel Iraqi President Saddam Hussein from Kuwait. "And when we do, the world community will have sent an enduring warning to any dictator or despot, present or future, who contemplates outlaw aggression," the President said.

"Our cause is just. Our cause is moral. Our cause is right. We are on course. Iraq's capacity to sustain war is being destroyed. Time will not be Saddam's salvation."

Addressing a joint session of the House and Senate girded by unprecedented security measures to thwart a possible terrorist attack, Bush presented a picture of unwavering determination to carry out what he called "the hard work of freedom"—in prosecuting the war with Iraq, in tackling U.S. domestic problems and in pursuing other U.S. interests around the world.

Seeking once again to leave no doubt about why he sent 500,000 soldiers, sailors, airmen, Marines

■ TEXT OF SPEECH: A11

and Coast Guardsmen to the Persian Gulf and unleashed the most furious bombardment in the history of warfare, Bush said:

"Saddam Hussein's unprovoked invasion—his ruthless, systematic rape of a peaceful neighbor—violated everything the community of nations holds dear. The world has said this aggression would not stand—and it will not stand."

The speech, delivered 13 days to the hour after he told the nation it was at war, found Bush at the most difficult moment of his presidency thus far, and with a particularly difficult task. Addressing a nation facing military combat for the first time in almost a generation, he sought to explain why he was asking thousands of young Americans to face the ultimate sacrifice.

"This is the burden of leadership—and the strength that has made America the beacon of freedom in a searching world," he said. "The cost of closing our eyes to aggression is beyond mankind's power to imagine."

Though Democrats command majorities in both houses of Congress and many had opposed going to war now, Bush's often eloquent address drew five standing ovations. And with his verbal salute to "every man and woman now serving in the Persian Gulf," the House and Senate, members of the Cabinet, diplomats and the Joint Chiefs of Staff stood as one, applauding for more than a minute. "What a fitting tribute to them," Bush said of the emotion-charged moment. "What a wonderful, fitting tribute to them."

Please see SPEECH, A10

Bush Seeks Leadership on Social Issues

By JAMES RISEN
TIMES STAFF WRITER

WASHINGTON—President Bush, seeking to reassert leadership on key social issues, proposed a wide variety of domestic initiatives Tuesday, ranging from programs for highways, energy, space and education to a plan to transfer billions of federal dollars to the states.

He proposed eliminating altogether the use of political action committees to finance political campaigns, pledged to step up enforcement of existing civil rights laws and renewed a proposal—rejected by Congress last year—to cut taxes on capital gains.

The full plate of domestic initiatives, contained in

Please see SOCIAL, A12

House Passes Agent Orange Claims Funding

By WILLIAM J. EATON
TIMES STAFF WRITER

WASHINGTON—Prodded by Iraq's threat to use chemical weapons in the Persian Gulf War, the House ended more than a decade of deadlock Tuesday and passed legislation to guarantee compensation for Vietnam veterans exposed to Agent Orange. The vote was 412 to 0.

One leading congressional advocate said that the Agent Orange measure would establish a process for deciding claims pressed by American military personnel exposed to possible chemical or biological substances used against U.S.-led forces by Iraqi President Saddam Hussein.

"Anybody looking at this issue has to conclude that we may be in the same situation with a whole new generation of veterans in a matter of months," said Sen. Thomas A. Daschle (D-S.D.).

Shortly after the Gulf War began, opponents of government benefits in Agent Orange cases yielded to pressure from veterans'

Please see ORANGE, A21

Saudi Truck Stop an Oasis for GIs on the Road to War

■ **Crossroads:** The service station-general store offers gas at 55 cents a gallon. Arab travelers stop to pray.

By JOHN BALZAR and DOUGLAS FRANTZ
TIMES STAFF WRITERS

ON THE ROAD TO KUWAIT, Saudi Arabia—It's like no other truck stop on no other highway.

This is where great armies of America and Britain and the other nations of the anti-Iraq coalition stop for a Pepsi or a radiator clamp or just a stretch of the legs on the advance north.

Arab travelers and farmers pause and pray during holy hours at the truck stop's ramshackle mosque annex. Nomadic Bedouin camel drivers pass by alone, seeming to need little, their exotic wandering herds of one-hump dromedaries posing more of a hazard for transportation convoys than Saddam Hussein's dispersing air force.

Here at the Al Buanain truck stop, a Saudi security agent can wash his car and get a haircut and a meal.

Spread across five acres of scrub and sand dunes of Eastern Saudi Arabia, this truck stop is to the 20th Century what the oasis was to travelers of the centuries before: the crossroads in a barren land.

It offers water and everything else—from gasoline at the equivalent of 55 cents-a-gallon to men's dress shoes that buyers pick out of a cardboard bin, hoping to find two the same. And surely someone buys the whole frozen catfish

Please see STOP, A16

INSIDE TODAY'S TIMES

South Africa's 2 Top Black Leaders Urge End to Strife

■ **Ethnic violence:** The summit between Mandela, Zulu Chief Buthelezi is first significant reconciliation attempt.

By SCOTT KRAFT
TIMES STAFF WRITER

DURBAN, South Africa—Nelson Mandela and Zulu Chief Mangosuthu Gatsha Buthelezi, in a historic accord aimed at ending one of South Africa's bloodiest conflicts, called on their supporters Tuesday to stop attacking each other.

"We have reached a breakthrough and we can only hope that [peace] will be the result," Mandela told a news conference after 10 hours of talks between the African National Congress and Buthelezi's Inkatha Freedom Party.

"You can see, not only from the warmth between us but from our body language, that the meeting was a complete success," said a smiling Buthelezi. "There was no acrimony whatsoever."

But Buthelezi cautioned that the agreement did not necessarily mean that the internecine violence will end immediately. "We don't think that we can just wave a magic wand" and make it stop, he said.

The summit between the two most powerful black leaders in South Africa, after more than a decade of bitter feuding between their organizations, marked the first significant attempt at a reconciliation between the ANC and Inkatha since the ANC was legalized and Mandela was freed from

Please see SOUTH AFRICA, A20

Troop Pay

Monthly pay rates for various ranks in most branches of the military. Service personnel in gulf receive an extra $110 in combat pay:

Sgt. 1st Class	$1,323--$2,338
Staff Sergeant	$1,139--$1,707
Sergeant	$999--$1,448
Corporal	$932--$1,167
Private 1st Class	$878--$1,001
Private:	$697--$845

Desert warrior: young Saudi national guardsman at remote outpost.

PATRICK DOWNS / Los Angeles Times

DAY IN THE GULF

Diplomacy: The allied assault on Iraq could end now if Iraqi President Saddam Hussein makes an "unequivocal commitment" to withdraw from Kuwait, the United States and Soviet Union declare, seemingly softening a previous U.S. insistence that only actual withdrawal would stop the war.

■ The joint statement is issued by the new Soviet foreign minister, Alexander A. Bessmertnykh, and Secretary of State James A. Baker III.

Military: The Pentagon says 10 more Iraqi planes have flown to Iran, bringing the total to more than 90.

■ British military officials say up to 80% of Iraq's oil refining capacity has been destroyed.

■ Allied warplanes catch an Iraqi military convoy moving across the desert and knock out 24 tanks, armored personnel carriers and supply vehicles.

International: French Socialist Defense Minister Jean-Pierre Chevenement, at the center of a controversy over his misgivings over the war with Iraq, resigns.

■ Germany promises an extra $5.5 billion to help cover war expenses and will send antiaircraft units to Turkey along with troops to operate them. It also promises to tighten export controls to limit the flow of military goods to Iraq.

Home front: U.S. law enforcement and intelligence agencies have detected more than 700 cases in which firms and individuals have tried to sell munitions and other goods to Iraq, government sources say.

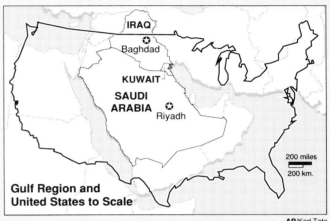

Gulf Region and United States to Scale

200 miles
200 km.

AP/Karl Tate

OUTRAGE OVER
POWS

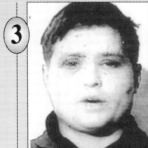

American POWs

The first seven U.S. POWs include four members of the Air Force, two Marine Corps officers and one Navy lieutenant. They are:

1. **Lt. Col. Clifford M. Acree, 39, Marines.**
2. **Chief Warrant Officer Guy L. Hunter, 46, Marines.**
3. **Lt. Jeffrey N. Zaun, 28, Navy.**
4. **Col. David W. Eberly, 43, Air Force.**
5. **Capt. Harry M. Roberts, 30, Air Force.**
6. **Maj. Jeffrey S. Tice, 35, Air Force.**
7. **Maj. Thomas E. Griffith Jr., 34, Air Force** (picture not available)

Unconfirmed reports from Iraq that a captured allied pilot was killed in allied bombing on a Ministry of Industry building in Baghdad has renewed outrage over Iraqi treatment of prisoners. Among the developments:

● **IRAQ'S** announcement that it would send captured airmen to strategic sites as human shields provoked an outcry of war crimes from the allied powers. Iraq now says that several POWs have been wounded in air raids, but did not identify them by name or nationality.

● **NUMBERS:** The allies say 28 airmen are missing or captured. The Pentagon said Iraq never produced formal notification that it holds POWs as required by the Geneva Convention, but seven Americans are listed now as prisoners of war.

● **RED CROSS** officials complain that Iraq has ignored pleas to inspect conditions of the allied prisoners as required under the Geneva Convention.

● **IRAQI PRISONERS:** Allied forces have captured more than 110 Iraqi POWs, most of whom have been inspected by the International Red Cross.

● **WAR CRIMES:** Accepted international regulations prohibit placing prisoners near targets, beating prisoners and parading them before Iraqi television, say American officials. President Bush and others have said Iraq's Saddam Hussein should be tried as a war criminal at the end of hostilities. Hussein said Bush and French President Francois Mitterrand should face charges.

The Geneva Convention Rules

In 1949, 164 countries signed agreement— known as the Geneva Convention— to set rules for treatment of prisoners. Among the agreements:

● Prisoners "must at all times be treated humanely" and "must at all times be protected."

● Prisoners are "entitled in all circumstances to respect for their persons and their honor."

● Prisoners are bound to give only name, rank, date of birth, and army serial number . . . No physical or mental torture, nor any other form of coercion, may be inflicted.

● Prisoners shall be evacuated, as soon as possible after their capture, to camps in an area far enough from the combat zone for them to be out of danger.

● No prisoner may be sent to areas where he may be exposed to the fire of the combat zone, nor may his presence be used to render certain points or areas immune from military operations.

Dealing With Captor's Tactics

U.S. forces receive special training on being prisoners of war. Among the methods that some specialists suggest for coping with captivity:

● Try to worry about buddy or country, instead of dwelling on own situation.

● Try to answer questions in ways that conceal useful information.

● The goal is to avoid being killed; each day is a new victory.

● Keep mind occupied with something that avoids dwelling on the situation.

● When reading statements, use words or emphasis that indicates it is not own phrasing.

● Try to maintain a feeling of control, perhaps by minor tricks pulled on guards.

● Resist as much as possible to help sense of self-worth.

SOURCE: Los Angeles Times, Associated Press, Knight-Ridder Newspapers

Allied Plans for POWs

● U.S. forces are constructing huge barbed-wire compounds in Saudi Arabia to house up to 30,000 prisoners of war.

● Initially, Iraqi prisoners will be kept in the open compounds. Later, tents may be set up.

● These compounds are intended as holding areas near the front while prisoners are readied for transport to the rear areas. The military hopes to move prisoners several hundred miles south within a few days of capture.

● Minor medical problems will be treated at the camps. Prisoners requiring more serious care will be sent farther south to military medical facilities.

● Military plans call for seized Iraqi gas masks to be distributed to the prisoners and for purchase of Saudi ration packs for a diet in accordance with Islamic law.

DAY 15

JANUARY 31, 1991

"What kind of weapon is this?" moaned Moshe Natayas. "Why didn't our jets shoot it down?"

An Israeli visiting his daughter in Los Angeles, he had left his 98-year-old mother in Tel Aviv, where she lived alone. For him, as for tens of thousands of other Israelis in Southern California, the first reports that Scud missiles had struck Tel Aviv triggered an instant dread, a sense of helplessness and an aching concern for loved ones.

Natayas dashed to a gray-metal public telephone at the corner of Fairfax and Rosewood, in the commercial heart of the Los Angeles Jewish community.

"I want to make a collect call to Tel Aviv! I want to make a collect call to Tel Aviv!" he repeated. Each time the phone rejected his call, he gathered his coins and, trembling, inserted them again.

Eventually, persistence paid off. Natayas heard his mother's reassuring voice. But those first frightening hours stripped him and his compatriots of their sense of strength, that no matter what the odds, they were still in control of their fate.

—Steve Braun, in Los Angeles

Los Angeles Times

CIRCULATION: 1,225,189 DAILY / 1,514,096 SUNDAY

THURSDAY, JANUARY 31, 1991

COPYRIGHT 1991 / THE TIMES MIRROR COMPANY / CC†† / 144 PAGES

DAILY 25¢ DESIGNATED AREAS HIGHER

Allies Battle for Saudi Town

Enemy Air Force No Longer a Factor: Schwarzkopf

COLUMN ONE

Direct Hit on Psyche of Israel

■ With Tel Aviv traumatized by Iraqi missiles, assumptions on how the country should defend itself have been turned topsy-turvy.

By DANIEL WILLIAMS and CAREY GOLDBERG
TIMES STAFF WRITERS

TEL AVIV—Always, in past wars, Tel Aviv was the carefree heartland that Israelis left behind when they went to defend the country in the far-off sands of the Sinai or the mountainous Golan Heights.

Now, suddenly, it is the front.

For the first time in 42 years of independence through five wars, an enemy has struck deep and consistently into Israeli cities. In physical terms, the damage has so far been light. But in terms of the Israeli psyche, it has been clear and immediate.

With Israel's coastal cities under repeated missile attack from Iraq, thousands of Israelis have become refugees in their homeland, fleeing to inland cities as far away as Eilat, a resort town on the Gulf of Aqaba in the far south.

It is not the soldiers called to duty who are in danger, but the families left behind. Dearly held assumptions of how Israel will defend itself have been turned topsy-turvy, and in Tel Aviv, a way of life has been profoundly disrupted.

"The ostrich is having to take its head out of the sand," said filmmaker Stuart Schottman, referring to the languorous coastal city. "And it's getting a real look at the Middle East."

Tel Aviv's trauma has become a point of national debate as tens of thousands of residents head up the highway toward Jerusalem. Mayor Shlomo Lahat sparked an uproar last weekend when he called his fleeing constituents "deserters."

"Someone who leaves Tel Aviv now would leave the country when times get hard. It's a direct connection," he said.

His criticism brought furious rejoinders from parents who left to take their children to safety and Tel Aviv residents who proclaimed their own right to decide where to weather the war.

"You scholars telling women and children what to do—what arrogance!" Chanah Ben-David, an official of the Naamat women's organization, nearly shouted at Lahat and a panel of professors and journalists who gathered Sunday to discuss the pros and cons of leaving

Please see ISRAEL, A18

Associated Press

A Saudi tank sits outside Khafji, where Iraq staged the first major ground assault of the war. Smoke rises from a destroyed Iraqi vehicle.

■ **Gulf War:** Coalition troops recapture much of Khafji after first major Iraqi ground assault. U.S. air strikes, gunfire destroy 24 tanks. Twelve Marines are killed.

By J. MICHAEL KENNEDY
TIMES STAFF WRITER

RIYADH, Saudi Arabia—Allied forces led by Saudi troops recaptured much of the Saudi town of Khafji early today after the first major Iraqi ground assault of the Persian Gulf War, a "hellacious" battle that began in the eerie glare of a full moon and took the lives of 12 Marines—the first U.S. ground troops killed in action.

The liberation drive began at 11 p.m. Wednesday, Saudi time. By early today, Saudi troops backed by U.S. Marines reportedly had taken control of all but one Khafji neighborhood where Iraqis with some 20 armored vehicles were holding out. Khafji had been in enemy hands for at least a full day. It was the first time Iraqis had captured Saudi territory since the war started.

After 15 minutes of heavy Marine artillery fire to soften up the Iraqi defenses, dozens of Saudi light armored personnel carriers, along with MAX-30 tanks from the Persian Gulf emirate of Qatar, roared toward the center of the town. Some Saudi forces made it—but others, including some of the Marines, were forced into a 50-mile-an-hour retreat when they were pelted by Iraqi rocket fire.

They regrouped and attacked again, and the Marines opened an artillery barrage on the holdout neighborhood, where the Iraqis were still said to be lurking in buildings.

Deserted since the beginning of the war, Khafji was occupied Wednesday by an estimated 50 to 150 Iraqis. U.S. troops said allied forces would fight until they won it back. "If they control the town for the moment, it's only going to be for the moment," said Marine Lt. Michael Ragoza, a platoon commander. Marine Maj. Craig Huddleston said, "They probably ought to call 911 right now."

The Iraqis began their ground assault Tuesday night in the northeast corner of Saudi Arabia. Under the full moon and flares that flashed with white light, they advanced with about 1,500 troops and 50 tanks in four attacks stretching from the shore of the Persian Gulf to about 25 miles west into the Saudi desert. Air strikes and ground fire beat virtually all of them back and destroyed about half their tanks. The fighting lasted through Tuesday night and into Wednesday.

Marine Lt. Col. Cliff Myers used one word to sum it up: "Hellacious."

In addition to the 12 Marines who were killed, at least two others were wounded, and two U.S. soldiers were trapped by Iraqi fire. A daring effort to rescue them was

Please see COMBAT, A6

MWD to Seek 31% Reduction in Water Use

By VIRGINIA ELLIS and JANE FRITSCH
TIMES STAFF WRITERS

SACRAMENTO—Threatening the most severe drought measures in its history, officials of the Metropolitan Water District said Wednesday they will ask their board in mid-February to order Southern California water agencies to cut consumption by 31%.

The threatened cutback, coupled with the "dismal" level of snowfall in the Sierra, has convinced Los Angeles Mayor Tom Bradley and key members of the City Council that mandatory rationing is necessary, sources in City Hall said. They plan to announce Friday that they will seek council authority to enact the rationing plan.

Bradley is said to want a "fair and reasonable" mandatory plan that will at first require a 10% reduction in water use from 1986 levels. But if the water supply situation continues to worsen or the MWD approves a drastic cutback, Bradley will push for more severe conservation measures, the sources said.

If the plan is approved by the City Council, it would be the first time since 1977 that mandatory rationing has been imposed in Los Angeles.

The city of Los Angeles is one of the water district's largest customers and this year is relying on the district for 60% of its water supply.

Officials in counties surrounding Los Angeles expressed surprise at

Please see DROUGHT, A24

General Gives Detailed, Upbeat Review of War

■ **Assessment:** He also says 75% of Iraq's command, control and communications facilities have been hit.

By J. MICHAEL KENNEDY
TIMES STAFF WRITER

RIYADH, Saudi Arabia—Operation Desert Storm's commanding general Wednesday provided an upbeat and thoroughly detailed accounting of the first two weeks of war, saying allied forces have gained absolute command of the air and are engaged in a methodical destruction of Saddam Hussein's military machine.

Gen. H. Norman Schwarzkopf told reporters that the Iraqi air force has been effectively eliminated as a factor in the fighting to liberate Kuwait, with 29 Iraqi jets shot down in air-to-air combat. Also, allied jets have hit 38 key airfields, some as many as four times.

Iraq's Republican Guards, the best of Hussein's army, have been the targets of massive raids by B-52 bombers, Schwarzkopf said,

■ **THE GENERAL STARS**
Schwarzkopf takes center stage to detail enemy losses. A8

adding that on Wednesday alone 28 B-52s dropped 470 tons of explosives on the elite troops' positions inside Kuwait.

The general, illustrating his briefing with charts and dramatic combat videos, said all fixed Scud missile launchers have been knocked out.

He added that allied warplanes have hit 75% of Iraq's command, control and communications facilities, forcing Hussein to resort to less effective and more easily targeted backup measures. Finally, he said, one-fourth of the nation's electric generating facilities have been "rendered inoperative."

Please see BRIEFING, A7

Allies Control Air; Picture on Land Is Unclear

By MELISSA HEALY and JOHN M. BRODER
TIMES STAFF WRITERS

WASHINGTON—Although the most intensive air campaign in history has won the U.S.-led coalition unchallenged mastery of the skies over Iraq and Kuwait, it remains unclear how much the more than 15,000 bombing runs have hurt Iraq's ground-fighting capability.

Enemy troops "certainly have a lot of fight left in them," said Gen.

NEWS ANALYSIS

H. Norman Schwarzkopf on Wednesday. Although his assessment of the progress of the battle to date was unqualifiedly upbeat, he could offer no concrete evidence

Please see ASSESS, A8

U.S. Denies It's Easing Terms for Ending War

By DOYLE McMANUS and ROBIN WRIGHT
TIMES STAFF WRITERS

WASHINGTON—The U.S.-Soviet statement proposing a Persian Gulf cease-fire if Iraq promises to pull out of Kuwait was intended as a gesture to keep Moscow from drifting away from the anti-Iraq coalition and not a softening of previous demands for total withdrawal, Bush Administration officials said Wednesday.

The statement, issued Tuesday evening after four days of U.S.-Soviet talks, said the allied assault on Iraq could end now if Saddam Hussein makes an "unequivocal commitment to withdraw from Kuwait" followed by "immediate, concrete steps" to carry out that promise.

Administration officials insisted Wednesday that those terms were no different from President Bush's previous position that Hussein must withdraw all his forces from Kuwait to end the war. "There's no change in policy," said White House Press Secretary Marlin Fitzwater.

But Soviet and Arab diplomats said they considered the U.S.-Soviet statement important because it implicitly endorsed Soviet President Mikhail S. Gorbachev's efforts to persuade Hussein to accept an early cease-fire in the war.

The tangled saga of the U.S.-Soviet statement has become perhaps the messiest hand-to-hand battle on a somewhat neglected front of

Please see POLICY, A20

THE TIMES POLL

Rationing, Slow Growth Favored to Offset Drought

By KEVIN RODERICK
TIMES STAFF WRITER

Californians regard the drought as the state's most pressing problem after crime and would accept mandatory water use rules, including a proposal to limit households to 300 gallons a day, according to Times Poll findings released Wednesday.

Yet as reservoirs fall near empty and a dry summer looms, the drought is not viewed as a simple failing of the weather. Four in 10 people blame excessive growth in Southern California for the worsening water shortage, and they feel new population should be discouraged by the government until more sources of water are found.

In a message to state officials, most people also say they oppose building more dams—or risking new damage to the sensitive environments of the Owens Valley, Mono Lake and Sacramento-San Joaquin River Delta—in order to get that additional water.

Instead, they favor looking outside California for new water, perhaps in the Pacific Northwest, and embracing technology such as desalination and sewage reclamation.

As for water use at home, more than 8 in 10 say they have cut their water use in response to the drought—most commonly by taking shorter showers—and 70% say it would be easy for them to comply if mandatory rationing is imposed.

With modern California itself a creation of massive transfers of water from the green north to the

Please see POLL, A26

INSIDE TODAY'S TIMES

■ WAR STORIES, PHOTOS: A5-21; F2

■ ANTI-TERRORIST EFFORT
Warnings and advisories have hampered international terrorist attacks backed by Iraq, a Philippine official said. A5

■ REFUGEES BLAME ALLIES
Allied bombing raids severed the main refugee trail out of the Iraqi war zone and left at least five people dead in the last two days, witnesses said. A9

■ OIL CLEANUP IN DOUBT
A U.S. Coast Guard official said there is little hope of fully clearing a massive oil spill from the Persian Gulf, amid reports of a second slick off Kuwait. A10

WEATHER: Mostly sunny today with high clouds tonight. Civic Center low/high: 46/74. Details: B5

■ TOP OF THE NEWS ON A2

Agence France-Presse

Soviet troops in Lithuania.

■ SOVIETS REMOVE TROOPS
Soviet officials said that most of the additional troops deployed in the three Baltic republics earlier this month have been withdrawn. A22

War Suddenly Becomes Real for Marine Families

■ **Camp Pendleton:** Base has sent thousands to Gulf. Those left behind can only speculate, hope, pray, wait.

By TOM GORMAN and RAY TESSLER
TIMES STAFF WRITERS

OCEANSIDE—The toughest thing here Wednesday was that nobody knew much of anything. They only knew a war that in some ways had seemed an unreal adventure at once had become quite real, quite lethal and quite frightening.

Twelve Marines had been killed in combat, U.S. officials announced early in the day. Not announced was what base these dead Marines came from—who they were, and who they had left behind. Here at Camp Pendleton, which has sent thousands of Marines to the front, the unanswered questions haunted everyone—wives and buddies, ministers and commanders.

All they could do was speculate and hope, pray and wait. It hardly seemed enough.

Joey Bailey, a laboratory technician at a medical building in Vista, went to work—but spent her lunch hour driving alone and listening to news accounts of the fighting. "And I just started crying. My chest hurts," she said.

Coralee Collins sought refuge by taking her two children for a walk on the Oceanside beach. She wore a Marine Corps sweat shirt emblazoned with the caricature of a bulldog.

"There's nothing more I can do," she said. "My husband's there. I

Please see PENDLETON, A15

AV-8B Harrier II

Both the United States and Britain have versions of the so-called jump jet, popularized during the Falklands War. The unusual fighter, produced for the U.S. Marine Corps, is capable of vertical takeoffs and landings, deliver thousands of pounds of ordnance, and then land vertically on an unimproved forward site.

Exhaust nozzle turns for vertical takeoff

Crew: one

Max speed: .88 Mach at sea level

Armament:
25-mm gun
Sidewinder air-to-air missiles
Maverick air-to-ground missile
Laser-guided and gravity bombs
Rocket launchers

1 Late Tuesday night, Iraqi mechanized battalion crosses border west of Wafra, and is forced to retreat after engagement by allied forces.

2 Just before midnight, another Iraqi mechanized battalion moves into the deserted Saudi town of Khafji.

3 Just after midnight, Iraqi infantry and tanks cross border northwest of Khafji. Allied planes force them to withdraw.

4 About noon Wednesday, a column of tanks crosses at Wafra. Allied air and ground fire force them to withdraw.

Ahmadi

TURKEY
SYRIA — IRAN
o Baghdad
IRAQ
o Basra
SAUDI ARABIA
Persian Gulf
KUWAIT
0   200
MILES

Wafra
KUWAIT
Persian Gulf
SAUDI ARABIA
Khafji
0   10
MILES

U.S. and allied forces battled a multipronged attack by Iraqi troops, the first major ground assault of the Gulf War. Twelve Marines died, the first American ground troops to be killed in action.

WHERE SITUATION STANDS

Allied forces led by Saudi troops tried to liberate the small Saudi town of Khafji, which was being held be an estimated 50 to 150 Iraqis.

The Iraqis began the ground assault Tuesday night, advancing about 1,500 troops and 50 tanks in four attacks from the shore of the Persian Gulf about 25 miles west into the Saudi desert. Air strikes and withering ground fire slowly beat back most of the invaders.

LOSSES

■ Twelve Marines killed, two wounded.
■ 2 Marine light armored vehicles reported lost.
■ About a dozen Iraqis captured.
■ At least 24 Iraqi tanks destroyed.

PURPOSE

The Iraqi objective was unclear, but officials speculated it was a response to recent heavy Marine fire on Iraqi positions north of the Kuwaiti border.

ANDERS RAMBERG / Los Angeles Times

Khafji: In a "hellacious" battle, U.S. Marines and allied forces recapture much of the frontier Saudi town of Khafji after the first major Iraqi ground assault of the war.
■ The Iraqis had advanced by moonlight with about 1,500 troops and 50 tanks.
■ U.S. officials say Iraqi casualties are heavy but give no count; Baghdad Radio says the Iraqi army is "wiping out" the "forces of the tyrants."
■ Allied troops engage Iraqi soldiers along a 25-mile-long front extending from Kuwait's Wafra oil field to Khafji; 12 Marines are reported killed; one of them is later listed as missing.

Military: Gen. H. Norman Schwarzkopf says two weeks of bombing raids have forced Iraq to abandon centralized control of its air defense. He declares allies have supremacy over Iraqi skies.
■ U.S. Marines capture a second Kuwaiti island, Umm al Maradim.
■ The number of Americans in the theater passes the half-million mark, bringing the total number of allied troops to more than 700,000. Iraq is estimated to have 545,000 troops in the field.
■ The United States is blanketing Iraqi troops from the air with at least 4 million leaflets telling them how to surrender.

Environment: A new oil slick appears in the Gulf, emanating from an Iraqi oil terminal.

Diplomacy: The Bush Administration says the U.S.-Soviet agreement proposing a cease-fire if Iraq promises to pull out of Kuwait is not a softening of previous demands for total withdrawal.

Jordan: Refugees fleeing Iraq say allied warplanes bombed and strafed civilian and military targets between Baghdad and the Jordanian border.

Home front: A poll by Times Mirror Center for the People and the Press shows President Bush with an overall 79% approval rating; 73% of those polled said the United States made the right decision in using force against Iraq.

A LOOK AT
IRAQI DEFENSES

With allied bombers mounting a concentrated air blitz on Iraqi supply lines and elite Republican Guard troops behind the front lines, U.S. military planners are setting the stage for what could prove to be a bloody but decisive confrontation between ground forces in the desert.

Conventional military wisdom calls for attackers to hold a 3-1 superiority in numbers before attempting to blast well-entrenched defenders out of their positions. But Pentagon planners are relying on U.S. technological superiority—which some experts describe as a World War III force seeking to overcome World War I-style fortifications—to rout the Iraqis.

SCENARIO:
The most likely scenario for the looming ground war, experts say, is a night-time, three-pronged allied attack — including land, air and sea elements. U.S. Army units, assisted by allied Arab

forces, would thrust into Iraq west of the Kuwaiti border. U.S. paratroopers would drop behind Iraqi lines while Marines launch an amphibious assault.

Each of these maneuvers would help support the main attack along Iraq's front line on the Kuwait-Saudi border.

POSSIBLE STRATEGIES
To punch holes in Iraqi defenses, some experts speculate that allied troops would:
▶ Start with massive artillery and bombing strikes. Heavy smoke might be used as a diversion to mask allied maneuvers.
▶ Employ repeated B-52, A-10 and Apache helicopter strikes.
▶ Use bulldozers and tanks with heavy rollers and exploding "line charges" to clear minefields.
▶ Use M-1A1 Abrams tanks to zip through the breach followed by Bradley fighting vehicles with infantrymen.

Triangular strongpoints
These large triangular forts are made of sand piled up to form walls about 10 feet high. The corners house companies consisting of infantrymen, tanks and artillery guns. Ramps made of sand and gaps in the walls are used to enter and exit.

Companies positioned in corners
2,000 meters

A typical layout of an Iraqi brigade position
8,000 - 12,000 meters

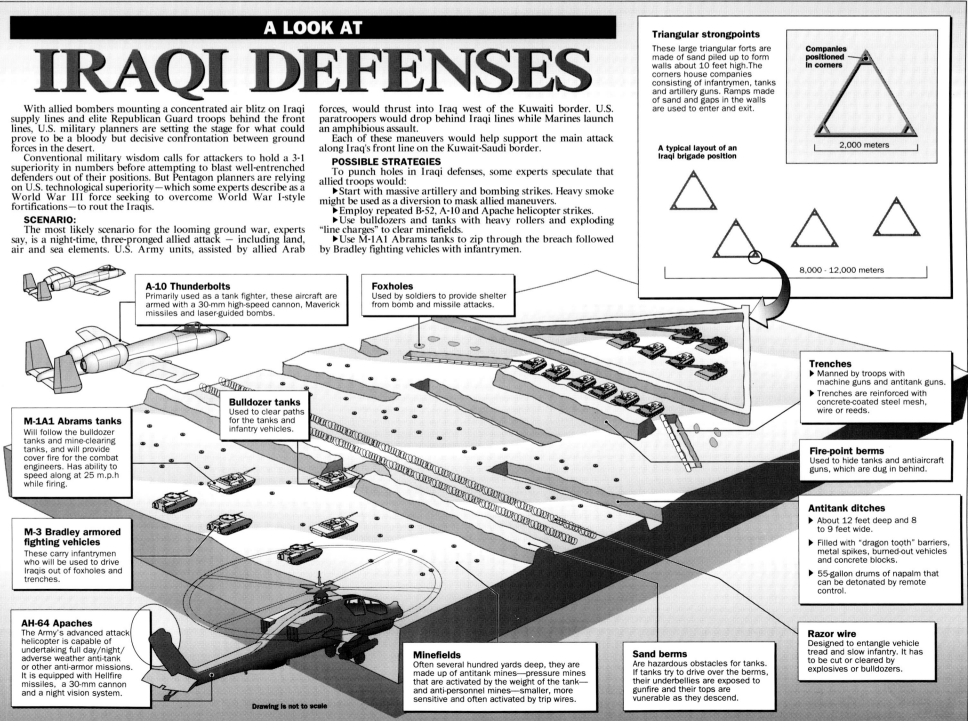

A-10 Thunderbolts
Primarily used as a tank fighter, these aircraft are armed with a 30-mm high-speed cannon, Maverick missiles and laser-guided bombs.

Foxholes
Used by soldiers to provide shelter from bomb and missile attacks.

M-1A1 Abrams tanks
Will follow the bulldozer tanks and mine-clearing tanks, and will provide cover fire for the combat engineers. Has ability to speed along at 25 m.p.h while firing.

Bulldozer tanks
Used to clear paths for the tanks and infantry vehicles.

M-3 Bradley armored fighting vehicles
These carry infantrymen who will be used to drive Iraqis out of foxholes and trenches.

AH-64 Apaches
The Army's advanced attack helicopter is capable of undertaking full day/night/ adverse weather and anti-armor missions. It is equipped with Hellfire missiles, a 30-mm cannon and a night vision system.

Trenches
▶ Manned by troops with machine guns and antitank guns.
▶ Trenches are reinforced with concrete-coated steel mesh, wire or reeds.

Fire-point berms
Used to hide tanks and antiaircraft guns, which are dug in behind.

Antitank ditches
▶ About 12 feet deep and 8 to 9 feet wide.
▶ Filled with "dragon tooth" barriers, metal spikes, burned-out vehicles and concrete blocks.
▶ 55-gallon drums of napalm that can be detonated by remote control.

Razor wire
Designed to entangle vehicle tread and slow infantry. It has to be cut or cleared by explosives or bulldozers.

Minefields
Often several hundred yards deep, they are made up of antitank mines—pressure mines that are activated by the weight of the tank— and anti-personnel mines—smaller, more sensitive and often activated by trip wires.

Sand berms
Are hazardous obstacles for tanks. If tanks try to drive over the berms, their underbellies are exposed to gunfire and their tops are vunerable as they descend.

Drawing is not to scale

SANDY KAY / Los Angeles Times

DAY 16

FEBRUARY 1, 1991

Hysteria over the threat of terrorism quickly entered the realm of the absurd, and more often than not, Arab-Americans were the victims.

In Long Beach, police pulled over a car driven by a woman in a veil and a Muslim headdress. She was driving home with a rented vacuum cleaner in the back seat. Apparently, someone had seen the two "barrels" of the vacuum cleaner peeping above the seat and called police to report that a suspicious-looking Arab was driving around town with a carload of shotguns.

Indeed, anti-Arab sentiment was common, and some of the nastiest examples occurred in public school classrooms. One Arab-American from Los Angeles angrily related that every time he'd pick his up his 6-year-old son from school, the boy's classmates would taunt him, saying, "Bye-bye, Saddam."

—Tammerlin Drummond, in Orange County

Los Angeles Times

CIRCULATION: 1,225,189 DAILY / 1,514,096 SUNDAY

FRIDAY, FEBRUARY 1, 1991

COPYRIGHT 1991 / THE TIMES MIRROR COMPANY / CC†† / 136 PAGES

DAILY 25¢ DESIGNATED AREAS HIGHER

COLUMN ONE

Stealth Jet: Tiny Town Flies High

■ Communities that are home to many of the nation's exotic weapons have a special perspective on the war. In Tonopah, Nev., citizens track the F-117A with pride and confidence.

By JENIFER WARREN
TIMES STAFF WRITER

TONOPAH, Nev.—When a mysterious black jet slipped past Iraqi radar detectors and bombed Baghdad with the opening shot of the Persian Gulf War, chests puffed up with pride all over this gritty desert town.

Tiny Tonopah is the home of the famed F-117A Stealth fighter plane, that once top-secret weapon designed to sneak undetected through even the most sophisticated enemy defenses.

"You're doggone right we feel pride," barked Fred Shepard, 57, a retired Tonopah casino worker. "That's our baby over there. It may have been born someplace else, but we raised it, right here in our back yard."

Peek into the most desolate reaches of the American West, into communities on the edge of military proving grounds and test ranges, and you'll find people with a special perspective on the Mideast war—people who have long enjoyed a ringside view of the exotic weaponry now proving its mettle in the Persian Gulf. With the ultimate test finally at hand, they are tracking the contest with passion and unwavering confidence.

In Ridgecrest, a Kern County city that hugs the giant China Lake Naval Weapons Center, locals scan the news for word of the Sidewinder missile, a deadly air-to-air weapon designed and developed at the hometown base.

Alamogordo, N. M., normally a sleepy place, is now abuzz with boastful talk of the now-famous Patriot missile, the all but invincible anti-Scud shield that has been tested at the neighboring White Sands Missile Range since 1986.

And in Barstow, residents who have watched the M-1 Abrams scoot across miles of Mojave Desert at Ft. Irwin debate how the squat, brown tank would fare in a ground war with Iraq.

Perhaps nowhere, however, is the bond between town and weapon as strong as it is in Tonopah. Located in a dusty valley halfway between Las Vegas and Reno, the community borders the Tonopah Test Range, a vast Air Force installation where the 59 Stealth planes of the 37th Tactical Fighter Wing are based. Close to one-third of the 4,000 townsfolk work at the so-called "TTR," and with mining and tourism—Tonopah's other main industries—so fickle, the U.S. military is cherished as the area's only steady employer.

But the relationship goes way beyond economics. This is a place where kids of 8 or 9 can tilt an ear skyward and tell you whether that's an F-16 or a Stealth screaming by. The elusive, angular jet is

Please see STEALTH, A26

Kuwait City Steels Itself for Big Battle

By EDWIN CHEN
TIMES STAFF WRITER

WASHINGTON—With a sense of foreboding, the hundreds of thousands of Kuwaiti civilians and Iraqi troops in Kuwait city are bracing for what could be the bloody, climactic battle of the Persian Gulf War in the streets of the ransacked capital.

According to Kuwaitis and Westerners who have maintained direct contact with people inside the occupied emirate, Iraqi troops are rounding up civilians, forcing some to give blood and possibly holding others as human shields. Iraqi soldiers have even donned

Please see KUWAIT, A10

Russia Objects to Using Troops to Patrol Streets

By MICHAEL PARKS
TIMES STAFF WRITER

MOSCOW—In a direct challenge to President Mikhail S. Gorbachev's emergency powers, the Russian Federation decided Thursday to question the constitutionality of his decree authorizing troops to patrol the streets of the country's cities, and it appealed to him to suspend the order to avoid further confrontations and possible bloodshed.

With the patrols scheduled to begin today, the Russian Legislature expressed concern that they could lead to clashes similar to those in the Baltic republics last month, when 21 people were killed, and that they could mask a right-wing takeover of the government.

"Who knows what might happen in the next 24 hours?" Russian President Boris N. Yeltsin, the maverick populist who has emerged as Gorbachev's most powerful critic, said during the debate.

The Russian Legislature warned in a resolution that "the use of armed soldiers on city streets can lead to further destabilization of the political situation and to a considerable curtailment or violation of rights and freedoms."

The lawmakers asked the Committee on Constitutional Compliance, which acts as the Soviet Union's constitutional court, to rule on the legality of Gorbachev's decree. They argued that the Soviet president had exceeded even the enhanced authority given him in December by the Congress of People's Deputies, the national Parliament.

Sergei S. Alexeyev, the chairman of the Constitutional Compliance Committee, has indicated that the panel already has begun to study the decree. As the Soviet Union's largest constituent republic, the Russian Federation has the weight to put the issue at the top of the committee's agenda.

Alexeyev, who is known to oppose the order, told friends this week that this could well become

Please see TROOPS, A39

Allies Drive Iraqis From Saudi Town and Take 167 Prisoners

Reuters

Marines in Khafji fire at Iraqi positions with a machine gun while helping to retake the Saudi border town.

■ **Gulf War:** Bush says he is not yet ready to deploy U.S. forces in a ground offensive. Hussein is rumored to mass troops for a second assault; heavy bombardment reported.

By J. MICHAEL KENNEDY and JOHN M. BRODER
TIMES STAFF WRITERS

RIYADH, Saudi Arabia—Saddam Hussein's troops took a severe beating as forces from Saudi Arabia, Qatar and the United States drove them from the Saudi town of Khafji, the allied military command said Thursday, adding that a rumored second ground assault by Iraqi soldiers would only lead them "into harm's way in a major way."

Army Lt. Gen. Thomas W. Kelly theorized that Hussein's ground attack on Khafji was an attempt "to draw us into something that we don't want to be drawn into right now." President Bush said Thursday that he is not yet ready to deploy U.S. troops in ground combat to force the Iraqis out of Kuwait.

The Pentagon would not comment on unconfirmed reports by allied troops and Iraqi radio that as many as 60,000 of Hussein's troops were massing near the Saudi border for a second, massive ground attack.

Early today, a pool report from a reporter with the British 4th Armoured Brigade said American B-52 bombers were pounding a column of 1,000 Iraqi vehicles stretching 10 miles. The commander of a squadron of American Harrier jump jets said the Iraqi column was heading through southern Kuwait toward the Saudi border.

The pool report, by Simon Clifford of the Southampton Evening Echo, a British paper, said he could hear the dull thud of bomb explosions as the B-52s, A-10 tank killing planes and Apache helicopters attacked the column. Clifford said the B-52s refueled in the air as they attacked over a 150-mile stretch of the border.

Another pool report early today said Iraqi forces had renewed their attack on Khafji. It said witnesses saw wounded being carried out of the city and said a route between Khafji and Kuwait remained open, giving the Iraqis an avenue of attack.

In repulsing the initial Iraqi incursion on Khafji late Wednesday and early Thursday, allied forces took 167 prisoners of war, destroyed 42 tanks and 35 other vehicles and killed an undetermined number of enemy troops during the battle, the Pentagon said.

"The Iraqis achieved nothing other than to be mauled badly," Kelly said. "When you take 167 prisoners, they didn't fight too hard."

In other developments:

• Two U.S. soldiers declared missing during the battle for Khafji were found, but the Pentagon would not comment about two other U.S. soldiers—a man and a woman—still missing near the Saudi-Kuwaiti border, saying only

Please see WAR, A6

Grieving Begins for Marines Killed in Gulf

■ **Casualties:** For families of 11 from Southland bases, a painful wait gives way to mourning and memories.

By RAY TESSLER and TOM GORMAN
TIMES STAFF WRITERS

OCEANSIDE—The cruel suspense ended for families and comrades Thursday as the names of 11 young Marines who are among America's first combat dead of the Gulf War reached their homes in hamlets and cities across the nation.

From the military bases of Camp Pendleton and Twentynine Palms in Southern California—where all 11 had been stationed—to their hometowns in tiny places such as Wood Lake, Minn., and giant ones, such as New York City, the unbearable wait ended and the grieving began.

The Marine Corps confirmed the identities of the Marines killed two days earlier during the first in a series of four Iraqi ground attacks Tuesday night and Wednesday morning along the Saudi Arabian border.

At Camp Pendleton, where 23-year-old Cpl. Stephen E. Bentzlin lived, his widow, Carol, recalled talking to him only last week. "Perhaps he had a premonition of this tragedy, because he wanted to talk about the details, should he not return," she said in a statement read by Marine officials.

"He tried to prepare me for this," said Bentzlin, who has three young children. "He said, 'Somebody's gonna get hurt, Babe.' But I didn't think it would be Steve."

In Bountiful, Utah, James T. Stephenson, a former Marine who served in Vietnam, choked with emotion while telling how President Bush had just telephoned to express his sorrow over the death of his son, Lance Cpl. Dion J. Stephenson, 22.

"He offered his condolences," said Stephenson. "I told him that we're 100% behind him. The President was definitely affected when I talked to him. He's a good man. He's my President.

"I want it to be known that my son's death was not in vain."

Across the country, families and friends recounted touching details about the men they had lost and sought fitting tributes for them.

Lance Cpl. Thomas A. Jenkins, 21, of Coulterville, Calif., of the 1st Combat Engineers at Camp Pendleton, had been a search and rescue volunteer in civilian life. In his honor, a flag at Yosemite National Park was lowered to half-staff.

Lance Cpl. Michael E. Linderman Jr., 19, of Douglas, Ore., served with the 3rd Light Armored Infantry Battalion at Twentynine Palms near Barstow in San Bernardino County. Friends remembered that he had surprised his music teachers by entering the military.

Please see MARINES, A18

Troops Caught Behind Lines, Spy on Enemy

By JOHN BALZAR
TIMES STAFF WRITER

EASTERN SAUDI ARABIA—The Iraqis were not alone for those 36 hours when they took and held the border town of Khafji. Lurking there among them, sometimes just footsteps away, were 12 U.S. reconnaissance Marines.

A day and a half of daring, of stealth, of close encounters of the breathless kind were described Thursday after the abandoned coastal city was retaken by Saudi forces and the two six-man Marine "recon" teams were withdrawn.

The Marine task force commander, Col. John Admire, recounted the behind-enemy-lines action to a correspondent, whose dispatch was passed through military censors and made available to all other reporters in the war zone.

Admire said the two six-man recon teams were on routine intelligence-gathering patrols in Khafji, about 10 miles from the Kuwaiti border. That was Tuesday. Suddenly, Iraqi tanks and foot soldiers swept into the deserted town—which in peaceful times had a population of 20,000.

The recon Marines held their ground, lay low and quietly radioed information on the rapid Iraqi advance.

"By the time they determined that they were surrounded, it was too late," Admire said.

Not such a strange condition, truly, for recon Marines, whose

Please see RECON, A16

Drought Taxes State Water Project Beyond Its Ability

■ **Crisis:** System was designed to prevent current scenario. Supplies to south could be cut 85%.

By KEVIN RODERICK and VIRGINIA ELLIS
TIMES STAFF WRITERS

With a snow survey Thursday confirming near-record dry conditions, California has come face to face with its most severe drought crisis in modern times—a scenario that the massive state Water Project conceived in the 1950s was supposed to prevent.

The project cost more than $2.5 billion to build, threw up dams across wild rivers in Northern California and today gulps more electric power than any city. But it looks as if the project will fail to stave off the painful effects of the longest and deepest drought in six decades.

Barring uncommonly hard falls of late winter snow and rain, state officials say they will have to reduce the flow of Northern California water into Southland cities by as much as 85%. Farms would get no state water this summer. At the tap, people will have to endure rationing in most Southern California cities.

Gov. Pete Wilson, who has the power to declare a drought emergency and order even more stringent steps, has called a press conference for today to address the drought.

Measuring crews delivered bad news from the Sierra Nevada above Owens Valley, 250 miles north of Los Angeles. They found

Please see DROUGHT, A3

INSIDE TODAY'S TIMES

■ **WAR STORIES, PHOTOS:** A5-29; B6,7; E1; F1

■ **PENTAGON CUTBACKS**
The Bush Administration is readying a defense budget that would continue cutbacks in spending, despite the war. **A5**

■ **PLO PROVOCATIONS**
Israel said Palestinian guerrillas are trying to open a new front in the Gulf War by launching attacks in the Israeli-held buffer zone in southern Lebanon. **A23**

■ **IRAN TO HOLD IRAQI PILOTS**
Iranian officials told a visiting top aide of Saddam Hussein that Iraqi pilots who landed in Iran and their planes will be held until the war ends. **A24**

Associated Press

Seidman at news conference

■ **NO FDIC BAILOUT**
L. William Seidman, chairman of the Federal Deposit Insurance Corp., said a taxpayer bailout of the deposit insurance fund will not be needed. **D1**

WEATHER: Variable high clouds today with light winds. Civic Center low/high: 51/77. Details: B5

■ TOP OF THE NEWS ON A2

Cult of Saddam Hussein Grows as War Drags On

■ **Third World:** The poor and oppressed need a hero, an analyst says. In Iraq's leader, they've found one.

By MARK FINEMAN
TIMES STAFF WRITER

RUWEISHED, Jordan—Samir Saad al-Din Nimr had little interest in politics until the Gulf War gave him a new hero two weeks ago.

Nimr, a cab driver, does the 550-mile run from Amman to the Iraqi capital of Baghdad over what is now the most deadly stretch of road on Earth. He dodges the allied strafing and bombing runs, going in empty in his Chevy van and running out overloaded with war refugees. And every day, he listens to news of the war and his new hero on the Mother of Battles radio station from Baghdad.

"Hey, did you hear?" Nimr called out to his fellow drivers and Jordanian friends when he emerged from the war zone about noon Wednesday to spread the news of the day.

"Saddam went 20 kilometers into Saudi Arabia. He took it and then gave it back. It was just to show he could do it."

"Saddam is God!" shouted Abdul Ahmad, another driver who made the run Wednesday. "Even if every single American comes here to fight, they cannot face him even standing alone."

Such is the stuff of the emerging cult of Iraqi President Saddam Hussein.

After two full weeks of bombing have battered Iraqi targets and driven much of Iraq's military elite

Please see CULT, A13

LAV-25

In the ground fighting near Khafji this week, the Marines reported losing at least two of their lightly armored vehicles. The LAV-25 is an 8-wheel, 15-ton lightly armored vehicle that carries a crew of three and six troops. It was developed specifically for the U.S. Marine Corps and is equipped with a 25-mm cannon. By contrast, the Army's Bradley troop carrier, weighing 25 tons, carries nine soldiers.

Speed: 62 m.p.h.
Range: 410 miles
Cross trenches up to: 6 ft. 9 in. wide
Amphibious speed: 6.2 m.p.h.

Khafji: Forces from Saudi Arabia and Qatar, supported by U.S. Marines, drive Iraqis from the Saudi town of Khafji, capturing 167 prisoners, destroying about 75 tanks and other vehicles, and killing an undetermined number of enemy troops.

■ A Pentagon briefer says the Iraqi ground attack appears to be an attempt to draw the allies into a ground war.

■ Baghdad Radio announces that Saddam Hussein had personally planned the Khafji attack. It broadcasts patriotic songs and claims Iraq scored a moral victory against U.S. ''infidels'' and their allies.

■ Officials reveal that 12 U.S. reconnaissance Marines had been radioing information from inside Khafji throughout the 36-hour battle.

■ Gen. H. Norman Schwarzkopf calls the Iraqi attack ''about as important as a mosquito on an elephant.''

Military: A pool report from a British correspondent says B-52 bombers were pounding a column of 1,000 Iraqi vehicles stretching 10 miles. An American commander says the column had been heading south toward the Kuwaiti border.

■ Two U.S. soldiers—a man and a woman—are confirmed to be missing near the Saudi-Kuwaiti border.

■ A four-engine U.S. AC-130 plane armed with cannons is reported missing behind enemy lines.

■ A Harrier pilot operating in southern Kuwait reports too many targets to choose from: ''It's almost like you flipped on the light in the kitchen at night and the cockroaches start scurrying.''

Missiles: A Scud missile lands on the West Bank. No injuries or damages are reported.

International: American B-52s are sent to an air base in Spain to launch raids over Iraq.

Terrorism: The State Department says about 70 acts of terrorism have been committed against American and allied interests since the war started—11 of them in the past 24 hours—but that Iraqi agents were involved in only three.

Huddled Iraq POWs dotted war theater after ground campaign.

PATRICK DOWNS / Los Angeles Times

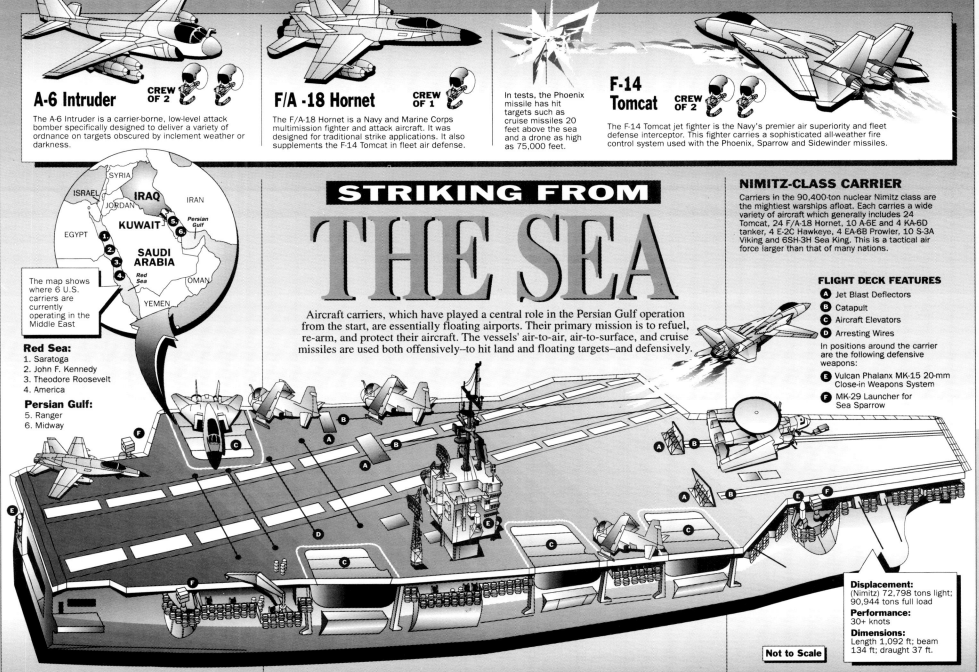

A-6 Intruder
CREW OF 2

The A-6 Intruder is a carrier-borne, low-level attack bomber specifically designed to deliver a variety of ordnance on targets obscured by inclement weather or darkness.

F/A-18 Hornet
CREW OF 1

The F/A-18 Hornet is a Navy and Marine Corps multimission fighter and attack aircraft. It was designed for traditional strike applications. It also supplements the F-14 Tomcat in fleet air defense.

In tests, the Phoenix missile has hit targets such as cruise missiles 20 feet above the sea and a drone as high as 75,000 feet.

F-14 Tomcat
CREW OF 2

The F-14 Tomcat jet fighter is the Navy's premier air superiority and fleet defense interceptor. This fighter carries a sophisticated all-weather fire control system used with the Phoenix, Sparrow and Sidewinder missiles.

STRIKING FROM
THE SEA

Aircraft carriers, which have played a central role in the Persian Gulf operation from the start, are essentially floating airports. Their primary mission is to refuel, re-arm, and protect their aircraft. The vessels' air-to-air, air-to-surface, and cruise missiles are used both offensively--to hit land and floating targets--and defensively.

The map shows where 6 U.S. carriers are currently operating in the Middle East

Red Sea:
1. Saratoga
2. John F. Kennedy
3. Theodore Roosevelt
4. America

Persian Gulf:
5. Ranger
6. Midway

NIMITZ-CLASS CARRIER

Carriers in the 90,400-ton nuclear Nimitz class are the mightiest warships afloat. Each carries a wide variety of aircraft which generally includes 24 Tomcat, 24 F/A-18 Hornet, 10 A-6E and 4 KA-6D tanker, 4 E-2C Hawkeye, 4 EA-6B Prowler, 10 S-3A Viking and 6 SH-3H Sea King. This is a tactical air force larger than that of many nations.

FLIGHT DECK FEATURES
A Jet Blast Deflectors
B Catapult
C Aircraft Elevators
D Arresting Wires

In positions around the carrier are the following defensive weapons:

E Vulcan Phalanx MK-15 20-mm Close-in Weapons System
F MK-29 Launcher for Sea Sparrow

Displacement:
(Nimitz) 72,798 tons light; 90,944 tons full load

Performance:
30+ knots

Dimensions:
Length 1,092 ft; beam 134 ft; draught 37 ft.

Not to Scale

JIM OWENS / Los Angeles Times

DAY 17

FEBRUARY 2, 1991

The war kept them from returning to their country, but the first Kuwaiti police officers to graduate from the Egyptian police academy still had a beat to pound—the disco beat.

The rich lifestyles of Kuwait's "five-star refugees"—so named because they spent their exile in the luxury of Cairo's five-star hotels—were clearly an embarrassment to their Egyptian hosts. But when the war began, behavior that had been merely embarrassing suddenly seemed scandalous.

"We could not allow these kids to behave like they were on vacation," a senior Kuwaiti official explained. "American soldiers and Arab troops were putting their lives on the line. . . . A small but conspicuous minority was giving the rest of us a bad name by dancing and drinking in the discos every night."

When warnings to the Kuwaiti exile community failed to have much effect, Egyptian officials agreed to allow several newly graduated Kuwaiti police cadets to go undercover in Cairo's crowded discotheques. Their role was to report misbehaving youths to the Kuwaiti Embassy. Officials would not say how many disco delinquents were collared in this way, but several Kuwaiti youths were deported to Saudi Arabia.

—Michael Ross, in Cairo

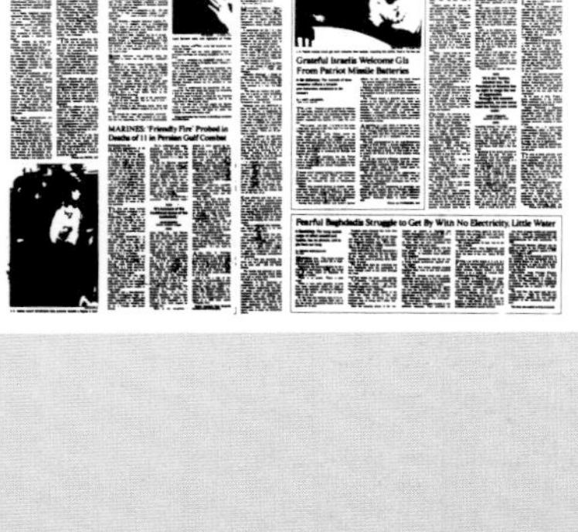

Los Angeles Times

CIRCULATION: 1,225,189 DAILY / 1,514,096 SUNDAY

SATURDAY, FEBRUARY 2, 1991

COPYRIGHT 1991 / THE TIMES MIRROR COMPANY / CC††† / 112 PAGES

DAILY 25¢

DESIGNATED AREAS HIGHER

Planes Collide at LAX; 12 Die

24 Injured in Runway Crash; 21 Unaccounted For

U.S. Planes Pummel Iraqis Along Border

■ **Gulf War:** Intent of enemy movements remains a puzzle. Allies report seizing 400 POWs in Khafji fighting.

By JOHN M. BRODER and J. MICHAEL KENNEDY
TIMES STAFF WRITERS

WASHINGTON—U.S. warplanes Friday pummeled Iraqi troops and armored vehicles moving along the Kuwaiti border with Saudi Arabia, but the aim of the Iraqi movement remained unclear.

U.S. and Saudi officials said allied forces seized at least 400 Iraqi prisoners of war in two days of clashes in and near the Saudi town of Khafji that ended Thursday night.

Also Friday, officials confirmed that an AC-130 Spectre gunship had been shot down in southern Iraq early Thursday. Search and rescue operations for the crew were called off Friday night, and the 14 crew members were listed as missing in action.

U.S. losses now total 11 killed, 9 wounded, 8 held prisoner and 23 missing, including the AC-130 crew. Thirteen American aircraft have been lost in the first 16 days of combat.

In other developments:

- A Michigan couple said the Pentagon has informed them that their daughter, an Army specialist, is missing in the war zone.
- France granted permission to U.S. B-52 bombers based in Britain to fly over its territory on bombing missions to the Persian Gulf. Neutral Switzerland said it will let U.S. medical evacuation aircraft cross its airspace for one week starting today "for humanitarian purposes." And Spanish defense officials acknowledged that Spain is allowing B-52s to use a joint Spanish-U.S. air base as a staging area for raids on Iraq.
- Military authorities in Saudi Arabia are investigating the deaths of 11 Marines in the fighting around Khafji to determine whether any were killed by allied "friendly" fire.
- Ground-hugging Tomahawk missiles fired from U.S. Navy warships struck Baghdad, Iraqi officials told Western journalists in the Iraqi capital. Two crashed in residential neighborhoods and narrowly missed the abandoned American Embassy, they said.
- President Bush, speaking to the cheering families of soldiers poised for combat in Saudi Arabia, told them that Iraqi President Saddam Hussein has an "endless appetite for evil" but that the U.S.-led military coalition will teach him a lesson.

Pool reports coming in from the front said that an Iraqi tank attack took place late Thursday night about 50 miles west of Khafji near the Kuwaiti border town of Umm Hujul. According to the reports, three Iraqi tanks were destroyed by elements of the 1st Marine Division in an area of open desert. No U.S. casualties were reported in the fighting.

Please see WAR, A6

'Friendly Fire' Is Probed in Battle Deaths

By JOHN BALZAR and HELAINE OLEN
TIMES STAFF WRITERS

DHAHRAN, Saudi Arabia—A glum front-line Marine commander said Friday that at least some of the first Marine ground combat casualties may have been the result of a missile fired by a U.S. battle-support aircraft—but only because of desperate, close-range fighting.

Officials at the Pentagon and at command headquarters in Saudi Arabia said military investigators are looking into the possibility that "friendly fire" killed some or all of the 11 Marines who died in the open-

Please see MARINES, A8

Saudis Praised After Their 1st Test in Combat

By DAVID LAMB
TIMES STAFF WRITER

EASTERN SAUDI ARABIA—Amid the hulks of burned-out armored vehicles and the skeletons of charred bodies, Saudi Arabian troops exulted Friday in crushing the Iraqi assault on Khafji. Never before in the modern history of the kingdom had the Saudis fought a land battle—either here or elsewhere in the Middle East.

The victorious troops cavorted through the streets of the northern border town, waving their national flag overhead and shouting, "*Allahu akbar!*" (God is great). They clutched one another in Arab embraces and swaggered about with chests extended, savoring a moment to be long remembered by a nation that had always considered

Please see SAUDIS, A6

ROBERT DURELL / Los Angeles Times

Twisted wreckage of USAir 737 jetliner on LAX runway. Tail section at left was partially torn away.

■ **Disaster:** USAir jetliner with 89 aboard burns with commuter craft stuck underneath. The FBI says there is no evidence of terrorism.

By ERIC MALNIC and RICHARD A. SERRANO
TIMES STAFF WRITERS

A USAir jetliner landing at Los Angeles International Airport collided on the ground with a a SkyWest commuter plane Friday night, creating a fiery tangle of wreckage. At least 12 people were killed, 24 were injured and 21 were missing, officials said.

The USAir Boeing 737—carrying 83 passengers and a crew of six—veered across a taxiway after the collision, apparently dragging the smaller plane beneath it, and slammed into an abandoned airport building, witnesses said.

The mangled wreckage of the smaller, twin-engine Fairchild Metroliner III with two pilots and 10 passengers aboard ended up beneath the burning fuselage of the USAir's Flight 1493.

A SkyWest spokesman said there were no survivors on the commuter plane.

Federal aviation officials said it was too early to determine how the accident occurred and precisely where on the ground the two planes collided.

Said SkyWest official Mikeil Callahan: "The information I have is that the USAir plane landed on top of the SkyWest plane."

An airport employee told reporters it appeared the commuter plane taxied into the jetliner's path.

The FBI said there was no evidence of terrorism.

As passengers swarmed from the jetliner, at least a dozen fire engines sped to the crash site on the north side of the airport's passenger terminals. Ambulances rushed the injured to nearby hospitals. Ten were reported to have suffered moderate to severe injuries, with another 14 suffering lesser injuries.

"It's amazing anybody is alive," said Los Angeles Police Officer Ken Brady, who was at the crash site. "It was a pretty grisly scene. It's amazing anybody walked away."

Hours later, several bodies remained pinned in the tangle of wreckage or scattered on the airport Tarmac. Five hours after the crash, relatives of as many as 10 USAir passengers were still awaiting word at the airport on their missing kin. Salvage crews were held back by leaking fuel, but they intended to explore the wreckage today.

One witness said the jetliner's landing gear was not lowered as the big plane approached the airport. But USAir contradicted that report, saying there was no initial information that anything was amiss. Fire officials said a survey of the wreckage showed the landing gear was down.

Federal Aviation Administration officials said the pilot of the jetliner

Please see PLANES, A31

De Klerk Calls for End to All Apartheid Laws

By SCOTT KRAFT
TIMES STAFF WRITER

CAPE TOWN, South Africa—President Frederik W. de Klerk, sweeping away the last legal pillars of apartheid, Friday announced government plans to scrap the laws that segregate housing, restrict black ownership of land and legally classify all citizens by race.

The president's decision put the country on the verge of meeting all five preconditions established by Congress for removing U.S. sanctions against Pretoria. Both the government and the African National Congress say they expect the final condition—the release of political prisoners—to be met by the end of April.

"The South African statute book will be devoid, within months, of the remnants of racially discriminatory legislation which have become known as the cornerstones of apartheid," De Klerk said in a speech opening South Africa's Parliament. The lawmaking body, which is controlled by the ruling National Party, is expected to approve the president's recommendations before it adjourns in June.

Foreign Minister Roelof (Pik) Botha told reporters the speech was "an important further step on the road to a return to international respectability."

"The process toward dismantling apartheid and fundamental change in South Africa is irreversible," Botha added. "After today, few can doubt that."

In Washington, State Department spokeswoman Margaret Tutwiler hailed De Klerk's steps, which she said brings South Africa "pretty close" to conditions required for lifting U.S. economic

Please see RACE, A26

Fed Lowers Key Discount Rate to 6% to Aid Economy

By OSWALD JOHNSTON
TIMES STAFF WRITER

WASHINGTON—The Federal Reserve Board, in an emergency move to prop up the steadily worsening economy, lowered its key discount rate to 6% Friday in hopes of bolstering consumer confidence and spurring more bank lending.

The reduction from 6.5% marked the second time in five weeks that the Fed has lowered its benchmark rate and sparked a rally in the bond market. It also prompted several of the nation's major banks to reduce their prime lending rates to 9% from 9.5%.

The discount rate is the interest charged by the Fed on overnight

Please see FED, A28

Survivors Tell of Smoke, Fire, Fear of Death

By JENIFER WARREN and SHERYL STOLBERG
TIMES STAFF WRITERS

Passenger Chul Hong was in seat 7F, flying into Los Angeles from Columbus, Ohio. He would recall later that the landing of the USAir Boeing 737 was smooth, that he felt "just a little bump."

"Then I heard a noise—I thought it was just the tires blowing off," said Hong, a 62-year-old physician from Canton, Ohio. "And then I see the flames, and everybody started screaming their heads off. I thought I was going to die."

Leaping through an exit just behind his seat, Hong dropped to the Tarmac and then sprinted from the plane, fearing it might explode at any time. After 100 yards, the slight, bespectacled man glanced back. He saw fire engines, paramedics and other vehicles streaming toward the scene.

And he saw the plane, engulfed in flames.

"Thanks to the Lord," said Hong, who is relocating to Los Angeles and had come west Friday to shop for a home. "I could be burned to death."

Wrapped in thin, blue blankets, looking weary and shellshocked, survivors of ill-fated USAir Flight 1493, which originated in Syracuse, N.Y., told a tale of horror Friday as they trickled from the airline lounge where they were taken

Please see ORDEAL, A30

Judges Urge Rejection of Edison-SDG&E Merger

■ **Utilities:** Their recommendation says the proposed $2.6-billion union would lessen competition in the state.

By PATRICK LEE and GREG JOHNSON
TIMES STAFF WRITERS

Dealing a major blow to a giant utility merger, two state administrative law judges on Friday recommended rejection of the proposed $2.6-billion combination of Southern California Edison Co. and San Diego Gas & Electric Co., arguing that the merger would lessen competition in the state.

The judges' ruling, which does not hold force of law, is not the final word on the controversial merger that would create the largest utility in California. Final approval lies with the Federal Energy Regulatory Commission and the state Public Utilities Commission.

Gov. Pete Wilson, a former San Diego mayor who has not taken a position on the merger, could play a role in determining the outcome. He has said he soon will fill two vacancies on the five-member PUC.

In their exhaustive, 1,300-page ruling released in San Francisco, Judges Lynn Carew and Brian Cragg concluded that the proposed merger would lessen competition for electricity, give the merged companies undue control over

MORE WAR COVERAGE

■ **WAR STORIES, PHOTOS: A5-19; D2; F1**

■ **IRAQ WARNS ON POWS**

Iraq said captured allied fliers will be treated as common criminals, not as prisoners of war, for allegedly carrying out attacks on civilians. **A8**

■ **WARM ISRAELI WELCOME**

U.S. soldiers who are manning Patriot missile batteries around Israel have been receiving a warm welcome. **A9**

■ **BUSH VISITS BASES**

President Bush visited three military bases in the East, delivering an upbeat, patriotic message in his first outing since the Gulf War began. **A11**

WEATHER: High cloudiness today with highs in the 70s. Civic Center low/high: 54/74. Details: B4

JAVIER MENDOZA / For The Times

Agent Lawler answers critics.

■ **FBI DEFENDS ACTIONS**

Lawrence Lawler, FBI chief in Los Angeles, expressed concern about "paranoia" and said only

Bradley Calls for Toughest Water Rationing in History

■ **Drought:** Residents would have to cut usage 10% on March 1 and 15% on May 1. Council must act on plan.

By JANE FRITSCH
TIMES STAFF WRITER

Calling Sierra Nevada snowpack figures "astonishing" and "frightening," Los Angeles Mayor Tom Bradley on Friday called for the toughest water-rationing measures in the city's history.

Bradley and Department of Water and Power officials said they want the measures enacted quickly so that on March 1, the 3.5 million residents of Los Angeles would be required to cut their water use by 10% from 1986 levels, and on May 1 by 15%. Those who fail to conserve would face stiff sur- make those cuts," Bradley said. "We don't have any choice."

The proposal is expected to win rapid approval of the City Council, which last summer rejected Bradley's plea for a 10% mandatory cutback.

Councilwoman Joan Milke Flores, who was instrumental in killing the mandatory plan, endorsed the tough new restrictions, as did council President John Ferraro.

"It's desperation time," Ferraro said. "We have to move ahead and do these things because it's going to be a long, hot summer. If we don't do it now, we're going to be in serious trouble."

B-52G Stratofortress

B-52G bombers have played an important role in air attacks on Iraq's elite Republican Guard. At least five of the giant Boeing-built bombers participated in Friday's sorties, carpet-bombing targets along the Saudi-Kuwait border.

The long-range planes, which entered service with the Strategic Air Command in 1955, were originally designed to carry nuclear bombs, but have since been adapted to carry other types of missiles and ordnance. The planes were used extensively during the latter part of the Vietnam War.

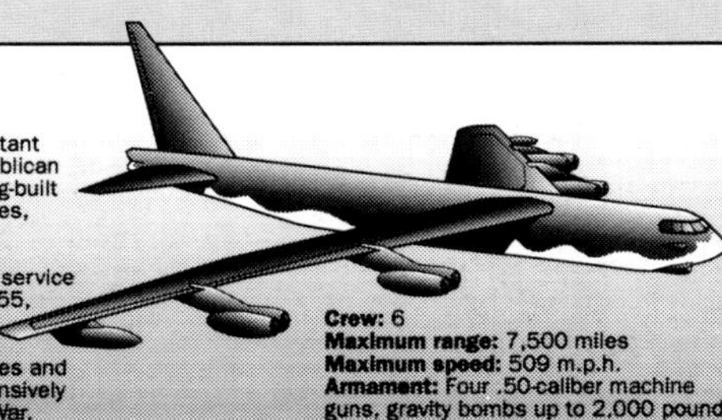

Crew: 6
Maximum range: 7,500 miles
Maximum speed: 509 m.p.h.
Armament: Four .50-caliber machine guns, gravity bombs up to 2,000 pounds each, and "smart" missiles

Military: Hundreds of planes, including U.S. B-52 bombers and British and French Jaguars, pound Iraqi troops and armored vehicles moving toward the Saudi-Kuwaiti border.

■ U.S. officials investigate the deaths of 11 Marines along the border to determine if they were killed by "friendly fire."

■ Tomahawk missiles fired from U.S. warships continue to strike Baghdad.

■ Word spreads among allied troops that Iraqi tanks at Khafji had turned their turrets backward in a sign of surrender, then moved closer to allied positions before opening fire.

White House: President Bush goes on a whirlwind tour of Southern military installations.

Iraq: Baghdad Radio says captured allied fliers will be treated as criminals, not as prisoners of war, for having carried out indiscriminate attacks on civilians.

■ The Baghdad government says Bush, British Prime Minister John Major, French President Francois Mitterrand and Saudi King Fahd are responsible for the deaths of innocent civilians. It vows to hunt down and punish them.

■ Iraq claims more than 180 coalition warplanes have been downed; the allies put aircraft lost in combat at 19.

■ Refugees arriving from Iraq say that claims of battlefield victory have boosted Iraqi morale. But the bodies of fallen soldiers begin to return home.

Iran: The Tehran government begins shipping food and medicine to Iraq, and opens diplomatic talks aimed at persuading the Iraqis to leave Kuwait.

Environment: The Gulf oil slick begins to break into pieces, but winds from the south give anti-pollution teams a break, pushing the slick away from Saudi desalination and power plants.

■ The U.S. military confirms that a second oil slick continues to spread off the coast of Iraq.

International: France agrees to allow U.S. B-52s based in Britain to fly over its territory.

PATRICK DOWNS / Los Angeles Times

Marines set off explosives to try to lure enemy into revealing himself.

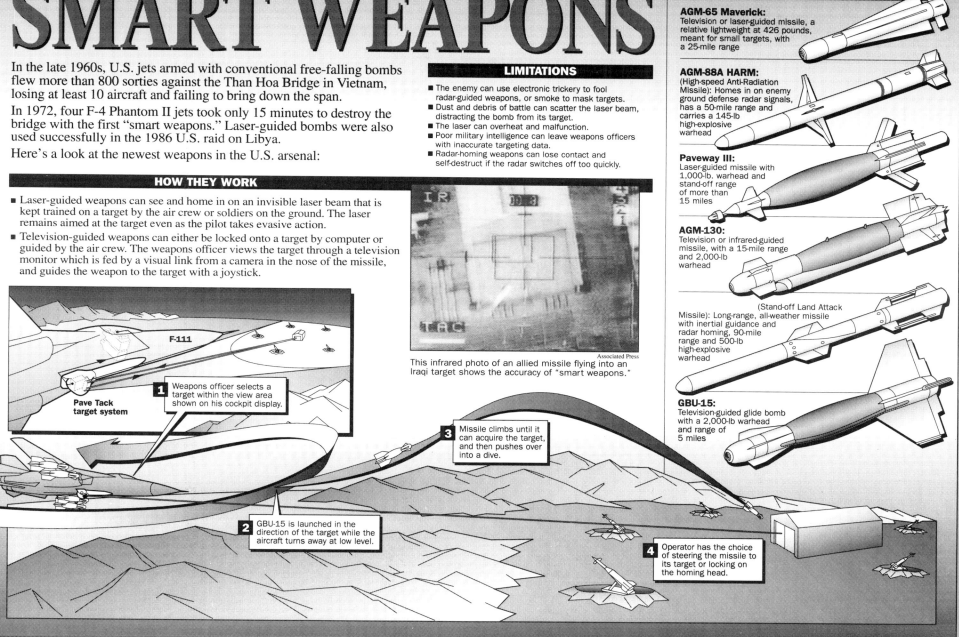

SMART WEAPONS

In the late 1960s, U.S. jets armed with conventional free-falling bombs flew more than 800 sorties against the Than Hoa Bridge in Vietnam, losing at least 10 aircraft and failing to bring down the span.

In 1972, four F-4 Phantom II jets took only 15 minutes to destroy the bridge with the first "smart weapons." Laser-guided bombs were also used successfully in the 1986 U.S. raid on Libya.

Here's a look at the newest weapons in the U.S. arsenal:

LIMITATIONS

■ The enemy can use electronic trickery to fool radar-guided weapons, or smoke to mask targets.
■ Dust and debris of battle can scatter the laser beam, distracting the bomb from its target.
■ The laser can overheat and malfunction.
■ Poor military intelligence can leave weapons officers with inaccurate targeting data.
■ Radar-homing weapons can lose contact and self-destruct if the radar switches off too quickly.

THE U.S. ARSENAL

AGM-65 Maverick: Television or laser-guided missile, a relative lightweight at 426 pounds, meant for small targets, with a 25-mile range

AGM-88A HARM: (High-speed Anti-Radiation Missile): Homes in on enemy ground defense radar signals, has a 50-mile range and carries a 145-lb high-explosive warhead

Paveway III: Laser-guided missile with 1,000-lb. warhead and stand-off range of more than 15 miles

AGM-130: Television or infrared-guided missile, with a 15-mile range and 2,000-lb warhead

(Stand-off Land Attack Missile): Long-range, all-weather missile with inertial guidance and radar homing, 90-mile range and 500-lb high-explosive warhead

GBU-15: Television-guided glide bomb with a 2,000-lb warhead and range of 5 miles

HOW THEY WORK

■ Laser-guided weapons can see and home in on an invisible laser beam that is kept trained on a target by the air crew or soldiers on the ground. The laser remains aimed at the target even as the pilot takes evasive action.

■ Television-guided weapons can either be locked onto a target by computer or guided by the air crew. The weapons officer views the target through a television monitor which is fed by a visual link from a camera in the nose of the missile, and guides the weapon to the target with a joystick.

Associated Press

This infrared photo of an allied missile flying into an Iraqi target shows the accuracy of "smart weapons."

F-111

Pave Tack target system

1 Weapons officer selects a target within the view area shown on his cockpit display.

2 GBU-15 is launched in the direction of the target while the aircraft turns away at low level.

3 Missile climbs until it can acquire the target, and then pushes over into a dive.

4 Operator has the choice of steering the missile to its target or locking on the homing head.

Sources: Jane's Weapon Systems, The Great Book of Modern Warplanes, Modern Airborne Missiles

JUAN THOMASSIE / Los Angeles Times

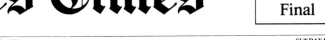

DAY 18

FEBRUARY 3, 1991

For days after U.S. Army Specialist Khiem Ta saw two friends burn to death when "friendly fire" hit the vehicle in which he and they were riding, everything Ta smelled or tasted was the same—"like things burning, maybe even human flesh."

"I've learned that war is serious," he said sadly in a hospital ward in Germany. "I was kind of fatalistic about war and casual about death. I was really naive and dumb. Unless you see war and death, you can't comprehend the emotions involved. I've learned that war is serious because death is serious. I've learned that death hurts the survivors who witness it.

"To me, everybody's brave back in the rear, safe and secure. It's when you come under fire that you find the true side of you, the guts."

—Janny Scott,
in Frankfurt, Germany

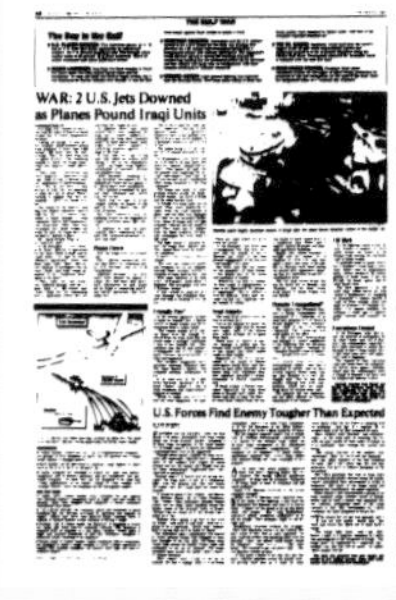

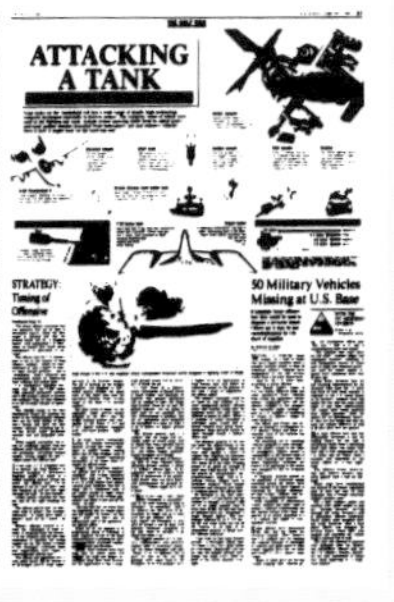

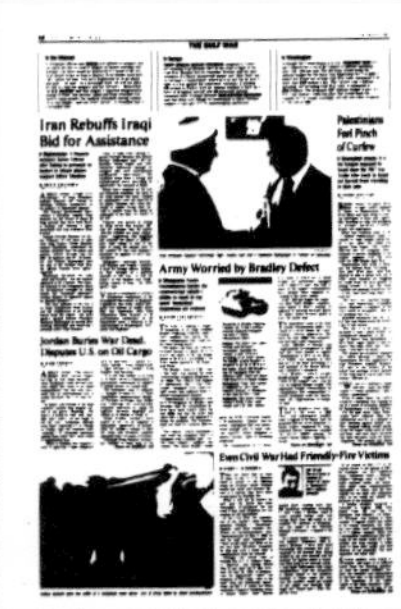

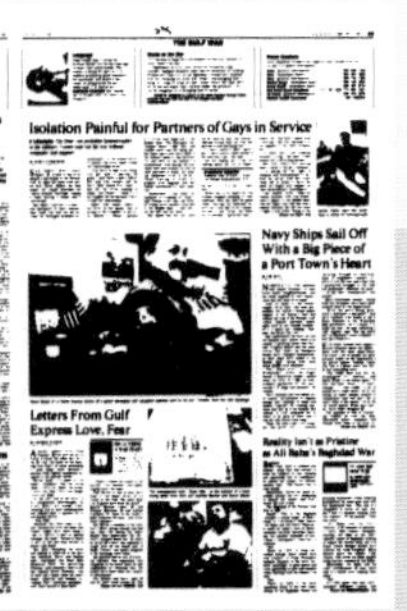

Los Angeles Times

Sunday Final

CIRCULATION: 1,225,189 DAILY / 1,514,096 SUNDAY

SUNDAY, FEBRUARY 3, 1991

COPYRIGHT 1991 THE TIMES MIRROR COMPANY CC† 466 PAGES

SUNDAY $1.25 DESIGNATED AREAS HIGHER

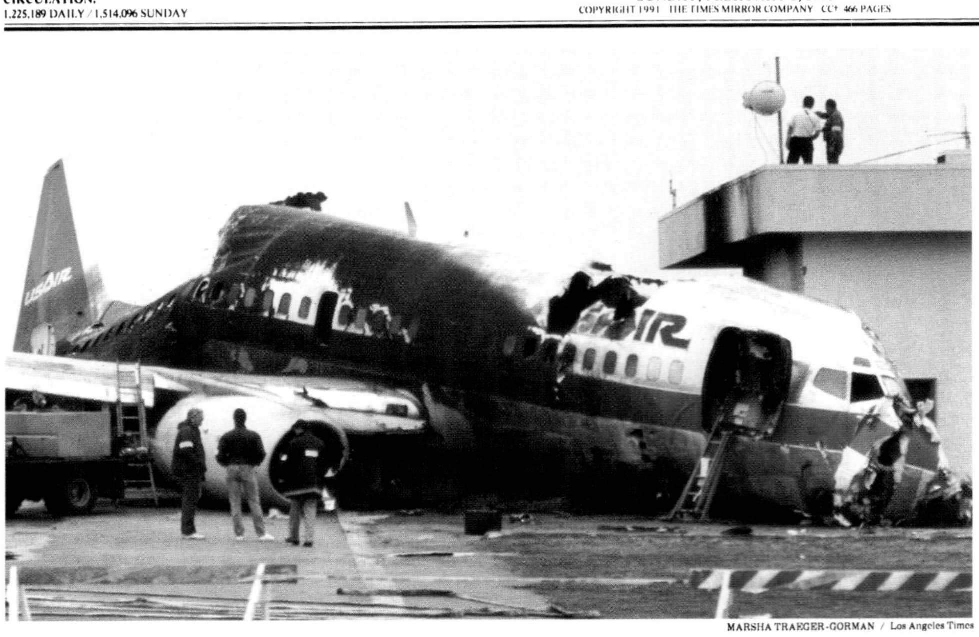

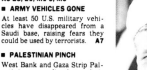

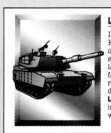

MARSHA TRAEGER-GORMAN / Los Angeles Times

Investigators examine charred hull of USAir 737 the morning after collision with a SkyWest commuter plane at LAX. At least 13 people died.

Air Controller's Error Blamed for Disaster at LAX

■ **Crash:** USAir 737 was given permission to land on a runway where SkyWest commuter plane was told to wait for takeoff, authorities say. Death toll may reach 33.

By ERIC MALNIC and TRACY WILKINSON, TIMES STAFF WRITERS

An air traffic controller cleared a USAir jetliner to land on the same Los Angeles International Airport runway where she had earlier directed a small commuter plane to await takeoff, leading to a collision that killed as many as 33 people, authorities announced Saturday.

The jetliner, a Boeing 737 out of Columbus, Ohio, carrying 83 passengers and a crew of six, plowed into the rear of the twin-engine SkyWest commuter and erupted in flames Friday night. Both aircraft then skidded 1,800 feet down the runway, across the Tarmac and into the side of an unoccupied airport fire station.

By Saturday, officials listed 13 people as confirmed dead—all 12 people on the commuter and the USAir pilot. The death toll is likely to climb, however: at least 20 people from the USAir flight remained unaccounted for and are feared dead. Twenty-five others were listed as injured.

James Burnett, an official with the National Transportation Safety Board, told a crowded press conference that investigators had listened to recordings of the conversation between the air traffic tower and the cockpit crews.

Burnett said the controller first told the SkyWest commuter, a Swearingen Metroliner, to wait on the runway for takeoff; one minute and 12 seconds later, she gave permission to the jetliner to land on the same runway.

One minute later, the two planes collided. The words "What the hell?" are then heard on the recording. It was not clear whether the expletive was exclaimed from the control tower or from one of the aircraft.

Burnett indicated the controller, who he did not identify, had shown signs of preoccupation and confusion, including "difficult communication" with an earlier Aeromexico flight.

Emergency crews, meanwhile, were struggling to remove bodies from the mangled wreckage Saturday, a task complicated by large

Please see CRASH, A28

The Crowded Ground Also Poses a Peril

By WILLIAM C. REMPEL and DAVID FREED
TIMES STAFF WRITERS

While the crowded skies above Los Angeles International Airport have been recognized as among the most hazardous in the nation, it is on the ground—in the airport's maze of runways and taxiways—where many accidents and harrowing near-misses have occurred in recent years, records show.

In June, 1989, a jetliner taxied onto Runway 25-Right for takeoff at the same time another jetliner was preparing to land on the same runway. The landing plane, which apparently was coming in on

Please see SAFE, A31

COLUMN ONE

Boning Up on Iraq's Way of War

■ U.S. military seeks clues to Hussein's next move by studying strategies used against Iran. By identifying strengths and failings, they hope to learn from Tehran's mistakes.

By DAVID FREED
TIMES STAFF WRITER

During a fight near Susangerd, they purposely bowed their lines, lured an enemy tank division into the trap and then slaughtered it.

At the battle of Fish Lake, they sent high-voltage currents surging through the water to electrocute enemy infantrymen fording the marshy shallows.

In retaking the port city of Al Faw, they caught the enemy off guard with an artillery barrage launched on a holy day, followed by an assault involving nearly 200,000 troops supported by helicopter gunships.

For eight years, from 1980 to 1988, Iraq waged savage war with Iran, ultimately winning it with stolid tactics and at times deadly innovation. By CIA estimates, no fewer than 550,000 Iraqis and 1 million Iranians were killed or wounded.

It was a war closed to all but a few outsiders, usually relegated to the back pages of most newspapers in the United States. Not even Soldier of Fortune magazine, whose stock in trade is luridly detailed combat journalism, was ever able to chronicle the butchery. "No one," associate editor Tom Slizewski conceded, "wanted to go."

Please see LESSONS, A22

Allied Ground Push in 20 Days Foreseen

■ **Strategy:** Officials say offensive can begin after air strikes destroy half of Iraq's combat vehicles, equipment.

By JOHN M. BRODER and MELISSA HEALY
TIMES STAFF WRITERS

WASHINGTON—U.S. military officials have concluded that the allied ground offensive against Iraqi troops can begin when half of the enemy's combat vehicles and equipment have been destroyed, a job that could be completed in as few as 10 days, Pentagon sources said Saturday.

The U.S.-led air campaign, which has just turned to the systematic bombardment of Iraqi forces in Kuwait and southern Iraq in the last five days, has had a "dramatic effect" on Iraq's 545,000 troops and their ground weapons, a senior official said.

The highly placed Pentagon official, who asked not to be named, said that unless the weather or some other factor disrupts the U.S. air war schedule, the Iraqi forces would be sufficiently softened up for an allied ground assault in 10 to 20 days.

His observations are the most precise assessment to date of the level of destruction that U.S. military planners want to inflict in Iraqi forces before commencing ground combat, and of the timetable they have laid out for achieving it.

The comments also project the Pentagon's increasing confidence that the air campaign is proceeding on schedule and meeting its key objectives, despite difficulties in determining the extent of damage and the need to divert hundreds of aircraft to the search for Scud missiles.

The task of disabling Saddam Hussein's ground forces has been made easier in recent days by the Iraqis, who have moved a large number of vehicles from protective shelters out into the open, where they have been subjected to relentless air attack.

Some U.S. military officials have speculated that the Iraqi movements, combined with recent border attacks, may be an attempt to draw allied units into a ground war prematurely. But the officials say the allies will not commit to massive ground combat until the air campaign has met its goals.

Please see STRATEGY, A7

Conservatives Step Up Attacks on Gorbachev

By MICHAEL PARKS
TIMES STAFF WRITER

MOSCOW—Conservatives in the leadership of the Soviet Communist Party are stepping up their pressure on President Mikhail S. Gorbachev, attacking *perestroika* as a setback for socialism, demanding a return to classic Marxist values and questioning his leadership of the party.

Ivan K. Polozkov, the first secretary of the Russian Communist Party, whose members make up about half of the Soviet party, told a meeting of the party leadership last week that *perestroika*, as Gorbachev's political and economic reforms are known, had long ago degenerated from an effort to renew socialism into an anti-commu-

Please see SOVIETS, A25

Allies Pound Iraqis; 2 U.S. Planes Downed

By J. MICHAEL KENNEDY and KIM MURPHY
TIMES STAFF WRITERS

RIYADH, Saudi Arabia—Allied warplanes raked Iraqi troops with some of the heaviest bombing of the Persian Gulf War on Saturday, scattering one unit of the elite Republican Guard and blowing up airfields, tanks and armored personnel carriers.

But the Iraqis, vowing to retaliate with everything from kitchen knives to "weapons of mass destruction," shot down two American planes—the first in two days. They used antiaircraft fire, but U.S. officers said it came from scattered guns and was not centrally controlled.

The officers noted that the Iraqi air force offered no resistance.

At the same time, a U.S. Marine was killed and two more were wounded in another possible instance of death by "friendly fire"—apparently when their convoy was hit in Saudi Arabia by cluster bombs dropped by an American aircraft.

This instance, like the deaths last week of 11 Marines, some of whom may have been struck by a missile from a U.S. battle-support aircraft, was being investigated by American officers. In Washington, Secretary of Defense Dick Cheney said, "We simply do not know what precisely happened."

In other developments:

• Iraq shot more conventionally armed Scud missiles into Israel and Saudi Arabia. No major injuries were reported.

• Gen. H. Norman Schwarzkopf, the top allied commander, said he has seen reports that Iraqi President Saddam Hussein is distraught and has had three doctors treating him with tranquilizers.

Please see WAR, A6

From All Walks of Life, Victims United in Death

By JENIFER WARREN and JOHN CHANDLER
TIMES STAFF WRITERS

They were a varied bunch. A businessman, a high school senior, even an air traffic controller returning home from a business trip to Atlantic City, N.J.

On Friday evening, just before 6, they came together at Los Angeles International Airport, clambering up a steep stairway into a slender Metroliner with two engines and 19 seats. The flight was SkyWest 5569, bound for Palmdale, 60 miles away.

Minutes later, before the 10 passengers buckled into the tiny craft even had a chance to get acquainted, their journey ended. A USAir Boeing 737, arriving from Columbus, Ohio, slammed into the small plane, flattening it in an explosion of flames.

Passengers on the larger aircraft had time to race for emergency exits, to make a frantic leap from a wing and flee to safety. There were no such opportunities for those flying with SkyWest. Only seconds after impact, the commuter plane had vanished, its wreckage buried beneath the smoking hulk of the USAir jet.

■ **MORE STORIES, PICTURES:** A3, A28-31

SkyWest's 10 passengers died instantly, as did the pilot, Andrew J. Lucas, and the first officer, Frank C. Prentice III, both based in San Luis Obispo.

As investigators prowled the charred wreckage of the two planes Saturday, relatives of the

Please see SKYWEST, A29

American Support Grows for Use of Nuclear Arms

■ **Weapons:** Heavy U.S. losses could boost pressure on Bush. Opponents warn of a wide backlash.

By ROBERT C. TOTH
TIMES STAFF WRITER

WASHINGTON—Should the United States use nuclear weapons in the Persian Gulf War?

Although the Bush Administration says it has no plans to do so, the possibility remains very real for many Americans.

New Gallup polls last week found 45% of Americans would favor the use of nuclear weapons "if it might save the lives of U.S. troops." Three weeks earlier, before the war began, only about half that proportion—24%—favored using nuclear weapons. About 72% were opposed.

The message is clear: If American losses were to mount into the thousands, and Iraq were to use chemical or nuclear weapons, President Bush would come under pressure to drop a nuclear bomb on Baghdad—or use smaller, tactical nuclear weapons—to save lives and shorten the war.

Increasing numbers of conservatives have been pushing that approach.

Former Texas Gov. John B. Connally, who fears that U.S. casualties in the Persian Gulf eventually could top 50,000, believes the United States should use nuclear weapons to shorten the war. "That's a cruel thing to say, but that's the most merciful thing to say," he said.

And Gen. Frederick J. Kroesen,

Please see NUCLEAR, A20

MORE WAR COVERAGE

■ **WAR STORIES, PHOTOS: A6-23; E1; M1-3, M6**

■ **ARMY VEHICLES GONE**

At least 50 U.S. military vehicles have disappeared from a Saudi base, raising fears they could be used by terrorists. **A7**

■ **PALESTINIAN PINCH**

West Bank and Gaza Strip Palestinians, confined to their homes under a curfew imposed by Israel on Jan. 18, are feeling an economic squeeze. **A8**

■ **TV BRINGS OPENNESS**

Round-the-clock news coverage has changed the tight censorship rules in the sheltered Arab states and has raised prospects of a social revolution. **A15**

WEATHER: Mostly sunny and warmer today. Civic Center low/high today: 47/75. Details: B2

■ TOP OF THE NEWS ON A2

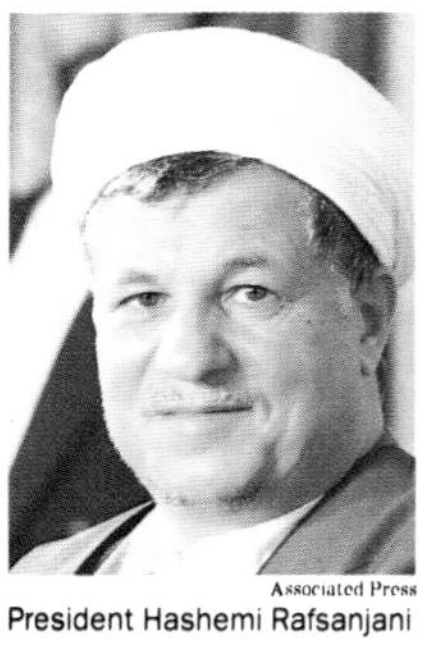

Associated Press

President Hashemi Rafsanjani

■ **IRAN REBUFFS HUSSEIN**

Iranian President Hashemi Rafsanjani refused a personal request from Saddam Hussein for the return of about 90 Iraqi aircraft flown to Iranian soil. **A8**

Prop. 140 Forces Exodus of Experts From Legislature

■ **Ballot measure:** Top Assembly, Senate staffers leaving because of voter initiative. Experience also lost.

By WILLIAM TROMBLEY
TIMES STAFF WRITER

SACRAMENTO—Waves of budget cutting, required by passage of Proposition 140 last November, swept over the California Legislature last week, carrying away many of its most talented staff members.

By Friday, more than 650 of the 2,500 consultants, lawyers, secretaries and others who work for the Legislature had left, helped on their way by severance pay or "golden handshake" pension credits.

Included were many of the most experienced and capable staffers for key Assembly and Senate committees, "in many ways, the core of this place," said state Sen. Becky Morgan (R-Los Altos Hills).

This leaves a smaller, younger, less experienced staff to cope not only with a heavy workload but with lobbyists, many of whom are vastly more experienced. In some cases, the new lobbyists are the old Assembly and Senate consultants.

The Assembly Ways and Means Committee, which handles more bills than any committee in either house, has lost its experts on public schools, social services, taxation, local government and toxic problems.

The number of consultants to the Senate Education Committee has been reduced from four to one. Bill Whiteneck, the survivor, was pre-

Please see PROP. 140, A32

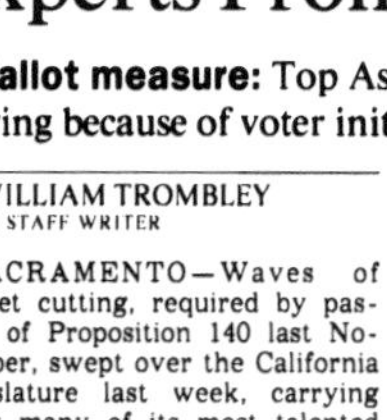

Language

Iraqi troops dug in along the Kuwait border are facing a barrage of more than allied bombs. The enemy is being hit daily by U.S. leaflets promising good treatment for surrender and death if they resist. In preparation for any defections, U.S. forces are **LEARNING PHRASES** like 'hands up" in Arabic and "lay down your weapons.'

Many Kuwaiti refugees were trapped, unable to return home.

PATRICK DOWNS / Los Angeles Times

DAY IN THE GULF

Military: Pentagon officials say the allied ground offensive can begin after air strikes destroy about half of Iraq's combat vehicles and equipment, which could take up to 20 more days.

■ Allied warplanes scatter a unit of the Republican Guard and blow up airfields, tanks and personnel carriers in one of the war's heaviest days of bombing.

■ Allied forces launch new bomb and missile attacks on the Iraqi port city of Basra and other parts of southern Iraq, with two huge blasts rocking Basra.

■ Gen. H. Norman Schwarzkopf says he has seen reports that Saddam Hussein is distraught and has three doctors treating him with tranquilizers.

■ At least 50 U.S. military vehicles disappear from a Saudi base.

■ Two American planes—an A-10 and an A-6—are shot down.

■ A Marine is killed, apparently by allied cluster bombs, bringing to 12 the number of Americans confirmed killed on the ground.

Missiles: Iraq fires two Scuds at Israel, but there are no reports of deaths or injuries.

■ A Patriot missile intercepts a Scud aimed at Riyadh. Debris damages an apartment building and injures 29.

■ Iraq has fired a total of 28 missiles at Saudi Arabia and the same number at Israel.

Iraq: Baghdad Radio says Iraq would use every kind of weapon, from knives to weapons of mass destruction and annihilation, to keep its hold on Kuwait.

Iran: Iraq's deputy prime minister winds up a mission to Tehran apparently empty-handed, failing to secure the return of Iraqi combat aircraft that have flown to Iran.

Environment: History's largest oil slick hits Saudi Arabia's northeast coast, polluting miles of sandy beach. A second slick, coming from Iraq, grows dramatically.

■ Germany sends environmental experts and 30 tons of equipment to Qatar to help it fight the oil slick.

ATTACKING A TANK

THE BATTLE AGAINST IRAQI ARMOR

Iraqi tanks on the battlefield will face a wide range of deadly high-technology weapons developed especially to destroy armor. The weapons, some of which were used in the fighting last week, include armor-piercing shells fired by allied tanks, anti-tank guided missiles launched from helicopters, jets and infantry vehicles. Here is how it might look on the receiving end:

AH-64 Apache
Heavily armed attack helicopter can maneuver nimbly on the battlefield, firing on tanks from many angles.

Maverick missile
Precision guided tactical missile homes in on tanks at supersonic speed using infrared, TV or laser guidance.

HEAT shell
High-explosive, anti-tank rounds are one of four different shells carried by M-1A1s (see inset). Only the newest Iraqi tanks have any chance of withstanding a hit.

Hellfire missile
Precision guided "fire and forget" missile can lock on to its target after firing, while the helicopter evades enemy fire.

TOW missile
Proven in Vietnam and the 1973 Middle East War, these missiles are guided to their targets by a wire tether that streams out the back of the missile as it flies.

Bradley
The infantry fighting vehicle is a cross between a light tank and armored personnel carrier. It carries TOW missiles and a 25mm cannon.

A-10 Thunderbolt II
Close-support "Warthog" jet streaks in at less than 100 feet above the battlefield, then pops up for a good shot.

M-1A1 Abrams main battle tank
Most modern version of America's best tank has improved crew protection, better suspension, and a 120mm gun.

TANK-PIERCING HEAT SHELL

Shell

A shaped charge detonates on impact, forcing a metallic penetrator through the armor.

Wall of tank

T-72 heavy tank
Iraq's best tank is big, fairly fast, Soviet-built, armed with a powerful 125mm main gun, and in some cases protected by HEAT-resisting Chobham-type ceramic-and-metal armor plating.

Dug-in tanks
In defensive fortifications, Iraq digs in tanks, half-burying them in the sand. Dug-in tanks cannot maneuver, but they are much harder to hit.

MAXIMUM RANGE OF ANTI-TANK ORDNANCE

Up to **25 miles** — Maverick
2.3 miles ← TOW
4.6 miles ← Hellfire
1.8 miles ← HEAT

Target   25 — *Miles* — 0

Sources: Jane's Armor and Artillery; Jane's Weapons Systems; Jane's All the World's Aircraft; Illustrated Guide to Modern Airborne Missiles; Great Book of Modern Warplanes; Combat Arms Modern Attack Aircraft; Atlas of Modern Warfare; Osprey Vanguard–The M1A1 Abrams Main Battle Tank; ARCO Guide to Modern Soviet Army Weapons; Land-Sea-Air Firepower

51

AP / Los Angeles Times

DAY 19

FEBRUARY 4, 1991

There were Americans who believed that President Bush was involving the United States in a war for economic motives. Many in the anti-war movement quickly adopted the slogan "No Blood for Oil." To make their point, one small group of protesters poured several quarts of motor oil and one pint of human blood on the marble steps of the downtown Los Angeles Federal Building.

They used the mess as a barrier. Then they sang songs and waited for arrest—and kept on waiting. The steps were so slippery that police called in a janitor to clear the way.

The janitor took one look and knew he needed something to soak up the blood and oil.

He used sand.

—Scott Harris, in Los Angeles

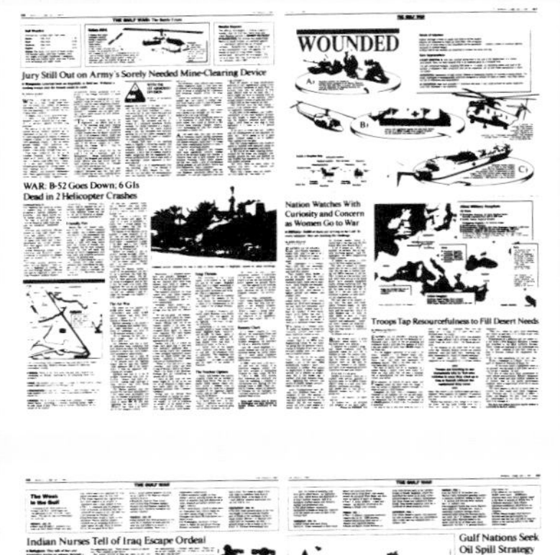

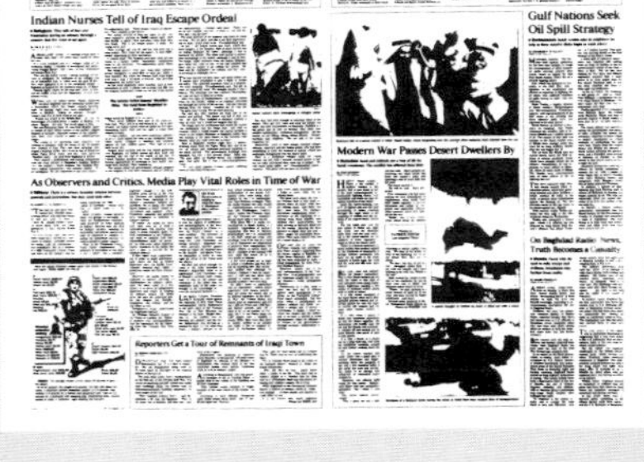

Los Angeles Times

CIRCULATION: 1,225,189 DAILY / 1,514,096 SUNDAY | MONDAY, FEBRUARY 4, 1991 | DAILY 25¢ DESIGNATED AREAS HIGHER

COPYRIGHT 1991 THE TIMES MIRROR COMPANY CC† 88 PAGES

COLUMN ONE

Cries for Help Go Unheeded

■ State and local governments are on the edge of a fiscal abyss. Much of the country is becoming meaner and harsher for those most desperate for assistance.

By SCOT J. PALTROW
TIMES STAFF WRITER

NEW YORK—State and city governments throughout the country are under financial siege, and as the crisis deepens, horror stories emerge from abstract budget numbers.

In San Diego County, a severely psychotic, homeless young man shouts at phantom voices as he sits starving in a public park. County mental health workers battle for weeks to admit him to a psychiatric ward. But the county's lack of funds means that no beds are available. Finally, they give up and load him onto a bus to New York, where his mother lives. They hope that through some miracle he will arrive there and find treatment.

In New York, two men burn to death in a house fire. The blaze is nine blocks from a fire station that was closed down only four days earlier under a city austerity plan. Early reports link their deaths to the delayed arrival of a pumper from a more distant station. At the same time, city transportation officials contemplate closing a crumbling elevated Manhattan highway that carries 90,000 vehicles per day. There is no money to repair it.

In Detroit, a city-funded soup kitchen that feeds up to 300 a day stopped receiving its regular payments from the city. One result: There was no Christmas dinner for the people it serves.

As fiscal disasters spread through state capitols and city halls, they have brought job freezes, massive layoffs of public employees and cuts in services. In much of the country, the cuts will be so deep that middle-class and wealthy citizens will notice them, if they haven't already. But budget experts say the cuts will have the hardest impact on inner cities and people most desperately in need of public services: inner city schoolchildren, battered children, the indigent, the homeless and the mentally ill.

The size of the crisis is staggering. In state after state, estimates of budget deficits are revised upward almost daily. In California, Gov. Pete Wilson has proposed an austerity budget intended to redress a potential state deficit of up to $10 billion over the next 18 months, which equals about 17% of the state's expected expenditures. New York state's deficit was put at $6 billion, or 20% of its budget. Connecticut, one of the few states without a state income tax, tallied up its revenues for the coming fiscal year and found itself fully 30% short.

The mayor of Connecticut's largest city, Bridgeport, last month took the extraordinary step of threatening publicly to take the city into bankruptcy proceedings. In Philadelphia, the city has been

Please see REVENUES, A16

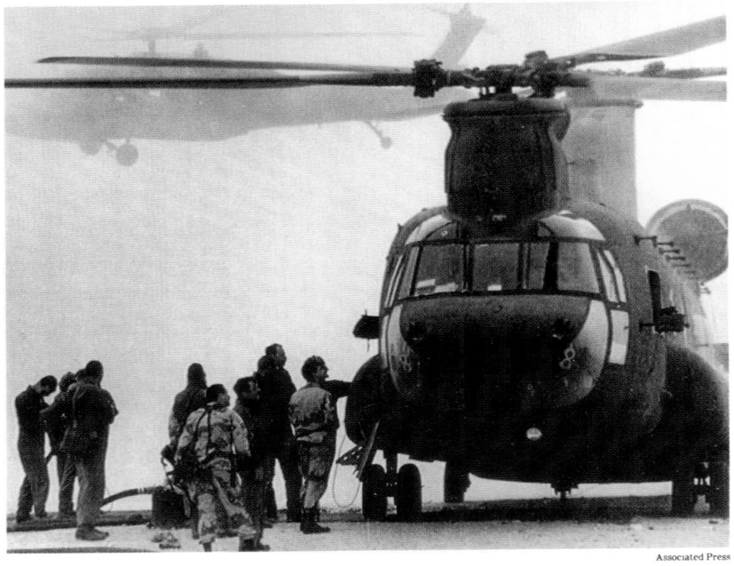

Associated Press

An Army Blackhawk helicopter flies overhead as soldiers refuel a CH-47 Chinook in Saudi Arabia. The Chinook chopper was transporting American troops and equipment to forward positions.

B-52 Goes Down in Ocean; 6 Dead in Copter Crashes

■ **Gulf War:** Mechanical failure blamed in loss of bomber that was returning from a mission. U.S. says eight Marines killed last week were victims of allied fire.

By J. MICHAEL KENNEDY, TIMES STAFF WRITER

RIYADH, Saudi Arabia—Six U.S. helicopter crewmen were killed in two separate crashes, and three airmen were reported missing after their B-52 crashed into the Indian Ocean while returning from a bombing run over Iraq, U.S. military officials said Sunday.

Also Sunday, Marine officials said seven of the 11 Leathernecks killed in a light armored vehicle last week and another Marine killed in a cluster-bomb attack Saturday were victims of so-called friendly fire.

All four crew members died in the crash of a Marine UH-1 helicopter on a noncombat mission in eastern Saudi Arabia, the U.S. Central Command said. No other details of the crash were immediately available.

In a second crash, two Cobra helicopter crewmen were killed when their gunship went down during an escort mission inside Saudi Arabia, officials said.

Three crew members were rescued from the B-52, which crashed late Saturday while on its way back to its base on the Indian Ocean island of Diego Garcia, 2,000 miles southeast of the Persian Gulf. Military investigators said there was no evidence that the crash of the eight-engine, $55-million Stratofortress was due to hostile fire, and they tentatively attributed it to mechanical failure.

The deaths of the six helicopter crewmen increased the number of servicemen killed since the war began to 18, while the missing B-52 crewmen raised the total of American missing to 26.

The crashes came as allied airmen flew more than 2,500 missions Sunday, concentrating almost exclusively on ground targets now that the U.S.-led coalition has claimed superiority in the air over Iraq and Kuwait and the waters of the Persian Gulf. A major target Sunday, as it has been for days now, was Iraq's crack Republican Guard, which was pounded with tons of explosives in round-the-clock bombing runs.

In other developments:

• State-run radio in neighboring

Please see WAR, A6

New Strategy May Bring End to Scud Threat

By J. MICHAEL KENNEDY
TIMES STAFF WRITER

RIYADH, Saudi Arabia—For weeks now, the most palpable fear on this side of the fighting has been of the Scud missile, that inaccurate but nevertheless deadly piece of supersonic machinery that has been aimed at Saudi Arabia and Israel since the fighting began.

The Scud comes only at night, when allied planes have more difficulty in targeting the missile and its launcher, and the announcement of the Scud approach has taken on a kind of routine—first the air raid sirens, then the sound of Patriot air-defense missiles leaving the ground in a whoosh, followed, almost always, by a

Please see SCUDS, A14

All 33 Bodies Found in L.A. Airport Collision

■ **Crash:** Ground radar was not working properly and controller's view may have been blocked, probers say.

By ERIC MALNIC
and JANET RAE-DUPREE
TIMES STAFF WRITERS

Picking through heaps of charred metal, rescue workers Sunday finished recovering the bodies of all 33 people killed in Friday's collision of a USAir jetliner and a SkyWest commuter plane, while investigators pieced together the sequence of events that led to the fiery crash.

The collision at Los Angeles International Airport occurred when an air traffic controller gave permission to the jetliner, with 89 people aboard, to land on the same runway where she had just directed the commuter plane to await takeoff, federal investigators say.

In new details released Sunday night, the investigators said that a ground radar system was not operating properly and that four light posts may have blocked the controller's view of the spot where the commuter plane sat on the runway.

"One of these structures was dead in the middle of the intersection," said one federal investigator.

All 12 people aboard the commuter were killed instantly when it was rear-ended and crushed by the jetliner, and 21 occupants of the USAir flight also died, airline officials and investigators said. Twenty-five people were treated at seven area hospitals for injuries ranging from burns to broken bones.

On Sunday, 27 bodies were recovered in a slow, tedious search through the wreckage. Twenty bodies came from the USAir flight—19 passengers and a flight attendant—and seven bodies were recovered from the commuter plane. On Friday, the bodies of five people who apparently had been hurled from the commuter were recovered from the Tarmac, and on Saturday the body of the USAir pilot was removed from the cockpit.

Throughout the day Sunday, emergency crews using a crane and non-sparking cutting tools dissected the twisted metal to clear the way for Los Angeles County coroner's officials to find and document bodies, their personal belongings and other means of identification like jewelry or purses.

Please see CRASH, A25

Air Controller Safety Issue Surfaces Again

By BOB BAKER
TIMES STAFF WRITER

Preliminary findings that an air traffic controller was at fault in the collision Friday between a SkyWest commuter plane and a USAir jetliner at Los Angeles International Airport have raised concerns once again about the quality and quantity of the nation's controllers.

Ever since President Reagan fired 11,400 of the Federal Aviation Administration's air traffic controllers during an illegal 1981 strike, air safety advocates have contended that the FAA did not move quickly enough to replenish its work force.

While the volume of air traffic continued to grow during the 1980s, America's airports were staffed by significantly fewer controllers during most of those years.

As late as 1986 there were 14,080

Please see CONTROLLERS, A3

Allies, Iraqis Trading Shots in Image War

By THOMAS B. ROSENSTIEL
TIMES STAFF WRITER

WASHINGTON—There is another war in the Persian Gulf—one not detailed in Pentagon briefings, the count of Scud attacks or videotape of surgical bombing sorties.

It is the battle for the mind.

Its weapons are radio reports from Baghdad, stories planted in foreign newspapers, images sent from Iraqi TV to the West via Cable News Network. It is an

NEWS ANALYSIS

element in everything from Iraq's Scud attacks on fellow Arabs in Saudi Arabia to the once-secular Iraqi government's decision to overlay the symbol of Islam on its flag the day before war began to the timing of U.S. military briefings in Washington.

Winning the psychological war could influence how long the shooting war lasts and will help determine the political landscape after the war has ended.

While many Iraqi claims and images may strike Americans as inept attempts at propaganda, each blow of psychological combat is evaluated for its impact on the troops of both sides, other Arab populations and citizens within the United States and Iraq.

So far, say the experts, the Gulf War allies have a basic advantage. The overwhelming evidence suggests that they are winning militarily. Should that continue, no propaganda will be able to deny it for long.

At the same time, Iraqi President Saddam Hussein's ability to depict himself as defying allied might is striking a chord in the Middle East, casting him as a hero in a region where the underdog can win merely by surviving.

But Iraq's efforts in the aspect of

Please see PROPAGANDA, A12

Battle Lines Drawn—but War Protests Are Gentler

By SCOTT HARRIS
TIMES STAFF WRITER

Midnight had passed on Los Angeles Street, and in front of the downtown federal building a new battle line had been drawn—antiwar protesters on one side, the Los Angeles Police Department on the other.

Then a large American flag abruptly appeared, held aloft by a man vehemently urging support for the troops in the Middle East. He strode into the crowd, and the protesters met his challenge, confronting him, surrounding him. Perhaps a half dozen started a chant.

"Burn it! Burn it! Burn it!"

The protesters surged toward the flag. So did reporters, photographers and a TV camera, its powerful light illuminating the scene. The police, immobile, watched as the flame of a cigarette lighter edged toward a corner of the cloth.

"Don't burn the flag!" another protester cried out. "We love the flag," someone else pleaded.

"Burn the [expletive] thing!" another man screamed.

There was a second of silence, and then a louder chant: "What do we want? PEACE! When do we want it? NOW!"

Just like that, a democratic spirit prevailed. The flag was spared. For the next half hour, the two sides engaged in a loud exercise of free speech. Still another hour passed before the crowd dwindled. Police arrested only three protesters who refused to budge.

In many respects, the peaceful outcome of that demonstration has proven typical. There have been exceptions—the torching of a

Please see PROTEST, A11

THE TIMES POLL

Wilson Popular but Some of His Proposals Aren't

By GEORGE SKELTON
TIMES SACRAMENTO BUREAU CHIEF

Californians highly regard their new governor, Pete Wilson, but they oppose his plans to cut benefits for welfare mothers and deny cost-of-living increases for schools, The Los Angeles Times Poll has found.

The public also objects to most of Wilson's tax increase ideas, accepting only his proposals to raise levies on liquor and extend the sales tax to candy and snack foods.

People obviously want it all—no spending cuts or major tax increases. They clearly will not be able to have that in a recession when tax revenues are falling far short of projections and state government is facing a deficit of up to $10 billion over the next 17 months.

Under the California Constitution, the state's annual budget must be balanced—unlike Washington's, where there is no constitutional requirement for a balanced federal budget. California citizens seem even more perplexed than their elected representatives about how to erase Sacramento's red ink.

Trying to "spread the pain," the new governor has suggested a wide range of program cuts coupled with tax and fee increases to balance a proposed $55.7-billion budget for the next fiscal year, which starts July 1.

Politically, Wilson is in a strong position. He is more popular now—one month into his governorship—than he was at the height of his election campaign last October, according to Times surveys.

Please see POLL, A24

INSIDE TODAY'S TIMES

■ **WAR STORIES, PHOTOS: A5-14; E1; F1-2**

■ **RED CROSS REBUFFED**

Red Cross officials said the agency has been stonewalled in its attempts to monitor the condition of Iraqi-held prisoners of war. **A5**

■ **DESERT CUSTOMS**

Despite the nearby rumble of modern warfare, the customs of Saudi Arabia's desert-dwellers endure. **A9**

■ **ADDING TO DEFICIT**

The cost of the Gulf War will add at least $15 billion to the fiscal 1992 deficit, according to Budget Director Richard G. Darman. **A11**

WEATHER: Sunny and warmer; morning coastal fog. Civic Center low/high: 46/67. Details: B2

■ TOP OF THE NEWS ON A2

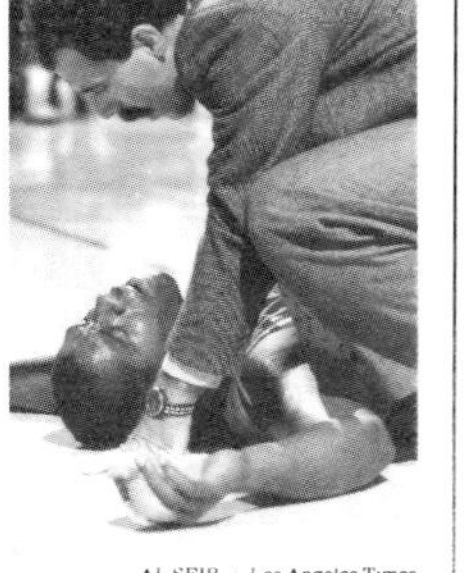

AL SEIB / Los Angeles Times

Trainer tends to Johnson.

MAGIC INJURED IN FALL

Magic Johnson fell and suffered a concussion as the Lakers defeated the Chicago Bulls, 99-86, the team's 15th consecutive victory. **C1**

Specter of Soviet Past Still Haunting Eastern Europe

■ **New democracies:** Many fear an invasion, and that Moscow's woes will spill over their borders, survey finds.

By ROBERT C. TOTH
TIMES STAFF WRITER

DEBRECEN, Hungary—The former Communist Party official was blunt and grave about his fears:

"All signs point to a strong military dictatorship emerging in the Soviet Union," he said. "Not only is Hungary afraid of this, but all the other countries of this region are afraid of this as well."

A politician in Budapest agreed. "The old empire still exists over there [in the Soviet Union]," he warned, "and it is still possible their military will appear on our horizon, possibly bringing back the old regimes in East Europe. This could be our 1991 nightmare."

Not just in Hungary but in Poland and Czechoslovakia as well, the specter of the Soviet past is sending fear sweeping across Eastern Europe.

While the West is still sighing with relief over the end of the Cold War, the emerging East European democracies are apprehensive. The Soviet Union—racked by its own

RELATED STORIES: A4, A19

internal problems, and involved in a crackdown in Lithuania and Latvia—is still "a menacing power," as a Hungarian stagehand put it.

Not only do the East Europeans fear a second round of Red Army invasions of their countries, but

Please see EAST, A19

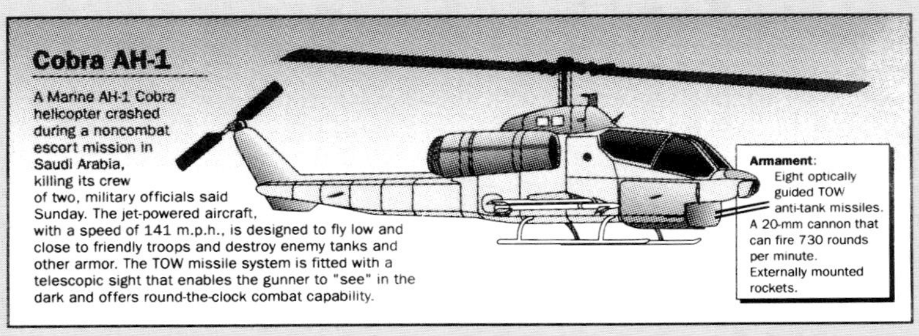

Cobra AH-1
A Marine AH-1 Cobra helicopter crashed during a noncombat escort mission in Saudi Arabia, killing its crew of two, military officials said Sunday. The jet-powered aircraft, with a speed of 141 m.p.h., is designed to fly low and close to friendly troops and destroy enemy tanks and other armor. The TOW missile system is fitted with a telescopic sight that enables the gunner to "see" in the dark and offers round-the-clock combat capability.
Armament:
Eight optically guided TOW anti-tank missiles.
A 20-mm cannon that can fire 730 rounds per minute.
Externally mounted rockets.

TREATING THE
WOUNDED
Kinds of Injuries:
■ Brain damage is likely to cause one-third of all the deaths.
■ Burns are expected to make up more than 10% of injuries.
■ One out of every three or four casualities will be psychiatric—soldiers unable to continue fighting because of combat fatique.
■ About half of war wounds are expected to involve the arms and legs.
New Approaches:
■ FLEET HOSPITAL 5: One new concept being tried in the Gulf is the deployment of a mobile, land-based, Navy-run field hospital that is as sophisticated as a hospital ship.
The self-contained hospital, including 500 beds in 14 wards, six operating tables and staff of 80 doctors, is shipped in 400 containers and can be un-packed, set up and made operational in about two weeks.
ANTIBIOTICS: Application of high concentrations of anitibiotics directly on wounds is being tested. The drugs, packaged in biodegradable polymers designed to release for days or weeks, may help reduce the risk of infections and amputations.
CT SCANNERS: High-tech portable CT scanners (full body X-ray) could provide far better diagnostic tools than standard X-ray machines.
A
Wounded soldiers are treated by medical teams assigned to all infantry platoons. The first hour after injury is crucial. The wounded must be stabilized, by stopping bleeding and providing intravenous fluids.
B
Victims with significant injuries are sent back toward the rear to a MASH (mobile Army surgical hospital) unit for antibiotics and skilled surgical care.
In Vietnam, the average delay between injury and hospital treatment was about two hours, thanks to the extensive use of helicopter evacuations. That compares to average delays of 5 hours in the Korean War and 10 hours during World War II.
Inside a Hospital Ship
Helicopter platform
Medical supplies
Sick call clinic
Recovery
Decontamination
Pharmacy
Lab
Medical repair
Water line
Casualty reception
Elevators
Wards
Operating rooms (12)
Elevators
Wards
C
Seriously injured soldiers go to a fleet or ship hospital, which has the capability to perform any operation short of open-heart or brain surgery. The most serious cases would be flown to hospitals in Europe or the U.S. The Air Force is capable of evacuating 1,000 patients a day to Germany.
Source: Jane's Ships, Department of Defense, Daily Telegraph, AP

PATRICIA MITCHELL AND DAVID PUCKETT / Los Angeles Times

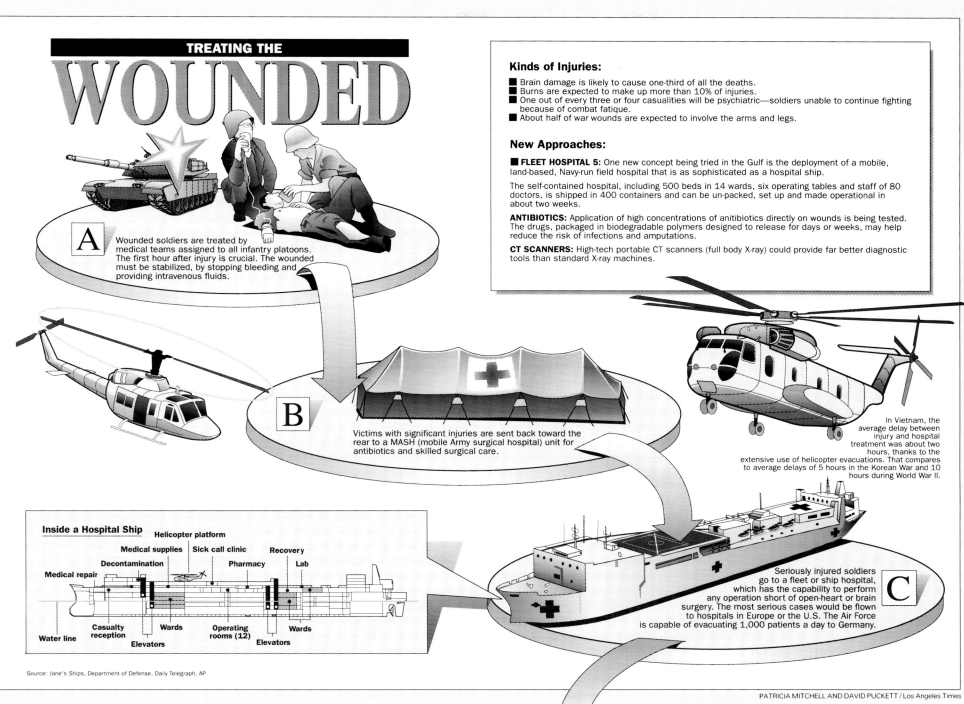

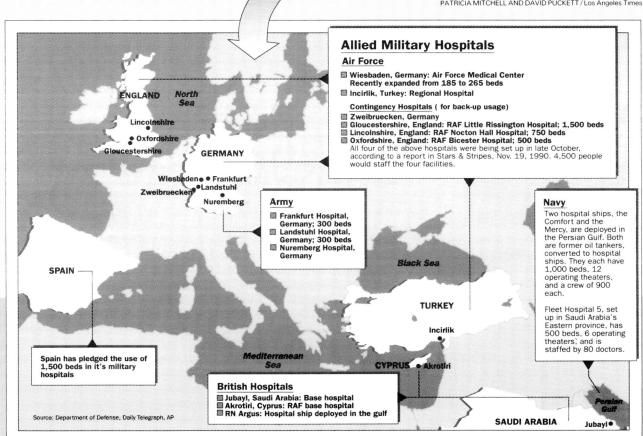

Allied Military Hospitals
Air Force
Wiesbaden, Germany: Air Force Medical Center Recently expanded from 185 to 265 beds
Incirlik, Turkey: Regional Hospital
Contingency Hospitals (for back-up usage)
Zweibruecken, Germany
Gloucestershire, England: RAF Little Rissington Hospital; 1,500 beds
Lincolnshire, England: RAF Nocton Hall Hospital; 750 beds
Oxfordshire, England: RAF Bicester Hospital; 500 beds
All four of the above hospitals were being set up in late October, according to a report in Stars & Stripes, Nov. 19, 1990. 4,500 people would staff the four facilities.
ENGLAND
North Sea
Lincolnshire
Oxfordshire
Gloucestershire
GERMANY
Wiesbaden
Frankfurt
Landstuhl
Zweibruecken
Nuremberg
Army
Frankfurt Hospital, Germany; 300 beds
Landstuhl Hospital, Germany; 300 beds
Nuremberg Hospital, Germany
Navy
Two hospital ships, the Comfort and the Mercy, are deployed in the Persian Gulf. Both are former oil tankers, converted to hospital ships. They each have 1,000 beds, 12 operating theaters, and a crew of 900 each.
Fleet Hospital 5, set up in Saudi Arabia's Eastern province, has 500 beds, 6 operating theaters, and is staffed by 80 doctors.
SPAIN
Black Sea
TURKEY
Incirlik
Spain has pledged the use of 1,500 beds in it's military hospitals
Mediterranean Sea
CYPRUS
Akrotiri
British Hospitals
Jubayl, Saudi Arabia: Base hospital
Akrotiri, Cyprus: RAF base hospital
RN Argus: Hospital ship deployed in the gulf
Persian Gulf
SAUDI ARABIA
Jubayl
Source: Department of Defense, Daily Telegraph, AP

PATRICIA MITCHELL / Los Angeles Times

DAY IN THE GULF

Military: An Air Force B-52 bomber returning from the Persian Gulf with a crew of six crashes in the Indian Ocean en route to a Diego Garcia air base, apparently because of a mechanical problem. Three crewmen are rescued; three are listed as missing.

■ Six U.S. helicopter crewmen die in two separate crashes.

■ The U.S. military says investigators have determined that seven Marines were killed by a missile fired by an American warplane during tank fighting along the Kuwaiti border the previous week.

■ The allied air war passes the 40,000-sortie mark.

Iraq: Baghdad Radio says American and Western interests worldwide will be targets in retaliation for alleged allied air attacks on civilian targets.

■ Former U.S. Atty. Gen. Ramsey Clark arrives in Baghdad and reportedly will meet with Saddam Hussein.

■ Iraq claims more than 180 allied aircraft downed, 320 civilians killed and 90 of its soldiers killed.

■ Red Cross officials say they have been blocked in their efforts to monitor the condition of Iraqi-held prisoners of war.

White House: Budget Director Richard G. Darman says the cost of the Gulf War will add at least $15 billion to the fiscal 1992 deficit.

Home front: Churchgoers heed President Bush's call for a day of prayer, flocking to services to hear songs of praise and sermons beseeching God to save lives.

■ The President and his family attend a service at Camp David, Md.

DAY 20

FEBRUARY 5, 1991

The threat of Iraqi-summoned terrorism emptied airports, hotels and city centers on more than one continent. In crossroads Turkey, bombs rattled American businesses, and terrorists killed two Americans and wounded another. Invited to breakfast with U.S. Ambassador Morton Abramowitz in Ankara, I found the embassy residence protected by fences and enough guards to have saved the Alamo.

Over coffee, Abramowitz portrayed the first outbreak of terrorism in Turkey as a natural by-product of American assertiveness in the Gulf. "There's bound to be more," he said.

Afterward, he offered me a lift in his armored black Cadillac.

"No thanks, I'll walk," I replied.

The ambassador seemed taken aback.

"You think walking's safer than riding with me?"

"I do."

Abramowitz laughed shortly.

"You're right," he said.

—William D. Montalbano, in Ankara, Turkey

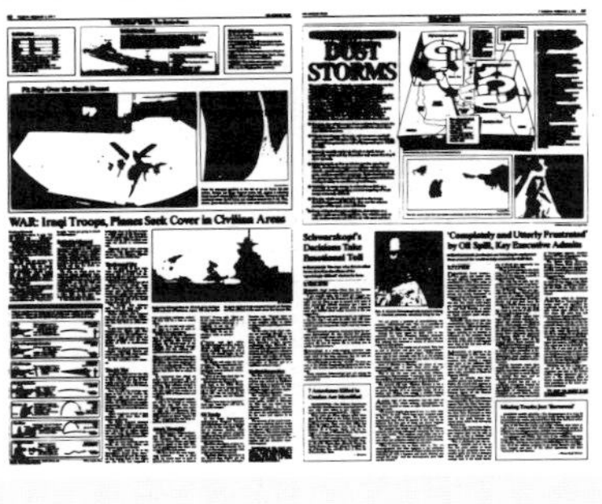

Los Angeles Times

CIRCULATION: 1,225,189 DAILY / 1,514,096 SUNDAY

TUESDAY, FEBRUARY 5, 1991

COPYRIGHT 1991 / THE TIMES MIRROR COMPANY / CC† / 108 PAGES

DAILY 25¢ DESIGNATED AREAS HIGHER

COLUMN ONE

High-Tech War Hopes Overdrawn

■ Policy-makers have celebrated advanced weaponry to win public support. Now they worry people may expect too much from technology. Its limits are profound.

By DAVID LAUTER
TIMES STAFF WRITER

WASHINGTON—How many tanks do the Iraqis have left? What planes have flown from Iraq into Iran? What is the condition of Saddam Hussein's troops in trenches in Kuwait?

Such questions come with regularity in Pentagon press briefings, congressional briefings, even barroom bets. And often, the queries open with the sort of premise posed by a reporter to Pentagon spokesman Pete Williams at a recent briefing: "With the satellite photographs that can read license plates, don't we have some indication. . . ?"

No society on Earth has had a greater, longer love affair with technology than America. "Technological utopianism"—the belief that any problem can be solved if only the right technology can be found and applied—has been a quintessential American belief for years, says Stanford University social historian Joseph Corn.

But now, for government policymakers in the Gulf War, the gap between the reality of technological limits and the public perception of the power of technology has become an object of both manipulation and anxiety.

On one hand, U.S. officials have tried to use the new technology to mold public opinion. Almost every day, freshly recorded military videotapes—never before released in the midst of an armed conflict—show bombs plunging into air shafts, swooping through doors and destroying bridges, all to drive home one overriding message: "This is not another Vietnam. This time American weapons work. American power will prevail."

At the same time, the same officials, from President Bush on down, openly worry that public misconceptions about the power of technology will lead Americans to expect too much—and ultimately could turn the country against the war at the slightest setback.

"Perhaps in the euphoria of the high-technology weapons and this sort of thing, we have lost sight of the fact that lives are being lost," the U.S. commander in the Gulf, Gen. H. Norman Schwarzkopf, mused during a recent Cable News Network interview.

"Somebody asked me about [whether] this is more like a computer game," Schwarzkopf added. "And I said, 'Not to me it's not. . . . There are human lives involved here, and war is going to kill people.' "

Indeed, for all the dramatic capability of modern weapons technology, its limits are profound.

High-technology bombs may crater a runway, but plain, low-technology shovels and asphalt can fill the holes back up.

Please see TECHNOLOGY, A18

Separated by War

Associated Press

Army Reserve medic Linda Osgood bids farewell to her 4-year-old son, Kaleb, in Auburn, Me. She and other members of her unit were called to duty in the wake of the Persian Gulf War.

2 Radar Systems Faulty in Collision on Runway

■ **Crash:** The equipment could have helped controller track planes before the disaster. Death toll rises to 34.

Two important radar systems that could have helped a controller keep track of a jetliner and a commuter plane before they collided in last week's Los Angeles airport disaster were not working properly, federal investigators said Monday.

The death toll in Friday night's runway crash climbed to 34 on Monday when an Ohio man who suffered massive burns died at Sherman Oaks Community Hospital. All 12 people aboard a SkyWest commuter plane died instantly and 18 passengers on a USAir jet were headed for exits when they died, said James Burnett, the National Transportation Safety Board member heading the investigation.

Burnett said one man died as he tried to climb over the seats toward an exit and a flight attendant died only a few feet from a doorway, apparently while trying to lead others to safety.

"I can't think of a recent accident where this many people have been up and out of their seats and didn't make it," Burnett said. He said part of the investigation will focus on why they were unable to escape.

The fiery crash occurred when a controller, who has not been identified, directed the USAir Boeing 737 jetliner with 89 people aboard to land on the same runway where she had positioned the SkyWest commuter plane to await takeoff, investigators said.

Please see CRASH, A26

Times staff writers Glenn F. Bunting, Rich Connell and Eric Malnic reported and wrote this story. Staff writers John Lee and Tracy Wood also contributed.

Farmers Dealt Double Blow on Water Supplies

By VIRGINIA ELLIS and DAVID SAVAGE
TIMES STAFF WRITERS

SACRAMENTO—The worsening drought hit the California farming industry on two fronts Monday as the state announced the suspension of all its agricultural water deliveries and Gov. Pete Wilson disclosed that federal deliveries would be cut by two-thirds.

Farming interests immediately predicted that the cutbacks would force more agricultural lands to go out of production and probably lead to steep increases in food prices as soon as next year.

Although some water will be available to farmers from under-

Please see FARMERS, A24

Iraqis Shelter Troops, Jets in Civilian Areas

■ **Gulf War:** Field headquarters are moved into schools and mosques to avoid air raids, a U.S. commander says. The battleship Missouri's big guns fire on bunkers.

By J. MICHAEL KENNEDY
TIMES STAFF WRITER

RIYADH, Saudi Arabia—Battle-shocked Iraqis are moving military field headquarters into schools and mosques and hiding warplanes on residential streets to take advantage of an allied pledge not to bomb civilian targets, a U.S. commander said Monday.

The Iraqi tactic is working, said Maj. Gen. Robert B. Johnston, chief of staff for the U.S. Central Command. But he said the allied command in the Persian Gulf War will not change its bombing policy. "We'll continue," Johnston said, "to scrupulously adhere to our policy that we will not target civilian areas."

Gen. H. Norman Schwarzkopf, commander of allied forces in the Gulf, stood firmly against civilian targeting. "It gives them [the Iraqis] an advantage," he declared in remarks to a small group of reporters. "But we are not going to reduce ourselves to that level of moral conduct just to even the score. . . . Guys in white hats don't do that." (Story, A7)

The Iraqi tactic, Gen. Johnston said, can have only limited success. "I'm not sure he [Iraq's President Saddam Hussein] can somehow put half a million troops and 5,000 tanks in a residential area," Johnston said. "I'm not being flip about it. He can hide a select part, I guess, of his military capability. But he can't hide it all."

There were these additional developments:

• On yet another day of relentless allied bombing, the U.S. battleship Missouri opened up with its 16-inch guns. It demolished prefabricated bunkers that the Iraqis were moving into place in Kuwait. It was the first time the Missouri has fired its big guns in anger since the Korean War.

• Possible terrorism began behind allied lines. In Jidda, Saudi Arabia, hundreds of miles from the battlefront, a sniper with a 9-millimeter pistol or rifle fired at a shuttle bus carrying three U.S. soldiers. Two were only slightly hurt by flying glass, but Johnston said that no serviceman is ever "totally safe."

• Saudi and American experts cautioned that the huge Persian Gulf oil spill is growing dramatically. Two jumbo jets full of oil spill-fighting equipment were scheduled to arrive today to help contain it. But an oil official said that cleanup crews were "completely and utterly frustrated."

The Iraqis warned that they would fight with "the hit-and-run tactics formulated by our ancestors"—the Arab raiders of old. Baghdad Radio said Iraqi troops were awaiting a signal to launch a "crushing offensive."

The broadcast included cryptic messages from a so-called "command center"—one of which was

Please see WAR, A6

Bush Budget Stays Within Deficit Limits

By JAMES RISEN
TIMES STAFF WRITER

WASHINGTON—President Bush on Monday proposed a $1.45-trillion federal budget for fiscal 1992 that seeks to live within the tight restrictions imposed by last fall's deficit-reduction accord, despite the mounting costs of the recession and the Persian Gulf War.

The Bush package, which covers the fiscal year that begins next Oct. 1, calls for a federal deficit of $280.9 billion, down only slightly from the deficit for fiscal 1991, which is expected to hit a record $318.1 billion as a result of the recession.

■ RELATED STORIES: A20,21; D1

The Administration's new deficit forecast dwarfs the $25 billion that the White House originally forecast for fiscal 1992, and surpasses the previous record deficit of $225 billion set in fiscal 1986.

The first budget that the White House has proposed under the new deficit-cutting framework forged last fall, the new spending plan contains few new domestic or military initiatives that might break that agreement and reopen a budget fight with Congress.

However, the new spending and deficit figures do not account for either the mounting costs of the Gulf War or the government's rescue of troubled banks and savings and loan institutions, either of which could bloat the deficit sharply.

The Administration expects the war to increase the deficit in 1992 by $15 billion, but officials conced-

Please see DEFICIT, A20

Overseas Travel to U.S. Falls by as Much as 40%

By DENISE GELLENE
TIMES STAFF WRITER

The Commerce Department said Monday that travel to the United States from some foreign countries has plunged as much as 40% since the Persian Gulf War began, providing fresh evidence of the deepening malaise afflicting the travel industry.

The report was issued amid growing signs that Americans also are putting off trips abroad. The U.S. airline industry is suffering record losses; travel agencies are laying off employees and, in some cases, closing down.

At a news briefing in Washington, Commerce Undersecretary Rockwell A. Schnabel cited the

Please see TRAVEL, A23

Marines Feel Pity as B-52s Pound Iraqis

By JOHN BALZAR
TIMES STAFF WRITER

EASTERN SAUDI ARABIA—At night, all night, Marines can hear the relentless rumbling. The skyline flickers hot orange. Through the soles of their boots, the Marines feel the sand quiver. Miles from ground zero, they stand in their bunkers and look toward Kuwait at one of the most fearsome sights of modern warfare—the carpet bombing by B-52s.

Mixed with their wonder, the Marines find themselves curiously twinged with pity.

"They're out there doing the same thing we are," said Lance Cpl. Gerald Childress, a 20-year-old from Spotsylvania, Va., whose wife is expecting

Please see PITY, A17

Refugees From Iraq Describe Hellish Scenes

By MARK FINEMAN
TIMES STAFF WRITER

AMMAN, Jordan—The massive allied bombardment of the Iraqi city of Basra has demolished every communications center in that strategic southern city, all major oil refineries, most government buildings, some civilian neighborhoods and hundreds of ammunition depots and food warehouses, according to eyewitnesses.

The result: a hellish nightmare of fires and smoke so dense that the witnesses say the sun hasn't been clearly visible for several days at a time.

In the besieged capital of Baghdad, witnesses say, air strikes continue to hit military targets, often for the second and third time, smashing key installations, destroying warehouses full of everything from medicine to the machinery of war—but also leveling some entire city blocks in civilian neighborhoods.

The result: bomb craters the size of football fields and an untold number of casualties.

Throughout war-torn Iraq, there is little water to drink, no civilian communications, intermittent power only from portable generators and a transportation network that has been chopped to bits by air attacks on bridges, highways and virtually every airfield. For drinking, residents are collecting rainwater from ponds and bomb craters and filtering it through shreds of cloth.

These are the images of the human and structural damage inflicted by the most massive aerial

Please see REFUGEES, A12

Forest Service Changing Image With New Policy

■ **Conservation:** The agency is emphasizing ecology and less logging. Environmentalists are skeptical.

By MARK A. STEIN
TIMES STAFF WRITER

KYBURZ, Calif.—Patricia Ferrell, a U.S. Forest Service timber management officer, has a new attitude toward logging in the El Dorado National Forest, and she advertises it on a badge pinned to her wool winter jacket.

The badge, borrowed from an anti-drug program, says, "Learn to Say No."

"In the past, our primary emphasis was on timber growth and yield only," she said during a recent visit to the upper reaches of the Sierra Nevada. "We are getting away from that now. If we clear-cut at all now, we'll leave more vigorous young trees and lots of dead [trees and branches]. It may look ugly to the public, but it's important to the overall forest ecology."

Less logging and more ecology once were frowned on by the Forest Service, but no more. Hundreds of other foresters now share Ferrell's philosophy, marking a significant change for the Forest Service and the 191 million acres of publicly owned timberland it manages, mainly in the West.

This promises to fundamentally alter the relationship between the agency and the wood products industry, historically its largest client.

What is emerging is a battle that may define the environmental

Please see POLICY, A29

INSIDE TODAY'S TIMES

■ WAR STORIES, PHOTOS: A5-19, E1, F1, F9, World Report

■ SPILL FIGHT PUSHED

Jumbo jets are flying oil-spilling fighting equipment into Saudi Arabia to try to control the world's largest oil spill as it spreads in the Persian Gulf. A7

■ ATTACK ON SOLDIERS

Two U.S. soldiers were hurt by flying glass when a gunman fired on a shuttle bus in Jidda, Saudi Arabia. A8

■ PEACE INITIATIVE

President Hashemi Rafsanjani of Iran offered to meet with Iraqi leader Saddam Hussein to try to mediate an end to the Persian Gulf War. A9

WEATHER: Cloudy with a slight chance of light rain. Civic Center low/high today: 51/68. Details: B5

■ TOP OF THE NEWS ON A2

Agence France-Presse

Mandela leaves courtroom.

■ WINNIE MANDELA ON TRIAL

The kidnaping and assault trial of Winnie Mandela opened in South Africa. The case stems from the death of a black youth allegedly beaten at her home. A4

GM to Slash Dividend, Jobs, Ask Suppliers to Cut Prices

■ **Autos:** Firm faces $1.4-billion loss in quarter, its worst ever. 15,000 white-collar positions will be eliminated.

By DONALD WOUTAT
TIMES STAFF WRITER

DETROIT—Struggling with an unexpectedly steep drop-off in sales and production and a river of red ink, General Motors Corp. on Monday announced that it will swing a multibillion-dollar ax through its ranks of shareholders, white-collar workers and suppliers.

GM said it was slashing its common-stock dividend by 47%, eliminating 15,000 salaried jobs over three years, demanding $2 billion in price cuts from suppliers and carving $500 million a year out of its capital spending.

Another retrenchment at GM—its second in just three months—had been widely expected as the recession deepened and car and truck sales tumbled. But the dividend cut was sooner and deeper than some expected, and the cut in capital spending raised eyebrows on Wall Street.

GM, the world's largest industrial company, is expected to report a $1.4-billion loss for the fourth quarter of 1990, its worst operating result ever. Although GM has major competitive problems, the chief culprit appears to be the condition of the U.S. economy.

Ford Motor Co., which surprised some analysts recently by deciding against a dividend cut, is expected to report a fourth-quarter loss in

Please see GM, A22

Battleship Missouri

The USS Missouri, which has fired cruise missiles at Baghdad, is now using its World War II guns to pound Iraqi defenses in occupied Kuwait. The battleship, which had been launching modern long-range Tomahawk cruise missiles at Iraq and other targets for two weeks, Monday fired seven massive shells at prefabricated bunkers that Iraq was moving into Kuwait. It is the first battle employment of the guns since the Korean War.

- **Guns:** Nine 16-inch gun turrets
- **Shells:** 2,700-pound weight; range of 23 miles
- **Missiles:** 32 Tomahawk cruise missiles
- **Crew:** More than 1,500
- **Launch:** January, 1944

BATTLEFIELD WEAPONS

Here is a guide to the basic types of weapons that ordinary soldiers use to fight a modern war. Examples of common U.S. models of each type are shown, along with the typical firing trajectory and effective range.

Rifle M-16A2
Most soldiers carry a rifle, but they are useful only for shooting at enemy troops you can see, an infrequent event.
DIRECT FIRE
1,300 ft.

Rifle with grenade launcher
Adding a grenade launcher to a rifle gives a soldier more explosive punch at close range.
DIRECT FIRE
800 ft.

Machine gun M-60
The main soldier-killer in World War I, useful against low-flying aircraft.
AREA FIRE
Up to 6,000 ft.

Rocket launcher AT-4
Light shoulder-fired rockets are potent weapons against light tanks.
DIRECT FIRE
1,000 ft.

Mortar M-19
By firing in a high arc, mortars can hit targets behind hills and obstacles, with closely spaced blasts.
INDIRECT FIRE
Range depends on ammunition

Howitzer M-114
Howitzers' low arc firing can deliver powerful shells fairly accurately over long ranges.
DIRECT OR INDIRECT FIRE
Up to 9 miles

Guided missile TOW
Guided weapons achieve accurate firing without wasting shots, but are very expensive.
GUIDED FIRE
200-12,000 ft.

Source: Jane's Infantry Weapons, Jane's Armour and Artillery, Jane's Weapon Systems

AP/Los Angeles Times

PATRICK DOWNS / Los Angeles Times

Mail call was the highlight of the Gulf soldier's day.

BRACING FOR

DUST STORMS

The possibility of a *shamal*—a major sandstorm on the Arabian Peninsula—has U.S. military strategists worried, because its dusty, blinding winds could ground allied warplanes and halt troop movements for hours or even days at a time. Although it is still early in the season, the military is on alert; early signs of a *shamal* were detected several times in January. "Basically, it would shut down operations at any [air] base that was affected," says Capt. Judy Dickey, a meteorologist for the 1st Tactical Fighter Wing in Saudi Arabia. Here are some facts about the *shamal*:

● **The hot, dry wind** sweeps from southern Iraq across the Saudi peninsula. Forecasters can predict its onset three days before it arrives.

● **Winds travel** up to 45 m.p.h. and can carve a path 60 miles long and 100 miles wide. In worst-case conditions, the storm can generate a wall of flying sand up to 14,000 feet high.

● **Shamals usually arrive** in March or April, but an unusually warm and dry December may mean that they'll show up early.

● **Stinging sand,** as fine as talcum powder, can clog air filters, overheat the engines on military vehicles and aircraft, scratch and erode rotor blades and other moving parts, and jam sensitive weaponry. Static electricity from the storms can also interfere with radio communications, making it tricky to coordinate ground forces.

● **Visibility** in some storms is reduced to as little as a sixteenth of a mile, making accurate targeting of Iraq's troops extremely difficult.

● **The dry winds** are physically hard on the troops. Besides being nearly blinding, they sear the mucous passages of the eyes, nose and throat.

● **Even without shamal conditions,** dust storms on a smaller scale are a daily problem. Any wind in such an arid, treeless terrain can fill the air with sand and dust.

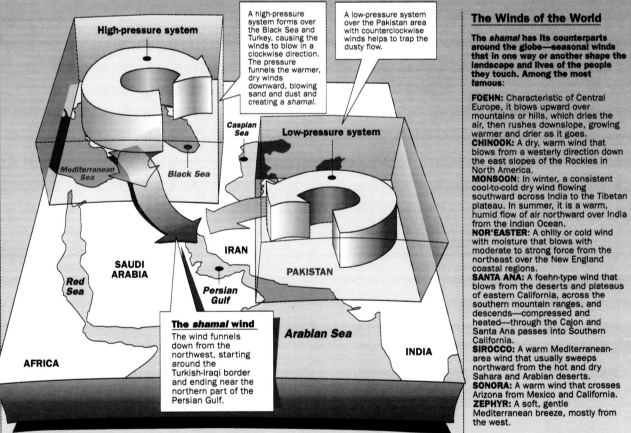

A high-pressure system forms over the Black Sea and Turkey, causing the winds to blow in a clockwise direction. The pressure funnels the warmer, dry winds downward, blowing sand and dust and creating a *shamal*.

A low-pressure system over the Pakistan area with counterclockwise winds helps to trap the dusty flow.

High-pressure system

Low-pressure system

Caspian Sea

Mediterranean Sea

Black Sea

IRAN

PAKISTAN

SAUDI ARABIA

Red Sea

Persian Gulf

Arabian Sea

INDIA

AFRICA

The shamal wind
The wind funnels down from the northwest, starting around the Turkish-Iraqi border and ending near the northern part of the Persian Gulf.

Source: WeatherData, Reuters, Financial Times, Encyclopedia Britannica

Associated Press
Two U.S. airmen make their way across a wind-swept, dusty street at an air base in Saudi Arabia.

The Winds of the World

The *shamal* has its counterparts around the globe—seasonal winds that in one way or another shape the landscape and lives of the people they touch. Among the most famous:

FOEHN: Characteristic of Central Europe, it blows upward over mountains or hills, which dries the air, then rushes downslope, growing warmer and drier as it goes.
CHINOOK: A dry, warm wind that blows from a westerly direction down the east slopes of the Rockies in North America.
MONSOON: In winter, a consistent cool-to-cold dry wind flowing southward across India to the Tibetan plateau. In summer, it is a warm, humid flow of air northward over India from the Indian Ocean.
NOR'EASTER: A chilly or cold wind with moisture that blows with moderate to strong force from the northeast over the New England coastal regions.
SANTA ANA: A foehn-type wind that blows from the deserts and plateaus of eastern California, across the southern mountain ranges, and descends—compressed and heated—through the Cajon and Santa Ana passes into Southern California.
SIROCCO: A warm Mediterranean-area wind that usually sweeps northward from the hot and dry Sahara and Arabian deserts.
SONORA: A warm wind that crosses Arizona from Mexico and California.
ZEPHYR: A soft, gentle Mediterranean breeze, mostly from the west.

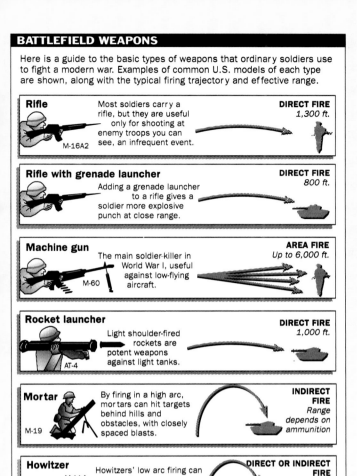

In the *shamal*, our faces chapped, while our eyelids, gone granular, seemed to creep back and bare our shrinking eyes.

T.E. Lawrence, known as "Lawrence of Arabia"

PATRICIA MITCHELL / Los Angeles Times

DAY 21

FEBRUARY 6, 1991

The Marines, the service with the most to lose bureaucratically in the Gulf War, eagerly encouraged the belief that they were going to land a massive amphibious assault to squeeze Iraqi forces from the east.

At Corps headquarters, on a hill overlooking the Pentagon, Marine spokesman Lt. Col. Fred Peck one day unloaded a spectacular amount of detail about amphibious landings. He even waxed poetic:

"The darker the moon and the higher the tide, the better it is for Marines to ride," he intoned.

Knowing that many analysts believed any amphibious landing to be a feint, I asked Peck how likely a landing really was.

"Oh, 95% certain," he assured me. "The only thing that could stop it would be if [Iraqi President] Saddam Hussein capitulates before we get there."

The landing never happened. But it was a real option, and the threat of it did keep five Iraqi divisions, about 80,000 Iraqi soldiers, pinned down. I think Peck believed almost all of what he told me that day, but the incident reminded me that in the military, there are wheels working within wheels.

—Melissa Healy, in Washington

Most U.S. Units Now Prepared to Begin Land War

STRATEGY: A Massive Aerial Pounding

Checklist for Cheney and Powell: Mission, Enemy, Terrain and Troops

AMPHIBIOUS ATTACK

MARINES: Future Could Be Determined on Beaches of Kuwait

First B-52s Land at Base West of London for Service in the Gulf

Saudis Arrest Sniper Suspects; Blast Kills 3 at U.S. Subsidiary in Peru

Jordan Looks to Syria for Oil Supplies

Scuds No Deterrent to Soviet Jews

Shamir Lists Terms for Scud Retaliation

Soviets, Iranians Await Signal From Iraq Before Putting Peace Proposals on Table

Los Angeles Times

CIRCULATION: 1,225,189 DAILY / 1,514,096 SUNDAY

WEDNESDAY, FEBRUARY 6, 1991

COPYRIGHT 1991 THE TIMES MIRROR COMPANY CC† / 92 PAGES

DAILY 50¢ DESIGNATED AREAS HIGHER

Land War Timing Up to Military, Bush Says

The President Speaks Out

On the Iraqis:

'We do not seek Iraq's destruction, nor do we seek to punish the Iraqi people for the decisions and policies of their leaders. . . . We are doing everything possible to minimize collateral damage . . .'

On a Ground War:

'Saddam Hussein will not set the timing for what comes next; we will do that. And I will have to make that decision if we go to ground forces. And I will do it upon the serious consideration of the recommendations of our military. . . .'

On the Draft:

'I have absolutely no intention of reinstating the draft. . . . We have an all-volunteer army that is totally capable of getting this job done.'

The President at Tuesday's White House press conference.

Associated Press

Allies Pour It On in Iraq and Kuwait

By J. MICHAEL KENNEDY
TIMES STAFF WRITER

RIYADH, Saudi Arabia—Allied warplanes, flying a mission a minute, bombed deeply into Iraq on Tuesday, taking special aim at the Republican Guard and at President Saddam Hussein's hometown of Tikrit, 90 miles north of Baghdad.

For a second day, the U.S. battleship Missouri slammed the Iraqis with shells from its 16-inch guns. Six rounds silenced a long-range artillery battery as it fired on allied troops. Another 28 rounds wiped out an Iraqi radar site. At midday, the huge guns on the big ship still were firing at targets on the coastline of occupied Kuwait.

But it was the incessant bombing that was most fearsome, and 10 more Iraqi planes, possibly as a result, fled to Iran. Marine Maj. Gen. Robert B. Johnston, chief of staff for the U.S. Central Command, said this brought the total now impounded by Iran to 110. He said that 25 more Iraqis surrendered to allied forces after hiding out in the border town of Khafji since the allies reclaimed it from Iraqi soldiers last week. This brought the allied count of Iraqi prisoners of war to 800.

In other developments:

- Syrian troops clashed with the Iraqis for the first time. Saudi military officers said Syrian artillery drove 30 intruders back into occupied Kuwait. But pool reports from the U.S. area of operations said the Iraqis overran a Syrian position in one attack and were pushed back by the Syrians in another.
- Iraqi Foreign Minister Tarik

Please see WAR, A5

Iraq Cuts Off Fuel Sales to Its People

By MARK FINEMAN
TIMES STAFF WRITER

AMMAN, Jordan—Iraq's economic and communications capability appeared all but gone Tuesday as the Iraqi leadership used Baghdad Radio to announce the suspension of all fuel sales to its people and to issue what military experts said were more coded instructions to Iraqi agents and terrorists outside the country.

Both of the orders issued on the state-run radio—which, after 20 days of allied air strikes, is now Iraq's only reliable link with the outside world—contained elements of desperation, analysts said.

And both were indications of the extent to which the allies have dismantled

Please see IRAQ, A11

■ **Desert Storm:** A ground assault may be unavoidable, the President declares. He will send Cheney and Powell to the Gulf for a status report.

By JACK NELSON
TIMES WASHINGTON BUREAU CHIEF

WASHINGTON—President Bush, declaring that a costly ground war may be unavoidable, said Tuesday he will rely solely on his military advisers in deciding any timetable for an assault on Saddam Hussein's Iraqi forces by U.S. and allied troops in Saudi Arabia.

Bush said he is dispatching Defense Secretary Dick Cheney and Gen. Colin L. Powell, chairman of the Joint Chiefs of Staff, to Saudi Arabia this week for a "firsthand status report" on the war and recommendations concerning a possible ground attack.

With Pentagon officials broadly agreeing that they will recommend a go-ahead for such an attack when the current air bombardment has destroyed 50% of Iraq's armored vehicles, some analysts now expect a ground war to begin within 10 or 20 days.

At that level of destruction, military analysts believe, Iraq's forces would be plunged into such chaos that they would no longer be able to function as an effective fighting force.

Brushing aside mounting congressional pressure to extend the air war to help minimize allied casualties, Bush said his decision will not be influenced by political opposition at home, anti-American sentiment in Arab countries or provocative actions by Iraq.

"Saddam Hussein will not set the timing for what comes next; we will do that," he told a press conference, raising his fist several times and speaking in blunt terms about U.S. military objectives and determination to prevail.

"And I will have to make that decision if we go to ground forces," he continued. "And I will do it upon serious consideration of the recommendations of our military," including Cheney, Powell and commanders in the field.

Bush also flatly ruled out any prospect that he might reinstate the draft. "I've heard no discussion from any of our people about the need to reinstate the draft," he said. "We have an all-volunteer Army that is totally capable of getting this job done."

In deciding the timetable for any ground assault, the President must worry about the potential for heavy casualties among allied forces if he moves too soon and about the possibility that the international anti-Iraq coalition will unravel if he delays too long.

Bush emphasized repeatedly, however, that in making his decision he will rely on advice from the military—Cheney, Powell and Gen. H. Norman Schwarzkopf, the U.S. commander in the Persian Gulf.

He said the trip by Cheney and Powell to Saudi Arabia to meet with Schwarzkopf and his staff will be a short one, and the two officials will return quickly to meet with

Please see BUSH, A12

COLUMN ONE

It's High Tide for the Marines

■ A massive U.S. landing on the beaches of Kuwait could be a turning point in the war. And the ability of the Corps to fight its way ashore may well determine its future.

By MELISSA HEALY and ROBERT W. STEWART
TIMES STAFF WRITERS

WASHINGTON—Some moonless night in mid-February, as the waters of the Persian Gulf lap high along the shoreline, the largest U.S. amphibious landing operation since the Korean War may begin on a remote stretch of beach in Kuwait.

And the future of the U.S. Marine Corps could hang in the balance.

In what will appear to be random attacks, warships will shell the beach and allied warplanes will drop bombs on Iraqi encampments along 100 miles of coastline. Marine reconnaissance teams and Navy commandos will probe the shore, attaching hidden explosives to all obstacles.

And when the tide reaches its peak, those charges will detonate, and Kuwait will echo with the ·ous burst of gunfire, and ·y over one three-mile stretch of beach will vibrate with the chatter of helicopters. The hour will have arrived.

If months of meticulous planning

Please see MARINES, A7

Treasury Urges Drastic Overhaul of Bank Laws

■ **Finance:** Institutions could market insurance and securities. U.S. protection of deposits would be curtailed.

By ROBERT A. ROSENBLATT
TIMES STAFF WRITER

WASHINGTON—The Bush Administration on Tuesday proposed the most drastic overhaul of financial laws since the Great Depression, giving banks complete freedom to move across state lines and to enter fully into the business of marketing insurance and securities.

The plan, aimed at reviving the ailing banking industry, also calls for limiting government protection of deposits for an individual to $200,000 in each bank. After five years, a more stringent ceiling would be adopted, restricting an individual's protection to $200,000 total—$100,000 in savings and $100,000 in retirement accounts.

Now, although every account is insured for a maximum of $100,000, there are no formal limits on the number of insured accounts, so the total amount insured can be many times higher.

The President's plan would shatter a longstanding separation of banking and commerce and permit big companies—such as Sears, Ford, or IBM—to own banks as part of an effort to bring badly needed new capital to the financial world.

"The laws that govern financial services should deal with the real world in which banks and other financial institutions operate," Treasury Secretary Nicholas F. Brady told a news conference.

For the first time since the Depression, a company engaged in banking could also operate insurance companies and securities firms. Walls against such mixed functions were created more than 50 years ago by an angry Congress after the stock market crash destroyed the value of shares in risky investment syndicates created by the banks. The banks had reaped profits twice, issuing the shares and providing loans to people to buy the stock.

The proposed reforms would require action by Congress, where the road to legislative success is long and uncertain. The two men

Please see BANKING, A18

Gun Law Forces Mental Hospitals to Name Patients

By CARL INGRAM
TIMES STAFF WRITER

SACRAMENTO—As an unexpected consequence of a gun control law that took effect Jan. 1, the names of people admitted for mental health treatment at California hospitals are being recorded in state law enforcement computers.

Although meant to keep firearms away from those who are considered dangerous to themselves or to society, the practice also applies to psychiatric patients who voluntarily check themselves in for treatment and have no history of violent behavior.

Their names, addresses and the fact that they were admitted to a hospital are being entered into the

Please see GUNS, A21

Fiercest Air Assault Ever Being Planned

By DAVID LAMB
TIMES STAFF WRITER

EASTERN SAUDI ARABIA—In the days before a ground assault begins, allied warplanes will unleash on Iraqi troops the fiercest concentration of bombing ever directed on an army, according to officers involved in the planning.

They have described for reporters here saturation bombing that will last around the clock for three or four days and be carried out by more than 2,000 planes, ranging from high-level, eight-engine B-52 bombers to two-seat F-15E Eagles capable of performing at Mach 2 (twice the speed of sound).

Allied planes already have flown more missions over Iraq and Ku-

Please see STRATEGY, A6

Bush's Signal: Iraqis Should Oust Hussein

By JIM MANN
TIMES STAFF WRITER

WASHINGTON—As he prepares to decide whether to commit American forces to a ground war, President Bush sent a signal to Iraqi military leaders Tuesday that they have a last chance to avoid huge casualties and a crushing defeat—by overthrowing Saddam Hussein.

During his televised press conference, the President went to considerable lengths to question Saddam Hussein's judgment and his compassion for Iraqi troops. At the same time, Bush refrained from criticizing the Iraqi officers and soldiers who are waging battle under Hussein's leadership.

While insisting that the United States has not added the overthrow of the Iraqi leader to its war objectives, Bush then quickly added: "Now, would I weep? Would I

NEWS ANALYSIS

mourn if somehow Saddam Hussein did not remain as head of his country? . . . There will be no sorrow if he is not there."

Moments later, the President stopped a questioner and returned to this same theme with more emphasis. "It would be a lot easier to see a successful conclusion [to the war], because I don't believe anybody other than Saddam Hussein is going to want to continue to subject his army to the pounding they are taking, or his people to the pounding that is going on."

These overtures call to mind the

Please see COUP, A12

Council Presses Reforms of Redevelopment Agency

■ **Government:** Members vote to give elected officials, public greater control over decisions and expenditures.

By JILL STEWART
TIMES STAFF WRITER

The Los Angeles City Council, after heated discussion Tuesday, backed extensive reforms designed to give the public and elected officials a more direct say in the activities of the beleaguered Community Redevelopment Agency.

The council's action followed blistering attacks by local lawmakers and homeowner groups on the agency's secret approval last December of a severance package totaling more than $1.5 million for outgoing administrator John Tuite.

Councilwoman Gloria Molina and Council President John Ferraro, sponsors of the reforms adopted by an 11-2 vote, predicted that redevelopment will more closely follow the desires of citizens and the pressing needs of the poor, with far less emphasis on building skyscrapers and luxury housing.

"What we are dealing with is the most resistant, arrogant city agency," Molina said of the CRA. "They are not going to pull their sneaky kinds of deals anymore."

Under the new policy, City Atty. James Hahn will be the CRA's general counsel, while City Controller Rick Tuttle will approve the agency's expenditures. The City Council will be empowered to reject a wide range of agency decisions and, by a two-thirds vote, remove any of the seven commissioners appointed by the mayor to

Please see CRA, A22

INSIDE TODAY'S TIMES

■ **WAR STORIES, PHOTOS: A5-14; D1-2; F1-3**

■ **U.S. UNITS READY**

Almost all U.S. military units needed for a ground assault have completed their desert training and are maneuvering into battle positions. **A6**

■ **TROUBLE FOR JORDAN**

Allied bombing of Iraqi highways has sharply cut back Jordan's oil imports, and its government is looking to Syria to fill the gap. **A8**

■ **SIGNAL SOUGHT FROM IRAQ**

Iranians and Soviets said they await a "signal" from Saddam Hussein before moving on proposals to end the war. **A9**

WEATHER: Coastal morning fog, otherwise sunny. Civic Center low/high today: 52/75. Details: B5

■ TOP OF THE NEWS ON A2

Agence France-Presse

Mikhail S. Gorbachev

■ **REFERENDUM NULLIFIED**

Soviet President Mikhail S. Gorbachev decreed that the results of a referendum on independence that Lithuania plans will have no legal standing. **A4**

U.S. Risking Its Hard-Won Stealth Secrets in Gulf War

■ **Aircraft:** But steps have been taken to protect much of the technology if one of the F-117A fighters goes down.

By RALPH VARTABEDIAN
TIMES STAFF WRITER

When a Lockheed F-117A crashed near Bakersfield in 1986, the Air Force cordoned off the site with armed guards, closed the airspace overhead and spent a month hauling away wreckage in a frantic effort to protect the secrecy of the aircraft.

But if an F-117A goes down in Iraq, where it has excelled in nearly 1,000 precision bombing missions, the world's most advanced combat jet would fall into the hands of the Iraqis and perhaps other potential adversaries curious about U.S. capabilities.

The U.S. military has spent billions of dollars to pioneer and dominate the technology of Stealth, which enables U.S. pilots to elude detection by enemy radar. While at other times in military history secret weapons have been held back, the United States has decided this time to deploy its most powerful technology despite the risks.

To protect the vast investments in Stealth, the secrets of the F-117A are known only to a few U.S. civilians and their military counterparts. The most critical information has been programmed into computers far from enemy lines, rather than put at the fingertips of military tacticians.

Indeed, the aircraft's innermost Stealth secrets have not been dis-

Please see STEALTH, A11

KC-130

These "flying gas stations" of the U.S. Marine Corps have been participating in allied bombing sorties since the start of the war, refueling the warplanes that are hitting targets in occupied Kuwait and Iraq. The Vietnam-vintage, propeller-driven aircraft is also considered one of the most reliable transports for troops and equipment. There are about a dozen KC-130s in the Middle East; six from the El Toro air station.

Tanker planes are able to transfer up to 11,000 gallons of fuel.

Manufacturer: Lockheed
Wingspan: 132 feet, 7 inches
Length: 97 feet, 7 inches
Max. cruising speed: 374 m.p.h.
Range with max. payload: 2,356 miles

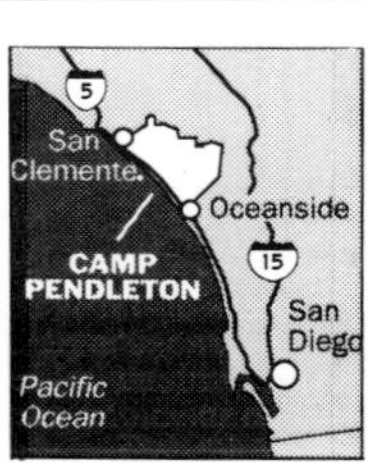

On the Map: Camp Pendleton

WHAT: Home base to 1st Marine Amphibious Force, 1st Marine Division, other supporting units.
BASE POPULATION: 45,000, including 32,000 active-duty Marines and 12,000 dependents (prewar levels).
WHERE: Northern San Diego County, bordered by San Clemente on the north and Oceanside on the south.
AREA: 125,000 acres
PERSONNEL IN MIDEAST: 30,000

Gary Olson of La Habra wore his patriotism on his roof.

JOE KENNEDY / Los Angeles Times

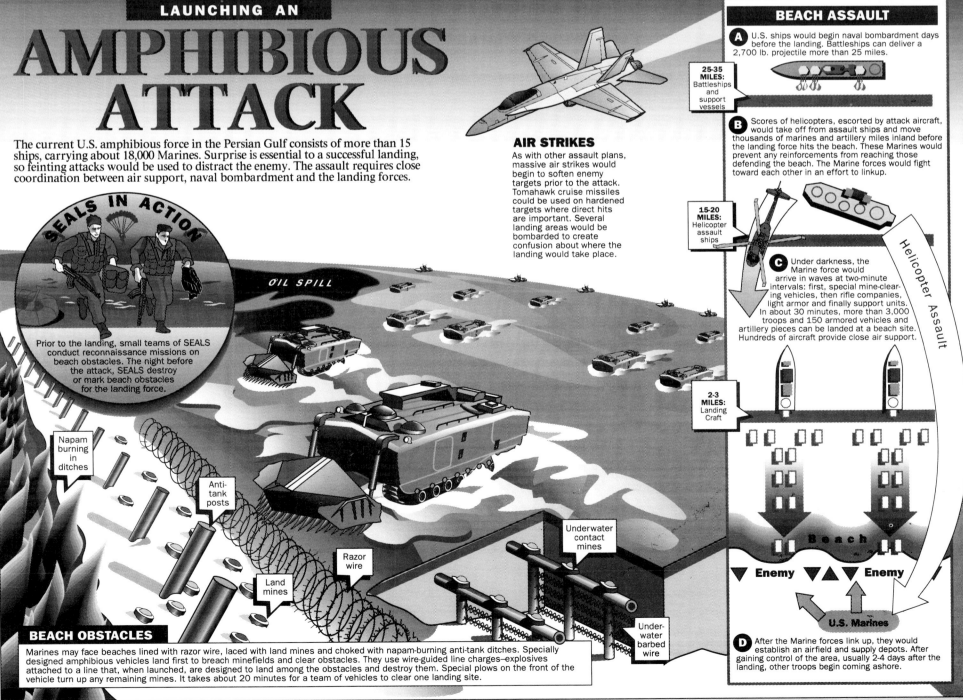

LAUNCHING AN
AMPHIBIOUS ATTACK

The current U.S. amphibious force in the Persian Gulf consists of more than 15 ships, carrying about 18,000 Marines. Surprise is essential to a successful landing, so feinting attacks would be used to distract the enemy. The assault requires close coordination between air support, naval bombardment and the landing forces.

SEALS IN ACTION

Prior to the landing, small teams of SEALS conduct reconnaissance missions on beach obstacles. The night before the attack, SEALS destroy or mark beach obstacles for the landing force.

AIR STRIKES

As with other assault plans, massive air strikes would begin to soften enemy targets prior to the attack. Tomahawk cruise missiles could be used on hardened targets where direct hits are important. Several landing areas would be bombarded to create confusion about where the landing would take place.

OIL SPILL

Napam burning in ditches

Anti-tank posts

Razor wire

Land mines

Underwater contact mines

Under-water barbed wire

BEACH OBSTACLES

Marines may face beaches lined with razor wire, laced with land mines and choked with napam-burning anti-tank ditches. Specially designed amphibious vehicles land first to breach minefields and clear obstacles. They use wire-guided line charges–explosives attached to a line that, when launched, are designed to land among the obstacles and destroy them. Special plows on the front of the vehicle turn up any remaining mines. It takes about 20 minutes for a team of vehicles to clear one landing site.

BEACH ASSAULT

A U.S. ships would begin naval bombardment days before the landing. Battleships can deliver a 2,700 lb. projectile more than 25 miles.

25-35 MILES: Battleships and support vessels

B Scores of helicopters, escorted by attack aircraft, would take off from assault ships and move thousands of marines and artillery miles inland before the landing force hits the beach. These Marines would prevent any reinforcements from reaching those defending the beach. The Marine forces would fight toward each other in an effort to linkup.

15-20 MILES: Helicopter assault ships

C Under darkness, the Marine force would arrive in waves at two-minute intervals: first, special mine-clearing vehicles, then rifle companies, light armor and finally support units. In about 30 minutes, more than 3,000 troops and 150 armored vehicles and artillery pieces can be landed at a beach site. Hundreds of aircraft provide close air support.

2-3 MILES: Landing Craft

Helicopter Assault

Beach

Enemy ▼ ▼ ▲ ▼ Enemy

U.S. Marines

D After the Marine forces link up, they would establish an airfield and supply depots. After gaining control of the area, usually 2-4 days after the landing, other troops begin coming ashore.

SCOTT BROWN / Los Angeles Times

57

DAY 22

FEBRUARY 7, 1991

In the desert, there is light and then there is blackness.

By day, the military sprawl across acres of sand sometimes seemed all within reach. But with camps scattered like homesteads across an uncharted frontier, the plunge into night brought baffling disorientation.

As the dusk deepened, my escort and I would race the sun, speeding toward home before home faded to nothingness. More than once, we found ourselves caught short. When that happened, navigation in our mud-covered Jeep Cherokee was mostly by touch. On a course set by a cheap compass, we rolled blind, seemingly weightless, hoping to bump into something familiar.

Sometimes, the sky came almost painfully alight, momentarily brilliant with missile-borne reminders of war. But mostly, we squinted to make out shapes in the black void.

Even success was two-edged, and we approached long-lost camps with trepidation. Nervous young sentries, their M-16s at the ready and the password forgotten, demanded to know who we were and what we wanted. We answered wearily: We were LID-squared: lost in desert, lost in dark.

—Douglas Jehl, in Saudi Arabia

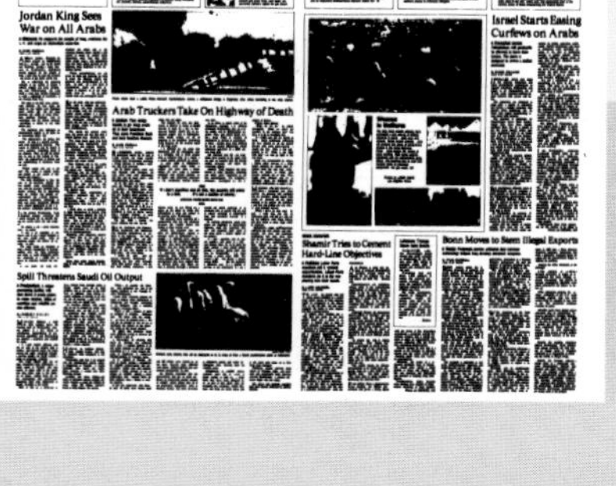

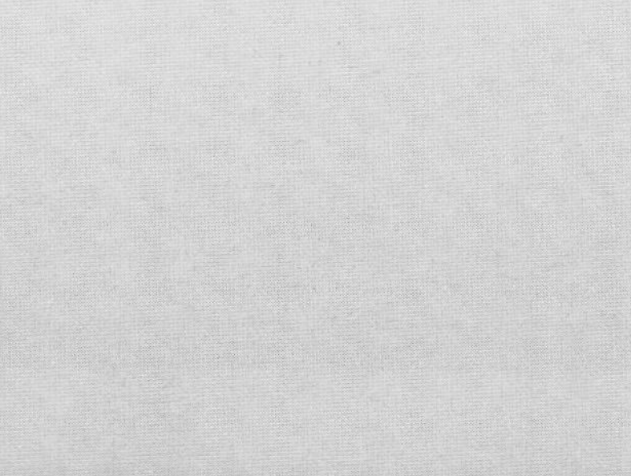

Los Angeles Times

CIRCULATION: 1,225,189 DAILY / 1,514,096 SUNDAY | THURSDAY, FEBRUARY 7, 1991 | M | DAILY 25¢ DESIGNATED AREAS HIGHER

COPYRIGHT 1991 / THE TIMES MIRROR COMPANY / CC† / 154 PAGES

COLUMN ONE

Housing Bias With a Twist

■ Complaints are increasing about immigrant landlords who close the door to renters who are not from their homeland.

By JUDY PASTERNAK
TIMES STAFF WRITER

In December, for the first time in her life, Patricia Leigh felt the stinging suspicion that she was a victim of racism. It was an odd, unsettling thought for a white American.

But to her mind, the evidence was there: She saw Asian applicants at a mid-Wilshire apartment building chat with the manager in their native language, fill out a form and hand over some cash. Next, Leigh was told coldly of a two- to four-year waiting list. Then she stepped aside and watched another Asian greeted with "much jolly talk," she says, and another exchange of paperwork for money.

"Why, it's a racial thing," she thought, shocked. "I'm not going to get a place because I am not Asian."

Fair housing officials say they are concerned about increasing complaints like Leigh's about immigrant landlords who prefer to rent to others from their homeland. Officials say they are also receiving accusations of immigrants who rent to white "outsiders" but not to blacks.

Immigrants are hardly responsible for the majority of the housing discrimination in the United States—"99% of the problems are caused by whites born here," says Shanna Smith, executive director of the National Fair Housing Alliance, an umbrella group based in Washington. But with immigrant bias becoming a more common complaint wherever newcomers cluster, "it needs airing," said Michael F. Dennis, compliance director for the Montgomery County Human Relations Commission in Maryland. "This is an up-and-coming problem."

California and federal laws prohibit discrimination by landlords on the basis of race, national origin or ancestry and religion, among other categories. The maximum penalty the state can levy is a fine of $1,000 per person per violation. In addition, renters can file suit.

Ferreting out discrimination and doing something about it are subtle, frustrating tasks, even in the best of circumstances. With immigrant landlords, fair housing activists say that cultural and language gaps make their work even more difficult. They worry, too, that rejected tenants develop prejudices of their own against the ethnic groups represented by managers who snub them—a reaction that adds to social tension.

Some activists in immigrant communities say there is no denying that, to varying degrees, biases are indulged by foreign-born apartment managers and owners, just as they are at times by American-born landlords. The reasons, they say, range from ignorance of

Please see HOUSING, A24

GIs Ambush Nighttime Iraqi Probes

By DOUGLAS FRANTZ
TIMES STAFF WRITER

NORTHERN SAUDI ARABIA—They lie silent on the ground all night, scanning the hostile terrain for anyone or anything coming or going, moving or waiting.

"You're cold and miserable and you just have to wait," said Lt. John Deedrick.

The Marietta, Ga., native was part of a U.S. Army patrol deployed on three knobs of rock-strewn desert, within sight of the Saudi-Kuwait border the other night. The patrol was waiting to ambush an Iraqi patrol expected to come through the valley that lay

Please see PATROLS, A7

U.S. Will Send Relief to Baltics, Skirt Moscow

By JAMES GERSTENZANG
TIMES STAFF WRITER

WASHINGTON—The Bush Administration announced Wednesday that it will begin sending relief supplies directly to the Baltics and the Ukraine, circumventing the Soviet central government in an apparent response to Moscow's violent crackdown on nationalist dissent.

White House officials stressed that the assistance was not intended to undercut the efforts of Soviet President Mikhail S. Gorbachev to reach a peaceful solution to the crisis posed by the secessionist movements. But it nevertheless establishes the first direct relationship between the United States and the three Baltic states that are seeking to break away from the Soviet Union.

For more than 40 years, the United States has steadfastly refused to recognize the Soviet Union's annexation of Latvia, Lithuania and Estonia.

White House Press Secretary Marlin Fitzwater said the shipments were discussed with Soviet officials, who were said to have raised no objections. He said Bush acted for humanitarian reasons and "to demonstrate U.S. concern for the situation in the Baltic states."

The President, however, spoke harshly Wednesday night about Soviet actions in the Baltics, calling them "repression" that threatens the warming course of U.S.-Soviet relations.

"When we see repression in the Baltics, it is very hard to have business as usual," Bush said, in a question-and-answer session after a speech to the New York Economic Club.

"We've got to see that no more force will be used," the President said. Otherwise, he said, not only will future U.S.-Soviet trade suffer, but also the overall relationship.

"I'm not in a position to say what we can do, more positive, while we

Please see BALTICS, A16

U.S., Allies Might Help Iraq Rebuild After War, Baker Says

Agence France-Presse

Iraqis sit guarded by Egyptians in Saudi desert. POWs have reported heavy desertion by Hussein's troops.

■ **Persian Gulf:** Secretary adds that Baghdad could face reparations after a bloody ground conflict. He also says Iran must have a key peacetime role.

By NORMAN KEMPSTER
TIMES STAFF WRITER

WASHINGTON—Secretary of State James A. Baker III said Wednesday that the United States and its allies might help rebuild postwar Iraq, but when pressed by members of Congress, he said reparations might be exacted if Iraq fights to the finish in a bloody ground war.

"The time of reconstruction and recovery should not be the occasion for vengeful actions against a nation forced to war by a dictator's ambition," Baker told the House Foreign Affairs Committee. "The secure and prosperous future everyone hopes to see in the Gulf must include Iraq."

With an eye to U.S. budgetary problems, he added, "Of necessity, most of the resources for reconstruction will be drawn from the Gulf [countries]."

Baker also said the postwar political order in the Gulf must make a place for Iraq, its territorial integrity intact. He said Iran also must be included in postwar planning.

Baker's comments, contained in his prepared text, seemed aimed less at his Capitol Hill audience than at mounting concern in the Middle East that the U.S.-led military assault will go beyond demolition of Iraqi military power and destroy Iraq as a viable country.

In a dinner speech Wednesday at the New York Economic Club, President Bush touched on the same theme, saying "the road to real peace will be long and tough. But we will prevail. And when we do, we will have before us an historic opportunity. From the confluence of the Tigris and Euphrates, where civilization began, civilized behavior can begin anew.

"In the final analysis, America and her partners will be measured not by how we wage war but how we make peace," Bush said.

But earlier in the day, most members of the House committee insisted that the United States exact harsh terms once it defeats Iraq, either demanding financial reparations or putting Iraqi leaders on trial for war crimes or both.

Although Baker cautioned against hardening U.S. war aims, he said the allies might be more inclined to exact reparations if the war ends in bitter fighting for every inch of Kuwait than if Iraq agrees to withdraw before it is forced out. The U.N. Security Council has already adopted a resolution holding Iraq financially responsible for damage to Kuwait and other states in the region.

"It depends on how the cessation of hostilities comes about—whether it's by a peace treaty or facts on the ground," Baker said.

He said Iran, as the largest country in the Persian Gulf region, must play a key role in the postwar security of the region. That is a

Please see BAKER, A10

U.S. Jets Down 2 Iraqi Planes Fleeing to Iran

■ **Gulf War:** Two others are 'possible kills.' Exotic fuel-air weapons join the American arsenal.

By J. MICHAEL KENNEDY and KIM MURPHY
TIMES STAFF WRITERS

RIYADH, Saudi Arabia—The United States stockpiled exotic fuel-air weapons Wednesday for possible use in the battle for Kuwait, and allied officers said American jets intercepted Iraqi warplanes for the first time as they tried to flee toward Iran. American officers said at least two Iraqi planes were destroyed.

As an amphibious assault force of 18,000 Marines positioned itself for a possible attack into occupied Kuwait, reporters touring a U.S. air base on the Gulf saw stockpiles of weapons capable of spreading fuel mist and igniting it to create an explosion that some say is similar to a tactical nuclear blast.

An officer at the base, Maj. James McClain, said fuel-air explosives were new to the war. Pentagon officials have said that Iraq has also developed such weapons, capable of delivering a detonation several miles wide. "We have the ability to use all kinds of weapons," McClain told reporters, "and that's just one of them."

The two downed Iraqi jets were described by Marine Brig. Gen. Richard I. Neal as Soviet-built SU-25s, among Iraq's top warplanes. A Saudi military spokesman said American F-15s shot down four of seven Iraqi jets as they tried to dash to sanctuary in Iran. But Neal confirmed just two kills. He listed two MIG-21s as "possible kills."

American officers said 10 Iraqi jets made it to Iran, raising the total that have sought refuge there to 120.

In other developments:

- A knowledgeable Pentagon official said allied warplanes are "tearing up" many units of Iraq's select Republican Guard and have caused damage of "way over" 50% in some isolated cases. But he said other units remain "virtually untouched" and that the force overall "still might be able to fight."
- Pilots who have been bombarding occupied Kuwait and Iraq for the past three weeks said they have run out of ready targets and have begun to cruise for targets of opportunity. They said the landscape has gotten so littered with battle damage that it takes as many as seven passes to find something worth destroying.
- Iran's national news agency said allied air raids have caused severe food shortages in Iraq, forcing residents to pay 800 dinars (about $2,560) for a sack of flour.

Please see WAR, A6

Iraq Army Units Under Strength, POWs Report

By KIM MURPHY
TIMES STAFF WRITER

DHAHRAN, Saudi Arabia—More than a quarter of the positions in Iraq's regular army in Kuwait are either deserted or unmanned, raising serious questions about Iraq's ability to defend against a ground assault, according to reports from allied officials who have debriefed Iraqi defectors in Saudi Arabia.

The interviews, according to a senior government source familiar with the reports, also reveal that the small Iraqi contingent that launched an ill-fated invasion on the Saudi border city of Khafji last week expected to be joined by a full army division.

The reports, which U.S. officials are reviewing with cautious skepticism, seem to indicate that command and control of Iraqi troops in southern Kuwait has been disrupted, although only some units are experiencing severe shortages of basic supplies, said the source, who spoke on condition of anonymity.

The prisoners reportedly have told allied officials that an estimated one-fourth to one-third of the troops in Iraq's regular army in Kuwait have either defected, been taken prisoner, suffered casualties or simply fled their positions. Many of them are reportedly returning to cities in Iraq from which they were

Please see PRISONERS, A14

Bettelheim Plagiarized Book Ideas, Scholar Says

■ **Authors:** The late child psychologist is accused of 'wholesale borrowing' for study of fairy tales.

By ANNE C. ROARK
TIMES STAFF WRITER

The legendary child psychologist Bruno Bettelheim, who before his suicide last year at age 86 had written some of the world's most influential books on children's development, plagiarized ideas and words in his award-winning book on fairy tales, according to a leading UC Berkeley scholar.

Writing in the latest issue of the Journal of American Folklore, Alan Dundes, a widely published expert on folklore and a 28-year veteran of Berkeley's anthropology department, details what he says is "wholesale borrowing," not only of "random passages" but also of "key ideas" in Bettelheim's 1976 book, "The Uses of Enchantment."

Widely read by teachers and parents, Bettelheim's book, which won the National Book Award and the National Book Critics Circle Award, includes detailed analyses of some of the world's best-known fairy tales, and contains the Austrian-born psychologist's passionate plea for retelling these stories to young children if they are to grow up to be emotionally healthy adults.

The disclosure that many of the ideas in the book may have been lifted from other sources—particularly the work of Dr. Julius E. Heuscher, a clinical professor of psychiatry at Stanford University's medical center—is causing a storm

Please see BETTELHEIM, A28

INSIDE TODAY'S TIMES

■ **WAR STORIES, PHOTOS: A5-15; E1; F1**

NEW CORONER FOR L.A.

Dr. Joshua A. Perper, chief medical examiner of Pittsburgh, has agreed to become L.A. County coroner. **B1**

■ **HAS ARMS, CROATIA SAYS**

Croatia's defense minister said his republic has a large arsenal of imported arms with which it could repel any attack by the federal Yugoslav army. **A18**

■ **UNOCAL SETTLES SUIT**

Unocal Corp. agreed to a $78-million settlement in a price-fixing lawsuit charging six firms with trying to cheat California and Long Beach. **D1**

WEATHER: Mostly sunny today. Fair Friday. Civic Center low/high today: 51/80. Details: B5

■ TOP OF THE NEWS ON A2

ROBERT GABRIEL / Los Angeles Times

Danny Thomas last year

■ **DANNY THOMAS DIES**

Entertainer Danny Thomas, who starred on television and was the benefactor of St. Jude's Children's Research Hospital in Memphis, died at 79. **B1**

Grass-Roots Army Forms to Aid Those Left Behind

■ **Home front:** Volunteers and local charities pick up the slack for overburdened military relief system.

By SHAWN HUBLER and LOUIS SAHAGUN
TIMES STAFF WRITERS

Never has the home front been this hectic for the graying warriors of American Legion Post 790.

Joe Chilelli, a retired plumber and Korean War veteran, is running a hot line for GIs' families out of his La Puente home. Past Commander Eileen Krizansky has been commandeering baby-sitters from all over town. Others from the West Covina post have been dispatched to mow lawns, fix washing machines and hang American flags.

As the Persian Gulf crisis enters its seventh month, grass-roots volunteers and hometown charities increasingly have been needed to buttress an overburdened military relief system struggling to handle an array of hardships—some mundane, others heart-rending—created when war tears families apart.

"We've done baby-sitting for two and I personally did a plumbing job for one," Chilelli said of his hot-line callers. A senior past commander of his post, he responds to as many as 40 calls a day, directed to him by San Francisco-based switchboard operators of the legion's new toll free hot line.

"One [caller] needed a psychologist for a 4-year-old," Chilelli said. "One needed a psychologist for herself. Four wanted American flags." Three callers were hus-

Please see AID, A11

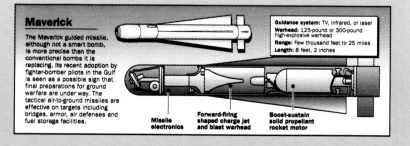

Maverick

The Maverick guided missile, although not a smart bomb, is more precise than the conventional bombs it is replacing. Its recent adoption by fighter-bomber pilots in the Gulf is seen as a possible sign that final preparations for ground warfare are under way. The tactical air-to-ground missiles are effective on targets including bridges, armor, air defenses and fuel storage facilities.

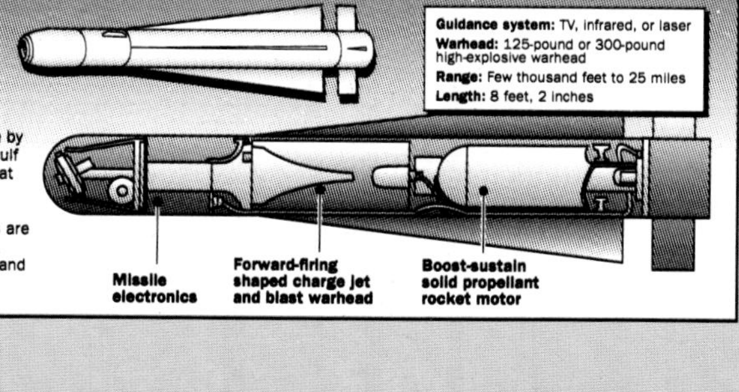
Guidance system: TV, infrared, or laser
Warhead: 125-pound or 300-pound high-explosive warhead
Range: Few thousand feet to 25 miles
Length: 8 feet, 2 inches
Missile electronics
Forward-firing shaped charge jet and blast warhead
Boost-sustain solid propellant rocket motor

Military: Debriefing of Iraqi defectors indicates that more than a quarter of the positions in Iraq's regular army in Kuwait are either deserted or unmanned; some units are experiencing severe shortages of basic supplies.

■ U.S. Air Force pilots said they swooped in behind four Iraqi jets — two SU-25s and two MIG-21s — and shot them down with air-to-air missiles as they tried to flee toward Iran.

■ American officers say 10 Iraqi jets made it to Iran, raising the total that have sought refuge there to 120.

■ An amphibious assault force of 18,000 Marines is positioned for a possible attack into occupied Kuwait.

■ Pentagon officials say warplanes are "tearing up" many units of the Republican Guard but other units remain "virtually untouched."

■ Pilots say they have run out of ready targets in Kuwait and Iraq and have begun to cruise for targets of opportunity.

Iraq: Iran's official news agency says air raids have caused severe food shortages in Iraq.

■ Iraq announces it is severing diplomatic relations with the United States, Britain, France, Italy, Egypt and Saudi Arabia.

State Department: Secretary of State James A. Baker III says the United States and its allies might help rebuild postwar Iraq. But when pressed by members of Congress, he says reparations might be exacted if Iraq fights to the finish in a bloody ground war.

Kuwait: Medical sources report the devastation of Kuwait's health-care system at the hands of Iraqi soldiers. They report that health workers have been arrested, tortured, raped and murdered.

Jordan: King Hussein expresses support for Iraq, criticizes the United Nations and urges an immediate cease-fire.

Marine tanks from Twentynine Palms, Calif., poised on the eve of war.

PATRICK DOWNS / Los Angeles Times

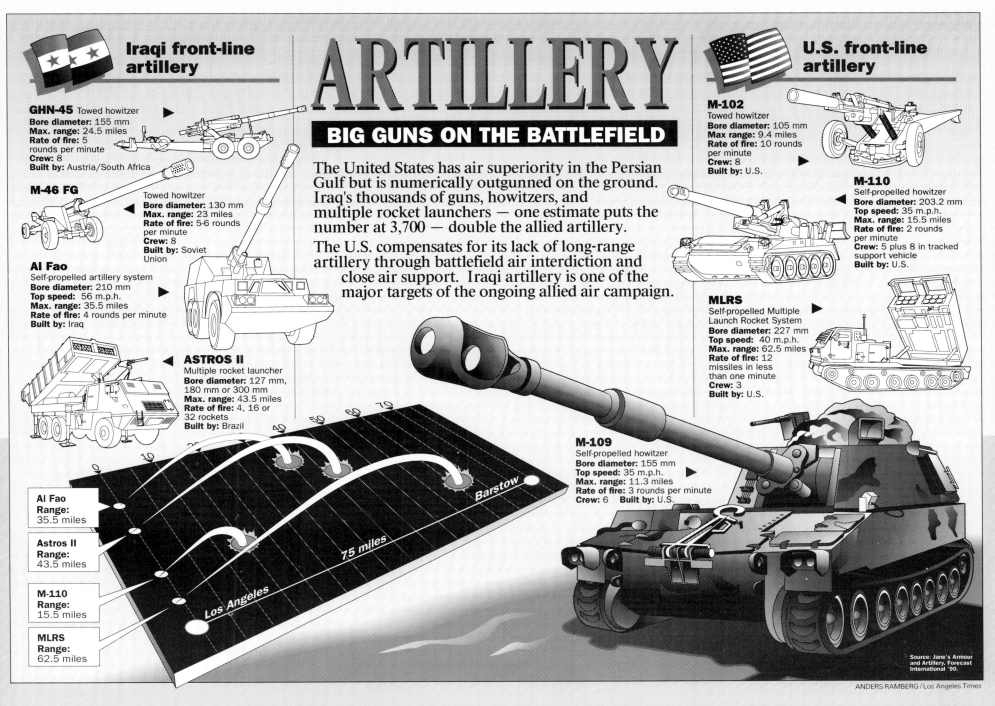

ARTILLERY

BIG GUNS ON THE BATTLEFIELD

The United States has air superiority in the Persian Gulf but is numerically outgunned on the ground. Iraq's thousands of guns, howitzers, and multiple rocket launchers — one estimate puts the number at 3,700 — double the allied artillery.

The U.S. compensates for its lack of long-range artillery through battlefield air interdiction and close air support. Iraqi artillery is one of the major targets of the ongoing allied air campaign.

Iraqi front-line artillery

GHN-45 Towed howitzer
Bore diameter: 155 mm
Max. range: 24.5 miles
Rate of fire: 5 rounds per minute
Crew: 8
Built by: Austria/South Africa

M-46 FG
Towed howitzer
Bore diameter: 130 mm
Max. range: 23 miles
Rate of fire: 5-6 rounds per minute
Crew: 8
Built by: Soviet Union

Al Fao
Self-propelled artillery system
Bore diameter: 210 mm
Top speed: 56 m.p.h.
Max. range: 35.5 miles
Rate of fire: 4 rounds per minute
Built by: Iraq

ASTROS II
Multiple rocket launcher
Bore diameter: 127 mm, 180 mm or 300 mm
Max. range: 43.5 miles
Rate of fire: 4, 16 or 32 rockets
Built by: Brazil

U.S. front-line artillery

M-102
Towed howitzer
Bore diameter: 105 mm
Max. range: 9.4 miles
Rate of fire: 10 rounds per minute
Crew: 8
Built by: U.S.

M-110
Self-propelled howitzer
Bore diameter: 203.2 mm
Top speed: 35 m.p.h.
Max. range: 15.5 miles
Rate of fire: 2 rounds per minute
Crew: 5 plus 8 in tracked support vehicle
Built by: U.S.

MLRS
Self-propelled Multiple Launch Rocket System
Bore diameter: 227 mm
Top speed: 40 m.p.h.
Max. range: 62.5 miles
Rate of fire: 12 missiles in less than one minute
Crew: 3
Built by: U.S.

M-109
Self-propelled howitzer
Bore diameter: 155 mm
Top speed: 35 m.p.h.
Max. range: 11.3 miles
Rate of fire: 3 rounds per minute
Crew: 6   **Built by:** U.S.

Al Fao Range: 35.5 miles

Astros II Range: 43.5 miles

M-110 Range: 15.5 miles

MLRS Range: 62.5 miles

Los Angeles   75 miles   Barstow

Source: Jane's Armour and Artillery, Forecast International '90.

ANDERS RAMBERG / Los Angeles Times

DAY 23

FEBRUARY 8, 1991

Nineteen-year-olds usually feel like they can't be killed, but Army Specialist Angel Alvarez of McAllen, Tex., knew better.

Alvarez, one of the first wounded soldiers to make it back from the Persian Gulf, met some of us from the press one afternoon at an indoor tennis court at Andrews Air Force Base, Md.. When they rolled his wheelchair into the circle of television lights, he was wearing a hospital bracelet and a Purple Heart and looking scared.

A thin youth with big, dark eyes, Alvarez told us how his unit was sent on a scouting mission, then bombarded with mortar rounds that struck him on both arms and legs and knocked him unconscious for two days.

How do you feel now about the war? I asked.

"I'll never do that again," said Alvarez, shaking his head. Then he looked around, perhaps noticed the dozen or so fellow soldiers hovering at the edge of the crowd of reporters, and added softly: "Unless I have to do it again."

—Paul Richter, in Washington

WAR: Cheney Hints at Land Offensive to Expose Iraqis
HELICOPTERS

Air Attack Caught Iraqis on Bridge
Baker Proposes Mideast Bank to Fund Postwar Repairs

Los Angeles Times

CIRCULATION: 1,225,189 DAILY 1,514,096 SUNDAY | FRIDAY, FEBRUARY 8, 1991 | COPYRIGHT 1991 THE TIMES MIRROR COMPANY CC† 152 PAGES | DAILY 50¢ DESIGNATED AREAS HIGHER

COLUMN ONE

War News: Blinding Effect?

■ U.S. preoccupation with Iraq has let other nations get away with controversial moves, some analysts say. Congress avoids other issues, and the media seem distracted.

By JIM MANN and THOMAS B. ROSENSTIEL
TIMES STAFF WRITERS

WASHINGTON—When Taiwanese-American dissident writer Henry Liu was gunned down in 1984 in the garage of his Bay Area home, American investigators painstakingly traced the murder from the killers up to Wang Hsi-Ling, then head of Taiwan's military intelligence.

Finally, amid considerable American prodding and intense press coverage, authorities in Taiwan convicted Wang and two associates of the American murder and sentenced them to life imprisonment. The sentence was later reduced to 15 years.

But this Jan. 21, less than a week after war broke out with Iraq, Taiwan quietly freed the three men from jail under a special amnesty. The men had spent only six years in prison.

The timing of the release may have been coincidental, yet the results were obvious: Few Americans noticed. Even though U.S. officials had drafted a statement deploring the release of the convicted intelligence chief, not a single member of the American media called to ask for it. No congressman took up the issue, either.

"I guess most people have lost interest," sighs Nat Bellocchi, head of the American Institute in Taiwan, the unofficial organization that has handled relations with Taiwan since the United States recognized China in 1979.

The freeing of the former intelligence chief is only one of the events here and around the world that have been lost, overshadowed or shunted aside as a result of the current American obsession with the war in Iraq.

Congress, the American news media and, in some instances, the Bush Administration itself have been so absorbed with the Persian Gulf that they have had far less interest than usual in developments elsewhere. Some analysts argue that certain foreign governments have taken advantage of the American preoccupation with Iraq to make moves that they knew the United States would have protested more vigorously in other times.

Such instances include:

—The recent crackdown by the Soviet military in the Baltic states. Developments in the Baltics call to mind events in 1956 when the Soviet Union resorted to tanks to crush the rebellion in Hungary. The Soviet action came when the West was consumed by the Suez crisis, in which Britain, France and Israel sought to regain control over the Suez Canal.

Although the tumultuous events in the Soviet Union have been covered in the American press,

Please see NEWS, A26

Los Angeles Times

Justice Allen E. Broussard

Liberal Justice Broussard to Retire in 1991

By PHILIP HAGER
TIMES LEGAL AFFAIRS WRITER

SAN FRANCISCO—Justice Allen E. Broussard, the leading dissenter and most liberal member of the conservative-led California Supreme Court, announced Thursday that he will retire from the bench this year.

The 61-year-old Broussard, a judge for 27 years, has spent nearly 10 years on the Supreme Court and is only its second black member in history. His impending retirement will enable Republican Gov. Pete Wilson to make his first appointment to the high court.

Broussard's departure will leave only one acknowledged liberal—Justice Stanley Mosk—on a court that has been controlled by a majority of five moderately conservative appointees of Republican Gov. George Deukmejian after the defeat of then-Chief Justice Rose Elizabeth Bird and two other liberals in the November, 1986, election.

"I know now what Thurgood Marshall must have felt like when William Brennan announced his retirement," said Mosk, referring to the two steadfast liberals on the conservative-dominated U.S. Supreme Court. "Justice Broussard has been a legal giant, in my estimation. His departure is going to be seen as a severe blow to the administration of justice in California."

Some close observers of the court expressed concern that Broussard's retirement could leave the court without the philosophical balance that all courts—whether liberal or conservative—need to produce thorough and well-reasoned decisions that have been tested against the views of the minority.

"His departure poses the threat of severely unbalancing the court by all but removing its liberal wing," said UC Berkeley law professor Stephen R. Barnett. "The court needs dissenters and it needs the ability to form a liberal-moderate majority in at least some cases. . . . There should be criticism and opposing views of what the majority is doing."

There were immediate calls for Wilson to name a minority-group member to replace Broussard. "It's very important to have that kind of diversity on the court," said Gerald F. Uelmen, dean of law at Santa Clara University. "It's going to be

Please see BROUSSARD, A41

Cheney Hints At an Early Ground War

■ **Gulf conflict:** Defense secretary says a land thrust could be used to drive Iraqi troops into the open. He and Powell dismiss suggestions of months of air strikes alone.

By MELISSA HEALY and JOHN BALZAR
TIMES STAFF WRITERS

RIYADH, Saudi Arabia—Defense Secretary Dick Cheney, offering the most direct indication to date of how and when a ground assault into Kuwait could begin, said early today that allied troops might launch a land offensive to draw Iraqi troops into a death trap well before warplanes have done their worst damage.

"We may reach the point where you could make the air campaign more effective by adding the other dimensions of the ground campaign, using ground forces to drive him [the enemy] out of his current positions, where they would become more vulnerable to air," Cheney told reporters flying with him to Saudi Arabia to assess progress in the Persian Gulf War.

Cheney and Gen. Colin L. Powell, chairman of the U.S. Joint Chiefs of Staff, who accompanied him, dismissed suggestions that America and its allies would continue aerial bombardment for months against Iraqi troops entrenched in occupied Kuwait and southern Iraq before launching a ground offensive. Powell said a ground assault would be part of a seamless plan.

"It is a single, integrated campaign," he said. "The air campaign will never end."

In other developments:

• Gen. H. Norman Schwarzkopf, commander of allied forces in the Gulf, told ABC News on Thursday that it was too soon to say whether a ground assault would be necessary to free Kuwait. He also said he

Please see WAR, A6

Controller Says She Confused Similar Planes

By ERIC MALNIC and TRACY WOOD
TIMES STAFF WRITERS

An air traffic controller told federal investigators that last week's Los Angeles airport disaster occurred after she mistook a commuter plane on a taxiway for a similar SkyWest plane that was sitting on a runway, officials reported Thursday.

The unidentified controller also told investigators in a three-hour interview Wednesday that she cleared a USAir Boeing 737 for landing on the same runway because she did not see the SkyWest plane.

In the first public account of her version of events, federal investigators said that missing paperwork

Please see CRASH, A46

IRA Shells Home of British Prime Minister

Agence France-Presse

Police watch the burning van from which mortar shells were fired at British Prime Minister John Major's residence. Four people were hurt.

■ **Terrorism:** Major and his War Cabinet are safe, and there is little damage when three mortars are fired from a van at No. 10 Downing St. Four others are only slightly hurt.

By WILLIAM TUOHY
TIMES STAFF WRITER

LONDON—Irish Republican Army terrorists fired three makeshift mortars at No. 10 Downing St., the official residence of British Prime Minister John Major, as he met with his War Cabinet on Thursday morning, but the apparent assassination attempt failed.

Major and the Cabinet members were shaken but unhurt when a mortar round exploded in the enclosed garden outside their meeting room.

Three policemen and a civil servant suffered minor injuries.

The shells were lofted through the roof of a van that was parked nearby among Great Britain's most important government buildings. Two of the shells landed on the nearby Foreign Office green and failed to detonate fully, Scotland Yard said, and the third shook the historic prime minister's residence and broke windows but did relatively little damage.

The van exploded after a man reportedly ran from it and fled on the back of a motorcycle.

As an icy blast from a rare snowstorm blew into the Cabinet room through sprung windows, Major reportedly said: "I think we'd better start again somewhere else."

The government ministers then moved to a more secure room in the building and finished their meeting, a spokeswoman said.

The IRA later released a statement in Dublin, claiming responsibility for the attack. A Scotland Yard official agreed that it was the work of the IRA.

Later, in a report to the House of Commons, Major declared that he had only contempt for the IRA terrorists and said the assault was "a deliberate attempt to kill the Cabinet and damage the democratic system."

"It's about time they learned that democracies cannot be intimidated by terrorism, and we rightly treat them with contempt," he said.

His views were seconded by Labor opposition leader Neil Kinnock, who declared: "These terrorist attacks are criminal, cowardly and pointless. They will change nothing, and the misery which the terrorists seek to cause is simply proof of their cruelty."

In a rare political comment as she appeared at a London hospital opening, Queen Elizabeth II also condemned the attack and said the bombers would never "undermine Britain's democratic system."

The IRA had previously tried to kill a prime minister, Margaret Thatcher, in 1984 by planting a bomb at the Grand Hotel in Brighton during a Conservative Party conference. Thatcher escaped but the blast killed five others—including a member of Parliament and the wife of another member—

Please see BRITAIN, A30

'Dumb' Bombs Cause Heavy Damage in Basra

■ **Air raids:** The weapons cannot be targeted precisely. In Baghdad, 'smart' bombs are aimed at military targets.

By JOHN M. BRODER
TIMES STAFF WRITER

WASHINGTON—Huge quantities of unguided "dumb" bombs have been used in the relentless U.S. air raids on Iraq's second-largest city, according to U.S. military officials, lending credence to growing reports of civilian casualties and extensive residential damage in the area.

The bombing of Basra, a critical nerve center for the Iraqi army, stands in contrast to that of Baghdad, where Pentagon officials have shown films of laser-guided "smart" bombs that hit military targets, bridges and industrial sites in and around the capital with little damage to nearby civilian sites.

The precise weapons, including Navy Tomahawk cruise missiles and bombs dropped by Air Force F-117 Stealth fighters, were favored there in part because they are virtually invulnerable to the heavy antiaircraft net protecting Iraq's capital.

The southern port city of Basra, by contrast, has relatively primitive air defenses and has therefore been assigned to less sophisticated carrier-based Navy A-6 attack planes, Air Force B-52s and F-111s dropping a combination of guided and unguided bombs, Pentagon officials said.

"These are clearly two different cities and two different areas," one senior officer said. "Baghdad is more heavily defended and that's why you use Stealth and stand-off weapons" such as cruise missiles. "Basra is more reachable by naval air and offers a lot more targets" that don't require the precision of the F-117 and Tomahawk, he added.

Former U.S. Atty. Gen. Ramsey Clark, who visited Basra this week, said Thursday that he found "no pinpoint bombing there . . . much greater destruction than [in] Baghdad." Clark said he saw residential areas, schools, a nightclub and a mosque that had been destroyed by the allied bombing of Basra.

Clark, a peace activist whose estimates of civilian casualties in the U.S. invasion of Panama ex-

Please see BASRA, A8

Wilson Budget Encounters Serious Trouble in Senate

■ **Politics:** Democrats want governor to revise his plan, back a $1.4-billion income tax hike aimed at the wealthy.

By DOUGLAS P. SHUIT
TIMES STAFF WRITER

SACRAMENTO—Gov. Pete Wilson's budget appeared to be in serious trouble in the Senate Thursday with majority-party Democrats saying they are unwilling to go forward with the governor's plan to cut welfare grants and establish new taxes on candy, snack foods, newspapers and magazines.

Senate President Pro Tem David A. Roberti (D-Los Angeles), after a closed-door meeting with fellow party members, said Senate Democrats instead will push the Republican governor to negotiate a minimum $1.4-billion income tax increase aimed at California's wealthiest taxpayers. Wilson has said he opposes any increase in the income tax.

In spelling out his terms, Roberti said that the first bill in Wilson's $1.7-billion tax-increase package is being put on hold because lawmakers believe it addresses only a small part of the budget problem.

The bill in question would impose a 6%-to-7% sales tax on candy, snack foods, newspapers and periodicals and raise about $300 million annually. But Roberti said that with the budget short by $7 billion to $10 billion over the next 17 months, the candy bill would hardly dent the problem. Wilson also has proposed boosting motor vehicle license fees, increas-

Please see BUDGET, A40

INSIDE TODAY'S TIMES

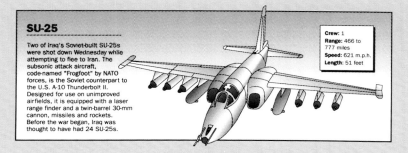

Agence France-Presse

Aristide at his inauguration

■ **HAITI LEADER SWORN IN**

The Rev. Jean Bertrand Aristide, a former slum priest, was sworn in by a jubilant Haiti as the nation's first democratically elected president. **A33**

■ **WAR STORIES, PHOTOS: A5-22; E1**

■ **DROUGHT RIPPLES**

Ripple effects from the state's drought, now in its fifth year, could change the face of agriculture in California. **A3**

■ **SPRING BREAK CURBS**

Palm Springs officials have passed several laws in an attempt to curb lewd and drunken behavior among Spring Break revelers in the desert resort. **A3**

■ **SOVIETS REASSURE U.S.**

Trying to retain good relations with the U.S., the Soviets said arms-control issues would be ironed out and asked for understanding in its Baltic crisis. **A4**

WEATHER: Mostly sunny today and Saturday. Civic Center low/high today: 53/71. Details: B5

■ TOP OF THE NEWS ON A2

Iraq POWs Treated Royally by Their Saudi Captors

■ **Camps:** The hosts view them as the neighbors of tomorrow. U.S. officials predict a flood of prisoners.

By KIM MURPHY and DOUGLAS FRANTZ
TIMES STAFF WRITERS

DHAHRAN, Saudi Arabia—It has become almost a morning ritual along the Saudi-Kuwaiti frontier: Three or four Iraqi soldiers creep across the border toward U.S. Marine positions, waving white T-shirts. Nearly always, they are hungry. Almost as often, they list their occupation as cooks.

"We've got 31 cooks and no food," one U.S. officer said wryly.

The trickle has yet to become the flood U.S. military officials are predicting in the allied offensive against Iraq. But the nearly 900 Iraqi soldiers already in custody, combined with the high rate of captured soldiers compared to casualties, has prompted some military analysts to predict that hundreds of thousands of Iraqis may eventually be in custody, rivaling the massive Italian surrender to the Allies in the North African desert in World War II.

"What we're presumably looking at is the possibility of having to look after as many as 300,000 or 400,000 men," said Andrew Duncan of London's International Institute for Strategic Studies. "Obviously, one hopes that most of them will surrender rather than have to be killed, but it will bring about tremendous logistic problems."

Already, U.S. forces have constructed two large holding facilities

Please see CAMPS, A18

SU-25

Two of Iraq's Soviet-built SU-25s were shot down Wednesday while attempting to flee to Iran. The subsonic attack aircraft, code-named "Frogfoot" by NATO forces, is the Soviet counterpart to the U.S. A-10 Thunderbolt II. Designed for use on unimproved airfields, it is equipped with a laser range finder and a twin-barrel 30-mm cannon, missiles and rockets. Before the war began, Iraq was thought to have had 24 SU-25s.

Crew: 1
Range: 466 to 777 miles
Speed: 621 m.p.h.
Length: 51 feet

Military: Allied warplanes concentrate on areas held by front-line Iraqi troops and territory to the rear held by the Republican Guard in what one officer calls "isolating and shaping the battlefield."
■ Britain's commander of Gulf forces, Lt. Gen. Peter de la Billiere, and French President Francois Mitterrand both say a ground war is inevitable.
■ The U.S. battleship Wisconsin fires its huge guns in action for the first time since the Korean War.
■ A U.S. Navy FA-18 is lost in the northern Persian Gulf as it returns from an apparently successful mission over enemy territory. A search for the pilot gets under way.
■ Two Iraqi helicopters are shot down by American planes.
■ France's new defense minister, Pierre Joxe, replaces the commander of its ground forces in Saudi Arabia, Gen. Jean-Claude Mouscardes, for medical reasons.

Iraq: A London newspaper cites sources saying that nearly 50 civilians died when allied bombers attacked a crowded bridge in the Iraqi city of Nasiriyah.
■ The Iraqi government says it is "waiting impatiently" for a ground war to begin in the Persian Gulf conflict and vows to send "tens of thousands" of Americans home in coffins.
■ Former U.S. Atty. Gen. Ramsey Clark says he saw many Iraqi civilian casualties in a visit to Baghdad.

Diplomacy: Secretary of State James A. Baker III proposes a new Middle East Bank for Reconstruction and Development to help rebuild that region following the Persian Gulf War.

Terrorism: An American who worked at the Incirlik Air Base in Turkey, from which U.S. aircraft are attacking Iraq, is shot dead by an unknown assailant in the Turkish city of Adana.

Famous "underachiever" shared triumphant allied drive.

PATRICK DOWNS / Los Angeles Times

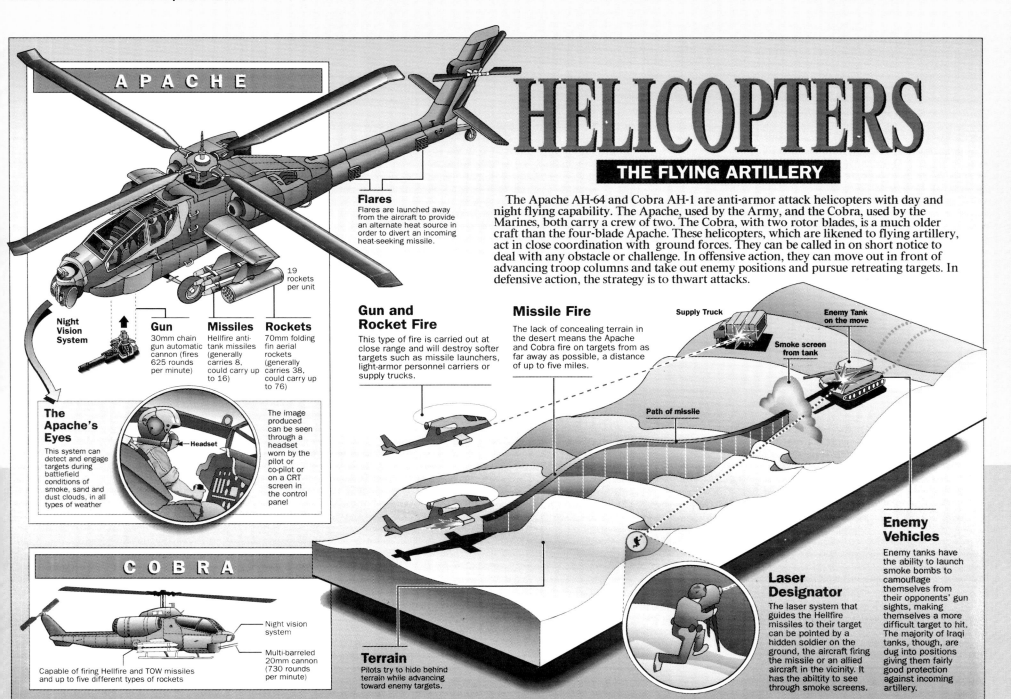

HELICOPTERS
THE FLYING ARTILLERY

The Apache AH-64 and Cobra AH-1 are anti-armor attack helicopters with day and night flying capability. The Apache, used by the Army, and the Cobra, used by the Marines, both carry a crew of two. The Cobra, with two rotor blades, is a much older craft than the four-blade Apache. These helicopters, which are likened to flying artillery, act in close coordination with ground forces. They can be called in on short notice to deal with any obstacle or challenge. In offensive action, they can move out in front of advancing troop columns and take out enemy positions and pursue retreating targets. In defensive action, the strategy is to thwart attacks.

APACHE

Flares
Flares are launched away from the aircraft to provide an alternate heat source in order to divert an incoming heat-seeking missile.

19 rockets per unit

Night Vision System

Gun
30mm chain gun automatic cannon (fires 625 rounds per minute)

Missiles
Hellfire anti-tank missiles (generally carries 8, could carry up to 16)

Rockets
70mm folding fin aerial rockets (generally carries 38, could carry up to 76)

The Apache's Eyes
This system can detect and engage targets during battlefield conditions of smoke, sand and dust clouds, in all types of weather

Headset

The image produced can be seen through a headset worn by the pilot or co-pilot or on a CRT screen in the control panel

COBRA

Capable of firing Hellfire and TOW missiles and up to five different types of rockets

Night vision system

Multi-barreled 20mm cannon (730 rounds per minute)

Gun and Rocket Fire
This type of fire is carried out at close range and will destroy softer targets such as missile launchers, light-armor personnel carriers or supply trucks.

Missile Fire
The lack of concealing terrain in the desert means the Apache and Cobra fire on targets from as far away as possible, a distance of up to five miles.

Supply Truck

Enemy Tank on the move

Smoke screen from tank

Path of missile

Terrain
Pilots try to hide behind terrain while advancing toward enemy targets.

Laser Designator
The laser system that guides the Hellfire missiles to their target can be pointed by a hidden soldier on the ground, the aircraft firing the missile or an allied aircraft in the vicinity. It has the abitlity to see through smoke screens.

Enemy Vehicles
Enemy tanks have the ability to launch smoke bombs to camouflage themselves from their opponents' gun sights, making themselves a more difficult target to hit. The majority of Iraqi tanks, though, are dug into positions giving them fairly good protection against incoming artillery.

Source: Modern Fighting Aircraft

DAVID PUCKETT / Los Angeles Times

DAY 24

FEBRUARY 9, 1991

For the most part, the Pentagon brass was pleased with the media's coverage of the war, but in a few cases they believed that military secrets were revealed. One case concerned a new way of targeting Iraqi tanks and armored vehicles dug into the desert.

After hundreds of unsuccessful air strikes against these targets, the Air Force discovered that at dusk the metal armor cooled more slowly than the surrounding sand and could easily be seen by thermal sights on U.S. aircraft. So, they switched to heat-seeking weapons and began knocking out the Iraqi tanks at a rate of nearly 100 a day.

Military officials hit the roof when ABC News reported the new technique. The report gave away valuable information to the enemy, they charged. Yet, the information, provided to numerous reporters, had come from senior officers eager to show off the prowess of their pilots and weapons.

—John M. Broder, in Washington

Los Angeles Times

CIRCULATION: 1,225,189 DAILY / 1,514,096 SUNDAY

SATURDAY, FEBRUARY 9, 1991

COPYRIGHT 1991 / THE TIMES MIRROR COMPANY / CC† / 108 PAGES

DAILY 25¢ DESIGNATED AREAS HIGHER

Allies Press Air War, Report 600 Tank Kills

Associated Press

Gen. Colin L. Powell, left, the chairman of the Joint Chiefs of Staff, confers with Gen. H. Norman Schwarzkopf at a Saudi air base.

■ **Persian Gulf:** Cheney, Powell exhort troops and begin consultations on a possible ground assault. An Iraqi Scud strikes Tel Aviv, injuring 20 and damaging apartment buildings.

By J. MICHAEL KENNEDY and MELISSA HEALY
TIMES STAFF WRITERS

RIYADH, Saudi Arabia—Allied warplanes screamed across blinding-blue desert skies to blitz Iraqi troops in the trenches and bunkers of Kuwait and southern Iraq on Friday, and a Saudi commander said the Iraqis have organized "execution battalions" to shoot any of their soldiers who might try to flee.

The allies focused their bombing extra tightly on the Kuwaiti theater of operations as Defense Secretary Dick Cheney and Gen. Colin L. Powell, chairman of the U.S. Joint Chiefs of Staff, visited U.S. troops and Powell exhorted them with his familiar battle cry about the Iraqi army of occupation in Kuwait.

"We'll get this over with a simple process," he said. "We'll cut it off and kill it."

Speaking of Iraqi President Saddam Hussein, Powell said, "He has seen what our Air Force can do, and he'll see a lot more of it in days and weeks ahead."

What the Air Force has done since the start of the Persian Gulf War was outlined at allied headquarters in Riyadh by Marine Maj. Gen. Robert B. Johnston, chief of staff for the U.S. Central Command, and another senior military official, who declined to be namcd. They said an estimated 600 of Iraq's 5,700 tanks and 400 of Iraq's 3,200 artillery pieces in Kuwait and Iraq have been destroyed.

These, however, are not necessarily enough kills, Johnston said, to encourage a ground campaign. "We have assigned no particular percentage," he said, "that will drive us to a decision [on launching a ground campaign]."

In other developments:

• Johnston said the number of Iraqi warplanes that have fled to Iran has increased to 147. The commander of allied naval operations said they include Iraq's deadliest anti-ship planes—and that they pose a greater danger now to ships in the Persian Gulf than they did when they were at home, because they are closer.

• The senior military official said air attacks have cut by 90% the flow of materiel to the more than 500,000 enemy troops in the Kuwaiti-southern Iraq theater. He also said that allied aircraft knocked out a mobile missile launcher just north of the Saudi-Kuwaiti border and that a British helicopter destroyed an Iraqi patrol boat.

• Iraq hit Tel Aviv with a Scud missile early today. An Israeli army spokesman said at least 20 people were hurt, none seriously. Several apartment buildings were damaged; one burned. The Scud was armed with a conventional warhead. It was not clear whether the incoming missile was hit by

Please see WAR, A4

COLUMN ONE

The Mob Against the Ropes

■ Prosecutors using new laws are cracking *omerta*—the code of silence—to jail hoodlums. The Mafia is still an ominous criminal force, but has lost much power.

By RONALD J. OSTROW
TIMES STAFF WRITER

WASHINGTON—The oath, uttered in Italian by would-be members of La Cosa Nostra, was terse—and stark: "I swear not to divulge this secret and to obey, with love and *omerta*"—the Code of Silence.

Then, in a centuries-old ritual, each inductee's trigger-finger was cut enough to draw blood. A holy card of the saint of the controlling family was burned and the men intoned the second part of the oath—again, in Italian: "As burns this saint, so will burn my soul. I enter alive into this organization and leave it dead."

What distinguished this initiation into La Cosa Nostra from hundreds of others that have been conducted in Mafia strongholds in Massachusetts, New York, Philadelphia, Milwaukee, Kansas City and elsewhere in the United States was that—despite the code of silence—the FBI secretly recorded it. "The final ignominy," as Atty. Gen. Dick Thornburgh puts it.

The government's ability to break *omerta* is instructive. Amid the popularity of movies such as "GoodFellas" and "The Godfather, Part III" the real Mafia is on the ropes in the United States, law enforcement officers say, emerging weaker as an underworld power than at any time since the days before Prohibition.

All across the country, stepped-up government enforcement efforts appear to have dealt severe blows to most of the 24 U.S. families of La Cosa Nostra (which means "This Thing of Ours" in Italian).

The mob, of course, remains a force to be reckoned with. Mafia-related units continue to exert a major influence on much of the nation's criminal activity—loan-sharking, gambling, narcotics trafficking, weapons possession, counterfeit credit cards, securities theft and money laundering. The impact on American life far exceeds the current estimated strength of 1,700 to 2,500 "made"—formally initiated—members.

But there's little doubt that prosecutors have gained ground. The key has been skillful use of the Racketeer-Influenced and Corrupt Organizations law, commonly referred to as RICO, under which prosecutors attack the mob as a criminal enterprise rather than filing cases on a mobster-by-mobster basis. The RICO approach often results in stiff sentences for those convicted. Federal wiretapping, undercover infiltration and witness-protection programs also have helped.

"RICO gives you the ability to pull together the various criminal acts committed by various persons in an organization [and present them] in one courtroom—before

Please see MOB, A22

Ship Retired

STEVE DYKES / Los Angeles Times

Marine trumpeter plays at ceremony decommissioning battleship New Jersey, the fourth time the ship has been mothballed. **B3**

Yugoslavia Near Breaking Point as Talks Fail

By CAROL J. WILLIAMS
TIMES STAFF WRITER

BELGRADE, Yugoslavia—Slovenia on Friday declared its intention to secede from Yugoslavia later this month while Croatia boycotted critical negotiations aimed at saving the federation, portending an ominous turn in relations among ethnic groups already poised for civil war.

All six Yugoslav republic presidents were to have met in Belgrade in an eleventh-hour attempt to avert a violent breakup of the federation.

But Croatian President Franjo Tudjman refused to attend the talks after Serbian Communists called a rally outside the meeting place to accuse Croats of plotting genocide. Slovenian President Milan Kucan stormed out of the session after the vitriolic demonstration by about 5,000 Serbian nationalists began, saying that nothing could be accomplished under such "impossible conditions."

Slovenia's prime minister then served notice on the Belgrade government that it is giving up on what were already slim prospects for continued affiliation with Yugoslavia.

Prime Minister Lojze Peterle said in Ljubljana that Slovenia's Parliament will annul all federal laws on Feb. 20, thereby withdrawing the republic from the Yugoslav state cobbled together in 1918 from the remnants of Ottoman Turkey and the Austro-Hungarian Empire.

Yugoslavia has been limping from crisis to crisis over the last month and tensions between Serbs and Croats have escalated to such a fevered state that the chance for a peaceful resolution is now considered minimal.

Croatia and the Serbian-dominated federal army only narrowly avoided an armed clash two weeks ago and the rift has widened since

Please see YUGOSLAVIA, A24

Bush Energy Plan Stresses Oil, A-Power

■ **Environment:** His proposal would open the Alaska National Wildlife Refuge to exploration and speed the licensing of new nuclear plants.

By RUDY ABRAMSON
TIMES STAFF WRITER

WASHINGTON—After 18 months of debate and deliberation, the Bush Administration will send to Congress within the next few days a national energy strategy proposing to expedite the exploration for oil and resuscitate the moribund nuclear power industry.

The massive plan, a draft of which was obtained 10 days before its scheduled unveiling by President Bush, appears certain to trigger major battles among environmentalists, conservationists, exploration advocates and other groups affected by its key provisions.

The plan includes a widely anticipated proposal to open 1.5 million acres of the Alaska National Wildlife Refuge to oil exploration and calls for commercial development of the Naval Petroleum Reserve in California's Elk Hills field. It would expedite the licensing of new nuclear power plants and seek a solution to the vexing problem of nuclear waste disposal.

Besides drawing fire for some of its more controversial proposals, the plan is expected to encounter considerable criticism for provisions it does not contain. The Administration strategy does not propose stiffer standards for automobile fuel efficiency or call for new taxes to encourage conservation, as advocated by some interest groups.

In a draft letter to congressional leaders, Energy Secretary James D. Watkins says the plan addresses four major themes developed in the course of numerous hearings and studies since 1989: increased energy and economic efficiency, securi-

Please see ENERGY, A19

Low Oil Prices, Moderation Seen for OPEC

By PATRICK LEE
TIMES STAFF WRITER

For now, nightly bombing raids over Baghdad and flaming oil fields in Kuwait have rendered the Organization of Petroleum Exporting Countries impotent to set the agenda for the world's oil market.

But, assuming allied forces prevail in the Persian Gulf War, it is likely that OPEC—with three-fourths of the world's proven oil reserves—will regain its grip on the global oil spigot after the last bomb is dropped, industry analysts and energy economists say.

Postwar OPEC, however, is likely to be dominated by moderate nations that favor stronger ties with the United States and other oil-consuming nations in the allied

Please see OPEC, A16

Allies Hope to Exploit Iraqi Lack of Mobility

■ **Ground war:** The strategy would be to strike the enemy fast and hard—and keep the battle moving.

By DAVID LAMB
TIMES STAFF WRITER

EASTERN SAUDI ARABIA—U.S. and allied commanders are laying the final plans for a ground war that will rely on speed and unprecedented violence to punch through Iraq's fortified lines and exploit Saddam Hussein's inability to adjust his fixed positions to the flow of battle.

Final preparations for the assault will be examined this weekend when Defense Secretary Dick Cheney and Gen. Colin L. Powell, chairman of the Joint Chiefs of Staff, meet in the Saudi capital of Riyadh with top U.S. commanders. But the framework for the offensive—and plans to deal with Hussein's formidable defenses—have been in place for weeks.

According to commanders at the front, the scope of the operation will be so large that entire corps will be moving across the battlefield simultaneously, supported by massive, close-in air support.

"We haven't seen elements of that size maneuvering since the North African campaign in World War II," said Col. Leroy Goff, a brigade commander with the Army's 3rd Armored Division.

The 3rd Armored sped across France and into Germany during that war, sometimes covering as much as 100 miles a day, as the vanguard for Gen. George S. Patton's attacking forces. No one expects it to match that feat in attempting to engage and destroy Iraq's estimable Republican Guard, but commanders say that maintaining momentum is essential even though Iraq has three elements that could slow the drive—mines, artillery and chemical weapons.

"We have to keep going forward. Don't get bogged down. Don't stop," said Col. Dana Robertson, who heads the division's engineering battalion, which would be called on to breach the antitank and antipersonnel minefields with a variety of devices, including

Please see STRATEGY, A12

Soldiers Get a Touch of Home on Videotapes

By DOUGLAS JEHL
TIMES STAFF WRITER

WITH U.S. FORCES, Saudi Arabia—In the gloomy Army tent, a television flickered and soldiers clutching cups of coffee to ward off the morning chill huddled in the corner to watch as home suddenly came to life.

There on the screen were their wives, their children, on sofas or on folding chairs, looking into the close-up lens and trying to find the words to tell their man how very much they missed him.

It was as if the soldiers could look into their living rooms, seeing even their own military portraits mounted on the wall, and their wives self-conscious, and the children fidgety, and all of it bringing a

Please see TAPES, A13

Indictment of Lawmakers Another Blow to Arizona

■ **Ethics:** Sting follows Mecham, King controversies. Case is one of series involving legislators around nation.

By PAUL FELDMAN
TIMES STAFF WRITER

PHOENIX—Nine minutes before stuffing what police say was $55,000 in cash into a gym bag, Arizona State Rep. Don Kenney sounded a bit nervous.

"You sure there isn't a camera?" Kenney asked J. Anthony Vincent, purportedly a deep-pocketed Las Vegas lobbyist seeking legalized casino gambling in Arizona. ". . . I remember those videotapes of the Abscam trial."

Kenney, chairman of the House Judiciary Committee, had greater intuition than he imagined.

Vincent was actually an ex-con named Joseph C. Stedino who was serving as a sting man for the Phoenix Police Department. And, despite Vincent's repeated denials, a hidden camera was indeed recording the action as Vincent counted and doled out the cash during a nearly two-hour meeting in his posh northeast Phoenix office last April.

In all, more than 200 video and 600 audiotapes of a yearlong series of sordid sessions are at the heart of a 102-count bribery and money-laundering indictment handed up this week against Kenney, six other Arizona state legislators and 10 lobbyists and political activists.

The Maricopa County grand jury action accuses the lawmakers of agreeing—often in B movie-style language—to support casino gam-

Please see ETHICS, A25

INSIDE TODAY'S TIMES

Associated Press

Roger Clemens

■ **CLEMENS STRIKES IT RICH**

Roger Clemens of the Boston Red Sox became baseball's highest-paid player when he agreed to a four-year contract extension worth $21,521,000. **C1**

■ **WAR STORIES, PHOTOS: A3-17; D1; F1**

■ **STORM BATTERS EUROPE**

A bitter winter storm buried much of Europe in snow, stranding thousands and causing at least four deaths. **A2**

■ **DROUGHT AID SOUGHT**

Legislation has been introduced to allow drought-stricken California communities to tap federal reservoirs and canals for relief. **A31**

■ **CHILD SLAVERY CHARGES**

After a two-year investigation, eight members of the Watts-based Ecclesia Athletic Assn. were indicted on child slavery charges. **B1**

WEATHER: Sunny and hazy. Civic Center low/high today: 49/72. Details: B4

■ INDEX TO FEATURES ON A2

Controller Was Stricken by Grief, Tears After Crash

■ **Disaster:** Co-workers spent hours after the accident counseling her and hid her from publicity for days.

Trembling in shock and smoking a cigarette, Robin Lee Wascher sat in a Los Angeles International Airport control tower office after guiding two airliners onto the same runway and seeing the ball of flame from the collision.

"I'm sorry. I'm sorry," the 38-year-old ground controller murmured over and over, tears spilling fitfully from her brown eyes.

Outside, firefighters were pumping flame-smothering foam into the smoldering wreck of a USAir Boeing 737 and pulling out victims. The Feb. 1 crash claimed 34 lives—all 12 people on a SkyWest Metroliner and 22 of the 89 aboard the larger USAir jet.

But in the minutes immediately after the accident, all Wascher knew was that there was a collision—and a fiery explosion. The eight-year veteran controller, known among pilots for her no-nonsense professionalism, was so anguished over the safety of the passengers that no one could tell her that a third of them had died in the wreckage.

This picture of grief and remorse was painted by another Los Angeles airport controller, one of the woman's many colleagues who

Please see CONTROLLER, A29

This article was reported by Times staff writers Rich Connell, Eric Malnic, John Mitchell, Mark Stein and Tracy Wood. It was written by Stein.

In the United Nations

Baghdad called for a U.N. probe of the allies' bombing Jan. 21 of what it called an **INFANT FORMULA FACTORY**. The allies say the factory produced biological weapons. **UNICEF** said it hopes to send a convoy from Iran to Baghdad next week with $500,000 in medical supplies for Iraqi women and children. U.N. Secretary General Javier Perez de Cuellar said reports of civilian casualties have filled him "with anguish and regret."

DRESSED FOR COMBAT

What the typical American soldier wears and carries while on maneuvers in the Persian Gulf region. **TOTAL COST: $1,452.10**

Desert helmet **$103.00**
Helmet cover **$2.50**
Desert hat **$4.90**

Desert coat **$15.48**
Suspenders **$6.95**
Brown undershirt **$2.40**
Night parka **$28.70**
Parka liner **$11.85**
Neckerchief **$4.10**

Field pack **$35.75**
Back frame **$23.85**
Shoulder straps **$5.30**
Strap pad **$11.30**
Sleeping bag **$64.25**

M16 rifle **$475.00**

Two-quart canteen **$5.45**
Canteen cover **$8.75**
Belt **$6.60**
Small arms case **$4.30**
Tool carrier **$2.00**
First aid case **$3.35**

Chemical protective clothing
Overgarment **$68.15**
Overshoe **$8.70**
Gloves **$7.85**
Helmet cover **$3.55**
Mask **$120.00**
Mask hood **$8.60**
Atropine kit **$14.00**
Detector kit **$49.07**

Desert trousers **$14.40**
Drawers **$1.50**
Night trousers **$19.50**

■ **ALSO:**
Fragmentation vest **$251.50**
Body armor cover **$24.65**

Boots **$33.20**
Socks **$1.65**

WEIGHT: The average soldier carries about 40 pounds of gear in the desert.
An M-16 assault rifle weights 8.8 pounds, the flak vest about the same. A chemical warfare protection system is 5.9 pounds. Add another 5.9 pounds for a helmet and equipment belt. Tack on 12.1 pounds for a backpack with sleeping bag, entrenching tooks, several quarts of water in canteens, night clothing and trousers.

Source: U.S. Army

AP/Los Angeles Times

DAY IN THE GULF

Military: Operation Desert Storm commanders throw hundreds of warplanes against new Iraqi front-line targets. They say the air war has knocked out about 600 Iraqi tanks.
■ At least 20 huge explosions, resulting from heavy bombing during the night in southern Iraq, shake buildings in the Iranian border cities of Khorramshahr and Abadan.
■ U.S. Marines mount a ground action, firing artillery shells across the border into Kuwait.
■ A British Royal Navy helicopter blows up an Iraqi patrol boat.
■ Defense Secretary Dick Cheney and Gen. Colin L. Powell arrive in Riyadh to meet with Gen. H. Norman Schwarzkopf on a two-day mission to determine when and how to pursue a ground war.

Iraq: POWs tell the allies of Iraqi "execution battalions" positioned behind the front lines. The units kill deserters and intimidate those considering fleeing the Iraqi forces.
■ Schwarzkopf says the military has reports that some of the Iraqi pilots defecting to Iran "actually bombed, you know, tried to bomb Saddam Hussein" in his presidential palace.
■ Soviet Deputy Foreign Minister Alexander M. Belonogov criticizes what he said was the deliberate destruction of Iraqi residential areas by allied air raids.

Missiles: The first Scud missile fired from Iraq in nearly a week strikes buildings in central Israel, and at least 15 people are injured.
■ U.S. bombers wreck one Iraqi mobile missile launcher in southern Iraq and damage or destroy three others in western Iraq overnight.
■ U.S. officials disclose that Iraq still has some fixed Scud launch sites in addition to the mobile launchers.

Congress: Thirty House Democrats sign an appeal to President Bush against further escalation of war against Iraq.

THE COST OF
A DAY OF WAR

Any war is expensive. Three month projections show that the Persian Gulf War, with its high-tech gadgetry and round-the-clock bombing sorties, will be one of the most expensive ever. Estimates of just how costly it will be start in the double-digit billions and soar skyward from there.

● The Congressional Budget Office estimated in early January that a war of longer than four weeks would cost about $87 billion — that amount added to what would already be spent for defense and troop support around the world. Then, on Tuesday, White House Budget Director Richard G. Darman suggested that a three-month war would add $67 billion to existing defense costs.

● Based on cost breakdowns in the CBO report and Darman's more recent estimate, a Los Angeles Times analyst has concluded that the tab for the war is running at $744.3 million a day.

● That figure takes into account various expenses that will continue after the war, such as maintaining an occupation force and extended medical care for disabled troops. Such costs are prorated into the daily figure. The numbers may also be inflated somewhat by the CBO's worst-case projections on the number of warplanes and ships lost.

**Total:
$744.3 million a day**
$31 million an hour
$516,875 a minute
$8,615 a second

MILITARY PERSONNEL COSTS
•Raising and maintaining 150,000 reservists
•400,000-plus troops receiving combat pay:

Total: **$70.4 million a day**

OPERATION AND MAINTENANCE COSTS
Fuel, food, supplies and maintenance costs incurred by the war. Everything troops may require while posted overseas. Example: Base post offices, tents etc.

Total: **$130.3 million a day**

REPLACING WEAPONS
•Aircraft: $130.3 million a day
•Tanks: $78.2 million a day
•Ships: $33.0 million a day

Total: **$241.5 million a day**

MISSILES AND AMMUNITION REPLACEMENT
•Aircraft attacking ground targets: $26.0 million a day
•Ammunition for Army troops and Marines on the ground: $104.2 million a day
•Antiaircraft missiles: $6.92 million a day
Navy munitions: $10.4 million a day

Total: **$147.5 million a day**

MEDICAL CARE
Immediate medical treatment and longer-term care and compensation

Total: **$33 million a day**

COST OF MAINTAINING TROOPS AFTER THE WAR
Cost of any occupation force, pro-rated.

Total: **$121.6 million a day**

Examples of replacement costs:

Patriot missile $500,000

F-14A Tomcat $71.9 million

M 109 $761,600

Not to scale

Source: Los Angeles Times; The Congressional Budget Office; Forecast International '90.

ANDERS RAMBERG / Los Angeles Times

DAY 25

FEBRUARY 10, 1991

Most of the Marines I talked to at Camp Pendleton were young, many only 19 or 20. But one, Cpl. Brett Doggett, was older—26. Doggett was serious and likeable. The war had interrupted his studies at Saddleback Community College in Orange County. He had seen active duty and been called up from the reserves. He was ready to go off to war, an old pro wanting to help the younger kids along. I mentioned him in a story.

A week after the fighting had ended, his father, Larry Garrett, phoned: "You did such a nice story on my son, I thought you'd like to know he stepped on a mine and lost his foot."

It had happened in Kuwait's Wafra Forest, days after the shooting was over. The explosion also badly injured Doggett's other foot. He faces his fifth operation. He wants to go back to college when he can.

—Ray Tessler, in north San Diego County

Los Angeles Times

Sunday Final

CIRCULATION: 1,225,189 DAILY / 1,514,096 SUNDAY

SUNDAY, FEBRUARY 10, 1991

COPYRIGHT 1991 / THE TIMES MIRROR COMPANY CC†/ 502 PAGES

SUNDAY $1.25 DESIGNATED AREAS HIGHER

Ground Attack Timing Is Next, Cheney Says

■ **Gulf War:** But air assault will continue—or even be stepped up. Hussein's army is still powerful, defense chief says, but 'there is nothing [he] can do at this point to . . . change the outcome.'

By JOHN BALZAR and MELISSA HEALY
TIMES STAFF WRITERS

RIYADH, Saudi Arabia—Defense Secretary Dick Cheney said early today that the Persian Gulf War "has gone extremely well to date" and that "the question is when" to begin a ground assault into Kuwait while continuing—and perhaps even stepping up—air attacks against the Iraqi army of occupation.

Iraqi President Saddam Hussein "retains a very significant part of the world's fourth-largest army . . . [and] nobody in a senior position wants to underestimate the size or capability of the forces left," Cheney said. Hussein may still have the capability to escalate the war through the use of poison gas warheads on Scud missiles, Cheney said, or to step up terror attacks or to send his remaining air forces on a "one-way attack."

But, Cheney said, speaking of ground troops, "at some point we would expect to bring other parts of our forces to bear on the problem of getting him out of Kuwait. The question is when—and what's the most effective use of coalition forces." There is nothing Hussein can do at this point, he said, "to fundamentally change the outcome."

Cheney said that outcome will be an allied victory.

He made the statements at a news conference before leaving Riyadh for Washington with Gen. Colin L. Powell, chairman of the Joint Chiefs of Staff. They will go to the White House on Monday and offer recommendations to President Bush, who has said he will decide whether and when to order a ground assault into Kuwait.

Cheney and Powell spent 8½ hours on Saturday—longer than expected—in a map-lined war room at the Saudi Defense Ministry with Gen. H. Norman Schwarzkopf, commander of allied forces in the Gulf, and others at the top of the Central Command. The commanders offered facts, analysis and hunches about whether Bush should order a ground assault—and what it might cost.

The defense secretary declined to specify what advice he and Powell would offer the President. But Marine Brig. Gen. Richard I. Neal, deputy operations director for the Central Command, described the mood of the military commanders who attended the Cheney-Powell briefing as "upbeat."

In other developments:

• U.S. officials in Washington disclosed that American warplanes last week began dropping a huge conventional bomb on Iraqi forces for the first time during this war. Known as the BLU-82, the bomb

Please see WAR, A6

COLUMN ONE

What Sort of Man Is Hussein?

■ Ruthless, enigmatic and unpredictable, the Iraqi leader has relentlessly pursued power and a place in history.

By STEPHEN BRAUN and TRACY WILKINSON
TIMES STAFF WRITERS

Saddam Hussein is everywhere and nowhere, as familiar as a face on a television screen, as elusive as rumor.

Staring impassively, blank as the head on a coin, he speaks to the world one moment from an anonymous house in the Baghdad suburbs and the next, in heated communiques from a front-line bunker. He dons public masks with an actor's flourish, each with its own wardrobe—the statesman's European-tailored business suits, the desert leader's flowing tribal *jellabas*, the commander's drab fatigues and black beret.

Unpredictability is his weapon—as integral to his survival as his penchant for secrecy and his reliance on violence as a tool of everyday business. Throughout his ascent to power—as a young Baath party conspirator, as a political prisoner, as a wily bureaucrat in the presidential palace and, now, as a leader at war—Saddam Hussein rarely has been pinned down.

To Americans, Hussein is both the personification of evil and an enigma. The rush of events has obscured his motivations; wartime blindness to his complexities has simplified and demonized his life.

"The West thinks he is an aberration," said Hani Fukaiki, an Iraqi political exile in London and former top official of Hussein's nationalist Arab Baath Socialist Party. "That is not true. For every Saddam Hussein who succeeds, there are 1,000 more who want to take his place."

From childhood, swaggering to school with a gun under his belt, to his present role as chosen enemy of the Western World, the common denominators in Hussein's life have been his pursuit of revolution, personal and political power and a place in history. Now 53 years old, he steeped himself in the tactics of insurrection, refining them over two decades of political carnage that shaped modern Iraq.

"The difference between us," he once lectured a visiting delegation of U.S. congressmen, "is that you came up through the over-ground. I came up through the underground."

If there is some childhood secret or shattering event in Hussein's past that goads him on in grim motivation, the scars are long buried under toughened skin. Like Stalin, his totalitarian model, Hussein has either eliminated or co-opted most of those who might shed light on his early life. He has replaced his obliterated past with one of his own making, reinventing himself as the one who can realize Iraqi dreams of leading the Muslim world and Arab yearnings for a seamless Mideast state.

What emerges in interviews with nearly 40 people—Iraqi exiles, scholars, diplomats, Congress

Please see HUSSEIN, A9

Bomb-Weary Baghdad Like 14th Century

By MARK FINEMAN
TIMES STAFF WRITER

AMMAN, Jordan—For the past two weeks in Baghdad, Dr. Rizek Jabr abu Kashef performed major surgery by candlelight.

He amputated legs of children without pain-killers, intravenous tubes or blood transfusions. He watched others die from infections for want of antibiotics or clean water for rehydration and, still others, simply from the cold.

In his little spare time, the Jordanian Red Crescent surgeon sat, freezing in a hospital with too little fuel for heat or consistent generator power; he read by candlelight about how to treat wounds from chemical and nuclear

Please see IRAQ, A20

Lithuania Votes 90% in Favor of Independence

By JOHN-THOR DAHLBURG
TIMES STAFF WRITER

VILNIUS, Soviet Union—Overwhelmingly rejecting President Mikhail S. Gorbachev's authority and his blueprint for a "common Soviet home," more than 2 million Lithuanians streamed to the polls on Saturday to confirm their will to be independent.

"The great majority of people in Lithuania no longer have any fear, and once again they have expressed their determination to the world," Vytautas Landsbergis, the Baltic republic's president, declared.

"They have said . . . what kind of Lithuania they want to create, what kind of Lithuania they will bequeath to their children."

At a late night press conference held inside Lithuania's barricaded Parliament building, election commission chairman Vaclovas Lipvinas said that preliminary returns showed 84.4% of 2.65 million voters cast ballots in Saturday's republic-wide referendum, with 90.4% in favor of "democratic, independent Lithuania."

Of the rest, 6.5% voted against independence, and the other ballots were invalidated because they were incorrectly marked, Lipvinas said.

Despite such an indisputable majority for independence, unofficial surveys tabulated by Lithuania's grass-roots nationalist movement Sajudis showed that the desire of the republic's ethnic minorities in Lithuania to remain part of the Soviet Union remains unshaken.

And that promises to be a major political headache for the Landsbergis leadership in upcoming negotiations with Moscow on the republic's political and economic future.

In Salcininku, where more than two-thirds of the population are ethnic Poles, turnout for the plebiscite was very low—only about 19%. According to Sajudis, more

Please see BALLOT, 28

Gorbachev to Send Envoy to Baghdad

■ **Diplomacy:** The Soviet president, warning that the allies may exceed U.N. mandate, will try to halt 'largest war in decades.'

By ELIZABETH SHOGREN and NICK B. WILLIAMS Jr.
TIMES STAFF WRITERS

MOSCOW—Soviet President Mikhail S. Gorbachev, warning that allied military actions in the Persian Gulf War threaten to destroy Iraq and thereby "exceed the mandate" set by the United Nations, announced Saturday that he will immediately send an envoy to Baghdad to try to end what he called the "largest war in recent decades."

Gorbachev reiterated his commitment to the U.N. Security Council resolution aimed at liberating Kuwait and expressed concern about the way the U.S.-led coalition in the Persian Gulf War has caused death and damage in Iraq.

"The logic of the military operations, the character of the military actions, threatens to exceed the mandate," Gorbachev said in a statement released by the official news agency Tass. "The number of casualties, including among the civilian population, is growing. Combat operations have already inflicted enormous material damage."

Although British Foreign Secretary Douglas Hurd sought to allay such concern, saying that the allies do not plan to expand their war aims to include the destruction of Iraq or the ouster of Iraqi President Saddam Hussein, both Iran and Pakistan, key nations bordering the Gulf region, tried to increase diplomatic pressure to end the war.

To that end, there were these developments:

• Iranian President Hashemi Rafsanjani met with Sadoun Hammadi, the deputy prime minister of Iraq, who carried a message from President Hussein.

• Immediately after delivering the message, Hammadi traveled to Amman, Jordan, and met with

Please see KREMLIN, A9

Central Coast, Hit Hard by Drought, Hunts for Water

By MILES CORWIN
TIMES STAFF WRITER

Morro Bay is the driest community in the driest region of the state during the driest period in almost 60 years—and every night, residents go to sleep not knowing if there will be enough water to get them through the next day.

The critical time is 7:30 a.m., when a city worker checks the 11 water storage tanks that are automatically refilled each night from nearby wells. If any of the wells, which are at dangerously low levels, dry up and the tanks are not refilled, residents face a crisis.

"If we don't get any rain, the

Please see DROUGHT, A36

J. ALBERT DIAZ / Los Angeles Times

Pallbearers carry coffin of Marine Lance Cpl. Thomas A. Jenkins.

Town Buries Marine With Pride and Sorrow

■ **War:** California hamlet remembers 21-year-old, one of the first combat casualties, as an American hero.

By DEAN E. MURPHY
TIMES STAFF WRITER

COULTERVILLE, Calif.—Thommy Jenkins was a seventh-generation resident of this Sierra foothill town, a rustic old place where young boys shoot guns and fight fires and learn not to cry when it hurts. But there were no such rules on Saturday.

Men with faces of steel broke down and wept in the warm morning sun as they listened to a young woman from nearby Jamestown sing the National Anthem and a bagpiper from Mariposa blow the melancholy notes of "Amazing Grace."

Marine Lance Cpl. Thomas A. Jenkins had left last summer for the Persian Gulf. He came home Saturday, all of 21 years old, in a shiny 18-gauge metal coffin.

Along with a Marine who was buried Saturday in White House, Tex., Jenkins preserved for himself a dark footnote in the young war's history—the first American combat casualties to be brought home and laid to rest.

About 500 people turned out for the service, conducted in a town park that had been decorated with flags usually reserved for the Fourth of July barbecue. There was no talk of "friendly fire" or wasted youth. Jenkins was remembered as an American hero.

"His unwavering devotion to duty, loyalty to country, faithfulness to his comrades at arms, and his love for his family and community are qualities that capture the essence of the spirit of this great nation," a Navy chaplain told the crowd, which came from all over the foothills and was twice as large as the town's population.

"Thomas Allen Jenkins," the chaplain said, addressing the coffin. "Your sacrifice will not be forgotten."

Marines were present to honor their fallen comrade with a formal military funeral, complete with a 21-gun salute and color guard. Jenkins died in a battle that began Jan. 29 near the Saudi-Kuwaiti border. He was one of the first 11 ground fatalities, of which seven are believed to have been killed by fire from a U.S. warplane.

No one here seems to know for sure whether Jenkins was one of those killed by so-called "friendly fire." That question, when raised, only produces hurtful looks.

"It would be kind of nice to know how it happened," said Jenkins'

Please see FUNERAL, A26

Air Traffic Controllers: Some Crave Job's Pressures

■ **Stress:** To succeed, you have to quickly solve three-dimensional puzzles—where mistakes can be fatal.

By BOB BAKER
TIMES LABOR WRITER

Scott Davies, an air traffic controller in the tower at Lindbergh Field in San Diego, doesn't feel as quick at noticing quirks of motion in the sky or on the ground. He believes his skills—the mastery of simultaneously watching, speaking, listening and writing—are deteriorating.

"As your age increases, so does your failure rate," he says soberly. "It's a young man's game."

Scott Davies is 32 years old.

The Feb. 1 ground collision in Los Angeles between a SkyWest commuter plane and a USAir jetliner, in which the tower controller apparently lost track of the position of the planes, left many people wondering why anybody would want to be a controller.

Simple.

With the right set of God-given skills, you can be making up to $70,000 a year by your late 20s, no college degree required. You can have the job security and benefits of the federal civil service. You succeed or fail on your own merits. You're challenged every day by an unpredictable array of three-dimensional puzzles. And you'll receive immediate gratification—by the minute in particularly hectic periods.

Of course, there's the workload, which increases constantly. And your schedule, which changes ev-

Please see CONTROLLER, A32

INSIDE TODAY'S TIMES

Associated Press

Leonard falls to the canvas.

■ **LEONARD LOSES**

Sugar Ray Leonard announced his retirement from boxing after he was knocked down twice and lost a unanimous 12-round decision to Terry Norris. **C1**

■ **WAR STORIES, PHOTOS: A6-26; B1; L3; M1-2,5**

■ **REAGAN PAPERS SHIELDED**

Not one sheet of the 54 million pages of documents in the Ronald Reagan Presidential Library will be available for public scrutiny until years after it opens. **A3**

■ **LOW-INCOME HOUSING**

Some cities have been reluctant to use redevelopment funds for low-income housing. State officials say that is wrong. **A3**

■ **DRUG TEST LAWSUIT**

The union representing LAPD officers is filing a lawsuit challenging the constitutionality of the department's new mandatory drug testing policy. **B1**

WEATHER: Mostly sunny and warm today. Civic Center low/high today: 52/81. Details: B2

■ TOP OF THE NEWS ON A2

U.S. War Plan on Track—but What About the Peace?

■ **Diplomacy:** The Bush Administration seems to have come up with the right questions but no answers.

By ROBIN WRIGHT
TIMES STAFF WRITER

WASHINGTON—The Bush Administration's efforts to spell out its postwar plans in the Persian Gulf have exacerbated, rather than allayed, concerns about its long-term diplomatic strategy for the region, according to government and private experts.

Secretary of State James A. Baker III was expected to provide at least an outline of the Administration's thinking on postwar policy in his two days of testimony before the Senate Foreign Relations Committee last week.

Instead, in contrast to meticulous U.S. military planning for Operation Desert Storm, Baker listed a series of unanswered questions and long-accepted generalities, such as the need to control the flow of arms to the region after the fighting has ended.

"It was appalling," lamented an official specializing in the Middle East. "Six months into this crisis,

NEWS ANALYSIS

and we really should be in the final stages of planning."

Judith Kipper, a Middle East specialist at the Brookings Institution, was equally blunt: "How can you know what your war aims are if you don't know what your peace aims are?"

Indeed, while the Administration

Please see DIPLOMACY, A8

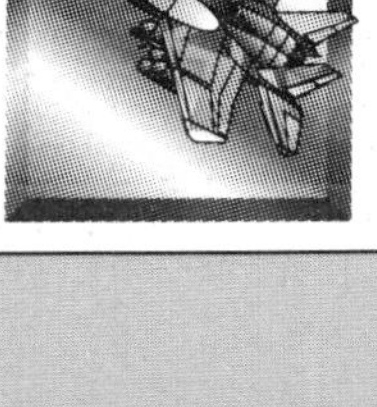

Sorties by the Numbers

The Defense Department defines sortie as "a sudden attack made from a defensive position" and "an operational flight by one aircraft." So when a briefing makes reference to "400 sorties," that number includes all the aircraft that might participate in the bombing runs--not just the bombers. This includes escorts planes, cover patrols, AWACS and refueling craft and reconnaissance flights.

Revenge: Kuwaiti pilot getting ready for bombing mission.

PATRICK DOWNS / Los Angeles Times

DAY IN THE GULF

Military: Secretary of Defense Dick Cheney, after a day of meetings with top U.S. brass in Saudi Arabia, says "the question is when" to begin a ground assault.
■ The U.S. command says that allied forces have conducted 57,000 combat and supply sorties in 24 days. It says 35 key highways and seven important railroad bridges have been attacked to cut supply routes from Baghdad.
■ An unidentified missile exploded within yards of a U.S. frigate in the northern Persian Gulf the previous week, causing slight shrapnel damage to the vessel but no injuries.
■ U.S. officials in Washington disclose that U.S. warplanes for the first time began dropping a huge conventional bomb on Iraqi forces, the BLU-82, a 12,600-pound explosive.
■ Despite poor weather, U.S. and allied pilots continue to pound positions in Kuwait and southern Iraq.
■ U.S. B-52 warplanes loaded with bombs leave an English air base on their first Gulf combat mission from Britain.

Diplomacy: Soviet President Mikhail S. Gorbachev says that military action by allied forces in the Persian Gulf risks exceeding the U.N. mandate to oust Iraq from Kuwait; he is sending a personal envoy to meet Saddam Hussein.
■ Iranian President Hashemi Rafsanjani meets with Sadoun Hammadi, the deputy prime minister of Iraq, who carries a message from Saddam Hussein.

Prisoners of war: Officials say 21 Iraqi soldiers deserted in three days, raising the total of Iraqi POWs to more than 900.

Turkey: Turkish President Turgut Ozal predicts the Gulf War will last only another six weeks and urges business people to gear up for "incredible economic activity."

HIGH "G" BARREL ROLL

One standard maneuver in an air-to-air engagement is called the High "G" Barrel Roll. In this example, the F-16–being pursued by an enemy MIG-23 fighter–suddenly loops around to drop behind the pursuer and attacks.

A DETECTION
Either through electronic or visual means, detection is usually the deciding factor in the outcome of air-to-air combat. The pilot who makes the first identification of an enemy enjoys a tremendous advantage.

B CLOSING IN
Altitude and speed are important factors in this phase; both translate into more options for the pilot who needs to move into a favorable attack position behind the enemy aircraft.

C ATTACK
Radar-guided missiles can be fired at distances from 5 to 62 miles away from the target, heat-seeking missiles are effective from 2 to 11 miles, and mounted guns can be used within 2,000 feet of the enemy plane. About 80% of victims are taken by surprise, but if the attacker fails to hit his target, the encounter moves to the next phase.

D MANEUVER
At this point, the pilot must employ his greatest skills as an aviator and decide whether to attack again or to disengage. Once in a dogfight situation, the advantage enjoyed by the pursuing pilot decreases dramatically.

E EXIT
The attacking pilot normally tries to exit within about 30 seconds to avoid a counterattack.

CLASHES IN THE SKY

Despite the destruction of about 30 Iraqi planes in the air in the Gulf War so far, only a few of the engagements have involved the close and complex aerial combat that characterizes dogfights. Many of the other enemy craft have been downed without the elaborate maneuvering that is associated with Top Gun-type flying. In one of the first dogfights of the war, U.S. F-15 pilot Capt. Steve Tate locked in on an Iraqi F-1 Mirage that was on the tail of another U.S. F-15. He destroyed the Mirage with a radar-guided missile. The top U.S. Air Force dogfighters include both F-15s and F-16s. A look at the five key phases of engaging the enemy in the air:

FIGHTER JARGON
Some of the terms pilots use in communicating with each other:

Bandit: enemy plane
Bingo: out of gas, need to go back
Bogey: unidentified, treated like a "Bandit" until identified as a "Friendly"
Bogey-gathering turn: an attention-getting aerial turn
Dogfight: planes engaged in air-to-air combat at close quarters
Friendly: one of our planes
Fur ball: hectic tangle in air-to-air combat
Joker: low on gas

F-15 EAGLE

F-16 FALCON

IRAQI MIG-23

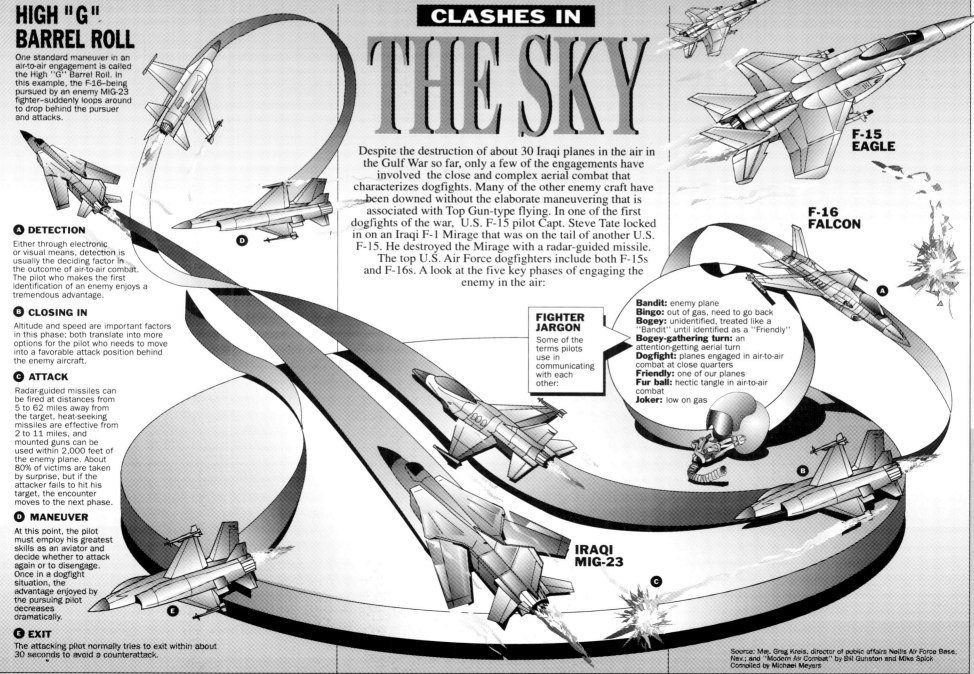

Source: Maj. Greg Kreis, director of public affairs Nellis Air Force Base, Nev.; and "Modern Air Combat" by Bill Gunston and Mike Spick
Compiled by Michael Meyers

JIM OWENS / Los Angeles Times

DAY 26

FEBRUARY 11, 1991

Flying home from Saudi Arabia, Defense Secretary Dick Cheney was ready with his advice to President Bush on when to start the ground war. He seemed extremely relaxed and was looking forward to a refueling stop at Shannon Airport in Ireland. That's where he and his party are regularly treated to a pint of beer or an Irish coffee at the airport bar.

After filing my story by phone, I joined Cheney and others for a quick drink. A freshly poured beer in hand, I glanced toward Cheney and his companions and made a quick toast: "To peace." It was intended to be non-controversial—when do Americans more cherish peace, I reasoned, than in the midst of war? But Cheney maintained a tight smile and stared at the floor, gently declining to acknowledge the toast. He clearly meant to complete his victory before drinking any toast to peace.

—Melissa Healy,
in Shannon, Ireland

Los Angeles Times

CIRCULATION: 1,225,189 DAILY / 1,514,096 SUNDAY

MONDAY, FEBRUARY 11, 1991

COPYRIGHT 1991 / THE TIMES MIRROR COMPANY / CC† / 106 PAGES

DAILY 25¢
DESIGNATED AREAS HIGHER

Cheney to Urge More Bombing Before Land War, Officials Say

Associated Press

Gen. Colin L. Powell, with Secretary of Defense Cheney, speaks to Stealth fighter unit at Saudi air base.

■ **Gulf conflict:** Area remains 'target-rich,' a general declares. U.S. loses first warplane in a week as raids on Iraqi troops in Kuwait are stepped up.

By MELISSA HEALY and J. MICHAEL KENNEDY
TIMES STAFF WRITERS

RIYADH, Saudi Arabia—Defense Secretary Dick Cheney will recommend to President Bush today that he allow warplanes to continue bombing Iraqi troops for a while longer before ordering a ground assault into occupied Kuwait, senior Bush Administration officials said.

The officials, who declined to be identified, made the statement Sunday as military officials said another two to four weeks of allied bombardment in the Persian Gulf may be needed before allied ground troops are sent against Iraqi forces across the Saudi-Kuwaiti border.

At allied military headquarters, Marine Brig. Gen. Richard I. Neal, deputy operations director of the Central Command, told reporters that there is no shortage of Iraqi targets for allied warplanes to hit.

"It remains a target-rich environment," Neal declared.

Cheney, who spent two days in Saudi Arabia being briefed by officers, will take recommendations for the timing of a ground attack to a meeting with Bush at the White House. Cheney said after his briefing that "the question is when" such an attack will be launched.

As Cheney departed for the United States, jets streaked low over the deserts of Iraq and Kuwait and stepped up the tempo of their attack on Iraqi troops in the Kuwaiti theater of operations. Allied pilots flew 2,800 sorties in 24 hours, an increase of 400 flights over previous days. This pushed their total so far to 59,000.

One American plane, a Marine AV-8 Harrier, was shot down in southern Kuwait, officers said. Its pilot was listed as missing and was not immediately identified. The aircraft was the first American warplane lost in combat in more than a week.

Because of the increased bombing, one U.S. officer said, airspace over Iraq and Kuwait got so crowded that traffic was harder to coordinate than in the skies of Los Angeles, Atlanta and Dallas combined. Each target destroyed, a British officer said, means fewer casualties when the ground offensive opens.

He said British planes hit four bridges, a Silkworm missile factory and two hardened aircraft shelters—one with a plane inside.

In addition, American officers said, 75 more Iraqi soldiers surrendered to allied forces. Some brought their AK-47 assault rifles with them, the Americans said. This pushed the total of Iraqi prisoners of war to more than 1,000.

In other developments:

• An Iraqi prisoner of war reportedly told U.S. officials that two POWs, a man and the only American woman to be taken prisoner by

Please see WAR, A6

COLUMN ONE

The Call to Arms That Jolts

■ When reservists are activated, their worlds can be turned upside down. They often must abruptly leave jobs, families, homes and financial obligations.

By DAVID FERRELL
TIMES STAFF WRITER

A happy Dan Chrastil was beginning a new life. The former U.S. Air Force man uprooted his wife and daughter from California, drove them along with three Labrador retrievers, two cats and 9,000 pounds of furniture across the country to his in-laws' home in Greenville, S.C., and went on alone to Virginia to start a new computer job.

For a week in late January he shopped for the family's next address—and he got lucky, really lucky. The place he found was a beautiful ranch house on three acres of forested mountainside. Chrastil signed the lease—$650 a month—and strolled out on the redwood deck, overlooking a snowy ski run below.

"This is fabulous!" he nearly shouted.

Then, while telephoning his wife with the great news, he got the word: His U.S. Air Force reserve unit, stationed at Norton Air Force base in San Bernardino County, was being called to action. The summons turned Chrastil's world upside down, just as it has for about 190,000 American armed forces reserves assigned to active duty.

All of a sudden, Chrastil, 37, is living in a sparse military apartment on the smoggy outskirts of Barstow while his distraught wife and daughter wait on the East Coast, fearing for his future. At the same air base, reservist Greg Darty frets over how he will make the payments on his Gardena home now that he can no longer report to work at the Los Angeles County Probation Department. As a full-time sergeant, he makes less than half what he is accustomed to as a county employee.

Lt. Col. Branden Morad, a soft-spoken dentist who invested $70,000 to open a private practice six weeks ago, fears the venture will be lost. He has laid off his two employees. He also wonders how he will continue to pay for that new $300,000 Mission Viejo home he bought a year ago.

Maj. Jeff Brann, a test pilot for McDonnell Douglas in Long Beach, is expecting to fly out this week in a C-141 cargo plane bound for the Persian Gulf. He has written a will and arranged with a bank to pay the mortgage on his Lakewood home with automatic withdrawals. The concerns of mowing the lawn and putting out the trash each week have given way to fears of Iraqi missiles and chemical weapons and the likelihood of having to transport the dead back to the United States.

Like reservists elsewhere, these members of the 445th Military Airlift Wing are paying a high price in personal hardship for serving in the allied forces in the Persian Gulf conflict. Reservists

Please see RESERVES, A20

Nature May Be Iraq Ally if War Stalls

By DEAN E. MURPHY
TIMES STAFF WRITER

If allied forces are unable to drive Iraqi troops from Kuwait before the end of next month, the forces of nature could weigh into the conflict on the side of Saddam Hussein by bogging down the war with blinding seasonal sandstorms and soaring desert temperatures.

Independent military analysts predict that the onset of spring and summer sandstorms—caused by hot, dry winds known as *shamals*—and gradually rising temperatures could complicate combat in the Arabian Desert and give Hussein an unexpected boost by dragging out the

Please see WEATHER, A8

Crash Raises Questions on Jet Evacuation

By SHERYL STOLBERG
TIMES STAFF WRITER

After the impact, with their jetliner skidding across the runway in flames, the cockpit crew of USAir Flight 1493 fought to bring the hulking aircraft to a halt. Capt. Colin F. Shaw cut the engines. Co-pilot David Kelly attempted to hit the brakes.

The Boeing 737 had just slammed into a small SkyWest commuter plane, crushing it like an aluminum can. In an instant, the SkyWest passengers and crew were dead. But in a twist that may earn the Feb. 1 collision a place in aviation safety textbooks, everyone on board the USAir jet—with the exception of the pilot—was alive when the wreckage came to rest.

They had less than two minutes to escape the dark, smoke-filled plane. Virtually all of those who became victims died while trying to get out.

Although the official cause of the crash may not be determined for weeks, government investigators have already identified a number of significant safety problems—including impediments to evacuation—that arose in the frantic minutes after the collision at Los Angeles International Airport.

The crash has raised questions about the workload in the air traffic control tower, the absence of a functioning ground radar system, and the fact that the pilot and co-pilot of the USAir jet were not able to see the SkyWest commuter—even though its rotating red beacon and navigational lights were illuminated as required.

The most significant questions, federal investigators say, may emerge from their examination of the evacuation of the USAir jet: Should the plane have been fitted with the latest fire-retardant wall and ceiling coverings? Do government aircraft evacuation tests accurately predict how long it will take passengers to escape? Could inflatable emergency chutes be bet-

Please see CRASH, A3

Iraq Rebuffs Iranian Plan for Peace in Gulf

■ **Diplomacy:** Baghdad insists it will not compromise. Hussein, in a broadcast, says U.S. power will not prevail.

By NICK B. WILLIAMS Jr.
TIMES STAFF WRITER

AMMAN, Jordan—Iran's week-old initiative to stop the Persian Gulf War foundered Sunday on continued Iraqi determination to hold on to Kuwait.

Baghdad Radio, Iraq's army newspaper and a traveling member of President Saddam Hussein's inner circle all insisted that the Iraqi regime will make no compromises on its claim to the conquered sheikdom and that it is awaiting a coming ground war with American-led forces.

Hussein himself was heard in a broadcast Sunday for the first time in about two weeks, and he said nothing to indicate that he would be receptive to a peace proposal from any quarter.

"Iraq is not ready to relinquish the role given to it by God," he said in a radio address to his people that the Iraqi News Agency had advertised as a "historic speech."

He said that Iraq would win the war and that "victory will restore to the Iraqis all the requirements for a free and honorable living that they will merit as a reward for their patience and steadfastness," according to the news agency's transcript of the speech.

"All of America's financial, military and economic power is not sufficient to fight the fortress of faith in Iraq," he said.

Asked about the speech, President Bush said in Washington: "I heard what Saddam Hussein said, and I didn't hear him say anything about him getting out of Kuwait. . . . Of course, that's what the whole world is wanting to hear."

Earlier, Baghdad's military newspaper, Al Qadissiyah, said: "The Iraqi people and army led by the unique leader Saddam Hussein will continue to wage the mother of battles to the end."

One of Hussein's aides, Deputy Prime Minister Sadoun Hammadi, arrived in Jordan on Saturday night after delivering Hussein's answer to the Iranian peace initiative in Tehran. He told a press conference here Sunday:

"We have explained to the Iranians that what is currently taking place is unrelated to Kuwait. The question now is a question of the American aggression, a violent and imperialist aggression, which is intended to destroy Iraq and subjugate the region. . . . The issue of Kuwait has been used as a cover for aggression."

The Iranian proposal, which President Hashemi Rafsanjani has not disclosed in detail, met initial enthusiasm in Moscow and some other capitals, although not in Washington. Rafsanjani offered to personally mediate a political solution between Baghdad and Wash-

Please see PEACE, A18

Big Guns Find Targets Thanks to Little Drones

By DOUGLAS FRANTZ
TIMES STAFF WRITER

EASTERN SAUDI ARABIA—When the U.S. battleship Wisconsin began pounding a marina on the Kuwaiti coast, its first 1,900-pound shells landed wide of the target. But infrared pictures from a small aircraft circling the beach allowed the battleship's gunners to adjust their aim.

The correction proved devastating. When the 30-round barrage from the Wisconsin's thundering 16-inch guns ended, the water was littered with the remains of 15 boats that Iraq could have used for raids against the Saudi coastline.

The episode last Thursday night was a graphic demonstration of the tactical effectiveness of remote piloted vehicles, or RPVs, in the Persian Gulf War. These small, unmanned aircraft—they resemble oversize model planes—broadcast live video pictures back to shipboard fire-control officers, who can then pinpoint targets and adjust aim almost instantly.

"To be able to hit a target, you have to be able to know within reason where the target is," said Capt. David S. Bill, the Wisconsin's commanding officer. "With our RPVs and our dominance in the air, we pretty much know exactly where our targets are, and we can spot our rounds precisely."

RPVs also are being used by Marines for aerial patrols along the

Please see DRONES, A7

Colorado River Deal Could Ease State's Drought Woes

■ **Water:** Official is optimistic that California's needs can be met. Dry spell still parches much of the West.

By KEVIN RODERICK
TIMES STAFF WRITER

The hero of California's last drought, the mighty Colorado River, is suffering its own water shortage this time due to a dry spell in the West that has left pockets of five states in Dust Bowl-like conditions and dropped Lake Powell—the river's jewel reservoir—to its lowest level in 15 years.

Nonetheless, California, facing the most widespread water shortage in the Western United States, is negotiating what could be an unprecedented deal that would again tap the Colorado River to ease some painful effects of drought on Southern California cities.

The deal, which needs the approval of the six other Western states that use the river, would not eliminate the need for water rationing. It would avert a worse

■ RELATED STORY: A3

shortage by taking water out of storage to give Southern California more than its yearly share of the river—in practice, withdrawing from savings to cover this year's bills.

"I think we're going to find a way for California's needs to be met this year," said Wayne Cook, executive director of the Upper

Please see DROUGHT, A26

INSIDE TODAY'S TIMES

■ **WAR STORIES, PHOTOS: A5-21; D1; F9**

■ **WARNING FOR GIs**

As ground war looms, experts are warning troops not to let surges of adrenaline in combat drive them to war crimes. **A7**

■ **ARABS ARRESTED**

The Israeli military said it arrested 350 Palestinian activists. Meanwhile, thousands of Arabs headed back to work in Israel as a rigid curfew ended. **A8**

■ **LOOKING FOR LOOPHOLES**

Both Congress and the White House are probing the new budget plan for ways around the spending caps imposed by the deficit-reduction agreement. **A4**

WEATHER: Some morning clouds, otherwise sunny today. Civic Center low/high: 54/79. Details: B2

■ TOP OF THE NEWS ON A2

Associated Press

Voters rejoice in Lithuania.

■ **LITHUANIA'S LONELY ROAD**

Lithuanians' landslide vote in favor of independence may be little more than a cry in the wilderness of a world divided by more far-reaching issues. **A4**

With Fighting, Gulf Letters Take on Sense of Urgency

■ **The front:** Soldiers tell of relief, worry now that war has begun. They seek to lessen fears of loved ones.

The letters come less frequently now that their writers are at war. But slowly, mail sent since the fighting began is trickling home from the sandy bivouacs of Saudi Arabia and the warships patrolling the Persian Gulf.

Whether on colorful stationery or rumpled notebook paper, in a youthful scrawl or the mature hand of men and women, the letters offer telling reflections on the first weeks of combat.

As in earlier correspondence, the pages carry expressions of love for those left behind, of confidence in eventual reunions, of longing for the safety of home. There are still requests for items at once trivial and important—send more cheese spread and a board game. And there are still dashes of humor.

But now there is a deeper urgency than before the shooting began—both in the way the words are written and the way they are read, over and over again. In letters shared with The Times, a young soldier makes contingency plans for a future that could be marred by injury; a mother worries about her young children growing up without her, and an older brother urges a younger one to stay

Please see LETTERS, A9

This story was reported and written by Times staff writers Scott Harris, Kevin Johnson and Nora Zamichow.

heep, normally banned from Kuwait city, were key food source.

PATRICK DOWNS / Los Angeles Times

DAY IN THE GULF

Military: A U.S. briefer in Saudi Arabia says there is no shortage of Iraqi targets for allied planes to hit. He calls it a "target-rich environment."

■ U.S.-led forces destroy a suspension bridge and damage another over the Tigris River that divides Baghdad.

■ A U.S. Harrier jump jet is lost over southern Kuwait and its two crew members are missing, the first loss of a U.S. warplane in combat in a week.

■ American pilots on "Scud patrol" claim likely hits on five Iraqi missile launchers in the previous two days.

Prisoners of war: U.S. military officials report that 75 more Iraqi soldiers have crossed into Saudi Arabia to surrender, bringing the number of Iraqi prisoners of war and deserters to more than 1,000.

Iraq: Iranian President Hashemi Rafsanjani says Iranian peace proposals got little positive response from Iraq.

■ Baghdad Radio and Iraqi officials insist that the Iraqi regime will make no compromise on its claim to the conquered sheikdom and that it is awaiting a ground war with American forces.

■ Saddam Hussein is heard on a broadcast for the first time in two weeks. He says, "Iraq is not ready to relinquish the role given it by God."

■ Deputy Prime Minister Sadoun Hammadi arrives in Jordan and accuses the United States of conducting "a violent and imperialistic aggression, which is intended to destroy Iraq and subjugate the region." He urges all Arab states to sever diplomatic ties with allied countries bombing Iraq.

Soviet Union: Soviet Marshal Sergei F. Akhromeyev predicts that any ground war is likely to take longer than the allies expect. "The Iraqi forces are not the kind of forces that are likely to flee the battlefield from the first blow," he says.

DECOYS

THE ART OF DISGUISE

In an age of ultra high-tech warfare, trickery similar to that used during the Trojan War 3,000 years ago still plays a part in the Persian Gulf War. Decoys–replicas of real equipment or weapons–from the sophisticated to the simplistic are employed. According to U.S. officials, Iraq has successfully deceived allied aircraft on bombing runs. The allied forces, according to at least one U.S. firm, also have a stock of decoys.

IRAQI TRICKS

Among the decoys and disguises believed in use by Saddam Hussein's forces:

■ Wooden tanks covered in tinfoil, to confuse radar into thinking a tank has been hit.

■ Buckets of oil ignited on tank dummies—or even on serviceable tanks—to imply the whole unit is on fire.

■ Decoy missile launchers and anti-aircraft positions made of cardboard, plywood and aluminum.

■ Netting in desert-style camouflage used to hide tanks, airplanes and strategic sites.

■ Italian-made, full-scale copies of tanks and planes—made of metal and fiberglass. Some possess a metallic mass, which would be picked up by radar. If furnished with a crude heat source, they would attract heat-seeking missiles.

■ Decoys packed with drums of oil to simulate exploding materiel.

■ Phony weapons factories or chemical arms plants, created by changing the contours of some non-essential buildings to look suspicious.

■ "Cratered" runways that are really intact, made by painting holes and pits on serviceable airfields to discourage more bombing. Conversely, destroyed runways have been papered over to look intact to encourage unneeded bombing.

■ Mock aircraft shelters and artillery, some of which emit fake electronics signals.

■ Missiles hidden in portable, innocent structures such as mosques.

Agence France-Presse

Workers transport inflatable replica of a Soviet-made T-72 tank, built by French firm as a training device and wartime decoy. Iraqis, who use T-72 tanks, are believed to have similar tank decoys.

MAKING AMERICAN FAKES

From 200 yards away, the vehicles look remarkably real–but on closer inspection, it turns out that the tanks and trucks turned out by TVI in Maryland are actually pictures painted on canvas and stretched over a collapsible metal frame. The components of one decoy, an M-1 tank:

Two- or three-dimensional.

Entire unit fits in a duffel bag.

Weighs about 25 to 50 pounds.

Can be assembled by one person in about three minutes.

Some tank decoys are embedded with panels that heat up when hooked to a portable generator, mimicking

Washington Post

Decoy allied soldier carried past likeness of armored vehicle.

the heat "signature" of a real tank. The aim is to fool a target-seeking infrared system.

A tape recorder and speakers added to the decoy can

disguise the number of personnel.

Tank decoys cost about $3,000 or $4,000, compared to $3 million for the real thing.

THE ALLIED DECOY ARSENAL

Maryland-based TVI produces sophisticated battlefield decoys, but Department of Defense restrictions prevent the firm from talking about its contributions–if any–to the war effort. Among the planned uses for its products:

■ Fake tanks, trucks, and jeeps designed to trick enemy gunners into firing at an erroneous target.

■ Phony equipment to deceive an enemy into believing it's up against an armored division instead of a handful of tanks.

■ Some look-alike tanks are used for target practice in training tank crews.

■ A British firm makes camouflage netting, fake tanks with thermal and radar "silhouettes," which are mostly used as targets for British pilots.

Washington Post

Sample of decoy military vehicle–canvas stretched on a frame–produced by U.S. firm

HISTORY

Dupery in warfare is nothing new. In the Trojan War, legend has it that the Greeks hid soldiers inside a huge wooden horse, which the curious Trojans dragged inside the gates of the city. Later, the Greeks crept out, let in their compatriots, and massacred the people. In World War II, the U.S. created a dummy army unit in southern Britain to misguide the Germans about the Normandy invasion. The Soviets have made great use of disguise, although in one case in the 1970s, a fake submarine was exposed when it bent in half. And decoys were believed widely used in the Iran-Iraq war.

Source: Los Angeles Times, Associated Press, Reuters, Washington Post

PAUL GONZALES / Los Angeles Times

DAY 27

FEBRUARY 12, 1991

There are thousands of neighborhoods like La Verne Avenue across the United States. They go about the rigors and joys of life beyond the glare of TV cameras and the curiosity of total strangers. But the residents of La Verne, a working-class barrio of wood and stucco homes in East Los Angeles, got an eye-opening education about the news media after reporters found out that five young men from a single block of the street were in the Gulf.

Some of the parents received as many as 75 calls a day from reporters, even at 2 a.m. And when the parents decided to disconnect their phones, reporters came unannounced to their doorsteps at the crack of dawn. Treasured roses were trampled, and neighborhood dogs were kicked in the stampede.

Despite all this unwelcome attention, the parents still proved to be parents. A Times reporter, a bachelor who spent many hours chronicling the war's effect on the street, was repeatedly introduced to eligible women from La Verne.

"You should be home with a wife," Rachel Reyes, whose son was abroad the carrier Saratoga in the Gulf, once lectured. "But since you're here so much, we'll find a wife here."

—George Ramos, in Los Angeles

Los Angeles Times

CIRCULATION: 1,225,189 DAILY / 1,514,096 SUNDAY | TUESDAY, FEBRUARY 12, 1991 | COPYRIGHT 1991 / THE TIMES MIRROR COMPANY / CC / 106 PAGES | DAILY 25¢ DESIGNATED AREAS HIGHER

Air Battle to Go On for Awhile, Bush Says; Silent on Land War

Associated Press

An F-117 Stealth fighter sits near its camouflaged hangar as crews prepare the jet for a raid against Iraq.

■ **Strategy:** White House worries that Iraqi reports of civilian casualties could risk support for allies. No decision on timing of ground assault has been made, official indicates.

By JAMES GERSTENZANG
TIMES STAFF WRITER

WASHINGTON—The massive aerial campaign against Iraq "will continue for awhile," President Bush said Monday after conferring with key military advisers just back from Saudi Arabia. But he drew a curtain of silence around the timing of a ground assault.

"We are going to take whatever time is necessary to sort out when a next stage might begin," Bush declared after discussions with Defense Secretary Dick Cheney and Gen. Colin L. Powell, chairman of the Joint Chiefs of Staff.

White House officials, meanwhile, demonstrated concern that Iraqi reports of civilian casualties were finding a sympathetic audience and could risk international support for the allied position. They cited Soviet President Mikhail S. Gorbachev's statement over the weekend that the allied effort may be going too far as evidence of the success of Saddam Hussein's "propaganda and [public relations] battle."

But most attention in Washington was focused Monday on whether—and when—a ground assault may begin. The decision appears to hinge on determining the point at which the three-week-old air assault has achieved maximum results.

Lt. Gen. Thomas W. Kelly, director of operations for the Joint Chiefs of Staff, seemed to signal that there are military reasons to continue the air campaign.

"We have not passed, I think, what's been referred to as a point of diminishing returns in the air campaign," he said.

The bombardment is being used to destroy, one by one, as many of Iraq's 4,200 tanks, 2,800 armored personnel carriers and 3,100 artillery pieces as possible before they can be used against allied forces on the ground.

Kelly said 750 tanks—and possibly twice that number—had been wiped out, along with 600 armored personnel carriers and 650 artillery pieces. He added that 90% of the lines of communication between headquarters in Baghdad and forces in the field have been cut.

Despite the notes of caution coming from the White House and the Pentagon about the timing of a ground war, military officials said over the weekend that the point of "diminishing returns" could be reached by early next week. For the last several days, allied war planes have been flying 750 bombing runs a day against Iraqi troops and armor in Kuwait and southern Iraq.

A White House official, speaking on the condition of anonymity, said that Bush was indicating that no decision on the start of the ground war had been made and that "we're not ready to do anything at this stage."

Please see STRATEGY, A12

COLUMN ONE

Forbidden Words on Campus

■ For decades, denial of free speech has provoked college protests. But now schools are split as student codes limit expression—at least when racial or sexual issues are involved.

By DAVID G. SAVAGE
TIMES STAFF WRITER

WASHINGTON—Campus humor can be a risky business these days.

In December, the editors of the Connector, the student newspaper at the state-run University of Lowell in Massachusetts, published a cartoon mocking what they considered overzealous protesters—both those who favor animal rights and those who favor the death penalty.

One side showed a drawing of an animal rights activist, with the caption: "Some of my best friends are laboratory rats." On the other was a big-bellied death-penalty advocate. "None of his best friends are young, black males," said the legend underneath.

But black students didn't find the cartoon funny and neither did university officials. They promptly charged the student editors with violating the student code by creating a "hostile environment" on campus and other "civil rights" abuses. Eventually, the editors found themselves facing university sanctions that included six months' probation and 30 hours of community service and removal from the newspaper's staff.

For decades, denial of free speech has provoked protests on campus. But these days the complaints are on the other side. Today, many students and liberal academics are urging limits on free speech—at least when the topic involves racial or sexual issues.

From Massachusetts to California, more than 200 colleges and universities—many of them the nation's most elite—have either revised their student codes of conduct or enacted new "speech codes" designed to prevent utterances on race, sex, religion, national origin or sexual preference that might offend some students.

"This is the new liberal *cause celebre*," says UC Berkeley law professor Robert C. Post. "It has forced a wedge between those devoted to civil rights and civil liberties."

University of Colorado Law School Dean Gene Nichol calls himself an "old-fashioned, free speech liberal" but now finds his views unpopular. "It is no longer 'politically correct' to take the free speech position," Nichol laments.

Examples abound:

—The University of Michigan has warned that it will discipline students for comments that "stigmatize or victimize" others based on race, sex, sexual orientation, ancestry or religion—including joke-telling or making fun of someone.

—The University of Wisconsin has revised its code of conduct to prohibit "discriminatory harassment"—including comments that

Please see LANGUAGE, A16

Bilingual Pupils Held to Do Well

By JENNIFER TOTH
TIMES STAFF WRITER

WASHINGTON—Spanish-speaking elementary school children in three different bilingual education programs excelled at the same rate as students in the general student population, according to a report released Monday by the Education Department.

The study, conducted over four years beginning in 1984, tracked about 2,000 Spanish-speaking students from kindergarten through the fourth grade who participated in three types of English-as-second-language programs in California, Texas, Florida, New York and New Jersey.

In one program, students were taught only in Eng-

Please see PUPILS, A18

Court Rejects 'Truth-in-Ads' Ballot Measure

By PHILIP HAGER
TIMES LEGAL AFFAIRS WRITER

SAN FRANCISCO—In the first ruling of its kind, a state appeals court on Monday struck down Proposition 105, a November, 1988, initiative requiring "truth in advertising" for ballot measures, hazardous products, health insurance and other areas.

The panel ruled 3 to 0 that the measure, known as the Public's Right to Know Act, violated a state constitutional provision limiting initiatives to a single subject.

The varying components of the initiative, the court said, did not meet the required standard of being "functionally related" or "reasonably germane" to one another or the objects of a single legislative goal.

The ruling marked the first time a court has invalidated a voter-approved initiative since the single-subject requirement was first applied to initiatives in 1948.

The decision followed other recent rulings in which courts appear to be giving increasingly closer scrutiny to ballot measures. The state Supreme Court, for example, last year struck down a key provision of Proposition 115, the anti-crime initiative, as a constitutional "revision" that could be accomplished only through the Legislature or a constitutional convention.

An attorney for sponsors of the initiative expressed hope that the state Supreme Court would overturn Monday's ruling and reinstate the initiative.

"The measure clearly is bound together by a common thread of requiring affirmative disclosure in advertising," said Jim Rogers of Oakland, representing Consumers United for Reform. "The voters by a solid margin felt more disclosure was needed in these areas."

If the court fails to salvage the initiative, Rogers said, the Legislature will be asked to enact the measure. However, lawmakers had previously rejected similar provi-

Please see BALLOT, A26

Carter Hawley Stores File for Bankruptcy

■ **Retailing:** West's biggest department chain is crippled by debt. Officials plan comeback but obstacles are many.

By STUART SILVERSTEIN
TIMES STAFF WRITER

Carter Hawley Hale Stores, crippled by the junk bond debt it took on four years ago to fend off corporate raiders, on Monday sought Chapter 11 bankruptcy protection from its creditors. It is one of the largest bankruptcy cases ever in California.

The Los Angeles-based company, parent of the Broadway-Southern California and the biggest department store organization in the West, now begins the complicated job of trying to get back on its feet financially.

Carter Hawley's fall, widely expected in recent days as word got out about its cash squeeze, marks another in the rash of retailing bankruptcies since early last year linked to junk bond-financed buy-

■ RELATED STORIES: D1, D5

outs and corporate overhauls. Analysts said Carter Hawley also fell victim to the slump in U.S. retail sales over the past two years and to more aggressive competitors that have taken away some of the company's customers.

Under Chapter 11, a company is shielded from creditors' lawsuits while it keeps operating and tries to work out its financial problems. Even if Carter Hawley reorganizes successfully, it is likely to remain under bankruptcy court supervision for at least 18 months and to emerge, some retailing analysts said, as a smaller company.

Carter Hawley executives said business is continuing as usual at its 88 stores. There are no plans, they said, for store closings or additional layoffs.

In addition to Broadway-Southern California—the Southland's biggest chain of department stores—Carter Hawley owns the

Please see CARTER, A20

The Broadway: Bright History, Uncertain Future

By MARTHA GROVES
TIMES STAFF WRITER

On Feb. 24, 1896, a British-born merchant named Arthur Letts opened the Broadway Department Store in a 40-by-100-foot building at 4th Street and Broadway, then the outskirts of Los Angeles. The business made Letts so rich that he bought up a huge chunk of ranch-land for $2 million and called it Holmby Hills. His son later built what is today the Playboy Mansion.

During the boom years after World War II, a visionary young Broadway president, Edward W. Carter, followed the freeway map and devised the idea of a suburban department store chain.

Please see BROADWAY, A21

Pilots Report Hundreds of Targets Left

By JOHN BALZAR
TIMES STAFF WRITER

RIYADH, Saudi Arabia—The desert sun broke through cloudy skies over the Persian Gulf on Monday, opening a devastating window through which allied air forces rained bombs on Iraq and occupied Kuwait with intensified ferocity, military officials said.

Pilots flying F-16 fighter-bombers against Iraqi positions said they were still seeing hundreds of military targets, indicating that a great deal more softening up is needed before ground troops from the multinational force launch an assault against dug-in Iraqi troops.

"I know everybody wants to get it over with and get home," said Lt. Col. Billy Diehl, 41, of Tampa, Fla. "But the longer they give us, the better it's going to be for our guys when they roll into Kuwait."

Marine Brig. Gen. Richard I. Neal said that civilian casualties could not be avoided in air strikes on the key port city of Basra, but he suggested that Iraq may nonetheless be faking some bomb damage. Neal said the Iraqis are leading television crews to areas of the city that were destroyed in the eight-year Iran-Iraq War and claiming the destruction was the result of allied bombing in the Gulf War.

Located in southeast Iraq and described as a key staging area for supplies heading south into Kuwait, Basra is "a military town in the truest sense of the word," said Neal. "There are a lot of military targets woven into the fabric of Basra itself."

Please see WAR, A6

Rookie Becomes First L.A. Policewoman Slain on Job

■ **Crime:** Her partner shoots to death the gunman, an illegal immigrant. Gates lashes out at the INS.

By LESLIE BERGER and STEPHEN BRAUN
TIMES STAFF WRITERS

A rookie Los Angeles policewoman was shot to death in Sun Valley early Monday morning by an assailant who in turn was fatally wounded during a brief gun battle with the officer's partner. Tina

■ RELATED STORIES: A3

Kerbrat, 34, was the department's first female officer killed in the line of duty.

Kerbrat, who stepped out of her black-and-white cruiser shortly after midnight to question two men drinking beer in public, had no

Please see SLAYING, A27

Tina Kerbrat

INSIDE TODAY'S TIMES

■ **WAR STORIES, PHOTOS: A5-12; E1; F1; World Report**

■ **LAND MINES OF GAS?**

A U.S. military official said land mines planted by Iraq in southern Kuwait may contain nerve and mustard gases. **A6**

■ **POSTWAR PERILS**

The entire Arab moral and political order could become a casualty of the fight to free Kuwait. Some predict a region-wide civil war. **In World Report**

■ **DOW CLIMBS 71**

The Dow Jones industrial average followed last week's gains with a 2.5% advance, fueled by investor fears of being left out of a big rally. **D1**

Associated Press

Mandelas arrive at court.

■ **MANDELA TRIAL DELAY**

The kidnaping trial of Winnie Mandela was abruptly postponed after the prosecution announced that one of its key witnesses had been abducted. **A4**

WEATHER: Variable high cloudiness. Civic Center low/high today: 54/81. Details: C9

■ TOP OF THE NEWS ON A2

Allied Planes Stacked Up for Runs on Iraqi Targets

■ **Air war:** Pilots must must wait their turn to deliver bombs. The already furious pace is expected to intensify.

By DAVID LAMB
TIMES STAFF WRITER

EASTERN SAUDI ARABIA—So many allied planes are stacked up over Kuwait and southern Iran that pilots often must wait 10 minutes or more for their turn to bomb, and air traffic controllers are worried about the possibility of midair collisions, U.S. commanders said Monday.

"It's mind-boggling how well orchestrated it [the air campaign] is," Marine Brig. Gen. Richard I. Neal said. "It's a busy place up there. It makes LAX [Los Angeles International Airport], Dallas and Atlanta combined look like kids on the block."

Allied planes from nine nations are averaging more than 600 combat missions a day over the Rhode-Island-sized chunk of desert where Iraq has concentrated its troops. That figure is likely to increase as the U.S.-led coalition intensifies its attacks in preparation for an expected ground offensive.

On Monday, U.S. planes flew 750 combat sorties against the Iraqi positions, including 200 against the Republican Guard, U.S. officials said. Altogether, good weather enabled the allied air forces to fly 2,900 sorties on Monday, making it one of the busiest days of the almost four-week-old war.

Those 2,900 missions mean about 5,800 takeoffs and landings, or about triple the 1,800 to 2,000

Please see SORTIES, A7

Westland Lynx 3

The Westland Lynx 3 is a British helicopter that has played a key role in the allied effort to neutralize the Iraqi naval presence in the northern Gulf. In a recent engagement, a Lynx from the destroyer Gloucester fired two surface-skimming Sea Skua missiles to knock out an Iraqi TNC-45 patrol boat believed armed with as many as four Exocet anti-ship missiles. The Lynx 3 is also used in ground warfare, fitted with antitank weapons.

JUAN THOMASSIE / Los Angeles Times

White House: President Bush says the massive aerial campaign "will continue for a while."
- He draws a curtain of silence around the timing of the ground assault.
- Officials say Iraqi claims that thousands of civilians have been killed are inflated propaganda and that civilian casualties have not "been very extensive."

Military: Officials say the round-the-clock bombing has inflicted such great casualties on front-line Iraqi troops that they have been forced to regroup.
- Improving weather over the Persian Gulf allows the air campaign to intensify.
- More than 140 Iraqi warplanes that have fled to safety in Iran were flown by inexperienced pilots and lack the maintenance support to pose a serious threat, reports say.
- About 300 guerrillas from Afghanistan arrive for deployment in the war zone.
- One pilot says hunting down from the air "every last tank is virtually impossible. There's just so much stuff out there."

Missiles: Six people are slightly injured when a Scud hits a residential area in Tel Aviv.
- Two people are slightly injured in a Scud attack on Riyadh; a Patriot destroys the Scud, but debris hits the ground.
- It is the 30th Scud fired toward Saudi Arabia and the 16th aimed at Riyadh.

Iraq: The Iraqi government announces that all 17-year-olds will be conscripted into the army.
- Baghdad Radio says Iraq would not accept a cease-fire "before total victory is achieved."
- Soviet envoy Yevgeny M. Primakov arrives in Baghdad for talks with Saddam Hussein.

Terrorism: U.S. officials report that about 100 terrorism incidents have been aimed at American interests and those of its allies since the war began.

Environment: Massive oil pollution in the Persian Gulf has devastated a once-vital fishing industry and a key source of food.

Oil fires turned Kuwait's days into nights; this was about 5 p.m.

PATRICK DOWNS / Los Angeles Times

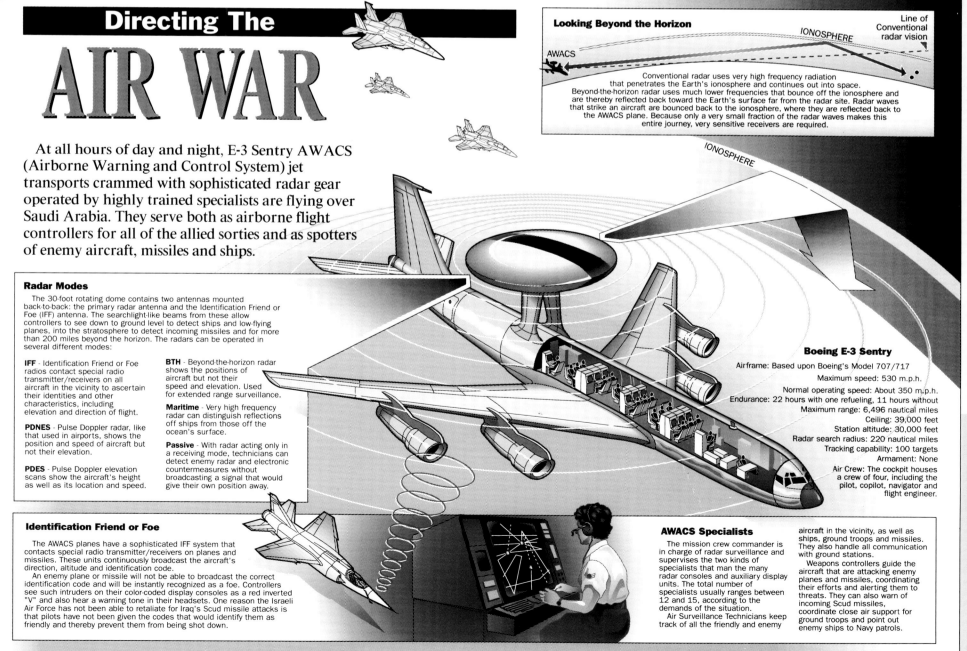

Directing The
AIR WAR

At all hours of day and night, E-3 Sentry AWACS (Airborne Warning and Control System) jet transports crammed with sophisticated radar gear operated by highly trained specialists are flying over Saudi Arabia. They serve both as airborne flight controllers for all of the allied sorties and as spotters of enemy aircraft, missiles and ships.

Looking Beyond the Horizon

Conventional radar uses very high frequency radiation that penetrates the Earth's ionosphere and continues out into space. Beyond-the-horizon radar uses much lower frequencies that bounce off the ionosphere and are thereby reflected back toward the Earth's surface far from the radar site. Radar waves that strike an aircraft are bounced back to the ionosphere, where they are reflected back to the AWACS plane. Because only a very small fraction of the radar waves makes this entire journey, very sensitive receivers are required.

Radar Modes

The 30-foot rotating dome contains two antennas mounted back-to-back: the primary radar antenna and the Identification Friend or Foe (IFF) antenna. The searchlight-like beams from these allow controllers to see down to ground level to detect ships and low-flying planes, into the stratosphere to detect incoming missiles and for more than 200 miles beyond the horizon. The radars can be operated in several different modes:

IFF - Identification Friend or Foe radios contact special radio transmitter/receivers on all aircraft in the vicinity to ascertain their identities and other characteristics, including elevation and direction of flight.

PDNES - Pulse Doppler radar, like that used in airports, shows the position and speed of aircraft but not their elevation.

PDES - Pulse Doppler elevation scans show the aircraft's height as well as its location and speed.

BTH - Beyond-the-horizon radar shows the positions of aircraft but not their speed and elevation. Used for extended range surveillance.

Maritime - Very high frequency radar can distinguish reflections off ships from those off the ocean's surface.

Passive - With radar acting only in a receiving mode, technicians can detect enemy radar and electronic countermeasures without broadcasting a signal that would give their own position away.

Boeing E-3 Sentry

Airframe: Based upon Boeing's Model 707/717

Maximum speed: 530 m.p.h.

Normal operating speed: About 350 m.p.h.

Endurance: 22 hours with one refueling, 11 hours without

Maximum range: 6,496 nautical miles

Ceiling: 39,000 feet

Station altitude: 30,000 feet

Radar search radius: 220 nautical miles

Tracking capability: 100 targets

Armament: None

Air Crew: The cockpit houses a crew of four, including the pilot, copilot, navigator and flight engineer.

Identification Friend or Foe

The AWACS planes have a sophisticated IFF system that contacts special radio transmitter/receivers on planes and missiles. These units continuously broadcast the aircraft's direction, altitude and identification code.

An enemy plane or missile will not be able to broadcast the correct identification code and will be instantly recognized as a foe. Controllers see such intruders on their color-coded display consoles as a red inverted "V" and also hear a warning tone in their headsets. One reason the Israeli Air Force has not been able to retaliate for Iraq's Scud missile attacks is that pilots have not been given the codes that would identify them as friendly and thereby prevent them from being shot down.

AWACS Specialists

The mission crew commander is in charge of radar surveillance and supervises the two kinds of specialists that man the many radar consoles and auxiliary display units. The total number of specialists usually ranges between 12 and 15, according to the demands of the situation.

Air Surveillance Technicians keep track of all the friendly and enemy aircraft in the vicinity, as well as ships, ground troops and missiles. They also handle all communication with ground stations.

Weapons controllers guide the aircraft that are attacking enemy planes and missiles, coordinating their efforts and alerting them to threats. They can also warn of incoming Scud missiles, coordinate close air support for ground troops and point out enemy ships to Navy patrols.

MICHAEL HALL / Los Angeles Times

DAY 28

FEBRUARY 13, 1991

My 5-year-old son Nick was on the other end of the telephone, asking hard questions through the crackling line.

"Why are they dropping bombs on you, Daddy?" he asked anxiously. He had been slipping into the family room and turning on the news himself, seeing things on television that my wife and I had decided he should not see.

Earlier, he had asked my wife about the videotapes of the "smart bombs" destroying buildings in Baghdad. Catherine assured him there were no people in the buildings.

"How do they know there are no people?" he asked.

—Douglas Frantz,
in Dhahran, Saudi Arabia

Los Angeles Times

CIRCULATION:
1,225,189 DAILY / 1,514,096 SUNDAY

WEDNESDAY, FEBRUARY 13, 1991

COPYRIGHT 1991 THE TIMES MIRROR COMPANY CC† 104 PAGES

DAILY 50¢
DESIGNATED AREAS HIGHER

COLUMN ONE

Iraq Arms: Big Help From U.S.

■ Technology was sold with approval—and encouragement—from the Commerce Department but often over Defense officials' objections.

By HENRY WEINSTEIN and WILLIAM C. REMPEL
TIMES STAFF WRITERS

WASHINGTON—The Commerce Department approved millions of dollars in high-technology exports to an Iraqi research center after a classified Pentagon report warned on Nov. 6, 1986, that the nine-acre complex north of Baghdad was secretly developing missiles and weapons of mass destruction, according to government sources familiar with the report.

In a letter the next day, the Pentagon objected to issuance of an export license to a New Jersey computer maker, citing the "high likelihood" that American computer equipment would be applied to secret Iraqi military research at tne complex called Saad 16.

Nonetheless, Commerce approved the sale "without condition."

In fact, Commerce approved $1.5 billion in exports to Iraq of American high technology and other equipment with potential military uses from 1985 to 1990—some of it shipped directly to such Iraqi agencies as the Ministry of Defense, Atomic Energy Commission and air force. Although most of the U S. government's Iraqi trade documents remain secret, the story emerging from glimpses of Baghdad's massive weapons procurement program reveals a U.S. export control system that seemed to be more sieve than barrier.

At Saad 16 alone, U.S. firms provided such products as: advanced computers, electronic instruments and high-grade graphics

First of two parts.

terminals for rocket testing and analysis; flight simulators and test equipment; microwave communications gear; radar maintenance equipment, and computer mapping systems.

The United States was not alone. In the years leading up to Iraq's invasion of Kuwait, other countries now aligned against Saddam Hussein also sold him billions of dollars in arms and the technology to bolster his military manufacturing capabilities. Until mid-1988, Iraq was at war with Iran, a conflict in which the United States and others tilted toward Baghdad.

If America and its allies in the Gulf want to see who turned Iraq into the world's fourth-largest military machine, "just look in the mirror," said Stephen D. Bryen, a former deputy assistant secretary of defense in charge of the Pentagon's technology security office.

But the reflected image is particularly painful for Americans, who now bear the heaviest burden of coalition forces in the Gulf War. Ironically, America also has been a leading critic of the spread of unconventional arms.

"We can't go on solving every

Please see ARMS, A7

Associated Press

U.S. Marines scramble toward helicopters during a troop deployment exercise in the Saudi desert.

Front-Line Enemy Troops Get Biggest Pounding of War

■ **Gulf conflict:** 50 oil fires are burning in Kuwait. Four mobile Scud launchers reportedly destroyed by U.S. jets.

By J. MICHAEL KENNEDY and MELISSA HEALY
TIMES STAFF WRITERS

RIYADH, Saudi Arabia—Allied forces battered Iraqi front-line positions along the Kuwaiti border from the land, air and sea Tuesday in the most extensive assault on forward positions by the multinational coalition since the beginning of the war.

Military officials also reported that more than 50 fires—possibly started by Iraqi sabotage or allied bombing—are burning at oil storage and related facilities throughout Kuwait.

Rear Adm. John (Mike) McConnell, director of intelligence for the Joint Chiefs of Staff, said the fires pose "a difficult problem" because they can obscure the gun sights of allied warplanes and reduce visibility.

In addition, American pilots reported knocking out four mobile Scud missile launchers, as well as a convoy of up to 50 vehicles in southern Kuwait.

Marine Brig. Gen. Richard I. Neal said at a press briefing here that the assault on the Iraqi front lines was launched by both the Saudis and the Americans against targets in southeastern Kuwait.

"We thought there was a good opportunity to take them on," said Neal, who described the targets as dug-in tanks, artillery and armored personnel carriers.

In other developments:

• Iraqi President Saddam Hussein appeared to open the way to dialogue on the crisis, announcing that he is willing to discuss "a peaceful, political, equitable and honorable solution" to the war. But he did not mention the key demand spelled out in United Nations resolutions—withdrawal from Kuwait—and American officials stressed that the demand has not changed.

• Allied air strikes reportedly demolished the headquarters of an Iraqi ministry headed by Hussein's

Please see WAR, A6

Bush Assails Iraqi 'Myths and Falsehoods'

By JAMES GERSTENZANG and NORMAN KEMPSTER
TIMES STAFF WRITERS

WASHINGTON—President Bush complained angrily on Tuesday of Baghdad's "one-sided propaganda machine cranking out a lot of myths and falsehoods" as concern mounted that public opinion may be influenced by reports of civilian casualties and urban damage.

"I don't think the world is buying it," Bush asserted.

Still, the Administration's moves to quickly counter Iraqi President Saddam Hussein's allegations reflect concern that public support could be jeopardized if the charges go unchallenged.

"It doesn't look serious yet, but you don't want to wake up in two weeks and find out it's run away from you and public support has evaporated. Is it a serious problem now? No. Would it be if he's allowed a free hand? Yes," a senior White House official said.

The official, speaking on the condition of anonymity, described Bush's remarks as a calculated "preemptive strike on a nascent problem that could get out of

Please see BUSH, A10

MWD Slashes Water Supplies to Agencies 31%

By JENIFER WARREN
TIMES STAFF WRITER

Faced with record low rainfall and no prospects for relief, the Metropolitan Water District declared a water emergency Tuesday and imposed a 31% cut in the amount of water it delivers to 27 agencies from Ventura to San Diego.

The 46-1 vote by the MWD's board of directors—a move widely dreaded but not unexpected—marked the most severe water cutback in the giant agency's history and signaled the increasing severity of the drought, now in its fifth year.

While conceding that the nearly one-third cut is dramatic and could prompt mandatory water rationing in many areas, MWD officials warned that harsher reductions may lie ahead for Southern California if dry conditions persist.

Many communities already are preparing for that day. The Los Angeles City Council is expected to approve a mandatory rationing plan next week, ordering a 10% reduction from the 1986 water use level on March 1 and a 15% reduction on May 1.

"If we can't get water from the heavens then we have to create it and the way we create it is to conserve," said director S. Dell Scott, who represents Los Angeles. "The message is conservation, and I have always believed that the guy who turns on the tap has got to pay the bill."

The board also agreed to allocate $30 million from the MWD's reserve fund to buy water from other sources around the state. Rice farmers in the Sacramento area may be willing to take some land out of production this year and sell their water to thirsty cities.

Realizing that public awareness

Please see MWD, A24

Bakker 45-Year Term Is Upset; Verdict Upheld

By DAVID G. SAVAGE
TIMES STAFF WRITER

WASHINGTON—A federal appeals court Tuesday overturned TV evangelist Jim Bakker's 45-year prison sentence because it said the judge at his trial had displayed a personal religious bias against the defrocked founder of the PTL ministry.

But the court upheld Bakker's 24-count conviction for conspiring to defraud his followers.

Under federal sentencing guidelines now in effect, Bakker would have received a 10- to 12-year prison sentence for his crimes. But on Oct. 24, 1989, U.S. District Judge

Please see BAKKER, A21

Suburban Life: Urban Ills Are Catching Up

By FAYE FIORE
TIMES STAFF WRITER

It's 4 a.m. and the caravan is already leaving Moreno Valley in Riverside County for the long, long drive to work. Six men in a van pool have learned to sleep sitting up. One woman puts in a cassette tape and practices self-hypnosis. They thank God that when the sun comes up it will not be in their eyes.

These are people who spend an average of three hours a day on the road while their children spend as much as 12 hours in day care. The drive home is usually worse than the drive in. But what waits for them is their reward—the house, typically a salmon stucco spread

Please see SUBURBS, A22

Missing Twain Manuscript Is Believed Found

By TRACY WILKINSON
TIMES STAFF WRITER

A century-old, handwritten manuscript purported to be a portion of the original text of Mark Twain's "Huckleberry Finn" has been found in a trunk in the attic of a 62-year-old librarian's home in Hollywood.

The 600-page manuscript is in the hands of the auction firm Sotheby's of New York, according to a Sotheby's spokeswoman in Beverly Hills who declined to release details, including who authenticated the document, pending an announcement today. Sotheby's has told Twain scholars in California and elsewhere that it is convinced that the manuscript is genuine.

Two Twain scholars in California who have been consulted on the manuscript but who have not examined it themselves believe it to be a section of the book that mysteriously disappeared in the late 19th Century.

"There is no question in my mind what it is," said one California-based expert who has studied Twain's letters, notebooks and manuscripts for two decades and who was given a detailed description of the find.

"This is the most important manuscript the man ever wrote," he added.

Another Twain scholar, John Seelye of the University of Florida, said he had not yet heard of the find, but speculated that it would be difficult to fake such a document because of the large volume of Twain handwriting samples that are available.

According to the Hollywood woman, the manuscript has rested for nearly 30 years in one of six trunks containing the papers of her grandfather, a Buffalo, N.Y., lawyer known to have corresponded

Please see FINN, A3

Islam's Holy Month Could Add to Political Problems

By KIM MURPHY
TIMES STAFF WRITER

DHAHRAN, Saudi Arabia—It was the 10th day of the Muslim holy fasting month of Ramadan in 1973, but Egyptian President Anwar Sadat already had decreed that his soldiers would be exempt from the fast as they prepared to launch a daring drive across the Suez Canal into the Sinai Desert.

The president was more than a little discomfited when he strode into the operations room before the first strike and found his senior commanders fasting. The operation, he sternly warned, needed their full concentration.

"I noticed they were very embarrassed," Sadat wrote in his autobiography. "So I ordered some tea for myself and lit my pipe—whereupon they began to smoke and order tea."

Now, nearly two decades later, the Arab world again finds itself at war. Once again, the rising of the crescent moon over the desert March 17 marks the debut of the holiest month in Islam—and a whole new set of potential political complications for the crisis in the Persian Gulf.

For Arab soldiers assembled in the Saudi desert, the Muslim tradition of shunning food, drink and tobacco during daylight hours will, as before, be optional. Saudi pilots will be required to eat and make up the fast after the war. But in any case, allied commanders are determined to press ahead with the campaign to dislodge Iraqi troops from Kuwait.

"Our religion teaches us to pray," said Col. Ahmed Robayan, spokesman for the Joint Arab Forces, "and also to fight."

Please see RAMADAN, A15

Widespread Monetary Plot to Oust Gorbachev Alleged

■ **Soviets:** Prime minister says coup was foiled. Skeptics see story as justification for unpopular currency seizure.

By ELIZABETH SHOGREN
TIMES STAFF WRITER

MOSCOW—The Soviet Union's new prime minister alleged Tuesday that his government had foiled a devilish multinational scheme to oust President Mikhail S. Gorbachev with an economic coup.

"Someone simply decided that President Gorbachev became a nuisance and had to be removed," Prime Minister Valentin S. Pavlov told the trade union newspaper Trud in an interview that seemed to come straight from the pages of a spy novel.- "Soviet banks and several private banks in Austria, Switzerland and Canada have all been involved in this."

Pavlov, 53, who was finance minister before being appointed prime minister by Gorbachev last month, said that huge amounts of Soviet money in large bills were being held in foreign banks, ready to be injected into the Soviet economy to cause massive inflation and economic ruin.

"There is nothing original about that plan," Pavlov said. "Such operations were conducted 'in many regions of the world when someone wanted to change the political system or overthrow unwanted political leaders."

But the coup attempt was prevented just in time by Gorbachev's highly unpopular decree three weeks ago withdrawing from circulation all 50- and 100-ruble

Please see SOVIETS, A18

INSIDE TODAY'S TIMES

■ **WAR STORIES, PHOTOS: A5-15; E1**

■ **SAUDIS STRAPPED?**
Oil-rich Saudi Arabia is facing short-term financial problems after spending billions on the Persian Gulf War, a Western diplomat said. **A9**

■ **2 DISSIDENTS GET PRISON**
China sentenced two influential dissidents to 13 years in prison for their roles in the Tian An Men Square protests. **A4**

■ **EUROPE TREATY CONFLICT**
Conflicting views of how weapons such as tanks are counted may jeopardize the European forces treaty talks between the U.S. and Soviet Union. **A19**

WEATHER: Morning low clouds, otherwise mostly sunny. Civic Center low/high: 55/73. Details: B5

■ TOP OF THE NEWS ON A2

Reuters

Jordanians rallying for Iraq

■ **PEACE TALKS HINTED**
Iraq's Saddam Hussein appeared to open the way for dialogue to settle the Gulf War, saying he is willing to discuss an "equitable" solution to the conflict. **A9**

Nation's Ammo Industry Suffering Despite the War

■ **Defense:** Pentagon cutbacks bite deeply into the business. Some worry about future capability.

By RALPH VARTABEDIAN
TIMES STAFF WRITER

Ammunition plants were the arsenals of democracy in World War II, but they play an anonymous and beleaguered part in the Persian Gulf War.

Along a grimy industrial strip in the Los Angeles suburb of Vernon, NI Industries, the nation's biggest producer of large-caliber ammunition, is cutting manufacturing capacity, laying off workers and auctioning machinery. A "For Sale" sign adorns one facility.

The problems confronting NI are symptomatic of the entire American ordnance industry, which is suffering through one of its worst slumps in history—despite the hot war in the Gulf. It is a low profit, heavy industry in an age when high technology wins the accolades.

Critics contend the industry's problems reflect broader Pentagon mismanagement of the nation's defense industrial base. Although contractors around the nation are pleading for a government policy of retaining key defense industry capabilities, the Pentagon wants to rely on the marketplace and "let the chips fall where they may," critics say.

Ammunition orders by the Army have dropped from about $4 billion annually during the mid-1980s to about $1 billion in the fiscal 1992 budget. Less than $1 billion will be

Please see AMMO, A13

GIANT VIPER
The Giant Viper, a British-made mine-clearing device, is designed to help allied troops cross Iraqi fortifications during a land assault. The device has never been tested in war.
How it works:
1 The Viper uses rockets to launch a 700-foot hose filled with plastic explosives over enemy minefields.
2 When the hose lands the charge is detonated, setting off the mines.
3 If the Viper works according to design, a 20-foot-wide path is cleared, allowing soldiers and vehicles to pass through.

DAY IN THE GULF

Military: Allied forces batter Saddam Hussein's troops from the air, sea and land in the most extensive attack on the Iraqi front lines so far in the war.

■ Air strikes reportedly destroy the headquarters of the Iraqi government ministry headed by Hussein's cousin.

■ Officials also believe that the incessant bombing has prevented Iraqi troops from taking care of their war machinery.

■ The Pentagon acknowledges that it is following Hussein by intelligence means, saying "we know he moves frequently" from place to place to avoid harm.

■ Allied planes hit Scud missile launchers in western Iraq, and pilots report that four may have been destroyed.

Environment: Military officials report more than 50 fires at oil facilities throughout Kuwait.

White House: President Bush complains angrily of Baghdad's "one-sided propaganda machine cranking out a lot of myths and falsehoods" as concern mounts that public opinion may be influenced by reports of civilian casualties and urban damage.

Iraq: Saddam Hussein appears to open the way to dialogue, announcing that he is willing to discuss "a peaceful, political, equitable and honorable solution" to the war. But he does not mention the key demand spelled out in U.N. resolutions: withdrawal from Kuwait.

Washington: The Pentagon invokes a Civil War-era law called the Feed and Forage Act, which permits the military to spend money during wartime beyond levels appropriated by Congress.

■ It plans to request a supplemental appropriation beyond the $69 billion that Congress approved for spending on "operations and maintenance" of U.S. troops and equipment.

TIMING A GROUND ATTACK

Several non-military factors may influence any decision on starting a land war. For instance, a moonless or half-moon night and high tide would be favorable elements for an amphibious landing. However, religious holidays such as the Muslim holy month of Ramadan might delay action by either side. But Muslim scholars also consider the 10th day of Ramadan to be a favorable day for attack because Mohammed, the prophet, emerged victorious from battle on that day.

Los Angeles Times

Where Iraq Got Its

WEAPONS

Throughout the 1980s, weapons and technology poured into Iraq from all over the industrialized world. Nations that enabled Saddam Hussein to create his war machine now find themselves among the allies doing battle with it.

In much of the past decade, Iraq—brimming with petrodollars and at war with Iran, an archenemy of the United States—found willing arms merchants wherever it turned.

The greatest amount of weaponry in Iraq's arsenal came from the Soviet Union. But other Western nations like France, Italy and West Germany sold weapons of every type. Even more disturbing is the export of U.S. high technology to Iraq that apparently occurred between 1985 and 1990, a whopping $1.5 billion worth. That technology is believed to have contributed to the development of Saad-16, a military-research complex that was part of Hussein's goal of building a home-grown weapons industry.

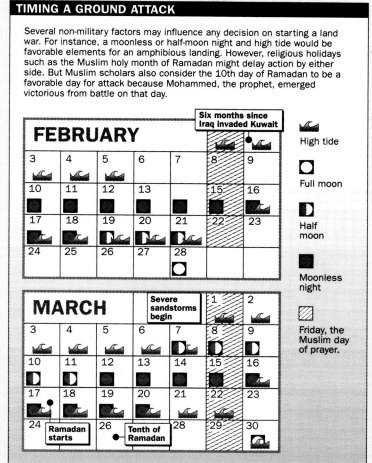

Mirage France

M-46 FG Soviet Union

GHN-45 Austria/South Africa

ASTROS II Brazil

SAAD-16: A Case Study

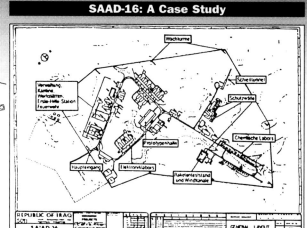

Saad-16, located in mountains near Mosul (north of Baghdad), was a military research and development center with 82 laboratories. Plans for the plant, above, were drawn up in Austria and show buildings and laboratories labeled in German.

Work in those labs was related to such areas as missile propellants, ballistics, chemical and nuclear weapons, composite metals, electronics, lasers and aircraft construction.

The United States provided much of the high-tech equipment that made the research possible. After repeated allied bombing attacks, U.S. government sources say, Saad-16 has been reduced to rubble.

A Sample of Products Exported to Saad-16 From U.S. Sources:

■ Electronic instruments for rocket testing
■ Computer graphic terminals for rocket research
■ Hybrid analog-digital computer for missile R&D
■ Flight test lab equipment
■ Microwave technology
■ Radar maintenance equipment
■ Computer mapping system

Some Services Exported to Saad-16 From Various Foreign Sources:

■ Plans and blueprints for the plant—Austria
■ Rocket motor nozzles—France
■ Gyroscopes for missile guidance systems—France
■ Machine tools and precision lathes—Britain
■ Chemical weapons lab facilities—Italy
■ Plant construction—West Germany
■ Non-echoing room for missile research and development—West Germany
■ Wind tunnel—West Germany
■ Chemical weapons test equipment—West Germany
■ Computers for simulating nuclear explosions—West Germany

BUILDING IRAQ'S ARSENAL: Countries and the Weapons They Sold

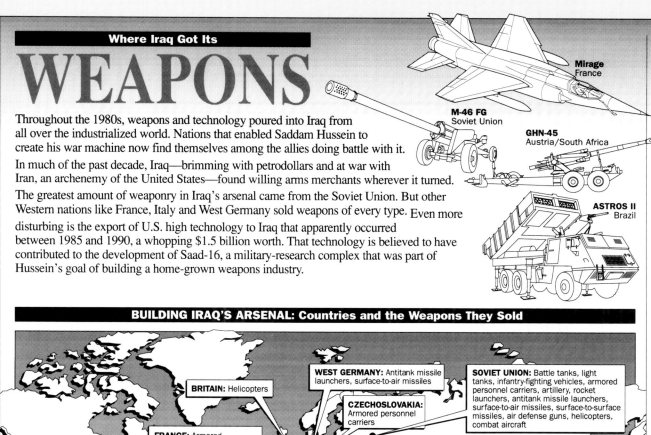

BRITAIN: Helicopters

WEST GERMANY: Antitank missile launchers, surface-to-air missiles

CZECHOSLOVAKIA: Armored personnel carriers

SOVIET UNION: Battle tanks, light tanks, infantry-fighting vehicles, armored personnel carriers, artillery, rocket launchers, antitank missile launchers, surface-to-air missiles, surface-to-surface missiles, air defense guns, helicopters, combat aircraft

FRANCE: Armored personnel carriers, artillery, antitank missile launchers, surface-to-air missiles, helicopters, combat aircraft

HUNGARY: Armored personnel carriers

UNITED STATES: Helicopters

AUSTRIA: Artillery

SPAIN: Helicopters, combat aircraft

ITALY: Artillery, helicopters

CHINA: Battle tanks, combat aircraft, armored personnel carriers

YUGOSLAVIA: Artillery

EGYPT: Antitank missile launchers

BRAZIL: Armored personnel carriers, rocket launchers

SOUTH AFRICA: Artillery

Sources: Various U.S. government agencies; Middle East Defense News

JUAN THOMASSIE / Los Angeles Times

DAY 29

FEBRUARY 14, 1991

Last time I wore a flak jacket with the U.S. Armed Forces, women were something to dream about, or someone to change your battle dressing at the field hospital in Da Nang. So, it was with curiosity that I headed to the front with the new unisex Army. How had women changed the coarse, manly realm of the warrior?

Answer: Not much, really.

The rich, ear-stinging profanity remains: "You [deleted], you really [deleted], didn't you, you [deleted]!" joked a woman pilot to a male colleague.

And likewise, a soldier's simple daydreams: "When I get home," a woman captain said offhandedly, "the second thing I'm going to do is start on a six-pack of beer and order a pizza."

And finally, two soldiers sat close together, sharing an old lament: "It's all right," the young man told the young woman, patting her on the back. "The mail's just screwed up. I'm sure the guy loves you more than anything and is writing every day. You'll see. . . . Otherwise, we'll get back to the world and bash his face in."

—John Balzar,
with the Army Airborne Corps

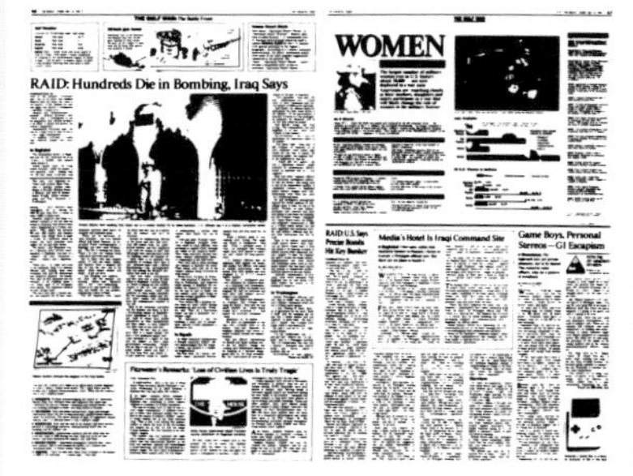

RAID: Hundreds Die in Bombing, Iraq Says
WOMEN
RAID: U.S. Says Precise Bombs Hit Key Bunker
Media's Hotel Is Iraqi Command Site
Game Boys, Personal Stereos—GI Escapism

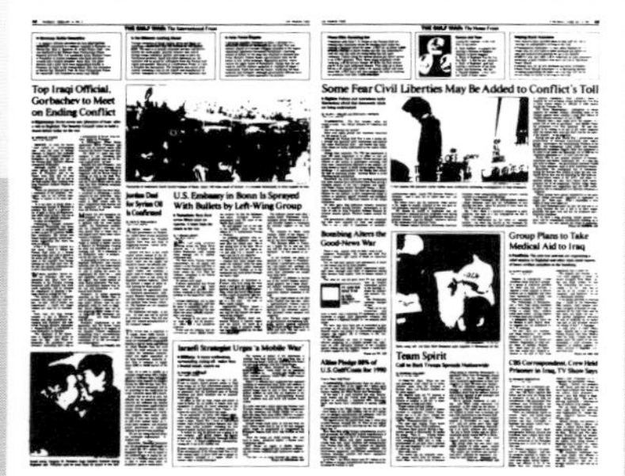

Top Iraqi Official, Gorbachev to Meet on Ending Conflict
Some Fear Civil Liberties May Be Added to Conflict's Toll

Los Angeles Times

CIRCULATION: 1,225,189 DAILY / 1,514,096 SUNDAY | THURSDAY, FEBRUARY 14, 1991 | DAILY 25¢ DESIGNATED AREAS HIGHER

COPYRIGHT 1991 / THE TIMES MIRROR COMPANY / CC† / 182 PAGES

Raid Kills Hundreds, Iraq Says

Claims Civilian Shelter Hit; U.S. Calls It Military Site

■ **Gulf War:** Hussein regime puts the death toll in attack on Baghdad at 500. Americans say it was precision bombing of a command-and-control bunker.

From Times Staff Writers

Hundreds of Iraqi civilians, many of them women and children, were reported killed Wednesday when two American bombs scored precision nighttime hits on what Baghdad called a residential bomb shelter and the United States called an Iraqi command-and-control bunker.

The bombs pierced the structure's hardened concrete shell and exploded inside. The Baghdad government said 500 people were killed. Videotape taken by Western journalists showed bodies, almost all of them charred or mutilated, being carried out of what had become a huge concrete grave.

Scores of corpses lined the pavement when the journalists arrived, under escort by officials from Iraq's Information Ministry. The facility was burning. Iraqi men beat their chests, sobbing uncontrollably and wailing, *"Allahu akbar!"*—God is great—as they searched desperately through the smoke and rubble for more victims.

The videotape showed that the facility was marked as a "Shelter" in English and Arabic, and Iraqi officials called the attack a crime. But at allied command headquarters in Riyadh, Saudi Arabia, U.S. Marine Brig. Gen. Richard I. Neal said American intelligence had identified the structure as a command-and-communications bunker. He said U.S. warplanes would not have attacked had the Americans known that the facility contained civilians.

In addition to these apparently contradictory explanations for the deaths, experts at Jane's military publications, considered to be an authoritative source of information, said the facility may have been a two-tiered structure—"a dual-purpose location," according to Paul Beaver, publisher of Jane's Defense Weekly.

"Civil on top, military underneath. . . ," he said.

In Washington, Marlin Fitzwater, President Bush's spokesman, suggested to reporters at the White House that Iraqi President Saddam Hussein had deliberately placed civilians at the site to prevent attacks or to reap propaganda points if allied bombing produced civilian casualties.

"We don't know why civilians

Please see RAID, A6

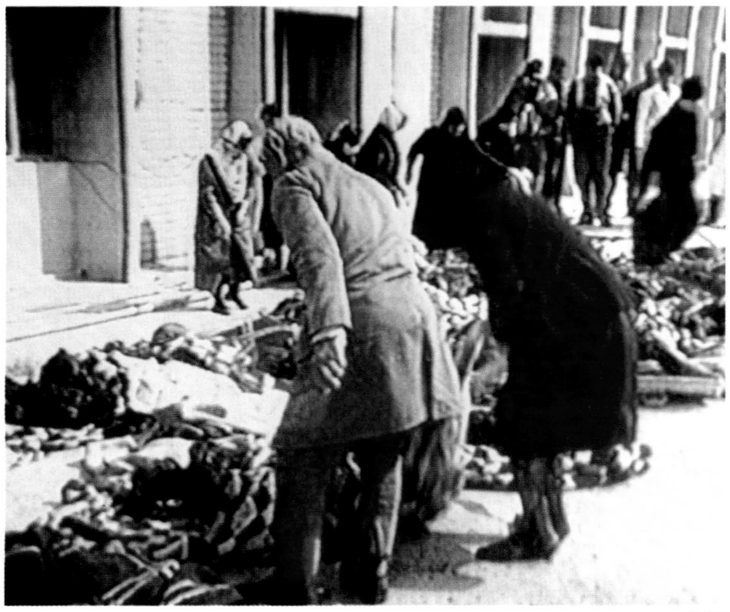

Reuters

Iraqis try to identify those killed during an allied bombing raid on Baghdad in which Iraq says 500 died.

Saudis Sharply Cut Estimates of 2 Oil Slicks

By KIM MURPHY
TIMES STAFF WRITER

DHAHRAN, Saudi Arabia—Saudi officials are dramatically reducing their estimates of the size of two giant oil slicks in the Persian Gulf, saying it now appears likely that 3 million barrels or less has been dumped from oil facilities and tankers off the coast of Kuwait.

Although authorities initially announced that the spills could reach 11 million barrels—the largest in history—a U.S. Coast Guard spokesman said Wednesday that the Saudi Meteorology and Environmental Protection Agency now believes the slicks range from 500,000 barrels to 3

Please see SLICKS, A13

COLUMN ONE

A Species No Longer in Danger

■ Interior Secretary Manuel Lujan Jr. has survived controversial gaffes and a host of skeptics. Now, he must confront a thorny environmental agenda.

By RUDY ABRAMSON
TIMES STAFF WRITER

WASHINGTON—Over the past two years, Secretary of the Interior Manuel Lujan Jr. may have amassed the most interesting job-performance record in the Cabinet:

Early in his term, he jolted staff aides by reacting with shock and indignation to news that off-road recreational vehicle racing in the California desert at Barstow was damaging the habitat of the endangered desert tortoise—only realizing later that ORVs actually were motorcycles, not full-sized Winnebago trailers and campers.

On two or three occasions, he has set environmentalists' blood boiling by wondering aloud why the United States must protect every subspecies of endangered species. Many are leery as well because they believe that he almost unfailingly will side against the majority of environmentalists on issues such as offshore oil drilling policies, old-growth timber, mining claims, irrigation contracts or grazing fees.

And knowledgeable sources confirm informally that an alert park ranger once caught him about to scratch his initials blithely in some of the ancient Indian carvings in one of the treasured petroglyphs areas outside Albuquerque.

Now, Lujan is heading into his third year of running the federal bureaucracy that controls a third of all the land in America, protects its wildlife, provides services for a million American Indians and hosts 265 million visitors a year to national parks, landmarks and monuments—and he is finding himself the Rodney Dangerfield of the Bush Administration: He don't get no respect.

His only salvation has been comparison with former Interior Secretary James G. Watt, whom some environmentalists regard as the *worst* secretary of the Interior in memory.

Even after he had been in office only a few months, Washington pundits began laying odds that Lujan would be the first Cabinet member to pack his bags. Rumors wafted about that he would be replaced by Sen. James A. McClure (R-Ida.).

Despite all the furor, however,

Please see LUJAN, A24

Bush Proposes $105-Billion Highway Plan

By ROBERT L. JACKSON
TIMES STAFF WRITER

WASHINGTON—The Bush Administration on Wednesday unveiled a five-year, $105-billion program to expand and improve the nation's deteriorating bridges and highways and to encourage construction of urban mass transit systems.

Billed as one of President Bush's major domestic initiatives, the proposed legislation would earmark $87 billion for highways and bridges, $16.3 billion for urban mass transit and $2.3 billion to promote safety programs, with a particular focus on combatting drunk driving.

A little more than $22 billion of the highway funds would be set aside in a special program that would allow states to spend their share of the money on transit systems, if they wish.

"The future of America's transportation rests on the new foundation that we're laying today," Bush said at a White House ceremony attended by Transportation Secretary Samuel K. Skinner. He called the proposed legislation, known as the Surface Transportation Assistance Act, the "first step on a long road that lies ahead."

Please see HIGHWAYS, A22

U.S. Forced to Defend Basic Targeting Goals

■ **Policy:** Bush set broad guidelines and left details to the generals. Their approach may be a problem.

By MELISSA HEALY
and MARK FINEMAN
TIMES STAFF WRITERS

NEWS ANALYSIS

WASHINGTON—With the U.S. bombing of Iraqi civilians huddled in a Baghdad structure, President Bush is beginning to confront the unhappy consequences of a strategy for conducting the Gulf War that was carefully designed to avoid the pitfalls of Vietnam—a strategy that, for the first month of the conflict, was judged highly successful.

Instead of imposing endless political constraints on the military, or directly involving himself in battlefield decisions as Lyndon B. Johnson and some other ill-starred predecessors did, Bush decided at the outset to lay down broad policy goals and then turn over fighting the war to the professionals.

"I don't think you would ever see George Bush going over targeting charts. He's not involved in that kind of micro-management," White House Press Secretary Marlin Fitzwater said in an interview last month, declaring that Bush is leaving "military tactics, logistics and analysis" to his generals.

"Never again will our armed forces be sent out to do a job with one hand tied behind their back," Bush himself told an audience of military reserve officers less than a week after the war began.

But now, while results from the battlefield have generally been positive, the relentless aerial assault on Iraq—with its horrifying images of civilian casualties—is beginning to reveal that Bush's approach may also bring with it increasingly difficult political and foreign policy problems.

"They're now in a new and trickier phase of the air war," said a Western analyst who is still based in the Persian Gulf region. "They're taking out secondary and tertiary targets—all with military justification, but most of them packed in close to civilian areas." And, U.S. officials acknowledge, some of those targets have had both civilian and military uses.

That point was driven home Wednesday as television screens across the country and around the world carried pictures of mangled civilian victims being removed from the ruins of the bunker outside Baghdad. U.S. officials insist that the bunker was a military

Please see TARGETS, A10

Images of Death Give Iraq a Boost in Propaganda War

By THOMAS B. ROSENSTIEL
TIMES STAFF WRITER

NEWS ANALYSIS

WASHINGTON—In the shadow war of the Persian Gulf—the battle for public sentiment—Iraq on Wednesday delivered the equivalent of a fuel-air explosive through the images of charred Iraqi women and children.

The pictures—men weeping, women stricken with grief, bodies mangled after an American bombing attack—led news broadcasts from Moscow to Tel Aviv to Paris to Amman, Jordan.

American officials could counter with only explanations in English, and some diagrams of the facility they said was really a military command center. In propaganda terms, such a response pales before the vivid telecasts from Baghdad.

The video images also landed in a context of believability, propaganda experts said, coming at a time when several world leaders already were expressing worries about Iraqi civilian casualties. In the Soviet Union, for instance, where President Mikhail S. Gorbachev spoke out earlier this week about civilian casualties, state-run television noted that innocent women and children are increasingly the victims of the American bombs.

"The worst fear of the Gulf War appears to have occurred in Baghdad," French anchorman Patrick Poivre d'Avor somberly announced to open the evening

Please see DEATH, A12

Library Apparently Will Get Twain Manuscript

■ **Literature:** Scholars hail 'Huckleberry Finn' discovery, saying it will shed light on the masterpiece.

By TRACY WILKINSON
and JANE HALL
TIMES STAFF WRITERS

A long-lost "Huckleberry Finn" manuscript discovered stashed away in a Hollywood attic appears to be destined for the Buffalo, N.Y., public library to which Mark Twain donated it more than a century ago.

Sotheby's of New York, in announcing the rare find Wednesday, said there are no plans to auction the priceless manuscript, and the Hollywood librarian who made the discovery said she probably will return the handwritten papers to Buffalo.

The move apparently defuses a brewing dispute over the rightful ownership of the manuscript, found in a musty old trunk, where it had been stored for at least 30 years.

The discovery sent excited tremors through the American literary world. Scholars said the manuscript will shed important light on Mark Twain's thoughts and intentions as he wrote "The Adventures of Huckleberry Finn," widely considered to be his masterpiece and one of the greatest works of American fiction.

"To find the actual handwritten text is just beyond anyone's dream," said noted Twain scholar Robert Hirst, general editor of the Mark Twain Papers Project at UC Berkeley.

The manuscript is a handwritten

Please see TWAIN, A40

INSIDE TODAY'S TIMES

■ **WAR STORIES, PHOTOS: A5-16; E1**

■ **HUSSEIN ACCUSED**

The U.S. accused Iraqi President Saddam Hussein of endangering relics by parking planes near an ancient temple. **A5**

■ **MISSION TO MOSCOW**

Iraq will send its foreign minister to Moscow this weekend for talks with President Mikhail S. Gorbachev on ending the Gulf War, Kremlin officials said. **A8**

■ **RIVERS OF FIRE**

Gasoline from a wrecked tanker truck ignited, creating fiery rivers that destroyed homes and forced evacuations in Carmichael, near Sacramento. **A3**

WEATHER: Scattered high clouds today and Friday. Civic Center low/high today: 54/78. Details: B5

■ TOP OF THE NEWS ON A2

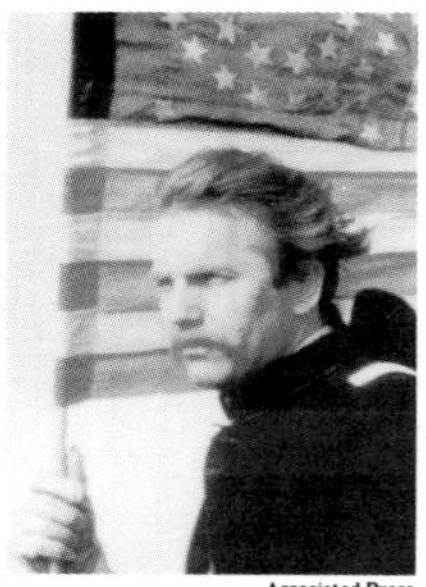

Associated Press

Costner in "Wolves."

■ **OSCAR NOMINEES**

Kevin Costner's "Dances With Wolves" led the 1990 Academy Award nominations with 12. "Dick Tracy" and "Godfather III" tied with seven apiece. **F1**

40 Die in Crush of Pilgrims Honoring Ash Wednesday

■ **Religion:** Some report pushing among the visitors to a Mexican town; others blame an attempted robbery.

By MARJORIE MILLER
TIMES STAFF WRITER

CHALMA, Mexico—At least 40 Indian pilgrims, most of them elderly women and children, were trampled to death in a crush of worshipers headed through a narrow marketplace to church for this town's Ash Wednesday celebration.

Another 35 people were injured in the crowd of thousands, which panicked for reasons that authorities did not clearly understand. Emergency workers said some people reported that the market grew too crowded in the early morning and that pilgrims at the back began to push; others told them that the melee may have been provoked by hoodlums trying to rob the worshipers.

"Something happened at the back of the crowd that set off the avalanche of people," said Eladio Briano Guerrero, one of the first paramedics on the scene. "Some of the people fell and others just ran over them."

Candida Arenillas, 51, was leaving the colonial church shortly before 8 a.m. when pandemonium broke out among the masses bearing flowers, incense and images of the Virgin of Guadalupe.

"We were leaving the church and suddenly someone yelled: 'Go back, go back!'" Arenillas said through tears. "All around me

Please see PILGRIMS, A21

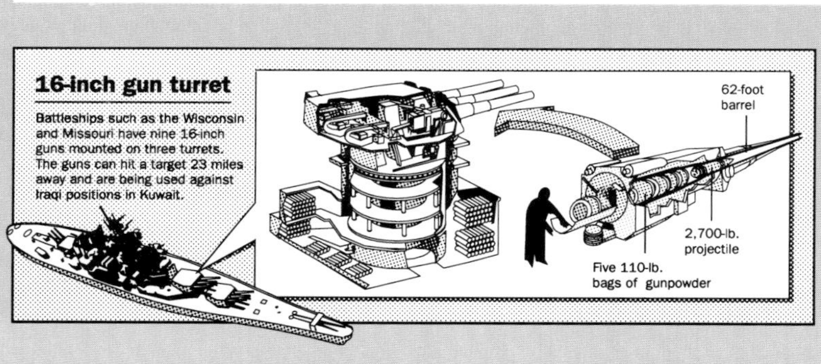

16-inch gun turret
Battleships such as the Wisconsin and Missouri have nine 16-inch guns mounted on three turrets. The guns can hit a target 23 miles away and are being used against Iraqi positions in Kuwait.
62-foot barrel
2,700-lb. projectile
Five 110-lb. bags of gunpowder

DAY IN THE GULF

Iraq: Two missiles pierced the entrance of an underground shelter in Baghdad and exploded inside, killing 500 people, the Baghdad government says. The United States says the bombed shelter was a bunker used as a military command-and-control center.

■ The scene of carnage is videotaped by Western journalists.

■ White House Press Secretary Marlin Fitzwater suggests that Saddam Hussein deliberately placed civilians at the site to prevent attacks or to score propaganda points if allied bombing produced casualties.

■ A Pentagon official also says the Iraqi military is operating a key command center from the basement of the Rashid Hotel, which houses Western reporters and other foreigners in Baghdad.

Military: The allies fly 2,600 sorties in 24 hours, bringing the total to 67,000 since the war began.

Pentagon: Defense Secretary Dick Cheney accuses Saddam Hussein of endangering one of the world's most precious archeological treasures, the ziggurat at Ur, by parking two warplanes near the ruins.

Diplomacy: Soviet envoy Yevgeny M. Primakov returns to Moscow and reports ''glimmers of hope for a resolution to the problem.''

■ Iraqi Foreign Minister Tarik Aziz discloses plans to meet with President Mikhail S. Gorbachev in Moscow.

■ Germany's foreign minister announces that Syria is ready to recognize Israel's right to exist as part of a postwar Middle East settlement.

■ The U.N. Security Council votes to debate the Persian Gulf crisis in a formal meeting closed to the press and the public.

Jordan: The Amman government obtains Syrian petroleum supplies to replace war-disrupted imports from Iraq and keep its staggering economy fueled.

THREATENED ARCHEOLOGICAL SITE

Temple, or ziggurat, at Ur was built about 2100 BC. It is regarded as one of the most spectacular archeological relics in Mesopotamia. United States says Iraq is stashing MIG-21 warplanes, such as the one below, at the site to avoid bombing.

Associated Press

DON CLEMENT / Los Angeles Times

WOMEN
IN THE GULF FORCE

Army Capt. Linda L. Bray, who led troops in a gun battle during the Panama invasion.

The largest number of military women ever in U.S. history — about 30,000 — are now deployed in a war zone. Americans are watching closely as their mothers, daughters and sisters participate in a war that will likely change the role of women in the military forever.

Army Spec. Tanya Miller in the Gulf

As It Stands

Since 1973 — when the draft was ended and replaced by the all-volunteer force — the number of women in the U.S. military has increased dramatically. No longer relegated to their traditional roles of nurse and secretary, military women today fill positions ranging from military police to Air Force pilots. They make up 6% of the 500,000-plus soldiers in the Gulf and 11% of the 2.1 million U.S. forces worldwide.

The Combat Question:

By law, American military women are excluded from combat in all branches of the service, which some argue effectively denies them higher pay and promotions.

•Women are not allowed in attack or fighter aircraft, or in artillery or infantry units, aboard subs or surface combat ships (except on temporary duty).

•The Pentagon says that 88% of all military job classifications are open to women, which amounts to about 56% of the total number of military assignments.

•But today's battlefield scenarios often do not distinguish between frontline combat assignments and rear support ones. Women in active war zones in certain jobs — for example, on supply lines — could become combatants, rendering existing job classifications artificial.

Panama Invasion, a Turning Point:

During the 1989 invasion of Panama, U.S. military women came under fire alongside their male comrades both on the ground and in the air.

•A female Army captain led her fellow military police into a gun battle with the Panama Defense Forces.

•Two female helicopter pilots, on noncombat aircraft, came under gunfire.

•Overall, 600 of the 24,500 troops in the invasion were women.

MIAs and POWs:

If U.S. military women become war casualties or POWs, it will not be a first:

•In the Gulf War, Army Spec. Melissa Rathbun-Nealy is listed as MIA.

•Eight American women died during the Vietnam War; one was killed by "hostile fire."

•During World War II, about 70 servicewomen were captured and interned as POWs by the Germans and Japanese.

Jobs Available

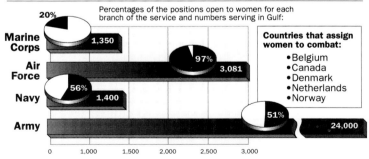

Percentages of the positions open to women for each branch of the service and numbers serving in Gulf:

Branch	% open	number in Gulf
Marine Corps	20%	1,350
Air Force	97%	3,081
Navy	56%	1,400
Army	51%	24,000

Countries that assign women to combat:
•Belgium
•Canada
•Denmark
•Netherlands
•Norway

All U.S. Women in Uniform

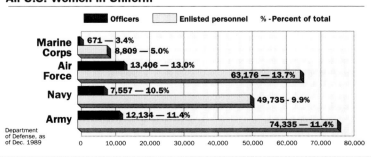

Officers ■   Enlisted personnel □   % - Percent of total

Branch	Officers	Enlisted personnel
Marine Corps	671 — 3.4%	8,809 — 5.0%
Air Force	13,406 — 13.0%	63,176 — 13.7%
Navy	7,557 — 10.5%	49,735 — 9.9%
Army	12,134 — 11.4%	74,335 — 11.4%

Department of Defense, as of Dec. 1989

Chronology

1901: Army establishes auxiliary of nurses. In 1908, Navy installs similar auxiliary.

World War I: Navy and Marines enlist women to fill clerical positions. After war, women are demobilized.

World War II: Army's WAC (Women's Army Corps), Navy's WAVES (Women Accepted for Voluntary Emergency Service), and parallel organizations established in other branches. Some women serve in war zones, but away from front. Overall, women make up 2.3% of military.

1948: Legislation is enacted banning women from combat. Ceiling of 2% placed on number of women in each branch. Army gives WAC permanent status.

1950: Congress temporarily lifts 2% limit during Korean War.

1967: 2% limit permanently removed, along with many restrictions on grades to which female officers could rise. Percentage of women in the military is still less than 1%.

1968: First major increase in number of women in services since 1953. About 7,500 women serve in Vietnam, but none in combat assignments.

1970: Two women promoted to rank of general, first time in U.S. history.

1972: Five-year program established to increase number of women in non-medical fields.

1975: Military academies ordered to open their doors to women.

1978: Women's Army Corps is dismantled, integrates its personnel into regular Army.

1983: Female pilots fly support helicopters during Grenada invasion.

1986: Four women co-pilot non-combat planes during Libyan mission.

1989: Army Capt. Linda Bray, leading 30 military police, engages in combat in Panama.

1990: Army rejects Pentagon advisory group's suggestion that women be allowed combat assignments on experimental basis.

1991: 30,000 women make up 6% of U.S. forces in Gulf War.

Sources: Congressional Quarterly's Research Reports, and the Department of Defense.

ANDERS RAMBERG / Los Angeles Times

DAY 30

FEBRUARY 15, 1991

Not long after the air war began, Edward Said, a Columbia University professor of English and the most prominent Palestinian spokesman in America, was deep in gloom. During a broad-ranging talk on the implications of the war, he kept returning to a disturbing theme: the destruction of Baghdad.

"This is a very difficult thing for Arabs to accept and understand," he said. "Baghdad is a symbol historically of such high civilization. It is a terrifying thing to consider this punishment from the air and this city in particular—something that few in the West would understand."

—Josh Getlin, in New York

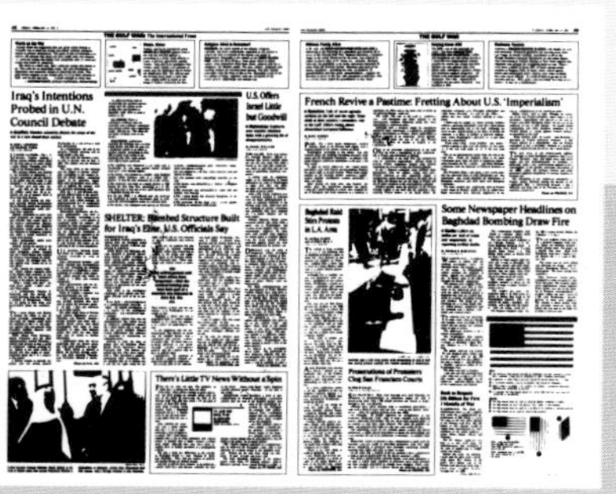

Los Angeles Times

CIRCULATION: 1,225,189 DAILY / 1,514,096 SUNDAY | FRIDAY, FEBRUARY 15, 1991 | DAILY 25¢ DESIGNATED AREAS HIGHER

COPYRIGHT 1991 / THE TIMES MIRROR COMPANY / CC† / 148 PAGES

COLUMN ONE

Pollution Is Price of Asia Boom

■ Unprecedented industrial growth in the '80s brought widespread damage to the water and air. Governments have been slow to deal with the threat.

By CHARLES P. WALLACE
TIMES STAFF WRITER

TAIPEI, Taiwan—More than 3,000 demonstrators gathered outside government offices in December in one of the largest protests Taiwan has witnessed in recent years. The protesters were not demanding political reforms, but freedom from pollution in a nation where all 45 rivers are contaminated with toxic wastes and water pumped from an underground well is so polluted it can be set on fire with a match.

In China, air pollution is so bad that the entire city of Benxi regularly disappears from satellite photographs because of the dense smoke billowing from the city's factories. Two years ago, an estimated 250,000 people died in Shanghai from an epidemic of hepatitis caused by contaminated drinking water.

In Thailand, vehicle exhaust has grown so noxious in Bangkok, where 10,000 new motor vehicles hit the streets every month, that a recent study showed newborn babies have more than twice as much lead in their blood as infants in the United States, raising the prospect of a generation with learning disabilities. A single huge coal-fired power complex being completed near the northern city of Chiang Mai is expected to emit more carbon dioxide than western Germany.

The 1980s were a decade of unprecedented economic boom for Asia, producing double-digit growth in a crescent of fast-developing countries stretching from Taiwan to Indonesia. Belatedly, the people of these countries are realizing that the boom also carried an enormous price in terms of damage to the environment.

"Asia is where America was in the 1950s—there is now widespread air pollution, water pollution, dumping of industrial waste and deforestation," said Erik Scarsborough, an environmental economist who recently did a pilot study on the region for the United Nations. "Environmental degradation is taking place so fast that it may restrain economic development."

Although environmental damage is not as great as in the worst areas of Eastern Europe, many more people are at risk from Asia's pollution. Rapid population growth and continued migration to the cities threaten to intensify environmental pressures.

Asian governments have been slow to act, in part because the top priority is frequently to promote industrial growth and boost employment. "The attractive thing about industry is that it can absorb labor where agriculture cannot. There are only so many guys you can put in a rice field," said Rezaul

Please see ASIA, A22

Training for Assault

Associated Press

Marines in Saudi Arabia charge barbed wire barriers in preparation for a ground war against Iraq. Allies reported 1,300 Iraqi tanks destroyed and said naval power in Gulf has been increased.

Higher Iraqi Tank Losses Reported; 4th Carrier in Gulf

■ **Attack options:** The United States will consider announcing bomb targets in advance to avoid killing civilians, general says after Baghdad air raid.

By MELISSA HEALY and J. MICHAEL KENNEDY, TIMES STAFF WRITERS

WASHINGTON—The United States declared significant gains Thursday in destroying Iraqi tanks and combat vehicles as an additional U.S. aircraft carrier moved into the Persian Gulf in preparation for a possible Marine amphibious landing soon.

The carrier America joined three other U.S. aircraft carriers in the narrow Gulf waterway, filling out a core naval force that would provide air support for an 18,000-man amphibious assault that could take place in days rather than weeks, defense officials said.

The officials, who asked to remain anonymous, said the battleship Missouri began shelling the coast of occupied Kuwait this week for the second time in the war. Minesweepers prepared to clear Kuwaiti coastal waters of planted explosives that could disrupt a Marine landing, one Pentagon official said.

As indications of coming ground action mounted, military officials in Washington and at Central Command headquarters in Riyadh, Saudi Arabia, said intense allied air attacks were taking a high toll on Iraqi armor, seen as the chief impediment to a ground assault from Saudi Arabia into occupied Kuwait.

Lt. Gen. Thomas W. Kelly, operations director for the Joint Chiefs of Staff at the Pentagon, called the status of Iraqi ground troops "precarious" and said that up to 45% of all Iraqi combat vehicles are now believed to be destroyed or disabled.

Military officials have said a ground offensive can begin when half of Iraq's combat vehicles and other equipment are destroyed. In recent days, however, they said an attack might come sooner if allied warplanes isolate Iraqi ground units from each other and from Baghdad.

In other developments:

• The United States said it will consider announcing bomb targets in advance to avoid killing civilians. Marine Brig. Gen. Richard I. Neal said this is "one of many options that we're exploring."

Please see WAR, A6

Iraqis Vow Revenge; Other Arabs Outraged

By MARK FINEMAN and NICK B. WILLIAMS Jr.
TIMES STAFF WRITERS

AMMAN, Jordan—Iraq vowed "severe revenge" Thursday for the U.S. air strike that reportedly left hundreds of civilians dead in a Baghdad structure, as outrage over the attack spread to the streets of neighboring Jordan and elsewhere in the Arab world.

Chanting "Death to America!" and "Saddam, Saddam, use the chemicals, Saddam!" hundreds of demonstrators splattered the wall of the U.S. Embassy in Amman with red paint and planted Iraqi flags outside it during a demonstration that began

Please see ARABS, A12

UC Regents Hike Fees a Record $650 to $2,274

■ **Education:** In the austerity move, they also voted to curb enrollment growth and cut 1,000 non-teaching jobs.

By LARRY GORDON
TIMES EDUCATION WRITER

SAN FRANCISCO—Heeding warnings about a state financial emergency, the University of California's Board of Regents voted overwhelmingly Thursday for a $650 fee increase, the largest in the 123-year history of UC, and moved to limit enrollment growth through tougher entrance standards.

The regents also voted to cut 1,000 non-teaching jobs, mainly through attrition and early retirements, and to delay by a couple of years planning for a new campus in the San Joaquin Valley.

Basic UC undergraduate fees for state residents will rise 40%, to $2,274 next year, not including room, board or activities charges, which differ among the nine campuses. UC officials pledged that extra financial aid will cover the fee increase for the needy, but student leaders angrily contended that many students still will suffer.

"There are no easy answers" to the budget shortfall, said Susan Polan, president of the UC Student Assn., a lobbying group that represents 166,500 students. "But we are disappointed that a fee increase of 40% is even an option, considering the devastating impact it will have on the university and the families of California."

She urged the regents to maintain the state policy of limiting annual fee increases to 10% and she called for investigation of other ways to save money, such as increasing professors' teaching loads and cutting back on agricultural research.

However, UC officials clearly wanted to protect the system's reputation for research and scholarship, even if fee increases and enrollment limits are the result. "The University of California may

Please see REGENTS, A36

U.S. Water for State Farmers Is Cut by 75%

By CARL INGRAM
and MARIA La GANGA
TIMES STAFF WRITERS

SACRAMENTO—In another indication of the severity of California's worsening drought, the federal government Thursday stripped farmers in the fertile Central Valley of three-fourths of their water allocations and also sharply curbed deliveries to two urban centers in Northern California.

The U.S. Bureau of Reclamation's announcement that it will reduce water deliveries for agriculture by 75% set off fearful speculation among farmers that crop prices will rise, workers will go idle and acres of land will fall out of production.

"We'll see 350,000 acres or so of

Please see DROUGHT, A32

Structure Built to Shelter Iraqi Elite, U.S. Says

By DOYLE McMANUS
and JAMES GERSTENZANG
TIMES STAFF WRITER

WASHINGTON—The Baghdad structure destroyed by U.S. bombs Wednesday was built as an air raid shelter for the families of Iraq's elite, American officials said Thursday, adding that among the civilians who died in it may have been officials of the ruling Baath Party, their spouses and children.

Western intelligence officers believe that the building also was linked to a neighboring compound of villas reserved for top officials and distinguished foreign visitors—including a house frequently used by Palestine Liberation Organization chief Yasser Arafat, who was in Baghdad during the bombing, one official said.

"We watched them build those things," said a U.S. official previously stationed in Baghdad. "Our understanding was that these were VIP shelters, built for government cadres and party people."

The reinforced concrete structure in the Baghdad suburb of Amariya was one of a number of such shelters built during Iraq's war with Iran in the 1980s but apparently never used until this year, the official said.

The structure that was bombed was modified and converted into a military command-and-communications center in the late 1980s and was used for that purpose since, Pentagon officials said.

However, the Bush Administration has decided to try to weather the outcry over the estimated sev-

Please see SHELTER, A8

Germany Was Hub of Iraq Arms Network in Europe

By TYLER MARSHALL
TIMES STAFF WRITER

BONN—It was the ideal marriage.

On one side, a dictator with a grudge, ready cash and a will to possess unchallenged military power; on the other, a nation with an advanced high-tech industry and a proud tradition of selling to any and all.

That connection, between an array of mainly German companies and the envoys of Saddam Hussein, underpinned a carefully constructed Iraqi purchasing network across Europe that operated for the better part of a decade.

Between the late 1970s and the time alarm bells began ringing in government offices across Western Europe 10 years later, this network had brought Hussein the richest, most frightening harvest of military technology ever assembled by a Third World country.

"The Iraqis operated a substantial front on two levels," commented Heino Kopitz, former weapons specialist and senior Middle East analyst at the London-based consulting firm Control Risks. "They wanted to maintain their war with Iran, but on the other hand they were looking far beyond that."

Although the French delivered weapons, the British machine tools,

Second of two parts

the Swedes trucks and the Belgians protective hangars, the German connection brought Hussein far more: the key ingredients to wage chemical and biological warfare, upgrade ballistic missiles and important components of nuclear

Please see WEAPONS, A16

2 S. African Blacks Find Freedom and Fear Coexist

■ **Reforms:** A prisoner gets his release. A shack dweller finds that violence has created a living hell.

By SCOTT KRAFT
TIMES STAFF WRITER

NEW BRIGHTON, South Africa—Fuzile Tsewu, doing six years' hard time for terrorism, watched the prison TV in disbelief a year ago when the government freed Nelson Mandela and promised, once and for all, to get rid of apartheid.

Tsewu was usually skeptical of South Africa's white leaders, but he couldn't help hoping for an early release. And he got his wish a few weeks ago when he boarded a ferry to leave the Robben Island penal colony and rejoin his family here in New Brighton township.

A thousand miles away, in a township known as Tokoza, James Dywili also had been cheered by the government's promise of a "new South Africa." Dywili hoped it would mean he could move out of his corrugated-iron shack and, he said, "lead a normal life."

But today Dywili's shack lies in ruins, burned to the ground in black fighting spawned in large part by those reforms.

Everything Dywili owned, from the vegetables and chickens in his corner store to his children's school uniforms, was destroyed. And he now walks the streets afraid for his life.

This is the story of two black men, a prisoner and a shack dweller, whose lives were touched by the most hopeful and violent year

Please see APARTHEID, A28

INSIDE TODAY'S TIMES

■ **WAR STORIES, PHOTOS: A5-19; D1; F1**

■ **EXECUTIONS IN KUWAIT**

At least 200 Kuwaitis have been executed since the start of the allied bombing of Iraq, a Kuwaiti official said. **A6**

■ **CLOUDS ON THE HORIZON**

The recent warming of U.S.-Israeli relations may not outlast the Gulf War, observers say. Disagreements on the Palestinian issue are far from ended. **A8**

■ **TAPPING INTO THE SEA**

Southern California utilities are studying plans for a desalination plant that would produce 100 million gallons of drinking water daily. **B1**

WEATHER: Morning coastal fog, otherwise high clouds. Civic Center low/high: 58/78. Details: B5

■ TOP OF THE NEWS ON A2

Asst. Chief Jesse A. Brewer

■ **NO. 2 OFFICER TO RETIRE**

Jesse A. Brewer, the assistant chief of police who said his first attempt to join the LAPD was rejected because he is black, will retire after 38 years. **B1**

Old Salts Coming Back to Help Move Cargo to Gulf

■ **Merchant marine:** Many return from years of retirement. In all, thousands are called back to sea duty.

By JEFF KAYE
SPECIAL TO THE TIMES

BREMERHAVEN, Germany—Dressed in clothing more appropriate for the Sunbelt than the numbing chill of this busy North Sea port, 75-year-old Guy Lipane tugs on the front of his thin blue sweater.

"I live in Florida," he says with a New York accent. "This is the warmest thing I've got."

Until a few weeks ago, the white-haired Lipane was a Ft. Lauderdale retiree. Today, he is chief engineer of the Cape Farewell, a mammoth cargo ship, sleek and gray, anchored here to pick up missiles, rockets, bombs, trucks and tanks for delivery to coalition troops in the Persian Gulf.

Plucked from 10 years of retirement and dropped into these incongruous surroundings, Lipane is one of thousands of American merchant seamen—and former merchant seamen—who have been called into service to keep the allied forces supplied.

They travel unarmed into the most dangerous waters in the world, usually carrying enough explosives to blow a fair-sized city to smithereens. Floating mines, Exocet missiles and chemical warfare attacks are their nemeses. As they enter the Gulf, the seamen hold tight to their gas masks and lower the lifeboats in preparation for abandoning ship. Many sleep on

Please see SEAMEN, A17

Water, Water

Turkey and Syria considered using **WATER AS A WEAPON** against Iraq in the war but decided against it, according to a senior Arab official in Cairo. A prewar agreement among Turkey, Iraq and Syria stipulates that Turkey must release a set amount of water into the Euphrates River below the Euphrates Dam. The official said the Syrians have made it clear that "they would suffer as much as the Iraqis if Turkey restricted the flow."

Suited up for the chemical attack that never came.

DAY IN THE GULF

Military: B-52s bomb a missile assembly and repair facility in Iraq. Other targets include troops and artillery along the Kuwaiti coastline, the key Iraqi supply-line city of Basra and depots in Kuwait.

■ U.S. officials say they are considering ways to avoid killing civilians in the air campaign, including announcing bombing targets in advance.

■ A U.S. command spokesman says the Iraqis have lost 1,300 of their 4,200 tanks, 1,100 of 3,100 artillery pieces and 800 of 2,800 armored vehicles.

■ A fourth U.S. aircraft carrier, the America, moves into the Persian Gulf, joining the Ranger, the Midway and the Theodore Roosevelt.

■ Two American airmen are killed in the crash of a U.S. EF-111A Raven electronic jamming and radar-detection jet, the first EF-111A lost in the Persian Gulf War.

■ Allied battlefield leaders report a surge in Iraqi soldiers crossing the Kuwaiti border to surrender, adding 350 to more than 1,000 already taken.

Missiles: Iraq makes its first Scud strike on a northern Saudi city, but the missiles apparently break up in flight.

Kuwait: Iraq has stepped up executions inside occupied Kuwait, killing at least 200 people since the allied air campaign began, a Kuwaiti official says.

■ Iraqi occupation troops in Kuwait have tortured and hanged 10 Kuwaiti women since Feb. 8 for aiding resistance forces, witnesses in Cairo say.

Iraq: Thousands of angry Iraqis march to a cemetery to bury fellow civilians killed in the U.S. bombing of a structure where they had taken shelter. The mourners cry out for revenge.

■ Palestine Liberation Organization Chairman Yasser Arafat pledges solidarity with Iraq.

Diplomacy: The U.N. Security Council opens debate on the Gulf War in its first closed-door session in 15 years, adjourns after 3½ hours of debate and plans to reconvene in the morning.

Congress: The Administration says it will ask Congress for $56 billion in supplemental assistance for the war—$41 billion of which would be defrayed by allied contributions.

CHEMICAL WARFARE

World War I saw the first use of chemical agents, and they were used in several conflicts through the 1930s. Although chemical weapons were not used in World War II, their use was suspected in Southeast Asia and Afghanistan in the early 1980s—and confirmed during the 8-year Iran-Iraq War.

Kurdish victims of 1988 Iraqi chemical attack.

PREVENTION AND CLEANUP

Gas Mask and Gas Hood

Gloves

Body Suit

Overboots

U.S. soldiers are well prepared for chemical attack. They wear both a gas mask and hood which protect the wearer's head and neck. To protect the body, the soldier wears gloves, overboots and a two-piece suit (an outer layer of nylon/cotton and an inner layer of charcoal-impregnated polyurethane foam).

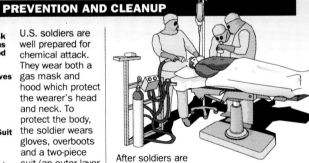

After soldiers are contaminated, they are taken to specially marked yellow tents beside hospital units. Medics cut off their chemical suits and wash them in a bleach-like liquid. Alternative treatments include applying fuller's earth, an absorbent clay, to soak up chemical agents or covering with charcoal-lined bags.

HISTORY

According to the Stockholm International Peace Research Institute, at one time as many as 38 countries were pursuing chemical weapons programs. However, in the 1980s that number dropped to about 16 nations, with only 10 having confirmed stockpiles.

■ **Confirmed Chemical Programs:**

1. U.S.
2. Soviet Union
3. France
4. Afghanistan
5. Iran
6. **Iraq**
7. Libya
8. Syria
9. Vietnam
10. N. Korea

▨ **Suspected Chemical Programs:**

11. Israel
12. Egypt
13. Ethiopia
14. Burma
15. Taiwan
16. China

Iraq and Chemical Warfare

Defying international bans, Iraq launched poison gas attacks against Iranian forces and Kurdish rebels in the mid-1980s. Iraq produced numerous deadly chemicals—including sophisticated nerve gases. Recent allied air strikes have been successful in destroying most of Iraq's ability to produce chemical agents, but reportedly large stockpiles remain intact.

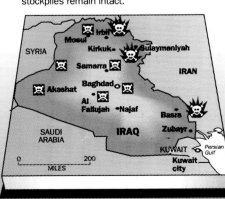

Iraqi Chemical & Biological Weapon Facilities   Past Chemical Attacks by Iraq

CHEMICAL WEAPONS AND HOW THEY AFFECT THE BODY

Nerve Agents
• **Entry:** Breathing, skin • **Effects:** Nervous system

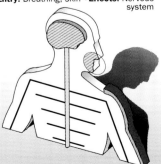

Inhaled or absorbed through the skin, these agents prevent the normal functioning of the nervous system. Death usually results from respiratory failure. Iraq is known to have Tabun, an early nerve gas and possibly Sarin, a much more sophisticated and deadly type.

Lung Agents
• **Entry:** Breathing • **Effects:** Lungs

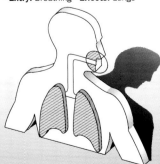

Inhaled into the lungs, agents such as chlorine gas cause massive irritation to the respiratory system. Drowning results as the damaged lungs fill with fluid. Gas masks provide adequate protection against some of these agents.

Blood Agents
• **Enter:** Breathing • **Effects:** Circulation system

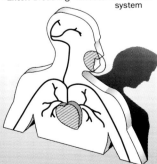

Absorbed primarily by breathing, blood agents such as hydrogen cyanide block the normal transfer of oxygen between blood and body tissue, resulting in suffocation. Gas masks are effective in blocking these types of agents.

Blister Agents
• **Entry:** Breathing, skin • **Effects:** Lungs, skin

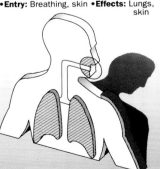

Blister agents, inhaled or absorbed through the skin, are insidious in action: there is little pain at contact, but after a short time the victim develops large blisters. Known as mustard gas, blister agents are seldom fatal, but permanently damage lungs and skin. Iraq used this gas extensively in its 8-year war with Iran.

Sources: U.S. Strategic Institute, Federation of American Scientists, Jane's NBC Protection Equipment, Associated Press

Written by SCOTT BROWN / Los Angeles Times

DENNIS LOWE / Los Angeles Times

DAY 31

FEBRUARY 16, 1991

What war ever evoked so much pity, soldier-to-soldier? Whether it was the Marine artillerymen lobbing shells onto Iraqi positions, or Air Force flyers pelting Iraqi bunkers with bombs, Americans waged war professionally, without the blood lust of passion.

All across the front, Americans found themselves wincing a little as the lopsided battle proceeded. These were fellow human beings dying over there, husbands and fathers and sons, unwilling soldiers many of them, themselves sad-sack victims of Iraqi President Saddam Hussein.

I spent what turned out to be the final night of the war with U.S. soldiers chasing retreating Iraqis. Under the bombing and shelling of the Americans, the ground vibrated almost like an airplane does as it pierces a storm. At 7:55 a.m. the last bomb fell and the earth felt rock solid again. Among the many emotions expressed that final morning was relief: Thank God for our sake, thank God for their's.

—John Balzar, in Iraq

Los Angeles Times

M

CIRCULATION: 1,225,189 DAILY / 1,514,096 SUNDAY | SATURDAY, FEBRUARY 16, 1991 | COPYRIGHT 1991 / THE TIMES MIRROR COMPANY / CC† / 118 PAGES | DAILY 50¢ DESIGNATED AREAS HIGHER

Bush Rejects Iraqis' Offer to Leave Kuwait as 'Cruel Hoax'

■ **Gulf War:** Baghdad offers to withdraw in return for an allied pullout, reparations and linkage to Mideast issues. The President urges overthrow of Saddam Hussein.

By NICK B. WILLIAMS Jr. and JAMES GERSTENZANG
TIMES STAFF WRITERS

AMMAN, Jordan—Iraq offered Friday to withdraw from Kuwait if the United States and its allies met several conditions, but President Bush said the offer was "dead on arrival" and rejected it as "a cruel hoax."

For the first time, Bush explicitly urged the Iraqi military and the people of Iraq to overthrow President Saddam Hussein.

"Until a massive withdrawal begins, with those troops visibly leaving Kuwait," Bush said, the United States and its allies will press the Persian Gulf War without letup. "But there's another way for the bloodshed to stop.

"And that is for the Iraqi military and the Iraqi people to take matters into their own hands, to force Saddam Hussein, the dictator, to step aside, and to comply with the United Nations resolutions, and then rejoin the family of peace-loving nations."

Iraq said it would abide by a U.N. resolution calling for unconditional withdrawal of its troops from Kuwait. But it then attached conditions, including a pullout of allied forces, Israeli withdrawal from occupied Arab territories, payment of allied war reparations to Iraq and replacement of Kuwait's ruling Sabah family with a new Kuwaiti government.

Hussein's offer, broadcast on Baghdad Radio at 2:30 p.m., brought a joyous demonstration on the streets of the Iraqi capital. People thought it meant the end of the war, which is heading into its second bloody month. Air raid sirens wailed, and Baghdadis fired rifles into the air. People gathered in excited groups to discuss the news.

But excitement in Baghdad and elsewhere ended as the United States made its response and as U.S. commanders began repositioning tens of thousands of Marines along the border of Kuwait and Saudi Arabia in preparation for a ground assault. Britain and France declared that Hussein's offer was not enough. British Prime Minister John Major called it "a bogus sham."

Soviet President Mikhail S. Gorbachev, however, welcomed the Iraqi proposal as "a positive signal" to be explored. And, while Bush publicly greeted Hussein's offer with pessimism, it was privately seen at the White House as a sign that Hussein is suffering from the pressure of unrelenting allied air attacks and might be preparing to give in.

While taking pains to avoid raising any expectations, one official noted that the offer marked the first time Hussein has spoken about leaving Kuwait—and that the

Please see WAR, A4

Ceremony at Arlington

Associated Press

Gayle Edwards holds hands with sons Bennett, left, and Spencer as daughter Adrianne looks on during the funeral for her husband, Capt. Jonathan R. Edwards, the first Gulf War casualty to be buried at Arlington National Cemetery. The Marine died flying a mission over Saudi Arabia.

COLUMN ONE

B-52 Fears Echo From a Past War

■ Vietnamese survivors of U.S. bombing recall the terror. But they also caution against underestimating the endurance of America's current enemy.

By SONNI EFRON and MARK FINEMAN
TIMES STAFF WRITERS

More than 15 years have passed since Vu Duy Thanh heard the train of death rumbling through the sky above, that dreadful drone of the American B-52s and the horrible few seconds that followed each time, as 1,000-pound bombs whistled down on his hometown of Haiphong.

"You do not forget this sound, ever," Thanh said. "North Vietnamese people, we know what is B-52." Thanh relived the memory just weeks ago in Iraq, where, as a road-crew worker, he observed the latest B-52 bombing sorties.

Truong Nhu Tang, a Viet Cong survivor of bombing along the Ho Chi Minh Trail, has similar memories. He pressed himself against a bunker floor during his first B-52 attack, feeling as though he "had been caught in the apocalypse."

"The terror was complete," he later wrote in memoirs. "One lost control of bodily functions as the mind screamed incomprehensible orders to get out."

Both men offer insight into what Saddam Hussein's troops may be experiencing as B-52s shower them with bombs day after day in the Kuwaiti war zone. There are probably many deaths. And if the Vietnam experience is a guide, some Iraqi soldiers are having nervous breakdowns. Others are suffering from ruptured eardrums, nosebleeds, speech impairments, long-lasting headaches, nausea and disorientation.

North Vietnamese and the Viet Cong recall the B-52s and their bombs as among the most terrifying weapons used against them, with potential for both physical and psychological devastation. The U.S. military is counting on that, relying on bombing by B-52s and other aircraft to sap the Republican Guards and other Iraqi front-line troops of both the strength and will to fight.

But there may be another lesson from Vietnam: B-52 bombing may fall short of accomplishing its goals. Vietnamese soldiers suffered under the shower of bombs, but they did not give up. Bunkers provided some physical protection; a certain stoicism gave them psychological support. Bombing strikes leveled acres of jungle but did not stop the flow of North Vietnamese troops, ammunition and supplies.

As a result, no one can predict whether B-52 bombing of Iraqi troops, protected by concrete and steel-reinforced bunkers deep beneath the desert sands, will bring a speedy conclusion to the war.

"No army has ever surrendered because they were subjected to heavy bombardment," said retired Rear Adm. Eugene J. Carroll Jr. "I

Please see BOMBER, A5

Iraqis Must Leave Arms, Military Says

By MELISSA HEALY
TIMES STAFF WRITER

WASHINGTON—Senior defense officials, responding to Saddam Hussein's new cease-fire proposal, warned Friday that any Iraqi troops participating in a withdrawal from Kuwait would have to leave their tanks, vehicles and weapons behind or be subject to continued allied attack.

The stern terms outlined by U.S. officials are intended to address serious concerns that even in capitulation, the Iraqi president could emerge with a formidable military machine that would pose a threat to other nations in the volatile

Please see ARMS, A17

Wilson Directs Plans Begin for 50% Water Cuts

By VIRGINIA ELLIS
TIMES STAFF WRITER

SACRAMENTO—Predicting that prolonged drought will have a dramatic impact on the California lifestyle, Gov. Pete Wilson directed local communities Friday to plan for a 50% cut in water supplies and proposed the creation of a $100-million fund to grapple with the crisis.

The governor, announcing his first concrete proposals for coping with the fifth year of drought, shied away from an outright declaration of emergency, suggesting instead a five-point program recommended by top water officials.

It included plans to establish a water bank to ease buying and selling of the precious resource among the water haves and have-nots and recommendations for saving fish and wildlife.

Wilson said he would ask that his proposal for a water fund be put on a "fast track" in the Legislature so state officials could begin making emergency loans to public and private agencies and provide technical help in finding new supply sources. He did not specify where the money would come from, but usually those types of funds come out of the state's emergency reserves.

"I will not kid you; a drought of this magnitude is going to change the way we live," said the grim-faced governor. "It will cause inconvenience. It will cause some very real pain. There is no getting around it; this is a time for sacrifice."

Wilson directed the state Department of Water Resources to monitor the actions of communities and report to him in two weeks on their progress. He said he would use the power and prestige of the governor's office to pressure any community that dragged its feet. If this failed, the governor said, he would be prepared to invoke his emergency powers. Those powers enable a governor to suspend rules, regulations and even state laws in crisis situations.

Please see DROUGHT, A35

Hussein Trying to Buy Time, Divide the Allies

■ **Strategy:** The maneuver to stave off a ground war and spare Iraqi forces won't work, U.S. officials insist.

By ROBIN WRIGHT
TIMES STAFF WRITER

WASHINGTON—On the brink of having to fight a ground war that he finally realized he could not win, Saddam Hussein has embarked on a last-ditch effort to generate negotiations that he hopes will buy him time and ensure the survival of his army and his regime.

And U.S. officials and Middle East analysts believe that his government's offer Friday to withdraw from Kuwait—hedged with

NEWS ANALYSIS

conditions Hussein knew Washington would instantly reject—was designed to entice the Soviet Union into serving as a wedge to split the coalition arrayed against Baghdad in the Persian Gulf. Iraqi Foreign Minister Tarik Aziz, scheduled to be in Moscow this weekend, will invite the Kremlin to play a mediator's role and bypass the United States, they predicted.

Yet prospects for success of the Iraqi maneuver are highly uncertain. And even if Hussein's proposal was intended as the opening ploy in a longer diplomatic gambit, it may not stave off a U.S.-led ground war against his war machine in Kuwait.

"Unless he eliminates his conditions, there will be a ground war. He has not bought any additional time," a Pentagon official said. "We ought to know within the next couple of days just how serious Saddam is."

"It's too little, too late," said Augustus Richard Norton of the International Peace Academy's new program on Gulf security.

President Bush declared publicly that absolutely no compromise is possible on the U.N. Security Council's terms for ending the war.

"Saddam either has to back off his conditions or the war will continue," a senior Administration official said. "There will be no compromise, no discussion of linkage" to other Mideast issues.

"And we will decide when we pull out, not Saddam," the official

Please see ASSESS, A21

Broadcast Gives Iraqis Fleeting Moment of Joy

By MARK FINEMAN
TIMES STAFF WRITER

AMMAN, Jordan—Air-raid sirens wailed and machine-gun fire filled the air throughout Iraq's besieged capital city just after 2:30 p.m. Friday, but for the first time in a month, these sounds of war were an emotional explosion of hope and relief.

"The war is over!" civil servants and militiamen were overheard shouting exultantly as they embraced in the streets after hearing Baghdad Radio's "historic" broadcast indicating that their leadership had finally decided to do what many of them had hoped for weeks ago: get out of Kuwait.

The celebration, of course, was short-lived. Tears of joy turned quickly to tears of frustration, fear and despair as President Bush and other allied leaders flatly rejected the heavily conditional withdrawal offer.

But the few moments of frenzied joy in the streets and cafes of Baghdad spoke volumes about the real motives behind the Iraqi leadership's offer to pull its hundreds of

Please see IRAQIS, A22

LAX Crash Prompts FAA Safety Rules for Runways

■ **Disaster:** Aircraft may no longer wait in intersections at night or if controllers' vision is obstructed.

By PAUL RICHTER
TIMES STAFF WRITER

WASHINGTON—In its first formal response to the crash two weeks ago that killed 34 people at Los Angeles International Airport, the Federal Aviation Administration announced new rules Friday that will keep aircraft from waiting in runway intersections before takeoff.

The rules, which take effect today, prevent air traffic controllers from allowing any aircraft to wait in runway intersections at night. They also bar controllers from allowing such waits during daylight hours when bad weather or any other obstructions keep controllers from clearly seeing the intersections.

Fred Farrar, an FAA spokesman, described the move as "one of many" changes that may be made to correct the hazards that contributed to the Feb. 1 crash and other ground accidents.

The disaster occurred when a USAir Boeing 737 landed on a smaller SkyWest Metroliner commuter aircraft that was in the same runway, killing all 12 people on the SkyWest aircraft and 22 on the USAir plane. Sixty-seven people survived the fiery accident.

Eight people died and 22 were injured in Detroit last Dec. 3 when two Northwest Airlines planes, a McDonnell-Douglas DC-9 and a Boeing 727, collided on a runway

Please see FAA, A31

INSIDE TODAY'S TIMES

■ **WAR STORIES, PHOTOS: A3-23; D1-2; F1, F18-19**

■ **CZECH-LITHUANIA TIES**

Czechoslovakia said it will set up diplomatic ties with Lithuania by opening an office in Vilnius. But the office may not have embassy status. **A2**

■ **REGULARS VS. RESERVES**

Friction is increasingly evident in the Gulf as the U.S. tries to meld military regulars and so-called weekend warriors. **A5**

■ **SLAIN OFFICER HONORED**

Tina Kerbrat, the first female LAPD officer killed in the line of duty, was remembered by family and colleagues in an emotional funeral service. **B1**

WEATHER: Cloudy with a chance of rain, clearing tonight. Civic Center low/high: 59/71. Details: B4

■ INDEX TO FEATURES ON A2

John A. McCone

■ **CIA PIONEER McCONE DIES**

John A. McCone, who helped form the Central Intelligence Agency and served as its director during the Cuban missile crisis in 1962, has died. **A34**

S. African Accord to End ANC's Guerrilla Activity

■ **Apartheid:** The agreement is seen as helping the peace process and speeding the release of political prisoners.

By SCOTT KRAFT
TIMES STAFF WRITER

JOHANNESBURG, South Africa—The African National Congress and the government, removing a serious threat to the South African peace process, ratified an agreement Friday that will end all ANC underground guerrilla activity and expedite the release of political prisoners.

The accord, heralded as a major breakthrough by both sides, was likely to significantly speed up the black-white negotiation process and pave the way for the removal of American sanctions against Pretoria.

"This will serve as a stimulus to the negotiation process," President Frederik W. de Klerk said. "Matters which stood in [our] way . . . have now been resolved."

De Klerk added that the spirit of the talks reflected "a genuine desire on both sides to solve difficult problems sensibly. It bodes well for the road ahead."

Pallo Jordan, chief ANC spokesman, said the pact was "a step in the right direction." And he agreed that it could "bring negotiations onto the agenda much more quickly than expected."

The agreement, ratified by the ANC and the government and released on Friday, was reached Tuesday in an all-day meeting between De Klerk and ANC Depu-

Please see ACCORD, A28

UH-1 Huey

Formally known as the Iroquois, the Huey was used extensively during the Vietnam War as a transport and escort helicopter. The twin-turbopowered helicopter, armed with two forward firing M-60 machine guns, was the military's first gunship. Since the beginning of the war in the Gulf, two Hueys have been lost, both in noncombat missions.

Crew: One, plus up to 14 troops
Max. Speed: 110 knots
Range: 237 miles
Load: 5,000 pounds (external load)

"IRAQ AMERICA'S MOST WANTED"

Marines played a major role in freeing Kuwait City.

PATRICK DOWNS / Los Angeles Times

RELYING ON

THE B-52

The great airborne Cold Warrior has taken on a new mission: blasting away at Saddam Hussein's vaunted Republican Guard and turning large parts of Iraq and Kuwait into moonscape. Built as intercontinental atomic bombers in the 1950s, the B-52s have been redesigned, reinforced and retrofitted through three decades of wars, both cold and hot. Although the planes are older than most of their pilots, they bring to this latest conflict a package of state-of-the-art electronics and smart weaponry.

Crew: 6 (includes pilot, copilot, navigator, radar navigator, ECM operator and gunner)
Length: 160 ft. 10.9 in.
Wingspan: 185 ft.
Maximum takeoff weight: 488,000 lbs.
Maximum speed: 595 m.p.h.
Maximum altitude: over 50,000 ft.
Range: 7,500 nautical miles

Brake parachute door

Remote control tail gun
Four 12.7-mm M-3 machine guns

TYPICAL PAYLOAD CONFIGURATIONS:

45 250-lb. gravity bombs	51 500-lb. gravity bombs	51 750-lb. gravity bombs	18 2,000-lb. gravity bombs
OR	OR	OR	

Low-light television scanner turret

Optional wing-mounted cruise missile pylon
Holds six missiles (AGM-86B Air Launch Cruise Missiles or AGM-69 SRAM air-to-ground missiles)

Pratt & Whitney J57-P-43WB turbojet engine

Fixed external fuel tank

THE B-52 IN THE GULF

▶ **NUMBERS:** The Gulf fleet is thought to comprise 33 to 45 aircraft. One has been lost at sea.

▶ **BOMBING RUNS:** The aircraft typically fly in formations of three at an altitude of six or seven miles. These "cells" drop their bomb loads—usually 40 to 60 tons per mission—in a box-shaped area about one mile long by a half-mile wide.

▶ **"CARPET BOMBING":** There is some technical debate over whether this is actually taking place. According to military experts, true carpet bombing is carried out by many planes in a tight formation, flying wingtip to wingtip and nose to tail. The term *saturation bombing* is used frequently in the Gulf.

▶ **BASES AND FLYOVERS:** With space for the B-52s in Saudi Arabia at a premium, the NATO airfield at Fairford, England, and the island of Diego Garcia in the Indian Ocean are the favored bases. Spain has provided a staging area at Moron de la Frontera. France is allowing B-52s to fly through its airspace as long as they are carrying conventional weapons.

▶ **MAINTENANCE:** For every hour a B-52 is in the sky, 30 to 50 hours of maintenance are required.

EFFECTIVENESS

▶ Even when its bombs are dropped from miles in the air, the B-52 is surprisingly accurate. The addition of sophisticated electronic defense systems and "smart" weapons enables the huge planes to fly low-level missions with comparative safety.

▶ Results of bombing Republican Guard strongholds have been mixed. Against troops and equipment spread out over a large area or targets that require a direct hit, effectiveness declines. A hardened bunker

must sustain a direct hit to be destroyed, and if the bunker is fortified with sand, even a direct hit may be ineffective.

▶ B-52 raids against Iraq's front lines are expected to be more effective than those against the dug-in Republican Guards because the front-line troops are more exposed and likely to be in concentrated formations.

BACKGROUND

▶ Designed in the late 1940s, there were 744 B-52s built between 1955 and 1962. The first were designed to carry four nuclear bombs a distance of 7,000 miles at maximum altitude—long enough to get to the Soviet Union without refueling. Until 1968, the Strategic Air Command kept some of the bombers airborne 24 hours a day against a surprise Soviet attack.

▶ In Vietnam, the B-52s were fitted with conventional bombs and flew hundreds of raids. Two dozen B-52s were lost, including 16 shot down in a two-week period in late 1972.

▶ Since then, the planes have been reinforced and retrofitted to make them less vulnerable to antiaircraft missiles.

▶ Of the original fleet, about 250 remain, 150 of which carry conventional weapons. SAC still has planes on round-the-clock ground alert.

▶ According to some estimates, the B-52 could remain in active service until 2035, when the aircraft will celebrate its 80th year.

THE ROUTE TO WAR

Because the giant planes are vulnerable on the ground, the Gulf's B-52 fleet is scattered among several bases as far as possible from the war zone. Bombing missions are taking off from Saudi Arabia, Spain, England, the island of Diego Garcia, even bases in the United States. The key refueling and maintenance stops are in southern England and on Diego Garcia. Bombers completing a mission over Iraq—at the midpoint between the two—may continue on to either base.

England · Spain · United States · Iraq · Saudi Arabia · Diego Garcia

Sources: Los Angeles Times; Press Assn. Ltd.; Times of London; Jane's All the World's Aircraft; Greg Grant, Center for Strategic and International Studies; Reuters.

SANDY KAY / Los Angeles Times

DAY 32

FEBRUARY 17, 1991

Like many people, President Bush is a creature of routine—in his case, frenetic routine— and it was amazing how faithfully he kept to it even during the war's most anxious moments. He needed those rituals then more than ever. On weekends, Bush continued to visit Camp David, Md., as much as possible. And he almost always took guests with him.

"He has a tendency, even if he goes away for the weekend—he doesn't want to be alone," said one White House aide. "If he wants to play checkers, they'll play checkers. If he wants to talk about dogs and hunting, they'll talk dogs and hunting."

For this man, "it's not solitude, but it's a way of building a wall between him and the Washington pressures," the aide said.

—James Gerstenzang,
in Washington

Los Angeles Times

Sunday Final

CIRCULATION:
1,225,189 DAILY / 1,514,096 SUNDAY

SUNDAY, FEBRUARY 17, 1991
COPYRIGHT 1991 / THE TIMES MIRROR COMPANY / CC† / 474 PAGES

SUNDAY $1.25
DESIGNATED AREAS HIGHER

Agence France-Presse
President Bush is accompanied by reporters during a chilly walk on the beach at Kennebunkport, Me.

Massive Land-Sea-Air Push Expected in Days

■ Onslaught: Unless Iraq surrenders or strikes a diplomatic deal, the President will order the assault this week, senior Pentagon officials predict.

By JOHN M. BRODER
TIMES STAFF WRITER

WASHINGTON—Barring an Iraqi surrender or a diplomatic deal in the next three days, the United States is planning to unleash this week a ground, air and sea assault of unprecedented ferocity against the half a million Iraqi troops in Kuwait and southern Iraq, senior Pentagon officials said Saturday.

U.S. ground and amphibious forces were given orders at the start of the war to be ready to mount a coordinated offensive any time after Feb. 15, and they are now ready, military officials said.

The final call on whether—and when—to launch a ground war will be made by President Bush, who has said in press conferences that he will reserve that decision for himself.

But "the table has been set," a senior Army officer said Saturday. "We are in position. We can go any time. We are very close to the level of destruction [of Iraqi troops and equipment] that the commanders wanted to see. This isn't video-game stuff anymore. This is real."

The intense, monthlong air campaign has cut the combat effectiveness of the Iraqi army virtually in half, one senior military operations officer said. "His army is close to 50% destroyed and the casualties are very high," he said.

Iraqi prisoners of war have reported that the Iraqi army is burying some of its dead in mass graves in Kuwait and hauling other bodies back to Iraq in refrigerator trucks, a Pentagon officer with access to sensitive data said.

Defense Secretary Dick Cheney said Saturday that continued air strikes would further weaken the Iraqi forces. But several senior defense officials said that U.S. commanders in the theater would be comfortable with an order to initiate the ground campaign at any time.

"Every day just makes it easier," one Army officer said. "We could fruitfully continue air operations for a month, but I don't think that's necessary. The troops are ready as they're going to get."

Commanders in Saudi Arabia have ordered a number of specific preparatory and diversionary operations over the next several days—the capture of an island off the Kuwaiti coast, naval bombardment of several possible amphibious landing zones, artillery and helicopter strikes across the Kuwaiti border and armed reconnaissance patrols into enemy territory.

The Air Force will step up its bombing over Kuwait and southern Iraq to wear down the enemy troops and keep the Iraqis guessing about when and where the ground attack will come, Pentagon officials said.

Warplanes will drop fuel-air explosives and giant 15,000-pound "daisy-cutter" bombs to clear

Please see ASSAULT, A28

Tide of Arms, Troops Flows Toward Front

■ Gulf War: U.S. reports loss of three planes. Iraqis claim more civilian deaths from allied bombing.

By J. MICHAEL KENNEDY
and JOHN M. BRODER
TIMES STAFF WRITERS

RIYADH, Saudi Arabia—As troops, war machinery and supply trucks, stretching from horizon to horizon, rolled into position Saturday for a long-awaited ground assault into Kuwait, U.S. and allied warplanes bombed Iraqi forces so hard just across the front lines that they rocked U.S. Marines in their foxholes.

While the allied planes mounted their thundering attack, the Iraqi government said British jets had swooped down on the central Iraqi town of Fallouja two days before, missed one of their targets and hit an apartment house and an outdoor market filled with civilians, killing 130 people and hurting another 78.

Neither British nor U.S. commanders in Riyadh said they knew of the deaths. But at the Pentagon, U.S. military officials said they have evidence that in another instance, the Iraqis damaged one of their own buildings so they could blame allied bombing. One official said it was a mosque in the city of Basra.

In other developments:

• Iraqi antiaircraft gunners shot down two U.S. A-10 Warthog anti-tank jets as they attacked Republican Guard positions in northwest Kuwait. Both pilots were listed as missing in action. An American

Please see WAR, A6

Iraq's Talk of Peace Replaced by Words of War

By MARK FINEMAN
TIMES STAFF WRITER

AMMAN, Jordan—The Iraqi leadership girded itself Saturday for a looming allied ground offensive to drive it from occupied Kuwait as Baghdad's talk of peace gave way to the rhetoric of war.

Top Iraqi generals boasted of their war preparations, baiting the allies to abandon their "cowardly" air war. And Iraq's Revolutionary Command Council, President Saddam Hussein's inner ruling circle, which announced a heavily conditional withdrawal offer just a day earlier, returned to its hard-line stand, even with its own people. The council announced that it is now a capital offense for Iraqi

Please see IRAQ, A7

Soviets Reject Iraq Conditions for Withdrawal

By JOHN-THOR DAHLBURG
and JOHN J. GOLDMAN
TIMES STAFF WRITERS

MOSCOW—As global diplomatic attention zeroed in on Moscow and the possibility of achieving a negotiated end here to the Persian Gulf War, the Soviet Union on Saturday stressed that, while Iraq may have opened a "path to peace," it still must get out of Kuwait and has no right to pose preconditions.

That position won praise from U.S. and European officials.

Based on statements carried by Tass, comments by Soviet President Mikhail S. Gorbachev to three visiting European Community foreign ministers and remarks by President Bush, the Soviets on Saturday appeared to be holding fast to the U.S. and allied stance on Iraqi compliance with the U.N. Security Council resolutions calling on Iraq to withdraw from Kuwait.

In Kennebunkport, Me., where the President is spending the weekend at his vacation home, Bush insisted that the anti-Iraq coalition remains "solid" and that his Administration has received "fresh" assurances from Gorbachev, supporting the allies.

"He's been very solid in support of the coalition," Bush said of Gorbachev. The Soviets have played "a constructive role," he said, adding, "Let's just put it this way: The United Nations' position is solid and there's no giving on that at all."

After meeting with Gorbachev,

Please see MOSCOW, A9

COLUMN ONE

Friendly Fire Lurks on the Front Lines

■ Such mistakes have been part of all conflicts and can devastate morale. New technology, coupled with Gulf conditions, could worsen the problem when ground battle begins.

By ALAN C. MILLER
TIMES STAFF WRITER

WASHINGTON—They call it "friendly fire," but the expression is misleading, almost mocking.

Last month, seven U.S. Marines—half of the confirmed U.S. combat fatalities in the Persian Gulf—were killed when an allied pilot apparently mistook their light armored car for an Iraqi vehicle during a night skirmish in Kuwait and destroyed it with a Maverick missile. Another Marine also died, apparently in an errant U.S. cluster-bomb attack.

Military experts say friendly fire—the inadvertent shelling or bombing of troops by their own side—often occurs because of just such mistakes in the chaos of war. An artillery unit misreads a map. A pilot misidentifies ground troops. A soldier—exhausted, wounded or new to combat—simply panics.

At other times, it happens because commanders have pushed their coordinated ground, air and artillery forces to the limit in an effort to reduce their own casualties and to maximize enemy damage. A combat unit that is in danger of being overrun may even call in fire on its own position.

"When you are forced to fight at close quarters, when you cannot control the fighting of the enemy,

Please see FRIENDLY, A12

Bush Waging Personal War, Associates Reveal

■ Motivation: He's out to get Hussein, as well as liberate Kuwait, they say. He's described as determined yet calm.

By JACK NELSON
TIMES WASHINGTON BUREAU CHIEF

WASHINGTON—In the privacy of the White House, President Bush refers to Saddam Hussein as "that lying s.o.b." and has vowed to associates that the Iraqi dictator will no longer pose a menace to the Gulf region or be able to claim a victory of any kind when the war finally ends.

The President has personalized the conflict in his own mind, sources who have counseled him say, because he is convinced it springs from "the evil work" of one man—Hussein.

Given that mind-set, some Bush advisers expect the President to settle for nothing less than Hussein's removal from power and the destruction of most of Baghdad's war-making capability—not just the liberation of Kuwait.

"He's not ready for this war to be over quite yet because there's still too much of Saddam's military machine left," one senior government official said.

Reflecting this unwavering determination to rain punishment on Hussein and his forces, the President has developed a stock reply to all proposals from within the Administration for a pause in the bombing: "Let's just stick to the plan," he says.

In private, according to sources close to him, Bush has grown increasingly quiet and reflective as the war has progressed. And while he may rail about Hussein and express frustration at the dictator's behavior, Bush is described as remarkably calm in approaching the most momentous decisions he has faced since entering the White House.

"The President is much quieter than any time that I've seen him over the past 10 years," one source said. "He's calm, too, but he's also angry. You can see the anger in his eyes."

"It's on the President's mind all the time," said another longtime Bush associate, who believes the war has preoccupied him like nothing else since he took office a little over two years ago. "He's totally focused and doesn't want to discuss anything but the war. Talking about the ground war, he'll say, 'We're not there yet, but we're getting there.'

"In the past, when making decisions on other things, he would say, 'Let's move slowly and look at all the options.' But not on the war. He's decisive and knows where he's going," the associate said.

The President, some advisers

Please see BUSH, A20

Plan Seeks U.S. Park Status for Wounded Knee

By RUDY ABRAMSON
TIMES STAFF WRITER

WASHINGTON—More than a century after the U.S. Cavalry killed 400 Sioux at Wounded Knee, S.D., ending the U.S.-Indian wars, the National Park Service has decided to begin taking steps to establish a national historical park on the site of the battle.

Park Service officials said Saturday that they plan to order a feasibility study designed to pave the way for possible acquisition of the land. Most of the 330 acres at the site where the massacre began are already part of the Pine Ridge Indian reservation.

David Simons, a staff member of

Please see PARK, A32

Saudis Losing Fight to Corral Huge Oil Slick

By KIM MURPHY
TIMES STAFF WRITER

DHAHRAN, Saudi Arabia—The battle against a massive oil slick in the Persian Gulf has become one of the latest casualties of war, with environmental officials admitting that they are not prepared to check much of its devastating progress southward along the Saudi coastline.

Saudi Arabia, already strapped for cash because of huge outlays for the war effort, has committed only a small fraction of the estimated $1 billion needed simply for initial containment and cleanup of the spill, according to diplomatic sources in the Saudi capital.

Please see SPILL, A9

Hospital or Family: Who Decides the Right to Die?

■ Medical ethics: Minneapolis facility seeks to disconnect a comatose patient's respirator in test case.

By ROBERT STEINBROOK
TIMES MEDICAL WRITER

MINNEAPOLIS—Since May, 87-year-old Helen Wanglie has lain unconscious and motionless at the Hennepin County Medical Center here. Although there is no hope for recovery, she is kept alive by a breathing machine, feedings through a stomach tube, and round-the-clock care.

In most such cases, physicians and family agree that further care is futile and quietly let the patient die. Not in the Wanglie case.

In what experts say is the first case of its kind, the hospital is seeking court permission to disconnect Wanglie's respirator while the family fights to continue her care.

The dispute is attracting national attention as a crucial test of whether physicians or patients and their families have the final word about the right to live or die.

At first glance, the situation appears to be the reverse of the case of Nancy Cruzan, the comatose Missouri woman whose family fought all the way to the U.S. Supreme Court for permission to stop her artificial feedings, despite the objections of physicians.

On closer inspection, both cases center on what ethicists call "patient autonomy." For this reason, the Wanglie family is actually attracting the support of leading right-to-die groups, among others.

"This hospital is trying to turn

Please see ETHICS, A40

INSIDE TODAY'S TIMES

■ WAR STORIES, PHOTOS: A6-30; E1

■ THE NEW DISNEYLAND

Walt Disney Co. land purchases in Anaheim have some analysts speculating about what the new Disneyland may look like. **A3**

■ MEDELLIN BOMB KILLS 15

A car bomb exploded as a crowd of about 10,000 left a bullring in Medellin, Colombia. Officials said at least 15 people were killed in the attack. **A4**

■ FACING THE ENEMY

American troops and some of their allies have already come face to face with the enemy—at a POW camp—and found them to be human. **A6**

WEATHER: Mostly sunny and breezy today. Civic Center low/high today: 54/66. Details: B2

■ TOP OF THE NEWS ON A2

Associated Press
Stevie Wonder sings a tribute.

■ GOSPEL FAREWELL

About 4,000 friends and admirers give a rousing and reverent farewell to the Rev. James Cleveland, acclaimed as the king of gospel music. **B4**

Causes of State's Drought Are as Elusive as Rainfall

■ Climate: Some scientists believe that no single event triggered each of the five years of the dry spell.

By MAURA DOLAN
TIMES ENVIRONMENTAL WRITER

Scientists are looking to ocean currents and temperatures, wind patterns and even volcanic eruptions to explain the causes of California's prolonged drought, but the answers remain elusive.

Theories that neatly accounted for the lack of rainfall in one year have failed to explain it in the next.

Some scientists believe that no single event triggered each of the five years of drought, saying that warm sea temperatures may have been to blame one year and that strong westerly winds from the central Pacific Ocean may be to blame in another. "I don't know of a simple, single causal mechanism that explains this," said Daniel Cayan, climate researcher at Scripps Institution of Oceanography in La Jolla.

Tree ring records suggest that the drought is simply a part of California's normal climate. What is not normal is decade after decade of heavy rainfall.

Although prolonged droughts were relatively rare in past centuries, shorter and more severe dry spells of one to two years were common, the records show.

Unfortunately, decisions about water use and distribution were made during a time span—1850 to 1950—that stands out as having the fewest short-term, severe droughts in nearly 2,100 years,

Please see DRY, A38

Nuclear Shadow

Iraq still has enough enriched uranium to build a **PRIMITIVE NUCLEAR BOMB** even though its nuclear reactors have been bombed, some officials and analysts believe. Israeli bombers destroyed a large reactor in 1981, and U.S. planes have bombed nuclear research facilities. But the whereabouts of an estimated 48 pounds of enriched uranium remains a mystery.

Marine tanks and tank crews silhouetted on ridge at sunset in northern Saudi Arabia.

PATRICK DOWNS / Los Angeles Times

JORDAN

A COUNTRY IN THE MIDDLE

QUESTION: Is Jordan's King Hussein siding with Saddam Hussein?

ANSWER: The Jordanian monarch has been trying to walk a difficult diplomatic tightrope of neutrality. In an impassioned Feb. 6 address to his nation, he expressed the strongest possible sympathy and support for the Iraqi people, particularly the civilians enduring relentless bombardment and critical shortages of food, fuel, heat and water. The personal solidarity the king expressed for the Iraqi people had two main motivations: The king's personal outrage over the destruction of any Arab nation and the massive popular pressure from his own subjects, among whom more than 50% are of Palestinian origin.

Q. What kind of relationship has the king historically had with Saddam?

A. King Hussein has never had as close a personal relationship with the Iraqi president as he has had with President Bush. There are basic philosophical disagreements between the king's government and Saddam's Arab Baath Socialist Party, and the relationship between the two leaders has been largely cool but cordial. Since the Gulf crisis began last August, though, there have been extensive contacts between Saddam Hussein and the king, who early in the crisis brokered a peace plan that would have allowed Iraq to retain two disputed islands from Kuwait and all of the vital Rumaila oil fields. That plan ultimately failed, but the king has been among the few world leaders capable of communicating with the Iraqi leader.

Q. What domestic considerations influence King Hussein's thinking?

A. Besides the economic considerations (see accompanying text), Jordanians of Palestinian origin make up more than half of the kingdom's 3.1 million population, and they are largely sympathetic to Saddam. Politically, King Hussein feels he must speak for the emotional outrage of all people in his kingdom

Q. Has the king turned on the United States, his longtime supporter?

A. The king has not turned on the United States but may feel that the United States has turned on him. He took equal pains in avoiding the mention of the United States or any other individual anti-Iraq coalition member in his Feb. 6 speech. Despite the fiery rhetoric about the demolition of Iraq, the king fully intended to continue walking his tightrope of neutrality, especially with the United States, with which he has extensive personal and bilateral ties (he is married to an American). However, the king is both upset and confused that the allied air strikes on his oil tankers on the Baghdad-Ruweished highway, Jordan's only lifeline for the fuel oil he imports from Iraq. He is also puzzled by what he sees as a deliberate U.S. attempt to push him off his neutral stance.

Agence-France Presse

Jordan's King Hussein, left, with Iraqi President Saddam Hussein in talks held last Aug. 3, the day after Iraq invaded Kuwait.

Q. How much aid does Jordan receive from the United States?

A. U.S. aid to Jordan totals about $55 million annually, money the kingdom needs just to keep its economy at the current, marginal levels. Moreover, King Hussein is also losing Iraqi aid, at about $50 million. Saddam Hussein also has helped Jordan militarily, donating 120 Chieftain battle tanks, captured from Iran during the eight-year war, to Jordan and helped to finance Jordanian arms purchases from the Soviet Union after the Amman government was rebuffed in its efforts to purchase American weaponry.

Q. What happens to King Hussein if Saddam loses the war and is deposed?

A. Regardless of the outcome of the allied war on Iraq, King Hussein is more than likely to remain in power, with or without a Saddam Hussein ruling next door. The king has survived 37 years of turmoil, conflict, civil war and crisis, and today's troubles are little compared to the storms he has weathered in the past.

— MARK FINEMAN, Times Staff Writer

AN ECONOMY IN CHAOS

Iraq was Jordan's main trading partner before the U.N.-imposed embargo that followed the invasion of Kuwait. During the 1980-88 Iran-Iraq War, as much as 80% of the traffic through Jordan's port of Aqaba was to or from Iraq. In addition, resource-poor Jordan imported most of its oil, at very cheap rates, from its eastern neighbor. Trade with Iraq accounted for 11% of Jordan's $4-billion economy in 1989.

Now, the Jordanian economy is basically in ruins. Milk, bread and sugar are already being rationed. The country's largest earner of foreign exchange, the phosphate industry, is on the critical list because of the high insurance rates for shipping from Aqaba. The World Bank forecasts the losses to the Jordanian economy from the Gulf War at more than $1.5 billion annually. With no export earnings, Jordan is facing a severe foreign exchange crisis and unemployment is soaring.

Associated Press

Destroyed truck on the Baghdad highway near the Jordanian border.

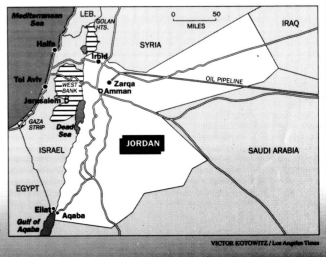

VICTOR KOTOWITZ / Los Angeles Times

DAY 33

FEBRUARY 18, 1991

The worst did not happen. Airliners were not blown out of the sky by terrorists maddened into waging war on the American traveler. But we did live in fear of it.

Travel became once more a matter of urgent necessity, not of pleasure. Like everyone else, I looked upon my fellow travelers, and their baggage, with fresh suspicion. I got angry when an airport security guard in Buffalo practically took apart the laptop computer of the man ahead of me but didn't so much as ask me to flip mine open. If he let me pass on through—because I was a woman, or for whatever reason—what was the chance he'd overlook the real thing?

Everybody was edgy. The war was just a few days old when, on a flight out of Atlanta, a bright flash exploded in the cabin. People practically burst out of their seat belts and turned to see what had happened. A woman behind me had taken a picture with a flash. Nobody thought it was funny.

—Patt Morrison,
in the United States

Los Angeles Times

CIRCULATION: 1,225,189 DAILY / 1,514,096 SUNDAY

MONDAY, FEBRUARY 18 1991

COPYRIGHT 1991 / THE TIMES MIRROR COMPANY / CC / 102 PAGES

DAILY 25¢
DESIGNATED AREAS HIGHER

Reuters

Rockets fired toward Iraqi positions by the U.S. 1st Cavalry in Saudi Arabia streak through the night sky.

U.S. Steps Up Combat, Launches 7 Firefights

■ **Gulf War:** Two soldiers killed, six wounded by 'friendly fire' from a U.S. helicopter in night attack. Warplanes 'shaping the battlefield' by focusing on southern Kuwait front.

By J. MICHAEL KENNEDY
TIMES STAFF WRITER

RIYADH, Saudi Arabia—U.S. forces launched seven firefights against Iraqi troops Sunday in a stepped-up pace of ground combat that saw two American soldiers killed and six wounded when their armored vehicles were hit by missiles from one of their own helicopters during night fighting.

The two soldiers were killed in one of the separate engagements along the border punctuated by heavy ground and helicopter fire against Iraqi patrols and positions.

Their deaths were the first American fatalities suffered by an Army unit while engaged in combat with the Iraqis, and the first involving helicopters flying in close support of U.S. ground troops, according to a spokesman for the 1st Infantry Division.

An AH-64 Apache helicopter launched Hellfire missiles on an M-2 Bradley Fighting Vehicle and on an armored personnel carrier carrying a ground surveillance radar, officials said.

Both vehicles were destroyed, killing the two crew members of the Bradley vehicle. Miraculously, although the six soldiers in the armored personnel carrier were injured, none of them was in serious condition, military officials said.

In the pre-dawn border raids Sunday, three Iraqi tanks, a multiple rocket launcher and two bunkers were destroyed, allied officials said. According to Marine Brig. Gen. Richard I. Neal, the Iraqi targets were patrols that were "apparently trying to determine the disposition of U.S. positions all along the border."

Neal said at a press briefing that the allies flew 2,600 sorties Sunday, bringing the total to 78,000 since the beginning of the air war. He said 800 of those were flown in the Kuwait theater of operations. Neal also said a Huey helicopter crashed in a noncombat accident, with slight injuries to the crew.

Over the last two weeks, allied warplanes have gradually shifted the focus of their attention to the southern Kuwait front in what has been described by the military as "shaping the battlefield."

"It's a transition to a ground offensive," said one knowledgeable military source.

In other developments:

• British military officials admitted that a "smart" bomb dropped from one of its warplanes veered off course and into the Iraqi town of Fallouja last week. Officials, however, said they had no evidence to support Iraq's report that civilians were killed there.

• In addition to hundreds of civilians that they say have been killed in Baghdad, Iraqi officials said a total of 585 more have died in allied raids on three other cities during the Gulf War's first month.

Please see WAR, A6

United Effort Stymied Iraqi Terror Threat

WASHINGTON—Unprecedented international cooperation and the expulsion of more than 100 Iraqi diplomats around the world have prevented Saddam Hussein from delivering on his threat to wage a campaign of terror against America and its allies, U.S. officials believe.

The expulsion of the diplomats and other Iraqi terrorist agents "clearly thwarted his operational capabilities," said one U.S. official. "We've been successful in getting the [suspect] Iraqis expelled, as well as general bad guys."

The official, who declined to be identified by name or agency, said no one country could claim credit for the apparently successful counterterrorism effort. "We worked together on identifying the bad guys through intelligence and diplomatic channels," he said.

In addition, terrorist experts said last week that lack of a favorable milieu has helped inhibit terrorism in the United States. They said relatively well-assimilated Middle Eastern ethnic groups are much less likely to give aid or protection to would-be terrorists than Arab or Palestinian groups in Europe.

Even so, counterterrorism officials are worried that widespread wrath over civilian casualties caused by last week's allied bombing of a structure in Baghdad could provoke incidents of terrorism by individual zealots—the hardest activity to prevent.

This story was reported and written by Times staff writers Ronald J. Ostrow, Kenneth Reich and Robin Wright.

"You don't need a secret cable from Baghdad" ordering individual terrorists to strike, one official said, noting that "the media serve as the conduit."

The disruption of Hussein's communications network by the intensive allied air strikes on Baghdad had been cited as a principal reason for the Iraqi leader's apparent inability to carry out his terrorist threats.

Although about 115 terrorist incidents have been reported worldwide since the U.S.-led coalition launched Operation Desert Storm a month ago, most have appeared isolated and relatively unsophisticated in nature, officials said.

"What we haven't seen is dedicated, highly trained, cellular terrorism in all the incidents that occurred so far," said William M. Baker, the assistant FBI director whose responsibilities include overseeing the bureau's counterterrorist efforts.

None of the incidents reported so far have been inside the United States. Counterterrorism experts attribute the nation's good fortune to the long lead time available to

Please see TERROR, A12

Bush's Church Services Jolted by Protester

By DAVID LAUTER
TIMES STAFF WRITER

KENNEBUNKPORT, Me.—Competing sounds of protest and patriotic song punctuated President Bush's Sunday morning church service here, as a longtime peace activist staged a demonstration that momentarily breached the distance that has separated the President and the public since he launched the war against Iraq.

"This is a time for repentance," the anti-war protester, John Schuchardt, called out. "This is a time to admit mistakes. We are called to be peacemakers. This is a vicious, immoral attack."

The congregation here in the Congregational Church responded by rising, spon-

Please see BUSH, A11

Aziz Arrives in Moscow; U.S. Stands Firm

By JIM MANN
TIMES STAFF WRITER

WASHINGTON—President Bush and his top advisers offered little hope Sunday for a diplomatic solution to the Gulf War as Iraqi Foreign Minister Tarik Aziz arrived in Moscow for talks today with Soviet President Mikhail S. Gorbachev.

Aziz and other Iraqi diplomats continued to press for negotiations on Baghdad's offer, made Friday, to withdraw from Kuwait if a series of conditions are met. Aziz said Sunday that he was not carrying any new proposal to Moscow.

"We have taken our step, and now is the turn of the other side to show its goodwill," Aziz told reporters in Tehran, according to Iran's official Islamic Republic News Agency. Aziz had traveled overland from Baghdad to Iran, where he boarded a Soviet Aeroflot jetliner bound for Moscow.

Also on Sunday, Abdul Razik Hashimi, Iraq's ambassador to France, said that the series of conditions attached to Baghdad's offer to pull out of Kuwait were intended, in effect, as an opening offer meant to lead to negotiations.

"You see, it's a package. It's a proposal," Hashimi said on CBS's "Face the Nation. "So those concerned, if they have questions, of course it's normal. They should sit [at] the negotiating table to ask these questions, and then Iraq will answer, and Iraq also [can ask] questions of the other side."

However, with U.S. military forces reported to be poised to

Please see DIPLOMACY, A7

COLUMN ONE

Fears Haunt the Brave New World

■ After years of state control, the hardships and uncertainty of reform have Eastern Europeans looking to the future with doubt and dread.

By CHARLES T. POWERS
TIMES STAFF WRITER

KOSICE, Czechoslovakia—The flatiron colors of winter roll on through village and hamlet, across the still fields and stands of forest, a landscape unaltered by the year of change in Eastern Europe.

The roads are lined with poplars, their wet limbs bare and black. The countryside settlements of East Slovakia, some of them hundreds of years old, are dumpy, wooden and as still as the fog hanging over the snowfields. The barnyards are cluttered—rusted implements, firewood, spavined wagons, muddy ruts— and watched over by foraging poultry and chained dogs. It cannot have looked much different 100 years ago.

And then, approaching through fog thickened by coal smoke, there is Kosice, its industrial stacks ghostly in the murk. Like most of the sizable cities of East Slovakia, if not all of Eastern Europe, this is a factory town, a Communist monument to blast furnaces and heavy-equipment manufacture, to the primacy of the worker in the workers' state.

The workers, a year after the revolution, are terrified. As the surrounding countryside seems frozen in time, the people of the cities, through much of Eastern Europe, seem paralyzed as well. As the past crumbles beneath them, the future is a vast question mark,

Please see FEARS, A22

Recession Hits State With Surprising Force

■ **Economy:** The war has brought no large benefits to defense industries. The jobless rate is at a high 7%.

By JONATHAN PETERSON
TIMES STAFF WRITER

An employer advertises 28 job openings and the result is pandemonium: Anxious applicants race to the plant at dawn the next day, jamming traffic on nearby streets. Within a week, almost 14,000 people—some with advanced college degrees—have asked for a job.

A tale from the Great Depression? Hardly. The employer was Los Angeles-based Arco, and the scene took place recently at its Carson oil refinery.

"I couldn't get in the front gate," Doug Elmets, an Arco spokesman, recalled of the mob scene. "Security people were directing traffic. It was quite a sight to see."

The national recession has hit California with surprising force, eroding the state's mystique as a haven from hard times, a place somehow exempt from the grinding turns of the business cycle. Last week's move by the Broadway department stores' parent company to seek bankruptcy protection is just the latest sign of malaise.

In recent months, the Golden State's unemployment rate has soared to 7%, third-highest among major industrial states. Weakness persists in construction, aerospace and retailing. A large deficit in the state budget threatens future problems. Consumer worries about the length of the Persian Gulf War and growing concerns over the state's drought round out the joyless picture.

Despite an unexpected gain in

Please see ECONOMY, A32

Anti-AIDS Workers Struggle to Get Message to Minorities

By CHARISSE JONES
TIMES STAFF WRITER

As the face of AIDS changes in Los Angeles County from white to African-American, Latino and Asian, dedicated men and women scour street corners, homes, gay bars and businesses within communities of color, determined to deliver a message many do not want to hear.

With each passing year, the message becomes more dangerous to ignore.

But many front-line workers say denial runs deep in minority communities, fueled by religious and cultural taboos against homosexuality, drug abuse and birth control, and made all the more insurmountable by the white, gay, middle-class image of AIDS in educational literature and the media. Money for programs is hard to come by. And the battle against AIDS must compete with the struggle to overcome poverty, inadequate health care and myriad other problems.

"People of color still don't face that it affects us," said Phillip Wilson, AIDS coordinator for the city of Los Angeles and an African-American. "You're talking about helping people to fight a disease that could kill them in 10 years, and they're dealing with drive-by shootings and hunger, which threatens to kill them every

Please see MINORITIES, A28

California Turns Seaward to Slake Thirst for Water

■ **Drought:** Despite their costliness, small desalination plants have opened and larger ones are planned.

By THOMAS H. MAUGH II
TIMES SCIENCE WRITER

Faced with growing populations and a devastating five-year drought, communities up and down the coast of California are gearing up for the desalting of seawater to augment their dwindling water supplies.

Desalination is a proven and effective technology that has been widely used in the Middle East and the Caribbean, but desalination of seawater has never been used in the continental United States because of its high cost compared to other sources of water.

That situation is rapidly changing, however. The first seawater desalination plant in the United States was opened by the U.S. Navy on San Nicolas Island last October and a second is scheduled to open on Santa Catalina Island in late April. Santa Barbara has contracted for a larger desalination plant that would supply a third of its water needs by 1992.

Marin County operated a pilot desalination plant for three months last year and residents are expected to vote this fall on whether to construct a permanent facility to treat bay water.

The Metropolitan Water District, which supplies water to much of Southern California, expects to have a 5-million-gallon-per-day pilot desalination plant on line within three to four years and to

Please see THIRST, A34

INSIDE TODAY'S TIMES

■ **WAR STORIES, PHOTOS: A5-20; B3; E1; F3**

■ **RED CROSS SNUBBED**
Allied prisoners of war in Iraq remain off-limits to the International Committee of the Red Cross despite many pleas. **A5**

■ **EYES ON THE GROUND**
During an invasion of occupied Kuwait, U.S. lives may well depend more on the eyes and ears of crack military spies than on high-tech snooping. **A6**

■ **VISION STILL UNCLEAR**
Saddam Hussein helped President Bush find a slogan for his Administration. But neither Bush nor anyone else can define "the new world order." **A9**

WEATHER: Clear skies today with a warming trend. Civic Center low/high: 50/75. Details: B2

■ TOP OF THE NEWS ON A2

ANACLETO RAPPING / Los Angeles Times

Ants on Santa Barbara foray.

■ **INVASION OF THE ANTS**
Droves of ants have invaded homes and other buildings throughout the Southland in search of a drink of water in this fifth year of drought. **A3**

Ancient Doctrine Guiding Futuristic Warfare in Gulf

■ **Strategy:** Sun Tzu's tiny book, written more than 2,500 years ago, is influencing U.S. and Iraqi tactics.

By PAUL RICHTER
TIMES STAFF WRITER

WASHINGTON—A general who long ago led troops with brass-tipped spears and rhinoceros-hide shields is today helping guide the high-tech missile and tank warfare in the Persian Gulf.

He is Sun Tzu, a shadowy figure of 6th-Century BC China who preached a military philosophy of subtlety and cunning in a tiny book called the "The Art of War." Long a revered text in Asian military academies, the volume of aphorisms has stirred new interest among the U.S. armed forces and contributed to a revolution in basic tactics in the U.S. Marine Corps.

Indeed, Sun Tzu's principles are even being applied by the Iraqis, who absorbed his ideas in the 1970s and 1980s from their Soviet military advisers, according to military analysts.

"You could say Sun Tzu's spirit is hovering above the whole conflict," says Col. Sam Gardiner, a retired Air Force officer who used to head a department at the National War College in Washington.

Sun Tzu's doctrine is the opposite of the thinking that some people associate with the U.S. military.

Rather than applying massive firepower, Sun Tzu argued that the successful military leader will outwit his adversary with deception, disinformation, lightning flank at-

Please see BOOK, A14

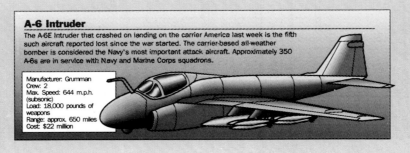

A-6 Intruder

The A-6E Intruder that crashed on landing on the carrier America last week is the fifth such aircraft reported lost since the war started. The carrier-based all-weather bomber is considered the Navy's most important attack aircraft. Approximately 350 A-6s are in service with Navy and Marine Corps squadrons.

Manufacturer: Grumman
Crew: 2
Max. Speed: 644 m.p.h. (subsonic)
Load: 18,000 pounds of weapons
Range: approx. 650 miles
Cost: $22 million

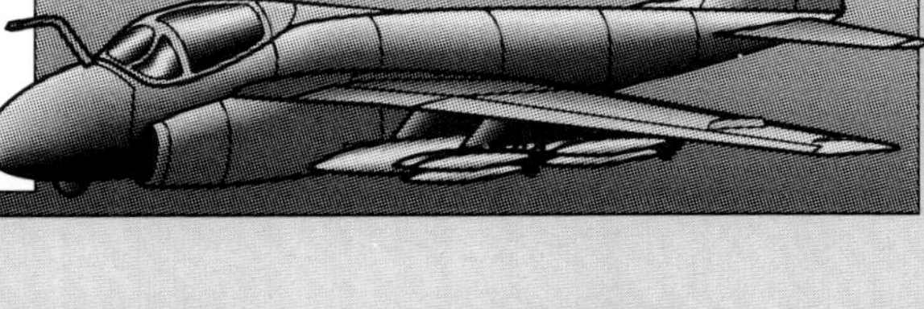

Military: A briefer says U.S. soldiers skirmished with Iraqi forces on the Saudi border, capturing 20 soldiers. Two Americans are killed and six wounded by "friendly fire" by an Army helicopter during one of seven border engagements overnight.
■ Baghdad experiences its quietest night since the war began, with no air raids. Heavy rain and a sandstorm buffet the capital, impairing visibility.
■ Allied troops take up new positions in remote border areas and test their tanks.
■ U.S. Navy supply ships in the Persian Gulf pour hundreds of tons of supplies an hour into warships; commanders say the four-day resupply effort is the biggest of its kind ever attempted.
■ British military officials admit that a "smart" bomb dropped from one of its warplanes veered off course and into the Iraqi town of Fallouja last week.

Diplomacy: Iraqi Foreign Minister Tarik Aziz arrives in Moscow but says he is not carrying any new proposals.
■ President Bush and his advisers offer little hope for a diplomatic solution to the war.
■ Abdul Razik Hashimi, Iraq's ambassador to France, says the conditions attached to Baghdad's pullout proposal are intended as an opening offer meant to lead to negotiations.

Terrorism: U.S. officials say unprecedented international cooperation and the expulsion of more than 100 Iraqi diplomats around the world prevented Saddam Hussein from delivering on his pledge to wage a campaign of terror against the allies.

Environment: Iran says oil fires in Iraq are causing a black rain that "has polluted the environment, water and agricultural resources in the region."
■ A southeasterly wind briefly halts a giant oil slick that had been moving toward vital water and industrial plants on the Saudi coast.

Home front: A protester stages a demonstration at a church service attended by President Bush.

First war, then insurrection: Iraqi refugees in the town of Safwan.

PATRICK DOWNS / Los Angeles Times

DEMANDS AND ISSUES

Many of Iraq's conditions for withdrawal from Kuwait reflect recurring issues in the region. Any eventual peace settlement will have to address them, including:

• **BOYCOTT:** Iraq wants an end to the embargo. However, the U.S. has suggested that the boycott will remain as long as Saddam Hussein is in power. The U.N. has tied ending the embargo to Iraq's withdrawal.

• **OCCUPATION:** If victorious, the allies would maintain an occupation force for a certain period. Under Iraq's terms, the U.S. and its and allies would withdraw forces within a month of Iraq's withdrawal from Kuwait. Who prevails will affect the ultimate balance of power in the region.

• **ISRAEL:** The United States has insisted that it would not talk about linkage, but the question of Israel and the occupied territories will almost certainly factor in peace talks.

• **TERRITORIAL RIGHTS:** Iraq has long claimed "historical rights on land and at sea" in Kuwait and the Gulf.

• **REPARATIONS:** Who will pay to rebuild Iraq? Iraq is insisting that the allies must rebuild targets they destroyed while the allies want Iraq to pay for damage to Kuwait.

Iraqi Foreign Minister Tarik Aziz

MISSION TO
MOSCOW

Soviet President Mikhail S. Gorbachev

Soviet President Mikhail S. Gorbachev's meeting today with Iraqi Foreign Minister Tarik Aziz was announced last week after Soviet envoy Yevgeny M. Primakov visited Baghdad. Iraq followed that announcement Friday by making an offer to withdraw from Kuwait–if a long list of conditions were met. Today's meeting is now seen as a way to measure Saddam Hussein's sincerity and to explore the conditions attached to his offer. Some of the issues that will be talked about will recur in subsequent attempts to reach a peace settlement.

• **MOSCOW:** Soviet officials have stressed that Iraq must leave Kuwait and has no right to pose preconditions, but added that it is not too late to make one more attempt at a diplomatic solution that would avert a bloody ground war.

• **BAGHDAD:** Iraqi leaders claim that their conditional offer to withdraw from Kuwait was made in response to Soviet diplomatic initiatives, and that Aziz's mission to Moscow will be a way of exploring reactions to last Friday's offer. Iraq's ambassador to France indicates that the list of conditions is meant merely as an opening offer.

• **WASHINGTON:** Bush Administration officials say they will be satisfied if Gorbachev can persuade Iraq to withdraw unconditionally from Kuwait. But they say the United States is not interested in any last-minute negotiations on conditions for withdrawal and will not disrupt its military planning for the Moscow meeting.

REACTION

• **JORDAN:** Jordanian officials have described the Iraqi proprosal as a "significant shift" that should bode well for peace.

• **FRANCE:** France has been in the forefront of allies urging negotiation but indicated Sunday that Iraq's offer to withdraw must be accompanied by deed. "We would begin to consider this seriously," said French Foreign Minister Roland Dumas, if Hussein begins withdrawing "massively, immediately and unconditionally."

• **ISRAEL:** Iraq's conditional offer is a sign that Hussein is beginning to realize that he is in serious trouble, said Israeli Defense Minister Moshe Arens.

• **VATICAN:** Pope John Paul II distanced himself from Italian leftists and pacifists, declaringSunday that he does not seek "peace at any cost."

• **IRAN:** Iranian President Hashemi Rafsanjani, a key player in efforts to end the Gulf War, said Iraq's offer has created a chance for peace. Tehran is sending a senior delegation to Iraq soon with a reply to an earlier message from Saddam Hussein. Pakistani Foreign Minister Sahabzada Yaqub Khan was due in Tehran for peace talks.

Iranian President Hashemi Rafsanjani

81

DAY 34

FEBRUARY 19, 1991

Before Petty Officer 2nd Class Arrington Leonard shipped out, he took an old, blue cotton shirt and made a pillow out of it for his 6-year-old son. With his father gone, Kenny slept wrapped around the "Daddy pillow." And when the boy was upset, he would grab for it.

I met Kenny when his father's ship, the destroyer tender Acadia, pulled out in September. He was screaming: "Daddy! Don't leave me!" It was the kind of scream that tugs at your guts.

After the war began, Kenny wrote his father a letter. In big capital letters, he scrawled: "BE BRAVE."

Every time I visited, Kenny's collection of GI Joe dolls had grown. He was gathering the dolls, Kenny explained, to form a rescue team headed for the Persian Gulf, where they would save his father.

—Nora Zamichow,
in San Diego County

Los Angeles Times

CIRCULATION: 1,225,189 DAILY / 1,514,096 SUNDAY

TUESDAY, FEBRUARY 19, 1991

COPYRIGHT 1991 / THE TIMES MIRROR COMPANY / CC / 102 PAGES

DAILY 25¢ DESIGNATED AREAS HIGHER

Gorbachev Plan Urges Kuwait Pullout, Pledges Iraq Survival

Associated Press

Soviet President Mikhail S. Gorbachev, right, Foreign Minister Alexander A. Bessmertnykh, center, and special Kremlin envoy Yevgeny Primakov listen to Iraqi Foreign Minister Tarik Aziz in Moscow.

■ **Diplomacy:** U.S. receives details but withholds comment. Aide to Hussein travels to Baghdad with Soviet proposal. Preparation for a land offensive continues.

By JOHN-THOR DAHLBURG
TIMES STAFF WRITER

MOSCOW—Soviet President Mikhail S. Gorbachev, in a surprise attempt to avert a fast-approaching ground war between Iraq and U.S.-led forces, delivered his own peace plan to a top Iraqi official on Monday.

Although details of the proposal were not immediately available, Soviet spokesmen said the plan is "fully in line" with United Nations demands for unconditional withdrawal of Saddam Hussein's troops from Kuwait, promising at the same time that the state of Iraq will survive.

White House officials said President Bush received a lengthy cable from Gorbachev that detailed the Moscow proposal.

But presidential Press Secretary Marlin Fitzwater said "the Soviets have asked that we treat the substance of this account as confidential. Thus we will not comment further on it."

Bush met late into the night with Secretary of State James A. Baker III and other top advisers, including Secretary of Defense Dick Cheney, National Security Adviser Brent Scowcroft, White House Chief of Staff John H. Sununu and Gen. Colin L. Powell, chairman of the Joint Chiefs of Staff.

Officials said that, barring a dramatic turnaround, allied forces will continue to prepare for a massive ground offensive against Iraqi forces in the near future.

"No change of mission has been given to Central Command," a Pentagon official said.

Fitzwater denied as "totally erroneous" reports that the Soviets had asked the United States to delay the start of a ground attack against Iraqi troops.

The Soviet proposal "doesn't require any response from us," he said. "This is between the Soviet Union and Iraq."

Soviet presidential spokesman Vitaly N. Ignatenko said Iraqi Foreign Minister Tarik Aziz received Gorbachev's plan "with interest and understanding" and left immediately for Baghdad, using a Soviet jetliner placed at his disposal. Aziz was expected to fly to Tehran, then travel overland from the Iranian capital to Baghdad.

"We are looking for a very speedy answer to the proposals that Mikhail Sergeyevich Gorbachev has made," Ignatenko emphasized. Soviet officials said they expected that Hussein would be briefed on the plan by today at the latest.

Declaring the Gorbachev-Aziz peace talks "a decisive turning point between war and peace," the Iraqi regime expressed optimism about them Monday while continuing to prepare its people for the devastation of a ground war.

Iraq's official media provided no

Please see PLAN, A14

COLUMN ONE

Sacrificing Lives, Not Lifestyles

■ Compared to other major U.S. wars, the conflict in the Gulf has had little financial impact on most Americans. A lengthy conflict, however, could change that.

By JONATHAN PETERSON
TIMES STAFF WRITER

The Persian Gulf War stands out from other U.S. wars in a vast chasm between the battlefield and the home front: Even as fighting rages, life in America goes on with little apparent sacrifice for most of the public.

Higher taxes do not appear likely, a departure from every major U.S. war this century. Consumers can shop for groceries and other goods unimpeded by special restrictions, unlike World War II. The cost to motorists actually has been going down. Oil, the commodity so central to the Gulf conflict, is glutting the market, and gasoline prices have fallen in recent days.

It may seem ironic to members of the armed forces and their loved ones, but in terms of normal, daily life, "most Americans have not been asked to sacrifice a thing," declares Robert B. Reich, a political economist at Harvard University's John F. Kennedy School of Government.

That state of affairs could change, of course. A lengthy war would strain the economy and exacerbate the U.S. budget deficit. Federal Reserve Chairman Alan Greenspan warned recently that if the war lasts longer than three months, the recession will get worse.

Unknowns about the postwar world—the level of terrorist threat, instability in the Middle East and reconstruction costs—threaten a different sort of toll that cannot yet be gauged. War-related anxieties already have eroded the confidence of U.S. consumers, leading to layoffs by auto makers, airlines and other beleaguered employers.

Yet for the moment at least, most Americans don't really feel the pinch. Odd as it may seem, economists say the U.S. economy has become so colossal, the defense sector so vast, that Americans typically face little inconvenience even as the battle goes on.

"The average person is untouched," said Martin Anderson, a senior fellow at the Hoover Institution and former domestic and economic policy adviser to President Reagan.

Unlike earlier wars, the United States entered the Gulf battle with a gigantic military arsenal in place, one originally meant for use against the Soviet Union. As a result, there has been no sudden need, say, for auto makers in Detroit to retool factories in a rush to make tanks or airplanes.

Consider the $1.35-million Tomahawk cruise missile, now being fired off U.S. ships toward targets in Kuwait and Iraq.

Since the war began, the United States has launched some 300 Tomahawks, according to the non-

Please see SACRIFICES, A10

Bombs Rip Rail Stations in London

By WILLIAM TUOHY
TIMES STAFF WRITER

LONDON—Central London was plunged into daylong transport chaos Monday when rail and subway services were drastically curtailed after two explosions in railroad stations killed one man and injured 43 others.

Later, the Irish Republican Army in an unsubstantiated telephone message claimed responsibility for the blasts—in what was the IRA's first major attack against obviously civilian targets since the bombing of Harrod's department store in 1983, which killed six people.

Please see BOMBS, A18

THE TIMES POLL

Most Wary but Will Support a Ground War

By RONALD BROWNSTEIN
TIMES POLITICAL WRITER

As military preparations intensify in the Middle East, Americans remain reluctant to immediately begin a potentially bloody ground war against Iraq but indicate they will rally behind President Bush if he decides to launch such an attack, a new Los Angeles Times Poll shows.

On the eve of what may be the decisive confrontation in the Gulf crisis, the poll finds America in a hesitantly hawkish mood, with a substantial majority rejecting any negotiations until Iraq has unconditionally withdrawn from Kuwait but simultaneously preferring to rely as long as possible on air attacks before subjecting U.S. troops to the unpredictable risks of a ground assault.

Neither the reports of civilian casualties in Baghdad, nor the flurry of diplomatic maneuvers by Iraq and the Soviet Union, have dented the public support for the war, the poll found. After one month of fighting, the public remains overwhelmingly committed: 81% of those surveyed said they backed the decision to fight, virtually unchanged from the war's first week, and 63% strongly support the war.

At the same time, 84% of those polled approve of Bush's handling of the crisis—down only minimally from the stratospheric 88% approval the President received in the war's euphoric first days. And despite deepening fears about the economy, 82% approved of Bush's overall performance as President—among the highest figures ever recorded for any President.

That public confidence represents, perhaps, the key political asset for Bush as he confronts America's jagged apprehensions about moving from a virtually unchallenged air war, which some have likened to a video game, into a ground conflict, which many fear could instead call to mind grue-

Please see POLL, A12

Mines Damage 2 U.S. Warships in the Gulf

■ **Conflict:** Allies press air campaign against Iraqis. F-16 pilot is plucked from Kuwait in a daring rescue.

By DAVID LAMB
TIMES STAFF WRITER

RIYADH, Saudi Arabia—Mines damaged two American warships in the northern Persian Gulf on Monday, ripping a 16-by-25-foot hole in one and slightly injuring seven sailors.

Allied forces, meanwhile, launched heavy air strikes against Iraqi troop positions on Monday, as well as initiating artillery duels across the Kuwaiti border. The United Arab Emirates joined the air battle, flying four missions with French-built Mirage 2000s against the Iraqis inside Kuwait.

The San Diego-based Tripoli, an amphibious assault carrier, was leading a minesweeping operation about 4:30 a.m. when a blast tore open the hole in its forward starboard hull, about 10 feet below the waterline, flooding several compartments.

About two hours later, the $1-billion guided-missile cruiser Princeton, based in Long Beach, was rocked by another mine as it steamed toward the Tripoli in response to what turned out to be a false alarm that two crewmen had been thrown overboard by the earlier explosion.

Marine Brig. Gen. Richard I. Neal said the Tripoli apparently hit a floating contact mine, but early indications were that the Princeton was damaged by a so-called "influence" mine—one that detonates without contact—because "surprisingly, there is no hole."

In the air action, a U.S. F-16 fighter was downed over Kuwait, but an American helicopter crew, with jet fighters providing cover overhead, made a daring rescue of the pilot, flying 40 miles into the occupied emirate to pluck him to safety.

Please see WAR, A6

Social Security Expects to Cut Services Sharply

By ROBERT A. ROSENBLATT
TIMES STAFF WRITER

WASHINGTON—Top officials of the Social Security Administration are privately predicting that sharply rising caseloads and expected budgetary restrictions will force them to cut services significantly this year.

Officials say their top priority will be getting the monthly Social Security checks out on time to the 42 million people who already receive benefits of one kind or another.

But everything else will take longer, from delays in changing a recipient's address to adjusting the check of a retired person who works part time or handling the

Please see SERVICES, A21

Soviet Official Calls for 60% Hike in Prices

By ELIZABETH SHOGREN
TIMES STAFF WRITER

MOSCOW—Soviet Prime Minister Valentin S. Pavlov on Monday proposed price increases averaging 60% on food and most consumer goods for the first time since World War II.

"There will be fixed prices set by the state for staples and vital commodities, and they will be allowed to grow under tight controls imposed by the state," Pavlov told Soviet legislators at the opening of a new session of the Supreme Soviet, the national legislature.

Although state-set price ceilings will govern prices for basic goods—like meat, milk, flour, bread and sugar—prices will be freed on 30% of all retail goods, including leather shoes, refrigerators, washing machines and candy.

The price hikes, however, will be compensated, Pavlov said, by substantial aid payments to wage earners, conscripts, pensioners, students and families with children. These compensations would offset 85% of the price increases, he contended.

The proposals, which need parliamentary approval, have apparently been endorsed by President Mikhail S. Gorbachev, who appointed Pavlov to his post last month.

It was not clear when the increases would take effect. The government has been struggling with how to raise prices since September, 1987, and rumors of price hikes last year sparked wide-

Please see SOVIETS, A20

Lessons of the 1970s Shape Water Rationing Plans

■ **Drought:** Users will respond if they believe the emergency is real and the cutback applies to everyone.

By JENIFER WARREN
TIMES STAFF WRITER

When Goleta launched its model mandatory water rationing program in 1989, the experts were skeptical. The drought, while serious, was not mainstream dinner table conversation, and many officials figured that consumers—including thousands of students packed into apartments near UC Santa Barbara—would rebel and refuse to conserve.

> ■ **RATIONING APPEALS**
> Many water districts grant most requests to be exempt. A3

Nonetheless, Goleta proceeded gamely, directing its 74,000 customers to cut water use and giving them the low-flow shower heads and other nifty devices to do it. The reaction was nothing short of astounding. Asked to reduce usage by 15%, the Central Coast community delivered twice that.

"The key here was that rather than telling people, 'Reduce water or we're going to punish you,' we said, 'Reduce water and here's how we're going to help you,'" said Larry Farwell, conservation coordinator for the Goleta Water District. "They believed the need to save was real, and just like people waving their little yellow ribbons in support of the war, everybody got on board."

With cloudless skies warning

Please see RATIONING, A22

INSIDE TODAY'S TIMES

■ **WAR STORIES, PHOTOS: A5-17; E1; World Report**

■ **PROTEST BY FIRE**
A man in Amherst, Mass., carrying a sign that said "peace" set himself on fire and died, refusing offers of help. **A12**

■ **TARGETING HUSSEIN**
The United States and many of its allies in the Gulf War want to force Saddam Hussein out of Iraq, as well as Kuwait. Can they succeed? **In World Report**

■ **VOW OF VENGEANCE**
Veterans of the anti-Sandinista army in Nicaragua vowed to take up arms again to avenge the slaying of ex-Contra chief Enrique Bermudez. **A4**

WEATHER: Sunny today with gusty canyon winds. Civic Center low/high: 54/81. Details: B2

■ TOP OF THE NEWS ON A2

ROBERT DURELL / Los Angeles Times

Unfurling the flag in Porterville.

■ **PROUD PORTERVILLE**
Yellow ribbons hang from every tree in Porterville, it seems. The Central California town has sent about 150 of its sons and daughters to fight in the Gulf. **A9**

Chinese Fascinated by Gulf War, Strongly Back U.S.

■ **Reaction:** The government maintains a neutral stance. But some in Beijing say Bush should get tougher.

By DAVID HOLLEY
TIMES STAFF WRITER

BEIJING—When a couple of peasant farmers from China's far northeast visited a friend here last month, they weren't interested in seeing the sights. All they cared about, their young Chinese host said, was keeping score on the Gulf War: Who had used what weapons and how many planes had been shot down?

"They treated the fighting like a soccer match," he lamented. "It was really shocking to me to see these people more excited about people dying than I had ever seen them before."

Since the first U.S. bombs fell on Baghdad, a curious kind of war fever has swept China, despite efforts by the state-run media to cool the excitement with low-key reporting.

Most public sentiment in Beijing is vehemently pro-American. In conversations, Chinese often say Iraqi President Saddam Hussein should be punished. Expressions of hope for still-fiercer attacks on Iraqi forces are common.

"[President] Bush is much too weak," a taxi driver complained. "He should go in there and get rid of Hussein with one nuclear bomb. Then this would all be over."

But beneath the surface, fascination with the war and the outpouring of support for the United States may reveal as much about China's

Please see CHINA, A16

T-72 Tank

Iraq's best tank, the Soviet-built T-72, is considered to be a match for the U.S.'s M-1A1 tank. Heavily armored and often manned by Saddam Hussein's vaunted Republican Guard troops. Most of Iraq's estimated 1,000 T-72s are in prepared defensive positions with overhead cover, making them hard to detect.

Crew: 3 or 4
Length: 23 feet
Top Speed: 50 m.p.h.
Weight: 45 tons
Armament: 125mm cannon, coaxial 7.62mm machine gun, and a 12.7mm turret-mounted antiaircraft machine gun.

Los Angeles Times

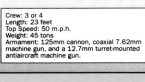

After the fighting, catching some rays and reading on an upturned tank.

PATRICK DOWNS / Los Angeles Times

FEEDING THE TROOPS

In the early 1800s, Napoleon's army was able to take advantage of a brand-new technology: canning. Since then, food for the troops has gotten steadily better. In the Persian Gulf, front-line soldiers have been eating the next best thing to home cooking—military version.

Generations of American soldiers knew them as C-rations: canned victuals that included such culinary delights as Spam, pork and beans and the beloved fruit cocktail. Today's U.S. combat troops dine from individual foil-lined plastic pouches called MREs (Meal, Ready-to-Eat) that feature entrees ranging from chicken ala king to spaghetti with meat sauce. Ideally, troops in the field eat only one MRE a day. Field kitchens serving large numbers of troops offer more menu variety. Soldiers in the desert heat must drink 4 to 6 gallons of water per day.

The military is also testing MOREs, (Meal, Ordered Ready-to-Eat) which are similar to microwavable meals found in supermarkets.

MREs:

Each foil-lined plastic pouch weighs 1 1/2 pounds and contains several smaller packages of precooked food, condiments, and other items. To avoid monotony and improve nutrition, the military tries not to feed troops MREs for longer than 10 days at a time, although they've been field-tested for up to 30.

American troops are served B-rations—hot meals that are a treat for soldiers in the field who sometimes eat cold rations called MREs.

Associated Press

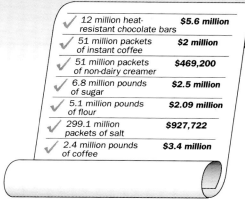

A U.S. soldier from the 1st Armred Division heats his MRE over a camping stove.

Reuters

Sample MRE:
- pork with rice in BBQ sauce
- applesauce
- jelly
- crackers
- cocoa beverage
- powder
- spoon
- accessory packet*

- Calories: 1,300
- Cost: $3.90
- Preparation: Ready-to-eat, can be heated in hot water, hot sand, on top of a hot engine or under the arm.
- Shelf life: 6 years

OTHER KINDS OF RATIONS

A-rations:
The best. Hot meals made with fresh meat, vegetables and fruit (being supplied by the Saudis) prepared at cafeterias away from the front. For those fortunate enough to be close to a hotel, the fare might include "Saudi Champagne:"

Saudi Champagne:
- 12-ounces of Perrier
- 12-ounces of apple juice
- sliced apples and oranges
- mixed in pitcher, served chilled

B-rations:
Also served hot. Meals primarily made from dehydrated meat and canned food, served aboard ship, at cafeterias or at mobile kitchens in the field. B-rations are often supplemented with fresh meat and produce.

T-rations (tray rations):
Available in 20 menus. One tray-pack provides enough food and utensils for 36 soldiers, supplying a better variety of food than MREs. Containers are placed in hot water and can be served buffet-style from temporary tents and mobile kitchens in the field. Tray Ration sample menu:

Sample Lunch/Dinner:
- chicken cacciatore
- potatoes diced in butter sauce
- green beans
- chocolate pudding
- lemon-lime beverage powder
- peanut butter, jelly
- 5-compartment plate
- 8-oz cup
- accessory packet*

*Accessory packet includes coffee, cream substitute, sugar, salt, matches, toilet tissue, chewing gum, towelette, candy or bottle of hot sauce.

THE FOOD BILL

The military is spending about $4.5 million per day to feed the troops in the Mideast. The total grocery bill since Iraq's invasion of Kuwait adds up to about $850 million. Food orders include:

✓ 12 million heat-resistant chocolate bars	**$5.6 million**
✓ 51 million packets of instant coffee	**$2 million**
✓ 51 million packets of non-dairy creamer	**$469,200**
✓ 6.8 million pounds of sugar	**$2.5 million**
✓ 5.1 million pounds of flour	**$2.09 million**
✓ 299.1 million packets of salt	**$927,722**
✓ 2.4 million pounds of coffee	**$3.4 million**

TOP FOOD CONTRACTORS

Almost a third of all the food budget is going to four companies.

$62 million   **Oregon Freeze Dry, Albany, Ore.:** Freeze-dried meat

$55 million   **Vanee Foods Co., Berkeley, Ill.:** Vacuum-packed "T-rations" that include canned pudding, sausage links and lasagna.

$44.6 million   **Geo. A. Hormel Co. Austin, Minn. (Top Shelf meals):** For use in MREs. Entrees include, beef sukiyaki and glazed breast of chicken.

$14 million   **Fisher Foods Ltd., Lincoln, Neb.:** Dehydrated scrambled eggs.

Associated Press

Lance Cpl. Cory Keeling of 1st Service Support Group, spoons "chili-mac" into insulated containers. Group prepares 22,000 hot meals a day.

83

JUAN THOMASSIE / Los Angeles Times

DAY 35

FEBRUARY 20, 1991

U.S. commanders were much more confident of a quick military victory than they were willing to admit publicly. A few days before the ground war began, I asked Desert Storm's U.S. commander, Gen. H. Norman Schwarzkopf, how prolonged and bloody the fighting would be.

"It won't be that prolonged or that bloody," he replied. Then he caught himself and added a string of qualifiers a yard long.

Afterwards, when I looked over my notes, I decided to err on the side of caution. In my report of the interview I did not even mention his assessment. Looking back now, I'm convinced the general knew exactly what bad shape the Iraqi forces were in. But he had learned the lessons of the Vietnam War: Prepare the public for the worst, not the best.

—David Lamb,
in Riyadh, Saudi Arabia

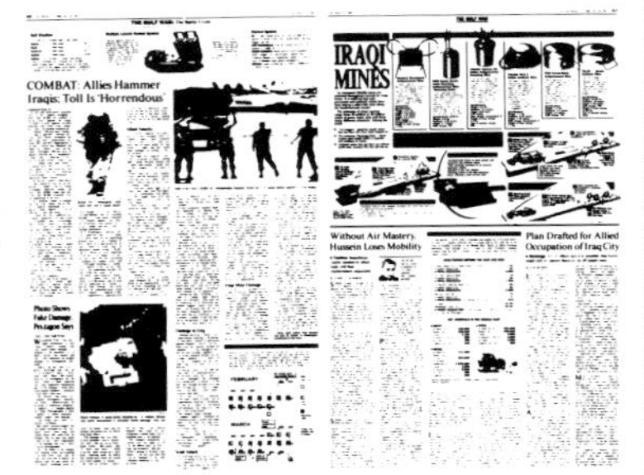

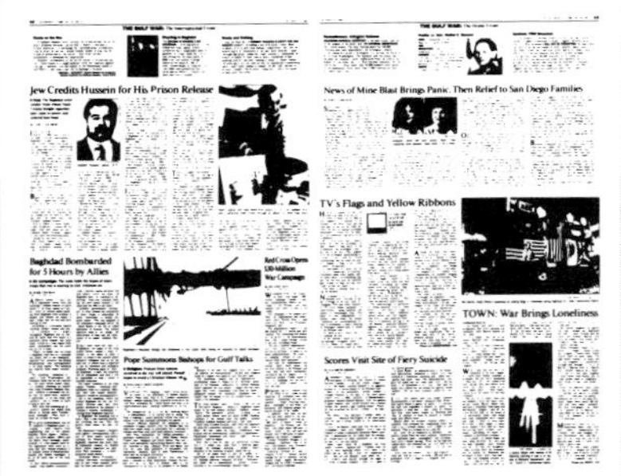

Los Angeles Times

CIRCULATION: 1,225,189 DAILY / 1,514,096 SUNDAY

WEDNESDAY, FEBRUARY 20, 1991
COPYRIGHT 1991 / THE TIMES MIRROR COMPANY / CC†† / 92 PAGES

DAILY 25¢
DESIGNATED AREAS HIGHER

COLUMN ONE

The Media Take a Pounding

■ Pentagon rules and instant communication have changed the way war is reported. Reporters come off as clumsy villains in the Gulf drama.

By THOMAS B. ROSENSTIEL
TIMES STAFF WRITER

WASHINGTON—It may have been the strongest signal yet of who is losing the political battle of the Persian Gulf war.

NBC's "Saturday Night Live" recently opened with a skit pointedly satirizing not Iraqi President Saddam Hussein, or President Bush, or U.S. commander Gen. H. Norman Schwarzkopf, or even Vice President Dan Quayle.

Instead, the skit shredded the American press corps. Every question that the red-eyed media horde asked at a mock Pentagon briefing seemed designed to help the enemy.

Being the butt of jokes on late-night television is not the only sign that the press has come to be seen as a clumsy villain in the Gulf War drama. Sen. Alan K. Simpson (R-Wyo.) recently accused Cable News Network's Baghdad correspondent Peter Arnett of being an Iraqi "sympathizer." Frankly, say CNN executives, Simpson was only piling on: Callers and letter writers to CNN have denounced Arnett from the beginning.

And polls show the public agrees with the military that there should be rigid restrictions on reporters in the Persian Gulf, rules most journalists say are limiting and perhaps even distorting public perception of the war.

A key factor, both military and press officials agree, is that the public is seeing the bulk of the reporting process as it happens, in military briefings. And gathering news, like making sausage or making laws, is not always an attractive sight.

Reporters shouting questions and trying to pry information often look rude, dense and disorganized on television—especially when going up against briefers trained to appear as officers and gentlemen and who can claim military security and saving lives whenever they refuse to answer a question.

And frankly, journalists admit, some questions are dumb. One reporter, for instance, recently asked briefers whether Iraqi optical antiaircraft artillery might change the course of the war. No, the officer said politely, this wouldn't help the enemy much. Optical targeting merely means the Iraqis had abandoned their ineffective radar and were aiming their guns by eyesight.

In addition to seeing news gathered, the public's ability to see the war from all sides instantly also has made the media far more a weapon—and a target—than in any previous war.

Iraq, for instance, followed its purported peace offer last week with another more private message to the West: It invited more U.S. news organizations to Baghdad, with the obvious intent that this would help tell the Iraqi side of the

Please see MEDIA, A16

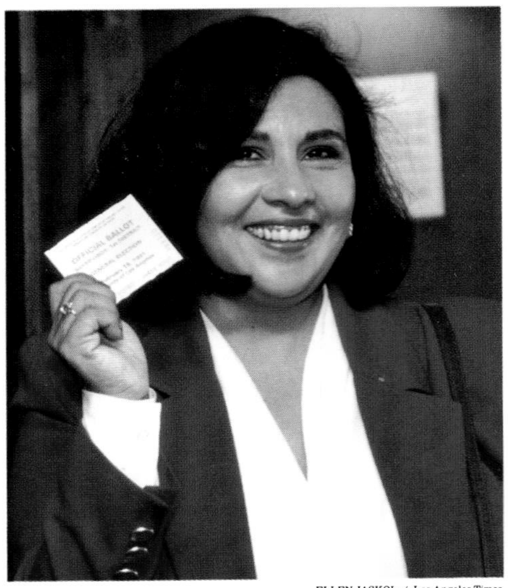

ELLEN JASKOL / Los Angeles Times

Gloria Molina displays her ballot stub after voting in 1st District race.

Molina Wins Historic Contest for Supervisor

■ **Politics:** The victory culminates a long struggle to put a Latino on board. She is first woman elected to panel.

By RICHARD SIMON
TIMES STAFF WRITER

Gloria Molina, a farm worker's daughter who rose from grass-roots politics to become a force in Los Angeles government, was elected Tuesday to the County Board of Supervisors, culminating a long struggle for Latino representation in county government.

Molina, a Los Angeles city councilwoman, defeated Democratic state Sen. Art Torres 55.4% to 44.6% to become the first Latino this century and first woman ever elected to the governing board of the nation's most populous county. Voter turnout in the historic 1st District race was 23%.

"I feel great, so great," Molina said, claiming victory at 10:05 p.m. "We went door to door talking to voters and conducted a grass-roots campaign, and that really made a difference."

At a packed East Los Angeles assembly hall, cheers filled the room and the crowd of about 700 supporters sang "Viva Gloria Molina" throughout the night. Molina walked through the crowd hugging and kissing supporters with her parents at her side. "It means people really care what happens in this district," Molina said. "I'm very proud to have their support."

Conceding defeat at 10:40 p.m., Torres said: "Gloria Molina, I gave you your first job. Gloria Molina, I supported you for the Legislature. Gloria Molina, you are the winner, and I congratulate you."

Torres had spent much of the night secluded with close political ally City Councilman Richard Alatorre in a private room at Stevens Steak House in the City of Commerce.

After conceding, the senator went to Molina's celebration, hugged her and raised her arm in a victory salute. "Let's all work together," he said.

Molina led Torres among Latino voters, 59% to 41% and among Anglos, 52% to 48%, according to an exit poll of about 1,000 voters commissioned by Spanish-language television station KMEX. Pollster Sergio Bendixen said that Molina also carried the women's vote, 60% to 40%, and the male vote, 54% to 46%. Molina led Torres in heavily Democratic East

Please see ELECTION, A18

■ THE REAL VICTORY
For those who brought the voting rights suit, the balloting was the real victory. B1

L.A. OKs Water Rationing; More Cutbacks Likely

By JANE FRITSCH
TIMES STAFF WRITER

Five years into a tenacious drought, the Los Angeles City Council on Tuesday imposed the toughest water-rationing measures in the city's history, and officials predicted that even more stringent measures may be necessary by the end of the year.

Beginning March 1, the city's 3.5 million residents will have to cut water use by 10% from 1986 levels and, on May 1, by an additional 5%. Those who fail to comply face stiff penalties.

"I don't think we can wait," said Councilwoman Joan Milke Flores. "We are in a desperate situation and we must act accordingly."

The 11-1 vote, with Councilman Nate Holden dissenting, came after

Please see WATER, A20

Soviet Peace Proposal Falls Short, Bush Says

Gorbachev Must Go, Yeltsin Says

By JOHN-THOR DAHLBURG
TIMES STAFF WRITER

MOSCOW—Exploding a political bombshell on live nationwide television, Boris N. Yeltsin issued an unprecedented call Tuesday night for Soviet President Mikhail S. Gorbachev's immediate resignation, charging that Gorbachev's reform drive has degenerated into a quest for boundless dictatorial powers.

In an announcement likely to rock this country's political world to its core, Yeltsin, president of the Russian Federation, the largest and most populous Soviet republic, said that he is severing all political ties with Gorbachev and called on Russians for their support.

"I am disassociating myself from the presidential position and policy and calling for his immediate resignation and the delegation of [his] powers to a collective body, namely the Council of the Federation," Yeltsin said, referring to the executive body to which he and the leaders of the other 14 republics belong.

As long as Gorbachev remains in office, Yeltsin charged, the Soviet people cannot hope for an easing of their nation's economic and social woes and there is no hope that local authorities can break Moscow's grip on their economies or politics.

Yeltsin's harsh words were a body blow to Gorbachev's efforts to calm this country's growing political crisis, a fact that was not lost on the Soviet television journalist who questioned Yeltsin during the 40-minute program.

Please see SOVIETS, A21

Schwarzkopf Sees Iraqis on Edge of Collapse

By DAVID LAMB
TIMES STAFF WRITER

RIYADH, Saudi Arabia—Gen. H. Norman Schwarzkopf said Tuesday the Iraqi military machine is on the verge of collapse and is losing about two battalions of tanks a day to allied air strikes, an attrition rate that no army can survive.

In assessing 34 days of warfare, Schwarzkopf, the U.S. commander of Operation Desert Storm, said Iraq's military capabilities were probably overrated in the first place.

Its performance, he said, is reflective of something that the allies knew intuitively last fall but seldom talked about publicly: After fighting Iran for eight years, the Iraqi army was

Please see WAR, A13

Iraqi Pullout Could Increase Gulf Instability

By ROBIN WRIGHT
TIMES STAFF WRITER

WASHINGTON—The possibility that Iraqi President Saddam Hussein might voluntarily withdraw from Kuwait and eliminate the need for a bloody ground war—a prospect raised by the Soviet Union's 11th-hour, weekend peace initiative—sent an understandable surge of hope through millions of Americans.

But an Iraqi withdrawal that permits Hussein to survive as head of a still-powerful military machine could leave the United States and its allies with a more difficult, even more volatile situation in the Persian Gulf than it faced before the war began, according to U.S. officials, foreign envoys and Middle East specialists.

While Baghdad's agreement to withdraw unconditionally before a ground war starts would probably spare hundreds, even thousands of lives, a settlement of the kind

NEWS ANALYSIS

being pressed by the Soviet Union and Iran could be even more costly in the long run.

"There's absolutely no question that Saddam's survival would make this incredibly messy, from a security standpoint, from a political standpoint, from virtually every standpoint you look at," said a leading U.S. military analyst.

"Many of the nascent plans for the postwar Middle East presumed tacitly that we'd be dealing with a different government in Baghdad,

Please see ANALYSIS, A12

Allied Aircraft Pound Iraqis in 'Turkey Shoot'

By J. MICHAEL KENNEDY
TIMES STAFF WRITER

RIYADH, Saudi Arabia—American helicopters and jets hammered Iraqi tanks, trucks and armored personnel carriers in what one pilot described Tuesday as a "turkey shoot," and a senior U.S. military source said the month-old air campaign is inflicting "horrendous casualties" on Saddam Hussein's forces.

Baghdad came under repeated bombardment overnight and French fighter-bombers attacked Hussein's artillery positions in Kuwait and Iraq as allied forces intensified their attempts to strip Iraqi troops of their will to fight in what many believe are the final hours before a massive, U.S.-led ground offensive.

Please see COMBAT, A6

■ **Diplomacy:** President is critical of the plan, but officials say it has not been rejected. Iraq's foreign minister is expected back in Moscow today.

By JAMES GERSTENZANG
TIMES STAFF WRITER

WASHINGTON—President Bush on Tuesday threw cold water on the new Soviet peace plan, saying "it falls well short of what would be required" to end the Gulf War.

His remarks—the first he has made in public on the secret proposal—appeared to dismiss what was seen as the last chance to avoid a brutal war on the ground to throw Iraq's occupying force out of Kuwait.

Nevertheless, the diplomatic flurry the plan spawned seemed to put the start of an offensive on hold for at least another day, and there remained some signs that the United States was not rejecting it out of hand.

"It would look bad to have a live thing on the table and go to a ground war," a White House official said. Also, the State Department insisted that the United States is not rejecting the plan at this point.

White House Press Secretary Marlin Fitzwater also put a positive spin on the U.S. reaction to the proposal by Soviet President Mikhail S. Gorbachev.

"We've said from the beginning that if President Gorbachev can be helpful in getting [Iraqi President] Saddam Hussein to pull out of Kuwait, so much the better," Fitzwater said.

He said the Kremlin initiative is still in progress and added: "Essentially, it could be helpful."

There was no official response Tuesday from Iraq to the Soviet proposal. But Yuli M. Vorontsov, the Soviet ambassador to the United Nations, said Iraqi Foreign Minister Tarik Aziz was expected back in the Soviet capital today. Aziz was given the proposal Monday by Gorbachev in Moscow and took it immediately to Baghdad.

Although details of the plan remain secret, the Soviets have described it as "fully in line" with the United Nations' demands for an unconditional Iraqi withdrawal from Kuwait. "The key element of the plan consists in securing a rapid start of a withdrawal of the Iraqi forces from Kuwait," Vorontsov said.

But the plan also reportedly offered assurances of no penalties for Iraq or its leadership, along with other controversial points.

The British response was negative, but France indicated the plan might be acceptable if the Iraqis accept it and pull out immediately.

At the United Nations, some diplomats predicted a fight in the Security Council if Hussein accepts the proposal and Bush rejects it. One Western diplomat predicted calls for a cease-fire in the council if Iraq agrees to the plan.

Bush, meeting with congressional leaders, said "as far as I'm concerned, there are no negotiations. The goals have been set out."

Please see PLAN, A14

Recession Lowers Prices of Luxury Homes, Slows Sales

■ **Economy:** The drag on a market that thrived in bad times shows this downturn may be worse than others.

By JUBE SHIVER Jr.
TIMES STAFF WRITER

In Orange, the asking price for a 30,000-square-foot mansion owned by the founder of the Clothestime women's apparel chain has been cut by nearly one-third to $14.95 million, but the home still has not attracted a buyer after nearly a year.

In Montecito near Santa Barbara, a Mediterranean-style villa owned by musician Kenny Loggins has languished on the market for more than six months, despite a $2-million price reduction.

In Bel-Air, a 6,500-square-foot home sold last month for about $1.5 million in a neighborhood where similar homes had brought $3 million just 18 months ago.

For years, the luxury home market defied economic gyrations and kept expanding through good times and bad. But now, even the wealthy are beginning to feel the chill of recession, as home prices tumble and houses go unsold for longer periods than at any time in the last 10 years.

The turn of fortunes at the upper end of the housing market is a sign that the current economic downturn—fueled by fading consumer confidence and uncertainty over the Persian Gulf War—may be cutting a wider swath than previous slumps. And a worldwide economic slowdown is adding to the

Please see LUXURY, A17

INSIDE TODAY'S TIMES

■ WAR STORIES, PHOTOS: A5-16; D1; F14

■ PROXY FIGHT
The Gulf War is almost a laboratory for a U.S.-Soviet conflict. The West uses U.S. equipment and doctrine, and the Iraqis depend on Soviet versions. A5

■ DROUGHT MEASURES
A lawmaker accused a federal agency of failing to promote water conservation among state farmers. Restraints on population growth are under study. A3

■ MILKEN'S SENTENCE
The judge who sentenced Michael Milken to 10 years in prison said she intended him to serve only 36 to 40 months. D2

WEATHER: Clear skies today through Thursday. Civic Center low/high today: 53/79. Details: B5

■ TOP OF THE NEWS ON A2

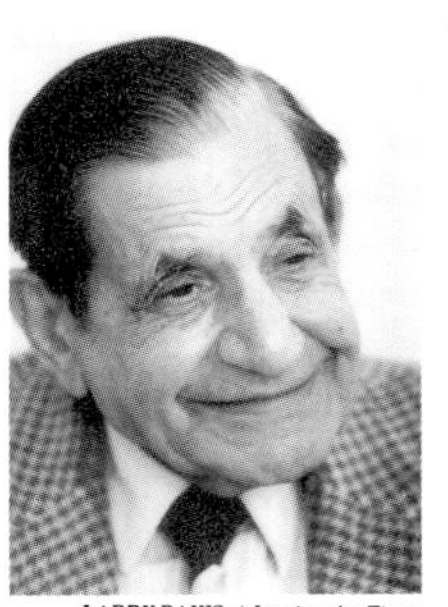

LARRY DAVIS / Los Angeles Times

Naim Twaina

■ HUSSEIN'S PAST
Naim Twaina, an Iraqi Jew now in Israel, recalls Saddam Hussein as the man who sold him cigarettes in Baghdad and later showed him mercy in prison. A8

Marine Town Fights Own Enemies: Loneliness, Fear

■ **Twentynine Palms:** Families say business is down, crime is up. They rely on toughness to get through war.

By SCOTT HARRIS
TIMES STAFF WRITER

TWENTYNINE PALMS, Calif.— Morning has come to the Bowladium, and since it's Thursday, so has the league that, inexplicably, changed its name this year from Desert Dolls to Desert Ladies.

On Lane 11, Peaches Oliva has rolled one right down the middle, the kind of ball that could spell triumph or disaster, a resounding strike or the dreaded 7-10 split.

It's a strike. Oliva claps as her teammates whoop and offer high-fives. Then she resumes the role of mommy. Two daughters, ages 4 and 2, are behind the ball rack and a third, age 13, is at school. The little ones are whining for candy, but they're a snap compared to her teen-ager.

"She's so rebellious," Oliva says. ". . . I just wish the ground war would happen so I'll know whether I'll have a husband or not."

In this isolated desert community next door to the massive Marine Corps Air Ground Combat Center, such fatalistic bravado is often preferable to outright expressions of pain and dread. War means not only anxiety to Twentynine Palms, but also loneliness, economic troubles and crime. Yet with suffering expected to mount, toughness is the order of the day.

So far, the war with Iraq has claimed the lives of seven young Marines who were based at Twen-

Please see TOWN, A9

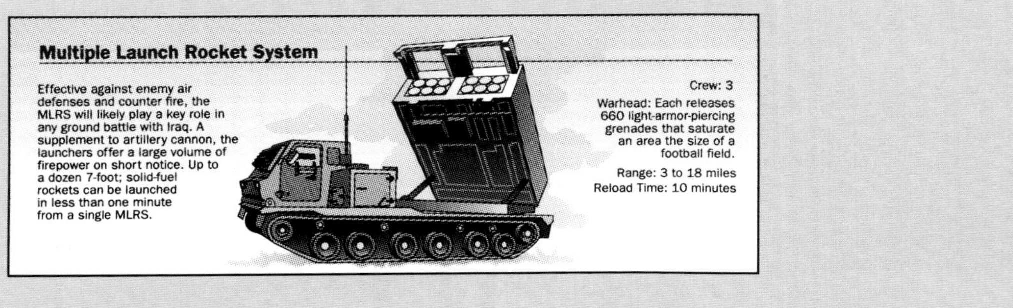

Multiple Launch Rocket System
Effective against enemy air defenses and counter fire, the MLRS will likely play a key role in any ground battle with Iraq. A supplement to artillery cannon, the launchers offer a large volume of firepower on short notice. Up to a dozen 7-foot; solid-fuel rockets can be launched in less than one minute from a single MLRS.
Crew: 3
Warhead: Each releases 660 light-armor-piercing grenades that saturate an area the size of a football field.
Range: 3 to 18 miles
Reload Time: 10 minutes

Thousands of land mines were recovered from Kuwaiti beaches.

PATRICK DOWNS / Los Angeles Times

Diplomacy: President Bush rejects a Soviet proposal to end the war in the Persian Gulf, saying there must be no negotiations and no concessions to gain Iraqi withdrawal from Kuwait.
■ The plan reportedly offers assurances of no penalties for Iraq or its leadership, along with other controversial points.

Military: Gen. H. Norman Schwarzkopf says in an interview that the Iraqi military machine is "on the verge of collapse" and is losing about two battalions of tanks a day.
■ American helicopters and jets hammer at Iraqi tanks, trucks and military equipment in what one pilot describes as a "turkey shoot."
■ The number of sorties flown by allies is now at 83,000.
■ The guided missile cruiser Princeton, one of two American warships to hit mines in the northern Persian Gulf, is towed to Bahrain.
■ An Iranian newspaper reports that more than 20,000 Iraqi troops have been killed and more than 60,000 wounded since the beginning of the war.
■ Lt. Gen. Thomas W. Kelly, director of operations for the Joint Chiefs of Staff, says the U.S. combat units are ready for the impending ground war.

Missiles: A Scud missile hits central Israel but causes no injuries.

Iraq: A military official in Baghdad says Iraq fired ground-to-ground missiles against concentrations of allied troops in Saudi Arabia, inflicting "heavy casualties." Allied military officials deny the report.
■ Baghdad is bombarded for five hours by the allies. The raids rattle the hopes of many Iraqis that the war is nearing its end.

Pentagon: Defense Secretary Dick Cheney says financial commitments by allies now total $41 million. The cost of the war to date is estimated at $56 billion.

Vatican: Pope John Paul II summons Roman Catholic bishops from countries involved in the Gulf War, including the United States and Iraq, to an unprecedented peace-seeking conference.

A DEADLY DANGER:
IRAQI MINES

An estimated 500,000 mines are scattered throughout Kuwait by Iraqi forces. It is believed that antipersonnel and antitank mines have been laid in a mile-wide zone along the Saudi-Kuwaiti border.

The estimates of Iraq's arsenal range from 10 million to 20 million mines of many types, sizes and from many different countries. Among the kinds:

▶ "Toe poppers," relatively simple mines that can blow off a foot when stepped on.

▶ The notorious "Bouncing Betty," which reaches chest height before it explodes and mutilates its victim.

▶ Antitank mines that can blow up a 60-ton battle tank, tossing it five feet into the air.

Inside the Iraqi Arsenal:

Cardoen Directional Antipersonnel Mine
• Chilean-made and created for defense and ambush.
• Curved rectangular body that can be installed on posts or trees or on the ground.
• Lethal within 52 feet over an arc 60 degrees wide; fragments can be dangerous within a range of 820 feet.
Approximate Specifications:
Weight: 3.47 lbs.
Length: 8.5 inches
Width: 1.37 inches
Height: 3.2 inches
Main charge: Composition C-4
Weight of main charge: 1.4 lbs.

OZM Series Soviet-made Bounding Antipersonnel Mine — "Bouncing Betty"
• Fires a grenade waist- or chest-high before exploding.
• Detonates by either remote electrical fire, pressure on a fuse or by pulling a wire attached to the fuse.
• Explodes 5 feet to 8 feet above the ground with an effective radius of 82 feet and can blow a person apart.
Specifications (OZM-3):
Weight: 6.6 lbs.
Diameter: 2.95 inches
Height: 4.7 inches
Main charge: TNT

Valsella Valmara 69 — Italian Antipersonnel Bounding Mine
• Cylindrical shape in plastic case with removable fuse mounted on top; spikes project out of top at angles.
• Bursts into more than 1,000 metal splinters. Lethal radius is at least 82 feet.
• Detonated by tripwire or by direct pressure on one or more of the fuse prongs.
• Fully waterproof.
Specifications:
Weight: 6.6 lbs.
Diameter: 5.1 inches
Height (with fuse): 8.07 inches
Main charge: Composition B
Weight of main charge: 0.9 lbs.
Type of booster charge: RDX

Valsella VS-2.2 — Italian Antitank Mine
• All plastic, waterproof, pressure-activated mine.
• Small, highly effective against main battle tank tracks and suspensions.
• Has anti-shock device that prevents accidental detonation.
• Iraq has these and comparable mines, not necessarily from Italy, but probably copies.
Specifications:
Weight: 7.7 lbs.
Diameter: 9.44 inches
Height: 4.72 inches
Main charge: Composition B
Weight of main charge: 4.7 lbs.

PMN Soviet-Made Antipersonnel Mine
• Most significant numerically and used extensively in combat throughout the world. Made of plastic with rubber cover.
• Hard to defuse.
• Detonates with pressure and can easely remove a leg.
• Estimated that hundred of thousands were deployed in Afghanistan.
Specifications:
Weight: 1.3 lbs.
Diameter: 4.4 inches
Height: 2.2 inches
Main charge: TNT

TM-46 — Soviet Antitank Mine
• Old technology, but Iraq has a lot of them.
• Metallic and laid either by hand or mechanically.
• Detonated by pressure.
• Versions are produced in Israel, China, Egypt and Bulgaria.
Specifications:
Weight: 19.55 lbs.
Diameter: 12 inches
Height: 4.33 inches
Main charge: TNT
Weight of main charge: 13.09 lbs.
Type of booster charge: Tetryl

Fighting the Threat
A variety of mine-clearing methods and equipment exist, from hand-held detectors to plows attached to armored tanks to sophisticated mine-explosive techniques. Among available methods, some of which may not be used in the gulf:

Giant Viper
A British made, 700-foot hose coiled in 2-ton box, 3-inch diameter, filled with plastic explosive.
B A cluster of eight rockets propels the hose.
C Three parachutes guide the tail as it straightens.
D Charge is fired electrically from towing vehicle and explodes, neutralizing mines.
The hose blasts a passage for vehicles at least 600 feet long and 24 feet wide.

Large plows are used by tanks and other fighting vehicles to clear path through the minefield

Fuel-air Explosives
1 21 mine-clearing rockets launched from an Assault Amphibious Vehicle
2 Parachute deploys at a pre-set time
3 Two-stage detonation spreads a fine mist of fuel in the air and then ignites it.
4 Shock waves detonate pressure-sensitive mines in the area.
1,000 feet-long by 66 feet-wide clearing

Aardvark Joint Services Flail Unit
• Scottish-built device to clear plastic antipersonnel and antitank mines.
• Flail assembly mounted on an armored half-track vehicle, attached to the rear chassis.
• Rotating action of the flail detonates mines, clearing a path 10 feet wide.

AN/PRS-8 Metallic and Non-metallic Mine Detectors
• Handheld detector with headset, equipped with solid-state electronics and signal-processing equipment.
• Can be used in any kind of soil.
• Once detected, the mine is marked and destroyed or later removed.
• Few U.S. versions available.

Mine-clearing Line Charge (MSLC) M-58A4
1 American-made linear charged-explosive-filled hose
2 The linear charge hose is launched by a 127-mm rocket. Forward travel is limited by a 206-foot arrest cable.
3 After reaching the minefield it explodes, detonating the mines.
4 The 355-foot long charge clears a path 45 feet wide and 330 feet long.

Source: Jane's Military Logistics; U.S. Army Weapons Systems; David Isby, Washington-based national security consultant.

ANDERS RAMBERG / Los Angeles Times

DAY 36

FEBRUARY 21, 1991

After weeks of watching Pentagon "smart-bomb" videos and hearing briefers talk of "a healthy day of bombing," the horror of war finally confronted me on a lonely road in northeastern Kuwait.

Ten days before, a retreating Iraqi military convoy had been slaughtered by allied bombers. On one truck, the driver's corpse still sat upright. Eight soldiers in the back were frozen in their final agony, each clutching the next. The last looked as if he had tried to curl up and hide behind the cab. All appeared to be in their teens.

—Bob Drogin, in Kuwait

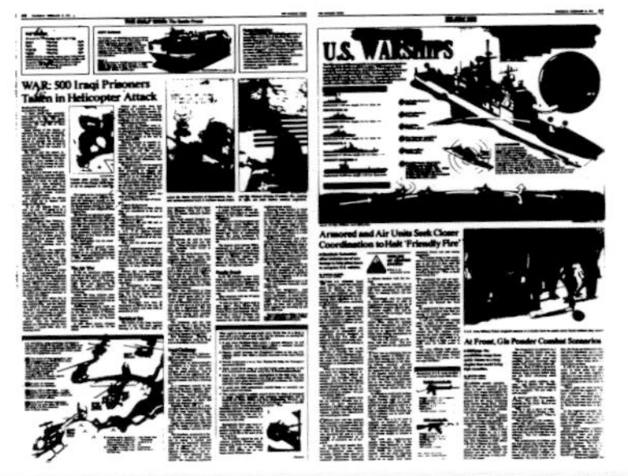

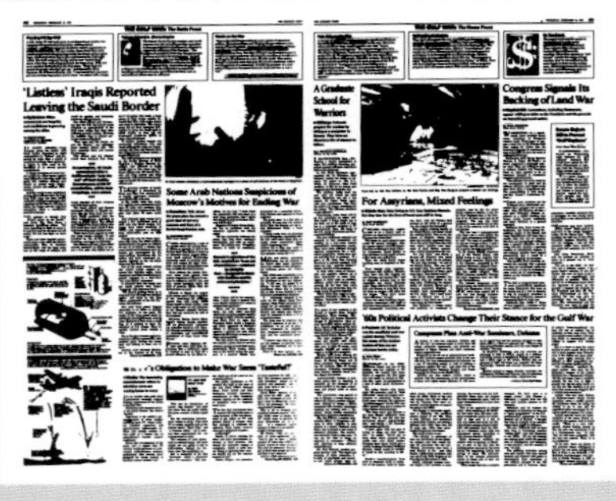

Los Angeles Times

CIRCULATION: 1,225,189 DAILY / 1,514,096 SUNDAY

THURSDAY, FEBRUARY 21, 1991

COPYRIGHT 1991 / THE TIMES MIRROR COMPANY / CC† / 148 PAGES

DAILY 25¢ DESIGNATED AREAS HIGHER

U.S. Copters Lead Attack on Iraqis; 500 Prisoners Taken

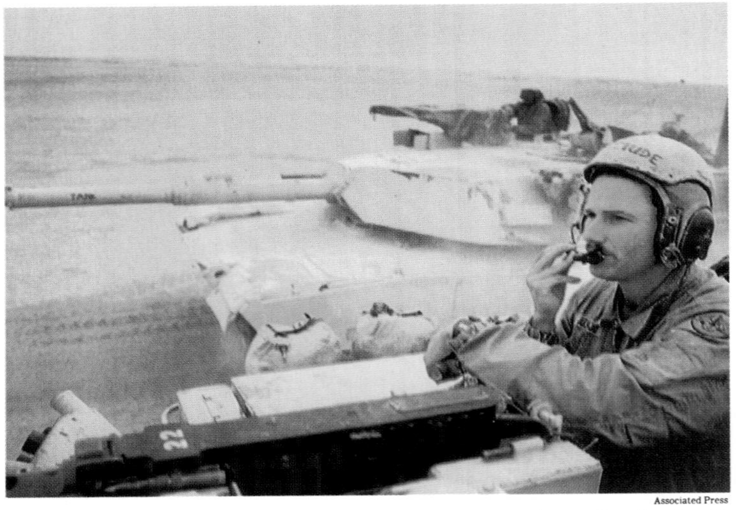

Associated Press

U.S. tank commander speaks into headset as he leads an armored column along northern Saudi border.

■ **Gulf War:** Skirmishes and a record number of air sorties mark an increasing tempo of action. Officials say traffic accidents are the leading killer of troops.

By J. MICHAEL KENNEDY
TIMES STAFF WRITER

RIYADH, Saudi Arabia—In the largest roundup of Iraqi prisoners of war to date, American Apache and Kiowa attack helicopters swarmed across the front lines on Wednesday and captured up to 500 enemy soldiers, U.S. commanders said.

Huge Chinook helicopters hauled them to prison camps in Saudi Arabia.

Almost simultaneously, military officials said, an American task force clashed with Iraqi forces south of the Saudi border. The Iraqis called in artillery that killed one American and wounded seven others. But, the officials said, the task force destroyed five Iraqi tanks and 20 artillery pieces and took seven additional prisoners.

The skirmishing plus 2,900 air sorties, the most on any day so far, marked a steadily increasing tempo in the Persian Gulf War as allied forces braced for orders to launch a ground assault into Iraqi-occupied Kuwait.

Pentagon officials in Washington gave some members of Congress detailed briefings on what such a ground assault would employ, including an array of American vehicles and artillery.

In other developments:

- American aircraft bombed a large Iraqi logistics support area containing about 300 vehicles, including tanks. More than 50 of the vehicles were destroyed, American commanders said.
- Crewmen from a British destroyer recovered the remains of Iraqi marines floating in the Persian Gulf and buried them at sea with full military honors. The Iraqis were thought to have been killed by allied attacks on Iraqi patrol boats.
- An Iraqi official challenged Gen. H. Norman Schwarzkopf, commander of U.S. forces in the Gulf, to "try his luck" on the battlefield if he thinks Iraqi forces are nearing a breakdown. The official accused Schwarzkopf of blustering when he told the Los Angeles Times that Iraq's military is "on the verge of collapse."
- Officials said traffic accidents on unpaved roads built through northern Saudi Arabia far outpace artillery, missiles and "friendly fire" as the leading killer of U.S. personnel. The hazardous but essential roadways are lifelines that link scattered military camps to each other and to supplies.

The helicopter roundup of Iraqi prisoners was reported by U.S. Marine Brig. Gen. Richard I. Neal, deputy operations director at the Central Command, who said two Apache and two Kiowa attack helicopters swarmed over a warren of at least 12 Iraqi bunkers dug into occupied Kuwait.

The Apaches and Kiowas fired at

Please see WAR, A6

COLUMN ONE

Miami, So Lovely and Bizarre

■ Bodies wash ashore. The mayor packs a Beretta. For robbers, it helps to be bilingual. A reporter reflects on 15 years of living amid beauty and covering the macabre.

By BARRY BEARAK
TIMES STAFF WRITER

MIAMI—The memories are mostly of beauty and weirdness, of sunbeams that made the bay waters sparkle like a carpet of gems and of news stories that seemed to warp toward the surreal in this city's subtropical heat.

At times, the beautiful and the bizarre layered over each other the way they would in a Salvador Dali painting. Always, the sky was the most luminous of blue; often, the world below the most haunting of dreamscapes.

There was the morning when dead Haitian boat people washed ashore onto the talcum-soft beaches behind the luxury high-rises, first five, then 10, then 20, until every shape in the mesmerizing surf seemed a corpse.

There were the evenings, woefully repeated, when racial combustion lit into ghastly towers of smoke. The police fanned out in riot gear, and the streets took on an unsteady pulse, the pinging of gunfire and the smashing of glass.

There was the night when a hurricane wind sent palm fronds rolling across the sand like tumbleweeds through a ghost town. Civil defense teams rushed to evacuate nursing homes near the oceanfront.

Without medication or caretakers, the confused residents were dispersed into the expedient shelter of a convention hall. I roamed among them with a spiral notebook. Four of them asked me the same question: "Are you my son?"

This has been my job, observer of other people's pleasures and pains, a newspaperman in Miami. Now, after 15 years, leaving for another place, there is an inevitable incompleteness and an urge to write a few final things.

Did I say the city is beautiful and weird?

□

Miami is an enchantress who comes on to you with hot breath and moist lips. She likes tourists the best and used to coax them onto the dance floor for a fox trot and a hora, though it is now more often a samba and a merengue.

A metropolitan knockout, the city is confident of its good looks and sunny disposition, yet, at important moments, it somehow manages to appear hideous.

Honchos of the National Hockey League recently met here, choosing sites for new franchises. Miami wanted one. Instead of showing off its pretty face, the city broke out in untimely hives, suffering its fifth riot in a decade.

The previous street rebellion had come in January, 1989, a week before Super Bowl XXIII, when 1,500 reporters were in town searching for a pregame angle.

Please see MIAMI, A22

Court Rules Amnesty Is Open to Suits

By DAVID G. SAVAGE
TIMES STAFF WRITER

WASHINGTON—The Supreme Court ruled Wednesday that aliens have a legal right to mount broad court challenges to how the government has implemented the massive amnesty program begun in 1986.

The 7-2 ruling was a major procedural victory for as many as 250,000 aliens who could be affected by pending class-action lawsuits against the Immigration and Naturalization Service.

The ruling will allow legal aid attorneys to contest policies under which thousands of aliens were reject-

Please see ALIENS, A23

Molina's First Goal—Expand County Board

By HECTOR TOBAR and RICHARD SIMON
TIMES STAFF WRITERS

Supervisor-elect Gloria Molina, claiming a mandate for political change, announced Wednesday that her first priority will be expansion of the Board of Supervisors to provide better representation for Los Angeles County's 8.8 million residents, especially minorities.

"The election was not only a mandate for me, but a mandate for the entire board about the things we could change," Molina, a city councilwoman, said the day after her victory over state Sen. Art Torres in the historic election that placed a Latino on the board.

Molina, a fiery Democrat and self-proclaimed political outsider, will join Supervisors Ed Edelman

■ **RELATED STORIES** and Election Tables: B2, B3

and Kenneth Hahn in forming a new liberal majority on the board. Her fellow liberals say that they already are dusting off proposals that were shot down by conservative supervisors, including a ballot measure to expand the board.

Molina said Wednesday that she will provide the swing vote authorizing a ballot measure that would enlarge the board from five to seven members and eventually to nine members.

In defeating Torres 55% to 45%—despite being outspent nearly 2 to 1—Molina became the first Latino elected to the board this century and the first woman ever elected supervisor. She has promised to push for campaign contribution limits, the hiring of more Latino county employees, increased funding for health and welfare programs and removal of the glass security barrier that separates supervisors from the public in the board chambers.

Though she joins two longtime liberals on the board, Molina is expected to set her own agenda and

Please see MOLINA, A3

Ground War Nears as Iraqi Reply Is Awaited

■ **Diplomacy:** Baghdad promises an answer 'soon' to a Soviet peace proposal. Allies see an attempt to 'buy time.'

By DAVID LAUTER and JOHN-THOR DAHLBURG
TIMES STAFF WRITERS

WASHINGTON—A massive ground attack against Iraqi troops grew imminent Wednesday as time began to run out on Soviet efforts to mediate a peaceful withdrawal of Saddam Hussein's troops from Kuwait.

Iraqi radio announced that Foreign Minister Tarik Aziz will travel to Moscow "soon" to deliver Hussein's response to Soviet President Mikhail S. Gorbachev's peace proposal. But allied officials dismissed such talk as a "desperate" attempt by Iraq to "buy time" to avert a total defeat.

Sources at the United Nations said that if a favorable Iraqi response is received in time, the Security Council might meet today at the request of the Soviet Union. And if Iraq agrees to abide by all 12 of the council's resolutions on the war, the Soviets might move for a cease-fire.

But statements from both sides Wednesday emphasized preparations for war, not the possibilities of peace.

"One way or another, the army of occupation of Iraq will leave Kuwait—soon," Secretary of State James A. Baker III declared. "Kuwait will be liberated—soon."

The U.N. mandate demanding Iraqi withdrawal "is crystal-clear, and there can be no negotiation over its meaning," said Baker, who made his remarks at a ceremony welcoming Denmark's Queen Margrethe II, here on a state visit.

For its part, Baghdad Radio insisted that Iraq's army is "impatiently waiting to take on the infidels."

Officials from France and Iran told reporters in Paris that Moscow has given Iraq until some time today to respond to its peace offer. But Administration officials said

Please see DIPLOMACY, A14

Slovenia Begins Secession, Voids Yugoslav Laws

By CAROL J. WILLIAMS
TIMES STAFF WRITER

LJUBLJANA, Yugoslavia—Fed up with fruitless efforts to prevent the breakup of Yugoslavia, Slovenia began the process of secession Wednesday by annulling all federal authority in the tiny republic.

The Slovenian Assembly also overwhelmingly approved a four-point Act of Dissociation, which the pro-independence media declared to be the end of the 72-year-old state of Yugoslavia.

Although the bold moves are aimed at fulfilling a dream of sovereignty for the 2 million residents of this affluent republic, they will also ratchet tensions up another notch in the volatile standoff

Please see SLOVENIA, A20

Bush Reported Unhappy With Gorbachev Bid

By JACK NELSON
TIMES WASHINGTON BUREAU CHIEF

WASHINGTON—Soviet President Mikhail S. Gorbachev has jeopardized his warm relations with the United States by pushing a last-ditch Gulf peace proposal that President Bush considers an ill-advised gesture to win greater Soviet influence in the Arab world at the expense of allied goals, government analysts said Wednesday.

Bush is "biting his lip" to contain his unhappiness with Gorbachev's diplomatic efforts, according to one analyst who said the Soviet president "has done more harm to himself [in Washington] in the past 72 hours than he did by all the head-knocking in the Baltics."

Administration officials say Gorbachev's initiative—which Bush has rejected as falling "well short of what is required" to end hostilities—complicates the allies' efforts to force an unconditional Iraqi withdrawal from Kuwait and remove Saddam Hussein as a future threat to Persian Gulf stability.

But they insist that the Soviet initiative is having no effect on the timetable for a ground attack on the Iraqi dictator's forces.

With some sources suggesting that a ground assault is imminent, a senior aide to the President said: "Bush just tells the staff, 'Don't worry. We've got a plan and we're not changing it.' And there's a feeling among the staff that we want to get on with it and get it over with."

Despite Moscow's support for the

Please see SOVIETS, A16

Quincy Jones, Prayers for Peace Prevail at Grammys

■ **Music:** Veteran entertainer becomes most honored pop artist. Julie Gold's 'From a Distance' is best song.

By ROBERT HILBURN
TIMES POP MUSIC CRITIC

NEW YORK—Quincy Jones became the most honored pop artist in the 33-year history of the record industry's Grammy Awards here Wednesday on a night when he and other key winners included prayers for peace in their acceptance speeches.

"Pray for peace on earth and when we get peace on earth, let's take care of the earth," Jones said after winning one of his six awards during the nationally televised ceremony at Radio City Music Hall.

Jones' awards, including citations for best album of the year and best producer, gave the veteran producer-arranger a career total of 25 Grammys, five more than the previous record of 20 held by composer-conductor Henry Mancini. He is surpassed only by Sir Georg Solti, who has won 28 in the classical field.

In accepting the best song award given her for "From a Distance," Julie Gold said: "To our soldiers, we pray for your speedy return. We pray for peace on earth."

Her song, a warmly philosophical plea for brotherhood, has been adopted by radio stations in recent weeks as a sort of informal anthem during the Persian Gulf crisis.

Backstage, Gold, who wrote the song five years ago, added: "I'm 35 years old and have lived through

Please see GRAMMYS, A20

INSIDE TODAY'S TIMES

■ **WAR STORIES, PHOTOS: A5-18; D1, D14; F1, F11**

■ **HALTING 'FRIENDLY FIRE'**

U.S. commanders are giving high priority to protecting troops from becoming victims of "friendly fire" if and when the ground war starts. **A7**

■ **NATION OF CITY DWELLERS**

A 1990 census report indicates that for the first time a majority of Americans live within one of the nation's 39 large metropolitan areas. **A3**

■ **GREENSPAN UPBEAT**

Federal Reserve Chairman Alan Greenspan predicted the recession will end soon and inflation will remain in check. **D1**

WEATHER: Hazy sunshine today and Friday. Civic Center low/high today: 53/74. Details: B5

■ TOP OF THE NEWS ON A2

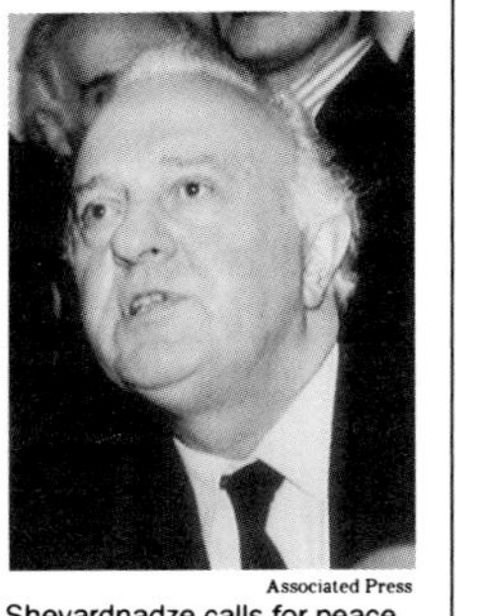

Associated Press

Shevardnadze calls for peace.

■ **YELTSIN UNDER ATTACK**

Soviet officials attacked Boris Yeltsin's demand that President Gorbachev resign as ex-Foreign Minister Eduard Shevardnadze tried to make peace. **A21**

Chemical Attack Would Escalate Allied Retaliation

■ **Tactics:** Iraqi use of poison gas could trigger a march on Baghdad to hunt down Hussein, officials warn.

By MELISSA HEALY
TIMES STAFF WRITER

WASHINGTON—U.S. and allied officials warned Wednesday that any significant Iraqi use of chemical weapons against coalition troops would lead to a major escalation of the war and could trigger a contingency plan for a march on Baghdad to hunt down Saddam Hussein.

Already, allied forces are attempting to discourage front-line Iraqi artillery crews from obeying future orders to fire chemical shells, notifying them in leaflets that they would be pursued individually after the war—much as some Nazi death camp guards have been brought to justice decades after World War II ended.

Major use of chemical weapons, a violation of international law, would cross a "red line beyond which all previous bets are off," said a senior Bush Administration official involved in the final preparations for a ground war.

"It's a red line that would compel the coalition to change its own objectives—adopting, for instance, a march on Baghdad to find Saddam and eliminate his regime," he said of the Iraqi president.

A senior Arab official confirmed Wednesday that the allies have prepared specific plans for retaliation if Iraq wages chemical war.

"We'll use the unimaginable, short of nuclear weapons," he said.

Please see CHEMICAL, A18

AAV7 Amtrack

The Amtrack—or Amphibious Assault Vehicle—would play a key role in the first waves of any allied amphibious assault against Iraqi forces. The full-tracked vehicles can handle seas of up to 10 feet, landing troops and supplies ashore. Although lightly armored, Amtracks can also be used for subsequent land operations.

Crew: 3
Load: 25 troops or 10,000 pounds of equipment
Speed: 40 m.p.h. on land, 8 m.p.h. in water
Range: 300 miles on land, 55 miles in water
Armament: .50-cal. machine gun

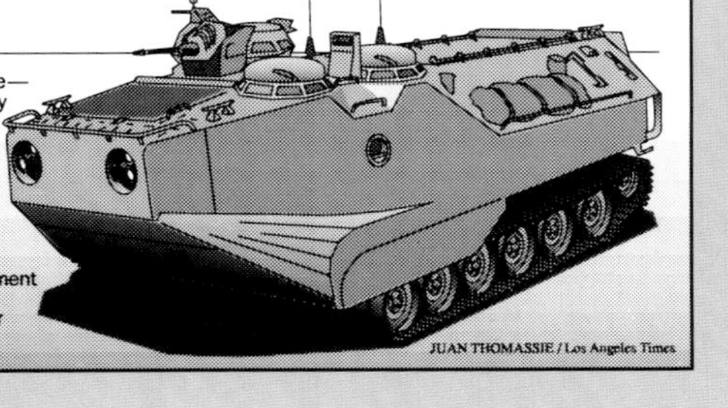

JUAN THOMASSIE / Los Angeles Times

DAY IN THE GULF

Military: In the largest roundup of Iraqi prisoners yet, American Apache and Kiowa attack helicopters swarm across the front lines and capture up to 500 enemy soldiers, U.S. commanders say.

■ An American task force clashes with Iraqi forces south of the Saudi border. One American is killed and seven are wounded. Five Iraqi tanks are destroyed.

■ The allies fly 2,900 air sorties, the most of any day so far.

■ U.S. aircraft bomb a large Iraqi logistics support area containing about 300 vehicles, including tanks. More than 50 of the vehicles are destroyed.

■ British officials give this tally of Iraqi warplanes: Of an estimated 700 at the start of hostilities, about 50 were destroyed; about 150 were flown away from air bases and 200 otherwise dispersed; and between 300 and 350 are still in bunkers ready to fly.

■ A U.S. F-16 fighter-bomber crashes because of engine trouble about a mile southwest of Diyarbakir, Turkey. The plane had taken off from the NATO air base at Incirlik. The pilot ejects and survives.

■ Bombing raids flatten installations on the Kuwaiti island of Faylakah, once used as a major Iraqi naval base.

Iraq: Baghdad Radio announces that Foreign Minister Tarik Aziz will travel to Moscow "soon" to deliver Hussein's response to the Soviet peace proposal.

■ An Iraqi official challenges a statement by Gen. H. Norman Schwarzkopf that Iraq's military is "on the verge of collapse," challenging the commander of the U.S. forces to "try his luck."

■ Iraqi troops along the border with Saudi Arabia have apparently begun to draw back as the likelihood of an all-out ground assault looms.

Diplomacy: Most Arab nations cautiously stick to previous positions and wait for other countries, namely the United States and Iraq, to make the final decisions.

Home front: The Senate defeats the "Gulf orphans" measure that would have asked the Defense Department to reassign from the Gulf single parents and military couples with children.

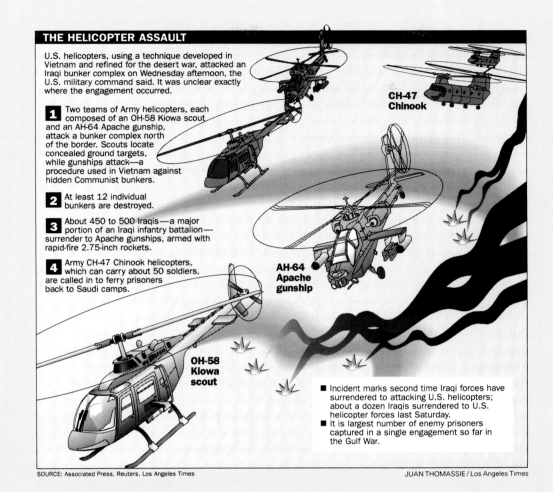

THE HELICOPTER ASSAULT

U.S. helicopters, using a technique developed in Vietnam and refined for the desert war, attacked an Iraqi bunker complex on Wednesday afternoon, the U.S. military command said. It was unclear exactly where the engagement occurred.

1 Two teams of Army helicopters, each composed of an OH-58 Kiowa scout and an AH-64 Apache gunship, attack a bunker complex north of the border. Scouts locate concealed ground targets, while gunships attack—a procedure used in Vietnam against hidden Communist bunkers.

2 At least 12 individual bunkers are destroyed.

3 About 450 to 500 Iraqis—a major portion of an Iraqi infantry battalion—surrender to Apache gunships, armed with rapid-fire 2.75-inch rockets.

4 Army CH-47 Chinook helicopters, which can carry about 50 soldiers, are called in to ferry prisoners back to Saudi camps.

CH-47 Chinook

AH-64 Apache gunship

OH-58 Kiowa scout

■ Incident marks second time Iraqi forces have surrendered to attacking U.S. helicopters; about a dozen Iraqis surrendered to U.S. helicopter forces last Saturday.

■ It is largest number of enemy prisoners captured in a single engagement so far in the Gulf War.

SOURCE: Associated Press, Reuters, Los Angeles Times

JUAN THOMASSIE / Los Angeles Times

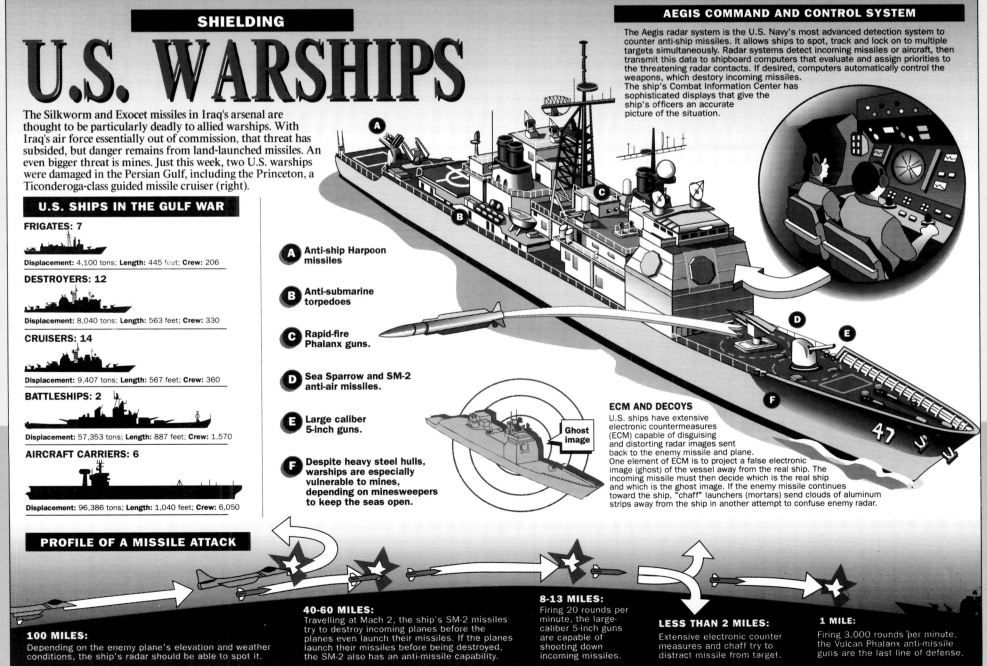

SHIELDING

U.S. WARSHIPS

The Silkworm and Exocet missiles in Iraq's arsenal are thought to be particularly deadly to allied warships. With Iraq's air force essentially out of commission, that threat has subsided, but danger remains from land-launched missiles. An even bigger threat is mines. Just this week, two U.S. warships were damaged in the Persian Gulf, including the Princeton, a Ticonderoga-class guided missile cruiser (right).

AEGIS COMMAND AND CONTROL SYSTEM

The Aegis radar system is the U.S. Navy's most advanced detection system to counter anti-ship missiles. It allows ships to spot, track and lock on to multiple targets simultaneously. Radar systems detect incoming missiles or aircraft, then transmit this data to shipboard computers that evaluate and assign priorities to the threatening radar contacts. If desired, computers automatically control the weapons, which destroy incoming missiles.
The ship's Combat Information Center has sophisticated displays that give the ship's officers an accurate picture of the situation.

U.S. SHIPS IN THE GULF WAR

FRIGATES: 7
Displacement: 4,100 tons; **Length:** 445 feet; **Crew:** 206

DESTROYERS: 12
Displacement: 8,040 tons; **Length:** 563 feet; **Crew:** 330

CRUISERS: 14
Displacement: 9,407 tons; **Length:** 567 feet; **Crew:** 360

BATTLESHIPS: 2
Displacement: 57,353 tons; **Length:** 887 feet; **Crew:** 1,570

AIRCRAFT CARRIERS: 6
Displacement: 96,386 tons; **Length:** 1,040 feet; **Crew:** 6,050

A Anti-ship Harpoon missiles

B Anti-submarine torpedoes

C Rapid-fire Phalanx guns.

D Sea Sparrow and SM-2 anti-air missiles.

E Large caliber 5-inch guns.

F Despite heavy steel hulls, warships are especially vulnerable to mines, depending on minesweepers to keep the seas open.

Ghost image

ECM AND DECOYS

U.S. ships have extensive electronic countermeasures (ECM) capable of disguising and distorting radar images sent back to the enemy missile and plane.
One element of ECM is to project a false electronic image (ghost) of the vessel away from the real ship. The incoming missile must then decide which is the real ship and which is the ghost image. If the enemy missile continues toward the ship, "chaff" launchers (mortars) send clouds of aluminum strips away from the ship in another attempt to confuse enemy radar.

PROFILE OF A MISSILE ATTACK

100 MILES:
Depending on the enemy plane's elevation and weather conditions, the ship's radar should be able to spot it.

40-60 MILES:
Travelling at Mach 2, the ship's SM-2 missiles try to destroy incoming planes before the planes even launch their missiles. If the planes launch their missiles before being destroyed, the SM-2 also has an anti-missile capability.

8-13 MILES:
Firing 20 rounds per minute, the large-caliber 5-inch guns are capable of shooting down incoming missiles.

LESS THAN 2 MILES:
Extensive electronic counter measures and chaff try to distract missile from target.

1 MILE:
Firing 3,000 rounds per minute, the Vulcan Phalanx anti-missile guns are the last line of defense.

Sources: U.S. Dept. of Defense, Jane's Fighting Ships

SCOTT BROWN / Los Angeles Times

DAY 37

FEBRUARY 22, 1991

When I checked in with the U.S. Central Command "Media Center" for my credentials, the young British officer and the U.S. Air Force lieutenant in charge of handling the press noted that I had come from California.

Seizing the opportunity, I said, "Yes, and I understand you have quite a few soldiers around here from California."

They laughed, rolling their eyes. "Oh, yeah," said the airman, who hailed from New York. "We can tell the Californians a mile away. They're the ones here to 'share the experience' with us."

—Tracy Wilkinson, in Riyadh, Saudi Arabia

Los Angeles Times

CIRCULATION: 1,225,189 DAILY 1,514,096 SUNDAY

FRIDAY, FEBRUARY 22, 1991
COPYRIGHT 1991 THE TIMES MIRROR COMPANY
CC† 130 PAGES

DAILY 25¢ DESIGNATED AREAS HIGHER

U.S. Cool to Gulf Peace Plan

Bush Has 'Serious Concerns' Over Soviet-Iraqi Bid

■ **Diplomacy:** Baghdad would withdraw from Kuwait two days after a cease-fire if U.N. resolutions are lifted and sanctions ended. War operations will continue.

By JOHN-THOR DAHLBURG and MARK FINEMAN
TIMES STAFF WRITERS

MOSCOW—The Soviet Union said early today that Iraq has agreed to withdraw its troops from Kuwait after a cease-fire in the Persian Gulf War if there is agreement to lift U.N. resolutions, including economic sanctions against Baghdad and a demand for war reparations. President Bush said he has "serious concerns" about the proposal but will study it.

In the meantime, a ground assault into occupied Kuwait "is a matter that is still under consideration," Bush said in a statement issued by his spokesman, Marlin Fitzwater. "There is no change at this point in our schedule for prosecution of the war."

The proposal, outlined in eight points, was announced by a spokesman for Soviet President Mikhail S. Gorbachev after the Soviet leader met for more than two hours at the Kremlin with Iraqi Foreign Minister Tarik Aziz to hear Iraq's response to a Soviet peace initiative. The Soviet spokesman, Vitaly N. Ignatenko, called the Iraqi response "positive" and said the Soviet-Iraqi proposal subsequently "evolved."

Gorbachev and Aziz "came to the conclusion," Ignatenko said, "that it was possible to find a way out of the military conflict."

But Bush, in the statement that Fitzwater read to reporters at the White House, said he will consult with his partners in the anti-Iraq military coalition before making a final decision on the Soviet-Iraqi proposal. Fitzwater said that decision could come sometime today, adding that "the war itself continues."

"We will continue to seek compliance with the U.N. resolutions," Fitzwater said, "and the President will make decisions concerning the ground war as appropriate."

As presented by Ignatenko, the new proposal agreed to a "full and unconditional" withdrawal from Kuwait "in a fixed time frame" and monitored by neutral nations. It called for the pullout to begin the "following day after the cessation of hostilities." But the proposal also called for an end to U.N. economic sanctions against Iraq when two-thirds of its troops have gone, and a cancellation of all other U.N. resolutions once withdrawal is complete.

The U.N. resolutions include one that holds Iraq responsible for all financial losses resulting from its invasion of Kuwait. The same resolution seeks evidence of human rights abuses in Kuwait by Iraqi troops.

Previous Iraqi peace proposals have tied any pullout from Kuwait to an Israeli withdrawal from occupied territories. The Soviet-Iraqi proposal, however, made no mention of Israel.

Gorbachev telephoned Bush personally to advance the new proposal. Fitzwater said the two leaders talked for 33 minutes. "President Bush thanked President Gorbachev for his intensive and useful efforts," Fitzwater reported. But he said Bush "raised serious concerns about several points of the plan."

"The President has indicated," Fitzwater said, "there could well be some difficulties here."

Fitzwater declined to spell out the points in question or the difficulties with them. He said Bush will have a more complete response to the proposal after consulting with other allied leaders. Bush was not available for comment.

After talking to Gorbachev and meeting with his advisers, the White House said, Bush went to Ford's Theater to see "Black Eagles," a play about black Air Force pilots in World War II.

He returned after the play and met with senior national security advisers until midnight. After the meeting, one White House official said that the group did not officially reject the new proposal but concluded that it is unacceptable because it imposed conditions on the Iraqi withdrawal from Kuwait.

"Our conclusion at this time," said the official, who requested not to be identified, "is that the Soviet proposal represents a conditional withdrawal." He said the White House planned to communicate this conclusion to its allied partners

Please see OFFER, A26

WHAT THE SOVIETS SAY IRAQ AGREED TO

The Soviets and Iraqis agreed on an eight-point plan:

- **WITHDRAWAL.** A full and unconditional withdrawal from Kuwait.
- **WHEN.** The pullout would begin the second day after hostilities end.
- **TIMETABLE.** Pullout on a fixed timetable.
- **EMBARGO.** U.N. economic sanctions would end after two-thirds of Iraqi forces leave Kuwait.
- **U.N.** After a full pullout, other resolutions adopted after Iraq's Aug. 2 invasion of Kuwait would cease to have a purpose.
- **POWS.** All prisoners would be released immediately after a cease-fire.
- **MONITORING.** Pullout would be monitored under the aegis of the United Nations by countries not directly involved in the war.
- **DETAILS**. They are to be worked out. Notification is to be made to the U.N. Security Council.

COLUMN ONE

Economy Without a Country

■ Kuwait is conducting business without oil, its lifeblood. But with an estimated $100-billion portfolio, it is nowhere near broke.

By MARIA L. La GANGA
TIMES STAFF WRITER

The closest thing to home these days is makeshift digs in a drab bank building in central London, 150 Cheapside EC2. A sentry stands guard at the door, walkie-talkie in hand. The nondescript structure houses the Kuwait Investment Office, where the financial strategies of an invaded nation are carried out behind locked doors.

Shrouded in secrecy, swirling with rumors, the Kuwaiti economy in exile operates without the oil that has been its lifeblood for decades. It is an economy without a country, an estimated $100-billion investment portfolio with no place to call home.

"We've had lots of governments in exile, but never had a case where the whole population and the economy are in exile," said Philip K. Verleger Jr., a visiting fellow with the Institute for International Economics in Washington.

Kuwait, of course, is nowhere near broke. The International Monetary Fund estimated that the nation earned $11.6 billion in oil revenues in 1989. In addition, there was $8 billion in income that year from foreign investments, mainly a wide network of refineries in Denmark, Holland and Italy, and the nation's "Q8" chain of 6,500 gas stations throughout Europe.

"In terms of new crude oil revenues, it would be safe to assume the Kuwaitis don't have any, but that will not break them," said Vahan Zanoyan, senior director at the Petroleum Finance Co., a Washington consulting firm. "Even without exporting any oil, they could survive easily. They are truly in an enviable position in that respect."

Kuwait has been among the richest countries in the world, ranked about 15th in gross national product per capita—even counting the 1.3 million foreigners who are not citizens but who worked there. Now, as an economy in exile with nothing more than income from investments—but no foreign workers to pay—Kuwait's GNP per capita ranks about 20th, in the neighborhood of Hong Kong, Singapore and Israel.

But even for wealthy Kuwait, financial burdens are piling up.

Please see KUWAIT, A24

Associated Press

Some of the 421 Iraqis who surrendered to allied troops wait at a POW processing center in Saudi Arabia.

Iraqi Turnabout Could Bedevil Bush's Strategy

■ **Dilemma:** Action could derail President's plan to humiliate Hussein and control the timetable of the war.

By DOYLE McMANUS and ROBIN WRIGHT
TIMES STAFF WRITERS

NEWS ANALYSIS

WASHINGTON—Saddam Hussein's abrupt embrace of Soviet President Mikhail S. Gorbachev's peace initiative—and President Bush's decision to discuss the plan with his allies instead of reject it outright—has suddenly turned the Persian Gulf War into a game of diplomatic maneuvering.

And that could derail Bush's military plans to cut Hussein down to size, especially if it leads to lengthy and ambiguous negotiations, U.S. officials and other analysts said. Bush has repeatedly vowed that the allies—not Hussein—would control the timetable for the war, but the onset of negotiations would make it hard for the President to sustain such mastery of events.

Hussein's move exploited the worst-kept secret of American policy in the Gulf—that U.S. war aims go beyond the formal U.N. goal of forcing Iraq's withdrawal from Kuwait.

Bush Administration officials privately acknowledge that they also want to humiliate the Iraqi president, to deprive him of his political prestige and perhaps deprive him of his job as well. Only then, they argue, can peace be assured in the Gulf and future aggression elsewhere in the world discouraged.

Please see DILEMMA, A22

U.S. Offers Plan to Reduce Lead Risk to Children

By MARLENE CIMONS
TIMES STAFF WRITER

WASHINGTON—Calling lead "the No. 1 environmental poison for children," the Bush Administration on Thursday proposed a long-term strategy to reduce exposure to the toxic substance.

As many as 3 million to 4 million American children under 6 have high enough levels of lead in their blood to cause mental and other health problems, said Health and Human Services Secretary Louis W. Sullivan. "Lead poisoning is entirely preventable, yet it is the most common and societally devastating environmental disease of

Please see LEAD, A34

Allies Pound Iraqis, Brace for Land War

By J. MICHAEL KENNEDY
TIMES STAFF WRITER

RIYADH, Saudi Arabia—The coalition against Iraq stepped up bombing runs, artillery barrages and reconnaissance patrols Thursday as 700,000 allied troops braced for what U.S. commanders said could be one of the greatest land battles in the history of war.

Speaking before the Soviet announcement of a possible peace agreement, Lt. Gen. Thomas W. Kelly, director of operations for the Joint Chiefs of Staff, told reporters at a Pentagon briefing in Washington that "it will be an intense battle . . . [that will] rank right up there with the best of them."

"We expect we will have to fight hard to win," Kelly said. "We will fight hard. We will win."

The general described U.S. forces arrayed along the border of Kuwait and offshore as "uptight and ready to go."

In other developments:

• Seven American soldiers were killed Thursday when an Army Blackhawk medical evacuation helicopter crashed while attempting to land in Saudi Arabia during bad weather. It was the deadliest noncombat accident since Operation Desert Storm began. Two other Americans were killed when their Army OH-58 scout helicopter crashed while returning from combat operations along the border.

Please see WAR, A6

Dame Margot Fonteyn, 71, Renowned Ballerina, Dies

■ **Dance:** A classical performer in a modern time, she forged a second career in 1960s with Rudolf Nureyev.

By BURT A. FOLKART
TIMES STAFF WRITER

Dame Margot Fonteyn, the seemingly ageless *prima ballerina assoluta*, died Thursday in a Panama City hospital of the cancer she had struggled against for several years.

Louis Martins, a longtime friend and government spokesman, said she was 71. "She died in Panama, where she wanted to die," he said.

Adjudged by many balletomanes the most pristine and refined technician of the mid- and late-20th Century, Dame Margot had lived since the 1950s on a beachfront ranch in western Panama she and her husband called "La Quinta

Please see FONTEYN, A31

Fonteyn in 1978 performance.

INSIDE TODAY'S TIMES

■ **WAR STORIES, PHOTOS: A5-26; D1-2; E1**

■ **CROATIA SECEDING**

The republic of Croatia joined Slovenia in taking steps to secede from the Yugoslav federation and warned that it would meet force with force. **A4**

■ **NEW OFFSHORE LEASES**

The Interior Department said it plans to sell up to 23 new offshore oil and gas leases in the outer continental shelf. **A33**

■ **SLUMLORD IN SCOTLAND**

Vijaynand Sharma, who fled Los Angeles after his conviction in the largest criminal case ever brought by the city against a landlord, is in Scotland. **B1**

WEATHER: Hazy afternoon sunshine. Civic Center low/high today: 53/74. Details: B5

■ TOP OF THE NEWS ON A2

AL STEPHENSON / For The Times

Prince Bandar ibn Sultan

■ **IRAQ ALLIES WARNED**

Prince Bandar ibn Sultan, the Saudi ambassador to the United States, said Yasser Arafat, King Hussein and others will pay dearly for backing Iraq. **A8**

State High Court Asked to Overturn Term Limits

■ **Proposition 140:** The broad legal assault is backed by Democratic and Republican lawmakers.

By PHILIP HAGER
TIMES LEGAL AFFAIRS WRITER

SAN FRANCISCO—The state Legislature launched a broad legal assault Thursday on Proposition 140, asking the California Supreme Court to strike down the landmark term-limitation measure as unconstitutional.

A suit backed by Democratic and Republican lawmakers said the initiative's tight restrictions on terms and sharp cutbacks in legislative staff and operating budgets had gravely damaged the Legislature's ability to function as a separate branch of government.

Supporters of the initiative, passed by 52% of the electorate last November, rejected the legal claims in the lawsuit and said they would urge the justices to refuse to hear the case.

Proposition 140, co-sponsored by Los Angeles County Supervisor Pete Schabarum, was offered by backers as a way to trim what they saw as excessive concentrations of legislative power, bloated and expensive staffs and an extravagant pension system.

Most prominently, the measure limited statewide officeholders and state senators to two terms of four years each and Assembly members to three terms of two years each.

The measure also imposed restrictions on legislative operational costs that thus far have forced about one-fourth of the Legisla-

Please see PROP. 140, A31

Diplomacy: The Soviet Union says Iraq has agreed to withdraw its troops from Kuwait after a cease-fire if there is an agreement to lift U.N. resolutions and demands for war reparations.
■ President Bush expresses "serious concerns" about the proposal but does not reject it out of hand. He says he will consult with partners in the alliance.

Military: Defense Secretary Dick Cheney says allied forces are preparing "one of the largest land assaults of modern times" but offers no hints of when a full-scale land war might begin.
■ Britain's 1st Armored Division engages in its heaviest artillery shelling of Iraqi positions.
■ The U.S. military reports intensified fighting along the Saudi frontier, including artillery duels and allied incursions into enemy territory.
■ The CIA estimates that 10% to 15% of Iraq's tanks and artillery in Kuwait have been destroyed by allied bombing, far below the Pentagon's 35% figure.
■ U.S. forces return to a bunker complex behind enemy lines where the day before they took 421 Iraqi prisoners. They take 14 more prisoners and find a locked bunker containing intelligence documents.

Missiles: Iraq launches five or six Scuds at Saudi Arabia and Bahrain, but all of them are apparently downed by Patriot interceptors. There are no reports of damage.

Iraq: Saddam Hussein declares in a 40-minute radio address that Iraq is willing and ready to fight a ground war if President Bush continues to reject his peace efforts.

Home front: Anti-war protests on campuses in Los Angeles draw scant crowds. About 100 students turn out at UCLA, which has 36,000 students.

One of the many Kuwaiti oil fires illuminated a junkyard.

PATRICK DOWNS / Los Angeles Times

FIRE
IN THE OIL FIELDS

The oil fields of Kuwait are ablaze with more than 50 fires, ignited by Iraqi forces in an effort to conceal their troop movements, or by allied bombs raining havoc on enemy positions. Many of the remainder of the country's wells—numbering more than 1,000—are likely to be blown up by Iraqi troops, making good on Saddam Hussein's threat to destroy Kuwait's wells and refineries. Whatever the cause, many of the fires will burn unchecked for the duration of the war. Here is a look at what weapons firefighters will bring to their battle with flame and smoke:

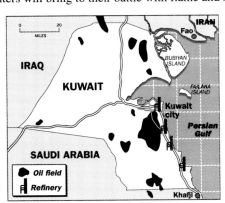

POTENTIAL PROBLEMS

■ The wells are likely to be booby-trapped, endangering crews attempting to put out the fires.

■ The longer the fires burn, the harder they are to extinguish because the wellheads erode.

■ Burning storage tanks are subject to "boil overs," the disastrous result of fiery oil hitting any water that may have pooled at the bottom of the tank. This could spread fire to adjacent tanks. Some of Kuwait's crude oil is known to have a high sulfur content, which could produce toxic fumes when burned.

HOW LONG WILL THEY BURN?

■ If oil is flowing freely from a wellhead under natural pressure and then ignites, it could burn for months.

■ Fire at a low-pressure well, where the oil must be pumped, is easier to control. If the pump is damaged or can be shut off, the fire will burn itself out when its supply of surface oil is gone.

■ Debris from the oil-bearing sands below the well might plug the well, shutting off the oil.

■ Since storage tanks contain a limited amount of oil, they can burn themselves out in several days or weeks.

FIRES AND THE ENVIRONMENT

■ Oil well fires produce comparatively little smoke because they burn efficiently—much like a Bunsen burner in a chemistry lab.

■ Burning storage tanks produce large volumes of smoke, but the fires burn themselves out comparatively quickly.

■ The massive volumes of smoke pumped into the air by oil fires are not expected to have an effect on global weather. Most scientists agree that the heavy soot will not soar high enough into the atmosphere to allow it to be spread around the world.

■ On a regional level, though, there are some serious environmental effects. For example, "black rain," a mixture of natural precipitation and soot from the Kuwait oil fires, has been reported falling on the Iran-Iraq frontier. The runoff can pollute water resources. Morever, refugees from Kuwait city have described an oily, sooty residue covering everything and say that the smoke makes breathing difficult.

FIREFIGHTING WEAPONS

WATER

■ Used to cool tanks that aren't burning.
■ A powerful stream of water can "blow out" a wellhead fire.
■ Like a heavy rain, a broad arc of water protects firefighters, enabling them to get near enough to shut off a valve or set an explosive charge.

EXPLOSIVES

A medium-size charge of dynamite is placed near the well. When it explodes, it's like blowing out a birthday candle. Firefighters must be able to get near enough to the wellhead source to place a charge.

FOAM

A layer spread on top of a well-confined fire, such as one in a storage tank, smothers it. The oil can then be drained from the lower part of the tank.

Sources: Los Angeles Times; Financial Times of London; Engineering News-Record; United Press International; University of Nevada, Reno; American Petroleum Institute; Oil & Gas Journal.

MATT MOODY / Los Angeles Times

DAY 38

FEBRUARY 23, 1991

The night the ground war began, I called the TV network executives in charge of coverage to ask their broadcast plans. They had no film or tape footage and hardly any audio, at that point, because of restrictions on the media. You could sense their frustration as they fell back on military analysts and Washington correspondents.

Bob Murphy, vice president of news coverage for ABC, epitomized their perplexed attitude about this unprecedented TV story: "We'll go back on the air as often as necessary until the ground war stabilizes," he said.

I asked him what he meant by "stabilizes" and he replied with apparent frustration:

"I don't know what that means. It's the first time we've ever had a live war on television."

—Rick Du Brow, in Los Angeles

Los Angeles Times

CIRCULATION: 1,225,189 DAILY / 1,514,096 SUNDAY | SATURDAY, FEBRUARY 23, 1991 | DAILY 25¢ DESIGNATED AREAS HIGHER

COPYRIGHT 1991 / THE TIMES MIRROR COMPANY / CC† / 108 PAGES

Bush Issues Ultimatum to Iraq

Warns of Land War if Pullout Doesn't Begin Today

COLUMN ONE

The Risk in Targeting Hussein

■ Assassinating Iraq's leader would end the war quickly, many believe. But finding and killing him wouldn't be easy, and political repercussions could be severe.

By ALAN C. MILLER
TIMES STAFF WRITER

WASHINGTON—Should the United States and its allies assassinate Iraqi President Saddam Hussein?

That question—always in the background since the Persian Gulf crisis began—has become more pertinent in recent days. Even if Iraq heeds President Bush's ultimatum to withdraw from Kuwait by noon EST today, the concern remains: Will the region be safe as long as Saddam Hussein lives?

The Bush Administration fears that even a militarily defeated Hussein would pose a continued threat to Western interests and Iraq's strategically vital neighbors. Still in power, Hussein could seek to cast himself as a hero in the Arab world, much as Egyptian President Gamal Abdel Nasser did when he regained the presidency following that country's drubbing by Israel in 1967. This could enable Hussein to wreak havoc through terrorism or sabotage and try to rebuild his still-substantial armed forces.

Indeed, some Western analysts believe that Hussein's death might mean an immediate end to the war—preventing the slaughter of hundreds, perhaps thousands, of American soldiers as well as innumerable Iraqis in a bloody ground conflict.

"One of the things we want is to be sure he doesn't repeat this adventure," says former CIA director William E. Colby. "The commander of the enemy force is a legitimate target. I would cheerfully have carried the bomb into Hitler's bunker."

At the same time, a direct attempt on Hussein's life is fraught with political risks, and travels over uncertain moral ground.

Political murder has a long and inglorious history, dating back through biblical times. Even the term "assassin" originated in the Mideast. Originally *hashshashin*, or hashish addict, it derived from the 11th-Century Ishmaili sect of the Shiite Muslims, whose method of terrorizing their enemies included murdering prominent adversaries.

Many assassinations have been linked directly with wars. In the

Please see ASSASSINATE, A20

Agence France-Presse

American troops sheltered behind ridge in Saudi Arabia watch smoke and flames following a U.S. bombing raid on Iraqi positions inside Kuwait.

■ **Diplomacy:** President accuses Hussein regime of setting Kuwait oil wells ablaze in a 'scorched earth policy.' Baghdad brands his message as 'shameful.'

By JAMES GERSTENZANG and ELIZABETH SHOGREN
TIMES STAFF WRITERS

WASHINGTON—President Bush on Friday gave Iraq until noon EST today to begin an "immediate and unconditional withdrawal" of its troops from Kuwait and seven days to complete it—or face the start of a ground war.

Iraq said the Bush ultimatum was "shameful" and gave no indication that President Saddam Hussein would comply.

With the shadow of an ever-closer ground assault hanging over the Persian Gulf, Bush accused the Iraqis of torching Kuwaiti oil wells in a "scorched earth policy" of warfare. Hussein's ruling Revolutionary Command Council denied the charge.

The Soviet Union, playing to the hilt its new role of middleman between Hussein and Bush, announced in Moscow that Iraqi Foreign Minister Tarik Aziz has agreed at the Kremlin to still another new plan for peace. The Soviets said this plan was awaiting final approval by Hussein.

The new Soviet-Iraqi proposal would commit Hussein to "an immediate and unconditional withdrawal" from Kuwait starting one day after a cease-fire. Instead of Bush's seven days, it would give Iraq three weeks to complete the pullout. The plan calls for an agreement to lift all U.N. resolutions against Iraq when the pullout is finished.

Bush was asked about this counterproposal to his high noon (9 a.m. PST) deadline as he bounded toward a Marine Corps helicopter taking him and Secretary of State James A. Baker III to Camp David, Md., for the weekend.

"We're just talking about it," he replied. "Don't know yet."

His spokesman, Marlin Fitzwater, said later: "If they [the Iraqis] can meet the Russian plan, they can meet the coalition plan. Our plan is the marker to meet. It [the counterproposal] doesn't quite meet our conditions. . . .

"It's a hard and fast date. Noon tomorrow. It's an ultimatum."

Bush's deadline met with strong approval from key Western and Arab allies in the anti-Iraq coalition, including Britain, France, Germany, Saudi Arabia and Kuwait.

French Foreign Minister Roland Dumas said the Bush ultimatum was the result of consultation among the allies. British Prime Minister John Major declared: "Iraq now knows precisely what it has to do."

Saudi and Kuwaiti officials expressed relief. Without the ultimatum, they had feared that the war would drag on for weeks longer.

The Bush deadline came early in a day of tense diplomacy as propos-

Please see GULF, A5

Yugoslavs Agree to Consider Splitting Nation

By CAROL J. WILLIAMS
TIMES STAFF WRITER

SARAJEVO, Yugoslavia—In this mountain resort where an act of violence led to the birth of Yugoslavia, leaders of the crisis-ridden federation agreed Friday to consider ways to grant the 72-year-old state a peaceful and dignified death.

At a closed session more remarkable for its absence of disaster than its accomplishments, presidents of the six fractious republics decided to appoint a committee to weigh the various options for Yugoslavia's future, including a controlled breakup.

Among the panel's tasks will be defining a legal procedure for secession by the republics, a position that appears to acknowledge determined moves toward independence already under way in the affluent northern republics of Slovenia and Croatia.

"At least, all the cards are on the table," Croatian President Franjo Tudjman conceded after the day-long session.

Stipe Mesic, Croatia's representative on the eight-man federal presidency, called the agreement

Please see YUGOSLAVIA, A28

Iraqis Torch Scores of Oil Facilities in Kuwait

■ **Gulf War:** At least 150 of the emirate's wells are set ablaze. Allies continue to hammer enemy forces.

By J. MICHAEL KENNEDY and MELISSA HEALY
TIMES STAFF WRITERS

RIYADH, Saudi Arabia—At least 150 of Kuwait's 950 oil wells have been set ablaze by Iraqi troops as part of a "scorched earth policy" that has blanketed a quarter of the occupied nation with smoke and cut off electricity and water, President Bush and Kuwaiti officials said Friday.

The torching of the wells came as allied forces continued to pour tons of bombs, missiles and artillery shells onto Saddam Hussein's military positions in Kuwait and southeastern Iraq in anticipation of a massive coalition ground attack, according to U.S. military officials.

Bush, who issued an ultimatum in Washington on Friday warning Iraq to commence a withdrawal from Kuwait by noon EST today or face a major allied ground assault, said Hussein started the fires "anticipating perhaps that he will be forced to leave. . . ."

"He is wantonly setting fire to and destroying the oil wells, the oil tanks, the export terminals and other installations of that small country," Bush said. "Indeed, they are destroying the entire oil production system of Kuwait."

In Baghdad, a spokesman for the ruling Revolutionary Command Council denied that Iraqi forces were burning Kuwaiti oil fields and called for a U.N. investigation of the allies' accusations.

In other developments:

• Baghdad Radio broadcast communiques to its front-line commanders contending that the allied ground offensive threatened by Bush has, in fact, already begun. The Iraqi claim was swiftly and emphatically denied by allied military officials.

• Saudi Arabian experts raised their estimates of the size of an oil slick that is clogging the Persian Gulf south of the Kuwait-Saudi border. The kingdom's Meteorology and Environmental Protection Administration said more than 138 million gallons of oil were fouling Gulf waters in that area. Earlier Saudi estimates had ranged from 21 million to 126 million gallons. The allies say Hussein deliberately dumped the oil into the Gulf; Iraq claims allied bombing caused the slick.

• Iraq launched a Scud missile toward the Dhahran area of Saudi Arabia, but it "exploded on its own

Please see WAR, A4

Deadline Ideal for Launching Night Attack

By JACK NELSON
TIMES WASHINGTON BUREAU CHIEF

WASHINGTON—A grim-faced President Bush, huddling at the White House with members of his war council in the early hours of Friday morning, decided on today's "high noon" deadline for Saddam Hussein because that would be nighttime in the Saudi Arabian desert, perfect for launching the massive ground war if Bush gives the final signal.

"The 12 noon deadline," a source familiar with the war strategy sessions said Friday, "was set on the basis that . . . that would allow the allies to take military action tomorrow night if Saddam Hussein doesn't pull out and Bush decides to go ahead with a ground attack."

Bush plunged into the discussion of how to respond to the surprise Soviet-Iraqi peace plan for ending the Gulf War immediately after returning to the White House about 10:20 p.m. Thursday from Ford's Theater, where he had watched a special performance of "Black Eagles," a play about black combat pilots in World War II.

Members of the war council had already been weighing the issue in

Please see DECISION, A22

Council Tentatively OKs Developer Fees for Art

■ **Urban affairs:** Builders would fund sculptures, murals, rehearsal spaces, theaters and music festivals.

By SAM ENRIQUEZ
TIMES STAFF WRITER

The Los Angeles City Council on Friday gave tentative approval to a public arts program that will require developers to pay millions of dollars annually to install artwork in commercial projects ranging from mini-malls to high-rise office buildings.

Supporters say that the public art program will enliven neighborhoods from the San Fernando Valley to South-Central Los Angeles, putting a new face on a cityscape that critics say is marred by dull architecture and graffiti.

The measure would require developers of non-residential projects costing more than $500,000 to spend as much as 1% of the construction value on "public art" such as sculpture and murals, as well as rehearsal space, parades, theaters and music festivals.

Developers can pay into a public art fund or spend an equivalent amount for art on their own buildings. City officials predict that most developers will prefer spending the money themselves.

The council voted 10 to 1 for the measure, meaning that it will come back to the council for a final vote March 1. Approval requires eight votes, and officials say they expect passage.

In addition to spawning public art projects, officials say that the measure will help integrate the

Please see ART, A31

INSIDE TODAY'S TIMES

■ **WAR STORIES, PHOTOS: A3-25; D1**

■ **SHOOTING IN ALBANIA**

Shooting erupted at a military academy in Tirana, Albania, where cadets were guarding a statue of Enver Hoxha. At least four people were killed. **A2**

■ **MWD FEARS CUTBACKS**

The MWD warned that the state may have to cut off all Southland water deliveries by March 1, forcing the district to cut deliveries 45% to 50%. **A30**

■ **KUWAIT DAMAGE**

Oil well fires and ruined facilities may impair Kuwait's ability to pump oil for months or years after the war, experts said. **D1**

WEATHER: Mostly sunny after morning low clouds. Civic Center low/high: 52/69. Details: B4

■ INDEX TO FEATURES ON A2

Associated Press

Martin after taking oath.

■ **NEW LABOR SECRETARY**

Lynn Martin was sworn in as labor secretary, and President Bush said she would become "a powerful force for good" in the American workplace. **A29**

Odd Couple Moscow and Tehran Drafted Peace Plan

■ **Mideast:** The joint effort was brought about by a shared anxiety over U.S. diplomatic gains in the Gulf.

By ROBIN WRIGHT and MICHAEL PARKS
TIMES STAFF WRITERS

NEWS ANALYSIS

MOSCOW—The surprise peace proposal unveiled by the Kremlin on Thursday was in fact a joint effort by the Soviet Union and Iran—a diplomatic odd-coupling of two of Washington's oldest foes with potential consequences that stretch well beyond the war in the Persian Gulf.

The extraordinary cooperation between Moscow and Tehran was brought on by a shared anxiety over U.S. diplomatic gains and long-term intentions in the Persian Gulf. But it is a pattern that could pose challenges for Washington elsewhere in the Middle East.

Although the Soviet Union has been given credit for the initiative, Soviet and U.S. officials said Tehran had played a crucial and almost equal role. "Everyone is making a big deal about the Soviets' leadership when Iran was just as much a part of this. It was really the Iranians who got the ball rolling and worked just as hard to sell it," said a senior U.S. official.

The effort, the only peace initiative since Iraq's Aug. 2 invasion of Kuwait to break the grim rhythm that was carrying events toward a full-scale ground war, evolved in early February from common con-

Please see IRAN, A7

Diplomacy: President Bush tells Saddam Hussein to begin withdrawing his forces from Kuwait by noon the next day if he wants to avoid a devastating ground war.
■ Bush also says he has evidence that Hussein had launched a ''scorched earth'' policy against Kuwait, setting fire to oil wells, tanks, export terminals and other installations.
■ Iraq calls the ultimatum ''shameful'' and gives no indication that Hussein will comply.
■ Baghdad Radio dismisses the deadline as ''desperate'' and calls Bush a ''madman.''
■ Bush's deadline meets with strong approval among key Western and Arab allies in the anti-Iraq coalition.
■ Soviet President Mikhail S. Gorbachev and Bush discuss the Moscow peace negotiations in a 90-minute telephone call.

Environment: A U.S. military briefer says well over 140 Kuwaiti oil wells had been set afire in the previous 24 hours. The Iraqis continue to destroy other wells; about 25% of the oil fields are covered with smoke.
■ Saudi Arabian experts raise their estimate of the size of the Persian Gulf oil slick to more than 3 million barrels.

Military: U.S. armored vehicles punch through sand berms on the Saudi Arabian border to clear pathways into Iraq.
■ Round-the-clock allied air attacks continue. Principal targets are Iraqi front-line forces, units of the elite Republican Guard and airfields. Meanwhile, big allied artillery guns relentlessly hammer targets in Iraq in one of the heaviest shellings since the war began.
■ Marine Harrier jets begin using napalm bombs to destroy the oil-filled trenches that Iraq has built to create smoke screens and tank hazards.
■ Allied planes carry out daylight bombing raids on the Baghdad area for the first time in nearly two weeks.

Iraq: Baghdad Radio broadcasts that allied forces launched ''the ground battle'' across the Saudi-Kuwait border. U.S. military commanders deny the claim.

Missile: Iraq fires a Scud missile at Saudi Arabia, but it explodes in the sky and falls into the desert.

An Iraqi gets a thorough search after surrendering to Americans.

PATRICK DOWNS / Los Angeles Times

COALITION DEMANDS

The list of specific demands as announced by White House Press Secretary Marlin Fitzwater:

■ Iraq must begin large-scale withdrawal from Kuwait by noon EST today.

■ Iraq must complete military withdrawal from Kuwait in one week.

■ Within the first 48 hours, Iraq must remove all forces from Kuwait city and allow for the prompt return of the legitimate government of Kuwait.

■ Iraq must withdraw from all prepared defenses along the Saudi-Kuwait and Saudi-Iraq borders, from Bubiyan and Warba islands and from the Rumaila oil fields.

■ Within the week, Iraq must return all forces to positions of Aug. 1.

■ Beginning immediately, Iraq must cooperate with the International Red Cross and release all prisoners of war and third-country civilians, and return the remains of killed service members within 48 hours.

■ Iraq must remove all explosives and booby traps, including those on Kuwaiti oil installations, and designate Iraqi military liaison officers to work with Kuwaiti and other coalition forces on the operational details related to Iraq's withdrawal—to include the provision of all data on the location and nature of any land or sea mines.

■ Iraq must cease combat aircraft flights over Iraq and Kuwait, except for transport aircraft carrying troops out of Kuwait, and allow coalition aircraft exclusive control and use of all Kuwaiti airspace.

■ Iraq must cease all destructive actions against Kuwaiti citizens and property and release all Kuwaiti detainees.

Fitzwater added:

"The United States and its coalition partners reiterate that their forces will not attack retreating Iraqi forces and, further, will exercise restraint so long as withdrawal proceeds in accordance with the above guidelines and there are no attacks on other countries. Any breach of these terms will bring an instant and sharp response from coalition forces, in accordance with U.N. Security Council Resolution 678."

Under the Bush plan:

All issues raised in the U.N. resolutions, including those relating to the embargo and reparations, would be dealt with separately by the United Nations.

COMPARING TERMS FOR AN

IRAQI PULLOUT

Agence France-Presse
George Bush at morning briefing.

Agence France-Presse
Mikhail S. Gorbachev at the Kremlin.

Within hours after President Bush said the allied coalition would give Saddam Hussein until noon today EST to begin immediate and unconditional withdrawal from Kuwait, the Soviet Union said it reached agreement with Iraqi Foreign Minister Tarik Aziz on a new six-point plan for withdrawal from Kuwait. Here is how the terms compare:

ABC News
Saddam Hussein meets with members of his Revolutionary Command Council Wednesday, as shown in TV photo released by Iraqi officials.

THE NEW SOVIET-IRAQI PLAN

The list of provisions agreed to by Iraq for an Iraqi withdrawal from Kuwait as announced by Kremlin spokesman Vitaly N. Ignatenko:

■ Iraq would implement U.N. Resolution 660, calling for an immediate withdrawal from Kuwait, without delay and without conditions.

■ The withdrawal would begin a day after a cease-fire.

■ The withdrawal would be completed 21 days after the cease-fire.

■ After withdrawal, all other Security Council resolutions, apparently including those relating to embargo and reparations, will "lose their meaning and be rescinded."

■ Prisoners of war would be released within 72 hours after the cease-fire begins.

■ Supervision of the withdrawal would be conducted by a peacekeeping force determined by the Security Council.

Ignatenko added:

The plan has been passed on to Baghdad. A final response to it from the Iraqi leadership was anticipated. Ignatenko said Soviet President Mikhail Gorbachev had spoken with Bush by telephone for 90 minutes just before the announcement.

UNITED NATIONS RESOLUTIONS

The Security Council resolutions, passed in the months after Iraq's Aug. 2 invasion of Kuwait, demand that Baghdad do the following:

■ Immediately and unconditionally withdraw its troops.

■ Restore the authority of the legitimate government of Kuwait.

■ Be held liable for war damages and economic losses.

■ Rescind its annexation of Kuwait and negotiate outstanding differences.

■ Observe all obligations under international conventions and laws regarding the conduct of an occupying power, the treatment of prisoners of war and the treatment of third-country nationals.

■ Ensure immediate access to food, water and basic services to Kuwaiti nationals and the nationals of all third states in Kuwait and Iraq.

■ Halt the mistreatment and oppression of Kuwaitis.

DAY 39

FEBRUARY 24, 1991

Pentagon spokesman Pete Williams believes his credibility hinges on never telling an outright falsehood, even to protect the security of a military operation.

A few minutes after the ground offensive officially began at 8 p.m. Washingtion time, but more than an hour before any public announcement, I phoned Williams and asked him directly, "Has the ground war started?"

There was silence on the line.

"Pete, I'm on deadline. You gotta help me," I pleaded.

"I just did," said Williams. "Have a good life." And he hung up.

—John M. Broder, in Washington

GULF: U.S., Allies Launch Ground Offensive
DEADLINE PASSED
GULF: U.S., Allies Launch Massive Ground Attack Against Iraq

U.S. Relocates Patriot Missiles to Repel Scuds in Ground War
Hopes and Prayers in the Southland
The Price of Peace: Hussein's Ouster
KUWAIT: Iraq's 'Campaign of Execution'
Kuwait Oil Well Fires Threaten Health, Crops
Ferocity of Air Attacks Said to Shock Hussein

Israeli Jews See Miracles in This War
Adding History
Objectors' Sincerity Doubted
East Coast Hospitals Gearing for Gulf Wounded
TV Scrambles for Any Bit of Scarce News
As the Ground War Begins, TV Is Left on the Sidelines
ORDNANCE: High Technology for Death, Destruction

Los Angeles Times

Sunday Final

CIRCULATION: 1,225,189 DAILY 1,514,096 SUNDAY

SUNDAY, FEBRUARY 24, 1991

COPYRIGHT 1991 THE TIMES MIRROR COMPANY CC† 466 PAGES

SUNDAY $1.25 DESIGNATED AREAS HIGHER

Ground War Launched

Bush Acts After Iraq Scorns Deadline

COLUMN ONE

Ordnance: High Tech's Gory Side

■ The new generation of weapons and ammunition, developed since the Vietnam War, can destroy tanks, penetrate bunkers and kill or maim troops with deadly precision.

By RALPH VARTABEDIAN
TIMES STAFF WRITER

They sound like a cast of cartoon characters: Adam, Beehive and Bouncing Betty. Yet they are among the most lethal ordnance ever deployed in battle.

Adam, a member of the Army's "family of scatterable mines," is packed with electronic detectors and a charge just large enough to puncture a liver. Beehive spews out 8,800 tiny flechettes—razor sharp darts that cause deep wounds. Bouncing Betty and its sister ordnance systems are designed to detonate at groin level, close to vital organs.

The Gulf War has raised public awareness of many high technology American weapons, such as Stealth fighters and Patriot missiles. But with much less fanfare, the Pentagon since the Vietnam War has developed a new generation of ordnance to destroy tanks, penetrate bunkers and kill troops with deadly effectiveness.

The mechanics of death and destruction are a grim affair. The military's scientific approach and its philosophies—for example, its preference for wounding vital organs over blowing off limbs—can be deeply disquieting to anybody who imagines such matters are left to chance. Many people would rather not know about the gruesome details.

"When my wife meets new friends and they ask, 'What does your husband do?' she tells them, 'He is a business executive at an ordnance manufacturer,' and they act horrified," one official lamented recently. "And they give her a very bad time. People don't like to think about ordnance."

People in the business of thinking up such weapons, fine-tuning them and producing them for maximum injury on the battlefield, are deeply committed to what they do. In war, the enemy must be destroyed. In the end, that will save American lives, they say.

In the Persian Gulf War, Saddam Hussein's notorious arsenal of ground weapons may be no match

Please see ORDNANCE, A10

An Iraqi soldier holds up his hands as he and other countrymen are taken prisoners of war by American forces in Saudi Arabia.

■ **Gulf conflict:** In a nationwide address, the President accuses Baghdad of redoubling its efforts to destroy Kuwait.

By JAMES GERSTENZANG and NICK B. WILLIAMS Jr.
TIMES STAFF WRITERS

WASHINGTON—One of the most violent battles in the history of modern warfare began on the wind-swept deserts beside the Persian Gulf today as the United States and its allies launched their long-threatened ground assault against Iraqi forces to drive them out of Kuwait.

"The liberation of Kuwait has now entered a final phase," President Bush announced at 10 p.m. EST Saturday at the White House.

Bush said he ordered the land assault because Iraqi President Saddam Hussein had ignored his deadline, Saturday at noon EST, to withdraw his troops from Kuwait and because Hussein had redoubled his efforts to destroy Kuwait and its people. Military officials said Iraqis had now torched 300 Kuwaiti oil wells and were raping, mutilating and executing thousands of Kuwaiti citizens.

"I have therefore directed Gen. Norman Schwarzkopf [commander of U.S. forces in the Gulf], in conjunction with coalition forces, to use all forces available, including ground forces, to eject the Iraqi army from Kuwait," the President said in a nationally televised statement. "Once again this was a decision made only after extensive consultation with our coalition partners. . . .

"I have complete confidence in the ability of coalition forces to swiftly and decisively accomplish their mission."

Bush made his announcement on a podium in the White House press room. He read his statement from notes. At one point, his left arm shook slightly in his gray suit jacket as he said to the American people:

"Tonight, as this coalition seeks to do that which is right and just, I ask only that all of you stop what you are doing and say a prayer for all the coalition forces, and especially for our men and women in uniform, who at this very moment are risking their lives for their country and all of us.

"May God bless and protect each and every one of them," Bush said, "and may God bless the United States of America."

At the United Nations, Iraq's deputy ambassador, Sabah Talat Kadrat, vowed: "The war will be long."

Defense Secretary Dick Cheney declared a blackout on information about the assault. He told reporters at the Pentagon that all military briefings in Washington and at allied headquarters in Saudi Arabia would be suspended until further notice. Cheney cited the safety of allied troops and the security of

Please see GULF, A6

Thai Military Seizes Power in Bloodless Coup

By CHARLES P. WALLACE
TIMES STAFF WRITER

BANGKOK, Thailand—Thailand's military Saturday ousted the country's civilian government, suspended the constitution and imposed martial law in a coup that could undermine one of Asia's fastest-growing economies.

Prime Minister Chatichai Choonhavan, a former army general who was the nation's first elected prime minister in 12 years, reportedly was taken from a military plane at gunpoint as he was about to leave a Bangkok airfield on a flight to attend the swearing-in of his new deputy defense minister. Other members of Chatichai's Cabinet also were detained.

The coup was carried out without apparent bloodshed and the capital showed little evidence of military activity. Weekend shoppers jammed downtown streets and malls as usual.

Troops in armored cars surrounded the buildings of Radio Thailand and the government-controlled television station. On the rival military station, an officer read a series of communiques from the new government, which is headed by Gen. Sunthorn Kongsompong, the supreme commander of the Thai military. The first

Please see THAILAND, A30

Allies Accuse Iraq of 'Execution Campaign'

■ **Atrocities:** U.S. military says Iraqi soldiers are killing Kuwaiti civilians to destroy evidence of torture.

By DAVID LAMB and JOHN BRODER
TIMES STAFF WRITERS

RIYADH, Saudi Arabia—Allied commanders accused Iraq on Saturday of conducting "a systematic campaign of execution" in occupied Kuwait, which a variety of reports suggested is suffering an intensifying devastation by the Iraqis.

"This is terrorism at its finest hour," said Marine Brig. Gen. Richard I. Neal, U.S. military spokesman in Riyadh, charging that Iraqi soldiers were killing Kuwaiti civilians previously subjected to torture. "They are executing people on a routine basis, people not connected with the resistance. They may think the game is up and they are trying to destroy the evidence [of torture], and that evidence is the people."

In Washington, Rear Adm. John (Mike) McConnell, director of intelligence for the Joint Chiefs of Staff, said that analysts estimated that 2,000 to 10,000 Kuwaitis had been arrested and in some cases raped, tortured and mutilated.

"The perpetrators of those crimes will have to answer for it," said Lt. Gen. Thomas W. Kelly, director of operations for the Joint Chiefs.

In Los Angeles, Kuwaitis in exile said reports from the resistance in their country had characterized the mood of citizens there as a mixture of dread and hope. The latest round of Iraqi atrocities was viewed by many Kuwaitis as the sad but expected prelude to freedom.

Besides the reports of the human toll of the Iraqi occupation, McCon-

Please see KUWAIT, A9

U.S. Officials Set Date for the Attack Nearly 2 Weeks Ago

By DAVID LAUTER
TIMES STAFF WRITER

WASHINGTON—For the scores of thousands of American and allied troops who launched the ground attack against Iraq early this morning and for their commanders, the last week of frantic diplomatic maneuverings in Moscow, Baghdad and the United Nations were a sideshow that might just as well never have taken place.

For nearly two weeks, the machinery to launch the assault proceeded like a vast train moving down the tracks. Only a massive

Please see TIMING, A24

Allied Assault Mapped to Rout Crippled Foe

By MELISSA HEALY and JOHN M. BRODER
TIMES STAFF WRITERS

WASHINGTON—The massive U.S.-led ground assault against the Iraqi army that began early today was designed months ago to be a campaign of speed, deception and seamless maneuver with just one goal, senior Pentagon officials said Saturday: to crush a crippled adversary.

It is a plan for surrounding and destroying the heart of the Iraqi military force, not merely to drive it from Kuwaiti soil.

The offensive, which envisions simultaneous air, land and amphibious attacks across the entire front, contains no intermediate objectives or "firebreaks" where action would pause to allow an orderly Iraqi withdrawal.

Instead, military planners said Saturday, the campaign is designed to do to the Iraqi army exactly what Gen. Colin L. Powell, chairman of the Joint Chiefs of Staff, promised it would: Cut it off and kill it.

Multiple attacks will force the Iraqis to defend at numerous points and will mask the main assault, a 150,000-man armored and airborne thrust which Pentagon officials call "the hammer."

And the attack will not stop until the hammer has fallen on the

Please see OFFENSIVE, A26

Who's Minding the Store at Big Department Chains?

■ **Business:** Retailers try new marketing tactics. Debt loads and demanding customers are hurdles in the '90s.

By MARTHA GROVES
TIMES STAFF WRITER

SAN FRANCISCO—If busy executives in Columbus, Ohio, hate to shop or cannot find the time, the Godfry's men's store will take its suits, ties and shirts to them.

Nordstrom employees are told: "If it makes sense, do it," and at least once it made sense to let a customer return a 3½-year-old pair of shoes.

Wal-Mart discount stores give customers who pay by check or credit card $1 if cashiers fail to call them by name and invite them back.

Welcome to the wonderful world of special touches and customer-driven retailing, where shopping is a pleasure, be it at folksy discount stores or service-minded specialty stores.

Unfortunately, a pleasant experience is not what shoppers have when they visit many of the nation's full-line department stores. Instead, customers often complain of indifferent—even inept—service and uninspired merchandise.

These are fretful times for department stores. Several are slogging through the recession hip-deep in debt. On top of last year's Chapter 11 filing by the owners of Bloomingdale's, Burdines and Jordan Marsh, the recent decision by Carter Hawley Hale Stores Inc., the West's only big department store company, to seek refuge from

Please see RETAILING, A32

INSIDE TODAY'S TIMES

■ **WAR STORIES, PHOTOS: A6-28; M1, M3, M5**

■ **OBJECTING TO OBJECTORS**

The military has doubts about the sincerity of 1,700 soldiers who have filed for conscientious objector status, pointing to the timing of their applications. **A11**

■ **RALLY FOR SOVIET UNITY**

Tens of thousands of marchers gathered near the Kremlin to show their support for keeping the Soviet Union intact. **A4**

■ **CHINESE REUNIFICATION**

A panel chaired by Taiwan's president proposed that the rival Chinese governments recognize each other as a first step toward reunification. **A5**

WEATHER: Patchy morning clouds near the coast. Civic Center low/high today: 53/75. Details: B2

■ TOP OF THE NEWS ON A2

Gov. Pete Wilson

■ **WILSON ATTACKS UNION**

Gov. Pete Wilson lashed out at the state's largest teachers union for an ad campaign opposing his proposed two-year, $2-billion reduction in school aid. **A3**

Apache Copters: Deadly Havoc in the Dark of Night

■ **Weapons:** Using night-vision sights, air cavalry visits devastation on Iraqi troops behind the lines.

By JOHN BALZAR
TIMES STAFF WRITER

WITH U.S. FORCES ON THE NORTHERN SAUDI BORDER—Through the powerful night-vision gun sights, they looked like ghostly sheep flushed from a pen—Iraqi infantrymen bewildered and terrified, jarred from sleep and fleeing their bunkers under a hellish fire.

One by one, they were cut down by attackers they could not see or understand. Some were blown to bits by bursts of 30-millimeter exploding cannon shells. One man dropped, writhed on the ground, then struggled to his feet; another burst of fire tore him apart. A compatriot twice emerged standing when shot at. As if in pity, the U.S. Army attackers turned and let him live.

For the Army's 18th Airborne Corps, the ground war had begun earlier. It was carried straight to the enemy in the blackness of night, at 50 feet above the sand, by the Army's longest punch: the fast, deadly and controversial AH-64 Apache attack helicopter.

Then, upon the Apaches' return to forward attack bases—like here, with the 5th Squadron of the 6th Cavalry, the Knight Raiders—the evidence of this early ground fighting is displayed in startling, sharp, intensely violent videotapes from gun cameras.

The $10-million-plus Apaches are night fighters and tank killers.

Please see APACHES, A28

War Costs

War with Iraq could **COST** the U.S. from $28 billion to $86 billion, a report has said. A Congressional Budget Office projection said the conflict would cost $17 billion to $35 billion this fiscal year, depending on its length and the severity of U.S. losses. The costs for future years would range between $11 billion and $51 billion.

Months of desert training preceded the 100-hour ground war.

PATRICK DOWNS / Los Angeles Times

White House: One of the most violent battles in the history of modern warfare begins about dawn as the United States and its allies launch the ground assault to drive Iraqi forces from Kuwait.
■ President Bush tells the nation "the liberation of Kuwait has entered a final phase."
■ He says he ordered the land assault after Iraqi President Saddam Hussein ignored the deadline to withdraw from Kuwait.
■ Prime Minister John Major says British forces will join the land drive, and President Francois Mitterrand orders French ground troops to engage "in the liberation of Kuwait."

Military: The ground battle pits more than 800,000 allied troops against about 500,000 Iraqis.
■ Spearhead units of U.S. troops and armor smash through Iraqi lines and wall defenses along the border.
■ American women helicopter pilots fly into combat areas for the first time.
■ Defense Secretary Dick Cheney declares a blackout on information about the assault.

Kuwait: A U.S. military briefer says Iraqi forces in Kuwait have been conducting "a systematic campaign of execution, particularly people who had been tortured." U.S. analysts estimate that 2,000 to 10,000 Kuwaitis have been arrested and in some cases raped, tortured and mutilated.

Missiles: Iraq launches Scud attacks at Saudi Arabia and Israel. One missile shot at eastern Saudi Arabia is hit by a Patriot missile, and a second breaks up in flight. The one fired at Israel is shot down by a Patriot. No damage is reported.

Iraq: Allied intelligence sources say that Saddam Hussein was stunned by the ferocity of allied attacks against him and that he accused the Soviet Union of not having warned him what the United States and its partners had in store.

As a tense world watched and waited, the noon deadline set by the United States for Iraq to begin withdrawing from Kuwait passed—and was ignored by Iraq.

About eight hours later, the 800,000- plus allied force launched its full-scale ground war on Iraq and occupied Kuwait, sources said.

In Washington, President Bush went on national television to declare, "The liberation of Kuwait has now entered a final phase." Asking Americans to pray for allied troops, he said: "I have complete confidence in the ability of coalition forces to swiftly and decisively accomplish their mission."

These developments earlier Saturday set the stage for the launch of the ground war:

In Moscow: Iraqi Foreign Minister Tarik Aziz, departing from Moscow, threw his support behind a Soviet plan that called for Iraq to pull out within three weeks of a cease-fire. But he did not mention the U.S. ultimatum.

At the United Nations: Just moments before the deadline, diplomats at the United Nations reported some last-minute overtures from the Iraqis, but the result was unclear. The Security Council made plans to meet later in the day—a meeting that adjourned quickly once word came that the ground attack had commenced.

In Baghdad: Izzat Ibrahim, deputy chairman of the ruling Iraqi Revolutionary Command Council, called Bush's demand "an aggressive ultimatum to which we will pay no attention."

SATURDAY, FEB. 23
THE DAY THE
DEADLINE PASSED

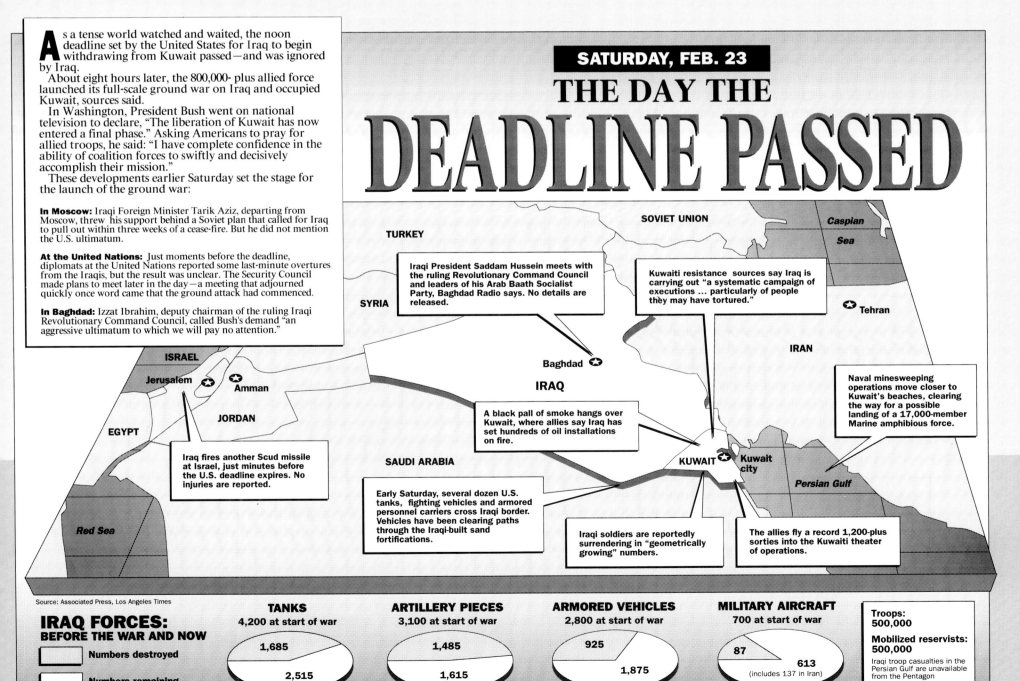

Iraqi President Saddam Hussein meets with the ruling Revolutionary Command Council and leaders of his Arab Baath Socialist Party, Baghdad Radio says. No details are released.

Kuwaiti resistance sources say Iraq is carrying out "a systematic campaign of executions ... particularly of people they may have tortured."

Naval minesweeping operations move closer to Kuwait's beaches, clearing the way for a possible landing of a 17,000-member Marine amphibious force.

A black pall of smoke hangs over Kuwait, where allies say Iraq has set hundreds of oil installations on fire.

Iraq fires another Scud missile at Israel, just minutes before the U.S. deadline expires. No injuries are reported.

Early Saturday, several dozen U.S. tanks, fighting vehicles and armored personnel carriers cross Iraqi border. Vehicles have been clearing paths through the Iraqi-built sand fortifications.

Iraqi soldiers are reportedly surrendering in "geometrically growing" numbers.

The allies fly a record 1,200-plus sorties into the Kuwaiti theater of operations.

SOVIET UNION · Caspian Sea · TURKEY · SYRIA · Tehran · IRAN · ISRAEL · Jerusalem · Amman · JORDAN · EGYPT · Baghdad · IRAQ · SAUDI ARABIA · KUWAIT · Kuwait city · Persian Gulf · Red Sea

Source: Associated Press, Los Angeles Times

IRAQ FORCES:
BEFORE THE WAR AND NOW

☐ Numbers destroyed
☐ Numbers remaining

TANKS	ARTILLERY PIECES	ARMORED VEHICLES	MILITARY AIRCRAFT
4,200 at start of war	3,100 at start of war	2,800 at start of war	700 at start of war
1,685	1,485	925	87
2,515	1,615	1,875	613 (includes 137 in Iran)

Troops: 500,000

Mobilized reservists: 500,000

Iraqi troop casualties in the Persian Gulf are unavailable from the Pentagon

SANDY KAY AND VICTOR KOTOWITZ / Los Angeles Times

93

DAY 40

FEBRUARY 25, 1991

I found the Iraqi I.D. card on a desk in a Kuwait city police station that Iraqi forces had used as a local headquarters. I've carried it with me ever since.

It shows a young Arab with a mustache, serious brown eyes, a little thin, looking as if he was trying to put on a pleasant face for the camera. He is Sgt. Taleb Hial Abed, service number 53431, blood type A-positive. The card was issued Sept. 28, 1980.

Every once in a while I've taken it out, just to look. Once, it was after I'd interviewed a family whose son was shot by the Iraqis on their doorstep. Once, it was when I saw the ruins of the emir's palace, horribly befouled. Often, it was when Kuwaitis told me how stupid the Iraqis are, how jealous they are of Kuwaiti wealth, how they would never achieve such riches even if they waited a million years, fought a million wars and died a million deaths.

I kept wondering if Sgt. Abed knew what was happening. If so, what did he think about it?

—Kim Murphy, in Kuwait city

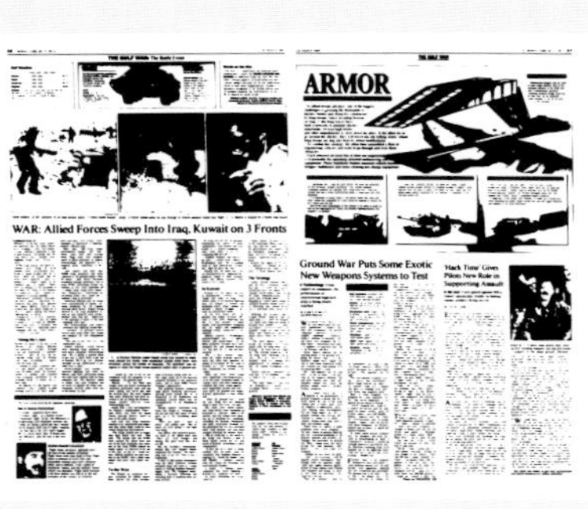

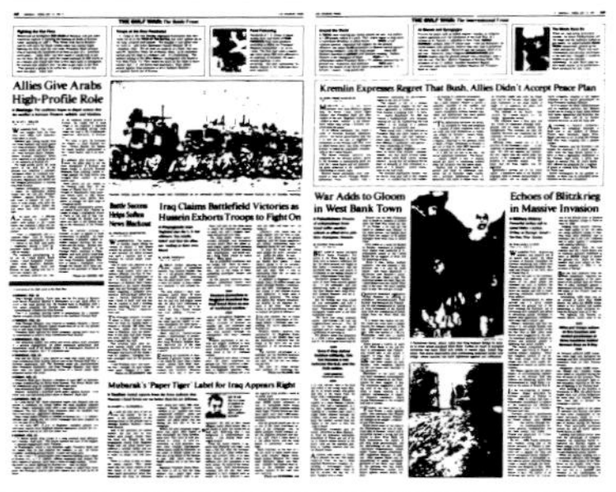

Los Angeles Times

CIRCULATION: 1,225,189 DAILY / 1,514,096 SUNDAY | MONDAY, FEBRUARY 25, 1991 | DAILY 25¢ DESIGNATED AREAS HIGHER

COPYRIGHT 1991 THE TIMES MIRROR COMPANY CC† 96 PAGES

Allies Push Ahead on 3 Fronts

10,000 Prisoners Reported Taken in Kuwait, Iraq

■ **Gulf War:** Gen. Schwarzkopf calls the offensive a 'dramatic success' so far. U.S. casualties are reported to be light.

By TRACY WILKINSON and JOHN M. BRODER
TIMES STAFF WRITERS

RIYADH, Saudi Arabia—Thrusting deeper into Iraq and Kuwait against little more than token resistance, U.S.-led ground forces pursued their swift campaign to rout Saddam Hussein's troops along a 300-mile front—taking at least 10,000 prisoners in the first 24 hours of the campaign and advancing toward the Kuwaiti capital, military commanders said Sunday.

"They are moving north with great speed," said Gen. H. Norman Schwarzkopf, commander of Operation Desert Storm. "So far, the offensive is progressing with dramatic success."

Allied forces achieved "all of their first-day objectives" within the first 12 hours after the operation began, in an unexpected downpour of pre-dawn rain, Schwarzkopf said.

Schwarzkopf described Iraqi resistance as sporadic and allied casualties as "remarkably light," but he gave no details. According to other sources, a total of three U.S. Marines, attached to the 1st and 2nd Marine divisions, were killed and 17 were wounded. Other sources reported a total of about two dozen U.S. troops wounded in the early hours of the ground offensive. Army officials said no Army personnel had been killed in the first 18 hours of the ground action.

Striking by land, sea and air, the allied offensive advanced along three fronts on the ground. To the east along the Persian Gulf coast, U.S. Marines pressed what was described as their largest land assault since World War II—smashing into Kuwait from the south along with Saudi and Kuwaiti armored troops.

To the west, American airborne troops pushed north into southwestern Kuwait, accompanied by helicopter gunships laying down a withering protective cover.

Still farther west, American, British and French armored forces struck directly into Iraqi territory, moving rapidly north in an apparent effort to cut off and encircle Iraq's vaunted Republican Guard.

Military spokesmen in Saudi Arabia said U.S. Marines aboard ships in the Persian Gulf rushed ashore in an amphibious landing with anti-tank weapons for their fellow Leathernecks pushing north from the border. Sources in Washington said U.S. Special Forces and paratroopers of the 82nd Airborne Division were dropped near Kuwait city in a bold maneuver, but they added that the capital had not been secured.

In other developments during the first day of the ground campaign:

• Iraq insisted that the ground

Please see WAR, A6

THE ALLIED GROUND OFFENSIVE

The long-anticipated ground war started as a massive, multi-pronged attack involving troops from 11 countries, mobile armor, airborne attacks and support from the sea. Military sources and press reports indicated that the land attacks struck in three directions. The common elements throughout were speed and mobility. Resistance was light, and thousands of Iraqi prisoners were taken:

1. British troops launched a major flanking attack from Saudi Arabia into Iraq. The British were believed to be pushing toward Basra, Iraq's second-largest city, or heading toward Kuwait city, encircling Iraqi troops in either case.

2. U.S. and French forces pushed into Iraq west of Kuwait. Reports had these armored troops at least 30 miles past the Saudi border.

3. U.S. airborne troops with quick-strike helicopter capability moved into southwest Kuwait.

4. Along the Gulf, U.S. Marines moved northward into Kuwait, along with Saudi Arabian and Kuwaiti armored elements.

5. Some U.S. forces were reported near Kuwait city. The quick recapture of the capital city is considered a high priority.

6. Early reports that U.S. Marines had taken the strategic island of Faylakah off Kuwait city were denied. Other unconfirmed reports said Marine amphibious troops had landed in Kuwait city suburbs.

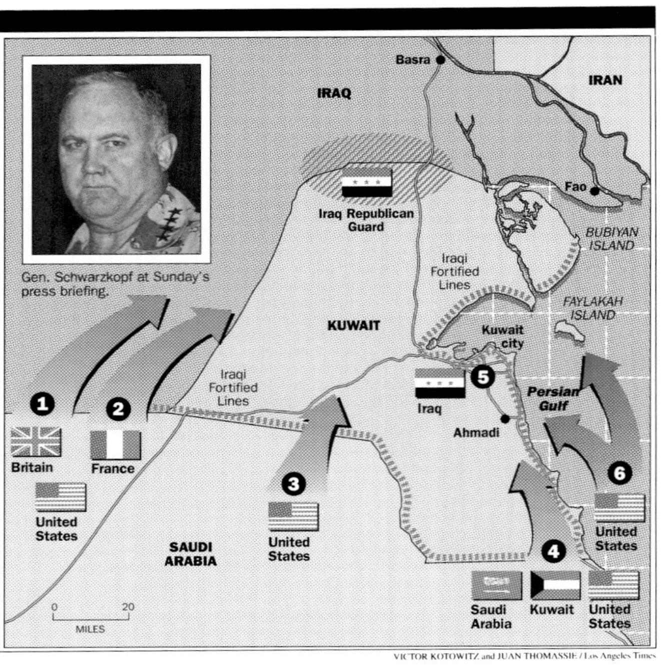

VICTOR KOTOWITZ and JUAN THOMASSIE / Los Angeles Times

COLUMN ONE

General Has Heart of a Romantic

■ Schwarzkopf, the soldiers' champion, is gruff, engaging and often quick-tempered. His men follow him with a loyalty that borders on idolatry.

By DAVID LAMB
TIMES STAFF WRITER

RIYADH, Saudi Arabia—Eighteen months ago, before a dinner honoring him in Kuwait, the general's hosts had suggested that appropriate dress would be the traditional *dishdasha* robe and he had thought to himself, "Holy smokes, Schwarzkopf is going to dress up like the Kuwaitis and all the Arabs are going to say, 'Who the hell does this guy think he is?'"

The general, though, was easily persuaded, and before dinner he took possession of a splendid embroidered *dishdasha* delivered to his hotel room. He slipped it over his bear-like frame and studied his image in the mirror, first from one perspective, then the other.

"It's wonderful," he said. And suddenly Gen. H. Norman Schwarzkopf was waltzing with his reflection, doing the same little three-step that T.E. Lawrence, widely known as Lawrence of Arabia, had done in the desert when he shed his British uniform for Arab robes and went on to form an alliance of Arabian tribes.

If Schwarzkopf is not Norman of Arabia, he is at least a soldier with the heart of a romantic, a man intrigued by Arab history and culture and a man who has followed his famous father's footsteps through the sands of the Middle East to lead a war that may shape the world into the 21st Century.

"The stakes," he says, "are higher than any conflict since World War II."

Gruff, engaging, sometimes hot-tempered, Schwarzkopf has a hearty laugh that can be heard down the corridor and a presence that fills the room. He is 6-foot-4, 240 pounds, with linebacker shoulders, upper arms as big as tree trunks—and a row of four stars on his collar. Sometimes he refers to himself in the third person. He seems to like privates as much as colonels and colonels more than politicians, and he makes his points with a furrowed brow and eyes that hold steady like a laser-guided bomb. No one ever left a meeting with him wondering who was in charge.

"What would I change about myself?" he asks. "I would probably"—he reaches for the words carefully—"want . . . a little more

Please see GENERAL, A16

Masses of Iraqi POWs Slowing Allied Advance

By PAUL RICHTER
TIMES STAFF WRITER

WASHINGTON—Allied soldiers who had expected to face flaming trenches and lethal minefields in the opening hours of the ground war found they had a quite different problem on their hands when the invasion actually began: a mass of surrendering Iraqis.

More than 10,000 Iraqis were reported to have given up during the first 24 hours of the ground offensive, slowing the allied advance and creating logistic snarls that Defense Secretary Dick Cheney described as "one of our biggest problems."

And Pentagon officials predicted they would be handling many more prisoners of war, perhaps as many as 100,000, as the campaign continues.

"Thousands of them are coming out of their holes," said a Pentagon official in Saudi Arabia. "We just hope they don't all surrender at once."

"They just keep coming and coming," said an amazed staff officer at 1st Marine Division headquarters. "I didn't know they had that many to give."

Pentagon officials had long expected that thousands of Iraqis

Please see POWS, A14

Allies Prepare Strategy to Force Out Hussein

■ **Policy:** Military defeat, continued sanctions and holding territory are seen as levers for change.

By DAVID LAUTER
TIMES STAFF WRITER

WASHINGTON—Buoyed by early reports of battlefield triumphs, senior Bush Administration officials Sunday for the first time sketched out extensive allied plans to seize and hold Iraqi territory as part of a strategy to force fundamental changes in Baghdad's government.

Key to that strategy, military sources say, is a drive deep into Iraq aimed at seizing control of Basra, Iraq's second-largest city and a strategic military center, as well as major points along the Euphrates River, the historic waterway that separates southern Iraq from the central part of the country.

Officials indicated they also intend to maintain economic sanctions on Iraq after the fighting ends to compel Baghdad to accept allied terms for ending the Gulf crisis.

The emerging allied strategy, coupled with the public statements by Administration officials Sunday, are the most direct evidence yet that one unofficial aim of the allied coalition is to force Saddam Hussein out of power.

Hussein "has demonstrated time and time again his character, and that is not compatible with a peaceful world," National Security Adviser Brent Scowcroft said. Scowcroft reiterated the official policy—that allied forces "have not made" eliminating Hussein a "goal for the success of the operation."

But he made clear that ending Hussein's rule will "absolutely" be the allied coalition's preference.

Bush and allied leaders hope that a combination of a devastating Iraqi military defeat, continued sanctions and allied occupation of a large sector of southern Iraq will provide enough leverage to force Iraq to sue for peace on allied terms, terms that are incompatible with continued rule by Hussein.

"One does not see how Saddam Hussein will mend his ways," French President Francois Mitterrand said Sunday in a Paris press conference. After an Iraqi military defeat, "the political authority and the military authority of Saddam Hussein would be considerably affected," Mitterrand said.

U.S. Defense Secretary Dick Cheney insisted that the allied coalition has "no interest in occu-

Please see STRATEGY, A21

'Saddam Line' Falls Easily to Marines

By BOB DROGIN
TIMES STAFF WRITER

EASTERN SAUDI ARABIA—Thoughout the desert night, the screaming jets hammered the enemy, some of them raining down fuel-air bombs that turned the skies a grisly orange. Loudspeakers blared, exhorting unseen Iraqi soldiers in Arabic to "surrender before it is too late." The artillery thundered, firing salvo after salvo.

Then, dressed in protective suits against chemicals, thousands of U.S. Marines launched the long-awaited allied attack into Kuwait on Sunday.

"G-Day," as the troops dubbed it, had the potential to be a nightmarish spectacle, filled with flaming oil ditches and deadly mists of biological and chemical gas. Iraqi President Saddam Hussein had repeatedly threatened that this was to be "the mother of all battles," with thousands of casualties.

It did not happen that way, as even the weather cooperated with the allies on Sunday. Unexpectedly this weekend, the wind shifted. Rain fell. The noxious smoke from burning Kuwaiti oil fields that had filled the sky for days, blotting out the sun and blackening the horizon, dispersed on G-Day.

Please see MARINES, A15

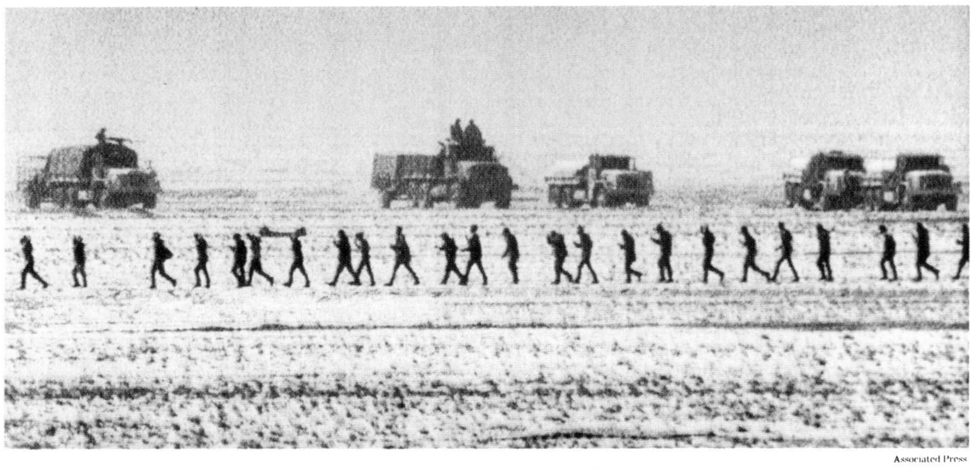

Associated Press

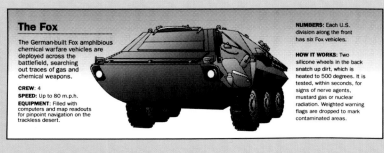

Captured Iraqi soldiers are marched through the desert in Kuwait past U.S. Marine 2nd Division vehicles as allied troops moved forward.

MORE WAR COVERAGE

The Fox

The German-built Fox amphibious chemical warfare vehicles are deployed across the battlefield, searching out traces of gas and chemical weapons.

CREW: 4

SPEED: Up to 80 m.p.h.

EQUIPMENT: Filled with computers and map readouts for pinpoint navigation on the trackless desert.

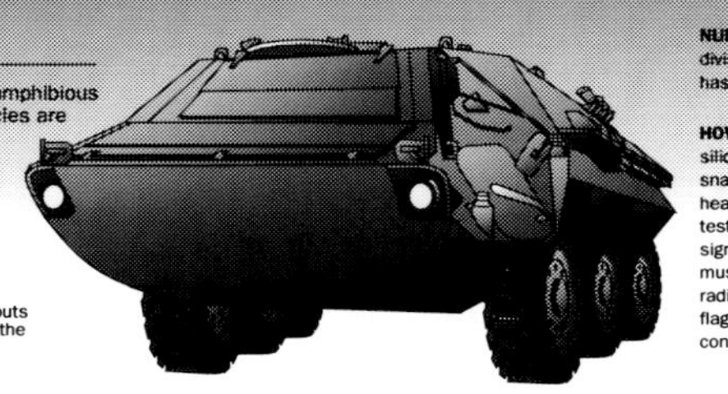

NUMBERS: Each U.S. division along the front has six Fox vehicles.

HOW IT WORKS: Two silicone wheels in the back snatch up dirt, which is heated to 500 degrees. It is tested, within seconds, for signs of nerve agents, mustard gas or nuclear radiation. Weighted warning flags are dropped to mark contaminated areas.

Military: U.S.-led ground forces advance toward Kuwait city against little more than token resistance and take at least 10,000 prisoners as the ground campaign extends along a 300-mile front.

■ Gen. H. Norman Schwarzkopf says allied forces have attained all objectives of the first day of the ground war and are "moving north with great speed." He describes allied casualties as "remarkably light."

■ Allied forces advance to the edges of Kuwait city, a senior U.S. military official says. There are unconfirmed reports of a deep drive into Kuwait and of Iraqis surrendering by the tens of thousands.

■ French Foreign Legion units spearheaded by light tanks speed into Iraqi territory west of Kuwait in an encircling movement designed to cut off supply lines to Iraqi forces.

■ Eight hours after the ground offensive begins, there are no reports that Iraqi forces have used chemical weapons.

Iraq: Baghdad Radio says Iraqi troops repulsed the U.S.-led ground offensive. "The offensive has so far totally failed, and the criminal aggressors are crying for help," it says.

Missiles: Iraq fires two Scuds at Saudi Arabia and two at Israel. None was believed to have caused any casualties or serious damage.

Diplomacy: The Soviet Union expresses regret that the Western allies began a land war against Iraqi troops and did not allow more time for diplomatic efforts.

International: Responses to the ground war split along expected lines. Nations with forces in the Gulf predict a swift victory. Nations outside the conflict, notably China, mark the escalation with "deep regret."

Trickle of Iraqi POWs turned into torrent of more than 60,000.

PATRICK DOWNS / Los Angeles Times

ARMOR

ON THE MOVE

As allied troops advance, one of the biggest challenges is crossing the thousands of ditches, berms and obstacles constructed by Iraqi troops. Since invading Kuwait on Aug. 2, the Iraqi forces have built a network of antitank ditches, minefields, 10-foot high berms and other impediments to slow down the allies. If the allies try to go around the ditches, they will travel into the killing zones, where Iraqi troops are dug into heavily armed fortifications.

To combat this strategy, the allies have assembled a fleet of engineering vehicles and tools to go through and over these obstacles.

Each armored division has at least one engineering battalion that is responsible for operating armored earthmoving and bridging equipment. These battalions feature armored-vehicle-launched bridges, bulldozers and mine-clearing line charge equipment.

M-60 TANK

Mechanized bridges may be used to span larger ditches. One of the principal vehicles is the M-60 tank, with a hydraulically operated unfolding scissors bridge spanning 63 feet that can be deployed in three minutes. It can be recovered in 10 to 60 minutes.

63 feet

M-9 COMBAT EARTHMOVER

To penetrate the 10-foot-tall sand berms, the army has developed the M-9 Armored Combat Earthmover. This combat bulldozer completely protects the operator from small arms fire in front-line combat and has a 9-foot earthmoving blade to move sand and other obstacles.

It is important to knock holes in the berms rather than drive over them, where the underbelly of a tank would be exposed to enemy fire as it came over the top.

One of the main advantages of this vehicle is its ability to travel as fast as the high-speed M-1 tanks and Bradley Fighting Vehicles that support it in combat.

PLASTIC TUBING (FASCINE)

To cross Iraq's antitank ditches, the allies will create a stable roadbed across smaller ditches by dropping bundles of plastic tubing (fascine) from the back of tanks. The tanks can then travel over the piping safely without exposing the top hatches or underbelly of the tanks to enemy fire.

M-88A1 RECOVERY VEHICLE

One of the most important tasks in front-line tank combat is to recover and repair immobilized tanks. Many tanks are not destroyed when hit by enemy missiles. Special vehicles, such as the M-88A1 Armored Recovery Vehicle, can retrieve damaged tanks that have toppled over, thrown tracks or sustained engine problems.

A large part of the Israeli tank inventory is made up of Soviet-built tanks recovered by Israeli troops during their war with Egypt following tank battles on the Sinai Peninsula.

PAUL GONZALES / Los Angeles Times

DAY 41

FEBRUARY 26, 1991

The videotape shows Frank Mitchell, ramrod straight in his Air Force uniform. His chin is out, his chest is proud and adorned with service ribbons, 30 years' worth. This was his retirement ceremony, less than a year ago. At his side, beaming with pride, is his daughter Adrienne.

Now, in their Moreno Valley home, Frank and his wife Sammie were trying to understand why war had taken their daughter. They hadn't wanted her to join the Army, but she had always been independent, and she had wanted to save for college.

For Frank, it had been 30 years without a scratch. Adrienne had been in for only five months. It made no sense. Why Adrienne and not him?

Nor could Frank explain why, when he turned on the TV that day, heard of the Scud missile attack and saw the wrecked and smoking barracks in Dhahran, he had said to Sammie, "Adrienne's in there."

"My mind wasn't working right," he recalled. "My mind was telling me something I didn't know about."

—Scott Harris, in Riverside

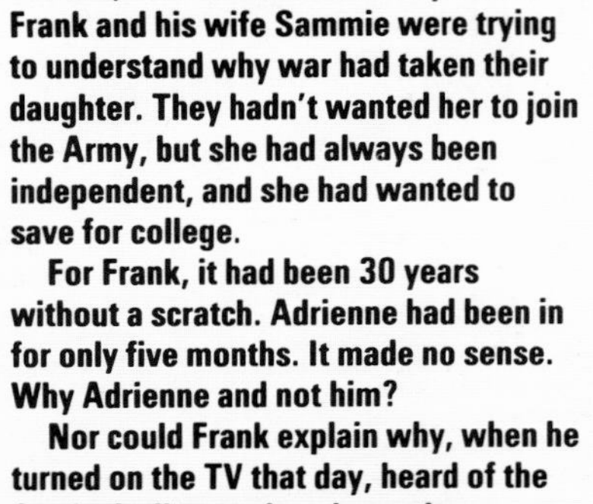

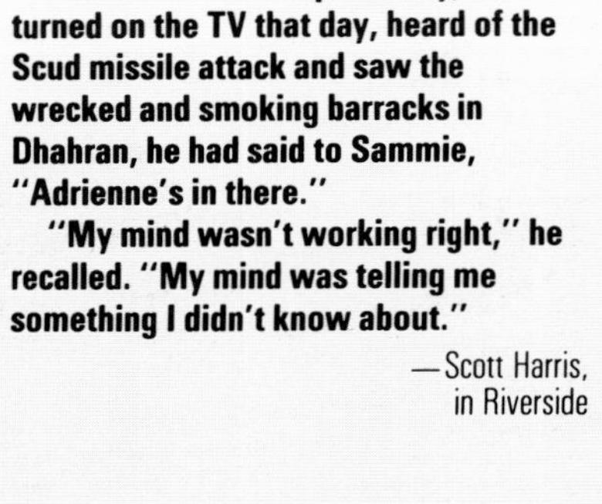

Los Angeles Times

CIRCULATION: 1,225,189 DAILY / 1,514,096 SUNDAY — TUESDAY, FEBRUARY 26, 1991 — COPYRIGHT 1991 / THE TIMES MIRROR COMPANY / CC†† / 110 PAGES — DAILY 25¢ DESIGNATED AREAS HIGHER

Iraq Orders Kuwait Pullout

U.S. Discounts Move, Sees No Change; War Pressed

■ **Gulf conflict:** Fitzwater says Hussein must publicly accept terms. Many Republican Guard tanks reported destroyed. Total of POWs put at 25,000.

By TRACY WILKINSON and NICK B. WILLIAMS Jr.
TIMES STAFF WRITERS

RIYADH, Saudi Arabia—Iraqi President Saddam Hussein's government ordered its forces to withdraw from Kuwait as allied troops pushed farther into Iraq and the occupied nation of Kuwait today in the third day of a massive ground offensive.

But the White House turned a cold shoulder to the withdrawal announcement broadcast over Baghdad Radio.

"We continue to prosecute the war. We have heard no reason to change that," President Bush's press secretary, Marlin Fitzwater, told reporters.

Before the U.N. Security Council met in a late-night session, Bush met Monday evening for about 75 minutes with his national security advisers. Fitzwater said afterward that the United States has seen "no evidence" to suggest the Iraqi army is withdrawing. "In fact," he noted, "Iraqi units are continuing to fight."

Fitzwater also tightened the conditions for ending the U.S.-led attack against Iraq, demanding public pronouncements from Hussein himself.

He said that for Hussein to persuade the allied coalition that his withdrawal announcement is serious, the Iraqi leader must "personally and publicly" agree to all U.S. demands contained in Bush's nine-point ultimatum of last Friday, including immediate withdrawal from Kuwait. Fitzwater said Hussein also must "publicly accept explicitly all relevant U.N. Security Council resolutions."

These include, in addition to an unconditional withdrawal from Kuwait, a renunciation by Hussein of his annexation of Kuwait and agreement to pay "compensation to Kuwait and others."

Fitzwater also said Bush would insist that Iraqi soldiers in Kuwait and Iraq must physically "lay down their arms" to show that they are retreating.

"We will not attack unarmed soldiers in retreat," Fitzwater said.

He also warned that U.S. forces would continue to attack any Iraqi troops that are still carrying or operating their weapons. "We will consider retreating combat units as a movement of war," he said.

A senior military officer in the Pentagon derided Baghdad Radio's announcement, telling the Associated Press: "They want us to pause. They want us to stop."

The Iraqi broadcast followed the U.S. military's announcement that allied forces had destroyed scores of Iraqi tanks Monday in the first significant combat with Hussein's top-rated Republican Guard.

Sources said that in other action, U.S. Marine and Saudi army battalions, backed by persistent air attacks, continued to press toward

Please see WAR, A6

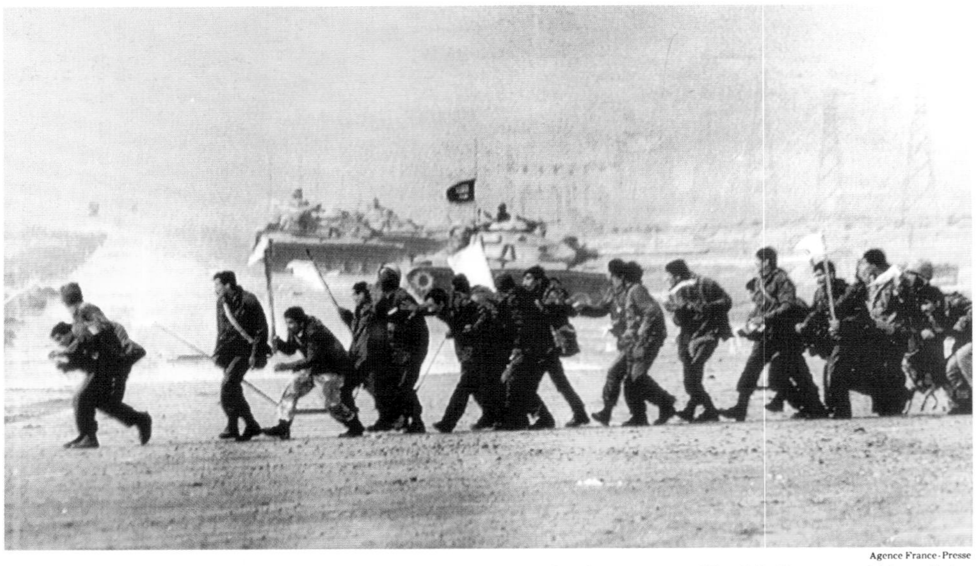

Agence France-Presse

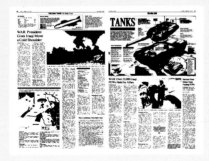

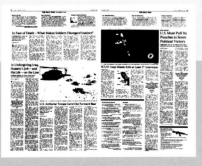

A group of Iraqi soldiers carrying white flags of surrender cross a highway in Kuwait as a convoy of Saudi Arabian army vehicles rolls by.

COLUMN ONE

Revisiting the Legacy of Nasser

■ The Egyptian walked away from military defeat in triumph. The chance that Hussein could emerge beaten but esteemed by other Arabs has affected the strategy of both sides.

By KIM MURPHY
TIMES STAFF WRITER

DHAHRAN, Saudi Arabia—The Arab world had been brought to its knees that day in 1967 when Egyptian President Gamal Abdel Nasser admitted that the pan-Arab army that was supposed to "drive Israel into the sea" had instead been overrun.

The fabled Sinai Peninsula was lost. So were Gaza City and the surrounding desert, Syria's Golan Heights, the West Bank of the Jordan River and one of the hearts of all Islam, Jerusalem's Old City. In all, 28,000 square miles had been lost in six days. The armies of Egypt, Jordan and Syria were in humiliating retreat.

Nasser, in a speech broadcast to millions all over the Arab world, glumly shouldered blame for the disaster and announced that he was abandoning the presidency.

Egyptians, however, would have none of it. Pandemonium erupted, and the next day the postal clerk's son who had sought to instill the checkerboard land between Morocco and the Persian Gulf with a defiant national identity far outside Egypt's borders exultantly rescinded his resignation.

"Nasser," his successor, Anwar Sadat, would say later, "was bigger than words."

It wasn't the first time that Nasser had walked away in triumph from military defeat. In 1956, after nationalizing the Suez Canal, Nasser's troops were crushed by the forces of Israel, Britain and France—yet he emerged as a revered advocate of Arab unity.

Now, in many ways, the outcome of one of the worst crises in the history of the Middle East rests on whether such magic can be worked again.

Iraqi President Saddam Hussein's decision late last week not to surrender Kuwait in the face of near-certain military devastation, holding on instead for what may be a swift but violent war, has much to do with Nasser's legacy—and the West's fears that the Iraqi leader could emerge from Kuwait defeated but triumphant in the eyes of the millions of Arabs who heard in Iraq's march into Kuwait echoes of Nasser's calls for Arab nationalism.

Please see LEGACY, A20

State to Shut Off Water Delivery to Southland

By VIRGINIA ELLIS and TED ROHRLICH
TIMES STAFF WRITERS

SACRAMENTO—Gov. Pete Wilson on Monday announced new and unprecedented cutbacks of state water deliveries so drastic that Southern California will be cut off from this traditional source of water by mid-March.

Wilson said heightened drought conditions had forced the state to notify all cities and industrial users served by the State Water Project

■ **RELATED STORIES:** A3

that they can expect to receive only 10% of normal deliveries for the rest of the year.

Because the Metropolitan Water District has already drawn that amount of water in January and February, officials said the announcement means that in March the state will effectively stop pumping water to Southern California.

"It's by far the most severe water restriction ever imposed," said George Baumli, executive director of the State Water Contractors Assn.

In Los Angeles, officials said the announcement means that water users may face cutbacks of up to 25% beginning May 1.

Wilson's announcement confirmed predictions made Friday by

Please see WATER, A28

Iraqi Missile Slams Into GIs' Barracks; 27 Killed

■ **Scud attack:** 98 are hurt in the deadliest such strike of the war. Quarters were for Pennsylvania reserve unit.

By BOB DROGIN and PATT MORRISON
TIMES STAFF WRITER

DHAHRAN, Saudi Arabia—Flaming debris from an Iraqi Scud missile slammed into a makeshift barracks full of U.S. troops near here Monday night, killing at least 27 soldiers and injuring 98 in a fierce explosion and fire, according to the U.S. military Central Command in Riyadh.

Eyewitnesses said a Patriot missile had intercepted the Scud overhead, but U.S. military officials in Riyadh said they could not confirm that a Patriot had been launched.

"Why did the Patriot have to hit it?" asked a dazed and weeping Specialist Robert Jacobs of Iowa, standing outside the twisted, flaming wreckage. "If it hadn't hit it, it would have passed on by."

This was the deadliest Scud attack of the war. The soldiers were the first Americans to be killed from the Scuds that Iraq has launched against Saudi Arabia and Israel.

Baghdad Radio hailed the attack, saying the missile struck "the coward traitors who mortgage the sacred places of the nation . . . and turn Arab youth into shields of flesh."

As air raid sirens wailed across Dhahran about 8:30 p.m., the incoming missile could be seen descending in a fiery arc against the cold desert night. It crashed in a roar of flame directly into the hangar-like, three-story former warehouse in Khobar city, just outside Dhahran.

"It came very slowly, then it fell and exploded, very loud," said Mohad Raies, a 34-year-old Indian construction worker who watched in fear through his gas mask as the missile landed 100 yards away. "It was a tremendous explosion. And then the fire. It is horrible."

Greg Seigle, a 25-year-old American free-lance journalist who arrived at the scene moments after the blast, said rescue helicopters and ambulances didn't arrive for 20 minutes to begin pulling the dead and wounded from the flames, bent steel girders and shredded tin walls and roofing.

"There was a huge fireball in the air, and huge pieces of flaming debris came raining down, like a Roman candle," he said. "The explosion shook the ground. Then there was a second, smaller explosion."

The deadly rain of fiery shrapnel caused several cars to collide on a nearby six-lane highway, and the air filled with the stench of sulfur, Seigle said. "The building itself was an inferno," he said. "All you could see was the skeleton frame, completely engulfed in flames."

Please see SCUD, A9

Arab Forces Wave Happily on Road North

By KIM MURPHY
TIMES STAFF WRITER

RAS AL ZOUR, Kuwait—The sign at the main border checkpoint into Kuwait says, "Welcome," but it tilts crazily to one side, and beyond it stretches newly liberated southern Kuwait: an eerie panorama of devastation and spring clover, of a sudden, fleeting violence that passed over the landscape and moved on.

On the coastal desert plains that frame the main highway from Saudi Arabia to Kuwait city, an occasional donkey grazes amid the blown-out wreckage of tanks and supply trucks. The road itself is, for long stretches, little more than a pile of asphalt chunks, churned up by Iraqi forces before they fled north from advancing allied forces.

Government buildings and way stations have been reduced to rubble over weeks of allied bombing raids; stinking oil trenches line the dugouts where Iraqi tanks crouched before falling back to the north, and roaring triumphantly across the battered landscape, hooting and waving, are dozens of Kuwaiti and Saudi soldiers straddling battle tanks still unscathed by war.

In this odd, turned-upside-down landscape, where a wealthy oil emirate looks like parts of the South Bronx and a warm afternoon sun breaks occasionally through the impermeable smoke haze of dozens of burning oil wells, even

Please see ARABS, A12

Census Finds Ethnic Boom in Suburbs, Rural Areas

■ **Population:** Asian and Hispanic growth exceeds expectations. State's white share continues to decline.

By FRANK CLIFFORD and ANNE C. ROARK
TIMES STAFF WRITERS

The face of California changed dramatically during the past decade, with suburbs and farm towns joining cities as entry ports for vast numbers of Hispanics and Asians migrating into the state.

According to 1990 U.S. census data released Monday, the most dramatic change in the state's ethnic makeup took place in the heartland city of Fresno, which experienced a 626% increase in its Asian population. Similarly, massive expansions of Hispanic and Asian populations were found in San Bernardino and Riverside counties.

Overall, the census found that one in four Californians is Hispanic and one in 10 is Asian.

"Clearly, we are seeing massive suburbanization of Asians and Hispanics," said Leo Estrada, UCLA professor of urban studies and a census adviser to the U.S. secretary of Commerce. "I've been hearing all day from officials in outlying areas who can't quite believe the figures they are seeing today. Places like Chino, Corona, Ontario, Rialto, Upland.

"They say the numbers can't be real. The size [of immigrant populations] are two or three times what they were estimating."

The numbers released Monday by the Census Bureau focused on

Please see CENSUS, A29

MORE WAR COVERAGE

■ **WAR STORIES, PHOTOS: A5-18; D1-2; F2**

■ **HUSSEIN'S REASONING**
Saddam Hussein's determination to stay in power is understandable. In Iraq's tradition, few leaders lose their jobs without losing their lives. **A8**

■ **WHY THEY FIGHT**
Why do soldiers in combat fight rather than flee? Most authorities agree that servicemen—and women—fight because of their loyalty to each other. **A8**

■ **POSTWAR CHALLENGE**
Operation Desert Storm is moving close to what may be the most difficult phase of all—the complex and delicate end-game in the political arena. **A9**

WEATHER: Mostly sunny with increasing high clouds. Civic Center low/high today: 51/73. Details: B5

■ TOP OF THE NEWS ON A2

■ **POWS AN OBSTACLE**
Marines pushing across the desert in the assault to free Kuwait are running into two major obstacles—minefields and surrendering Iraqi troops. **A7**

■ **TORTURE AND TERROR**
Tales of torture and terror by Iraqi forces against Kuwaitis were told by refugees who managed to flee to Jordan just before the land battle began. **A10**

■ **BISHOPS SPLIT OVER WAR**
The nation's Catholic bishops lack a "clear consensus" to declare the Gulf War morally unjustified, a spokesman for the American prelates said. **A11**

■ **HUSSEIN'S SURVIVAL**
Can Saddam Hussein survive the war? Some say it depends on whether he's willing to follow his people down the road to martyrdom. **In World Report**

25% of Kuwaitis May Be Casualties, U.S. Believes

■ **Aftermath:** Providing food, water and medical care 'will stretch world relief organizations' to the maximum.

By DAVID LAUTER
TIMES STAFF WRITER

WASHINGTON—As much as 25% of Kuwait's civilian population may be dead, injured or suffering from such diseases as cholera and dysentery by the time the country is free of Iraqi troops, U.S. Army analysts predict.

The analysis, contained in a detailed report prepared by Army civil affairs units to guide allied forces that will occupy Kuwait, paints a picture of a ravaged country whose capital city could be virtually razed if Iraqi defenders put up a fight against allied troops.

Providing food, water and rudimentary medical care to the roughly 800,000 people still in Kuwait "will stretch world relief organizations to their maximum capacities," the report estimates. A copy of the unclassified document was obtained by The Times.

Already, the plans say, dysentery has become "commonplace" among civilian Kuwaitis, 40% of whom are under the age of 15.

"Large numbers of children may be lost" to epidemics of viral disease spread by unsanitary conditions, and tens of thousands more could die if Iraqi troops battle to hold the city, according to the planners.

Even more civilians could die once formal fighting stops because "terrorist action is expected from stay-behind Palestinian or Iraqi

Please see TOLL, A10

Silkworm Missile

Two Iraqi Silkworm missiles were fired at allied warships Monday, believed to be the first use of the large anti-ship missiles in the Gulf War. One was knocked out by British missiles and the other fell into the sea. The Silkworm is the Chinese version of the 30-year-old Soviet Styx, a relatively crude radar-guided missile. However, it is considered a potent naval threat.

Launch: By ship or mobile launcher.
Range: 50 miles
Attack: Cruises at 100 feet above water, dropping to 50 feet for the attack.
Height: 23.9 feet
Weight: 5,060 lbs.
Diameter: 2.6 feet

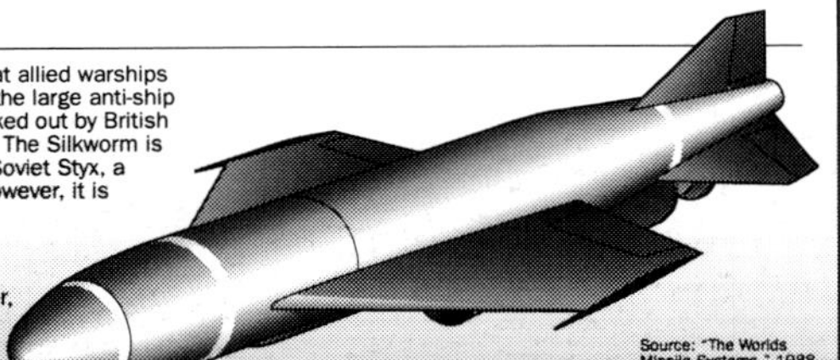

Source: "The Worlds Missile Systems," 1988

ANDERS RAMBERG / Los Angeles Times

Allied bombers caught Iraqi convoys fleeing Kuwait City.

PATRICK DOWNS / Los Angeles Times

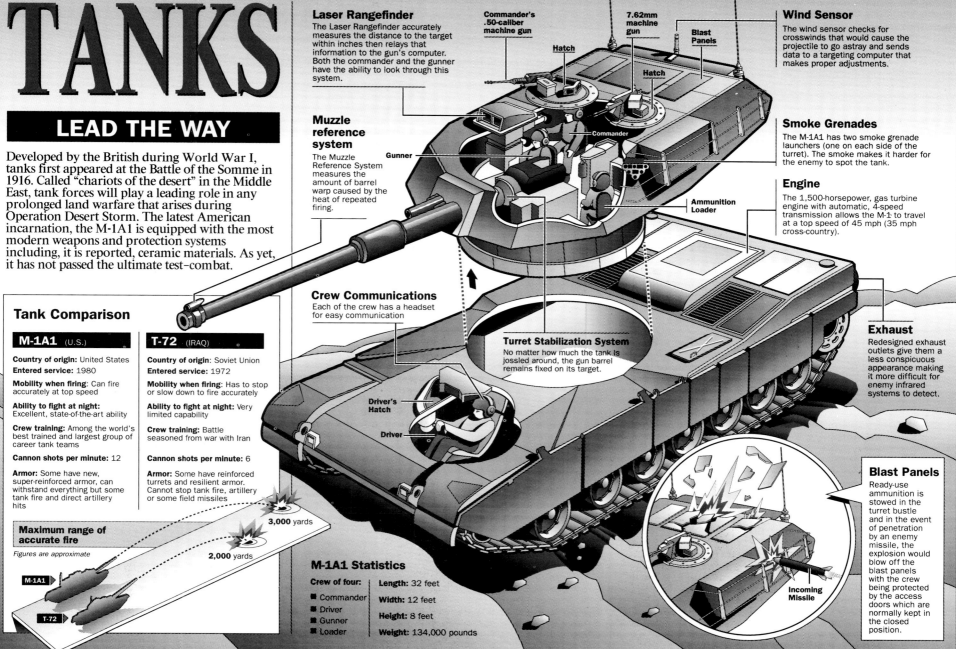

TANKS

LEAD THE WAY

Developed by the British during World War I, tanks first appeared at the Battle of the Somme in 1916. Called "chariots of the desert" in the Middle East, tank forces will play a leading role in any prolonged land warfare that arises during Operation Desert Storm. The latest American incarnation, the M-1A1 is equipped with the most modern weapons and protection systems including, it is reported, ceramic materials. As yet, it has not passed the ultimate test–combat.

Tank Comparison

M-1A1 (U.S.)	T-72 (IRAQ)
Country of origin: United States	**Country of origin:** Soviet Union
Entered service: 1980	**Entered service:** 1972
Mobility when firing: Can fire accurately at top speed	**Mobility when firing:** Has to stop or slow down to fire accurately
Ability to fight at night: Excellent, state-of-the-art ability	**Ability to fight at night:** Very limited capability
Crew training: Among the world's best trained and largest group of career tank teams	**Crew training:** Battle seasoned from war with Iran
Cannon shots per minute: 12	**Cannon shots per minute:** 6
Armor: Some have new, super-reinforced armor, can withstand everything but some tank fire and direct artillery hits	**Armor:** Some have reinforced turrets and resilient armor. Cannot stop tank fire, artillery or some field missiles

Maximum range of accurate fire

Figures are approximate

3,000 yards
2,000 yards

M-1A1
T-72

Laser Rangefinder
The Laser Rangefinder accurately measures the distance to the target within inches then relays that information to the gun's computer. Both the commander and the gunner have the ability to look through this system.

Muzzle reference system
The Muzzle Reference System measures the amount of barrel warp caused by the heat of repeated firing.

Gunner

Commander

Crew Communications
Each of the crew has a headset for easy communication

Commander's .50-caliber machine gun

Hatch

7.62mm machine gun

Hatch

Blast Panels

Wind Sensor
The wind sensor checks for crosswinds that would cause the projectile to go astray and sends data to a targeting computer that makes proper adjustments.

Smoke Grenades
The M-1A1 has two smoke grenade launchers (one on each side of the turret). The smoke makes it harder for the enemy to spot the tank.

Engine
The 1,500-horsepower, gas turbine engine with automatic, 4-speed transmission allows the M-1 to travel at a top speed of 45 mph (35 mph cross-country).

Ammunition Loader

Turret Stabilization System
No matter how much the tank is jossled around, the gun barrel remains fixed on its target.

Driver's Hatch

Driver

Exhaust
Redesigned exhaust outlets give them a less conspicuous appearance making it more difficult for enemy infrared systems to detect.

M-1A1 Statistics

Crew of four:
■ Commander
■ Driver
■ Gunner
■ Loader

Length: 32 feet	
Width: 12 feet	
Height: 8 feet	
Weight: 134,000 pounds	

Blast Panels
Ready-use ammunition is stowed in the turret bustle and in the event of penetration by an enemy missile, the explosion would blow off the blast panels with the crew being protected by the access doors which are normally kept in the closed position.

Incoming Missile

Sources: Modern Tanks, Knight-Ridder Tribune News, Jane's Armor and Artillery, Modern American Armour

DAVID PUCKETT / Los Angeles Times

DAY 42

FEBRUARY 27, 1991

The end brought eerie silence to a battlefield still smoldering from the war's final barrage. For four days, the American attack had seemed a constant din, a cacophony of armored clank, rocketed thunder and then—an ominous sound of head-to-head combat—the sure, dull, percussion of a tank's main gun. Near the front of the charge, from inside a Bradley Fighting Vehicle, I had clutched tight to my radio-helmet and strained to listen in over the deafening roar.

Yet, now it was 8 in the morning, and the radios had come alive with the order to cease fire. We sat almost stunned with disbelief, then slowly climbed outside to take measure. All around there lay the wreckage of war: an Iraqi base reduced to chaos, its tanks blackened hulks, its bunkers broken by bombs.

But now the guns were mute, and the fierce wind became suddenly audible, a reassertion by the long-disturbed desert. And as soldiers clambered out of their hatches to hoist trophies of triumph, the only new sound was that of flags flapping, Stars and Stripes over Iraqi soil.

—Douglas Jehl,
in southern Iraq

Los Angeles Times

CIRCULATION: 1,225,189 DAILY / 1,514,096 SUNDAY — WEDNESDAY, FEBRUARY 27, 1991 — COPYRIGHT 1991 / THE TIMES MIRROR COMPANY / CC†/ 92 PAGES — DAILY 25¢ DESIGNATED AREAS HIGHER

Iraqis in Full Retreat, U.S. Says

Marines in Kuwait City; Bush Demands Surrender

COLUMN ONE

A Flawless Strategy for Victory

■ The U.S.-led coalition's careful military planning and effective economic sanctions against Iraq turned the 'mother of all battles' into an allied rout.

By MELISSA HEALY and EDWIN CHEN
TIMES STAFF WRITERS

WASHINGTON—Iraqi dictator Saddam Hussein warned that it would be the "mother of all battles." Instead, it has become the "mother of all surrenders."

After months of allied concern over Iraq's battle-hardened million-man army, thousands of tanks and artillery pieces, chemical weapons and fearsome defenses, the attack against Iraqi forces by the 28-country U.N. coalition appears to have turned into a full-fledged rout.

As of Tuesday night, more than 30,000 Iraqi troops had surrendered—virtually without incident—to U.S. and other coalition forces, some even trying to give themselves up to small teams of journalists who were advancing on Kuwait city.

What happened to enable the allied forces to achieve what appears to be such a sweeping victory?

Experts and military commanders cite these developments:

- Although Iraq had amassed huge numbers of tanks and artillery, they apparently were inadequate to compensate for Baghdad's glaring deficiency in aircraft, electronic warfare gear and other high-tech weaponry, which left Iraq without a complete weapons system with which to fight.
- Shortcomings in Baghdad's war machine made the Iraqi army a hapless victim of its own vulnerabilities, seemingly enabling the allies to turn many of Iraq's initial strengths into major weaknesses.

For example, although Baghdad had erected elaborate fortifications, they eventually became a prison for immobilized Iraqi combat vehicles, making them more vulnerable than ever to allied air attacks, experts said. Hussein's insistence that his army rely heavily on orders from central command became a formula for chaos when allied warplanes destroyed Iraqi communications centers. And Iraq virtually squandered its million-man army by sending raw recruits to lead the defense in this past week's ground war.

- The Iraqis also apparently fell this week for a massive, months-long allied deception that caused

Please see ROUT, A18

Sky TV via Reuters

A group of Kuwaiti soldiers raise their country's flag just outside Kuwait city, signaling the end of the occupation of the capital by Iraq.

■ **Gulf War:** Republican Guard is cut off and attacked by allies. One elite division is reported 'virtually destroyed.' Two others try to flee.

By TRACY WILKINSON
TIMES STAFF WRITER

RIYADH, Saudi Arabia—U.S. Marines entered the capital of Kuwait, and coalition forces cut off the main body of Iraq's elite Republican Guard on Tuesday as Saddam Hussein's armies reeled and fled before a massive allied air and land offensive.

"The Iraqi army is in full retreat, although there is some fighting going on," Lt. Gen. Thomas W. Kelly, chief of operations for the Joint Chiefs of Staff, said in Washington. "Tomorrow, when the sun comes up, the question in my mind is whether the enemy is going to be there."

The Marines—a force composed of small reconnaissance units—moved into Kuwait city after a daylong advance through wind-swept rain along the Persian Gulf coast. Kuwaiti troops joined them in the capital soon afterward, raising their national flag in the center of town.

The advances in Kuwait came as allied forces launched the climactic battle of the Gulf War late Tuesday, sending U.S. airborne divisions, British tank forces and the heaviest concentration of American armor since World War II against Iraq's elite Republican Guard near the southeastern Iraqi city of Basra.

Scarcely four days into the massive ground war, coalition troops had pushed deeply into Kuwait and Iraq on three major fronts—along the coast, along the western Kuwaiti border and farther west, up through southeastern Iraq.

By dawn today, the allies had destroyed or neutralized 27 Iraqi divisions—a total of more than 270,000 men, or roughly half of the troops Hussein had deployed in Kuwait and southeastern Iraq, according to Marine Brig. Gen. Richard I. Neal. More than 30,000 others had surrendered, and still more began retreating to the north.

But just because some of Hussein's troops were moving out of Kuwait did not mean they were abandoning their weapons or giving up the fight entirely, the U.S. Central Command said. Instead, some appeared to be pulling back to regroup.

"Through the night and into the day tomorrow, we will continue to press the battle," Gen. Kelly told a Pentagon briefing Tuesday afternoon. "We are still engaged in combat, and we will not let up."

Kelly said that since the beginning of the war, coalition forces had destroyed 2,085 Iraqi tanks, about 50% of Hussein's original complement; 962 armored vehicles, or about one-third, and 1,505 artillery pieces, or about 48%.

U.S. casualties in the ground war held at four dead and 21 wounded. Among the joint Arab forces, the death toll rose to 13 with 43

Please see WAR, A6

U.S. Forging Sanctions Plan to Oust Hussein

By DOYLE McMANUS and NORMAN KEMPSTER
TIMES STAFF WRITERS

WASHINGTON—The Bush Administration, increasingly convinced that Saddam Hussein will hold onto power even after the rout of his forces, is quietly forging a strategy to prompt a coup in Baghdad by preventing the Iraqi president from rebuilding his shattered economy and offering a brighter future to his war-weary people.

Senior U.S. officials said Tuesday that the United States intends to maintain the economic sanctions that block Iraqi oil exports, depriving Hussein of the money his country will desperately need to recover from thousands of allied bombing raids. They hope that the further deterioration of life inside Iraq—and the bleakness of the country's prospects—will spark a revolt against Hussein's leadership in a matter of weeks or months.

"We will present Iraqis with the prospect of a future in which this leader will just drag them further and further down," a senior official said.

Asked whether the Administration foresaw Hussein being forced out of power within a year, the official replied: "We wouldn't want him around for that long."

At the same time, the Administration plans to ask the United Nations to maintain its embargo on sales of military and other "strate-

Please see POSTWAR, A10

President Tells Iraqis to Lay Down Weapons

■ **Diplomacy:** Bush scornfully rejects Hussein's effort to save face. His tough stand is criticized by the Soviets but is supported by Congress and the allies.

By DAVID LAUTER and MARK FINEMAN
TIMES STAFF WRITERS

WASHINGTON—President Bush vowed Tuesday that Saddam Hussein will fail in his attempt to "save the remnants of power and control" and ordered Iraqi troops to "lay down their arms" to avoid annihilation.

Bush's statement, coming shortly after the Iraqi president tried in a radio broadcast to claim a shred of victory in retreat, amounted to a demand for unconditional surrender and was clear notice that Iraq will not be able to withdraw from Kuwait on its own terms.

Hussein, announcing his army's withdrawal from the occupied sheikdom, argued that his "brave forces" have withstood an unprecedented assault by 30 nations and praised his soldiers, declaring they have "planted seeds" in the "mother of battles" that would be "harvested within the coming period."

Bush scornfully rejected the Iraqi leader's attempt to save face, saying that Hussein "is trying to claim victory in the midst of a rout." Hussein "is not interested in peace, but only to regroup and fight another day," Bush said.

Bush's uncompromising stand drew criticism from the Soviet Union but support from members of Congress and from key allies.

On a visit to the western Soviet Union, Soviet President Mikhail S. Gorbachev warned that superpower relations could suffer unless "responsible behavior" guides U.S. efforts to end the war.

"It is vital to end this conflict and put on the agenda of the world community resolution of the broader question of the Middle East," the Tass news agency quoted Gorbachev as saying. "There must be no more bloodshed."

But with some U.S. military officials privately predicting that the remainder of Iraq's army would be smashed within 48 hours, a majority of the 12-member U.N. Security Council meeting in closed session backed the United States in rejecting a cease-fire for now.

No cease-fire should be offered until Hussein's government provides a written acceptance of all U.N. resolutions regarding Kuwait, including the resolutions calling for payment of reparations, Security Council members agreed.

And at a meeting with congressional leaders in the Oval Office, both Democrats and Republicans offered support for Bush's position.

"Don't let Saddam Hussein off the hook," Senate Republican leader Bob Dole of Kansas told reporters he had advised Bush. "I think that's the view of most

Please see BUSH, A11

Fleeing Iraqis a 'Jackpot' for Navy's Pilots

By BOB DROGIN
TIMES STAFF WRITER

EASTERN SAUDI ARABIA—Again and again on Tuesday, loudspeakers on the carrier Ranger blared Rossini's "William Tell Overture"—the rousing theme song for the carrier pilots aboard, as well as for the Lone Ranger.

Each time—instead of a "Hi-yo, Silver, awaaay!"—another strike force of A-6 Intruder jets spurted flame into the cold night and roared off the flight deck to bomb what one pilot called "The Jackpot"—the roads north of Kuwait city, clogged with retreating Iraqi trucks and armored vehicles.

"This morning it was bumper-to-bumper," said Lt. Brian Kasperbauer, 30, a pilot based in Guam. "It was the road to Daytona Beach at spring break. Just bumper-to-bumper. Spring break's over."

Lt. Armando Segarra, 26, a bombardier of Floral Park, N.Y., agreed, saying: "We hit the jackpot!"

The giant carrier's skipper, Capt. Ernest Christensen Jr., said he had received orders to extend the sorties from 10 a.m., the scheduled stopping point, into the afternoon to better destroy the fleeing army.

"It looks like the Iraqis are moving out, and we're hitting them hard," Christensen told his crew. "It's not going to take too many more days until there's nothing left of them."

Please see JACKPOT, A14

War Shows Extraordinary Ability to Unite the Public

■ **Patriotism:** Pessimism fades and Americans rally around the flag, a contrast to reaction to domestic crises.

By RONALD BROWNSTEIN
TIMES POLITICAL WRITER

Flag sales are swelling. Blood drives are oversubscribed. Yellow ribbons flutter from car aerials and billboards and offices. In January, the Marines and Army—the services that are facing the greatest risk in the ground war with Iraq—exceeded their recruitment goals.

Polls show President Bush with near-record approval ratings. More than four in five Americans say they back his decision to go to war. In a matter of weeks, the mood of the country has reversed: Polls now find a majority of Americans consider the country to be on the right track, a startling reversal from December, when most considered the nation off in the wrong direction.

This emotional surge has graphically demonstrated that, even in an era of skepticism about government, war still has an extraordinary ability to unite the public—at least before bad news, and casualties, mount.

In recent years, many analysts have wondered whether the nation has become too segmented and disillusioned with its leaders to be united behind any purpose. Their pessimism seemed to be validated in the gridlock that has persisted for a decade between the Democratic Congress and Republican White House on corrosive domestic problems—from crime and poverty

Please see PATRIOTISM, A22

MORE WAR COVERAGE

■ **WAR STORIES, PHOTOS: A5-22; D1, D5; E1**

■ **A DISPIRITED ARMY**

"It's now obvious to Saddam and the world that the heart of the Iraqi army just isn't in this fight," a military analyst said after Hussein's speech. **A5**

■ **KUWAITI OFFICIALS**

Kuwaiti exile officials in Saudi Arabia said most of their capital has been liberated and they are eager to rebuild. **A9**

■ **WAR CRIMES TRIALS**

The allies are being pressured to try Iraqi soldiers as well as Saddam Hussein for war crimes. A Pentagon legal team is already collecting evidence. **A10**

Associated Press

Iraqi soldier surrenders.

■ **SMILING PRISONERS**

Allied forces are finding that many Iraqi prisoners are smiling men who appear glad to be captives instead of bearing signs of defeat. **A9**

WEATHER: Cloudy and breezy today with rain likely. Civic Center low/high: 56/66. Details: B5

■ TOP OF THE NEWS ON A2

War's Climax: Big Battle Against Iraq's Elite Units

■ **Strategy:** The allied assault is modeled on a 'hammer and anvil.' It is the centerpiece of Desert Storm.

By JOHN M. BRODER
TIMES STAFF WRITER

WASHINGTON—By throwing the heaviest concentration of armor since World War II against Saddam Hussein's vaunted Republican Guard, trapping it between a lethal "hammer and anvil," allied forces have launched the climactic battle of the Persian Gulf War.

The engagement is the centerpiece of Operation Desert Storm, the objective of a seven-month political and military campaign that began Aug. 6 when the United States dispatched the first squadron of fighter planes to Saudi Arabia, U.S. officials said Tuesday.

Pentagon strategists said they expect the combination of U.S., British and French forces to trap and crush the 150,000-man guard, considered the backbone of Hussein's power. Once the guard is disabled, Iraqi armed resistance will effectively cease, they said.

U.S. commanders have orders to press the attack until the entire Republican Guard force is demolished, officials in Washington said, but it was not clear how much resistance Iraq's elite units would offer.

Allied commanders, capitalizing on unexpected early successes in the ground war, moved up the attack on the Republican Guard by a full day and initiated assaults even before they had completed the planned encirclement of the

Please see GUARD, A15

M-16A2

Weight: 8.9 lbs.
Cartridge: 5.56-millimeter
Operation: gas-, air-cooled, selective fire; semi-automatic with 3-shot bursts
Range: 1,800 feet
Magazine capacity: 30 rounds
Cost: $420

Primary combat rifle issued to U.S. front-line soldiers in the Gulf. It is an improved version of the M-16A1, which during the Vietnam War was often criticized for its tendency to jam. First used in 1987, the M-16A2 has greater accuracy, heavier barrel and uses standard NATO ammunition. Soviet-made counterpart; the AK-47 assault rifle.

Military: U.S. Marines enter the capital of Kuwait, and coalition forces cut off the main body of Iraq's Republican Guard.
■ Kuwaiti troops join the Marines and raise their national flag in the center of town.
■ "The Iraqi army is in full retreat," the Pentagon's senior briefer says.
■ By dawn, the allies have destroyed or neutralized 27 Iraqi divisions.
■ Coalition forces destroy about 2,000 tanks, or half the original complement; almost 1,000 armored vehicles, or one-third, and 1,500 artillery pieces, about half.
■ U.S. casualties in the ground war are four dead, 21 wounded.
■ A French tank division cuts off the Republican Guard, stopping it from escaping to the west; one guard division is "virtually destroyed" by the U.S. Army's VII Corps, and two divisions attempt to flee, caught between a "hammer and anvil."
■ The Pentagon says an amphibious assault on the Kuwaiti coast is not needed.
■ Officials have stopped counting Iraqi POWs, but the figure is estimated at 30,000.

Iraq: On Baghdad Radio, President Saddam Hussein orders his troops to withdraw from Kuwait but takes pains to make clear that it is not a surrender and vows that his forces will, one day, fight again.
■ "Cheer for your victory, brothers," he exhorts.

White House: President Bush calls Hussein's radio speech "an outrage," charging that the Iraqi leader had refused to renounce territorial claims on Kuwait, had offered no "evidence of remorse for Iraq's aggression" and had said nothing about prisoners of war or the destruction of Kuwait.
■ He says the coalition will prosecute the war with "undiminished intensity."

Media: The liberation of Kuwait is televised live by American news correspondents who had violated Pentagon rules and taken to the battlefield unsupervised, carrying portable satellite "uplinks."

After seven months of occupation, Kuwaitis rejoiced at liberation.

PATRICK DOWNS / Los Angeles Times

THE BATTLE

Associated Press

U.S. Marines clear the way through minefields on the drive north toward Kuwait city.

Coalition Troops

The U.S. Command in Riyadh said U.S. Marines were engaging Iraqi tank forces in an intense battle at Kuwait airport and were apparently winning the day. But the command did not say that the city had been liberated. The lightly-armored Marines drove from Saudi Arabia in under three days through border defenses and defeated a heavy-armor Iraqi division. The first Kuwaiti troops of the multinational force entered the city and prepared to raise their national flag to celebrate the liberation of the capital.

The Resistance

After Iraqi soldiers beat a hasty retreat, Kuwaiti resistance leaders were attempting to take control of a battered Kuwait city, moving into police stations and other bases used by the Iraqis and searching through their equipment, Kuwaiti and press accounts said. Small groups of armed Kuwaitis were acting as a militia force.

The Retreat

Pilots aboard the U.S. warship Ranger told pool reporters that Iraqi troops had fled Kuwait city "bumper to bumper" and were attacked on the way out by A-6 Intruders and other aircraft. They said the Iraqis were fleeing north toward the city of Basra in Iraq, presenting a bounty of targets. Iraqi movements were described both as "a withdrawal and a retreat."

FIGHTING FOR

KUWAIT CITY

The first U.S. forces entered the capital city of Kuwait. There was fierce fighting near the Kuwait International Airport between Iraqis and U.S. Marines. Hassan Sanad, the Kuwaiti Information Ministry deputy director, said simply: "We confirm that Kuwait city is free." U.S. officials remained cautious, however. There were immediate signs of joy and a hint of the problems ahead:

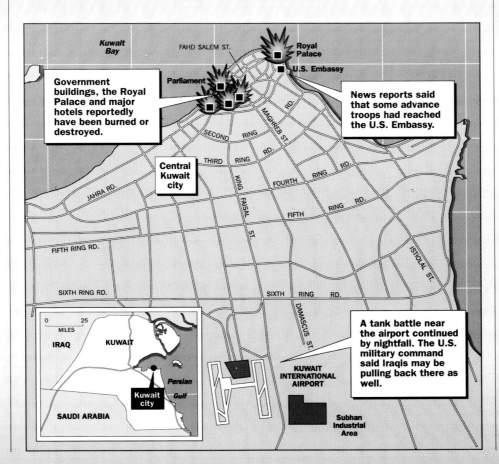

Government buildings, the Royal Palace and major hotels reportedly have been burned or destroyed.

News reports said that some advance troops had reached the U.S. Embassy.

Central Kuwait city

A tank battle near the airport continued by nightfall. The U.S. military command said Iraqis may be pulling back there as well.

THE CITY

News reports said that Kuwait city had been freed.

Entering the City

CBS News, in a live telecast from Kuwait city, showed Kuwaitis in the city waving flags and singing patriotic songs. Correspondent Bob McKeown described a scene of burned-out Iraqi tanks and other military vehicles as he drove into the city.

The Scene

Iraqi military vehicles in the city were either destroyed or abandoned, some with clothes strewn about, indicating a hasty retreat. There was no electricity and very little water in the city.

Martial Law

The emirate's exiled emir declared martial law throughout Kuwait. Sheik Jabbar al Ahmed al Sabah said a state of martial law would exist for three months. The decree, issued in the Saudi city of Taif — seat of Kuwait's exiled government since August — appointed Crown Prince and Prime Minister Sheik Saad al Abdullah al Sabah as martial governor-general.

The Government

The emir escaped to Saudi Arabia when Iraqi troops overran his country Aug. 2. Allied forces launched an air war against Iraq on Jan. 17 after President Saddam Hussein ignored a U.N. deadline to leave the emirate.

The Damage

Kuwait city government buildings and hotels have been destroyed in the last three days by Iraqi troops using tanks and artillery, Col. Abu Fahad, a member of the Kuwaiti resistance in Kuwait city, said. "It was unbelievable. No nation in the world saw what we've seen here," he said by telephone. "I have seen, by eyes, a lot of my friends and some of our guys executed in front of their families and their houses for nothing, just being in the country."

ANDERS RAMBERG, VICTOR KOTOWITZ AND DON CLEMENT / Los Angeles Times

DAY 43

FEBRUARY 28, 1991

For three painful hours, Mary Hunter thought her Marine husband was dead. Military officials had released the last list of freed POWs, and Chief Warrant Officer Guy L. Hunter was not on it. The Iraqis had displayed him on television but that had been many weeks, and thousands of allied bombs, ago.

Then she turned on the officials: "You tell them to get in there and count again. Guy must be there."

"I know the feeling of death in your heart, and I hadn't had it for Guy Hunter," she explained to me later.

When the officials corrected the list, her spirits soared. Clutching my hands tightly, her eyes filled with tears as she said: "I want you to meet him."

Guy L. Hunter came home to the United States five days later.

—Nora Zamichow, in San Diego County

Los Angeles Times

CIRCULATION: 1,225,189 DAILY / 1,514,096 SUNDAY | THURSDAY, FEBRUARY 28, 1991 | COPYRIGHT 1991 / THE TIMES MIRROR COMPANY / CC†/ 156 PAGES | DAILY 25¢ DESIGNATED AREAS HIGHER

Bush Halts Combat
'War Is Now Behind Us,' He Says

■ **Gulf conflict:** The President lays out conditions for a permanent cease-fire. Iraq must immediately free all prisoners and comply with U.N. resolutions.

By JAMES GERSTENZANG and NICK B. WILLIAMS Jr.
TIMES STAFF WRITERS

WASHINGTON—President Bush announced a suspension of hostilities in the Persian Gulf War Wednesday night, declaring to the nation and the world: "Kuwait is liberated. Iraq's army is defeated. Our military objectives are met."

Speaking from the Oval Office just 97 hours after U.S. and allied forces stormed into Iraq and Kuwait, the President said the coalition would suspend all offensive combat operations at midnight EST, and laid out conditions that Iraq must satisfy to make the suspension permanent.

"We must now begin to look beyond victory in war," Bush said. "This war is now behind us. Ahead of us is the difficult task of securing a potentially historic peace."

Bush said the next steps are up to Iraqi President Saddam Hussein. He said Iraq must:

- Return immediately all coalition prisoners of war it holds, any citizens from other countries, and the remains of U.S. and allied soldiers killed in the conflict.
- Release all Kuwaitis it has seized. According to some reports, the number is in the thousands.
- Inform Kuwaiti authorities about the location and characteristics of any mines its forces planted at sea or on land.
- Comply fully with each of the "relevant" resolutions passed by the U.N. Security Council in an effort to force the Iraqi occupiers out of Kuwait.

Among the resolutions, Bush said, were those demanding that Iraq rescind its annexation of Kuwait as its 19th province, and requiring it to pay compensation to Kuwait for the destruction it caused during the occupation.

Late Wednesday, Iraq's U.N. ambassador received a letter from his nation's foreign minister, Tarik Aziz, authorizing him to tell the Security Council that Iraq is prepared to accept all 12 resolutions the council adopted after Iraq invaded Kuwait last Aug. 2.

The letter was received before President Bush's address and does not speak to the issue of prisoners held by Iraq, particularly the thousands of Kuwaiti citizens taken to Iraq by Saddam Hussein's soldiers.

■ **BUSH TEXT:** A25

According to diplomatic sources, U.S. officials will take the position that Iraq has come a long way in complying with the demands of the Bush Administration, but that the new Aziz letter is still deficient and further clarifications are needed.

Bush's declaration suspending hostilities—coming 209 days after Hussein sent his troops into Kuwait—brought the United States to the brink of an achievement it has not seen in nearly half a century: unquestioned victory in war.

But success was not without its price:

Please see BUSH, A20

COLUMN ONE
Feeling on Top of the World

■ The prevailing sentiment across the country is that the nation showed its greatness in standing up to Saddam Hussein. But some still doubt whether war was necessary or wise.

By BARRY BEARAK
TIMES STAFF WRITER

And so the war had come to this, few Americans killed, the enemy turned tail, the "mother of all battles" no more than a shrinking violet easily plowed under.

Wednesday, exactly six weeks after the fighting began, people across the nation took stock of what had occurred and by and large felt darned good about it.

"I tell you, at school we say the pledge of allegiance every day, but those kids lately, they say it like they mean it," said Vernon Paul, high school principal in the tiny West Texas town of Seminole.

Frances Trigo, a bookkeeper in Costa Mesa, pounded her hand down on a table as if a platoon of Iraqi soldiers were scattering underneath. "They know we mean business now," she said.

Sea to shining sea, the prevailing sentiment was much the same: Hooray for us! We kicked butt! America the Great! We take no guff from no one no more no how.

And what of George Bush? Certainly, the tag "wimp" has been swept over by the desert sand. Now the President is spoken of as something of a John Wayne with an Ivy League diploma.

"When [Bush] ran for office, I wasn't for him; I always thought he was weak," said Mary Baldimar, owner of a small flower shop in Honolulu. She thought his wife was the tougher of the two. Now that makes her chuckle.

Bush really stood up to the Butcher of Baghdad, she said: "And he didn't let anyone else push him around either, not even Congress."

This week, the images being imprinted in the American psyche seem largely ones of a gutsy, resourceful nation. America is no longer the aging slugger who can't get the bat around on a fast ball. It is a lithe warrior and a cunning strategist and a heroic liberator.

Of course, that is not everyone's view. To some, the new world order has merely turned out to be as murderous as the old. And America is arrogant and foolhardy

Please see MOOD, A24

ON THE LIBERATION OF KUWAIT

In Washington

BERNIE BOSTON / Los Angeles Times

In Riyadh

Associated Press

President Bush announces a halt in combat, Gen. H. Norman Schwarzkopf outlines allied strategy, and joy fills the streets in Kuwait city.

In Kuwait city

Agence France-Presse

Iraqi Guard Mauled in Tank Battle

By TRACY WILKINSON
TIMES STAFF WRITER

RIYADH, Saudi Arabia—American tank crews, on the attack in one of the biggest armored battles since World War II, were ordered today to halt offensive fire against badly mauled Republican Guard tank divisions in southeastern Iraq.

The order to American troops came eight hours after as many as 800 tanks from the 1st and 3rd Armored divisions of the U.S. Army's VII Corps were reported battling two armored divisions of the Republican Guard about 50 miles west of the city of Basra.

Even before President

Please see BATTLE, A6

POWs Begging Not to Be Sent Back to Hussein's Iraq

By PAUL RICHTER and EDWIN CHEN
TIMES STAFF WRITERS

WASHINGTON—As the number of Iraqi prisoners of war swelled Wednesday to more than 50,000, allied officials and relief organizations confronted the urgent question of what to do with POWs who are afraid to return to a country still controlled by Saddam Hussein.

Allied forces say many Iraqi POWs are begging their captors not to repatriate them, and their fears may be understandable. They know Hussein as a man who executed officers for retreating during the Iran-Iraq War, and who more recently dispatched execution squads to shoot front-line soldiers who would not fight allied forces.

"They have reason to fear him, because Saddam's record on this kind of thing has been terrible," said David Korn, a former State Department official who last year wrote a book on rights abuses in Iraq for the group Human Rights Watch.

Although Hussein's future is anything but clear, the allies soon may be forced to look for other countries willing to provide homes for many of his long-suffering soldiers—and may find them hard to come by, some analysts say. Some could wind up in the United States.

"It is amazing how many of them said they wanted to go and live in the United States," said a member of the 1st Armored Division, which has been taking prisoners in Iraqi territory.

"We're now getting prepared to face this problem," said Francois zen Ruffinen, a delegate to the

Please see POWS, A17

Crowds Cheer Liberation Day in Kuwait City

By KIM MURPHY and BOB DROGIN
TIMES STAFF WRITERS

KUWAIT CITY—Kuwait's liberation army paraded into the nation's capital Wednesday on rumbling chariots of armor as thousands of cheering, chanting Kuwaitis poured into the streets in celebration.

"Blood for Freedom: Welcome Allied Forces," read a banner draped over the main highway into Kuwait, which was choked by midday with dozens of allied tanks, supply trucks and a honking stream of Mercedes-Benzes, BMWs and Chevrolets in a city come suddenly to life after seven months of occupation.

"We are very happy today. We thank all of you who helped by

Please see KUWAIT, A26

Schwarzkopf's War Plan Based on Deception

By JOHN M. BRODER
TIMES STAFF WRITER

WASHINGTON—The battle plan for vanquishing the Iraqi army mapped out by Gen. H. Norman Schwarzkopf was one of the most complex military campaigns ever devised, yet it rested upon a fundamental principle as old as human conflict—deception.

From the opening minutes of the air war in the pre-dawn hours of Jan. 17 to the climactic battle with

■ **BATTLE PLAN GRAPHIC:** A7

the Republican Guard, the plan was to render Iraq's army deaf and blind, deceive it on the allies' true intentions, and then suddenly—and violently—encircle and annihilate it.

Like all successful military undertakings, the U.S.-allied strategy incorporated a set of calculated

Please see PLAN, A18

Ethics Panel Says Cranston Broke Rules in Keating Ties

■ **Thrifts:** He is the only one of the five senators involved in the case who is judged to be in violation.

By SARA FRITZ
TIMES STAFF WRITER

WASHINGTON—The Senate Ethics Committee ruled Wednesday that Sen. Alan Cranston (D-Calif.) engaged in "an impermissible pattern of conduct" by intervening with federal regulators on behalf of Lincoln Savings & Loan while soliciting large contributions from its former owner, Charles H. Keating Jr.

Cranston, 76, who already has announced plans to retire at the end of his fourth term in 1992, was the only one of the "Keating Five" senators whose actions were judged to be in violation of Senate rules. His case is expected to be referred to the full Senate after he is given one more opportunity to reply to the charges.

The Ethics Committee concluded that there was "substantial credible evidence" that Cranston engaged in improper conduct by soliciting $994,000 in political contributions from Keating during the mid-1980s while agreeing to intervene on his behalf with officials of the Federal Home Loan Bank Board, which was investigating mismanagement at Lincoln.

The senator was in California recuperating from treatment for prostate cancer. But his office in Washington responded to the committee action with a one-sentence statement that did not indicate how

Please see CRANSTON, A28

MORE WAR COVERAGE

■ **WAR STORIES, PHOTOS: A5-26; D1-3**

■ **DESPERATE HUSSEIN BID**

Saddam Hussein played a final political card in a bid for survival, attempting to cast his nation as the invaded rather than the invader. **A5**

■ **CHEMICAL MYSTERY**

The United States and its allies are puzzled about why Saddam Hussein did not use his fearsome chemical arsenal. **A12**

■ **MARINE FRUSTRATION**

Members of the Marines' amphibious assault force proved an effective diversion for Iraqi forces, but they were hoping for a piece of the action. **A12**

WEATHER: Occasional showers. Civic Center low/high today: 55/62. Details: B5

■ TOP OF THE NEWS ON A2

Associated Press

Scud victim Christine Mayes.

■ **WAR DEAD MOURNED**

The Greensburg, Pa., area mourned 10 Army Reservists, including Christine Mayes, killed in Saudi Arabia by an Iraqi missile. **A22**

Special Forces: U.S. 'Eyes' Deep in Enemy Territory

■ **Commandos:** Elite troops use high-tech equipment and deception to operate effectively behind Iraqi lines.

By MELISSA HEALY
TIMES STAFF WRITER

WASHINGTON—Using high-tech parachutes to drift through the night sky above Iraqi positions, sometimes traveling 30 miles or more, American Special Forces teams equipped with night-vision goggles and special radios reported from midair on enemy formations below.

Green Berets, living in sandy burrows for days at a time to escape detection, infiltrated deep behind Iraqi lines—into the very heart of Saddam Hussein's most fearsome ground units. They fed vital intelligence to allied commanders weeks before the ground war began.

Other Special Operations units disabled communications towers and water wells, used lasers to target Scud missile launchers and tank emplacements for aerial attack and placed explosive charges on bridges to cut off future avenues of retreat for Iraq's Republican Guard troops.

These and countless other Special Operations forces "were the eyes that were out there," said Gen. H. Norman Schwarzkopf, commander of U.S. forces in Operation Desert Storm—the eyes and also the claws that penetrated the skin of Iraq's elite forces and helped sow the seeds of their destruction.

U.S. commando teams even

Please see COMMANDOS, A14

SCHWARZKOPF'S

STRATEGY

The strategy was launched Aug. 7, just six days after Iraq's invasion of Kuwait. It was relentlessly executed through months of U.N. negotiation, six weeks of allied bombing and five days of lightning-fast ground war against experienced Iraqi forces that greatly outnumbered allied combat troops. While pockets of Iraqi resistance remain, the Iraqi army is effectively out of commission.

White House: President Bush announces a suspension of hostilities and declares the war won after 100 hours of ground fighting.
■ He tells the nation: "Kuwait is liberated. Iraq's army is defeated. Our military objectives are met."
■ He says Saddam Hussein must comply with a series of steps to secure a truce.

Iraq: Baghdad Radio announces that, in exchange for a cease-fire, Iraq would accept U.N. resolutions declaring the annexation of Kuwait null and void, and calling for documentation of human rights violations and assessment of economic damage to Kuwait. It also offers to free all prisoners of war after a cease-fire.
■ Britain immediately announces the offer is deficient; no comment from Washington.

Military: A "classic tank battle" rages in Iraq, pitting more than 700 American tanks and armored vehicles from the Army's VII Corps against the 250 to 300 tanks of a Republican Guard division.
■ Allied paratroopers land at an air base near Nasiriyah on the Euphrates River, and troops of the U.S. 101st Airborne Division stand less than 100 miles from Baghdad.
■ A U.S. Marine armored force defeats Iraqi tanks at Kuwait International Airport.
■ Britain reports nine of its troops were killed by "friendly fire" from a U.S. warplane.
■ Gen. H. Norman Schwarzkopf discloses that the battle plan against Iraqi troops in Kuwait relied on deception to make Saddam Hussein think the allies planned an amphibious attack, which allowed allied commanders to move their forces into position to attack on the western front.
■ Schwarzkopf also displays charts: Allied forces destroyed about 3,000 of Iraq's 4,200 tanks, 1,900 of its 2,800 armored vehicles, and 2,100 of its 3,100 artillery pieces; he says these numbers are growing.
■ U.S. casualty totals are put at 79 dead—including 28 in the Scud attack on Dhahran, Saudi Arabia—213 wounded and 44 missing, Schwarzkopf says.
■ Schwarzkopf says the number of Iraqi dead is "very large;" prisoners of war are estimated at more than 80,000.

Aug. 7, 1990–Jan. 17, 1991: DECEPTION

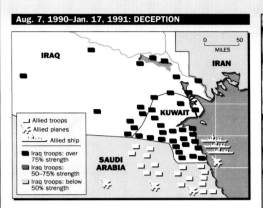

In early August, a limited defense force was put in place behind a Saudi task force along Saudi Arabia's border with Kuwait and Iraq. By November, in response to massive numbers of Iraqi troops pouring south to the border, U.S. and Arab forces were built up in defensive positions aligned north against Iraqi positions in Kuwait. At the same time, the U.S. Navy built up a conspicuous presence in the Gulf. When diplomatic efforts failed, a massive air war was begun to weaken the Iraqi forces, particularly along the border.

The Strategy: Make the Iraqis think that their main engagement with the allies would occur along the Kuwaiti border, forcing them to concentrate troops there. Lead them to expect an amphibious assault, something they greatly feared. Isolate Kuwait, preventing Iraq from resupplying, reinforcing or communicating with troops. Put as many Iraqi units out of commission as possible.

Gen. Schwarzkopf and his troops.

Associated Press

Saturday, Jan. 23, 1991: THE 'HAIL MARY'

Schwarzkopf and other allied commanders evaluated the number of Iraqi divisions still functioning after more than five weeks of bombing and saw much better odds than what existed in August. The destruction of their air force left the Iraqis blind to what the allies were doing. Schwarzkopf launched what he called his "Hail Mary" play—moving a massive number of troops and tons of materiel far to the west at blitzkrieg speed, knowing that the dug-in Iraqis were essentially immobilized along the Kuwaiti border.

The Strategy: The allies along the Kuwait border faced units at only 50% to 75% of their original strength. And they were then in position to flank the Iraqis on the west, while the Iraqis still expected the assault at the Kuwaiti border.

Sunday morning: THE FEINT

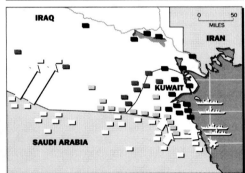

Against a background of amphibious maneuvers and naval gunfire, the 1st and 2nd Marine divisions and Saudi forces launched attacks and breached the barriers in the south. The Iraqis apparently believed that they had guessed right, and they were totally unaware of what was going on to the west: A deep thrust by French armored and U.S. airborne divisions to take an Iraqi airfield at Al Salman. At the same time, the U.S. 101st Airborne established an forward base deep inside Iraq.

The Strategy: To rivet the Iraqis' attention on the assault in Kuwait while establishing a left flank deep in Iraqi territory. That would allow allied troops to move through areas with little to no opposition to positions behind the dug-in Iraqis.

Schwarzkopf's Quotes
Here are notable quotes from Wednesday's briefing:

"As far as Saddam Hussein being a great military strategist, he is neither a strategist, nor is he schooled in the operational arts, nor is he a tactician, nor is he a general, nor is he as a soldier. Other than that, he's a great military man, I want you to know that."

"This was absolutely an extraordinary move. ... It was absolutely a gigantic accomplishment."
— Referring to the scale of the move inside Iraq, saying it was unprecedented in military history.

"They're not part of the same human race, the people who did that, as the rest of us are."
— Referring to atrocities committed by Iraqis in Kuwait.

"The war is not over. You've got to remember that people are still dying out there. And those people who are dying are my troops."

"Ladies and gentleman ... we were 150 miles from Baghdad and there was nothing between us and Baghdad."

Sunday afternoon: MOVING ON THREE FRONTS

1 The U.S. 1st and 3rd Armored Divisions and 2nd Armored Cavalry Division thrust north, encountering minimal Iraqi resistance. The 101st Airborne drove further into Iraq. At this point, allied troops were within just 150 miles of Baghdad.

2 The U.S. VII Corps breached the barriers and pushed into Iraq, followed by the British 1st Armored Division.

3 In what Schwarzkopf called a "superb operation," the Marines pushed ahead toward Kuwait city, encountering heavy artillery fire, mines, barbed wire, booby traps and fire-filled trenches. They were met with thousands of surrendering Iraqis. Arab forces penetrated the border defenses in southern and southwestern Kuwait.

The Strategy: The deception continued to work: The Iraqis believed the allies were mounting an all-out assault in the east while U.S., French and British forces quickly went around enemy fortifications and blocked the Iraqis on the west. For the Marines, strategy gave way to the hard work of capturing Kuwait city.

Monday and Tuesday: TIGHTENING THE NOOSE

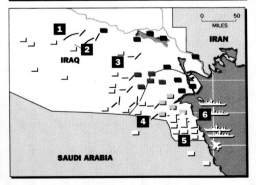

1 The 24th Infantry Divison punched all the way through to the Tigris and Euphrates Valley, blocking any escape route along the rivers by the Republican Guard.

2 The 101st Airborne also helped seal off northern positions, while the French set up a defensive flank to the west.

3 British forces and the VII Corps turned east to fight Iraqi forces from behind.

4 Arab troops turned east to meet up with the forces closing in on Kuwait city.

5 The Saudis and Marines pressed on north toward Kuwait city.

6 Special Forces teams cleared mines in the Gulf and performed other small-boat maneuvers that might precede an amphibious landing.

The Strategy: To finally trap the Iraqis on all sides.

Wednesday and Today: 'CLOSING THE GATES'

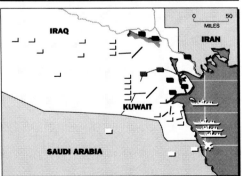

The 18th Airborne Corps has created solid wall across the north, with the VII Corps just to the south. Both are attacking the Republican Guard directly to the east. Arab and Kuwaiti forces are securing Kuwait city and the 1st Marine Division holds the airport there. The 2nd Marines are blocking escape routes out of the city. In Schwarzkopf's words, "and the gates are closed"

JUAN THOMASSIE / Los Angeles Times

101

Los Angeles Times

CIRCULATION 1,225,189 DAILY / 1,514,096 SUNDAY — FRIDAY, MARCH 1, 1991 — COPYRIGHT 1991 THE TIMES MIRROR COMPANY / CC/135 PAGES — DESIGNATED AREAS HIGHER — DAILY 25¢

Iraq Accepts Cease-Fire Talks
U.S. Wants Quick POW Release, Formal End of War

COLUMN ONE

Doomsday for War Forecasts

■ For months, analysts spelled out the disaster scenarios. But good planning, deft diplomacy, military skill—and some luck—produced a remarkable success.

By DOYLE McMANUS
TIMES STAFF WRITER

WASHINGTON—The doomsday predictions were seemingly endless.

■ Diplomacy: Washington plans a U.N. move that could ease some economic sanctions against Baghdad. But the allies expect the arms embargo to continue while Hussein remains.

By DAVID LAUTER
TIMES STAFF WRITER

Driven to Defeat

The scorched remains of civilian and military vehicles litter the main highway leading from Kuwait city to Basra and Baghdad.

No Place to Hide—Guard Pays the Price

By EDWIN CHEN
TIMES STAFF WRITER

As Truce Seems to Hold, Troops Think of Home

■ Gulf forces: Hundreds of thousands in anti-Iraqi coalition shift to defensive positions, stay on alert.

By TRACY WILKINSON and MELISSA HEALY
TIMES STAFF WRITERS

Gulf Pullout to Take Longer Than Buildup

By JOHN M. BRODER and MELISSA HEALY
TIMES STAFF WRITERS

Armed Resistance Governs Chaotic Kuwaiti Capital

By KIM MURPHY
TIMES STAFF WRITER

Southland Drivers Skid Into Wet-Weather Form

■ Rain: Once again, storms turn freeways into a tragicomic collection of crashes and jams.

By JESSE KATZ
TIMES STAFF WRITER

Kuwaiti Doctors, Nurses Recount Litany of Horror

■ Atrocities: They remain stunned by savagery of Iraqi troops. Torture and executions were common, they say.

By BOB DROGIN
TIMES STAFF WRITER

Los Angeles Times

CIRCULATION 1,225,189 DAILY / 1,514,096 SUNDAY — SATURDAY, MARCH 2, 1991 — COPYRIGHT 1991 THE TIMES MIRROR COMPANY / CC135 PAGES — DESIGNATED AREAS HIGHER — DAILY 25¢

COLUMN ONE

A Rallying Point for Iraqi Exiles

■ In the aftermath of war, their world is alive with possibilities. Many are trying to overcome rivalries—even hatred—to oust Hussein and shape their homeland's future.

By LAURIE BECKLUND and STEPHEN BRAUN
TIMES STAFF WRITERS

Kuwait's Rebels Vow to Speak Out

By KIM MURPHY
TIMES STAFF WRITER

Allies and Iraqis Plan Talks
Sunday on Cease-Fire, POWs

■ Diplomacy: The meeting of military commanders is delayed for one day, Cheney says. He says the war will be resumed if Baghdad makes new, hostile gestures.

By JAMES GERSTENZANG
TIMES STAFF WRITER

White House Backs Waivers of Job Bias Suits

By DAVID LAUTER
TIMES STAFF WRITER

2 Americans Killed on Still-Risky Battlefield

■ Aftermath: Doctor and medical aide are victims of mines. Thousands of Iraqi troops still roam the desert.

By TRACY WILKINSON
TIMES STAFF WRITER

U.S. Shakes Off Torment of Vietnam

By EDWIN CHEN and PAUL RICHTER
TIMES STAFF WRITERS

Images of War: Carnage, the Last Push, Nightmares

■ On the road: Bodies of Iraqi soldiers lie beside the booty they tried to take.

By BOB DROGIN

■ On the battlefield: There was elation—and anger—when fighting was halted.

By DOUGLAS JEHL

■ In the hospital: Injured Americans recall horror of seeing friends die in battle.

By JANNY SCOTT

Dead Iraqi soldiers lie near a destroyed tank following combat with U.S. forces.

Los Angeles Times

CIRCULATION 1,225,189 DAILY / 1,514,096 SUNDAY — SUNDAY, MARCH 3, 1991 — COPYRIGHT 1991 THE TIMES MIRROR COMPANY / CC135 PAGES — DESIGNATED AREAS HIGHER — SUNDAY $1.25

Sunday Final

COLUMN ONE

Flashbacks to Images of the War

■ Faces of ordinary people have been imprinted on the public mind. Their pathos, grief, frustration and solace reveal the conflict's impact on the spirit of the nation.

By PATT MORRISON and DEAN E. MURPHY
TIMES STAFF WRITERS

U.S. Troops Crush Iraqi Tank Column

■ Clash: The armored unit stumbles into American forces and opens fire. Basra, Iraq's second-largest city, is reported in turmoil.

By TRACY WILKINSON
TIMES STAFF WRITER

Bush Laying Plans for Broad Mideast Peace

■ Diplomacy: The President hopes to use the allied victory to forge a comprehensive settlement of long-intractable issues that have plagued the region, top officials say.

By DOYLE McMANUS
TIMES STAFF WRITER

Oil worker prays in sunlight of burning oil field near Kuwait city.

Kuwaiti Rulers Plan to Return, Restore Control

By KIM MURPHY
TIMES STAFF WRITER

An elderly Iraqi POW walks away from allied troops who freed him.

Iraqi POWs Tell Why They Refused to Fight

■ Prisoners: Threats of death, lack of food, fear for families are recounted in interviews with U.S. troops.

By BOB DROGIN
TIMES STAFF WRITER

Yugoslav Troops Sent to Quell Croatia Violence

By CAROL J. WILLIAMS
TIMES STAFF WRITER

Response to Drought Will Be Watershed for Wilson

■ Crises: The record deficit can be resolved, observers say. But divvying up the state's water is more difficult.

By GEORGE SKELTON
TIMES STAFF WRITER

U.S. Military Finding Key Deficiencies Amid Victory

■ Lessons: Much went right, planners say. But there are problems with fast, long-range deployment.

By JOHN M. BRODER
TIMES STAFF WRITER

Los Angeles Times

CIRCULATION 1,225,189 DAILY / 1,514,096 SUNDAY — MONDAY, MARCH 4, 1991 — COPYRIGHT 1991 THE TIMES MIRROR COMPANY / CC135 PAGES — DESIGNATED AREAS HIGHER — DAILY 25¢

Iraq Accepts Terms, U.S. Says
Speedy Prisoner Exchange Planned: Schwarzkopf

COLUMN ONE

Money for a 6-Pack on Welfare?

■ Gov. Wilson said his proposed cuts in aid would leave less for luxuries. But less than $700 a month to support a couple of children doesn't stretch far.

By VIRGINIA ELLIS
TIMES STAFF WRITER

■ Cease-fire talks: Maps are given to allies to help clear away mines and booby-traps. Baghdad sends a letter to the U.N. announcing acceptance of the latest resolution.

By EDWIN CHEN
TIMES STAFF WRITER

U.S. Gen. H. Norman Schwarzkopf, the allied commander in the Gulf, far left, and Lt. Gen. Prince Khalid bin Sultan of Saudi Arabia sit across table from their Iraqi counterparts. They include Lt. Gen. Sultan Hashim Ahmad, Iraqi deputy chief of staff, second from right.

Cold Capsules Are Recalled After 2 Deaths

By MARLENE CIMONS
TIMES STAFF WRITER

1,400 Iraqis Seized on Isle Off Kuwait Coast

■ Mop-up: Faylakah is last piece of enemy-held territory. Anti-Hussein protests reported in four cities.

By TRACY WILKINSON
TIMES STAFF WRITER

Signs of U.S. Victory Greet Iraqi Generals

By EDWIN CHEN
TIMES STAFF WRITER

Jetliner Crashes Near Colorado Airport; 25 Die

By CAROL PERRUSO and RONALD J. SOBLE
TIMES STAFF WRITERS

Seminar Rules Out 80% of Words Attributed to Jesus

■ Religion: Provocative appraisal of biblical scholars ends six years of voting on authenticity of the Gospels.

Gulf Crisis Rewrites the Policy-Makers' Guidelines

■ Stability: The allied campaign is seen as a hopeful precedent. But it may not be easy to duplicate.

By ROBIN WRIGHT
TIMES STAFF WRITER

PATRICK DOWNS / Los Angeles Times

U.S. Marines led the allied assault on Kuwait city's airport.

As Desert Storm commander Gen. H. Norman Schwarzkopf waited at the dusty, wind-swept Safwan airfield, in southern Iraq, for Iraqi generals to hear his cease-fire terms, he took shelter in a tent. But he emerged several times to greet other allied military commanders. When the Kuwaiti commander, Maj. Gen. Jabbar Khalid al Sabah, showed up, the two brawny generals exchanged powerful bearhugs. The reunion brought tears to Schwarzkopf's eyes.

It was a poignant moment. But many of the journalists swarming around the two men mistook Gen. Jabbar for Schwarzkopf's Iraqi counterpart. Why had they greeted one another so warmly? "Where do you know one another from?" one journalist shouted.

"From Kuwait, of course," said a misty-eyed Schwarzkopf.

—Edwin Chen,
in southern Iraq

Los Angeles Times

CIRCULATION: 1,225,189 DAILY / 1,514,096 SUNDAY   TUESDAY, MARCH 5, 1991   DAILY 25¢

COLUMN ONE

Chronicles of Loss and Resistance

■ The voices of Kuwaitis are full of outrage—telling tales of rape and murder, of invaders plundering their country. But they recall acts of courage too.

By KIM MURPHY
TIMES STAFF WRITER

KUWAIT CITY—It may be best to tell the seven-month agony of Kuwait in the voices of its people.

Royal Heir Home; Role Uncertain

By KIM MURPHY
TIMES STAFF WRITER

KUWAIT CITY—Crown Prince Sheik Saad al Abdullah al Sabah returned Monday to a capital city alive with celebratory gunfire, even as Kuwaitis vowed that the powerful ruling family would never again enjoy pre-eminence over one of the world's wealthiest oil sheikdoms.

Please see PRINCE, A14

Uprising Spreads Anarchy in South Iraq, Refugees Report

Specialist Melissa Rathbun-Nealy of Newaygo, Iraq to Jordan. With her are Specialist David Lock-Mich., leads a group of allied POWs as they leave ell, center, and Italian pilot Maurizio Cocciolone.

■ **Rebellion:** Seven cities are said to be under control of fundamentalist Muslims and other foes of Hussein. The Pentagon says there may be fighting between military units.

By BOB DROGIN
TIMES STAFF WRITER

SAFWAN, Iraq—Rebelling villagers have emptied political prisons and executed loyalists of Iraqi President Saddam Hussein.

Justices Uphold Large Punitive Damage Awards

By DAVID G. SAVAGE

WASHINGTON—The Supreme Court dealt big business a major setback Monday, ruling that the Constitution permits juries to punish corporations with multimillion-dollar verdicts, even if the award far exceeds the injury.

6 Americans Among First 10 POWs Freed

■ **Prisoners:** Group includes a U.S. female soldier. Allies plan to reciprocate by releasing 300 Iraqis.

By NICK B. WILLIAMS Jr.
TIMES STAFF WRITER

AMMAN, Jordan—Six American prisoners of war and four others from Britain and Italy were freed Monday by the Iraqi government, reaching Jordan after a seven-hour Red Cross road convoy from Baghdad.

Deep in Iraq, Perils Temper GIs' Jubilation

By DOUGLAS JEHL
TIMES STAFF WRITER

WITH U.S. FORCES, Iraq—The rifle pointed, nose down, into the battle-trampled sand, a helmet perched atop it, a pair of empty boots behind. A battalion of soldiers stood at stiff attention in a fierce desert wind as a first sergeant called out the roll to his assembled scout platoon.

Workfare Plan Falls Short as Relief Rolls Lengthen

■ **Welfare:** The program to move recipients into jobs is hit by shrinking budgets and failing confidence in it.

By RICHARD C. PADDOCK

SACRAMENTO—Law Van Dyken, a mother of two on welfare, was fast becoming a model of the state's new philosophy.

MWD to Slash Deliveries to Water Agencies by 50%

■ **Drought:** The district's board of directors also votes to cut the allocation for agricultural users by 90%.

By HECTOR TOBAR
TIMES STAFF WRITER

Adopting the most drastic conservation measures in its history, the Metropolitan Water District voted Monday to cut by 50% water deliveries to agencies serving 15 million people.

Los Angeles Times

CIRCULATION: 1,225,189 DAILY / 1,514,096 SUNDAY   WEDNESDAY, MARCH 6, 1991   DAILY 25¢

COLUMN ONE

Political Moves in Defense

■ Southern California loses as the aerospace industry locates plants in the districts of powerful politicians.

By BOB DROGIN and MARK FINEMAN
TIMES STAFF WRITERS

Kuwait Oil Fires: Year to Put Out?

By BOB DROGIN
TIMES STAFF WRITER

KUWAIT CITY—It may take a year or longer to extinguish about 500 Kuwaiti oil wells fire-bombed or damaged by retreating Iraqi troops.

Hussein Forces Counterattack in Basra; Many Flee Fighting

Scores of cars and trucks filled with refugees fleeing the unrest in Iraq line the highway to Kuwait city.

■ **Uprising:** Sources say the Republican Guard has retaken much of the port. But half a dozen other cities reportedly remain under opposition control.

By KIM MURPHY and MARK FINEMAN
TIMES STAFF WRITERS

SAFWAN, Iraq—Thousands of refugees fled worsening violence in southern Iraq on Tuesday.

Iraq Hands Over 15 More U.S. Prisoners

By RALPH VARTABEDIAN
TIMES STAFF WRITER

Iraqi Revolt Starting to Worry White House

■ **Policy:** The unrest could leave a weakened Hussein in power or install a radical Islamic regime, they fear.

By JAMES GERSTENZANG and MICHAEL ROSS
TIMES STAFF WRITERS

WASHINGTON—The Bush Administration viewed the Iraqi insurrection against Saddam Hussein with growing unease Tuesday.

Refugees Flee Iraq, but Some Find No Escape

By KIM MURPHY
TIMES STAFF WRITER

Kadafi Building Chemical Warfare Facility, U.S. Says

By JIM MANN
TIMES STAFF WRITER

Towing's 'Bird-Doggers' Race Streets for Business

■ **Traffic:** Officials link unlicensed operators to accidents and fraud. Drivers say they are entrepreneurs.

By JESSE KATZ
TIMES STAFF WRITER

Tape of L.A. Police Beating Suspect Stirs Public Furor

■ **Law enforcement:** Mayor says he's 'outraged.' The department, FBI and district attorney are investigating.

By HECTOR TOBAR and LESLIE BERGER
TIMES STAFF WRITERS

Los Angeles Times

CIRCULATION: 1,225,189 DAILY / 1,514,096 SUNDAY   THURSDAY, MARCH 7, 1991   DAILY 25¢

Maj. Rhonda Cornum is greeted by Gen. H. Norman Schwarzkopf as allied POWs arrive in Saudi Arabia.

Bush Calls for End to Arab-Israeli Conflict

Iraqi Purge Launched as Revolt Wanes

By BOB DROGIN and MARK FINEMAN
TIMES STAFF WRITERS

SAFWAN, Iraq—With a ruthless campaign of purges and rewards, President Saddam Hussein struggled Wednesday to suppress Iraq's postwar insurrections.

Coalition Arabs OK Plan for Gulf Security

By NICK B. WILLIAMS Jr.
TIMES STAFF WRITER

DAMASCUS, Syria—The Arab nations that backed the United States and its Western allies in the war against Iraq agreed Wednesday to consolidate their position in the Persian Gulf with a security system built around Egyptian and Syrian forces.

■ **Policy:** President salutes U.S. forces who fought 'with honor and valor.' He also tells a cheering Congress that the first wave of returnees will begin arriving today.

By JAMES GERSTENZANG
TIMES STAFF WRITER

WASHINGTON—Seeking to turn the momentum of the allied victory in the Persian Gulf War into a campaign for peace throughout the troubled Middle East, President Bush declared Wednesday that it is time "to put an end to the Arab-Israeli conflict."

COLUMN ONE

In Canada, Hockey Is a Game of Life

■ It's more than a Canadian national pastime; it's a passion. But many citizens complain about the mongrelizing influence of the United States.

By MARY WILLIAMS WALSH
TIMES STAFF WRITER

Ex-POWs on Hospital Ship; 3 Report Abuse

By JOHN BALZAR and TRACY WILKINSON
TIMES STAFF WRITERS

MANAMA, Bahrain—Fifteen freed American prisoners of war arrived at a U.S. hospital ship here Wednesday—thin, hungry and tired but generally in high spirits.

Cyanide-Tainted Sudafed Spawns Wave of Fear

By LOUIS SAHAGUN
TIMES STAFF WRITER

U.S. Inspectors Sent to State's Nursing Homes

By ROBERT A. ROSENBLATT and GEORGE SKELTON
TIMES STAFF WRITERS

WASHINGTON—The federal government is sending large numbers of inspectors into California nursing homes in a bitter dispute with the state over the standards of care for the state's elderly residents.

Town's Rationing Plan— 10 Gallons a Person Daily

■ **Drought:** Orange Cove, which relies solely on federal water sources, will get only 10% of its normal supply.

By MILES CORWIN
TIMES STAFF WRITER

Beating Victim Says He Obeyed Police

■ **Law enforcement:** He is freed from jail. D.A. files no charges against him.

By TRACY WOOD and FAYE FIORE
TIMES STAFF WRITERS

Los Angeles Times

CIRCULATION: 1,225,189 DAILY / 1,514,096 SUNDAY   FRIDAY, MARCH 8, 1991   DAILY 25¢

COLUMN ONE

Africa Hit by 'Donor Fatigue'

■ The developed world is contributing a smaller share of relief needs amid a sense of futility about the recurring famine, corruption and economic mismanagement.

By MICHAEL A. HILTZIK
TIMES STAFF WRITER

NAIROBI, Kenya—With the economic crisis in a recession, Mozambique's leaders were wary last year of asking for too much emergency aid.

Soldiers with 24th Infantry Division wave as they prepare to board plane in Saudi Arabia for flight home.

First U.S. Troops Return; Pullout Will Take Months

■ **Homecoming:** Cheering crowds greets 24th Division GIs in Georgia. Southland units are among those scheduled to begin arriving home this weekend.

By LEE MAY and DAVID FREED
TIMES STAFF WRITERS

HUNTER ARMY AIRFIELD, Georgia—The first planeload of the nation's returning Gulf War soldiers touched down here early this morning and a cheering, flag-waving crowd welcomed them home.

Baker to Urge New Steps to Mideast Peace

By DOYLE McMANUS
TIMES STAFF WRITER

Gates Wants 3 Officers Prosecuted in Beating

■ **Police:** Chief calls incident an aberration caused by 'total human failure.' Bradley also presses investigation.

By HECTOR TOBAR and SHERYL STOLBERG
TIMES STAFF WRITERS

Hundreds of Kuwaitis Are Freed by Iraq

By KIM MURPHY and TRACY WILKINSON
TIMES STAFF WRITERS

Palestinians Tell of Abuse From Resentful Kuwaitis

By KIM MURPHY
TIMES STAFF WRITER

Surgeons Being Voluntarily Tested for AIDS Virus

By ANNE C. ROARK and ROBERT STEINBROOK
TIMES STAFF WRITERS

Doctor Describes Aiding Cancer Patient's Suicide

■ **Ethics:** Many authorities support physician. But he could face charges of second-degree manslaughter.

By SHARI ROAN
TIMES STAFF WRITER

States Finding California Defense Firms Easy Targets

■ **Aerospace:** Many companies, offered sweet deals, are leaving Southland. Standard of living, labor costs cited.

By RALPH VARTABEDIAN
TIMES STAFF WRITER

Oil worker prays in sight of burning oil field near Kuwait city.

I was helicoptered aboard the Navy command ship La Salle one morning and rode it into the Kuwaiti port of Shauiba to cover the reopening of the badly damaged harbor. It was 9 a.m., but smoke from the oil-well fires made it as dark as dusk, 10 times worse than any air pollution you could imagine. A sailor asked me where I was from.

Los Angeles, I replied.

''You must be used to this,'' he said.

—David Freed,
in Kuwait

105

Los Angeles Times

CIRCULATION: 1,225,189 DAILY / 1,514,096 SUNDAY SATURDAY, MARCH 9, 1991 DAILY 25¢

COLUMN ONE

Forces Face Unkindest Cuts of All

■ The military is riding high after its stunning victory in the Gulf. But now the Pentagon is heading into a round of serious budget trimming, and personnel levels will be reduced markedly.

By ALAN C. MILLER and MELISSA HEALY
TIMES STAFF WRITERS

WASHINGTON—U.S. military commanders won more than just the war with their stunning success in the Persian Gulf. They have fully regained the hearts and minds of many of their fellow Americans that they lost during the Vietnam War.

Spirit of Iraq Also a Casualty of War, Revolt

By MARK FINEMAN
TIMES STAFF WRITER

AMMAN, Jordan—It was just before midnight Wednesday when the midlevel Iraqi bureaucrat wandered into the fifth-floor press room at Baghdad's Rashid Hotel, the headquarters of CBS Television's news operation in the Iraqi capital.

Jobless Rate Up in State Amid Hopeful Signs

By JESUS SANCHEZ
TIMES STAFF WRITER

The California jobless rate soared to 7.4% in February—the highest level since October, 1985—but some economists say other employment figures released Friday may offer a glimmer of hope in an otherwise bleak economic picture.

2 More American POWs Freed; Iraq Beset by Turmoil

■ Postwar disorder: Hundreds of Kuwaitis and 40 journalists also are released. Fighting is reported spreading in the north and south of the country.

By NICK B. WILLIAMS Jr. and TRACY WILKINSON
TIMES STAFF WRITERS

AMMAN, Jordan—Baghdad released hundreds of Kuwaiti prisoners of war and 40 journalists Friday in a display of postwar order that clashed with persistent evidence that the regime of Iraqi President Saddam Hussein is confronted with the chaos of defeat.

1,181 Kuwaiti Hostages Are Returned Home

By BOB DROGIN

SAFWAN, Iraq—Waving and cheering, and bedraggled but safe, 1,181 Kuwaitis who had been abducted as hostages by Iraqi troops were bused on Friday from Iraq's border to their homes in Kuwait city.

Soldiers with the Army's 24th Mechanized Infantry Division and the ribbon-festooned jet that brought them home to Savannah, Ga.

Thousands Return to Clamorous Celebration

Military: 'Everybody coming back's a hero,' an Air Force officer says. 'But there's some quiet inside us. . . .'

By MELISSA HEALY and JERRY LELLAW
TIMES STAFF WRITERS

TRAVIS AIR FORCE BASE, Calif.—Thousands of American GIs returning from the Persian Gulf escaped the pageant of transport planes and climbed out of cockpits Friday as the first full day of nonstop homecomings rolled across the country, launching a weekend of festivities in virtually every American time zone.

Italian Officials Move to Control Flood of Albanians

By WILLIAM D. MONTALBANO
TIMES STAFF WRITER

ROME—A stunned and overwhelmed, the Italian government scrambled Friday to control and reverse an unruly influx of refugees fleeing the collapse of communism in destitute Albania.

Right Wing Seeks Bold Bid by Bush on Domestic Issues

By ROBERT SHOGAN
TIMES POLITICAL WRITER

WASHINGTON—As President Bush turns from the triumph of the Persian Gulf War to the challenges of America's domestic problems he faces a potential collision not just with the Democratic majority in Congress but with the conservative wing of his own party.

Impact of Beating Deals a Blow to Officers' Image

Law enforcement: Many say they are embarrassed and humiliated by the nationally publicized incident.

By GREG KRIKORIAN and DAVID FERRELL
TIMES STAFF WRITERS

Aerospace Moves: Hidden Costs Often Negate Gains

Defense firms: Few states have L.A.'s pool of skilled workers, trade and technical schools, and weather.

By RALPH VARTABEDIAN
TIMES STAFF WRITER

INSIDE TODAY'S TIMES

Los Angeles Times | Sunday Final

CIRCULATION: 1,225,189 DAILY / 1,514,096 SUNDAY SUNDAY, MARCH 10, 1991 DAILY $1.25

COLUMN ONE

A People Problem in the Air

■ Technology and engineering advances have made the machinery of air travel safer. But federal records disclose a vast array of procedural blunders by pilots and air traffic controllers.

By DEAN E. MURPHY
TIMES STAFF WRITER

SEATTLE—In the cockpit of a Boeing 747 jumbo jet approaching Madrid in the fall of 1983, a recorded voice sounded urgently from the flight controls. "Pull up! Pull up!"

Hussein Steps Up Attacks to Crush Widespread Revolt

■ Postwar turmoil: Massive artillery and rocket attacks are reported. U.S. warns Iraq that air strikes may be resumed if chemical weapons are used on rebels.

By MARK FINEMAN and DOYLE McMANUS
TIMES STAFF WRITERS

AMMAN, Jordan—Iraqi President Saddam Hussein, his army rife with bitterness and fear, has intensified artillery and rocket assaults to regain control of chunks of the war-torn nation his regime, various sources said Saturday.

Bush Rules Out 'Uncle Sucker' Mideast Role

By STANLEY MEISLER
TIMES STAFF WRITER

WASHINGTON—Vowing that the United States will not be "Uncle Sucker," President Bush said in an interview released Saturday that Iraq must rebuild its own devastated infrastructure and that other Arab nations must undertake the job of ensuring peace and economic development in the postwar Persian Gulf.

Patti Gonzales made sure her son, Marine Lance Cpl. Eric Phillips, would find her among the throngs at Norton Air Force Base, her sign was emblazoned with his name, a large arrow and the word "Mom."

THE TIMES POLL

Majority Says Police Brutality Is Common

By TED ROHRLICH
TIMES STAFF WRITER

A Los Angeles residents overwhelmingly believe that police use excessive force in arresting Rodney G. King and that instances of police brutality are common.

Outpouring of Love, Emotion Greets Marines

By DEAN E. MURPHY and SEAN McHURLEY
TIMES STAFF WRITERS

Tanks, Troops Move in After Yugoslav Riots

By MICHAEL MONTGOMERY and CAROL J. WILLIAMS
SPECIAL TO THE TIMES

BELGRADE, Yugoslavia—Federal army tanks rolled into central Belgrade late Saturday to quell anti-Communist rioting that killed two people and injured nearly 80 in the worst unrest in the Yugoslav capital since the Communist takeover in 1945.

On Forgotten Kuwait Road, 60 Miles of Wounds of War

By BOB DROGIN
TIMES STAFF WRITER

ON THE ROAD TO UMM QASR, Kuwait—Two days after an informal cease-fire, desolation and death crowd the terrible wounded war road.

Rampage in Westwood: Hundreds Loot Stores

Riot: Officials seek answers after theater turns away youths. Police beating of black motorist cited by some.

By ELAINE WOO and IRENE CHANG
TIMES STAFF WRITERS

Old Troubles Cast Shadow on New 'Star Wars' Image

Defense: The Pentagon has offered a scaled-down plan. Many experts question its economics, efficiency.

By RALPH VARTABEDIAN
TIMES STAFF WRITER

INSIDE TODAY'S TIMES

Los Angeles Times

CIRCULATION: 1,225,189 DAILY / 1,514,096 SUNDAY MONDAY, MARCH 11, 1991 DAILY 25¢

COLUMN ONE

The Man Who Loves the RTD

■ Board President Nick Patsaouras loves hard promoting ridership and gives pep talks to the staff. Some observers see him as an opportunist who has designs on mayor's office.

By BETTINA BOXALL
TIMES STAFF WRITER

It was 5:30 a.m. and still dark at the RTD bus yard in West Hollywood, but it was too early for Nick Patsaouras to grab a microphone and rattle off a few inspirational words to the mechanics and bus drivers drifting in for the early-morning shift.

Ex-POW Sgt. Daniel J. Stamaris Jr. salutes during ceremonies as wife Nena wipes eyes.

Huge Rallies Demand Ouster of Gorbachev

By ELIZABETH SHOGREN
TIMES STAFF WRITER

MOSCOW—Hundreds of thousands of Russians in more than a dozen cities flocked to rallies Sunday to call for the resignation of Soviet President Mikhail S. Gorbachev and urge creation of a popular party to back the reformist leader Boris N. Yeltsin.

Asian, Latino Numbers Soar in U.S. Census

By FRANK CLIFFORD
TIMES STAFF WRITER

ANDREWS AIR FORCE BASE, Md.—Twenty-one former prisoners of war returned to America Sunday from their "unreturnable and dread" in Iraq and found themselves welcomed in a groove and giddy ceremony.

Top Pentagon Officials, Kin Greet Ex-POWs

By STANLEY MEISLER
TIMES STAFF WRITER

Quebec Liberals Vote to Join Push for Sovereignty

By MARY WILLIAMS WALSH
TIMES STAFF WRITER

MONTREAL—In the biggest challenge yet to Canada's future as a unified nation, the governing Liberal Party of Quebec voted to attempt a massive power transfer that would, in essence, make the Francophone province into a sovereign nation.

8 Arab Allies Back Bush's Initiative for Mideast Peace

Diplomacy: Baker terms it a 'signal' and says he'll press Israel to show more flexibility. He also may meet with Palestinians reportedly approved by the PLO.

By DOYLE McMANUS
TIMES STAFF WRITER

RIYADH, Saudi Arabia—Eight Arab countries gave a general endorsement to President Bush's Middle East peace initiative on Sunday, and Secretary of State James A. Baker III said their move should prompt Israel to show more flexibility.

In 'Message to Baker,' Arab Kills 4 Israelis

By DANIEL WILLIAMS
TIMES STAFF WRITER

JERUSALEM—A lone Palestinian fatally stabbed four Israeli women at a suburban bus stop Sunday, and police said he meant it as a "message" to Secretary of State James A. Baker III.

Iraqi Rebels Claim Gains Against Hussein's Forces

By NICK B. WILLIAMS Jr.
TIMES STAFF WRITER

AMMAN, Jordan—Widespread rebellion and unrest in Iraq claimed Sunday to have consolidated control of Shiite religious leaders in the south.

Tower Workloads Often Cited After Near Disasters

Aviation: Officials are warned of staff shortages. FAA data shows California is the near-miss capital of the U.S.

From Times Staff Writers

In 7 Months, Iraqis Stole 'the Very Soul' of Kuwait

Culture: Museums were looted, 200 animals were killed. And what wasn't taken was destroyed.

By BOB DROGIN
TIMES STAFF WRITER

KUWAIT CITY—Iraq's seven-month rape of Kuwait's culture and economy was a grisly affair.

INSIDE TODAY'S TIMES

Los Angeles Times

CIRCULATION: 1,225,189 DAILY / 1,514,096 SUNDAY TUESDAY, MARCH 12, 1991 DAILY 25¢

COLUMN ONE

Disposable Articles of Faith

■ Plastic or paper? Throwaway diapers or not? Long-held beliefs are being tested — and acrimony among environmentalists is one result.

By MAURA DOLAN
TIMES STAFF WRITER

For years, consumers have been guided by certain environmental articles of faith. Paper is better than plastic, biodegradable is good, disposable is bad.

$1 Billion in Annenberg Art for N.Y.

By SUZANNE MUCHNIC
TIMES STAFF WRITER

Walter H. Annenberg, publisher, philanthropist and former ambassador to Great Britain, has decided to bequeath his celebrated art collection to the Metropolitan Museum of Art in New York. The collection of more than 50 paintings, which is one of the most valuable in private hands, is said to be worth about $1 billion.

Palestinians and Baker to Confer

Diplomacy: The secretary will meet with West Bank and Gaza Strip leaders. But the U.S. insists the talks do not constitute a dialogue with the PLO.

By DOYLE McMANUS and DANIEL WILLIAMS
TIMES STAFF WRITERS

JERUSALEM—Secretary of State James A. Baker III pushed headlong into the convoluted world of Palestinian politics Monday, declaring that he will meet today with West Bank and Gaza Strip leaders.

Iraq to Return Remains of 14 Allied Dead

By TRACY WILKINSON and NICK B. WILLIAMS Jr.
TIMES STAFF WRITERS

RIYADH, Saudi Arabia—Iraq will turn over the bodies of 14 allied servicemen killed in the Persian Gulf War, U.S. military officials said Monday.

Officials Find L.A. Ethics Law Sows Confusion

By GLENN F. BUNTING
TIMES STAFF WRITER

Women in Jerusalem cry over grave of sister, one of four women slain by an Arab on eve of Secretary of State James A. Baker III's Israel trip.

McDonnell Unlikely to Build Jet in Long Beach

Industry: Concerned about costs at existing complex, company studies out-of-state sites for $3-billion project.

By RALPH VARTABEDIAN
TIMES STAFF WRITER

Pan Am Wins Reprieve; Route Sale to Proceed

By ROBERT E. DALLOS and OSWALD JOHNSTON
TIMES STAFF WRITERS

NEW YORK—After nearly a year of bitter negotiating, British Airways and U.S. Transportation authorities reached an agreement Monday that will enable troubled Pan American World Airways to sell its routes.

Noise Abatement Causing Near Misses, Pilots Charge

Aviation: Flight maneuvers that reduce sound are called hazardous. Reports criticize John Wayne Airport.

From Times Staff Writers

Conditions Go From Bad to Worse in Kuwait City

By KIM MURPHY
TIMES STAFF WRITER

KUWAIT CITY—The line for lentils, sugar, cooking oil and flour snakes for a block around the corner.

Failed 'System for Choice' Serves as Lesson to Schools

Education: A highly touted reform program has put Bay Area's Richmond district in state of bankruptcy.

Iraqi troops ravaged the emirate's capital, looting and wrecking.

Relentless allied bombing turns areas of Baghdad to rubble.

The myth of a single Arab nation stretching from North Africa to the Persian Gulf was just that, a myth. Reality wasn't accepted until the Iraqi invasion of Kuwait revealed the Arab world as a collection of splintered nations and tribes all desperately following their own self-interests.

How else to explain the division within the Arab world over the invasion itself, a division sharpened when even the massive intervention of supposedly hated outsiders against an Arab brother failed to bring united action?

Any doubts about the death of Arab nationalism must have evaporated when Libya's Moammar Kadafi stayed aligned with Syria's Hafez Assad and Egypt's Hosni Mubarak even after they indicated that Israel did not have to fear attack if it retaliated against another Arab state, Iraq.

—Kenneth Freed,
in Cairo

Hundreds of oil-field fires darkened Kuwait skies.

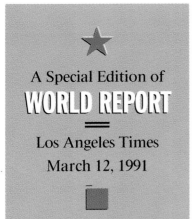

A Special Edition of
WORLD REPORT
=
Los Angeles Times
March 12, 1991

WITNESS TO WAR

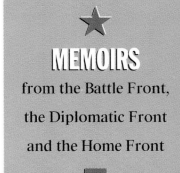

MEMOIRS
from the Battle Front,
the Diplomatic Front
and the Home Front

Images From the Gulf: Jets and Fury, Sand and Death, Flags and Victory

History has a way of seeming inevitable.

Looking back from the comfortable vantage point of victory, the Gulf War appears from the very beginning to have been a towering mismatch with but one possible outcome:

An isolated and almost-friendless developing nation was propelled by the ignorance of its despotic leader into a full-scale war against the largest, most technologically advanced military machine on Earth. Saddam Hussein—ignorant of the West, misunderstanding the power of technological war, misconceiving his appeal to the masses of the Arab world—confronted George Bush, a President determined to rid his nation of the "Vietnam Syndrome," intent on establishing new ground rules for a post-Cold War world, convinced of the moral rightness of his cause.

Hussein would not blink. Bush would not be swayed. The destruction of Iraqi power was, it seems, bound to follow.

It didn't all look so inevitable as the drama unfolded, of course. And even in hindsight, it's easy to see many moments when things might have gone wrong, when at the very least the human cost of the war could have been much higher.

How could it be otherwise when more than a million warriors, armed with some of the most devastating weaponry known to exist, square off in a desert offering little place to hide? This was the heaviest concentration of hostile firepower since World War II. It was war against an adversary who had already proven himself ready to use the most ruthless tactics, not only against enemies but against his own people.

On hand, too, were those professional witnesses to war: the correspondents who record what they can at the time, but whose images of conflict change subtly and become more powerful as they reflect on the fullness of the experience.

Those images, of chaos and fury, confusion and exhaustion, brilliance and folly, come alive in the memoirs of those correspondents.

Associated Press

'The mother of battles will be our battle of victory and martyrdom . . . . They want us to surrender, but of course they will be disappointed.'

SADDAM HUSSEIN
In speech announcing withdrawal from Kuwait

More than 60,000 Iraqis were seized or surrendered, often with an eagerness that surprised their captors.

PATRICK DOWNS / Los Angeles Times

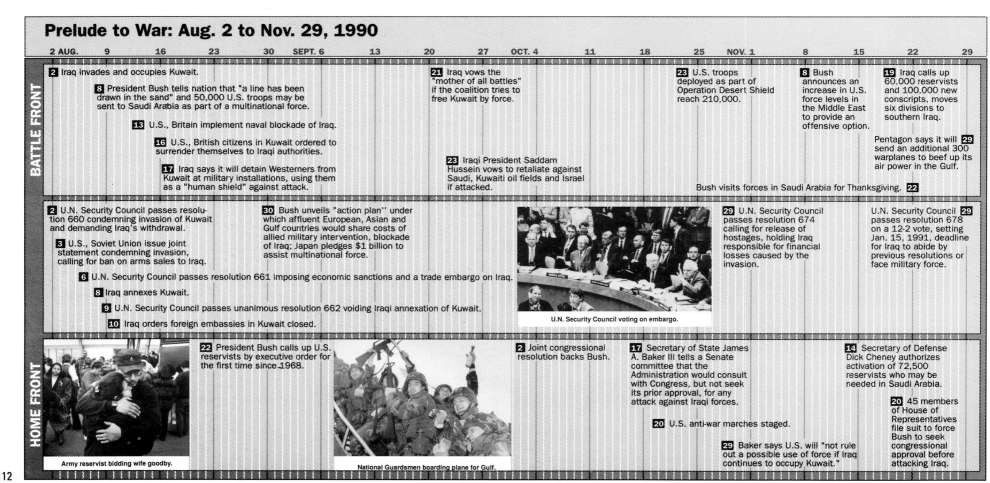

Prelude to War: Aug. 2 to Nov. 29, 1990

2 AUG. 9 16 23 30 SEPT. 6 13 20 27 OCT. 4 11 18 25 NOV. 1 8 15 22 29

BATTLE FRONT

2 Iraq invades and occupies Kuwait.

8 President Bush tells nation that "a line has been drawn in the sand" and 50,000 U.S. troops may be sent to Saudi Arabia as part of a multinational force.

13 U.S., Britain implement naval blockade of Iraq.

16 U.S., British citizens in Kuwait ordered to surrender themselves to Iraqi authorities.

17 Iraq says it will detain Westerners from Kuwait at military installations, using them as a "human shield" against attack.

21 Iraq vows the "mother of all battles" if the coalition tries to free Kuwait by force.

23 Iraqi President Saddam Hussein vows to retaliate against Saudi, Kuwaiti oil fields and Israel if attacked.

23 U.S. troops deployed as part of Operation Desert Shield reach 210,000.

8 Bush announces an increase in U.S. force levels in the Middle East to provide an offensive option.

19 Iraq calls up 60,000 reservists and 100,000 new conscripts, moves six divisions to southern Iraq.

29 Pentagon says it will send an additional 300 warplanes to beef up its air power in the Gulf.

Bush visits forces in Saudi Arabia for Thanksgiving. **22**

HOME FRONT

2 U.N. Security Council passes resolution 660 condemning invasion of Kuwait and demanding Iraq's withdrawal.

3 U.S., Soviet Union issue joint statement condemning invasion, calling for ban on arms sales to Iraq.

6 U.N. Security Council passes resolution 661 imposing economic sanctions and a trade embargo on Iraq.

8 Iraq annexes Kuwait.

9 U.N. Security Council passes unanimous resolution 662 voiding Iraqi annexation of Kuwait.

10 Iraq orders foreign embassies in Kuwait closed.

30 Bush unveils "action plan" under which affluent European, Asian and Gulf countries would share costs of allied military intervention, blockade of Iraq; Japan pledges $1 billion to assist multinational force.

U.N. Security Council voting on embargo.

29 U.N. Security Council passes resolution 674 calling for release of hostages, holding Iraq responsible for financial losses caused by the invasion.

29 U.N. Security Council passes resolution 678 on a 12-2 vote, setting Jan. 15, 1991, deadline for Iraq to abide by previous resolutions or face military force.

22 President Bush calls up U.S. reservists by executive order for the first time since 1968.

Army reservist bidding wife goodby.

National Guardsmen boarding plane for Gulf.

2 Joint congressional resolution backs Bush.

17 Secretary of State James A. Baker III tells a Senate committee that the Administration would consult with Congress, but not seek its prior approval, for any attack against Iraqi forces.

20 U.S. anti-war marches staged.

29 Baker says U.S. will "not rule out a possible use of force if Iraq continues to occupy Kuwait."

14 Secretary of Defense Dick Cheney authorizes activation of 72,500 reservists who may be needed in Saudi Arabia.

20 45 members of House of Representatives file suit to force Bush to seek congressional approval before attacking Iraq.

The Middle East: Breeding Ground For Instability

The Middle East has long been a region of shifting allegiances and borders. Here are just three arrangements that have come and gone during this century. Saddam Hussein tried to change the map once more by annexing Kuwait. He failed, but the world once more sees the different — and sometimes conflicting — interests of those countries with a stake in the region. As Secretary of State James A. Baker III tours the area this week, here is a look at some of those agendas:

PRE WORLD WAR I: 1914
■ British protectorates

Ottoman Empire
IRAN
KUWAIT
Hijaz
EGYPT
0   400
MILES

POST WORLD WAR I: 1920
▨ British mandate
■ Other British protectorates
▨ French mandate
H British-backed Hashemite rulers

TURKEY
IRAN
KUWAIT
H
Hijaz
Neutral zones
EGYPT
H

POST WORLD WAR II: 1948
■ British protectorates
■ Disputed areas

TURKEY
LEBANON
SYRIA
ISRAEL
IRAQ
IRAN
KUWAIT
JORDAN
SAUDI ARABIA
EGYPT

THE UNITED STATES wants political stability, friendship with both Israel and the Arabs and a reliable supply of oil at a price that will neither suppress economic growth nor price U.S. producers out of the market. Baker's talks are to focus on security agreements, a ban on chemical and nuclear weapons, the future of the Palestinians and economic aid.

THE SOVIET UNION wants back some of its old prestige as a superpower, as well as political stability in an area that is only 250 miles from its own Muslim republics.

SAUDI ARABIA and KUWAIT want a new security structure to protect their rich but under-defended countries against hun- grier and more powerful neighbors like Iraq and Iran. In the short run, that means they want Saddam Hussein out of power; in the long run, they want to be able to count on the United States coming to their aid if the events of 1990 are repeated.

IRAN is not on Baker's itinerary, but as the largest military power on the Persian Gulf it will have to be included in the deliberations sooner or later. Tehran wants to reduce Iraq's armed forces so they can no longer threaten Iran.

ISRAEL wants to see a diminished Arab threat so that it can devote a greater share of its resources to such national goals as absorbing new Soviet Jewish immigrants and less to security. But, as always since the Jewish state's founding in 1948, there is little sign that the two sides can agree on the future of the Palestinians or other issues.

SYRIA wants a role as a major political player in the Arab world as well as massive economic aid from the wealthy Gulf states. President Hafez Assad has given signals that he is ready to make peace with Israel, but only if he can obtain a favorable settlement for the Palestinians.

NOTE: Present borders are indicated on each map.
SOURCES: Atlas of the Islamic World; Times Atlas of World History; Cambridge Atlas of the Middle East and North Africa; National Geographic Society

THE MIDDLE EAST TODAY

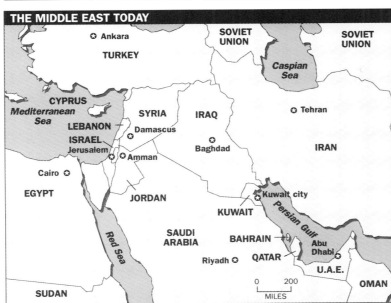

Ankara
SOVIET UNION
TURKEY
SOVIET UNION
Caspian Sea
CYPRUS
Mediterranean Sea
SYRIA
LEBANON
Damascus
IRAQ
Tehran
ISRAEL
Jerusalem
Amman
Baghdad
IRAN
Cairo
JORDAN
EGYPT
Red Sea
SAUDI ARABIA
Kuwait city
KUWAIT
Persian Gulf
BAHRAIN
Abu Dhabi
Riyadh
QATAR
U.A.E.
SUDAN
OMAN
0   200
MILES

IRAQ is not negotiating anything but cease-fire arrangments at the moment. Saddam Hussein wants the United Nations to lift its economic and arms embargoes, but the United States will block any relaxation. If Saddam falls, the new Baghdad government will need to reach political, military and economic understandings with its neighbors.

JORDAN wants forgiveness — and resumed aid — from Saudi Arabia, Kuwait and the United States, mainly because King Hussein wants to keep his present job.

EGYPT wants many of the same things Syria does, only more of them. President Hosni Mubarak has already won recognition as one of the Arab world's premier leaders and the forgiveness of American loans. But his country needs more economic growth.

THE PALESTINIANS want an independent state, but beyond that they don't agree among themselves on details. Most Pales- tinians still insist that Yasser Arafat and his Palestine Liberation Organization are legitimate representatives, despite Arafat's politically disastrous decision to back Iraq.

JUAN THOMASSIE / Los Angeles Times

Reuters
After seven harrowing months, Kuwait rejoiced—and U.S. prestige soared.

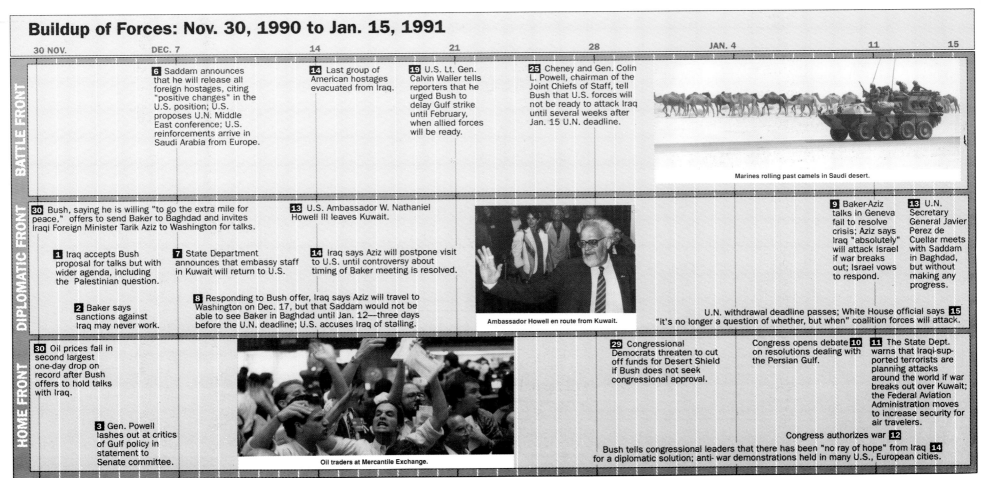

Buildup of Forces: Nov. 30, 1990 to Jan. 15, 1991

30 NOV.   DEC. 7   14   21   28   JAN. 4   11   15

BATTLE FRONT

6 Saddam announces that he will release all foreign hostages, citing "positive changes" in the U.S. position; U.S. proposes U.N. Middle East conference; U.S. reinforcements arrive in Saudi Arabia from Europe.

14 Last group of American hostages evacuated from Iraq.

19 U.S. Lt. Gen. Calvin Waller tells reporters that he urged Bush to delay Gulf strike until February, when allied forces will be ready.

25 Cheney and Gen. Colin L. Powell, chairman of the Joint Chiefs of Staff, tell Bush that U.S. forces will not be ready to attack Iraq until several weeks after Jan. 15 U.N. deadline.

Marines rolling past camels in Saudi desert.

DIPLOMATIC FRONT

30 Bush, saying he is willing "to go the extra mile for peace," offers to send Baker to Baghdad and invites Iraqi Foreign Minister Tarik Aziz to Washington for talks.

13 U.S. Ambassador W. Nathaniel Howell III leaves Kuwait.

9 Baker-Aziz talks in Geneva fail to resolve crisis; Aziz says Iraq "absolutely" will attack Israel if war breaks out; Israel vows to respond.

13 U.N. Secretary General Javier Perez de Cuellar meets with Saddam in Baghdad, but without making any progress.

1 Iraq accepts Bush proposal for talks but with wider agenda, including the Palestinian question.

7 State Department announces that embassy staff in Kuwait will return to U.S.

14 Iraq says Aziz will postpone visit to U.S. until controversy about timing of Baker meeting is resolved.

2 Baker says sanctions against Iraq may never work.

8 Responding to Bush offer, Iraq says Aziz will travel to Washington on Dec. 17, but that Saddam would not be able to see Baker in Baghdad until Jan. 12—three days before the U.N. deadline; U.S. accuses Iraq of stalling.

Ambassador Howell en route from Kuwait.

U.N. withdrawal deadline passes; White House official says **15** "it's no longer a question of whether, but when" coalition forces will attack.

HOME FRONT

30 Oil prices fall in second largest one-day drop on record after Bush offers to hold talks with Iraq.

3 Gen. Powell lashes out at critics of Gulf policy in statement to Senate committee.

Oil traders at Mercantile Exchange.

29 Congressional Democrats threaten to cut off funds for Desert Shield if Bush does not seek congressional approval.

Congress opens debate **10** on resolutions dealing with the Persian Gulf.

11 The State Dept. warns that Iraqi-sup-ported terrorists are planning attacks around the world if war breaks out over Kuwait; the Federal Aviation Administration moves to increase security for air travelers.

Congress authorizes war **12**

Bush tells congressional leaders that there has been "no ray of hope" from Iraq **14** for a diplomatic solution; anti-war demonstrations held in many U.S., European cities.

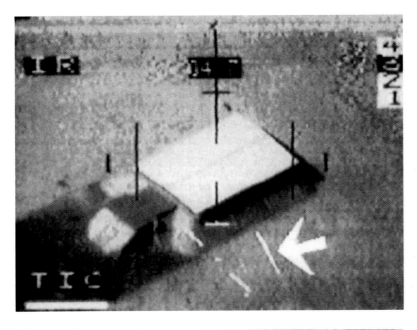
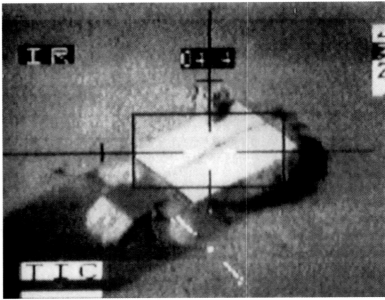
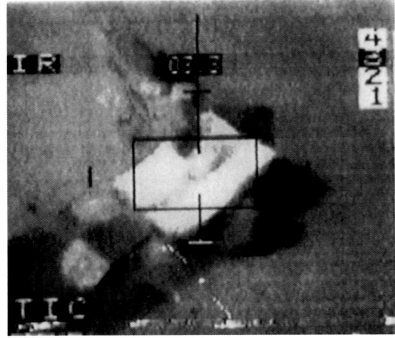
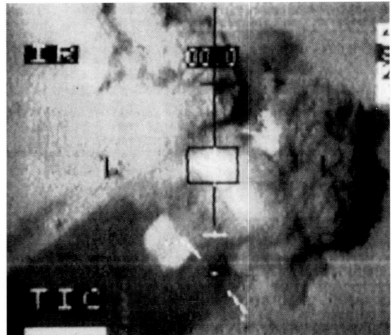

Associated Press

Video of an allied attack shows a ''smart bomb,'' marked by arrow at top left, closing in on its target and various stages of explosion and target's destruction.

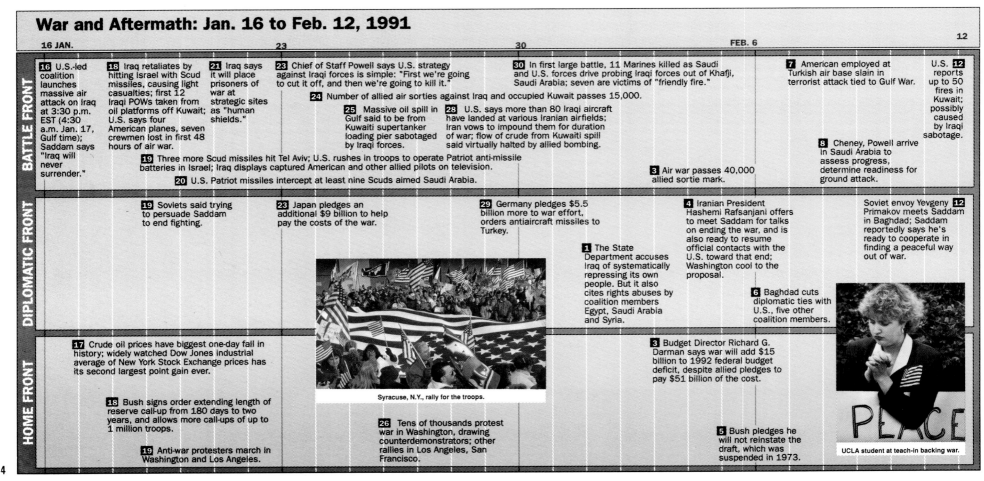

War and Aftermath: Jan. 16 to Feb. 12, 1991

16 JAN.   23   30   FEB. 6   12

BATTLE FRONT

16 U.S.-led coalition launches massive air attack on Iraq at 3:30 p.m. EST (4:30 a.m. Jan. 17, Gulf time); Saddam says "Iraq will never surrender."

18 Iraq retaliates by hitting Israel with Scud missiles, causing light casualties; first 12 Iraqi POWs taken from oil platforms off Kuwait; U.S. says four American planes, seven crewmen lost in first 48 hours of air war.

21 Iraq says it will place prisoners of war at strategic sites as "human shields."

23 Chief of Staff Powell says U.S. strategy against Iraqi forces is simple: "First we're going to cut it off, and then we're going to kill it."

24 Number of allied air sorties against Iraq and occupied Kuwait passes 15,000.

25 Massive oil spill in Gulf said to be from Kuwaiti supertanker loading pier sabotaged by Iraqi forces.

28 U.S. says more than 80 Iraqi aircraft have landed at various Iranian airfields; Iran vows to impound them for duration of war; flow of crude from Kuwaiti spill said virtually halted by allied bombing.

30 In first large battle, 11 Marines killed as Saudi and U.S. forces drive probing Iraqi forces out of Khafji, Saudi Arabia; seven are victims of "friendly fire."

7 American employed at Turkish air base slain in terrorist attack tied to Gulf War.

12 U.S. reports up to 50 fires in Kuwait; possibly caused by Iraqi sabotage.

19 Three more Scud missiles hit Tel Aviv; U.S. rushes in troops to operate Patriot anti-missile batteries in Israel; Iraq displays captured American and other allied pilots on television.

20 U.S. Patriot missiles intercept at least nine Scuds aimed Saudi Arabia.

3 Air war passes 40,000 allied sortie mark.

8 Cheney, Powell arrive in Saudi Arabia to assess progress, determine readiness for ground attack.

DIPLOMATIC FRONT

19 Soviets said trying to persuade Saddam to end fighting.

23 Japan pledges an additional $9 billion to help pay the costs of the war.

29 Germany pledges $5.5 billion more to war effort, orders antiaircraft missiles to Turkey.

1 The State Department accuses Iraq of systematically repressing its own people. But it also cites rights abuses by coalition members Egypt, Saudi Arabia and Syria.

4 Iranian President Hashemi Rafsanjani offers to meet Saddam for talks on ending the war, and is also ready to resume official contacts with the U.S. toward that end; Washington cool to the proposal.

6 Baghdad cuts diplomatic ties with U.S., five other coalition members.

12 Soviet envoy Yevgeny Primakov meets Saddam in Baghdad; Saddam reportedly says he's ready to cooperate in finding a peaceful way out of war.

HOME FRONT

17 Crude oil prices have biggest one-day fall in history; widely watched Dow Jones industrial average of New York Stock Exchange prices has its second largest point gain ever.

18 Bush signs order extending length of reserve call-up from 180 days to two years, and allows more call-ups of up to 1 million troops.

19 Anti-war protesters march in Washington and Los Angeles.

Syracuse, N.Y., rally for the troops.

26 Tens of thousands protest war in Washington, drawing counterdemonstrators; other rallies in Los Angeles, San Francisco.

3 Budget Director Richard G. Darman says war will add $15 billion to 1992 federal budget deficit, despite allied pledges to pay $51 billion of the cost.

5 Bush pledges he will not reinstate the draft, which was suspended in 1973.

UCLA student at teach-in backing war.

PATRICK DOWNS / Los Angeles Times

Following a pounding air campaign, U.S. Marines were able to barrel across the Kuwait border to savor victory.

War and Aftermath: Feb. 13 to March 11, 1991

13 FEB.	20		27	MAR. 6

BATTLE FRONT

13 Iraqi officials say 500 civilians killed in bombing attack on what U.S. says was command-and-control bunker in Baghdad; U.S. troops deployed in Operation Desert Storm reach 514,000.

14 Kuwaiti official says Iraqis have executed at least 200 Kuwaitis since air war began.

16 Pentagon officials say U.S. forces poised to launch ground, air and sea assault when Bush gives the word.

20 Senior Arab official says allied air raids may have killed or wounded more than 75,000 Iraqi soldiers.

23 Allied forces launch massive ground operation against Iraqi troops at 5 p.m. (4 a.m. Feb. 24, Gulf time); U.S. command says allied forces had already destroyed 39% of Iraqi tanks in region, 32% of its armored vehicles and 48% of its artillery.

24 Gen. H. Norman Schwarzkopf says allied casualties on first day of ground campaign were "remarkably light"; Iraq says offensive "so far has totally failed."

25 Baghdad Radio says Saddam has ordered his forces to withdraw from Kuwait in accordance with Soviet peace proposal; Scud warhead falls on U.S. barracks near Dhahran, killing 28 Americans; allies say more than 600 fires are burning in Kuwait, including more than half the country's 1,000 oil wells.

26 Iraqi forces in Kuwait and southern Iraq virtually surrounded; Marines enter Kuwait city.

27 Bush declares victory over Iraq, says Kuwait liberated and orders allied combat suspended at midnight EST (8 a.m. Feb. 28, Gulf time); permanent cease-fire said to depend on Iraq's release of POWs, compliance with all U.N. resolutions.

28 Iraq accepts Bush's terms.

3 Allied, Iraqi commanders meet in Iraqi airfield, lay groundwork for official cease-fire.

4 Iraq frees first 10 POWs, including six Americans. Refugees report rebellion against Hussein in several southern Iraqi cities.

5 Iraq frees 35 more POWs, including 15 Americans. Thousands of Iraqis flee unrest.

8 Iraq frees 1,181 Kuwaitis abducted as hostages, 40 foreign journalists and two more U.S. prisoners of war.

DIPLOMATIC FRONT

14 U.N. Security Council opens private debate on Gulf War.

15 Iraq offers a strings-attached plan to withdraw troops from Kuwait, but Bush dismisses it as a "cruel hoax."

18 Aziz visits Moscow, where President Mikhail S. Gorbachev offers plan for ending war.

19 Bush rejects Soviet proposal as "inadequate."

22 Bush gives Saddam ultimatum: Withdraw by noon EST Feb. 23, or face a ground war. Bush charges Iraqi leader with launching a "scorched-earth" policy against Kuwait; Baghdad calls U.S. demand "shameful"; Soviet-Iraqi talks continue.

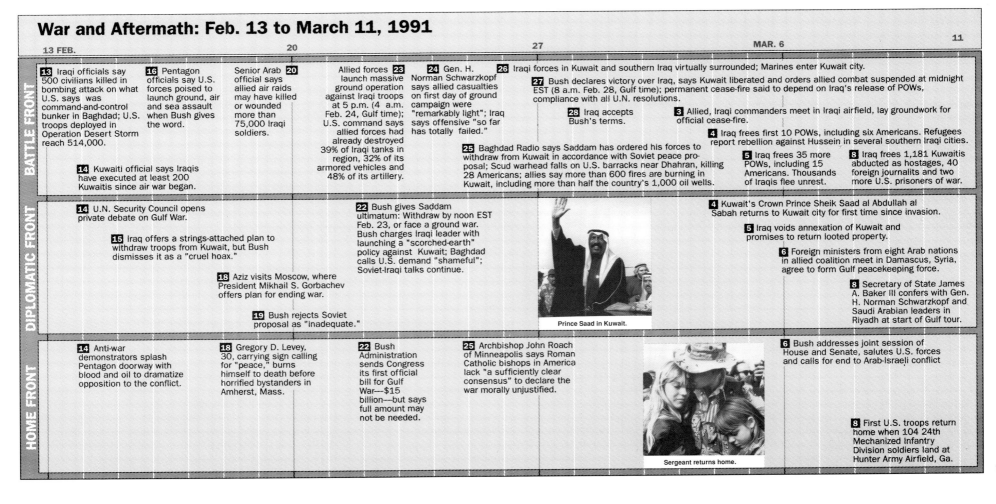

Prince Saad in Kuwait.

4 Kuwait's Crown Prince Sheik Saad al Abdullah al Sabah returns to Kuwait city for first time since invasion.

5 Iraq voids annexation of Kuwait and promises to return looted property.

6 Foreign ministers from eight Arab nations in allied coalition meet in Damascus, Syria, agree to form Gulf peacekeeping force.

8 Secretary of State James A. Baker III confers with Gen. H. Norman Schwarzkopf and Saudi Arabian leaders in Riyadh at start of Gulf tour.

HOME FRONT

14 Anti-war demonstrators splash Pentagon doorway with blood and oil to dramatize opposition to the conflict.

18 Gregory D. Levey, 30, carrying sign calling for "peace," burns himself to death before horrified bystanders in Amherst, Mass.

22 Bush Administration sends Congress its first official bill for Gulf War—$15 billion—but says full amount may not be needed.

25 Archbishop John Roach of Minneapolis says Roman Catholic bishops in America lack "a sufficiently clear consensus" to declare the war morally unjustified.

Sergeant returns home.

6 Bush addresses joint session of House and Senate, salutes U.S. forces and calls for end to Arab-Israeli conflict

8 First U.S. troops return home when 104 24th Mechanized Infantry Division soldiers land at Hunter Army Airfield, Ga.

Beyond the Line in the Sand

To most Americans, all's well that ends well. Support for the President has hit 90% in the polls, making George Bush the most popular U.S. President ever—more popular, even, than Harry S. Truman at the end of World War II.

From an American point of view, this war turned out to have most everything going for it. Its outcome was unequivocal, its technology awesome, its strategy brilliant. Good and evil never traded uniforms to confuse people.

Even the soldiers who fought it saw another side, however. They winced at the death and destruction rained on a large but clearly outgunned enemy force. Left behind in the Gulf are two countries in chaos, a region in a potentially dangerous state of flux.

Also lurking behind the current homecoming celebrations are unsolved domestic problems. America has yet to emerge from the muddy trench of its recession. When it does, there will still be millions of the sick to heal and the poor to feed. There will be cities to resurrect and waters to clean.

These are some of the problems that remain on this side of the line in the sand.

Iraq was battered with missiles from land and sea. From the Gulf, a Tomahawk missile streaked through the night from the battleship Wisconsin.

The Strategy:
Feint and Fury

WHAT WAS LEARNED

■ The AirLand battle doctrine initially worked out by U.S. strategists for use by NATO against Soviet forces passed its first test in actual wartime conditions—spectacularly.

■ A battle mockup discovered behind enemy lines shows that Iraqi forces anticipated an allied amphibious landing and deployed their forces to stop it—indicating that U.S. efforts to deceive the enemy strategically were successful.

WHAT IS STILL UNKNOWN

■ How to obtain speedy battle-damage reports in the face of bad weather and heavy smoke damage.

■ Why the allies were unable or unwilling to silence Baghdad Radio.

■ Whether the Iraqis' unused coastal defenses in Kuwait were any better than their land defenses.

White House photo

President Bush and advisers meet at Camp David on Jan. 19. From left: Gen. Colin L. Powell, chairman of the Joint Chiefs of Staff; Secretary of State James A. Baker III; Secretary of Defense Dick Cheney; Vice President Dan Quayle; National Security Adviser Brent Scowcroft; Bush, White House Chief of Staff John H. Sununu.

Smart Bombs and Chemical Weapons:
Accuracy and Fear

WHAT WAS LEARNED

■ Ultra-high-technology weapons such as "smart bombs" and cruise missiles managed to hit military targets without damaging civilian sites nearby.

■ Unguided "dumb" bombs were no more effective than in past wars in attacking point targets such as bridges and tanks.

■ Patriot missiles are very effective in homing in on the body of an incoming Scud or similar tactical ballistic missile. But you can't count on it to destroy the warhead.

WHAT IS STILL UNKNOWN

■ Why Iraq never used its chemical and biological weapons against allied troops, even though it had them in ample supply.

■ How well the chemical-protection suits used by American forces would have worked had Iraq used these weapons.

■ What the actual rate of accuracy of the U.S. "smart" weapons was.

■ Whether Iraq would have been able to mount chemical weapons on Scud missiles.

■ Whether Iraq still possesses any Scud missiles, and if so, how many.

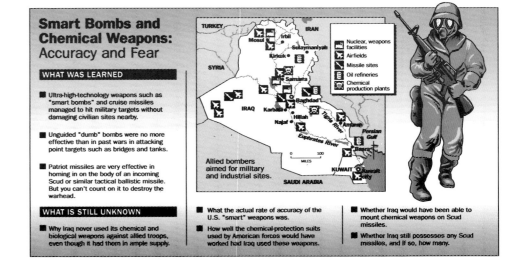

Allied bombers aimed for military and industrial sites.

Nuclear, weapons facilities
Airfields
Missile sites
Oil refineries
Chemical production plants

TURKEY   IRAN
SYRIA   Mosul Irbil Sulaymaniyah
Kirkuk
Samarra
IRAQ   Baghdad
Karbala   Hilla
Najaf   Euphrates River   Amarah   Persian Gulf
SAUDI ARABIA   KUWAIT   Kuwait City

Associated Press

The Air War:
Raining Terror

WHAT WAS LEARNED

■ Weeks of heavy bombing of military targets and supply-lines before the start of a ground offensive can seriously cripple an enemy force, but it can't win the war alone. A ground attack is necessary to bring about total victory.

■ The controversial Apache attack helicopter, once disparaged as likely to encounter too many technological problems, works well in desert conditions.

■ Early U.S. strikes on Iraqi air defense systems prevented enemy commanders from challenging allied air attacks.

■ Stealth technology works. The F-117 fighter flew thousands of missions over Iraq's most heavily defended sites and was never scratched by enemy fire. In fact, Air Force officials say, it was never even seen.

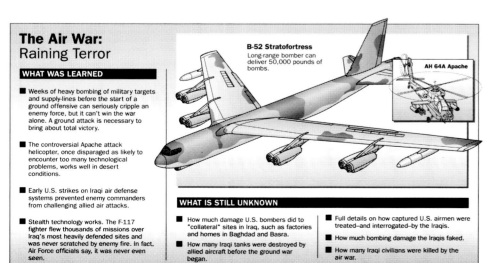

B-52 Stratofortress
Long-range bomber can deliver 50,000 pounds of bombs.

AH 64A Apache

WHAT IS STILL UNKNOWN

■ How much damage U.S. bombers did to "collateral" sites in Iraq, such as factories and homes in Baghdad and Basra.

■ How many Iraqi tanks were destroyed by allied aircraft before the ground war began.

■ Full details on how captured U.S. airmen were treated–and interrogated–by the Iraqis.

■ How much bombing damage the Iraqis faked.

■ How many Iraqi civilians were killed by the air war.

The Ground War:
Lightning Pace

WHAT WAS LEARNED

■ U.S. ground forces barreled through Iraqi defenses, defeating the vaunted Iraqi infantry and armored units quickly and decisively.

■ U.S. forces moved far more rapidly than planned in flanking Iraqi positions from the west and then enveloping the disorganized units.

■ American forces sustained 119 killed in action during the Gulf War.

■ American Marines were able to clear passages through Iraqi minefields in their frontal assault on Iraqi lines.

M-60 Tank
deploying a mechanized bridge

M-1 Abrams

WHAT IS STILL UNKNOWN

■ How many Iraqi soldiers were wounded or killed during the air war and succeeding ground action.

■ Details of any of the major ground engagements, including some in which American servicemen and women were wounded.

■ How U.S. forces would have saved the Apache helicopters that had run out of fuel during the thrust into southern Iraq. The

choppers were grounded while the battles still raged.

■ How U.S. forces and Kuwaiti authorities will clear the hundreds of thousands of mines still embedded in the sands of Kuwait.

PAUL GONZALES / Los Angeles Times

For Kuwaitis, cheering soon gave way to travails of rebuilding.

THE DESERT STORM COALITION COUNTRIES

According to the Pentagon, 34 coalition allies, including the United States, contributed materials or manpower to Operation Desert Storm.

- Afghanistan
- Argentina
- Australia
- Austria
- Bahrain
- Bangladesh
- Belgium
- Britain
- Canada
- Czechoslovakia
- Denmark
- Egypt
- France
- Germany
- Greece
- Italy
- Kuwait
- Morocco
- Netherlands
- New Zealand
- Niger
- Norway
- Oman
- Pakistan
- Poland
- Qatar
- Saudi Arabia
- Senegal
- South Korea
- Spain
- Syria
- United Arab Emirates
- Turkey
- United States

THE COUNTRIES COMMITTING FORCES

This is how things stood on the eve of the land battle in the Gulf, following 36 days of heavy bombing that had failed to force Iraqi troops out of Kuwait. Iraq and the U.S.-led alliance had more than 1 million troops facing off. The balance of military and support forces in the region:

THE COALITION MEMBERS

■ **UNITED STATES:** More than 527,000 troops, including more than 295,000 Army, 94,000 Marines, 82,000 Navy, 56,000 Air Force.

Navy: More than 100 warships, including battleships Missouri and Wisconsin and aircraft carriers Midway, Ranger, Saratoga, John F. Kennedy, America and Theodore Roosevelt.

Air power: More than 1,800 Air Force, Navy and Marine fighters, bombers and other warplanes, ranging from radar-eluding F-117A Stealth fighters to B-52 bombers. More than 1,700 U.S. helicopters.

Armor: More than 1,200 tanks and 2,200 armored personnel carriers, including large number of M-1A1 front-line tanks.

■ **BRITAIN:** 43,000 troops, with about 25,000 in army's 1st Armored Division, equipped with about 170 Challenger tanks; up to 72 fighter planes, reconnaissance aircraft and helicopters; 16 warships.

■ **FRANCE:** 16,000 troops, including 12,000 army, 2,000 air force and 2,000 naval; 40 warplanes, 120 antitank helicopters; 40 battle tanks plus light tanks and field guns.

■ **TURKEY:** About 100,000 regular troops near the Iraqi border, backed by 35,000 paramilitary gendarmes and police; 50 tanks; estimated 50 jet fighters, The United States had an undisclosed number of F-15 fighters, 24 F-16s as well as 14 F-111 bombers at Incirlik base, and NATO had 42 aircraft from its allied mobile force.

■ **ARGENTINA:** One frigate and a corvette.

■ **AUSTRALIA:** A guided-missile destroyer, a frigate and a supply ship.

■ **BANGLADESH:** 2,000 troops.

■ **BELGIUM:** Two minesweepers and a support ship.

■ **CANADA:** 1,700 troops on three warships; squadron of Hornet fighter jets.

■ **CZECHOSLOVAKIA:** Anti-chemical warfare unit of 200.

■ **DENMARK:** One corvette.

■ **GREECE:** One frigate.

■ **ITALY:** Three frigates, an amphibious assault ship and eight fighter planes.

■ **NETHERLANDS:** Two frigates and a navy supply ship.

■ **NEW ZEALAND:** Two Hercules transport planes.

■ **NIGER:** About 500 troops.

■ **NORWAY:** One coast guard ship.

■ **PAKISTAN:** 11,000 troops.

■ **POLAND:** Two rescue ships.

■ **SENEGAL:** 500 troops.

■ **SOUTH KOREA:** Five C-130 planes and 150 air force pilots.

■ **SPAIN:** One frigate and two corvettes.

THE ARAB ALLIES

■ **SAUDI ARABIA:** About 118,000 troops, including 38,000 army, 56,000 paramilitary national guard, 7,200 navy and 16,500 air force; 550 tanks; 180 combat planes; 8 frigates.

■ **EGYPT:** Estimated 40,000 troops, equipped with tanks and missiles.

■ **UNITED ARAB EMIRATES:** 40,000 troops; more than 200 tanks; air force of 1,500 with 80 combat planes; navy of 1,500 with 15 ships.

■ **OMAN:** 25,500 troops with Scorpion, Chieftain and M-60 tanks; 63 combat planes; at least 4 Exocet-armed missile boats.

■ **MOROCCO:** 1,300 troops.

■ **BAHRAIN:** Army of 2,300; air force of 450; navy of 600.

OTHERS

■ **SOVIET UNION:** Two warships.

■ **ROMANIA:** Mobile field hospital team; 180 military experts on countering chemical warfare.

■ **SINGAPORE:** 30-member medical team serving in British hospital.

THE CHIEF WEAPONS OF THE GULF WAR

The allied air war against Iraq introduced Americans to a new generation of weaponry—the Patriot missile, Stealth fighters, smart bombs and many more:

GROUND WEAPONS

■ **M-1A1 Abrams tank:** The Army's main battle tank, equipped with a 120-millimeter cannon that fires an arrow-shaped dart—made of depleted uranium, and designed to punch through any known tank armor—at nearly 5,000 feet per second. Also three machine guns. Laser range-finder; top speed of 40 m.p.h.; cooling system designed to protect four-member crew from biological and chemical weapons attack. Cost $2.3 million. The Army has 3,300 of an earlier version.

■ **M-60 tank:** Predecessor to the M-1, equipped with a 105-millimeter cannon that fires a high-explosive antitank round. Cost: $1.2 million.

■ **TOW missile:** Tube-launched, optically tracked, wire-guided missile—the infantry's most powerful antitank weapon. Can be fired from helicopter, ground vehicle or from a tripod. Three-foot-long missile carries 13-pound warhead that can penetrate armor of heaviest tanks. Range is over two miles. Latest version is designed to go up in the air and come down on top of tanks, where armor is thinnest. Cost: $12,000.

■ **Bradley Fighting Vehicle:** Tank-like armored personnel carrier with three-member crew can carry 6 infantrymen into battle. Cruising range of 300 miles. Equipped with 25-millimeter cannon, machine gun and TOW antitank missiles; also has 6 rifles mounted in gun ports so that infantrymen can fight from inside. Cost: $1.5 million.

■ **Self-propelled howitzer:** Tank-like motorized gun with six-member crew. 155-millimeter cannon can fire shell over 13 miles. Cost: $760,000.

■ **LAV-25:** Marine Corps light-armored vehicle with three-member crew can carry 4 infantrymen. Cruising range of 400 miles. Top speed of 60 m.p.h. Equipped with a 25-millimeter armor-piercing gun. Cost: $973,000.

INFANTRY EQUIPMENT

■ **M-16A2 rifle:** Army's primary combat rifle, it weighs less than 10 pounds and holds 30 rounds that can be fired accurately at over 800 yards. Cost: $506.

■ **Night-vision goggles:** Worn by helicopter pilots or ground troops, these devices turn night into day by amplifying light from the stars or moon. Cost: $4,300 for troops, $10,000 for pilots.

■ **AT4 lightweight multipurpose weapon:** Shoulder-fired recoilless weapon that weighs less than 15 pounds. Fires an 18-inch armor-piercing shell with range of up to 1,600 feet. Used once and then discarded. Cost: $900.

■ **Stinger:** Shoulder-fired, heat-seeking antiaircraft missile. 35-pound weapon has range of several miles. Cost: $50,000.

■ **81-millimeter mortar:** Muzzle-loaded, tube-launched weapon that can lob a 9-pound high-explosive fragmentation shell nearly three miles. The blast sends fragments flying in a lethal zone that is 60 feet across. Cost: $23,000.

■ **Squad Automatic Weapon:** The SAW is a one-man portable machine gun that weighs just over 16 pounds and can fire 750 rounds a minute about half a mile. Cost: $1,360.

PLANES AND HELICOPTERS

■ **AH-64A Apache:** Army's primary attack helicopter. Its two-member crew is equipped with a night-vision sensor and up to 16 armor-piercing Hellfire missiles that home in on a laser spot projected onto a tank or other target. The laser can be aimed by ground observers, another aircraft or the Apache itself, and it enables the Apache in some cases to launch its missiles without seeing its target. Also has 30-millimeter gun. Army has more than 600 Apaches. Cost: $10 million.

■ **A-10 Thunderbolt:** Air Force's primary tank-killer. Has 30-millimeter guns in the nose and engines high above the wings. Nicknamed "The Warthog." Carries up to 16,000 pounds of ordnance. Cost: $8.7 million.

■ **AV-8B Harrier II:** Marines' vertical and short takeoff aircraft. Its short takeoff ability allows Marines to base plane near troops; with night-vision goggles, pilot can identify and track targets. It can carry 16 500-pound bombs. Cost: $21.9 million.

■ **Cobra:** Marines' attack helicopter. Two-member crew can fire TOW anti-tank missiles, 20-millimeter gun, Hellfire missiles. Also air-to-air Sidewinder missiles that can shoot down planes. Cost: $10 million.

Here are the 12 resolutions adopted by the U.N. Security Council after Iraq invaded Kuwait.

AUG. 2: The day after Iraq invaded Kuwait, the Security Council voted 14-0 to condemn the invasion and demand the immediate and unconditional withdrawal of Iraq's troops. Yemen, the only Arab member of the council, did not vote on **Resolution 660.**

AUG. 6: The council voted 13-0 to order a trade and financial embargo of Iraq and occupied Kuwait. Cuba and Yemen abstained on **Resolution 661.**

AUG. 9: In **Resolution 662,** the council voted 15-0 to declare Iraq's annexation of Kuwait null and void under international law.

AUG. 18: In **Resolution 664,** the council voted 15-0 to demand that Iraq free all detained foreigners.

AUG. 25: The council voted 13-0 to give the United States and other naval powers the right to enforce the economic embargo against Iraq and Kuwait by halting shipping to those countries. Cuba and Yemen abstained on **Resolution 665.**

SEPT. 13: The council voted 13-2 to allow humanitarian food aid into Iraq or Kuwait ''to relieve human suffering,'' and said only the council could decide when those circumstances exist. Cuba and Yemen voted against **Resolution 666.**

SEPT. 16: The council voted 15-0 on **Resolution 667** to condemn Iraq's aggressive acts against diplomatic missions in Kuwait, including the abduction of foreigners in the buildings.

SEPT. 24: On **Resolution 669,** the council voted 15-0 to stress that only its Sanctions Committee had the power to permit food, medicine or other humanitarian aid to be sent into Iraq or occupied Kuwait.

SEPT. 25: The council voted 14-1 to explicitly expand its economic embargo to include all air cargo traffic in or out of Iraq and Kuwait, except for cargoes of humanitarian aid specifically authorized by its Sanctions Committee. It also called on U.N. member nations to detain any Iraqi ships used to break the naval embargo. Cuba voted against **Resolution 670.**

OCT. 29: The council voted 13-0 to hold Iraq liable for war damages and economic losses, to demand that the Western embassies in Kuwait city be restocked with food and water and to demand that all hostages be released. Cuba and Yemen abstained on **Resolution 674.**

NOV. 28: The council voted 15-0 on **Resolution 677** to condemn Iraq's alleged attempts to drive out Kuwaitis and repopulate their country, and it asked the U.N. to take possession of Kuwait's census and citizenship records.

NOV. 29: The council voted 12-2, with one abstention, to give Baghdad ''one final opportunity'' until Jan. 15 to comply with all previous resolutions. After that date, nations allied with Kuwait were authorized ''to use all necessary means'' to force Iraq to withdraw and honor the resolutions, a phrase that all council members agreed would permit military action. China abstained on **Resolution 678;** Cuba and Yemen voted against it.

—Associated Press

Confirmed by the Pentagon as killed or missing in action in the Persian Gulf War.

KILLED IN ACTION (NON-CALIFORNIANS)

- Army Spec. Andy Alaniz, 20, Corpus Christi, Tex.
- Marine Lance Cpl. Frank C. Allen, 22, Waianae, Hawaii.
- Army Sgt. Tony R. Applegate, 28, Portsmouth, Ohio.
- Army Spec. Steven E. Atherton, 26, Nurmine, Pa.
- Army Cpl. Stanley W. Bartusiak, 34, Romulus, Mich.
- Army Spec. Cindy M. Beaudoin, 19, Plainfield, Conn.
- Army Sgt. Lee A. Belas, 22, Port Orchard, Wash.
- Marine Cpl. Stephen E. Bentzlin, 23, Yellow Meadow, Minn.
- Air Force 1st Lt. Thomas Clifford Bland Jr., 26, Gaithersburg, Md.
- Air Force Staff Sgt. John P. Blessinger, 33, Suffolk, NY.
- Army Spec. John A. Boliver, 27, Monongahela, Pa.
- Army Spec. Joseph P. Bongiorni, 20, Morgantown, W.Va.
- Army Sgt. John T. Boxler, 44, Johnstown, Pa.
- Air Force Capt. Douglas L. Bradt, 29, Houston.
- Army Sgt. Roger P. Brilinski Jr., 24, Ossineke, Mich.
- Air Force Senior Master Sgt. Paul G. Buege, 43, Milwaukee, Wis.
- Army Spec. Tommy D. Butler, 22, Amarillo, Tex.
- Army Staff Sgt. William T. Butts, 30, Waterford, Conn.
- Army Sgt. Jason C. Carr, 24, Halifax, Va.
- Army Spec. Clarence A. Cash, 20, Ashland, Ohio.
- Air Force Sgt. Barry M. Clark, 26, Hurlburt Field, Fla.
- Army Spec. Beverly C. Clark, 23, Armagh, Pa.
- Army Pfc. Melford R. Collins, 34, Uhland, Tex.
- Army Pfc. Ardon B. Cooper, 23, Seattle, Wash.
- Navy Lt. Patrick K. Conner, 25, Columbia, Mo.
- Army Maj. Mark A. Connelly, 34, Lancaster, Pa.
- Navy Lt. William Costen, 27, St. Louis, Mo.
- Marine Cpl. Ismael Cotto, 27, Bronx, NY.
- Army Sgt. Alan B. Craver, 32, Penn Hills, Pa.
- Army Pfc. Michael C. Dailey Jr., 19, Klamath Falls, Ore.
- Army Spec. Roy T. Damian Jr., 21, Toto, Guam.
- Army Spec. Michael D. Daniels, 20, Ft. Leavenworth, Ka.
- Army Spec. Manual A. Davila, 22, Gillette, Wyo.
- Army Pfc. Marty R. Davis, 19, Salina, Kan.
- Army Cpl. Rolando A. Delagneau, 30, Gretna, La.
- Army Spec. Luis Delgado, 30, Laredo, Tex.
- Army Sgt. Young Dillon, 27, Aurora, Colo.
- Army Sgt. David Q. Douthit, 24, Tacoma, Wash.
- Navy Lt. Robert J. Dwyer, 32, Worthington, Ohio.
- Air Force Capt. Paul R. Eichenlaub II, 29, Bentonville, Ark.
- Army Capt. Mario Fajardo, 29, Flushing, N.Y.
- Army Spec. Steven P. Farnen, 22, Columbia, Mo.
- Marine Lance Cpl. Eliseo Felix, 19, Avondale, Ariz.
- Army Spec. Douglas L. Fielder, 22, Nashville, Tenn.
- Army Chief Warrant Officer Phillip M. Garvey, 39, Pensacola, Fla.
- Army Sgt. Kenneth B. Gentry, 32, Ringgold, Va.
- Army Chief Warrant Officer Robert G. Godfrey, 32, Phenix City, Ala.
- Army 1st Lt. Daniel E. Graybeal, 25, Johnson City, Tenn.
- Marine Lance Cpl. Troy L. Gregory, 21, Richmond, Va.
- Air Force Capt. William D. Grimm, 28, Manhattan, Ka.
- Army Staff Sgt. Steven Hanson, 28, Ludington, Mich.
- Army Sgt. Michael A. Harris Jr., 26, Pollocksville, N.C.
- Air Force Staff Sgt. Timothy R. Harrison, 31, Maxwell, Iowa.
- Marine Sgt. James D. Hawthorne, 24, Stinnett, Tex.
- Army Warrent Officer Kerry P. Hein, 28, Sound Beach, NY.
- Army Spec. Timothy Hill, 23, Detroit, Mich.
- Air Force Tech. Sgt. Robert K. Hodges, 28, Hurlburt Field, Fla.
- Air Force Maj. Donnie R. Holland, 42, Bastrop, La.
- Army Spec. Duane W. Hollen Jr., 24, Bellwood, Pa.
- Army Pfc. Aaron W. Howard, 20, Battle Creek, Mich.
- Army Pfc. John W. Hutto, 19, Andalusia, Ala.
- Army Spec. Glen D. Jones, 21, Grand Rapids, Mich.
- Marine Cpl. Phllip J. Jones, 21, Atlanta, Ga.
- Army Sgt. Jonathan H. Kamm, 25, Mason, Ohio.
- Army Spec. Frank S. Keough, 22, North Huntington, Pa.
- Army Spec. Anthony W. Kidd, 21, Lima, Ohio.
- Army Capt. Joseph G. Kime III, 38, Charlestown, W.Va.
- Army Pfc. Jerry L. King, 20, Winston-Salem, N.C.
- Air Force Maj. Thomas F. Koritz, 37, Davenport, Iowa.
- Marine Lance Cpl. Brian L. Lane, 20, Bedford, Ind.
- Marine Lance Cpl. Michael E. Linderman Jr., 19, Roseburg, Ore.
- Marine Lance Cpl. James H. Lumpkins, 22, New Richmond, Ohio.
- Army Spec. Anthony Madison, 27, Monessen, Pa.
- Army Spec. Steven G. Mason, 23, Paragould, Ark.
- Air Force Master Sgt. James B. May II, 30, Jonesboro, Tenn.
- Army Spec. Christine L. Mayes, 23, Rochester Mills, Pa.
- Army Cpl. James R. McCoy, 29, Wilmington, Del.
- Army Spec. Jeffrey T. Middleton, 26, Oxford, Kan.
- Army Spec. James R. Miller Jr., 20, Decatur, Ind.
- Army Spec. Michael W. Mills, 23, Jefferson, Iowa.
- Army Sgt. Nels A. Moller, 23, Paul, Ida.
- Marine Sgt. Garett A. Mongrella, 25, Belvidere, N.J.
- Marine Sgt. Candelario Montalvo, 25, Eagle Pass, Tex.
- Army Warrant Officer John K. Morgan, 28, Bellevue, Wash.
- Army Pfc. James C. Murray Jr., 20, Conroe, Tex.
- Air Force Staff Sgt. John L. Oelschlager, 28, Niceville, Fla.
- Air Force 1st Lt. Patrick B. Olson, 25, Washington, N.C.
- Army Sgt. Patbouvier E. Ortiz, 27, Ridgewood, N.Y.
- Marine Cpl. Aaron A. Pack, 22, Phoenix, Ariz.
- Army Spec. William E. Palmer, 23, Hillsdale, Mich.
- Air Force Capt. Stephan R. Phillis, 30, Rock Island, Ill.
- Army Warrant Officer David G. Plasch, 23, Portsmouth, N.H.
- Army 1st Lt. Terry Plunk, 25, Vinton, Va.
- Marine Lance Cpl. Christian J. Porter, 20, Wood Dale, Ill.
- Army Sgt. Dodge R. Powell, 28, Hollywood, Fla.
- Army Sgt. Ronald M. Randazzo, 24, Glen Burnie, Md.
- Army Chief Warrant Officer Hal H. Reichle, 27, Marietta, Ga.
- Army Spec. Ronald D. Rennison, 21, Dubuque, Iowa.
- Army Sgt. Michael R. Robson, 30, Seminole, Fl.
- Air Force Staff Sgt. Mark J. Schmauss, 30, Waggaman, La.
- Marine Pfc. Scott A. Schroeder, 20, Milwaukee, Wis.
- Army Sgt. Brian P. Scott, 22, Park Falls, Wis.
- Army Pfc. Timothy A. Shaw, 21, Suitland, Md.
- Army Spec. Stephen J. Siko, 24, Latrobe, Pa.
- Army Capt. Brian K. Simpson, 22, Indianapolis, Ind.
- Army Sgt. Russell G. Smith Jr., 44, Fall River, Mass.
- Marine Lance Cpl. David T. Snyder, 21, Kenmore, N.Y.
- Marine Capt. David Spellacy, 28, Columbus, Ohio
- Army Staff Sgt. Christopher H. Stephens, 27, Houston, Tex.
- Marine Pfc. Dion J. Stephenson, 22, Bountiful, Utah.
- Army Spec. Thomas G. Stone, 20, Falconer, N.Y.
- Army Sgt. Gary E. Streeter, 39, Manhattan, Kan.
- Army Sgt. William A. Strehlow, 27, Kenosha, Wis.
- Army Pfc. Robert D. Talley, 18, Newark, N.J.
- Army Spec. James D. Tatum, 22, Athens, Tenn.
- Army 1st Lt. Donaldson P. Tillar III, 25, Miller School, Va.
- Navy Lt. Charles J. Turner, 29, Richfield, Minn.
- Marine Capt. Reginald C. Underwood, 27, Lexington, Ky.
- Army Pvt. Roger E. Valentine, 19, Memphis, Tenn.
- Army Pfc. Robert C. Wade, 21, Hackensack, N.J.
- Marine Lance Cpl. James E. Waldron, 25, Jeannette, Pa.
- Army Spec. Frank J. Walls, 20, Hawthorne, Pa.
- Marine Lance Cpl. Daniel B. Walker, 20, Whitehouse, Tex.
- Air Force Capt. Dixon L. Walters Jr., 29, Columbia, S.C.
- Air Force Maj. Paul J. Weaver, 34, Navarre, Fla.
- Army Spec. Troy M. Wedgwood, 22, The Dalles, Ore.
- Marine Capt. James N. Wilbourn, 29, Huntsville, Ala.
- Army Cpl. Jonathan M. Williams, 23, Portsmouth, Va.
- Army Pfc. Corey L. Winkle, 21, Lubbock, Tex.
- Army Staff Sgt. Harold P. Witzke III, 28, Caroga Lake, N.Y.
- Army Spec. Richard V. Wolverton, 22, Latrobe, Pa.
- Army Spec. James E. Worthy, 22, Albany, Ga.
- Army Maj. Thomas C.M. Zeugner, 36, Petersburg, Va.

CALIFORNIANS KILLED IN ACTION

- Army Sgt. David R. Crumby Jr., 26, Long Beach.
- Air Force Capt. Arthur Galvan, 33, Navarre, Fla.
- Army Sgt. Jimmy Dewayne Haws, 28, Traver.
- Marine Lance Cpl. Thomas A. Jenkins, 20, Mariposa.
- Air Force Sgt. Damon V. Kanuha, 28, San Diego.
- Army Pfc. David W. Kramer, 20, Palm Desert.
- Army Sgt. Edwin B. Kutz, 26, Sunnymead.
- Army Spec. Scott J. Lindsey, 27, Diamond Springs.
- Army Sgt. Cheryl L. O'Brien, 24, Long Beach
- Army Pfc. Adrienne L. Mitchell, 20, Moreno Valley.
- Army Sgt. Adrian Stokes, 20, Riverside.
- Army Warrent Officer George R. Swartzendruber, 25, San Diego.

MISSING IN ACTION

- Navy Lt. Cmdr. Barry T. Cooke, 35, Virginia Beach, Va.
- Navy Lt. Cmdr. Michael Scott Speicher, 33, Jacksonville, Fla.

PATRICK DOWNS / Los Angeles Times

The number of Iraqi soldiers killed may never be known.

PATRICK DOWNS / Los Angeles Times